THE DAWN OF UNIVERSAL HISTORY

THE DAWN OF UNIVERSAL HISTORY

Selected Essays from a Witness of the Twentieth Century

RAYMOND ARON

Translated by Barbara Bray
Edited by Yair Reiner
With an Introduction by Tony Judt

BASIC
BOOKS

A Member of the Perseus Books Group

The essays in this book were originally published in 1996 in France as part of
Une histoire du XXᵉ siècle by Éditions Plon
Translation copyright © 2002 by Raymond Aron

Published by Basic Books,
A Member of the Perseus Books Group

All rights reserved. Printed in the United States of America. No part of this book may be reproduced in any manner whatsoever without written permission except in the case of brief quotations embodied in critical articles and reviews. For information, address Basic Books, 387 Park Avenue South, New York, NY 10016-8810.

Designed by *Trish Wilkinson*
Set in 11.5 AGaramond by the Perseus Books Group

Library of Congress Cataloging-in-Publication Data
Aron, Raymond, 1905–1983
    [Histoire du vingtieáme siáecle. English Selections]
    The dawn of universal history : selected essays from a witness of the twentieth century / by Raymond Aron ; translated by Barbara Bray ; edited by Yair Reiner ; with an introduction by Tony Judt.
        p.   cm.
    "The essays in this book were originally published in 1996 in France as part of *Une historie du XXᵉ siècle* . . ."—T.p. verso.
    Includes bibliographical references and index.
    ISBN 0-465-00407-5
    1. History, Modern—20th century. I. Reiner, Yair. II. Title.
D20 .A6713 2002
909.82—dc21   2002004405

02 03 04 05/10 9 8 7 6 5 4 3 2 1

CONTENTS

INTRODUCTION

*by Tony Judt**

R aymond Aron was one of the "golden" generation of twentieth-
century French intellectuals: Born in 1905, he was a little younger
than André Malraux and Claude Lévi-Strauss, a little older than Maurice
Merleau-Ponty and Simone de Beauvoir, and the exact contemporary of
Jean-Paul Sartre. He attended the best Parisian schools and graduated, like
his friend Sartre, from the École Normale Supérieure. His formal training
was in philosophy—he placed first in the competitive national examination, the *agrégation*. Aron's natural trajectory—toward a teaching post in
the French University—was cut short, however, by the outbreak of war
in 1939. A Jew and a socialist, he left France following the establishment of
the puppet regime at Vichy and joined Charles de Gaulle's Free French organization in London.

Upon returning to France Aron served briefly in André Malraux's postwar Ministry of Information before returning to the university world to
teach sociology, at the same time taking up what proved to be a lifelong parallel career as a journalist and political commentator. In 1954 he accepted a
chair in sociology at the Sorbonne and taught there and at the École des
Hautes Etudes en Sciences Sociales until being named to the Collège de

*Tony Judt is Director of the Remarque Institute at New York University. His books in-
clude *Marxism and the French Left* (1986), *Past Imperfect: French Intellectuals 1944–1956*
(1992) and *The Burden of Responsibility: Blum, Camus, Aron and the French Twentieth Century* (1998).

France in 1971. By the time of his death in 1983, at the age of seventy-eight, he was widely regarded, in the words of his colleague François Furet, as "not just a great professor, but the greatest professor in the French University."[1]

Aron was distinguished from his peers in a number of ways. Unlike most specialized scholars he had a remarkable range. He was trained as a philosopher—his doctoral dissertation addressed complex epistemological problems in the philosophy of history. His academic appointments were in sociology, and he published influential, important studies of social thought and industrial society. His interests and publications spread across international relations, intellectual history, military theory, and comparative politics. In all of these areas he became a recognized international authority.

Raymond Aron's catholicity of interests and his prolific output marked him as one of France's leading public intellectuals. But unlike most of his French intellectual contemporaries, Aron made a virtue of being truly knowledgeable in everything that he wrote about—and refused to write about matters on which he was ignorant. In this sense he was both an engaged intellectual, commenting on a wide range of public events, and a specialized expert in the social sciences—a most unusual combination for a French scholar of his era. Moreover, although his initial political sympathies were on the Left and he cofounded (with Sartre and Merleau-Ponty) the influential left-wing cultural periodical *Les Temps Modernes,* Aron resolutely espoused the Western position in the Cold War, at a time when many of his Parisian contemporaries were either neutralist or else tempted by the appeal of communism.

In these ways, and in his broad international following in Europe and North America, Aron was distinctly atypical. Of course he was, as he always insisted, a product of his time and his place: a classically educated Frenchman who lived through two world wars, the Great Depression, fascism, communism, and the atomic age. This experience shaped his outlook and his interests no less than those of most other French intellectuals. But in Aron's case it led him away from abstract speculation and radical political affiliation—the characteristic path of most of his intellectual contemporaries; indeed, it is clear in retrospect that Aron was the only prominent French thinker of his generation to take a consistent liberal stand against all the totalitarian temptations of the age, of Right and Left alike. At the same time, he brought to his political writings and his commentaries on public affairs a distinctively French point of view, as we shall see. It is this unique mix that made Aron's work so distinctive in its day. And it accounts for the enduring appeal of his books and essays to today's readers.

The essays and excerpts gathered here are a representative cross section of Aron's writings during and about the Cold War era. They cover four broad themes: the Cold War itself and Great-Power relations in the first decades of the atomic age; the international history of the twentieth century; the theory and practice of totalitarianism; and imperialism and decolonization. With two exceptions all the material here dates from the 1950s: One article (on Nazism) was written in 1939, and the section on the United States is drawn from Aron's book *La République Impériale*, first published in France in 1973.

These works are thus contemporary reflections on public affairs as they were unfolding, and they lack the benefit of hindsight. We now know, as Aron could not, how the conflicts and dilemmas he discusses were to unfold—at least so far. But Aron's essays have the virtue of this defect: They offer an invaluable insight into the way things seemed, in the postwar years, to an unusually insightful Parisian observer. In those days no one knew how the U.S.–Soviet confrontation might end. No one could foresee the future of the Soviet Union, much less its eventual disappearance.

Furthermore, and despite being published in very different places and for quite different audiences, the essays form a natural unity. Aron understood how international affairs, domestic politics, colonial crises, and Marxist doctrine were interrelated and interdependent in the second half of the twentieth century. These and other matters needed to be presented separately for the sake of clarity, but they could not be understood in isolation. In Aron's view there were no longer local histories that could be described and explained without reference to outside developments. The rise of the superpowers had put an end to that. And for the same reason, international power struggles and ideological conflicts could not be understood except in a common framework.

Aron brought to his writings two overarching considerations that give them point and coherence. The first was a well-honed political prudence. As a graduate student Aron had lived in Weimar Germany during its death throes. He had witnessed the collapse of democracy and the rise of dictatorship. He had tried and failed to convince his French contemporaries of the seriousness of what was taking place across the Rhine. He had lived through the decline of the French Third Republic and observed firsthand the corrupt maneuverings that led to Philippe Pétain's seizure of power in 1940 in the aftermath of German victory.

In consequence, Aron was absorbed with, perhaps even obsessed by, the fragility of liberal polities and the ever-present threat of anarchy and despotism. This concern marked his writings in a way that nothing about his comfortable childhood and youth could have predicted, and it sets him apart from most French intellectuals of his generation. It explains his remarkable prescience during the 1930s, when most French politicians and intellectuals alike were tragically slow to grasp the meaning of Hitler's revolution, and his response to almost every major crisis in postwar French life, from the turmoil of the Liberation to the events of May 1968.

In Aron's view, democracy and freedom are the preconditions of civil society, but they are fragile. There will always be men, sometimes men of goodwill, tempted to overthrow or undermine a free society in the name of a better, purer, stronger, more "authentic" alternative. The first task of the intellectual is to speak out against this temptation and in defense of liberty. It was above all for this reason that he took very seriously the responsibility of intellectuals to be involved in important public debates. In a time of troubles it is not enough merely to observe and record: As Aron noted in his memoirs apropos his own support for the U.S. presence in Vietnam, one cannot restrict oneself to the role of "the observer of the follies and disasters of mankind."

Thus, Aron was a vigorous critic of those who sought a "catastrophic" solution to the social woes of postwar France (or anywhere else). As he recognized, this taste for violent, "definitive" solutions, as though the road to utopia necessarily lay through destruction, was in part born of the experience of war in our century. But he opposed it energetically, and when France came as near as it ever has in the twentieth century to a real peacetime civil conflict, at the time of the Communist-led strikes of 1948, Aron took a hard line: "The inevitable struggle will be muted only to the extent that the state has strengthened its means of action. It is just not acceptable that in the mines and electrical plants of France people are more afraid of the Communists than of engineers, directors, and ministers combined."[2]

The link in Aron's thought between political stability, civil order, and public liberties is thus clear—and as with Alexis de Tocqueville, whom he greatly admired, it was a product of experience and observation rather than theory. The correlation sheds light on his way of thinking about liberty in general, and the totalitarian threat to it. Unlike social commentators in the United States, for example, Aron was not an especially enthusiastic advocate of the term "totalitarian" as a general category covering various modern threats to a free society. His distaste for grand theory extended to anti-Communist rhetoric as well, and his thoughts about totalitarianism derived in the first instance from his concern for its opposite—the partial, always imperfect reality of liberty, constrained and threatened by necessity and history. If the United States was to be preferred in the global conflicts of the day, it was not because it represented some higher or more logically satisfying order of life, but because it stood as the guarantor, however defective, of public liberties. The lesson of totalitarianism, in short, was the importance of order and authority under law—not as a compromise with freedom, nor as the condition of higher freedoms to come, but simply as the best way to protect those already secured.

The second aspect of Aron's approach was what one might, for convenience, call a disenchanted realism. The two, of course, are related. It was because he had experienced the twentieth century as a series of threats to the fragile Western heritage of individual freedom and legal order that Aron accorded such importance to realism: We must look at the world not as we wish it to be but as it is. This duty was incumbent, he believed, on observers and practitioners alike.

Thus commentators, social scientists, and historians must begin by trying to understand the real-world constraints upon those whose acts they seek to assess. As he wrote of Max Weber, "He was prepared at any moment to answer the question that disconcerts all our amateur politicians: 'What would you do if you were a Cabinet minister?'"[3] It was for this reason that he had set out to educate himself in disciplines far removed from those he had studied as a young man. As early as 1937 he spelled out his motives: "It isn't every day that a Dreyfus affair allows you to invoke truth against error. If intellectuals want to offer their opinions on a daily basis, they will need knowledge of economics, diplomacy, politics, etc. Whether it concerns deflation and inflation, Russian alliance or entente cordiale, collective contracts or wage rates, the point at issue is less about justice than about effectiveness."[4]

Aron thus took his distance from all efforts to invest political or historical analysis with moral evaluation. Even Vichy, a preeminently emotive topic in French public debate, required in Aron's view a cooler assessment:

Vichy in his eyes was less a crime than an error, a mistake of political judgment. The pétainist fault lay in supposing that Vichy might benefit from its place in Hitler's Europe—a dangerous and ultimately tragic misjudgment, but one that needed to be understood in the context of the events of 1940. The point was to acknowledge the facts, however uncomfortable or inconvenient—"the analyst doesn't create the history that he interprets."[5]

For the same reason, he refused to share the widespread enthusiasm aroused in the mid-1950s by the first post-Stalinist whiffs of détente. He even welcomed the gloomy presence of Mr. Molotov: In Aron's eyes the inscrutable Mr. Molotov was a useful prophylactic against a return to interwar illusions—the idea that "peace depends on words rather than on the courage of men and the balance of forces." Writing in 1956, after the upheavals in Poland but before the repression of the Hungarian revolution, Aron reminded his readers that "if the Soviets felt truly threatened, they would return to the rigidity of earlier years. . . . Let us not mistake our dreams for near reality."[6]

But Raymond Aron was not at all a "realist" in the sense people mean today when they speak of "realpolitik"—the practice of making political judgments derived exclusively from a calculation of possibilities, interests, and outcomes based on past experience or a priori reasoning. He had no time for that sort of "theoretical realism," which led in practice to unrealistic decisions like that of Neville Chamberlain at Munich. His objection to this mode of thought lay partly in its frequently misguided conclusions, but above all in its rigidity, with the result that what begins as empirical calculation nearly always ends up as rule-bound dogma: "In my opinion, pseudocertainty, based on the relationship between the stakes and the risks, on some rational calculation ascribed to a likely aggressor, is of no more value than the dogmatism of the Maginot Line."[7]

To appreciate what was distinctive about Aron's writings on international affairs it helps to think of his method as a series of approaches that ran against the grain of his time. In the first place, he was a social scientist who thought historically. In his essays and lectures on nations and empires, or on the development of international relations since 1914, Aron broke with contemporary fashion. His understanding of interstate relations was unabashedly traditional. In his words, "The division of humanity into sovereign states preceded capitalism and will outlive it."[8] There were limits to what even the Great Powers could do, but there were equally limits to what could be done to prevent them from doing as they wished—hence his mildly skeptical attitude toward the United Nations and other international agencies.

The same emphasis upon continuity shaped his critique of grand claims about the need to rethink military and diplomatic strategy in the nuclear age. Raymond Aron saw very early on, well before most professional military theorists, the limits to the diplomatic and military uses of nuclear weaponry. In 1957, ten years before the British retreat from east of Suez, he pointed out that the British military's growing reliance on atomic weapons and its reduced expenditure on conventional arms would undercut its freedom of military and therefore diplomatic maneuver without doing anything to improve its security. Two years later he made the same point about the French *force de frappe*. French nuclear weapons only made sense in the hypothetical context of a conflict between NATO and the USSR, whereas for France's real problems in Africa or the Middle East they would be of absolutely no use whatsoever.

Despite his emphasis upon the main U.S.–USSR confrontation, Aron was thus alert to the changes already taking place in the postwar world from the late 1950s. Even in 1954 he had warned against betting all one's military budget and calculations on a single weapon; the wars of the future were likely to be quite different from those of the past and would require a very different sort of arsenal. Moreover, such local wars need not lead to international conflicts on a nuclear scale—on the contrary, if the nuclear "umbrella" secured anything, it was the space for greater and lesser powers to engage in old-style local or partial conflicts without putting "peace" at risk. The traditional logic of power politics remained in force, and with it the need to think militarily in a variety of keys and not just that of nuclear devastation. "One does not increase the risk of total war by accepting the obligations of local wars," he pointed out.[9]

In the second place, Raymond Aron was a realist who took ideas seriously. This is still an unusual combination. From Henry Kissinger down, most contemporary "realists" are contemptuously dismissive of moralizers and others who claim that politicians and statesmen are or should be moved by abstract goals or ethical ambitions. Ideas, ideals, and dogmas, from historical materialism to human rights, are, they suggest, the ephemera of political discourse; at best abstractions that cannot readily be taken into account when making hard political choices, at worst (and more commonly) excuses for actions undertaken for other reasons.

Aron thought otherwise. In his account, reality encompassed not only interests and power but also ideas. Like Clausewitz, he took it for granted that *Glaubensache*—beliefs of all kinds—constitute a social fact. Human beings have beliefs and are moved by them in various ways, and this phenomenon is as much a part of reality as the disposition of armaments or the forms of production. "Realism," in Aron's view, was simply unrealistic if it ignored the moral judgments that citizens pass on governments, or the real and imagined moral interests of all actors in a society.

It is for this reason that Raymond Aron's realism was so much better at explaining and predicting events in his time than the "realist" commentaries and prognostications of Sovietologists and others who shared his concerns but not his breadth of understanding. Thus, for example, in the late 1940s Aron laid out a "two-track" explanation of Soviet international strategy that would become conventional wisdom by the 1970s but was original and provocative in its time. According to his analysis there was a fundamental continuity of Soviet goals, but these might be sought either by the tactic of alliances, as in the era of the Popular Front (or for a brief moment after Hitler's defeat) or else by confrontational attitudes at appropriate times and in vulnerable places. Those who dismissed or downplayed the doctrinal reasoning that lay behind this Soviet strategy simply missed an important truth about the world in which they lived.

If Aron saw things in this light it was because—and this is the third distinctive feature in his approach—he was an anti-Communist who took Marxism very seriously. He was certainly in no doubt as to the dangers presented by the Soviet Union. As the essays in this book make clear, his assessment of the postwar international situation drew on his overwhelming concern with the Soviet Union and the threat it posed. He was one of the first European commentators to recognize, as early as 1945, the role that would be played by the USSR after Hitler's defeat, and everything he wrote was side-shadowed by this fact.

But his obsession with the Soviet threat was driven above all by his insight into the attraction of communism, which gave the USSR an appeal and a leverage far beyond that of a conventional Great Power. Aron was a lifelong student of Marxist thought and was far better informed on this subject than many self-styled Marxists. His interest in Karl Marx began with his early work on philosophies of history and was sustained both by his professional interest in nineteenth-century social thought and his polemics with

Marxist and *marxisant* contemporaries. Of his engagement with Marx, Aron had this to say: "Like the friends of my youth I never separated philosophy from politics, nor thought from commitment; but I devoted rather more time than them to the study of economic and social mechanisms. In this sense I believe I was more faithful to Marx than they were."[10]

For Aron, the distinction between Marx and his Marxist heirs was important—though not sufficient to absolve Marx himself of all responsibility for the actions and opinions of those claiming to follow his precepts. Marxism (like other twentieth-century radical dogmas of extreme Left and extreme Right alike) was what Aron called a "secular religion." Here, too, he was ahead of his time. The idea that extremist claims and projects of Left and Right had much in common with each other—in their appeal and in the threat they posed to liberty—was unfashionable and unpopular when Aron proposed it in the postwar decades. Today, in the aftermath of the fall of the Soviet Union and with greater attention paid to the crimes of Nazism and communism alike, we are more disposed to see the twentieth century in this light.

Aron's reading of Marxism as a secular religion made him few friends. American specialists on Soviet affairs preferred to analyze Marxist regimes in functional terms, whereas European and especially French Marxists and students of Marxism were deeply offended by Aron's refusal to take their ideas seriously *on their terms*. We forget today how willing many on the European Left were to give even Stalin the benefit of the doubt. Aron was merciless in his skewering of such illusions: Writing in 1950, at a time when the appeal of Stalin extended well beyond the boundaries of those parties and countries under his direct control, Aron commented, "The ludicrous surprise is that the European Left has taken a pyramid-builder for its God."[11]

One aspect of Aron's interests that brought him rather closer to contemporary American specialists was the attention he paid to modern economies and their apparent convergence. But here, too (and this is my fourth example of Aron's distinctive approach), he stood a little aside from conventional wisdom. Like many American sociologists of the late 1950s, Aron was struck by the apparently converging character of industrial societies. But unlike them, he was never led by this observation to suppose that they would all eventually merge into a single social model.

For most European social theorists and sociologists of Aron's time, of Left and Right alike, society was either capitalist or socialist: Forms of production and property ownership determined all other features. The Soviet Union and the West were categorically different systems, and there was widespread agreement across the European political spectrum that it was a serious political mistake, as well as an analytical error, to suggest that two such antagonistic political systems could share fundamental modern features in common.

Aron took a rather different position. He regretted the neglect of a question that had preoccupied early nineteenth-century writers at the dawn of modernity: What is the meaning, what is the nature of a society shaped by science and by industry? Unlike a number of "industrial society" theorists in the United States, however, he did not want to claim that East and West were somehow one, their distinctive ideological disagreements cast in the shade by a common drive toward the social, managerial, and rationalist goals of an industrial economy. He was too conscious of politics—of the contrast between societies where state and society were collapsed into one and those where they were distinct—and too well informed about the place of ideology in Soviet thinking to make this elementary mistake.

In his view, scholars who made this error were merely reflecting the complementary Marxist mistake of deriving political assumptions from economic forms: Comparable "forces of production," so the claim ran, must needs give birth to similar political institutions and beliefs. But why should this follow? From as early as 1936 Aron had already observed an original aspect of the Soviet "experiment." In the West, freedom and private enterprise had been the essential preconditions for industrialization and growth. But the latter might now happen under Soviet-style conditions of planning and public ownership. The USSR might be politically and socially dystopic, but it was no less a technically "advanced" society for that.

Technological modernity, then, was a fact of the contemporary world, and Aron was caustically dismissive of those French critics who fondly imagined that the rationalist and economistic traits of all modern (Western) societies were something gratuitously foisted upon Europeans by the United States for its own purposes. In his view the problems of modernity could no longer be cast in the simple old ways: private property versus public ownership, capitalist exploitation versus social equality, market anarchy versus planned distribution. These themes of socialist doctrine and Left-Right polemic had largely lost their meaning.

Aron's insight into the ways in which modern industrial society transcended the old doctrinal categories without necessarily leading to the blur-
ring of political forms put him in a singular position: someone who shared
some aspects of French and American social thought and political assessment but agreed wholeheartedly with neither. This lonely stance is echoed
in his writings on decolonization, a fifth arena in which the characteristic
Aronian perspective can be seen at work.

As the essays in this collection suggest, Raymond Aron was a critic of
French colonialism. Like many of his contemporaries on the Left, he favored French withdrawal first from Indochina and then from North Africa
and especially Algeria in the years following the Arab revolt of 1954. But
unlike almost everyone else in the anticolonial camp, he opposed the
French presence, in Algeria especially, not out of moral distaste or from
radical precept but on strictly "realist" grounds.

Raymond Aron was not against French colonies on principle. He resented the American and British failure to assist the embattled French
forces in Vietnam and shared the view, widespread in the political class of
his time, that France's identity was intimately bound up with its worldwide
possessions and influence. France has a duty, he wrote in *Le Figaro* in October 1955, to try and keep North Africa "in the sphere of modern civilization."[12] But lacking any personal ties to North Africa, he felt no emotional
attachment to the Maghreb and came to see his country's embroilment
there as costly and pointless. The rebellion in Algeria made it depressingly
clear that France could retain control of the country only by the application of considerable force.

Accordingly, as Aron argued in two trenchant pamphlets published in
1957 and 1958 (from which the excerpts in this book are drawn), the time
had come to give the Algerians their independence. He based this conclusion on characteristically Aronian grounds. To improve the condition of the
indigenous population of Algeria to a level compatible with equal membership of the French nation, and to provide Arabs and Berbers with equal political rights and representation, as proposed by liberal-minded defenders of
the status quo, would be hugely expensive (and therefore unpopular with
the taxpaying citizenry). It would also entail an Algerian presence in French
political life—projecting ahead the far higher growth rates of the Arab population—that would likely prove unacceptable to the metropolitan French
themselves. In short, the French were deluding themselves, not to speak of

misleading the Arabs, when they promised equality and equal representation in the future, having steadfastly refused it in the past.

Moreover, although it was true that the Arab Algerians would be better off if they stayed under French rule, this was not a factor that they could be expected to take into account. "It is a denial of the experience of our century," Aron wrote, "to suppose that men will sacrifice their passions to their interests." While he held no brief for the nationalist case, Aron understood its power to move millions, and the foolhardiness of opposing it. And he saw no point in debating whether or not there truly was an "Algerian nation" with claims to self-government and the like, as though the assertion that "Algerianness" was a modern invention would somehow undermine the case for independence. "It hardly matters whether this nationalism is the expression of a real or an imaginary nation. Nationalism is a passion, resolved to create the entity it invokes."

Once it was clear that the only mutually acceptable solution to the Algerian imbroglio was a parting of the ways—and by 1957 this outcome was obvious to Aron—it made absolutely no sense to wait. "The multiplication of would-be sovereign states, lacking the intellectual, economic, and administrative resources necessary for the exercise of sovereignty, is not inherently desirable. I am not a fanatic for the 'abandonment of sovereignty.' But I am more opposed to colonial wars than to the abandonment of sovereignty, because the former anyway produces the latter—under the worst possible conditions."

Note that Aron is not invoking historical inevitability here, much less a theory of necessary progress. The Algerian War need not have happened. The interests of its participants were not best served by the goals they sought. And even if the end result was in one sense foreordained, if only by French colonial malpractice, that did not make it "right." But the French had failed to hold on to North Africa, and the time had come to recognize this fact and act accordingly. Reasonable men might disagree on this; as Aron wrote with reference to the events of 1940, "faced with this tragic dilemma men of equal patriotism might make utterly opposed choices." No one had a monopoly of right.

Raymond Aron thus came down in favor of Algerian independence, like the overwhelming majority of other French intellectuals. But his arguments were quite unlike theirs. He did not seek to prove the legitimacy of the Arab claim to independence. He was not interested, for these purposes, in the moral debt the French had inherited from their colonial past that could only be liquidated by the abandonment of colonial power. He never invoked the course of history or the "natural" move to a postcolonial world. And, above all, he did not refer to the emotive issue of French military and police practices in Algeria itself, the use of torture to extract confessions from suspected terrorists, and the price that was being paid for these crimes in the soul of the French Republic. The Algerian tragedy, for Aron, lay not in the moral dilemma posed to individuals caught in the "dirty war," but in the absence of a satisfactory third alternative to a continuing conflict or a "catastrophic" independence. "Political action," he wrote, "is a response to circumstances, not a theoretical disquisition or the expression of feelings."

Aron was accused at the time of having neglected the "moral" dimension of France's Algerian crisis, of failing to grasp the true heart of the tragedy in his frozen concern with logic. His reply, when this charge was put to him again many years later, is revealing. Why did he not add his voice to those who were speaking out against the use of torture? "But what would I have achieved by proclaiming my opposition to torture? I have never met anyone who is in favor of torture." And, more generally, why did he not invoke moral criteria in his case for Algerian independence? Others were doing that already, he replied, and anyone who was open to that sort of argument was probably already convinced. "The important thing" was "to convince those who were arguing the opposite position."[13]

I have described at some length Aron's response to the Algerian crisis because it neatly encapsulates not just his views on colonialism but his distinctive, "cool" approach to the analysis of a political crisis. Here was Aronian realism at work, applied in this case to decolonization but present throughout his writings on postwar political and moral dilemmas. Some goals are desirable, others are not. But the point is always to ask what is possible in the circumstances in which men find themselves and to proceed—whether as observer or actor—from that starting point.

One final dimension of Aron's contribution to twentieth-century political analysis is worth mentioning. Raymond Aron was a Frenchman. As he himself never failed to insist, he saw the world from Paris. But Aron was an unusual Frenchman. He read and spoke fluent English and German, and unlike most French commentators of his era he saw very clearly just what the rise of the superpowers and the advent of atomic weapons meant for the international standing of his country. For these reasons his interpretation of twentieth-century international developments was unusual, perhaps unique.

That Raymond Aron was always and above all a Frenchman is crucial to an appreciation of his writings. His patriotism is palpable—he once described his two passions in politics as France and freedom, and it is clear that in important ways the two were for him but one. On more than one occasion in the 1950s his feelings as a Frenchman were deeply offended by international criticism of his country. In one angry commentary on Third World attacks at the United Nations, he wrote, "We have had enough of being lectured to by governments that do not apply and have no intention of applying the ideas they got from us and in whose name they condemn us."[14]

This wounded national sentiment occasionally colored his judgments, too. His dislike for Nasser ("the Egyptian Führer") led him at the time of the 1956 Suez Crisis to make implausible and misleading analogies with Munich, and utterly to misread American interests and intentions ("Forced to choose, Washington will not opt for Nasser's Egypt against Great Britain and France"—which is, of course, just what Eisenhower did). He even ventured wild and unsupported predictions of disaster in the event of Nasser's victory, which he initially saw as a catastrophe for France: "If pan-Islamism pushes the British out of the Near East and the French out of North Africa, it will not be long before the Americans are chased out of Europe."[15]

Aron's identification with France and its interests brought him close to General de Gaulle, though he was never a Gaullist (one fellow member of the Free French community describes him as the "only nonpassionate anti-Gaullist in wartime London"[16]). In the immediate postwar years he supported the General, recognizing in him a man who had, in Aron's words, all the qualities and all the defects of Machiavelli's Prince. He offered his guarded support again when de Gaulle returned to power as a result of the Algerian crisis of 1958. During the 1950s he even shared de Gaulle's own views on the hypocrisy of U.S. policy toward the Third World: "The Americans don't have a bad conscience when oil companies pay feudal rulers millions of dollars to support sordid regimes; but they would feel bad if their influence or their money helped the North Africans (French and Muslim) to build together a community shaped by the spirit of Western civilization."[17]

But his relationship with de Gaulle was always a difficult one. Aron regarded the Gaullist approach to foreign policy, nuclear arms, and the Atlantic alliance as cavalier, contradictory, and at times irresponsible. He remained a firm critic of Gaullist international illusions long after the General's departure from the scene: In April 1981 he reminded readers of *l'Express* that the French attitude toward the USSR—born of fantasies about playing a role between and independent of the "two hegemonies"—was the unfortunate legacy of de Gaulle. It was he, wrote Aron, who must take responsibility for bequeathing to his successors the illusion that France had some special place in the hearts and policies of Soviet leaders.

If Aron could distance himself from conventional French perspectives on international relations it was in part because of his distinctive intellectual affinities. Raymond Aron was an admirer of Montesquieu and Tocqueville, whom (following Elie Halevy) he affectionately referred to as the "English school of French political thought." His high regard for these thinkers, then out of fashion, was in some measure fueled by his frustration with German thinkers like Max Weber, whose work he knew well but of whose grand-scale, "bird's-eye view" of social processes he retained a certain suspicion.[18]

What distinguished Montesquieu and his heirs for Aron, by contrast, was their understanding of the political and their willingness to accord politics an autonomous and important place in social and historical explanation. With this appreciation of politics came that dispassionate realism that Aron valued so highly. In contrast, what was wrong with de Gaulle and his left-wing critics, in Aron's view, was their resolute unwillingness to look facts in the face and see France's situation as it truly was.

Not surprisingly, Aron's detached and objective way of being a French patriot did not endear him to either side. His situation—that of a Frenchman better understood and more appreciated abroad than at home—reminded him of the discomforts of the tradition in which he had chosen to place himself. In Alexis de Tocqueville's isolation amid the ideological currents of the nineteenth century, Aron detected a foretaste of the difficulties of the liberal thinker in a later age: "Too liberal for the side from which he came, not enthusiastic enough about new ideas for the republicans, he was taken up neither by the Right nor the Left, but remained suspect to them all. Such is the fate reserved in France to the English or Anglo-American school."[19]

Raymond Aron's situation, at least until the last years of his life, was thus in some measure a lonely one. He was certainly not without friends, quite the contrary: His years with the Free French in wartime London, his decades of political journalism, and his professional links to many universities and scholars across the globe had all provided him with a broad range of contacts and colleagues throughout the upper reaches of Western public life. Indeed it was his unusually good connections in government, public administration, and parts of the business world, for example, that gave Aron's editorial writings their authority and conviction.

Nonetheless, Aron was not part of any one community of thinkers. He was too "American" for most French colleagues; too French to fit easily into the world of 1950s American social science; and too liberal and free-thinking to be wholly at ease in the polarized scholarly and political sects molded by the Cold War era. His interests in industrial society, military strategy, and Great-Power relations were unfamiliar to much of his French audience, and his way of writing about these subjects demonstrated an interest in ideas and belief systems not yet commonplace in British or American policy networks and academies.

Intellectual autonomy has its advantages, however. Raymond Aron was largely detached from contemporary analytical conventions while being resolutely engaged in the affairs of his time. It is this combination, I believe, which makes him well worth our attention today. He not only commented insightfully on a world that has moved on but anticipated some of the issues and challenges of the twenty-first century. To take but one example: In his account of international affairs, Aron paid sustained attention to states and their traditional interests. He understood the changes wrought by the emergence of superpowers and the development of nuclear weapons, of course, but was not misled by the scale of change—as some were—into believing that the rules of international relations had changed in some mysterious, fundamental way.

He was therefore properly skeptical of the limits of international entities, whether the United Nations or the newly forming European Community. Like it or not, he argued, we live in a world of states and must make the best of this reality. Whereas if there were to be sustained attempts at forging larger units, for the purpose of securing peace or achieving prosperity, then these units must perforce acquire some of the characteristics of states, without which their prospects are illusory.

He thus appreciated from an early stage something that is only now dawning upon the political and administrative leadership of the European Union: that without a common foreign policy, and a European defense force to back it up, Europe lacks the fundamental building blocks of any sovereign entity and must remain at the mercy of its separate interests. Until this situation changes, international political and military crises will continue to be addressed not by some present or future "European Assembly" but by the national powers directly involved. This observation is as pertinent today as it was when Aron first made it in the context of a crisis in NATO's leadership in 1959.[20]

—

If Raymond Aron transcended his era and is of interest to today's reader, it is, I think, because of his distinctively tragic vision. By this I do not mean that he was a pessimist, much less someone given to predicting terrible futures. On the contrary, Aron's grasp of reality led him as early as September 1947 to the view, as he famously put it, that peace might be impossible, but war was improbable—which turned out to be a pretty fair description of the next forty years of world history. But his was a tragic view of history in a different, deeper sense.

Unlike most of his contemporaries, Aron held out no great hope for the radical transformation of the human condition—whether by revolution, technical invention, or indefinite economic growth. He despised the Soviet "model" but found little to admire in its main competitor—"the U.S. economy seems to me a model neither for humanity nor for the West." His own preference was of course for the West, but he did not share the illusion widespread among many "Cold Warriors" of both sides that History might in due course come to an End.

Aron had no time for such nonsense. The most that could be hoped for, in his view, was constant vigilance to limit the risks and damage of confrontation. This opinion placed him at odds with the dominant sensibility of his era, which held that the object of international relations was somehow to put an end to all wars—whether through nuclear stalemate, the negotiation of a definitive "peace settlement," or else a final victory by one side or the other. For all his vigorous anticommunism, Aron was strikingly moderate, not unlike George Kennan in later years. He believed that the Soviet Union would never deliberately push the world to the brink of war but instead would continue to pursue its objectives through subtle pressure—hence the alternating styles of compromise and confrontation.

This combination of moderation and worldly wisdom turns out to have been not only an accurate insight into the way things were but also an interesting anticipation of the mood of our own times. The Cold War ended and for the moment, at least, the great systems-builders and utopian models are behind us. There is much that is amiss today, but no informed observer imagines that it can or even should be set to rights through a monopoly on power or knowledge. In Aron's words, "Modern society . . . is a democratic society to be observed without transports of enthusiasm or indignation."[21] His "icy clarity" (François Mauriac) has served him well.

Raymond Aron was a trenchant critic of "systems" of any kind. His distaste for the monist doctrinaires of the Left was matched by his dismissal of dogmatic free-marketeers or minimal-state advocates of the Right. In the 1950s and 1960s this stance set him apart. Today Aron, like Isaiah Berlin, another defender of political and intellectual pluralism, has come into his own: He was an economic liberal who abhorred Hayekian system-building (while admiring the Austrian's nonconformist courage); a critic of the establishment who evinced deep distaste for all forms of disorder and confusion, mental and social alike; an anti-Communist who took Marxism seriously; a realist who acknowledged men's political beliefs; a French patriot who recognized and accepted the fact of American imperial power.

Like Berlin, Aron accepted and welcomed a multiplicity of conflicting opinions and objectives: "Theoretical elaboration, in our view, should serve to sharpen awareness of the plurality of goals and aims, rather than favoring the tendency to monoconceptual interpretations, always arbitrary and partisan."[22] It is for this reason that Aron's reading of the history of the twentieth century can still speak to us—because it was never in thrall to the prejudices and aspirations that shaped the story as it was unfolding.

He was, as he once described himself, *le spectateur engagé*, the committed observer, whose cool, dispassionate tone and disabused acceptance of the realities of life in the atomic age hid from sight his deep commitment to the fragile values of an open society. As he described himself when he was admitted to the Académie des Sciences Morales et Politiques, Raymond Aron was a "man without a party, whose opinions offend first one side and then another, who is all the more unbearable because he takes his moderation to excess and hides his passions under his arguments."[23] But his commitment was unmistakable and the passion real. To read Aron now is to be reminded of what was at stake in the great confrontations of the twentieth century and why it mattered so much.

NOTES

1. François Furet, "Raymond Aron, 1905–1983: Histoire et Politique," *Commentaire* 28–29 (1985): 52.

2. "La Cité déchirée: L'Etat et les Communistes," *Le Figaro*, April 11, 1948.

3. Aron, *German Sociology* (New York: Free Press, 1964), p. 86; originally published in 1936 as *La Sociologie allemande contemporaine*. See also *Commentaire* 28–29 (1985): 394, 402. Note, too, the observation in Aron's memoirs: "For a half-century I have restricted my own criticisms by posing this question—'what would I do in their place?'" (Aron, *Memoires: 50 ans de réfléxions politiques* [Paris: Julliard, 1983], p. 632).

4. Aron, "Reflexions sur les problemes economiques français," *Revue de metaphysique et morale*, November 1937, pp. 793–822, quotation from p. 794.

5. Aron, *Penser la guerre: Clausewitz*, vol. 1 (Paris: Gallimard, 1976), p. 53. For an example of the bemusement of his wartime colleagues at Aron's cool dispassion, see Daniel Cordier's remarks in *Commentaire* 28–29 (1985): 24–27.

6. "Conférence sans surprise," *Le Figaro*, July 27, 1955; "Apres Poznan détente sans reniement," *Le Figaro*, July 3, 1956; "Reprise de la guerre froide," *Le Figaro*, June 28, 1958.

7. Aron, *Penser la guerre. Clausewitz*, 2 vols. (Paris: Gallimard, 1976), vol. 2, p. 179.

8. Aron, *D'Une Sainte Famille a l'autre: Essais sur les marxismes imaginaires* (Paris: Gallimard, 1969), p. 13.

9. "Neutralite ou engagement," presentation to Congress for Cultural Freedom in Berlin, July 1950, in Aron, *Polémiques* (Paris: Gallimard, 1955), pp. 199–217.

10. See Aron, *Le Spectateur engagé* (Paris: Julliard, 1981), pp. 10–11, 300.

11. See "Fidélité des apostats" (1950), in Aron, *Polémiques*, p. 81.

12. See "L'unité francaise en peril," *Le Figaro*, October 15, 1955.

13. *Le Spectateur engagé*, pp. 193, 210.

14. "Le scandale de l'O.N.U," *Le Figaro*, October 4, 1955.

15. See "L'unité Atlantique: Enjeu de la crise de Suez," *Le Figaro*, August 8, 1956; "La démonstration necessaire," *Le Figaro*, September 13, 1956; "La Force n'est qu'un moyen," *Le Figaro*, November 2, 1956.

16. Jean-Louis Cremieux-Brilhac, *La France Libre* (Paris: Gallimard, 1996), pp. 192, 389.

17. "L'unite francaise en peril," *Le Figaro*, October 15, 1955.

18. See Aron, *German Sociology*, p. 51. Commenting elsewhere on the airy reflections by André Malraux and others about postindustrial society, the end of a civilization, and the like, Aron remarked, "These vast bird's-eye perspectives terrify me. I plead ignorance." See Aron, *La Revolution introuvable* (Paris: Fayard, 1968), p. 46.

19. Aron, *Les Etapes de la pensée sociologique* (Paris: Gallimard, 1967), p. 18.

20. "Force de frappe européenne," in *Le Figaro*, December 10, 1959.

21. Aron, *Etapes de la pensée sociologique*, p. 296.

22. Aron, "Apropos de la théorie politique," in *Revue française de science politique* XII, (1962), rpt. in Aron, *Etudes politiques* (Paris: Gallimard, 1972), p. 168.

23. Quoted in Nicolas Baverez, *Raymond Aron* (Paris: Flammarion, 1993), p. 338.

NATIONS
AND EMPIRES

There is no historic present without both memory and presentiment. In the middle of the twentieth century, the political universe cannot be grasped in the passing moment alone, for in that moment we encounter not only traces of the events we have lived through previously but also signs of what is to come. Moreover, a person's historical consciousness, his awareness of the present, varies according to the continent, country, and party to which he belongs.

In the case of Europeans, our sense of the present is dominated by two major phenomena: on the one hand the great wars that lately ravaged the Old World, and on the other the disintegration of the empires, built up over centuries, that once caused the Union Jack and the French tricolor to fly over New Delhi and Saigon, central Africa and the distant islands of the Pacific. Might not our understanding be distorted by this "Eurocentrism"? Apparently not.

Our evaluation of past upheavals naturally depends on the point of view from which we survey them. Whereas a European may lament the decline in Western power that resulted from the apocalyptic "great" wars of the twentieth century, a Chinese or Indian observer will rejoice that those conflicts hastened the end of an unnatural tyranny. Westerners remember the benefits they brought to non-Westerners; non-Westerners still resent the humiliations they suffered. One side talks of the breakup of empires, the other of the liberation of nations. But verbal differences should not prevent us from agreeing on essential facts.

Perhaps, in the future, American, Russian, Chinese, and Indian historians will see the European wars of the twentieth century quite differently and accord no more importance to those last convulsions of a dying civilization than this "little cape of Asia" warrants. Without the genius of Thucydides, the Peloponnesian War might have loomed no larger in the works of Roman historians than did the drowsy Greek cities in the Roman

Empire itself. And posterity may well modify the significance we ourselves attribute to episodes in our tumultuous century. So, although we cannot escape our own time and all that goes with it, nor must we exclude from our assessments the points of view of other observers appraising events from latitudes different from our own. Any appraisal is and must be related to a date and a place.

However, to be Europe-oriented in the middle of the twentieth century brings with it more benefits than disadvantages. Plainly, what has happened in Europe has largely determined what has happened in the rest of the world. It may be plausibly argued that India was bound to become independent sooner or later: But the Republic of India, a member of the Commonwealth governed by Jawaharlal Nehru, emerged out of the two European wars. We tend to think that whatever happened, China, after the troubled period resulting from the decline of the Manchu dynasty and the effects of Western influence, would eventually have become a strong power again and embarked on a policy of industrialization: But the China of Mao Tse-tung, of the Five-Year Plans, and Marxism-Leninism can be understood only in relation to events and to the evolution of ideas in Europe—to the 1917 revolution, to the assassination of an archduke in an obscure corner of the Austro-Hungarian Empire, to Hegel and Marx. People often dig up quotations from Alexis de Tocqueville to show that the rise of both Russia and the United States was written down in advance in the book of fate. And perhaps such developments really were inevitable on both those continents because of the vast spaces they had at their disposal, whereas Europe was divided up into jealous individual states. Nonetheless, it took two threats of German hegemony to make the United States aware of its own enormous power. And not until the European nations were exhausted did the Soviet Union come to seem invincible both to itself and to others. Even if they did not actually create them, Europe's two twentieth-century wars revealed the forces that dominate the world today.

They were world wars not only because their repercussions were felt to the ends of the earth; because Senegalese and Indians came and died in the Flanders mud; because the English beat a path through the Malaysian jungles; because the Solomon Islands provided a setting for the conflict between Americans and Japanese. What have become known as World Wars I and II were fought with weapons and in the name of values (and words) that had their source in the civilization of Europe. Forty years separated the taxis of the Marne from the atomic bomb—a transition between two distinct eras of military capabilities and industrialization. Now more than at any other time, armies, in both their structure and their equipment, are reflections of their society. The preeminence of the European nations was doomed to collapse as soon as the human masses of Asia acquired the same means of production and the same weapons of war as those that had conferred power and prosperity on the Europeans.

The Europeans exported their ideas at the same time as their machines. A century ago they saw no contradiction between the principle of nationalities they themselves espoused and the distant conquests they embarked on with such clear consciences. They believed that as "superior nations" they had the right to rule over "inferior" ones. But this implicit racism could not survive indefinitely the discovery on the one hand of the greatness of other civilizations and on the other the realization of how precarious Europe's supremacy really was. The wars brought out the contradiction between the principle on which order in Europe was based and the principle on which European empires outside Europe reposed. France and Britain fought or pretended to fight for a nation's right to self-determination but refused to grant the benefits of this right to the peoples of Africa and Asia. It is no accident that the concepts of *nation* and *empire* have gained currency all over the world and seem to embody an antithesis between good and evil. The widespread use of these two terms has given rise to much ambiguity and confusion.

The ideal type of a national state is a political unit all of whose citizens belong to the same culture and wish to live in an autonomous community. An imperial state is one that is imposed, usually by conquest, on peoples of different languages and cultures. We should probably add to this list at least a third ideal type—that of the federal state (Switzerland, for example), which involves neither homogeneity of culture nor imposed power. Moreover, our first two ideal types are never completely put into practice, and it is difficult to assign cases that fall between the two categories to either one or the other.

Even within a national state such as France there are minorities whose languages (Basque, Celtic, and so on) and cultures are not those of the majority. A homogeneous culture is the result of history—in other words, often of a series of conquests. Finally, de facto membership in a culture does not always carry with it a wish to belong to the corresponding political unit. In 1871 the people of Alsace spoke a Germanic dialect. They had been incorporated into the Holy Roman Empire, a Germanic state, in the Middle Ages, but in 1871, despite the Prussian victory, they still wanted to be French. The principle of nationalities could be interpreted in various ways, with emphasis placed on the free choice of the individual (as in the French version) or on the idea of an essential nation to which people belonged even if in practice they rejected it (a version to which German ideology tended).

The notion of empire is equally hard to pin down. Tsarist Russia, together with its heir, the Soviet Union, was the result of a series of military conquests. Many peoples, of various languages and cultures, were subjected to the rule of Moscow. Before he came to power himself, Lenin denounced the imperialism of the tsars and their acquisition of foreign territories. The right of secession for nonnative nationalities formed part of the Bolshevik program, and it is still, in the middle of the twentieth century, extant in official Soviet documents. Might the nationalities concerned have made use of the right of secession at the time of the revolution? Would they do so today if they were allowed? One could speculate forever about what might have happened or might still happen, but such speculation is pointless. Let us merely note that there are still imperial states in existence today that are made up of communities subscribing to a number of different cultures. We cannot exclude the possibility of a kind of imperial patriotism, whether Tsarist or Soviet, that might command the loyalty of even a large section of nonnative populations. There is no point in abstract discussion of the right of cultural communities to exercise political sovereignty.

The words *nationalism* and *imperialism,* as used in propaganda, are even more equivocal than *nation* and *empire.* The nationalism of the Tunisians and the Moroccans is bound up with their claim to independence. But what is meant by the nationalism of the French or the Germans once their respective countries are securely established as national units? Does the word convey a grandiose conception of the role of the nation, or merely an attachment to the particular values each country embodies? In one case we are dealing with a will to power that expresses itself in a desire for expansion, and in the other with a patriotism without which the state itself could not survive. Under the influence of revolution or religion, or in the name of universality or particularism, all the great exponents of nationalism have eventually come to accept conquest, inconsistent though it is, in theory, with the idea of nationality. The Jacobins spread liberty at the point of the bayonet; the Pan-Germanists dreamed of uniting all Germans in one state even before Hitler and his followers proclaimed the right of the master race to enslave "inferior" races. The messianism of the "Third Rome"[1] was a forerunner of the ideology that called for the liberation of the proletariat.

All this explains why "our" nationalism is seen as imperialist by "others"—a confusion compounded by the fact that when national states replaced monarchies they accepted their predecessors' diplomatic practices. As long as aggrandizement was seen as a natural law governing the conduct of all states, nationalism easily became imperialism and ideology seemed the legitimate servant of the will to power. In 1848, and again in 1918, the desire for nationhood, taken together with the liberal ideal, was seen by optimists to promise peace with liberty. But in both 1848 and 1939, and throughout the history of the twentieth century, the struggle for hegemony emerged as the dominant theme, even if German unity and the liberation of the national entities of central and eastern Europe are regarded as motivating ideas rather than merely the arguments of jurists and philosophers.

Outside Europe, imperialism seems easily recognizable when it appears in the form of European domination. But while political imperialism, symbolized by the annexation of sovereignty, may be clearly enough defined, where does economic imperialism begin and end? Lenin's book[2] popularized the theory that the countries of Europe were forced by the inconsistencies inherent in capitalism to look abroad for new markets, raw materials, and profits. But whatever the true causes of European expansion, that expansion preceded "monopoly capitalism." The Indian Empire was created and North America populated before capitalism reached its final stages, and in 1914 the African colonies occupied only a modest place in the world economy.

One need not subscribe to the whole of Lenin's thesis to understand why the economic superiority of the West was seen by the peoples of Asia and the Middle East as imperialism, even when it did not actually lead to the establishment of a colonial regime. The exploitation of raw materials without any attempt to create local industry; the destruction of native crafts and the stunted growth of industrial development that resulted from the influx of European goods; high interest rates on loans; ownership of major businesses by foreign capitalists—all these were dubbed imperialistic even when unaccompanied by political pressure, whether open or covert, on the governments of the independent countries concerned. This extension of the meaning of *imperialism* can be explained in terms of the emotional reactions involved, which, even if not always justified, were at least understandable. But in the interest of clarity we need to distinguish between three different interpretations of the word: the imperialism that leads to the legal establishment of a colonial regime or protectorate; that which takes the form of a de facto domination by a strong state over a weaker one; and that which functions on the plane of economics alone and consists in unilateral influence brought to bear by a major economy on a minor one.

These last two forms of imperialism seem as ineradicable as unequal power and unequal economic development among states. A country that expects to derive a third or a half of its income from tin, copper, or coffee depends on its main buyer more than the buyer depends on a supplier who doesn't possess a monopoly. A country that wants to attract foreign capital has to accept either that some of its businesses will belong to foreigners or that some of its resources will have to come from loans or gifts. We may speak of dollar or ruble imperialism when U.S. or Soviet capital opens up other countries to technicians, ideas, or influences originating in one or other of the two giant states, but it does not follow that the beneficiaries of such interested generosity need see themselves as victims. The more primitive forms of exploitation are tending to die out.

The changes that have occurred on the world scene in the past half-century are plain for all to see. If we take iron and steel production as a rough guide to military potential, the Soviet Union, with 4.2 million metric tons, was outclassed in 1913 by Germany (14.3 metric tons) and Great Britain (7.8 metric tons). In 1955, iron and steel production in the USSR equaled that of Great Britain and Germany put together (20.1 and 24.7 metric tons, respectively). Similarly, in Asia, Japan's military superiority is a thing of the past. In one generation China's Five-Year Plans will provide it with industrial resources that, mobilized for war, would be considerably greater than those available to Japan when it set out to create a sphere of coprosperity.

But even though, as regards the balance of power, a relatively clear provisional pattern emerges for the first half of the twentieth century, the significance of the international system as a whole remains obscure. Are we witnessing nothing more than the replacement of dying empires by younger ones, in an unbroken sequence of violence and injustice? Have the nations of Europe, like the cities of ancient Greece, had to abdicate from their former power because they clung to an outmoded principle of political organization? What kind of order is now being brought into being by the fighting techniques, the modes of production, and the passions of men?

I. THE DESTRUCTION OF THE EUROPEAN SYSTEM

The suggestion, now commonplace, that nations and nationalisms were responsible for Europe's decline is either self-evident or debatable according to the meaning one ascribes to the words themselves. Europe was once divided up into nations in the same way that ancient Greece was divided up into cities. If, following Albert Thibaudet, we compare the conflict that began in 1914 with the Peloponnesian War, we will easily conclude that modern Europe was the victim of rivalry between nations just as ancient Greece was the victim of rivalry between cities. But we still need to ask why such rivalries, a century earlier seen by Leopold von Ranke as consonant with the mission and favorable to the greatness of Europe, are now regarded as having been fatal. And because the provisional outcome of history largely accounts for our judgments, we are bound to wonder if we really should hold the various kinds of nationalism responsible for the ravages wrought in the twentieth century by the rivalry itself.

The case for the prosecution, which is encountered more or less everywhere, is impressive. The 1914 war arose out of quarrels in the Balkans over claims to nationhood. It was to counter the threat to the dualist monarchy of the Austro-Hungarian Empire, embodied in Serbian propaganda and addressed to the Southern Slavs, that the Austro-Hungarian ministers took the measures (the ultimatum to Serbia, the shelling of Belgrade) that sowed the seeds of a European war. It was Slav solidarity that prevented the government in St. Petersburg from allowing Serbian independence to be destroyed and from letting the Austro-Hungarian Empire win a diplomatic victory. It was national pride, the belief that the fatherland was destined to be a global power and that German culture should shine its luminosity throughout the world, that aroused the enthusiasm of the masses in the empire of Wilhelm II in 1914 and made the workers forget their former socialism. It was the will to survive as a Great Power and to recover their lost provinces that suddenly united the French and sustained them through years of tribulation.

During the first months of the war, nationalist passions reached an extreme, almost pathological degree of intensity both in Germany and in France. Rereading now the literature in which great writers reacted to events at the time, one cannot help feeling embarrassed, sometimes even ashamed. But in certain circumstances national unity is indispensable. A community cannot survive unless its members forget their quarrels when they have to confront an enemy from without. And while the attachment to national values shown on both banks of the Rhine before 1914 may in retrospect seem to us excessive and dangerously close to the rantings of propaganda, was the diplomacy that led up to the war really inspired by the violent emotions felt by the Germans as Germans or the French as Frenchmen?

Although such questions cannot be answered with a categorical yes or no, we can say that in the decades preceding the final explosion and the outbreak of hostilities, diplomatic activity was no different from what it had been in the past. Two coalitions were shaping up, with the central empires on the one hand and Tsarist Russia and the Anglo-French Entente on the other. But not every country was drawn in. Some, like Italy, remained noncommittal and did not break off relations with members of either camp. Neither Russia nor Britain refused to negotiate eventually with Germany. An interview between the tsar and the kaiser, and an English proposal about the Portuguese colonies,[3] remind us, if we needed reminding, that in pre-1914 Europe the two opposing sides were nothing like as rigid and clearly defined as the two blocs left facing one another after World War II.

The makeup of the coalitions formed before World War I was not dictated by the real or supposed extremes of British or German or French pride, or by the Pan-German or Pan-Slav doctrines that were stirring up unrest in some circles inside the Russian and German Empires. Ever since 1870, France had automatically been opposed to Germany. But although the yearning for a turning of the tables, the hope that Alsace-Lorraine would one day be part of France again, might have prevented any complete reconciliation with Germany, these feelings did not call for active hostility, still less for outright war. Traditional regard for the national interest and the desire to maintain the balance of power meant that allies must be sought in order to make up for the disparity between the strength of the German and French armies. Great Britain ranged itself on the side of Germany's enemies: Neither public opinion nor government circles compared the merits of the cultures involved or were motivated by collective pride. Britain felt threatened not so much by Germany's commercial expansion as by its building of a rival fleet. As Alfred T. Mahan put it,[4] the geopolitical situation of the two countries was such that the defense of Britain's very existence incidentally involved control of the sea-lanes leading to and from Germany. This being so, any challenge on the part of Germany to the Royal Navy's mastery of the seas was bound to seem like an attempt to strike at the very heart of Britain. Seen from England, Germany's naval policy seemed aggressive even though it was designed to be defensive, and conversely, seen from Germany, Britain's desire for maritime supremacy looked imperialistic.

Relations between Russia and Germany were, however, more influenced by popular sentiment. Wilhelm II did not renew the treaty of reassurance by which Bismarck had set such store. But in the long run he would have had to choose between St. Petersburg and Vienna. The alliance between the conservative regimes was undermined not so much by German ambitions as by the conflicts between Austria and Russia in the Balkans. In this sense, nationalism—not in the form of mass enthusiasm within established national states, but rather in the form of calls for independence on the part of national groups incorporated into the multinational empires—was one of the historical causes of World War I. The disintegration of the Ottoman Empire looked like both a precedent and a threat to the Austro-Hungarian monarchy. The empire was indeed troubled by conflicts between nationalities, and these conflicts go a long way toward explaining the diplomatic policy adopted by the cabinet in Vienna in 1914.

It would be wrong, with hindsight, however, to oversimplify the course of events and to imagine the peoples of central and eastern Europe chafing against their oppressor and eager to throw off the Viennese yoke. Although there seems to be no doubt that the Poles longed to see their country become an independent state again, neither the Czechs nor the Slavs were unanimously hostile to the continuation of Austro-Hungarian rule. Before 1914, a federal-type solution might have managed to settle quarrels in which the bones of contention—electoral, educational, and linguistic equality—strike us, at this distance in time, as curiously undramatic. When in 1917, while the war was still going on, Tomas G. Masaryk and Eduard Benes persuaded the Allies to accept as one of their war aims the liberation of oppressed nationalities, and consequently the dissolution of the Hapsburg Empire, not all the Czech protests in Prague were made under constraint.

In the nineteenth century the movement of nationalities had ended in German and Italian unity. These two large states had managed to form and to insert themselves into the European system without provoking wars like those that had arisen out of the revolution and the empire, or even out of French and Spanish hegemony. But in the twentieth century the movement of nationalities tended not toward integration but rather toward the breaking down of political units. The Germans, brought together at last in a national state, repudiated the principle they had recently invoked by denying the Poles the right to political sovereignty. If political units needed the cement of a common culture or a common will to bind them together, the Turkish Empire was doomed, and the Austro-Hungarian Empire, if it was to survive, would have needed to win the voluntary loyalty of its culturally and linguistically diverse citizens. But the miracle of the nineteenth century, which had solved the problems of integration posed by the movement of nationalities, was not repeated in the twentieth, when the disintegration or restructuring of political units arising out of the movement of nationalities unleashed a general war that in its scale and its consequences far outstripped the events that brought it about. War itself became the main fact, for which the conflicts of nationalities merely provided an occasion. From the day the guns began to speak, the whole status of Europe itself was at stake. Once again people were confronted with a choice between hegemony and equilibrium, as in the revolutionary wars, the wars of Spanish supremacy, and the Peloponnesian Wars. Whatever its aims had been in July 1914, a victorious Germany would have dominated Europe just as Athens, if it had vanquished Sparta, would have suppressed the liberties of the other Greek cities.

The retrospective polemics over responsibility for the war are significant. Pacifist sentiment and ideology, which in democratic societies can coexist with extremes of belligerency, do not completely explain the indictments of the judge-historians charged with seeking out culprits, as if it were a matter of conscience to condemn those responsible for starting the war. The targets had to be people whose crimes were in proportion to the catastrophe itself. The intentions of statesmen were assumed to be as monstrous as the battles and the devastation of the war. But no hard and fast explanation was possible: Historical events are too ambiguous for that. Even if a unanimous verdict could have been reached as to the diplomatic responsibilities involved during the weeks between the assassination of the archduke and Germany's declaration of war on France, it would still have left prosecutors and juries alike dubious and disappointed. For this was a war no one wanted.

Austria's ultimatum to Serbia, the rejection of Serbia's reply, the shelling of Belgrade, the blank check the German ministers gave more or less openly to their Viennese counterparts at the beginning of July—all these Austro-German initiatives constituted, as was clearly understood in the capitals of the Central Powers, a throwing down of the gauntlet to Russia and indirectly to the Entente. The scale of the hostilities would not have been greater if the Allies had declined to take up the challenge and allowed the central empires to enjoy a diplomatic victory. The leaders of the Central Powers had all recognized the danger and decided to take the risk. Some members of the Viennese cabinet and the German general staff hoped the Allies *would* take up the challenge. But both Russia and France did so with such resolution that historians refuse to acknowledge any essential difference between the psychology of the statesmen on either side. Neither of the two camps condemned war *absolutely* as a means of resolving differences between states; neither side foresaw what kind of war they were getting themselves into. The German and Austrian leaders were the first to make the fateful decisions; in 1914 the war party was stronger in Berlin and Vienna than in Paris or London. But forty years later such observations are of little interest.

But all the general staffs were surprised by the course hostilities took. None of them had foreseen a long war; none had made arrangements to mobilize their economy; none had built up stocks to cover more than a few months' fighting. All were equally unprepared, an anomaly that saved face all round and enabled opportunists like Emil Rathenau or Albert Thomas, whether industrialists or militant socialists, to make up for the shortcomings of the military establishment.

But why had the army chiefs failed to learn the lesson taught by long conflicts such as the American Civil War, perhaps the first modern war of logistics? Why did they think the issue would be decided by the first few battles? The error is perhaps less excusable in the Allies than in the Central Powers. It is conceivable that the latter might have been able to win in the first clash of arms, whereas the former would always have had to rely for eventual victory on their potentially superior forces, their mastery of the seas, and the possibility of blockading the enemy into exhaustion and submission.

The Germans lost their chance of a quick victory on the Marne in September 1914. Once the western front was stabilized, no local successes, however spectacular, were decisive. All the countries involved were discovering with horror the vastness of the material means that modern democratic and industrial societies could make available for war. The fact that the opposing forces were roughly equal, together with the temporary superiority of defense rather than attack as a favored policy, helped make the strategy of attrition imposed by circumstance find symbolic expression in trench warfare.

The war had begun before any of the individual belligerents or coalitions had clearly defined their aims. The hostilities themselves called forth not only historic claims, which had remained latent so long as the last word still rested with the diplomats, but also precise objectives hitherto consigned to secret treaties as well as grandiose and undefinable ideologies such as democracy, popular liberties, and justice. The French, who had never renounced their claim to Alsace-Lorraine but did not really want to go to war to recover it, would have seen a peace based on the status quo antebellum as a defeat. In order to bring the Italians into the war, the Entente had signed a secret treaty promising Italy territorial gains that could not all be justified in terms of the principles of nationality (these included Trentino [Cisalpine], Tyrol as far as the Brenner Pass, Trieste, Istria, part of the Dalmatian coast, plus some islands, and parts of the Ottoman Empire in Asia Minor and of the German colonies in Africa). In reply to a German proposal for negotiations at the end of 1916, the Entente made known its own conditions, which included the restoration of independence to Belgium, Serbia, and Montenegro, the evacuation of all occupied territories, the restitution of Alsace-Lorraine, the freeing of Italians, Slavs, Romanians, and Czechs from foreign domination, and the liberation of the peoples subjected to "the bloodthirsty tyranny of the Turks." The references to the liberation of Slavs and Czechs seemed to imply the destruction of the Austro-Hungarian Empire.

But it would not be right to say that even in 1916 the diplomats of the Entente regarded the destruction of the dualist monarchy as a war aim. This possibility was a matter of ideology rather than an actual policy, although it was then that the Masaryk-Benes committee gained influence in French political circles. In 1917, when Emperor Charles I tried to obtain a separate peace, the Allied powers did not yet feel committed to "liberating the Czechs." But the efforts of Franz-Joseph's successor came to nothing because of Italy's demands, the defeat at Caporetto, and hesitation on the part of both France and Britain.

Hostilities gave rise to apparent inconsistencies on both sides: Lofty ideas were proclaimed at the same time as diplomats drew up agreements that conformed to the usual cynicism of power politics. By a secret agreement made in February 1917, the French government obtained the promise of Russian support for the return of Alsace-Lorraine, the annexation of the Saar Basin, and the creation of an autonomous state on the left bank of the Rhine. France in exchange would leave its cosignatory free to fix its own western frontier—in other words, France abandoned Poland to Russia. England was determined not to give Germany back its former colonies and in June 1916 made an agreement with Russia and France whereby they divided the Middle East up between them into zones of influence. The other side did not consign its ambitions to secret documents, but as late as April 1917 the German military was demanding large territorial gains in the East, in Courland and Lithuania, and a form of protectorate over Poland. Belgium was to remain under German control: Liège and the Belgian coast were to be under military occupation for ninety-nine years, and the Briey-Longwy Basin was to be annexed.

In every country the patriotic unanimity of the early days had gradually been eroded by suffering and disillusion. From 1916 on, all the belligerents experienced labor unrest and strikes. At the beginning of the war, in Germany as well as in France, the socialists had joined the *union sacrée,* or movement of national unity, but a growing number of them now broke away. The war was undermining the unanimity of national states at the same time as it strengthened the demands of nationalist groups in central and eastern Europe. The dualist monarchy of Austria-Hungary fell victim to a war that some of its leaders had hoped would save it.

Judged by appearances, the outcome of World War I might be seen as the logical consequence of the circumstances that had started it: Austria-Hungary, torn by nationalist conflicts, had sought in foreign adventure the federal-style solution that could be brought about only by internal reform. The Allied victory gave all the oppressed nationalities the independence that had been denied them by the moribund Ottoman and Austro-Hungarian Empires. But this interpretation of events was merely an illusion.

Because of the way the peoples concerned were intermingled, it was to all intents and purposes impossible to apply the principle of nationalities in

Central Europe. Czechoslovakia, the main successor to Austria-Hungary, was no less multinational a state than the former dual empire. In Poland, too, minorities made up almost a third of the population. Nowhere had it been possible to use the principle of nationalities alone as a guide. The Czechs had acquired sovereignty over the territory of the Sudetens through geographical and military considerations. Poland's western frontier had been determined as the result of war. The Polish government laid claim to the lands east of the Curzon Line in the name of historic rights rather than on the basis of debatable statistics relating to nationalities. None of the new frontiers had been accepted definitively: Romania and Hungary were at loggerheads over Transylvania, Czechoslovakia and Poland were at odds over Teschen territory, while Romania disagreed with Bulgaria over Dobruja. Wherever the peasants spoke one language and the ruling class another, or a historically and geographically determined unit included a mixture of different nationalities, majority rule could not provide an adequate answer for a problem insoluble by its very nature.

But the Europe of nationalities, as it emerged from the Treaty of Versailles, was at risk from another and even more marked inconsistency. Quarrels over nationality had been the cause or occasion of the original explosion, and the liberation of oppressed national groups had been a theme of Allied propaganda before it actually came about under the pressure of events in 1918. What had been at stake in the war itself was the status of the Old Continent as a whole: Would the conflict result in the hegemony of Germany or in the triumph of maritime power, aided by continental allies too weak to stand alone against the dominant territorial power? Whatever part France and Russia may have played in land battles, victory on the historical plane belonged once again to maritime power. The mastery of the seas that had enabled the Allies to blockade the Central Powers had finally overcome the European country that possessed the best army. Wilhelm II was defeated in the same way as Louis XIV and Napoleon had been before him.

Events confirmed Mahan's famous theories, but the confirmation was difficult and slow in coming. Britain had to increase its contribution to the fighting on land. Armies, their mobility increased now that transport could be provided by automobiles as well as railways, came to play a more important part in the war than navies. Logistics on a continental scale were no longer too much for the technical and administrative resources available, as they had been in Napoleon's day. The new factor, which must have impressed contemporaries and determined the conduct of the politicians, was not the ultimate triumph of maritime power but the need for American troops to intervene on the front in France in order to decide the outcome.

European history has never taken place in isolation, nor has recourse to a non-European ally been the monopoly of any one state. For at least two centuries the course of European politics had been greatly influenced by the relations between the Old Continent and the other parts of the world, by the possibilities for emigration offered by hitherto unsettled territories, and by the resources that Britain could call on when at war from its overseas possessions and its trade with Asia and the Americas. But the role played by the U.S. Army in 1918 symbolized the beginning of a new age: The United States was becoming the arbiter of European wars because, in the earlier context, Germany was becoming too powerful, and German hegemony was unacceptable not only to Britain but also, through an Anglo-Saxon solidarity that came into play in times of crisis, to the United States.

The territorial arrangements made at Versailles, imperfect as they were, and although they created as many new demands as they settled old ones, might be regarded as logical enough in terms of the ideologies that had been bandied about and the passions that had been aroused. But they contradicted the conclusions any observer might have drawn from the course of the fighting. Germany had succumbed to a coalition made up of Russia, France, and the two English-speaking countries, Britain and the United States. The latter, whose hegemony was the inexorable outcome of World War I, was now losing interest in European affairs, and this withdrawal was to be as fatal for peace and equilibrium as any thirst for conquest. Russia, taken over by the Bolshevik party, no longer played its traditional role. There was no reason why it should defend an order—involving the independence of the Baltic states, Poland's western border, and Romanian Bessarabia—that had been established without its assent and against its interests. Britain and France, the only members of the victorious coalition that might have been expected to agree on maintaining the status quo, never managed to follow a common policy either on Germany or on Eastern Europe. The territorial arrangements set down in the Treaty of Versailles did not reflect the balance of power: It was the result of an exceptional situation arising from the temporary helplessness of the two great continental powers, Russia and Germany. Defeat and humiliation had made the latter more hungry than ever for conquest and more convinced than before of its unique greatness. When a rearmed Germany reoccupied the west bank of the Rhine it possessed a de facto hegemony over Central and Eastern Europe, between the frontiers of Russia and France. In September 1938, through threats and cunning and without firing a shot, Hitler obtained what had been denied to the Germany of Wilhelm II. A year later he deliberately unleashed a war to transform that hegemony into an empire.

Meanwhile, thanks to an economic depression of unprecedented proportions, a revolution had taken place, and both Britain and France underestimated the significance of this turn of events in Germany. In the long run, no German regime would have accepted the territorial arrangements laid down at Versailles. But a moderate, monarchical, or parliamentary one would not have cherished extravagant ambitions; it would have feared that in a second world war the same coalition as before, of Russia, Britain, and the United States, would re-form to crush the German Reich. But Hitler was beyond such calculations: Although he exploited national passions and appealed to the past, his racist ideology and plans for a New Order left behind the previous age of nationalities. The ideas of the kaiser's Germany were influenced by Pan-Germanism, ordinary expansionism, and a desire for hegemony or an international role: Diplomatic tradition and collective pride intermingled without producing a definite program. But the leaders of the Third Reich wanted to unify Europe and subject each of its constituent nations to a regime tailored to suit its place in the racial hierarchy. As soon as war came, the harshness of German occupation varied from East to West. The Slavs were treated as subhuman, the Poles had a "federal government" imposed on them, the Czechs a "protectorate"; France was supposed to retain a nominal sovereignty; the Jews were exterminated.

In a way, the stakes were the same in World War II as in World War I: The choice was between German hegemony and the balance of power. But in the later conflict the threat to the independence of nations was greater than it had been twenty years before. The openly proclaimed imperialism of Hitler's Germany marked a historic change. In most countries, national unity was weaker than it had been in 1914. France, in 1939, saw nothing like the *union sacrée*, the union of all Frenchmen against the enemy that Raymond Poincaré had spoken of at the beginning of World War I: Frenchmen now did not rise as one above their partisan quarrels. Some were paralyzed by the absurdity of the idea that the whole of Europe might be involved in a ruinous war; others so hated communism or democracy that they came to sympathize with fascism or National Socialism. Certain minorities of various sizes were half won over by the New Order before the first shot was fired. But despite some legends it seems that fifth columns did not play much part in the German victories of 1939–1941, which can be accounted for simply by the superiority of the Wehrmacht. After France was defeated, the ranks of the fifth columns were swelled by opportunists and fascists because the armistice, concluded by a legitimate government, had released them from having to treat the Third Reich as an enemy. Germany encouraged such "collaborators" with varying degrees of enthusiasm according to the countries in which they operated.

During World War I the German government, which until 1917 was against restoring Belgium's independence and territorial integrity, had favored the constitution proposed by the Council of Flanders, which broke with the monarchy, set up a customs union with Germany, and appointed a representative committee to act as a kind of provisional government. During World War II, the German authorities supported such parties and men in the occupied countries as were willing to govern them in accordance with the ideas and interests of the Third Reich. They hoped by so doing to establish the nucleus of a French, Dutch, and Norwegian National Socialist elite that would emerge in the Europe of the future.

But this policy of breaking up nations in order to form an empire was not implemented clearly or firmly. Historians have been struck by the inadequacy of the moral and material help that General Vlassov received from the German government, despite the distinguished role he had played when fighting for Russia before he turned against the Soviet regime. The Nazis clung so fiercely to the doctrine that other peoples were inferior to the Germans, and were so avid to impose themselves as the master race, that they threw away the chance of winning over to their side the Russians who hated Stalin and communism. Even in the West, where it would not have been impossible to carry out a policy of destroying national identities, the actions of the German authorities were divided because of the conflicting requirements of the army leaders, who wished above all to maintain order; of the economic planners, who were anxious to maximize the labor force; and of the officials responsible for propaganda and infiltration.

In certain European countries the weakening of nationalist passion was equally evident on the Right and on the Left. Among the privileged classes and in conservative circles, some had been led by their own anti-Communist sentiments to show a degree of indulgence toward Hitler. In occupied France some intellectuals and politicians declared themselves in favor of the New Order. But the majority of those who followed Marshal Philippe Pétain in 1940 saw in the old soldier both the symbol of their homeland and a promise of its restoration. At the other end of the spectrum, the workers, mindful of the propaganda directed against the "imperialist war" in 1939–1940, did not wish to see France defeated. When the line taken by the Communist Party coincided with their patriotic instincts and the interests of France, they showed by their heroism how glad they were to be able to reconcile their two loyalties. But when there was a conflict, most militant Communists, whatever the state of their conscience, put their party first.

At the end of World War II, Europe presented a complex and contradictory picture of the nature of national units and the structures behind the balance of power. In terms of frontiers as shown on maps, the Europe of today, even more than that of 1918, is a Europe of nationalities. The states brought into being at Versailles are still there. Both multinational empires—Turkey and Austria-Hungary—disappeared. Turkey renounced the idea of the Ottoman Empire and turned itself into a national state. Out of the Austro-Hungarian Empire came the national states of Austria and Hungary. The principle of nationalities was applied with pitiless severity through the transfer of populations. The Czechs expelled the Sudeten Germans, called in by the kings of Bohemia four centuries earlier. The Poles flowed back from the territories east of the Curzon Line and drove the Germans out of the lands east of the Oder-Neisse. Yugoslavia survived as a federal republic. The new Czech, Hungarian, and Romanian frontiers conformed more closely than the old to the notion of nationalism.

Rivalry between national states had faded, however, because Soviet power was so dominant east of the Iron Curtain and European countries to the west of it felt so dependent on the United States. Political entities, as they existed according to international law, were national in nature. Military entities, as they existed in fact, were imperial. NATO set the seal on occidental military integration, joining together Western Europe and North America. The common headquarters set up by Moscow in reply simply formalized the bloc represented by the presence of Soviet divisions in Germany and the power of the Communist parties in the popular democracies of Eastern Europe.

Germany was the main victim of the contradiction between the national entities and the imperialist military ones. As the country responsible for the war that had delivered the coup de grace to the old European system, it lost territories in the East that had been German for centuries and was divided into two pieces, each attached to one of the victorious coalitions—that is, into two countries, one of which declared itself a popular democracy while the other became a federal republic.

Although Germany was physically divided, other countries, in particular France and Italy, were split morally. A minority of the electorate voted for the party that supported internationalism, though that idea was really bound up with the fate of a foreign country. The Communists spoke and acted as if they put ideology before nationality. Those who claimed to defend their own national independence against Soviet domination felt vaguely uneasy at the thought that their country's fate was imposed on it rather than created from within: Some hankered after greater territory, comparable to what had existed earlier in the century, while others rebelled against an alliance made to look like serfdom by their own relative weakness. In the West as a whole the labor parties' conversion to reformism, and the refusal to accept an Internationale manipulated by an empire, reconciled most of the proletariat to their countries and to democratic socialism. But the reconciliation was incomplete, especially in France and Italy; it had more of resignation in it than enthusiasm, demonstrating that ideological passions were worn out.

On the other side of the Iron Curtain neither Russian domination nor communist-type regimes were accepted by the great majority of the population. The sacrifices demanded by the rapid construction of heavy industries, together with the suppression of civil liberties, were held against governments who owed their power to the Russian army. How strong would national feeling prove, and how attractive a federal order, if the countries of Eastern Europe, created at Versailles and illusorily restored in 1944–1945, were to become masters of their own fate again? The question could not be answered so long as the Russian and American armies faced one another along the demarcation line, splitting into two military blocs a Europe legally divided up into nations.

2. THE SETTING UP OF THE ASIATIC BLOC

The first so-called World War was really a European conflict. The operations carried out in Africa against the German colonies were no more than
an extension of the battles in the north. They provided the Allies with
guarantees. The campaigns in the Middle East arose, on the one hand, out
of the alliance between the Sublime Porte and the Central Powers, and on
the other out of Britain's desire to destroy the Ottoman Empire. Japan entered the conflict in order to get hold of Germany's possessions in the Pacific (the Caroline, Mariana, and Marshall Islands and Kiaochow). Although the intervention of the United States enlarged the zone of
hostilities, it did not fundamentally change the character of the struggle or
alter the stakes. The Entente would have had to make peace if it had not
been able to call upon the resources of the New World. The United States,
having tipped the balance in favor of the Allies, soon left the French and
the English to manage the common victory. It was possible for the nations
of Europe to think they were still the main players and that the sending of
an American expeditionary force was merely an isolated episode. In 1945
such a delusion was no longer possible.

The war became a world war at the end of 1941. Under cover of
Hitler's adventure, Japan set out to build an Asian empire on its own account. Events in the Far East were linked in many ways to those in Europe.
But the war in the Pacific, in which the main protagonists were Japan and
the United States, had neither the same origin nor the same meaning as the
war in Europe, although the use of the same words (fascism, imperialism,
and so on), the diplomatic partnerships (the German-Japanese alliance),
the force of the military operations, and the ultimately decisive action of
the Soviet Union and the United States all reflected a gradual if partial unification of world diplomacy.

Whatever debate there may be about President Franklin D. Roosevelt's
intentions and decisions in the months leading up to the attack on Pearl
Harbor, the cause of the war is plain for all to see. Hitler wanted to create
by force of arms a New Order in Europe and Africa, perhaps throughout
the whole world. Japan, engaged since 1937 in an exhausting attempt to
subjugate China, in 1941 launched an attack on the United States and
Britain. The generals who ruled in Tokyo would probably not have come
to this decision if Britain had not been struggling with Hitler's Germany

and if they had not assumed that at least some American forces would be tied up in Europe. The wars in Europe did not cause Japanese imperialism: They did provide it with an opportunity, however.

It is not such an easy matter to explain Japanese imperialism. It is astonishing that a country that for two centuries had cut itself off from the rest of the world, practically excluding all foreign contacts, should have embarked on the path of conquest as soon as it decided to borrow the secret of power from the West.

Japan, China, and India, the three main countries in Asia, cannot be easily likened historically to the type of state found in Europe. Arnold Toynbee saw each of them as a civilization in itself. Indeed, in terms of size, as well as of diversity of languages and cultures, India is more like the whole of Europe than like any of the single countries that make it up. China is not so heterogeneous with regard to either politics or culture, though the Kingdom of the Middle did include crowds of different religions and ways of life. But the unity of the 2,000-year-old empire was felt as the natural order, and ideographic writing made communications easy among the educated classes. Finally, Japan, just before the arrival of Commander Matthew C. Perry in 1853,[5] was a remarkably homogeneous country, perhaps more so than any country in Europe, though past wars over the central authority of the state had caused rifts that were not forgotten. But the peoples of the main countries of Asia had never experienced *national wars* because they had never created nations in the sense that the word had been used in Europe since the French Revolution.

In the era known as the Tokugawa shogunate, the Japanese nobility was under the power of the shogun of Kyoto, who kept the country at peace. It was a hierarchical society in which the upper classes alone had the right to bear arms: Before westernization, the middle classes, merchants, and artisans never acquired enough economic strength to play a historical role comparable to that of their counterparts in Europe. In China, the educated classes, civil servants, and landed proprietors were organized in a hierarchy with the emperor reigning at its head. Under the Manchu dynasty the country remained set in the culture and administrative systems of the past. The people were aware of China's greatness, but the conditions that fostered national consciousness in Europe were absent in Asia until the twentieth century. There was no bourgeois or popular revolution against the aristocracy, nor any peasant uprising against great foreign landowners (as in eastern Europe), nor even any gathering together of a whole people against an enemy from without.

Not that Asia lived in peace until the present. The Chinese Empire had had to defend itself against the Mongols and the Manchus—the "Barbarians" from the north. As soon as the various dynasties were established they used their armies to extend the area they ruled over. The emperors in Peking laid claim to a kind of protectorate over minor monarchs in Korea and Tonkin. But the important wars were those fought in troubled times when the unity of the empire was at stake. In the past, the Japanese had launched expeditions against the island of Formosa in the south and against Korea on the mainland. But though they had clashed with the Chinese several times, they had never dreamed, or been in a position to dream, of conquering China. A European type of policy based on nationalities was ruled out not only by the geography of Asia but also by the social and political composition of the countries involved.

The attempt to create an empire known as a "sphere of coprosperity" arose primarily out of the Japanese and Chinese Empires' different reactions to Western influence. Until the middle of the nineteenth century the Japanese Empire resisted the demands of foreign trade. But when Commander Perry forced his way into its harbors and the Japanese realized they had to choose not between isolation and contact with the outside world but between independence and subjection to a humiliating protectorate, a revolution took place, led by a section of the ruling classes. The abolition of the shogunate and the restoration of the emperor opened the way for a determined policy that aimed at uncovering and making use of the technical, administrative, and intellectual secrets of military force. From then on, economic expansion increased at a remarkable rate (about 3 percent per annum between 1870 and 1930). The Malthusianism of the Tokugawas gave way to a conscious attempt to increase the population. Japan borrowed from the West not only universal education, machines, conscription, parliamentary government, and legislation appropriate to the industrial era, but also the will to power and the idea that aggrandizement is the law by which all states are ruled, and the proof of their greatness.

Whereas in Japan the military aristocracy carried out the task of westernization, China remained weak and divided from the middle of the nineteenth century until the middle of the twentieth. The Manchu dynasty was incapable of imposing reforms comparable to those that allowed Japan to become a Great Power. In 1895, China was defeated by Japan, which annexed Formosa. In 1900 the Boxer Rebellion ended in another humiliation: A small army made up of contingents from all over Europe, under the command of a German general, advanced without undue difficulty as far as Peking and relieved the besieged foreign embassies. A few years later Japan won a military victory over Russia that had great repercussions throughout Asia. In an age of imperialism, when the dividing up of China into spheres of influence seemed waiting to happen, the unprecedented contrast between Japanese power and Chinese impotence was bound to act as an invitation to conquest.

But although in some respects industrialization in Japan was comparable to that in Germany, it was not accompanied by similar moves toward middle-class ideas and liberal institutions. In the case of Japan, technological civilization was incorporated into the structures of a hierarchical society in which authority was derived from above and the warrior aristocracy occupied the highest rank. Admittedly, the Empire of the Rising Sun, like the Reich, had introduced parliamentarianism. But in Japan sovereignty remained legally linked to the person of the emperor, and the supreme values of the community were those of the nobility rather than those of producers or parliamentarians.

As the first country in Asia to acquire, by its own efforts, the equipment of a Western power, Japan was able to enjoy an uninterrupted series of successes, from the annexation of Formosa to the beginning of the "China incident" in 1937, and including meanwhile the victory over Russia, the annexation of Korea, and the creation of the puppet kingdom of Manchukuo, in theory independent but in fact governed from Tokyo. Japanese diplomacy had shown astonishing skill in taking advantage of circumstances. An alliance with England made it possible for Japan to isolate Russia in Asia and to destroy the common front presented by the countries of Continental Europe. Two years after the Treaty of Portsmouth, Japan agreed with its recent enemy to divide Manchuria up into zones of influence. Under cover of World War I, Japan conquered bases in the Pacific and extended its influence in northern China. In 1931 Britain was not ready to join the United States in intervening to prevent the separation of Manchuria. In 1937, again, the United States protested against Japan's undeclared war on China but did not decide on effective rearmament. American diplomatic opposition to Japan's expansionist policy, combined with the absence of military action, encouraged the Japanese leadership to be in-transigent. In Asia as well as Europe, the United States was the dominant power, at least at sea and in the air, but its mixture of moral declarations with a refusal to mobilize encouraged the extremist parties in both Tokyo and Berlin.

So Japan's decision of 1941 becomes intelligible, absurd though it seems in retrospect to the historian, who can study the motives and means involved on either side and compare the resources and ambitions of the aggressor with the potential of the countries that were attacked. For decades Japan had proceeded from one victory to another, and pride had evolved into a determination to soar to the very top: not merely to rival the countries of the West, but to exclude them from the sphere of Asian coprosperity. To military leaders dreaming of conquest and community, National Socialism offered encouragement and example. A growing population and the obstacles put in the way of exporting manufactured goods provided arguments for those who preached the need for "living space." The countries of Europe were busy fighting one another. The China incident was turning into a war of attrition, with no end in sight so long as the government of Chiang Kai-shek went on receiving foreign aid. The Japanese army's initial successes—the taking of Hong Kong, Malaysia, the Philippines, and Indonesia—seemed to provide the war party with justification. But in fact even a German victory over Russia—and Tokyo could not count on that—would not have done away with the disparity between the forces involved. Japan's iron and steel production was barely a tenth of that of the United States. On a world scale, Japan, as an industrial society, belonged quantitatively, and even more qualitatively, in the second class. By defying China and the whole of the West simultaneously Tokyo was embarking on an adventure doomed to failure. But even the most passionate enthusiasts in Japan did not hope to beat the United States. They hoped the United States would not bother to win, and that out of weariness its leaders would sign a compromise peace. They forgot that the democracies, though slow to anger, would not stop short of total victory.

To win their initial successes they had to take the enemy by surprise. How could the Americans fail to exact a resounding revenge for Pearl Harbor? They may be peaceful by nature but when roused they strike hard. The destruction of the U.S. fleet at its moorings—a repetition of the attack Japan made on Russia's ships at Port Arthur, in the absence of any declaration of war—gave the Japanese navy temporary command of the seas from the Kurile to the Sunda Islands. But three years later the Japanese fleet no longer existed and U.S. planes and submarines had sunk almost all the merchant vessels that had maintained links between the various parts of the sphere of coprosperity. Japan, vanquished, was ready to make peace before the U.S. bombers had started to raze its cities to the ground, long before the atomic bomb had destroyed Hiroshima and Nagasaki. By the end of 1944, after the fall of General Hideki Tojo and the militarist clan, the Japanese government, under Prince Fumimaro Konoe, tried to enter into contact with the U.S. government to negotiate a peace. Naively and in vain, they addressed the Soviet leaders, too.

As a practical consequence of the Japanese defeat, the Empire of the Rising Sun lost its status as a major power once and for all, and this at a time when the European nations, which less than fifty years before had dreamed of dividing China up into zones of influence, were themselves disappearing from the scene.

Japan imports almost all its raw materials, including even coke. In peacetime the export of manufactured goods is for the nation a matter of life and death; in wartime it is as vulnerable to blockade as Britain. Cut off from the continents of Asia and the Americas and from the islands of the South Pacific, it would be unable to supply its factories and its people without trade. The population had tripled since the beginning of the Meiji era, and in the ten years that followed the war it was swelled by soldiers and civilians returning from the conquered territories. A reduction in the death rate, partly due to health measures introduced by the occupying Americans, also added to the number of mouths to feed. A Japan of 90 million inhabitants, without any colonies, was no longer a first-class or even a second-class power: It was only a satellite to the continental power or to the dominant maritime power.

The reforms imposed by the United States weakened both Japan's ruling classes and its militarist ideologies. The emperor, who had had to humble himself before the victors; the army and navy chiefs, who had started the war and lost it; the aristocracy, who had taken charge of industrialization and been able, thanks to foreign successes, to maintain the national traditions— all these conservative forces were shaken by a sudden break, to which Japanese history could offer earlier parallels. Public opinion turned away from power and glory and dreamed of being supreme in peace and democracy instead. But what will ultimately become of Japanese democracy? How far has the soul of the country changed, as distinct from the mask it wears? Do people's beliefs correspond to their words, and what will the beliefs disseminated by American "re-education" finally turn out to mean? One could debate such questions at length, but some things seem certain.

The prestige of the nobility, in Japan as in Germany, has been damaged for a long time to come. Japan lacks the material resources to rebuild a military force exercised primarily at sea and in the air. The parliamentary regime imposed by the victors reduces further the resources available for national defense. Ten years after the armistice, opposition to rearmament is still strong, and the clause in the Constitution that seems to forbid it has not been modified. In Japan and federal Germany alike, the economic and social foundations of the military class have been destroyed.

Japan wanted, through war, to gain control over China before it acquired a strong government and an industry of its own. But the war was not merely lost: It also has hastened what Japan had tried to prevent—the westernization of an independent China that would take Japan's place as the primary power in the region. Any stable regime in China would have built factories and trained a large army to end a century of subservience. The collapse of the Kuomintang and Mao Tse-tung's triumph made Communist doctrine, born in the West and transformed by Soviet practice, the official ideology of the new dynasty.

Seen from Asia the two giants of the twentieth century seem to have features in common. Both appear to worship machines and to be eager to wrest from technological progress all the power and well-being that it can yield. Both contain vast spaces, urban concentrations, millions of workers forming industrial armies. Despite the contrast between atheism and Christianity, both the godless and the believers are concerned about social service and profess, as far as words are concerned, the same goodwill toward their fellowmen. The antithesis between a one-party system and parliamentary institutions, between imposed orthodoxy and intellectual pluralism, is one that affects the basic values of a community. But to the rulers of Asia, conscious of the poverty of the masses and eager to wipe out the humiliations of yesterday, the main thing is to choose the most efficient method of industrialization.

In 1955, the balance of power between Japan and China is the reverse of what it was fifty years ago. China has become a Great Power again, while

Japan in its turn has sunk back into weakness. But the new balance is less unnatural than the previous one. China is still behind Japan in terms of economic development, whether calculated on the basis of the value of production per capita or the distribution of workers among the three sectors. In absolute figures, Japan's iron and steel production is still greater than China's. But China's output is growing: It stood at 4.5 million metric tons in 1956, but in five years' time it is due to reach 17 million metric tons—almost as much as Britain today and the same as Russia in 1938. The restoration of a strong state in Japan would not be enough to reverse the present balance of power. The islands of Japan, like those of Britain, can only aspire to Great-Power status by ensuring that their command of the seas extends at least as far as its sources of supply. The only way Japan could shake American domination would be by joining up with China—that is, by abandoning a policy independent of that pursued by the country dominating the mainland. China, through the extent of its territories, the size of its population, the energy of its ruling class, and soon by its industrial production, is in the process of recovering the supremacy it used to exercise between the frontier of the Soviet Union and the peninsulas of South Asia.

Is the phase of Japanese imperialism closing merely to usher in that of Chinese imperialism? It might be so, but we cannot be sure. Through all the ups and downs of imperial greatness and decline, Asia seems to be moving toward the creation of a system of states that, though unlike the European model, will differ profoundly from the exceptional situation of the turn of the century, when the nations of Europe, sometimes conspiring together and sometimes as rivals, reduced the states of Asia (Japan excepted) to the status of objects.

At present the autonomy of the Asiatic system is in fact limited by the presence of the two superpowers and the opposition between their ideologies and aims. The end of the Chinese civil war, after that of World War II, brought about a paradoxical reversal of alliances. Japan, the former enemy, has become an ally of the United States; China, the erstwhile ally, has become an enemy. China, whose stability had been the main object of American diplomacy in Asia for half a century, now found itself on the wrong side of the barricade. Newly democratized Japan was now on the right side.

The confrontation in Asia between the Communist countries and the United States is currently producing phenomena comparable to those we have already seen in Europe: Korea, a buffer kingdom between Japan and

China, which could only be independent if its two neighbors were equally strong or equally weak, is now, after a ruinous three-year war, divided up into two different countries (like Germany). The dividing line between the two coalitions, instead of passing through the middle, follows geographical realities. The United States, a maritime power in Asia, now has only bridgeheads on the mainland, though the islands (Japan, Formosa, the Philippines) still come within its sphere of influence. On the mainland, Sino-Soviet influence predominates. In such a context one might expect to find military blocs confronting one another, superimposed on the independence of national states. But that is less likely in Asia than in Europe.

Not that, militarily speaking, the absence of a local equilibrium is not equally evident here: U.S. allies and protégés are even weaker in Asia than they are in Europe. Nor do I consider the combination of China and Russia uncertain: On the contrary, their shared ideology reinforces their shared interests. The refusal of the United States to recognize the Communist regime in Peking leaves the latter no margin for maneuver, at least for the moment. But China is not occupied by Russian divisions, or ruled by men who arrive in Red Army trucks, who would be unable to cling to power if Moscow's support were withdrawn. The influence of Russian technology, ideas, and politics has made enormous progress thanks to the communization of China. This communization also marks the beginning of a new and different era, distinct both from the nineteenth century—when Asia was dominated by the European nations—and from its traditional past.

The collapse of the European empires—Dutch, French, and British—has brought a number of countries into being to the south of China, most of which take the nation-state as a model (though in fact they vary in structure and almost all have a multinational population). All are jealous of their own independence, though all, to different degrees, are fragile and incapable of much resistance.

The Asian states share a desire to throw off European and any other Western domination and to make progress along the path of economic development. They are divided by local quarrels (such as the dispute between India and Pakistan over Kashmir), which are comparable to local quarrels between the nations of Eastern Europe, and by their attitude toward the rivalry between the two superpowers: Some sympathize with the Communist bloc, others with the United States, and still others are neutral and nonengaged, though more or less in favor of one of the two sides. Amid all these shared interests, local quarrels, and different views of world diplomacy, what is the most important factor as far as the Asian system is concerned? The answer probably depends on China.

If, on the one hand, Communist China continues to confine its ambitions within the bounds of the Middle Empire as defined by its history, the Asian system will acquire an increasingly important autonomy. On the other hand, attempts on the part of China at military or even merely ideological expansion would amplify within Asia the repercussions of world conflict. The age of empires created by the henchmen of some lucky soldier is over. Even if we imagine Southeast Asia and India as taken over by communism, it is hard to see Moscow or Peking as the center of an empire stretching as far as Singapore and Madras. In Asia even more than in Europe, Communists are and will be *national*.

3. THE BREAKUP OF THE EUROPEAN EMPIRES

A nation that does not colonize is inevitably doomed to socialism and to the war between the rich and the poor. There is nothing shocking about the conquest of a country of inferior race by a superior race that settles in it in order to govern it. England practices this kind of colonization in India, to the great advantage of India, of humanity at large, and of itself. Just as conquest between equal races is to be condemned, so the regeneration of inferior or debased races by the superior races is in the providential order of humanity . . . *Regere imperio populos*, that is our vocation.*

These lines by Renan, written in the second half of the nineteenth century, still express in all its harshness—one is tempted to say in all its naïveté—the doctrine that Europeans have implicitly subscribed to for five centuries: the right of national entities in Europe to independence, and the right of European states to conquest in other continents. In South America, Europe's first concern was to divide up the various territorial zones between the Spaniards and the Portuguese. In North America, wars waged

---

*Ernest Renan, *La Réforme intellectuelle et morale de la France* (The Intellectual and moral reformation of France), in *Oeuvres complètes* (Complete works) (Paris: Calmann-Lévy, 1947; originally published in 1871), p. 390.

[Ed. Note: All footnotes in this book are Raymond Aron's own notes to his texts, translated from *Une histoire du XXᵉ siècle*.]

simultaneously at sea and in both Europe and the New World ended in the supremacy of England. Frenchmen and Englishmen fought on the other side of the world for the Indian Empire. In the twentieth century the two trends, contradictory in their essential significance, led to a dual crisis: While Germany tried to subject the rest of Europe to an imperialistic domination, the peoples of Asia threw off their yoke and seized the right to set up independent states.

These days few European historians would disagree with their colleagues in India, China, and Japan on one thing: Whether one is thinking in terms of the past or the future, the situation in 1900, not that in 1955, is to be regarded as abnormal. It is more difficult now to understand how tiny England was able to carve out a worldwide empire for itself than to explain how India or Indonesia came to achieve independence.

There has never been an empire that was not founded in the first instance on military force, and the European empires are no exception. The Indians of North America and the civilizations of Central America were all doomed by the technological equipment at the disposal of the Europeans. Europe's military and industrial superiority over Asia was recent and did not long endure, but while it lasted, superiority at sea facilitated the advances of the Portuguese, the Spaniards, the Dutch, the French, and the English. India was split up into many different states, of which the strongest, the Mogul Empire, was in decline. A single battle was enough to establish the supremacy of the English army. What had started out as a commercial enterprise was transformed into an empire, as much by the force of circumstance as by deliberate design. The loss of military superiority brought about the end of a European domination that had begun in the days when frigates could bombard their way into any ports that resisted.

In this context Japan's victories in 1904, the equally balanced fighting between the Chinese Communist army and the U.S. Army in 1950–1951, and the local but spectacular success of the Vietminh army at Dien Bien Phu are symbolic. Renan himself bracketed the mission to command with the mission to fight. Throughout history, dominant peoples have always attributed their military triumphs to their own virtue, and in this respect the Europeans are neither better nor worse than the empire-builders who preceded them. Artillery, like the more primitive ballistics of the legions 2,000 years earlier, illustrated the maxim *Regere imperio populos,* which fell into disuse when the ownership of ordnance was shared out more equally.

A primary role was played in the breakup of empires by an old and now reinvented military phenomenon—guerrilla warfare. Civilized peoples tend to organize war at the same time as they organize their own states. Regular armies channel spontaneous violence, excluding civilians from fighting and so preserving them. In the eighteenth century, and the nineteenth, too, after the French Revolution and Empire, the legislation governing civil rights did more and more to protect noncombatants and reduce the ravages of armed conflict: Only soldiers were allowed to fight, and those who were not in uniform were not to be molested. Twice during the imperial wars—in Spain and in Russia—the peasantry attacked the soldiers, either out of an elementary reflex of patriotism or out of hatred of the conqueror, or because the exactions of the invading armies were too much to be borne in countries already on the brink of famine. There was practically no guerrilla warfare in Europe during World War I, though it emerged throughout Europe during World War II, either spontaneously or by order. All over the world it became the typical military instrument of revolution.

In Russia it was organized by the Soviet army in the rear of the German army. Modern techniques, using aircraft and parachutes, made it possible for local and general headquarters to keep in touch with partisans behind the lines. In the vast spaces involved, small groups could carry out surprise raids and withdrawals. In the West, the ranks of the maquis increased when the German authorities tried to recruit workers for factories in the Reich. Like the conscription of army recruits earlier, the drafting of workers produced large numbers of evaders. But however one assesses its importance, guerrilla warfare played only a secondary part in World War II; it did not decide the outcome. Even without it the Third Reich would have been crushed beneath the weight of the Russian, British, and U.S. armies.

Things are very different when national independence or social revolution is at stake. A guerrilla army may not destroy the regular force, but nor does the regular army wipe out the partisans. It might be said that permanent insecurity represents the victory of the rebels over the pacifying forces. The job of the latter is to ensure the safety of people and property; the aim of their adversaries is to show that the old order has become impossible. The rebels win if they manage to survive. The pacifying forces lose unless they gain complete victory.

In China and Indochina guerrilla war was only the first stage of civil war. In China the formation of a regular army came quickly, thanks to the establishment of a revolutionary government in a remote province of that vast country. The divisions of Indochina's Vietminh were formed and trained in China. Militarily speaking, now as in the past, regular armies are required for victory. But sometimes a long guerrilla war can win political victory. In order to end the conflict the colonial power has to treat with the leaders of the so-called nationalist movement, who alone can restore peace. Such negotiations always end sooner or later in independence for territories that were formerly colonies or protectorates.

But it would be wrong to look at the disintegration of the European empires from the military point of view alone. It bears repeating that Europe exported its ideas at the same time as it exported its modes of production and warfare. Just as revolutionary France provoked or awakened nationalist sentiments that were late turned against France itself, so, outside Europe, the Europeans provoked or awakened patriotic sentiments whose first and legitimate aim would be to drive out erstwhile masters of a different race and color. Perhaps the mechanism of revolt can be reduced to three typical causes.

Whatever legal form it took, European colonization provided a minority of young men from among the local population with a Western education. To such graduates emerging from European or American universities, the English offered openings in the public services. The French, who exported their own trained officials everywhere, kept most posts, and not only the best, for themselves. This policy was bound to swell the ranks of nationalist parties: The latter could not but exist; their memberships could only increase. An empire created from afar by a mother country that itself subscribes to democratic ideas is by nature precarious and full of contradictions, doomed either to rapid change or to collapse. Unless the colonial power concerned means to maintain a permanent policy of ruthless repression, an empire, if it is to last, must gradually get rid of the inequalities arising out of conquest: Roman citizenship, and Russian citizenship, whether under the tsar or under the Soviets, implies equality, if not for all then at least for the privileged minority, whether they come from the master population or from among the natives. But the two nations of Western Europe were prevented, one by pride of race and the other by the practices of direct administration, from applying the principle of equality that the home countries, though governed by authoritarian methods, find less difficult to honor.

Incapable of incorporating their scattered colonies and protectorates into their respective "home" countries, the Western imperial powers, democratic within but overbearing without, were led, in their dependencies, to keep alive or restore traditional powers that were not at all in keeping with a democratic ideology. Britain's domination in India helped to strengthen the native princes who were allies. Its policy in the Middle East was based on tribal chiefs and absolute monarchs who governed in a style frequently though incorrectly described by present-day propaganda as feudal. It is easy to criticize after the event; but the whole undertaking was in itself full of inconsistencies. The imperial powers, lacking the nerve to adopt an out-and-out policy of integration or to abolish certain time-honored customs (it was Tunisia's first government after independence that outlawed polygamy), found it easy to justify the retention of anachronistic institutions in terms of their own respect—sometimes genuine—for foreign cultures. The division between Western and traditional elements was accentuated; the "feudal" element was favored at the expense of the "intellectuals" who opposed them, having emerged from our own universities and from the middle classes created in their own country as a result of economic development.

Everywhere (except in black Africa), Western dominance, the abolition or reduction of famine, the establishment of peace and order, and the dissemination, though incomplete, of medical and hygienic knowledge combined to accelerate population growth. And almost everywhere, resources failed to keep pace with this increase. Development, though often efficient, was or seemed to be motivated only by profit or the interests of the home country. The destruction of local crafts through imports of English cotton goods; the exploitation of mineral deposits and oil wells without any corresponding development of local industry; the toleration, in rural areas, of large landowners and money-lenders—all these are familiar charges in the case against economic colonialism.

Demographic pressure, stunted growth in industrialization, the growth of a nationalist minority that in the name of Western ideas condemns both European domination and traditional authorities—these are typical features that are to be found everywhere, irrespective of the material results of the European presence. No one doubts that World War I, then the Russian Revolution, then World War II precipitated the breakup of the European empires. But we must not forget the main fact: Any empire under a home country that claims to be a democratic nation is a contradiction in terms because the imperial power concerned can only remain in power by denying itself.

In Asia the decisive moment came when Britain granted independence to India. The way the struggle for independence evolved was as significant as the transfer of power itself. In 1941 Britain had tried to get the Congress Party to collaborate voluntarily in the war effort in exchange for a promise of independence when hostilities ceased. But the mission, entrusted to Sir Stafford Cripps, failed because he met with a demand for an independent government not in the indefinite future but at once. The imperial power, which had at its disposal an Indian administration and army trained and managed by British officers and executives, was still capable of mobilizing India's forces and resources in the struggle against Germany and Japan. A few Nationalist leaders were imprisoned; the people as a whole remained passive. When the war was over, the British, under pressure from both the United States and Russia, kept their promise and fixed a date for handing over sovereignty. They negotiated with the leaders of the Nationalist Party.

The Nationalists had adopted a policy of noncooperation rather than violence. It bore no grudge against those members of the ruling classes—businessmen or civil servants—who up till the last moment had collaborated with the British Raj. When the British troops departed from India they left behind the administrative and legal system that had given unity to what seemed more like a continent than a country. Power had been handed over to people trained in the school of British statesmanship who had learned to like and respect British institutions. But though little blood had been spilled in the struggle against the conqueror, it was shed in torrents when the empire over which Queen Victoria had reigned was succeeded by two new countries, one of which was based on religion. The birth of India and Pakistan was marked by huge transfers of population; millions of Muslims and Hindus were massacred. Since those early troubles, the republic of India has managed for nearly ten years to progress along the lines marked out by its founders. A parliamentary regime, the rule of law, economic development—these three elements of Western democracy as understood in the middle of the twentieth century are to be found (with some imperfections, but who is without them?) in a country still ruled by Mahatma Gandhi's chief disciple, Jawaharlal Nehru. Nehru, a Brahmin from Kashmir, educated at Cambridge, a left-wing intellectual in Europe who rediscovered the age-old culture of his own country, often unfair to Westerners but steeped in Western ideas, is a striking embodiment of the kind of man who can govern one of the new states of Asia without breaking with the democracies of Europe and the United States. Those who have ruled China since the failure of the Kuomintang have modeled themselves on Russia. Whatever the proportions of the influence exercised on their ideas and actions by Soviet communism on the one hand and by essentially Chinese ways of thinking on the other, they lack the wisdom that allows tradition to generate freedom.

Events in Burma and Ceylon followed morally and materially from what had happened in India. Britain had been a Great Power in India thanks both to the Royal Navy and to the Indian Army. We might even echo K. M. Pannikar and say that India under the British Raj was, on behalf of and for the benefit of the Raj itself, *the* great power in Asia. Burma and Ceylon had the same claim to independence as India, but in the two smaller countries the transfer of sovereignty did not present the same difficulties as on the so-called subcontinent itself.

The British example and American pressure forced Holland, too, to withdraw on the imperial front, after several years of unrest and two attempts to restore the colonial regime by force. In Indonesia during World War II the Japanese had interned all Dutch citizens, civilians as well as servicemen, and set up a government consisting of members of the Nationalist Party, which for a long while collaborated with the occupying authorities. But the restoration of the old regime would have met with opposition from the Nationalists and the guerrilla fighters even if there had been no external intervention. Holland, criticized both by the United States and the Soviet Union, gave in and negotiated a treaty with the Nationalist leaders that opened the way for a federal union. But the treaty was never put into practice, and Indonesia became a sovereign state. The government in Djakarta did not shrink from using force to create a centralized state, repressing any impulses toward independence or autonomy in Sumatra and the other islands.

In Indochina the situation was different from that of either Indonesia or India. Japanese troops had been stationed in Indochina since 1940. After France's defeat, the French authorities could offer no resistance against Japan, especially in light of the fact that the United States and Britain had informed the French government that they neither would nor could intervene.

On March 9, 1945, the Japanese authorities suddenly abolished the French administration, interned all French soldiers and civil servants, and declared Annam and Tonkin to be independent. However, most of the Nationalists refused to collaborate with the occupier and took to the maquis. After the capitulation of Japan, the southern part of the country was occupied by British troops and the north by the Chinese troops of Chiang Kai-shek. The French expeditionary force, which was supposed to take part in the final assault on Japan, reoccupied the south of the country easily enough, but in the north the French troops did not arrive in Tonkin until after an agreement had been signed between General Jacques Philippe Leclerc and Ho Chi Minh, an old militant of the Communist Party and a hero of the independence struggle. After the failure of Ho Chi Minh's negotiations in Paris and Dalat to establish an autonomous government in Cochin-China, and after the French artillery bombardment of Haiphong, war broke out in November 1946. Vietminh troops made a surprise attack on Hanoi, but it failed: French troops got the upper hand in the towns, and the Vietminh embarked on a partisan struggle that was to last eight years. As the Vietminh leaders were Communists, the French government, and gradually, after the Korean campaign, some of the American leaders, saw the war in Vietnam as an episode in the struggle against Soviet and Communist expansion in Asia. The Vietnamese, especially in the north, saw the Vietminh as the party of independence. The regime installed in the south by the French, and intended to serve as a rallying point for non-Communist nationalists, was only partly successful, either because of the personality of Bao Dai, the ex-emperor of Annam, or because of French reluctance to grant the Vietnamese government in Saigon either the reality or the symbols of sovereignty. After the Vietminh's victory at Dien Bien Phu, an international conference in Geneva reached an agreement recognizing the existence of both North and South Vietnam as completely independent states.

The anti-imperialist movement gradually gathered strength, emboldened by its own successes and the weakening of the former colonial powers of Europe. Imperial Britain had been able to do without compulsory military service; bereft of an empire it had, like the continental countries, introduced conscription, though this belated break with tradition failed to restore the nation's lost capacity for action. It was as ruler of India that Britain had exercised hegemony from the Persian Gulf to the eastern Mediterranean. Without the Indian Army, and at a time when naval power is in decline, it can no longer lay down the law over the vast Middle East, where the Arab populations are stirring and which is the source of the scores of millions of tons of oil essential to Europe's prosperity.

As a result of the disintegration of the Ottoman Empire after World War I, part of the region formerly known as Asia Minor was divided up into separate states—Syria, Lebanon, Iraq, and Palestine, then Jordan and Saudi Arabia, though none of them was really a national state. Syria and Lebanon were placed under French mandate. Palestine, where, through the Balfour Declaration, Britain had promised to create a national home for the Jews, was under British mandate.

The European countries, though they were critical enough of the Ottoman Empire, had not sincerely tried to promote the emergence of national entities there (how could they have done so in a place where national entities and identities did not exist?). France, Britain, and Italy had all taken advantage of the vacuum left by Turkey's collapse to increase their own dominance and influence as best they could. Some British officials and politicians who had encouraged or led the revolt in the desert were in favor of an Arab kingdom that would have included Iraq, Syria, Lebanon, and Palestine. But rivalry between the European powers, on the one hand, and the various Arab dynasties, on the other, resulted in a territorial arrangement that was no more and no less artificial than many others that might been put forward. The frontiers henceforth defining the layout of the Middle East were drawn in accordance with diplomatic convenience and the temporary fortunes of war rather than with the wishes or cultural affinities of the people concerned.

None of these states was homogeneous: Languages, religions, and cultures intermingled in Syria, Lebanon, and Iraq. In Palestine the growth of the Jewish minority would gradually lead to a latent civil war that the mandatory civil power could neither pacify nor repress. The Arab states were like the Muslim states of the past—created by force of arms, superimposed on a multitude of tribes, and lacking the equivalent of Europe's middle classes, that is, members of a bourgeoisie such as civil servants and intellectuals who might be capable of running a constitutional state.

In the interval between the two wars, at a time when the Arab states were still far from becoming effective political entities, the nationalism within their gates continued to grow in the form of a negative attitude largely defined in terms of a longing to be independent of the imperial or tutelary power. In Syria, with Britain's blessing, it turned against France. In Palestine, it turned against Britain, which was judged guilty of not forbidding Jewish immigration. In the other Arab states London's policy, in the short term, seemed a successful combination of respect for local sovereignties with the maintenance of British influence and the promotion of British interests.

The two sons of Hussein, the emir of Hejaz (who had been promised the kingdom of Arabia), were given the thrones of Iraq and Jordan, the latter detached from Palestine. Faisal became king of Iraq and Abdullah was made king of Jordan. In 1930 Britain gave up its mandate and recognized Iraq's independence, though it held on to bases there. In Jordan the Arab Legion was the only army, and its weapons, officers, and funding were supplied from London. Arabia itself had been unified under Ibn Saud, leader of the Wahabite sect. But Britain had come to terms with Ibn Saud's victory and encircled Saudi Arabia by means of its own protectorates in Aden, Kuwait, and the Hadramaut. Thus British policy seemed to be succeeding where French mandatory policy was failing. The creation of nominally independent states, support for the Arab League, and backing for the idea of Arab unity all helped Britain to increase its practical influence while retaining its access to the oil reserves, which held a fabulous potential for exploitation that was gradually becoming apparent.

The National Socialists tried, with some success, to set Arab nationalism against the imperialists, and especially against the British. Hitler's anti-Semitic slogans found an echo among the masses anxious about Jewish immigration into Palestine, which had increased as a result of the persecution suffered by the Jews in Germany. An anti-British revolt in Iraq, fomented by German machinations in 1941, was quickly put down. The region was consigned to the firm grip of the British troops. But the end of the French mandate in Syria, made inevitable by the defeat of France and the clash between the Free French and forces loyal to the government of Marshal Pétain, signaled the end of Britain's long-term plans. After World War II and the withdrawal from India, the method that had worked twenty years earlier worked no longer. Negative nationalism turned against the British; legal independence was not enough now to make people forget or accept de facto dependence.

The three stages of this development were marked by the end of the British mandate in Palestine and the creation of the state of Israel; the evacuation of British troops from the Suez Canal Zone; and the crisis that followed the nationalization of the Suez Canal Company. During the 1914–1918 war, Britain had made contradictory promises to the Jews and the Arabs. And the measures taken to limit immigration after the Nazis came to power had managed to anger the Jews without appeasing the Arabs. The struggle between Arab and Jewish terrorism, one against the other and both against the mandatory power, ended—after a pause during World War II when the Jews formed a brigade that fought in the British army—in a stalemate. The problem was submitted to the United Nations, which suggested a plan for partition that was accepted by the Jewish Agency but rejected by the Arabs. War broke out, and large numbers of the Arab population fled from their homes at the instigation of their leaders, who thought they would be able to return after a few days. After a few weeks of indecisive fighting, the United Nations imposed a month's truce. But during a second phase of the war the Jewish army, having received supplies of arms from abroad, was clearly getting the best of it, and its success was stopped only through the intervention of the superpowers and the United Nations. The existence of the state of Israel was seen by the Arabs as a permanent insult. A million refugees forbade either forgiveness or resignation. Although some of the arms used by the Israeli army were of Soviet origin, it was the British, who had permitted the setting up of a Jewish homeland, and the Americans, who were helping to fund the new state, who were included in the Arabs' hatred of Israel.

The revolution that drove King Farouk from his throne and brought to power a junta of officers arose out of the defeats suffered by the Egyptian army in 1948. Colonel Gamal Nasser, now commander in chief, negotiated a settlement of the Sudanese question with the British, who also agreed to withdraw their troops from the Canal Zone in advance of the date set by the 1936 treaty. How useful would the British base on the canal have been in the case of another world war? Military experts debate the question: The existence of atomic weapons creates so much uncertainty that no dogmatic answer is possible. But in peacetime the British military presence was an important factor in maintaining stability. No Middle Eastern government would have thought lightly of confronting the two British divisions stationed in the Canal Zone. Everyone knew it would be difficult both technically and politically to mount a military intervention from bases in Libya, Cyprus, or Malta. The last British troops left Egyptian soil in 1956. Britain gave up its last means of exercising force just as its former network of influence was finally breaking up.

Not long before, the king of Jordan had dismissed Glubb Pasha, founder and commander of the Arab Legion. Army officers inspired by the example of Colonel Nasser, or won over to his cause, now filled the senior ranks. The Baghdad Pact linking together Britain, Turkey, Iran, and Pakistan had aroused violent opposition from both Saudi Arabia and Egypt. The United States neither signed the pact nor expressed disapproval of it. Egypt, which in 1955 had signed an agreement with the Soviet Union, was spending a large part of its budget on arms. In 1956, as a riposte to Britain and the United States because of their refusal to finance the Aswan Dam, Colonel Nasser decided to nationalize the Suez Canal Company and take over its installations.

The collapse of Britain's positions in the Middle East was a direct result of its withdrawal from India: The British army in India, together with its main forces, had been able to maintain the *pax britannica*. But there are political as well as military reasons for the change. London's former policy was to support traditional rulers in the region, or rather to provide them with kingdoms made to measure for them. The few hundreds of thousands of Arabs or Bedouins scattered over the territory that came to be known as Jordan were not much affected when it was made into a kingdom. The 3 million Iraqis, divided into hostile religious sects (the Sunnis and the Shiites), did not acquire a national consciousness in the space of a few years. But earlier ways of life have been inevitably eroded by Western influence, by economic development, however meager, and by the considerable amounts of money handed over by the oil companies to the rulers of the countries concerned.

After World War II the British and the Americans would have liked to find rulers well-disposed toward them who were both popular and capable of promoting progress. But such rulers were not to be found. So, being mainly interested in oil, they made do with paying royalties to rulers who would at least give them temporary assurances of peace and quiet. In this way Ibn Saud and his successor, and the emirs of Kuwait and Bahrain, pocket hundreds of millions of dollars that are spent according to the whims of potentates of a bygone age. Meanwhile, the masses, the ordinary people whose lives do not improve and whose customs are being undermined, blame their poverty on imperialism. And the middle classes—graduates of

Western universities, clerks, civil servants, technicians—also accuse imperialism and call for independence, even in the emirates where huge oil production and a tiny population result in a high standard of living.

Incompetent as they may be, and sooner or later unpopular, the traditional rulers are nonetheless as nationalist, in their hostility toward Israel and sometimes toward the "imperialists," as revolutionary leaders such as those in Egypt. The latter are undoubtedly inspired by a sincere desire for progress. But the poverty of the people and the growth of the population are such that the rulers are too often tempted to seek rapid and sensational successes rather than the slow and difficult gains of real economic growth. The revolutionary leaders are acclaimed first and foremost for their belligerent words and deeds. They proclaim their hatred of Israel in violent terms, profess themselves hostile to westerners, and claim to be friendly to the Russians; but it is difficult to see how much of all this is genuine and how much mere blackmail.

The crisis of renewal that all the Islamic countries are going through in the Middle East explains the form that nationalism has taken in lands that are not and never have been nations. Soviet propaganda, including the myth of the Soviet Union as the country that rose all alone against the West at the height of its power, seems to constitute one of the influences creating hostility to the West in the region, especially as the Communists always conceal their long-term aims behind anti-imperialist slogans.

The breakup of British positions in the Middle East is taking place in countries where Britain itself has encouraged independence as groups or individuals hostile to Western influence come to power. The breakup of the French Empire in North Africa is also in progress, with former protectorates (such as Tunisia and Morocco) gaining independence. In 1956, Algeria, which was legally a part of the French Republic and, like France itself, divided up into departments, has become the setting for a conflict in which 350,000 French soldiers are trying to end a guerrilla campaign being fought by a few thousand rebels and patriots.

All the typical reasons for nationalist movements to arise against the European empires are to be found gathered together in North Africa: demographic pressure (the birthrate in Algeria grows at the rate of 2.5 percent annually, and in Tunisia and Morocco it is not much lower); lack of natural resources, together with slow industrialization (especially in Algeria); the undermining of ancient customs, accompanied by anti-Western and antimodern attitudes among traditionalists and in religious circles; the growth of an intellectual minority won over to French ideas and thus to the right of self-determination; the presence of a French population—settlers, civil servants, businessmen, executives, junior and senior clerks—all richer than or not so poor as most of the native inhabitants; the protecting power's loss of prestige after the defeat of France in 1940, and perhaps even more after the defeat in Indochina; the encouragement given to the nationalists by Soviet propaganda and the perceived attitudes of the American public; and finally, direct aid from other Islamic countries, in particular Egypt. Nevertheless, it is evident that many educated Tunisians, Algerians, and Moroccans, including the nationalist leaders, are still attached to France and to French culture. And personal relations between French people and Muslims often remain good.

For a long time French policy wavered between two alternatives: on the one hand, negotiation with the nationalists (with the Neo-Destour Party in Tunisia and the Istiqlal in Morocco), whose ultimate objective, if not their immediate claim, was independence for the protectorates; on the other hand, repression of the nationalist movements and the introduction of reforms in collaboration with those Tunisians and Moroccans who accepted a measure of joint Franco-Tunisian or Franco-Moroccan government, as it had evolved, in fact, over and above the terms of protectorate treaties. In 1951 Robert Schuman contemplated adopting the first alternative and included Neo-Destour ministers in the cabinet. But by the end of the year, resistance from various sources in Paris and opposition from French circles in Tunisia brought about a volte-face, and the Neo-Destour leaders were dismissed, imprisoned, or deported. In 1954 Pierre Mendès of France opted definitively for entente with the nationalists. Agreements granting internal autonomy to Tunisia were negotiated and approved by the French Parliament. But scarcely had these agreements come into force than events in Morocco called everything into question again. In Morocco, too, the second alternative had been chosen after the war. The deposition of the sultan, which Marshal Alphonse Juin had considered some years earlier, was ultimately provoked by Moroccan traditionalist circles and some members of the French administration. Terrorism broke out in the towns. To end it, and to reestablish contact with the nationalists, the French government sought, more or less sincerely, a compromise solution. But in reality, as soon as Sultan Ben Arafa had left the throne, the return of Mohammed V became inevitable, and this so threatened the law and order guaranteed by the French that independence was promised to the sultan as soon as he returned from exile in Madagascar.

The outcome of the crisis would probably have been the same in both Tunisia and Morocco in any case. The terms *independence* and *national sovereignty* have a magical force in the twentieth century. In the long run, it was impossible to govern in collaboration with the representatives of traditional Morocco, which Marshal Louis Hubert Lyautey had wanted to respect but which economic modernization inexorably relegated to the past. However, the representatives of modern Morocco, though few in number, were fiercely nationalist, and independence was their prime objective. If the French government had been able or willing to decide on a long-term policy, they themselves could have fixed the modalities of the process of liberation. Probably, in their heart of hearts, the Moroccan nationalists themselves might have preferred that France would remain responsible for keeping order during the years of apprenticeship and transition. Morocco's modern economy is entirely a French creation: All the businessmen and engineers are French, as is all the capital. If the economy should ever founder as a result of a French withdrawal, the disappointment of the masses, who expected independence to improve their lot, might well turn to anger.

Algeria, unlike Tunisia and even more unlike Morocco, has no history as a separate state. It has suffered many invasions and never been unified under an authority that the various Arab and Kabyle populations would have recognized as belonging to them. The Algerian nation is in the process of being born in revolt against the authority of France.

Black Africa, too, is affected by the nationalist movement, as understood in all the countries that once were part of the European empires. The revolt against the whites is perhaps more racial than national. It takes many different forms: almost primitive in Kenya, almost parliamentary on the Gold Coast and in Nigeria. There again, in West Africa, the British are trying to hand over power to states based on the European model. France in turn is taking the same path, preparing within the framework of the French Union to grant at least domestic autonomy to its territories in West Africa. Where the white minorities are relatively large, the main problem is racial relations. Where there are no settled white minorities, the problem concerns the fate of such European institutions as parties, elections, and legislative assemblies, and the issue of how the more or less westernized elite class will be able to create single nations out of diverse populations which have never been welded over time into unity by a shared political existence.

4. THE VARIETIES OF NATIONALISM

One might be tempted to summarize one of the lessons of the recent past by saying that what the Europeans have exported to the rest of the world is *nationalisms* rather than nations. The states newly created as a result of the decomposition of the European empires are nationalist against their former masters, but either they are not yet national or they are distinctly multinational. In Europe, and more widely in the West as a whole, the question is whether nation-states have left the nationalist stage behind them once and for all. In Asia, the Middle East, and Africa, the question is whether nations can be formed out of nationalisms.

As we have seen, the nation-states of Europe have to adapt themselves now to a system of international relations radically different from that which obtained at the beginning of the twentieth century. Then they were or seemed to be the subjects of historical decisions; today they are only their objects. They used to be great powers in their own right; now they form part of coalitions led by countries that are partly or wholly outside Europe. In time of peace they relinquish their military autonomy. This may seem only a temporary state of affairs: Atomic weapons, which accentuate the essential difference between nation-states and superpowers, will be available to all in ten or twenty years. The overall trend toward separate nationalisms will be irreversible so long as areas as vast as the United States, the Soviet Union, China, and India remain single political units. If the Indian subcontinent is unified as one country and North America made into three, Western Europe, in order to be on the same scale as the giants of the twentieth century, would have to become *one,* at least from the Atlantic to the Elbe (or to the Oder or the Vistula).

The rivalry as to power and ideology that runs through the middle of Germany, cutting Europe in two, temporarily forbids any such continental unity. But we may well wonder whether the nations of Europe might one day agree to merge into a federation, and whether they would submit to the law of a super-state.

True, chauvinism is less in evidence in the opposing camps since World War II. The dispute over the Saar has not given rise to violent passions either in Germany or in France. German and French officers have met together in Atlantic headquarters without anger or embarrassment. Parties that appeal to nationalist ardor have met with little success on either side of the Rhine. But it is important for us to identify the various components of this real or imaginary lull. The frontiers of the states of which Europe consists follow fairly closely the principle of nationality; none of these states can now claim material preponderance; and the Soviet threat, which hangs over them all, makes absurd any quarrels over boundaries, more appropriately regarded today as party walls. Memories of the still recent war tend to produce a turning away from militarism, especially in Germany. National feeling is unlikely to grow, or to degenerate, into nationalism unless forced into such extremity by foreign domination or swept along in a collective desire for power.

Nevertheless, there is as of yet no sign of a new kind of national feeling, a European one, in the process of coming into being. Empires have been built by force without the tribes or peoples concerned wishing to live in the kind of community imposed on them by the conqueror. But a federal state calls for something more than passive consent. And national feelings seem, after all, stronger than continental ones.

Fanatical advocates of the European ideal regard nationalist feelings and movements as negative because they hinder the realization of that ideal. They also oppose communism on the grounds that its spread would be synonymous with the expansion of the Russian Empire. For nationalist sentiments are an obstacle not only to a democratic federation of the states of Western Europe but also to the communism of the Soviets, whose verbal universalism conceals the absolutist role played by the Russian state. Nationalist feelings are for the moment conservative in nature, and therefore irritating to all who look to the future. They have ceased to be completely satisfying because nation-states have been relegated to secondary status and people still hanker for an international or supranational order. But such feelings are aroused again as soon as people feel threatened or oppressed. On the other side of the Iron Curtain, they are ranged against Russian domination, which is held responsible for the most hateful features of the new regime. In the West they are mobilized against transfers of sovereignty and American "leadership" in world affairs.

People's views on what is to be done vary in accordance with their views of the world and of the future. On the political level there are, in the abstract, three schools of thought. The first holds that communism provides the only valid answer to the problems of industrial society. It encourages nationalist feelings and movements, as long as they are directed against the European empires or Atlantic solidarity, but subordinates them to the interests of the ideological cause and ultimately envisages central planning on a supranational scale. Individual states, all subscribing to the same doctrine, would retain a certain amount of political and cultural autonomy. The second school of thought regards communism as the mortal enemy of Western civilization and wants to see a strengthening of Atlantic solidarity, and in particular the creation of a European federation large enough and with sufficient resources to counterbalance the Soviet bloc. The third school of thought is against all blocs—that is, all supranational military entities—and hopes for a more peaceful era ushered in by a return to a flexible system of relations between many different political units. The present situation is dominated by the confrontation between the first two schools of thought. The third could only prevail through the simultaneous defeat of the first two, which would presuppose a loosening of the links between Russia and the countries of Eastern Europe on the one hand, and between the United States and the countries of Western Europe on the other.

Even if this scenario should take place, object the advocates of Communist or of Atlantic unity, the European states would be too old-fashioned and too small to provide a suitable structure for a twentieth-century industrial economy. The argument that bigger is better was used during the last war by Nazi propaganda and has since then been revived by parties favoring European unity. It contains an element of truth: It is easier to exploit technology to the full on a large scale. But some small countries, such as Sweden and Switzerland, are among the richest in the world. The dimensions of a politico-economic unit is only one of the factors in productivity. Even if the European states are too small, a group of them—the six of Western Europe, for example—may, for obvious reasons or from necessity, still emerge as a significant force. In theory, extensive units of economic activity may be formed in two ways: through free trade, which may lead to an international community of labor, and through planning on a world scale. By intensifying their trade with one another, countries can come to resemble a supranational community without giving up their sovereignty.

In the twentieth century, the technologies of production and war all favor large units (although cheap production of atomic weapons is likely, in ten or twenty years from now, to give small countries unprecedented possibilities for action). But the units that exist now came into being over the course of centuries, through a slow apprenticeship in life lived in common. We may entertain the hope that, in the future, autonomy will no longer seem inseparable from absolute sovereignty. For the present, nations continue to exist, torn between the attraction of large spaces and the appeal of universal ideas and age-old loyalties—and perhaps, because of their very coherence, readier for future regroupings than the states that succeeded the European empires.

The peoples of Britain, France, Germany, Russia, and Spain each have a different idea of what constitutes a nation, their nation. France has no equivalent for the U.K. distinction between British on the one hand and English, Welsh, and Scottish on the other. The concept of a United Kingdom and the existence of the dominions have freed the British consciousness from its native provincialism and linked it to a civilization rather than to a nation in the French sense of the word. In Germany the idea of the nation has for centuries been attached to the idea of empire. As a people Germans have become imbued with their own uniqueness, not only from philosophical tradition but also in reaction against the multiplicity of states of which Germany is made up. The people must have had a singular soul in its own right, even if it had not acquired a state. In France, the desire to live together as a people defined the nation; history itself seemed to suggest this. In the United States, which had to overcome the fact that immigrants from many different origins settled there, the idea of the nation has been merged with ideologies and practices peculiar to American society. Anyone who betrays this Americanism becomes a "non-American."

The same variety of ideas about nationhood is to be found in Asia, the Middle East, and Africa. Japan, the country in this geographical category that is closest to the European type, has leapt in one century from being a feudal structure to being a mass industrial society without passing through the equivalent of our fifteenth to twentieth centuries, which in the West saw the development of rationalist thought and the industrial and mercantile middle classes, those typical elements in our idea of a nation. Universal education, urbanization, the introduction of democratic institutions, together with the decline of the aristocracy and its lofty values, have made the

Japanese nation resemble those of Europe more closely. But overpopulation, the loss of empire, existential difficulties, and ideological radicalism, by giving rise to dissent on the subject of nationhood, especially among the educated classes, bring Japan closest to the most nationally minded of all European nations: France.

In China, awareness of national unity has been strong for thousands of years among the educated classes. And measures taken by the Communist government—compulsory education, phonetic writing, the use of one dialect as a common language—have helped to spread this awareness among the masses. Thus the Communist regime, while subscribing to an internationalist ideology and aiming to replace capitalism, accords priority to objectives that in Europe were invented by the bourgeoisie: the creation of industry and the education of the people.

The case of India is altogether different. There the task is to build a nation on the foundation of anti-British nationalism. Not that the object must be to impose unity of culture, religion, customs, and language. But India, before the English, had never been totally unified. It was Britain, the occupying power, which after the decline and destruction of the Mogul Empire subjected the whole vast country to a single administration. The Indian republic has now succeeded the British Empire, inheriting both its light and its darkness, its terrible poverty but also an efficient bureaucracy speaking a common language, English.

Asian nationalism presents three different questions. Can unitary states, such as were created by the Europeans and taken over by nationalist parties, survive intact, or will they gradually be undermined by centrifugal forces, linguistic, religious, or ethnic? Must the independent states of Asia, the Middle East, and Africa, after their European mentors have left, acquire in their turn a thirst for power and set themselves one against the other? Lastly, will the same old combination of nationalism and imperialism—the strongest nation gaining its ends by exploiting the grievances of national minorities elsewhere—be repeated on the other continents?

At present all the Asian countries contain the equivalent of what in Europe used to be called national minorities. In Southeast Asia, the minority is Chinese. In Burma, the Karens have fought the central government for autonomy. In Indonesia, the central government has no real authority over all the islands of the Sunda archipelago. It has already had to send in troops against autonomist and separatist movements in, for example, the Moluccas.

The unity of India (excluding the two parts of Pakistan) is not for the moment threatened. But the feeling that contributed to the destruction of some multinational states in Europe is already present: The masses are calling for homogeneous states based on language. The new borders between the member states of the India Federal Republic were the result of long deliberations, but there are signs of resistance, sometimes taking the form of riots. For the moment this linguistic nationalism shows no tendency at all toward separatism. The unity of the Congress Party, the administration, and the army remains intact. But it seems that Hindi is not accepted as the national language by everyone. English is often still the only common means of communication between civil servants. The sense of a shared culture, however, will blossom into the desire to be a nation—an ambitious task, unavoidable for a regime that wants to be democratic in the Western sense of the word.

The countries of Asia are now familiar with local quarrels over boundaries or the future of some province; for example, the dispute between India and Pakistan over Kashmir, and that between Pakistan and Afghanistan over Baluchistan. Neither is all well on the Indochinese peninsula, where Cambodia is afraid of Vietnam and anxious to keep its sovereignty intact. But it seems unlikely that such local conflicts could take on alarming proportions in Asia. The two major states, China and India, are so big that neighbors' squabbles leave them unmoved. And Asia could not reproduce the dangerous combination that Europe once knew, of countries closely linked to one another but torn by permanent rivalry over power and prestige.

Nevertheless, if Communist China were to set itself foreign objectives it could, like Hitler's Germany, make use of the nationalist elements within its own borders to realize its ambitions and break up the other states over which it wanted to extend its domination. The Chinese minorities in Siam and Indonesia provide the same sort of pretext as the German minorities did in central and eastern Europe. It is a striking fact that in India the Communist Party is the one that has most ardently advocated homogeneous linguistic states, inciting to violence groups who rejected solutions suggested by the commission in charge of administrative reorganization.

In the Middle East, the states were created before the nations. The population is still passive; Islamic solidarity disregards frontiers; national consciousness is confined to the governmental or privileged minority. The middle classes, especially the university graduates, excluded or rejected by the traditional establishment, seek another faith to replace Islam and often find it in communism. So little are they involved in any political community, they make relatively easy recruits for a supranational ideology.

Nations exist even less in black Africa, where the first countries were born out of institutions resembling Western ones (with elections, parties, parliaments, and so on). What will these countries be like, though, once white domination is no more? How will they all get on together, the different tribes with their disparate religious beliefs, now mixed with political practices borrowed from Europe? No one has the answers to such questions. But it is important to understand the terms in which the problem presents itself in various places. The Europeans did not destroy already existing nations in black Africa, nor, if they left tomorrow, would they leave any behind them. But as a return to scattered tribes, balanced by unstable empires, is unlikely, the African peoples' education in national existence will continue well beyond the end of white domination.

We may even wonder how far a Western-type state is capable of completing such an education in nationhood. A state of this kind is in theory secular, unconnected with any transcendent belief or church, equally fair and just to all groups, indifferent to private matters, including religion, provided its citizens obey the laws and take their due part in public affairs. This ideal is far from being put into practice in all European countries: In all of them, one church is closer to state recognition than the others. The separation of temporal and spiritual powers is probably one of the most original features of European civilization, and one of the causes of its vitality and endless flexibility. But it is a duality that tends toward radical separation without ever achieving it. For a state to be really neutral its people must have a strong sense of their own unity. But a state that declines to be linked either to a religion or to an ideology is the work of centuries, not of a decision by the United Nations or by some imperial authority about to withdraw voluntarily or under compulsion.

The contrast between India and Pakistan is a striking illustration of one aspect of the problem facing the heirs to the European empires. In the absence of any agreement between the Congress Party and the Muslim League—in fact, between two men, Jawaharlal Nehru and Mohammed Ali Jinnah—the British fixed a date for the transfer of sovereignty to the two states, India and Pakistan, the latter of which declares itself to be essentially secular, while the former has in fact a religious basis. But there are still some

30 million Muslims in India, free and equal citizens of a lay republic. And there are about a million Hindus in Pakistan, inevitably second-class citizens in a country that rejected union with India because the Muslims feared they would be unfairly treated there. East Pakistan is a part of Bengal. The language spoken there is the same as that spoken in the other half of Bengal, West Pakistan. Apart from religion, Pakistan's Muslims have less in common with their compatriots in West Pakistan than with Pakistan's Indians.

It is common these days in Europe to point to the ravages of nationalism and hope that the evil will not spread to other continents. Any idea that has or has seemed to have been a cause of major wars is discredited when, with hindsight, people see the death and destruction wrought by violence. We cannot help smiling at the way every nation sees itself as the salt of the earth. We disapprove when we see minorities being denied human rights. The desire for conquest, in the name of some universal mission or racial superiority, unleashes great slaughter. But nationalist movements are not to be confused with such instances of vanity, discrimination, and fanaticism. Now that political units are no longer focused on a dynasty, a tradition, or a church, they rest on human will or a common culture. When human will and the community concur, a state is the work of both the living and the dead; it has been ripened by time, yet is kept alive by the ardor of the present. So long as the human race is divided up into sovereign units, those units will need a dynastic, religious, or national principle, and that principle, whatever it is, may cause conflict and be condemned by those who claim to know better. Everything that unites individuals also divides groups against one another. Men have fought as often in the name of universal religions as they have in the cause of nations.

But there are a number of ways in which nationalism, educator of a nation, can degenerate. The leaders of a newly independent state can turn the disappointments of the people against their erstwhile mentor. Foreigners are an easy target for resentment and failure. In the case of small countries, an obsession with sovereignty can paralyze economic development. Cambodia, Laos, Tunisia, and even Morocco need foreign help in the form of capital and experts. Independence, even if it is total from the juridical point of view, will always be limited in practice by lack of manpower and resources. And there is another danger that may be even more serious: Hitler's imperialism emerged from a Europe of nationalities; will other imperialisms arise out of the worldwide spread of nationalisms?

At present there seems not to be any example outside Europe of the paradoxical situation we have seen in Europe, where nation-states coincide with supranational military blocs. But the causes of that situation could recur elsewhere. The nationalisms of Asia, Islam, and Africa are strong only against their former or present mentors. They are weak against the attraction of a universalist ideology like that of communism. The latter has only been able to expand in Europe thanks to advances by the Red Army. In China, the victory of the Communist Party and its army has been won with less help from the Russians than America gave to Chiang Kai-shek. In Southeast Asia and in the Middle East, China and the Soviet Union, respectively, are capable of eliminating Western influence, inflaming nationalist feeling, and putting Communist parties in power without any direct intervention. Countries where that happened would continue to exist legally, but in reality their independence would be subordinated to the will of the leaders of Chinese or Russian communism.

It has become commonplace to see Soviet communism as a harsh method of industrialization especially suited to the needs of so-called underdeveloped countries. The political function that communism seems to have performed is less often noticed. That is, it tries to create a nation—a feeling of community, participation in public affairs, the formation of a middle class—on the basis of nationalism. It aims at reconciling national feeling, considered in the age we live in as an elementary force, with a desire for socialism and territorial expansion. The ideological unity of the Communist universe should in theory make it possible both to respect and to limit particular sovereignties. The state would be secular without being indifferent. It would tolerate religious though not ideological diversity.

The United States, for its part, tries both at home and abroad to combine nationalism and territorial expansion. Considered as a political unit, the states are neither a nation in the same sense as France or Italy nor an empire in the same sense as the Soviet Union. The American population is made up of immigrants from all the nations of Europe merged into one— varied in race, religion, and country of origin, but all inspired by the same view of life. In the United States patriotism depends on ideology less than in the Soviet Union but more than in France or Britain. Abroad, American diplomacy favors anti-European nationalisms as far as is compatible with the Atlantic alliance. It also attempts to turn the nationalisms of Asia and Africa against the Soviet Empire. In this it is not entirely successful, for outside Europe the Europeans of the West are regarded as much more imperialistic than the Russians, although Russia itself is a conglomeration of different peoples brought together through conquest (the Soviet Union now contains the world's largest Islamic minorities).

Where nationalism—a people's desire for independence—feels threatened by the spread of communism, which seems to be the case in part of Southeast Asia (where in any case communism is identified with China rather than with the Soviet Union), the Western combination of nationalisms with economic expansion produces additional difficulties. The exploitation of private capital gives rise to an accusation of economic imperialism. Government aid is thought to be dictated by ulterior motives and accompanied by unacceptable conditions. The universalist ideology of communism does not abolish the conflict between nationalism and expansion but it does tend to reduce it, whereas the national absolutism of the West may increase it.

Whether we talk of nations or nationalisms, empires or imperialisms, the world at present is full of differing phenomena called by the same name and similar phenomena called by different ones. Empires—gatherings of peoples of different cultures through conquest, where the nonnative peoples have no right of secession and the centralized state does not become a federal one—still exist. The European imperialisms are declining, though it would be going too far to say that imperialisms are a thing of the past: Universalist ideologies provide them with a pretext or justification. The disparity in strength between states makes domination by the Great Powers inevitable, though it may well be indirect or disguised. Modern technologies of production and war call for operations on the grand scale, which, though not incompatible with the legal independence of states, whether of Communist or democratic alignment, may in both cases inhibit certain national aspirations. Each side's propaganda denounces the other's imperialism. But there is a danger that, in some parts of the world, excessive concern with independence may hinder the necessarily international development of the economy, whereas in other places the danger is that tribal, linguistic, religious, or ethnic diversity will retard the formation of national communities, that indispensable stage between the small home and the vast human race as a whole.

Perhaps, to end this survey of nations and empires, we should look at the two most interesting cases the twentieth century has to show: the transformation of the Ottoman Empire into a nation-state, and the creation of the state of Israel on the basis of a typically modern European idea of a nation, mythically combined with the biblical idea of the Jewish people.

The application of the principle of nationalities after World War I led to a large-scale transfer of populations. More than a million Greeks from Asia Minor, whose ancestors had been settled there for 2,000 years, making a significant contribution to the spread of Greek culture and the greatness of the Byzantine Empire, left their homes and returned to Greece to live among those who spoke their language. The move, which entailed terrible suffering, was seen as an example of modern barbarity. In a part of the world where nationalities and religions were intermingled, where the different communities fulfilled complementary functions and plied complementary trades, was it not absurd to rearrange people into nationally homogeneous units? Yes, indeed, but in the long term the influx of Greeks from Asia Minor turned out be a source of enrichment for the Greek nation. And Kemal Ataturk's Turkey, having abandoned the Ottoman Empire and adopted the national model, recovered its youth and will to live.

Ataturk's achievement remains unique in that the separation of church and state was accompanied by a decision to abstain from ruling over other peoples. Turkey wanted to be a secular state, like those in Europe. It adopted the Western alphabet. Although, during the revolutionary period, it had temporary recourse to one-party rule, it decided to adopt Western political institutions as well as Western technology. Having opposed Western imperialism, and after the death of the Ottoman Empire, Ataturk set out to create a Turkish nation. In Tunisia the Neo-Destour Party, under Habib Bourgiba, seems to be following the same path, aiming at a secular state, European-style institutions, and a Tunisian nation.

The Zionist adventure is even more extraordinary. The first settlers and founding fathers of Zionism were not believers and did not regard themselves as a chosen people. Persecuted in Eastern Europe and treated as foreigners by anti-Semites, they turned what was intended as an insult into an advantage. They aimed at a state of their own, in which they would play as full a part as the French in France and the Russians in Russia. They entertained a number of different socialist ideologies—return to nature, living in strictly egalitarian communes. The stages Israel went through in the course of its formation are well known: agricultural settlements, the Balfour Declaration, the Hitler regime in Germany, terrorism and counterterrorism, war of liberation, and finally, in 1948, the proclamation of the state of Israel. Since the official recognition of its independence, its population has almost tripled. Jews from all the Islamic countries have, voluntarily or under compulsion, flocked to live there. The population of Israel belongs to several different races: Neither color nor nation of origin nor level of culture are the same for all its citizens. They are creating a nation out of a half-religious, half-mythological nationalism. People talk as if the Israelis were descended from the subjects of Solomon and David, but for most of them this is not so (a Yemeni Jew is of the same race as a non-Jewish Yemeni, not the same as a French or an English Jew). Every immigrant and every child is given one language—Hebrew; one past—that of the Bible; and one country—Israel, which they learn to know and to serve in the army.

The state of Israel is not, as Toynbee thinks, a fossilized relic of Syriac civilization. It is a European-type nation, created by the faith of a few and a unique set of circumstances. Is it a miracle of willpower? A historical miracle? The frontiers of this strange state are no less arbitrary than those of the free kingdom of Jerusalem.

5. HISTORICAL CYCLES AND A UNIQUE SET OF CIRCUMSTANCES

It may be that the contemporary historical situation is less novel than we like to think, but it is certain that the historical consciousness of the present age is without precedent. No civilization can now ignore the fact that it is one among many, that it came into being long ages ago, and that it may be doomed to die. Men are discovering the uniqueness of each of their societies just as those societies make contact with one another as never before. So our historical consciousness mixes together and contrasts a number of points of view: fatalistic ones, which claim that everything repeats itself; melancholy ones, according to which the age of European predominance is coming to an end; and optimistic ones, claiming that the present is as much a beginning as an end. The exploration of our planet is complete; with the help of science its riches have become inexhaustible. Together, the peoples of the world are about to embark at last on a universal history.

It is not impossible to explain the events of the past half-century in such terms. From the sixteenth century on, Spain and France took turns trying to dominate Europe. Philip II, Louis XIV, and Napoleon all failed, basically for the same reason: Europe had been opened up and the wealth of the outside world was available, partly at least, to whichever power had command of the seas. Britain achieved what Venice and Holland failed to do because they were too vulnerable. Far enough from the continent to be safe from invasion, near enough to be able to intervene there when necessary, Britain foiled the European ambitions of the Spanish and French kings while at the same time making sure it got the lion's share of imperial conquests in Asia, Africa, and America. Insofar as they were European wars, the wars of the twentieth century have resulted from Germany's repetition of France's and Spain's earlier attempts at hegemony. Whether or not the leaders of the Second Reich realized that this was what they were doing is of little importance: From the moment when the guns opened fire in August 1914, what was at stake once again was the supremacy of one European state over the rest of the continent.

None of these attempts at supremacy worked out the same way, and from one century to another, each coalition of forces that overcame the terrestrial power seeking supremacy was different. Russia and Prussia did not come onto the scene until the eighteenth century. But despite changes in the details over the four centuries in question, the fundamental pattern was the same. The country with the best army could not prevail permanently because of the help its weaker rivals received, sometimes from the power that had command of the seas and sometimes from countries bordering Europe—first the Turkish Empire, then that of the tsars.

Although the wars of the twentieth century have been fought for stakes similar to those of the seventeenth and late eighteenth centuries, their results have been very different because of the scale of the destruction wrought by modern warfare and of its repercussions in Europe and beyond. Russia, England, and their allies were able to beat Napoleon's France in the end without seeing Europe run out of men or lose its preeminence over the rest of the world; nor did troops of other races or from other continents join in to decide the issue. But as early as 1914 the Allies had to mobilize the economic reserves of the New World and called on black troops from Africa and yellow troops from Asia, the Indian Army, and French colonial troops to help them subdue their European rival. Finally, after the collapse of Russia, the U.S. Army had to intervene to tip the scales. As early as 1918, according to Max Weber, the hegemony of the United States was as inevitable as that of Rome after the Second Punic War.

The voluntary abstention of the United States and the establishment of territorial arrangements contrary to the interests of Russia and Germany paved the way for a repetition, in a more extreme form, of the war for hegemony. This time, in the West, the United States was not only the victor but also, quite plainly, the main combatant. In the East, the outcome of World War II was the same as it would have been for World War I if the Tsarist regime had survived. As soon as Germany was eliminated, the contested areas of Eastern Europe fell under Russian domination. They were occupied by Soviet troops and turned into popular democracies. In the twentieth century, armies are accompanied by regimes and ideologies.

We can also discern the precedents for the Asian crisis of our own day. For about a century China had been going through troubled times. The Manchu dynasty was already in decline when the white barbarians came on the scene. Half a century separates the occupation of Peking by European troops and the clash between the Chinese Communist army and the U.S. Army. The interval between the end of one dynasty and the beginning of another was filled by the disintegration of the Empire, the weakness of the republic, the warlords, and the precarious reign of the Kuomintang.

There was no equivalent there to Japan's attempt to conquer China or America's intervention in the Chinese civil war, nor to the meeting between Russian and American soldiers on the Elbe. Such incidents symbolize the difference between a mere repetition of the European struggle for hegemony, or a troubled period ending in a new Chinese dynasty, on the one hand, and the present state of world affairs, on the other. In both Europe and Asia a familiar process led to a completely new situation. We have to survey the scene from a loftier viewpoint in order to identify a larger periodicity.

Oswald Spengler and Arnold Toynbee have popularized interpretations of these events that have become part of the historical consciousness of our age. One foresaw the great wars that would ravage Europe as it entered the final phase of civilization. The other was struck by the similarity between the Peloponnesian War and that of 1914. A merciless struggle between political units of a certain type brings ruin on all the belligerents. Whichever city is apparently victorious, a generation later all of them fall under the domination of a semi-barbarous kingdom. In the same way the only choice left to the nations of Europe, all emerging vanquished from the wars of the twentieth century, is the choice of their protector.

But such facile comparisons finally lead to more questions than answers. Is the war of 1914 really comparable to the Peloponnesian War, as Toynbee suggested, or does it belong to a later stage in Western civilization, to a period more like that of the struggles that marked the end of the Roman Empire? Has the universal empire come into being already in the form of the Atlantic alliance, a military force under American command, or is the alliance only a first step toward the abolition of national sovereignties? In any case, Western civilization, assuming it constitutes a definite reality, ultimately is entering into an unprecedented situation marked by the creation of a genuinely worldwide politics.

None of these fashionable comparisons helps us to understand the present structure of international relations and the rivalry between the two superpowers. Not that we have not already witnessed battles between two cities or two men, each striving to rule their world. But the present rivalry between the United States and the Soviet Union does not parallel the classic scheme of Athens and Sparta or Rome and Carthage. Not that, in relation to what Sir Halford John Mackinder called "the world island"—the mass of Europe, Asia, and Africa—the United States does not appear as the maritime power, operating on external lines, in contrast to the Soviet Union, which operates on internal ones. But because of its very dimensions the conflict is *quantitavely* different from those recorded by the classical historians. Rome and Carthage were political units of the same type and the same order of magnitude as those contemporary with them. There was then no equivalent of the more or less westernized continents that have emerged from European domination and whose fate preoccupies Moscow and Washington more than the partition of Germany. The states of Asia could be the beneficiaries of a fight to the death between the United States and the Soviet Union, just as these two Great Powers were the beneficiaries of the fight to the death between the countries of Europe.

Perhaps the chief consequence of the European wars is not so much the division of Europe into two military blocs as the acceleration of the process, in itself inevitable, described both as the disintegration of the Western empires and as the liberation of colored peoples. Neither the wearing out of the Greek cities by the Peloponnesian War, nor the hegemony enjoyed by Rome as a result of the destruction of Carthage, nor Augustus's triumph over his rivals had comparable effects. In their European aspect, the wars of the twentieth century arose out of Germany's conscious or unconscious attempts at hegemony. On a world scale, they mark the end of European predominance.

Already historians of Asia are studying, as if it were a closed chapter, the centuries between the first appearance of Portuguese ships off the coasts of India and the departure of the last British and French troops from Malaya and Indochina. Four hundred years of European naval supremacy in Asia are drawing to a close. A century after China and Japan opened up to trade with the West, the troubled times in the former and the coprosperity venture of the latter ended with the establishment of a Communist regime in Peking and lethal bombing of the Japanese Empire. At one and the same time we are witnessing not only the end of the Ottoman Empire's two centuries of decay but also the close of the century during which the Europeans carved out empires for themselves in regions where Islamic civilization was either frozen or in decline. And soon, independent states will be coming into being in black Africa, marking the end of white domination.

But Europe's withdrawal, at the close of the period of expansion inaugurated by the great discoveries, does not necessarily alter the permanent conditions in which men try to live together in society. There are no more empty spaces left in the world; the times when millions of men could emigrate peacefully are over; the advantages Europeans enjoyed in the nineteenth century no longer exist. And yet, thanks to science, man is able as never before to exploit natural resources *intensively*. American historians, seeing democratic institutions as doomed because the vast frontiers are no more, dogmatize on another question: To what extent does increased production (in respect to land and industrial output) offer humankind new possibilities comparable to those once opened up by sparsely populated continents? This question points to the novelty of the present situation, over and above the ebb and flow of empires. Peoples, states, and civilizations exchange goods, ideas, diplomats, and inventions; everywhere aims and institutions are adopted that were once exclusive to Europe but now belong to the human race as a whole. They include economic growth, industrial development, and an improved standard of well-being for all.

Neither a fatalistic vision of history, colored to a greater or lesser extent by a biological philosophy of the life and death of states and cultures or by

Machiavellian pessimism, can account for the singularity of the present. True, empires, individual states, and civilizations are no more likely to last forever now than they ever were. The pace at which populations and wealth increase and multiply varies from one country to another; so power relations inevitably change. And as technological inequality between countries decreases, God tends more and more to take the side of the big battalions. There is little to suggest that men will not use technology to kill one another.

Nonetheless, a country's or an empire's relative decline no longer implies that it must become materially impoverished or intellectually sterile. Europe has never had such a large population, nor been so prosperous, as it is today. There have never been so many Frenchmen or Englishmen, and they have never before enjoyed, on average, such a high standard of living. It may be objected that statistics on demography or on prices and incomes tell us little about the quality of a culture or the virtues of any particular state. That is true, but never has it been so necessary to distinguish between prosperity and power; never have the spoils of victory been so derisory in comparison with the fruits of peaceful effort; never before has mankind, all of its members embarked together on the same venture, had so much to lose from wars and so much to gain from peace.

A Marxist school of thought gives a simple and apparently coherent interpretation of the present singular situation. The upheavals of the past half-century settle into a meaningful pattern if the Soviet regime is regarded as the end to which the industrial economy naturally tends; if the European wars are seen as the result of the contradictions inherent in capitalism; if European imperialism was bound to drag down all other imperialisms with it; and if conflict among states with the same doctrine and the same political and economic organization is inconceivable.

It is not difficult to see the difference between, on the one hand, things as they would have been if this interpretation were correct, and, on the other, the real course of events. Those who believed that war is fundamentally caused by opposing economic interests lost no opportunity to point to the conflict between Britain and the United States—though it ultimately found expression in a close and permanent alliance. And it was the construction of the German fleet much more than competition for foreign markets that brought Britain and Germany, who were economically dependent on one another, into a confrontation. Colonial affairs caused a number of diplomatic incidents; but it was in Europe, in connection with nationalities and the status of the Balkans, that the explosion took place. Europe did not wait for "monopoly capitalism" before embarking on the conquest of other continents, nor for "unequal development" before tearing itself to pieces in wars over hegemony.

True or false, this Marxist interpretation is still an integral part of current developments. It has been adopted by millions of people who expect prosperity and peace from their Communist regimes and the collective ownership of the means of production and the planning of all labor. But while this interpretation is unquestionably accepted by so many, it is also rejected by other hundreds of millions of the world's inhabitants. The conflict between the two views of world history is one aspect of the rivalry that exists not only between the two superpowers but also between and within other countries and empires.

The Marxist interpretation of history can only promise reconciliation in the not too distant future if it falls short of its own principles. According to the theory itself, economic and political regimes are a function of the development of the forces of production. But how can regimes keep pace with and resemble one another if their economies are going through different phases of growth? It is true that, contrary to theories accepted fifty years ago, so-called socialist regimes may coincide temporarily with backward countries (even in the Soviet Union almost half the work force is still employed in agriculture). Both for Marxists and non-Marxists, the huge disparity between productive capacity and people's earnings offers a partial explanation of differences between states, even though the same industrial technology is progressing everywhere.

If even a monistic explanation of the present situation, allowing for inequalities in economic development, makes current political and economic diversity intelligible, so much the more to the purpose is a pluralistic interpretation such as I have put forward in the preceding pages, though we must not conclude without emphasizing *the heterogeneity of the states that are now for the first time living together.* Nations and nationalisms, empires and imperialisms, are words much bandied about. But today's nations, forged in the crucible of the ages, are searching for an organization that will both outstrip and respect them. In some places, masters from foreign races have been or are being driven out, but the new states that succeed them, built on the European secular model, have to maintain or create loyalty among citizens, religions, and customs that are not European at all. They must create nations out of tribal or religious groups brought together only by revolt against the conqueror. Like the economies, the political bodies of our day have reached different ages. (Perhaps the very idea that they must all evolve in accordance with the same rules is only an illusion.)

But it is not the juxtaposition of different kinds of states, some very large (several hundred million souls) and others very small (Iceland has only a few hundred thousand inhabitants), that is new. The unprecedented factor is that this diversity is now accompanied by closer relations than ever before, and by verbal support for a unique view of political organization. The diversity stands out because the human race is on its way to unity, and everywhere people use the same words. China under Mao Tse-tung is probably less distant from Europe than it has ever been in the past, but never in the past did it subscribe to a philosophy developed in Germany, France, and England and put into practice in Russia.

In economics, politics, and ideology alike there is the same contradiction between closeness and distance. People everywhere are moving toward the same economic system, but the gap between the average income of a South American, an Asian, a European, and a North American has grown wider. People everywhere subscribe to the principle of nationalities, but nation-states are still in the majority. The rest are multinational, because they have recently succeeded empires established by force, or infra-national, groups of small collectivities with no experience of living together. People everywhere proclaim their attachment to democratic values, egalitarianism, and universal well-being, but the advocates of the rival ideologies are or think they are engaged in a fight to the death. The struggle over the way industrial society should be organized arouses passions all the more because the choice of a system involves joining one side or the other and choosing between a faith and a pseudo-religion.

Political unity and diversity, however, are complementary rather than contrasting features of the world today. The same fundamental forces produce not only the trend toward industrialization but also the huge differences in standards of living, the omnipresence of nationalism and the heterogeneity of states, the universality of democratic values, and the contrasts that exist between them and certain doctrines that make the same claims. People everywhere now belong to the same universe, but to ancient differences of religion, custom, and race our shared civilization to-day adds contrasts in wealth, power, and ideology.

In the middle of the twentieth century one is struck as much by the countless occasions of conflict as by the convincing arguments for peace. But we may hope that the present resolution of these contradictions will last: Countless as the conflicts may be, they are limited. In a diplomatic context that covers the whole planet, perhaps the absence of a great war will strike historians of the future as the equivalent of a great peace.

FROM SARAJEVO
TO HIROSHIMA

CHAPTER I

THE TECHNOLOGICAL SURPRISE

Frederick II left it to his jurists to justify his conquests retrospectively. In the eighteenth century the people took little part in the limited wars of the day, and professional soldiers, recruited from the lower classes, felt no need to know what they were fighting for. But in the twentieth century soldiers and civilians overlap, and the people as a whole, regarding themselves as peace-loving, call their rulers to account. So it becomes an affair of state to show that the enemy is to blame when things go wrong. Historians and intellectuals on all sides do their best to bolster their country's morale by helping not only the fighting forces, but even more the nation as a whole, to have a clear conscience.

Between 1914 and 1918 and even after the war was won, analysis of its causes was for propaganda purposes constrained by a kind of rebellion against the facts. Bourgeois Europe, proud of its civilization and with an unquestioning faith in progress, looked on war as a monstrous anachronism surviving from another age. The officials who drew up the Treaty of Versailles imposed reparations on Germany not because the verdict of arms had gone against Germany and it had been defeated (the Germans, well aware of what they themselves would have done had they been the victors, would probably have accepted that attitude without demur), but because Germany was held to have been the aggressor. The causes of the war were studied in a spirit not of sober inquiry but of moralizing. Who were the criminals who had hurtled Europe into the abyss of violence? What untoward happenings had made the most mature continent revert to the horrors of the past?

So historical examination produced only limited results; it could not abolish uncertainty. Inevitably it disappointed pacifists and passers of judgment alike.

A historian trying to identify the causes of an event asks two questions: Both are legitimate, but they need to be distinguished carefully from one another. First, why did the thing happen at that particular moment, and, given the situation, who were the people and what were the circumstances that actually gave rise to the event? And second, how did the situation come about in which the event occurred? The first question relates to what are usually called the immediate causes of the event, and the second to what are usually called the underlying causes. The significance historians attribute to the first category varies in accordance with both their individual philosophies and the results of their inquiry. If they conclude that the historical situation made the event inevitable, the immediate causes naturally become less important.

In the case of the 1914 war, historians were passionately keen to investigate its immediate causes. Reality provided them with a carefully limited field of inquiry. Before the assassination of the Archduke Franz-Ferdinand, Europe was living in a state of armed peace, but no one expected everything to explode without any warning. After the assassination, and especially after Austria's ultimatum to Serbia, the chancelleries and the peoples of Europe all started to fear imminent disaster.

Countless books, articles, and eyewitness accounts have been devoted to the week between July 23, the date of the Austrian ultimatum to Serbia, and July 30, when Russia announced that it was mobilizing its forces. In Vienna, Berlin, St. Petersburg, and Paris, archives have been gone through, the people involved have published their memoirs, and historians have reconstructed conversations, negotiations, and interviews. But the very quantity of documentation available has only further confounded the confusion.

The confusion is more apparent than real, however, and arises from mixing up three different lines of inquiry. What are the actions that made war possible, probable, or inevitable? How far were those actions morally or politically justifiable? And what were the intentions of the people who carried them out?

No one doubts today, just as no one doubted at the time, that the Austrian ultimatum introduced a possibility not only of war but of a general war. The politicians in Vienna were aware of the risk, and German politicians had acknowledged that the danger existed at conversations in Berlin early in July. Russia, which saw itself as protector of the Southern Slavs in the Balkans, was not going to let Serbia be crushed: It would not stand by and see the independent kingdom transformed into a kind of protectorate of the dual monarchy. The ultimatum was a challenge to Russia. All Europe saw that the threat originated in Vienna, and the plan would not have worked unless Berlin had promised to support it.

If to the ultimatum itself we add the refusal to accept the moderate Serbian reply as it stood (though it rejected Austrian participation in the assassination inquiry), the severance of diplomatic relations, and the bombing of Belgrade, we are contemplating a series of actions that may be attributed to Austrian diplomacy (and indirectly to German diplomacy), and which in the European context of 1914 made a general war more or less probable.

Retrospective arguments have centered in the first place on how far the course of action adopted by Austria's diplomats can be justified. To what extent did the behavior of the Serbian government warrant the exorbitant demands made by the Austrians in the name of human rights? However seriously some Serbian officials and politicians might have been involved in the assassination, the facts known at the time were not sufficient to implicate the government in Belgrade, nor, this being so, to permit the government in Vienna to make demands that encroached on Serbian sovereignty. Moreover, it seems very probable that the Austrian diplomats neither wished nor expected their ultimatum just to be accepted without more ado. They wanted to "teach a lesson" to the small country that dared to bother its powerful neighbor by tolerating or even supporting the "liberation" propaganda of the Southern Slavs. And the men in Vienna who were determined to administer this rebuke were quite ready to accept the possible consequences, even if these should include a general war.

The real question now becomes: Should we speak of those consequences as possible, probable, or inevitable? It is very unlikely that such a question will receive a unanimous answer. Although a historian, contemplating a galaxy of events, may legitimately examine the nature of the link that connects one of them with another, the conclusions he arrives at can never be beyond dispute. In this case all we can say is that the Central Powers had created conditions that made war probable. Would it have taken a miracle to avoid it, or merely more patience and diplomatic invention on the part of their opponents? We can go on wondering forever about what might have been.

The same kind of debate went on about the Russian mobilization, which predated the Austrian call-up but did not become public knowledge until after the latter had been decided. Was not the Russian move justifiable as a riposte to the first operations against Serbia? Even the German army chiefs regarded Russian mobilization as a special case, because it took Russia so long to marshal its forces. And was not the die already cast when Russia took the first step toward doing so, with the general staffs in the various capitals all eager to trigger a mechanism that would leave diplomacy no more scope for action?

So long as our examination is confined to questions of causality and legitimacy we are obliged to modify but not fundamentally to change the Allies' version of events. The Viennese cabinet had taken steps that the rest of Europe regarded as aggressive. It had thrown the gauntlet to Serbia, and so to Russia; it had wanted to win a prestigious success even if that meant a general war. Germany, having given Vienna carte blanche, shared the responsibility, whatever private reservations its leaders may have had. Even if it were shown that the Entente, and in particular Russia, had been too ready to take up the challenge, the main guilt, on the plane of diplomacy and in terms of actions and reactions, would continue to lie with the "instigators."

But there was no comparison between this so to speak diplomatic, positive, and limited culpability and that which was conjured up by popular passions. Public opinion was not looking for one particular minister bent on foiling the "irredentist" propaganda of the Southern Slavs; it wanted to get at the men who had deliberately unleashed the aggression. But there were no clear villains, at least not the kind that appear in bedtime stories.

The search for motives and incentives gives rise to endless controversy. Taking only some of the evidence into account, one might conclude that German policymakers were deliberately trying to hasten the arrival of a war regarded by others as inevitable. One could quote, for example, what Wilhelm II said to the king of the Belgians. It was thought certain, in some military circles, that the reorganization of the Russian army would not be complete until 1917 and that the French lacked machine guns and heavy artillery. Such considerations, reinforcing the confidence of the senior staff, must have influenced the attitude adopted by the generals at the talks held early in July. But extensive study of the archives reveals that German policymakers were not so sure of themselves. Berlin did accept the idea of a general war, but it cannot be said that the German statesmen involved consciously tried to use the Austro-Serbian dispute to start it. Such a thought certainly crossed some of their minds at some time or another, but it did not continually govern the behavior of the chancellor, the emperor, or the ambassadors.

In other words, when it comes to intentions, the crude image of aggressors on one side and victims on the other does not stand up to scrutiny. It is true we find even less desire for war among French politicians, while the tsar and many (though not all) of the Russian leaders feared war, perhaps even more for the sake of the regime than in itself. But the Allies were determined not to tolerate an Austrian coup in the Balkans—just as determined as the diplomats in Vienna were to use a coup to win prestige at Serbia's expense. On both sides the desire for peace was conditional, not absolute. Given the situation in Europe in 1914, it was highly improbable that a conflict could be contained, but both Berlin and Vienna would have been satisfied if they had attained their local objectives without triggering off a general war.

Europe was not made up of some states that were wolves and others that were sheep, but of sovereign states all equally resolved to hold on to their power and glory. In France and Britain there were no equivalents of the Pan-Germanists or the romantic theorists of violence: Both countries tended to be conservative and to relinquish old dreams of conquest. The Germany of Wilhelm II, in the midst of expansion, was more inclined to war and contemplated a recourse to arms with less reluctance than the bourgeois democracies. Nonetheless, the explosion of 1914 was first and foremost the result of a diplomatic bungle.

For a century Europe had enjoyed relative stability. Neither the Crimean War nor the Franco-Prussian War had become general. The wars in the Balkans had, with more difficulty, been halted without irreparable damage to European equilibrium. The "monster of war" that had put fear into the continent from 1792 to 1815 had been subdued. But in August 1914 it broke out again.

As soon as one goes beyond the limited context of the assassination of the archduke, the declarations of war, and the crisis of June–July 1914, it becomes apparent that there is no definite date at which one may stop and say that it marks the "very beginning" of the historical situation that ultimately gave rise to the 1914 war. The hostility between Germany and France points us at least as far back as the treaty of Frankfurt; and the animosity between Germany and Russia goes at least as far back as the young Emperor Wilhelm II's withdrawal from the treaty of mutual security. Unless an investigator means to scrutinize the entire diplomatic history of the previous half century, he must confine himself to a few well-defined questions.

Observers, looking back at the extraordinary rapidity of events—whereby a relatively remote outrage against a relatively minor royalty set the whole of Europe on fire—have wondered why the continent was so ready to explode and why so many people, politicians, and men on the street sensed that a storm was about to break over them.

Although points of detail have been keenly debated, the answers historians have put forward have in general been remarkably simple—so much so as to disturb anyone who scorns merely superficial data and prefers to look for the forces at work at deeper levels, unbeknownst to those involved in the action.

In obedience to an unwritten law of European diplomacy, Germany's strength was enough in itself to cause other states capable of standing up to it to join forces. The course the war took is ample proof that Britain, France, and Russia, even as allies, had no surplus of manpower or other resources at their disposal. The fact that the alliance was necessary to maintain the balance of power is not enough to explain why it was formed, however. It was not in place at the end of the nineteenth century, though the circumstances then were similar enough to have made it equally necessary. All I am trying to emphasize here is that the banding together of major European countries in more or less close alliances was nothing new or farfetched, and neither calls for elaborate explanations nor suggests that there must have been a guilty party.

According to an old tradition, France, having overcome the defeat of 1870, was naturally bound to look to the East for a counterbalance. The Franco-Russian rapprochement may have been encouraged or accelerated by mistakes made on the Wilhelmstrasse. But in the long run it would have been difficult for Germany to keep up a close friendship with both Russia and Austria-Hungary simultaneously. By deciding in favor of the latter Germany inevitably provoked the rapprochement between Paris and St. Petersburg. As for Britain, it could not but fear a German victory that would remove France from the ranks of the major powers and give the Reich almost unlimited hegemony over the continent. But perhaps Britain's diplomats would not have become so alive to the danger and to their country's fundamental interests if the Second Reich, by building an oceangoing fleet, had not issued the kind of challenge that the British Empire had to take up.

At the beginning of the twentieth century, however, the "fronts" were still far from definitively fixed. Contacts between the courts in Berlin and St. Petersburg were frequent right up to the eve of the rupture. Wilhelm II tried several times to use his personal influence over Nicolas II for political ends. The agreement signed by both emperors at Björkö in July 1905 was not forgotten, though the tsar's ministers refused to consider it. Quite apart from the dynastic links, relations between London and Berlin were not those of deadly enemies, even up to just before the catastrophe. As late as 1914 some British ministers thought to quell German ambitions by negotiating a division of the Portuguese colonies. But despite the efforts of French diplomacy the British government never formally accepted any of the proposals. The agreements made at the staff level left the cabinet in London free to ratify or reject them.

The division of the chief countries in Europe into two camps did not in itself mean war was inevitable. What it did mean was that if two of the major powers went to war with each other the conflict was bound to become general. But ever since a German Empire had come into being in the middle of Europe, with a population more than half as large again as that of France, the greatest industrial strength on the continent, and the dualist monarchy for an ally, a war like that of 1870 had no longer been possible. Neither Russia nor Britain would have looked on passively at a victory that would have made Germany not merely the dominant country in Europe but rather the ruler of a new European Empire.

The two sides were not doomed by some mysterious fatality to fight one another to the death. As a matter of fact, relations between the two blocs had gradually become so strained that farsighted observers had no illusions as to how the armed peace would end. But under what circumstances would that result come about? And through whose fault? There have been heated debates about it all. On the one side people have accused the insufferable behavior of the German diplomats, the demand for Théophile Delcassé's withdrawal, the spectacular voyage to Tangiers, the dispatch of a gunboat to Agadir, and the annexation of Bosnia-Herzegovina. On the other side, it has been pointed out that Germany, during the half century when it was the most powerful country in Europe, had enlarged its overseas possessions less than war-weakened France had done and had profited less than France through force of arms or negotiation. Germany made itself intolerable through the violence of its actions, the pride it flaunted, and the ambitions it made others suspect. But according to the rules of diplomacy it was still entitled to demand compensation when France claimed Morocco as a protectorate. Germany had to recognize that international conferences had done it no favors.

No doubt some will say that the occasion of the conflict is of no great importance and that war could just as well have broken out in 1911 as in 1914. Easily said but difficult to prove. The fact is, it was the disputes in the Balkans that brought about the final break, just as they had helped to destroy the stabilizing pact that continued to link the kaiser and the tsar despite their countries' diverging alliances. The cause of the clash between Russia and Austria-Hungary was partly diplomatic. Russia, frustrated in Asia after its defeat in 1905, reacted in traditional fashion by refocusing its interests and ambitions on Europe once more. But a deeper cause of the clash lay in the evolution of feelings and ideas. Two supranational empires still existed in Europe in the age of nationalities. Even before the Ottoman Empire was eliminated, diplomats already looked forward with apprehension to the day when the problem of the Austria-Hungarian succession would arise.

In this context, Vienna's diplomatic policy becomes more comprehensible. It was not so much a question of avenging an archduke who favored a trialist solution[1] and who many people in high places were glad to see removed from the picture. The object was to get rid of, once and for all, the nationalist propaganda that called into question the very existence of Austria-Hungary. For this reason alone, even in the absence of any others, Russia could not allow the Viennese government a free hand. The quarrel between the chancelleries also involved their peoples. Into the Europe that had emerged from the Congress of Vienna, European diplomacy had managed to incorporate, without a general war, a united Germany and a united Italy. But such a feat could not be repeated in the twentieth century. It was nationalist conflicts in Eastern Europe that now unleashed a general war.

Our search for the causes of the war does not allow us to proscribe either countries or individuals. But it does bring out clearly, at its early stages, the significance of the conflict. The immediate and the underlying causes are to a large extent indistinguishable. The reasons for the hostility between the various countries in Europe were many and complex. Alliances and balances of power made partial conflicts impossible. Germany's increasing power, with France fearing its predominance while Britain was alarmed by its oceangoing fleet, brought about what the group of countries surrounding it claimed to be a defensive counterbalance but what German propaganda denounced as an attempt at encirclement. Each side was apprehensive about the other and tried to calm its fears by arming itself. A series of incidents created a tense atmosphere and made everyone think catastrophe was imminent. The explosion finally occurred in Eastern Europe, where the opposing interests of Russia and Austria-Hungary clashed. There, the principle of nationalities was just finishing off its destruction of the Ottoman Empire and starting to undermine the still imposing edifice of the Austro-Hungarian Empire.

Wars are by nature unpredictable. But the wars of the twentieth century have been much more unpredictable than those of the past. And the way they unfold turns the situations that gave rise to them upside down. It is the fighting itself and not the origin of the conflict or the peace treaty that is the chief factor and has the most far-reaching consequences.

One has to smile at the plans prepared by the French general staff before hostilities began. For ammunition, they thought in terms of a daily output of 13,600 75mm shells, 465 155mm shells, 2,470,000 cartridges, and 24 metric tons of gunpowder; these were to be produced by 50,000 workers in thirty factories. Full production was to be reached on the eighty-first day after general mobilization.

But by September 19 the general staff was asking the minister responsible not for 13,600 shells but for 50,000. They got these in March 1915, but in the meantime, by January 1915 their request had gone up to 80,000. These were supplied in September 1915, by which time the demand was for 150,000—more than ten times the prewar estimates. This increase in the demand for ammunition for the artillery is symbolic of the overall pattern.

In both France and Germany people expected to obtain decisive successes in the first few weeks of the war. It was assumed that stocks of equipment and ammunition built up during the peace would be sufficient to

maintain the fighting and achieve victory. The result of this strange optimism was that by September 15, France's arms depots had only 120,000
75mm shells left. Over half the supplies had been used up in thirty days'
operations. In October, if both sides had not almost simultaneously exhausted their peacetime reserves, the lack of ammunition might have been
enough to bring about the decision vainly sought in the field. During the
first two years of the war, France managed to resupply guns of one caliber
with ammunition only at the expense of those of another caliber. It was not
until 1917 that supplies more or less met the ever-increasing demands of
the battlefield. Instead of 50,000 workers, 1.6 million workers were toiling
in Ministry of Defense factories, to which should be added the workers in
the United States whose labors were contributing directly or indirectly to
the Allied war machine. The ministers and their military advisers had
thought they were embarking on an "ordinary" war that would be decided
by a few all-out battles. But they were really taking their peoples into a long
war of attrition. Between anticipation and outcome had appeared what I
propose to call "the technological surprise."

In the nineteenth century the American Civil War had presented an
image corresponding quite closely to what we call total war, with its ruthless mobilization of national resources and race for new inventions.* The
period of peace in Europe, which extended from 1871 to the Balkan wars,
had been characterized by rapid progress in the field of arms and ammuni-
tions. Underwater mines, torpedoes, and submarines revolutionized naval
tactics. On land the general use of small-caliber automatic rifles, the development of the machine gun, and the introduction of rapid-firing ordnance
gave unprecedented firepower to armies made up of millions of men.

The technological surprise was the culmination of a gradual process in
which the wars of the French Revolution and Empire represented a decisive

---

*J.-F.-C. Fuller, in *Armament and History: The Influence of Armament on History from the
Dawn of Classical Warfare to the End of the Second World War* (New York: Scribner, 1945),
p. 119, wrote: "A magazine-loading rifle and a machine gun were invented. Torpedoes, land
mines, submarine mines, the field telegraph, lamp and flag signalling, wire entanglements,
wooden wire-bound mortars, hand-grenades, winged-grenades, rockets and many forms of
booby traps were tried out. Armoured trains were used; balloons were employed by both
sides. Explosive bullets are mentioned, searchlights and 'stink-shell' to cause 'suffocating effect' were asked for. The use of flame-projectors was proposed and the *U.S.S. Housatonic*
was sunk on February 17, 1864, by a small man-propelled Confederate submarine."

phase, if not the starting point. National wars are fought not by professional armies but by whole peoples, and what is at stake is not a few dynastic interests or the future of a province but the destiny of the community or of its ideals. In the age of democracy (in other words, of conscription) and of industry (that is, of serial production and destruction), wars tend naturally to expand into total wars. What calls for explanation is not that the 1914 war, spread over the whole continent of Europe through the system of alliances, should have become hyperbolical, but that the nineteenth century should have escaped the joint consequences of the French Revolution and the Industrial Revolution.

In fact, in the nineteenth century Europe was protected by various strokes of good luck. Diplomacy was able to contain conflicts because none of them threatened to destroy once and for all the overall balance of power. Neither the victory of France and Britain over Russia, nor that of France over Austria, nor that of Germany over Austria and then over France, seemed to represent a major menace to the powers looking on. They modified the situation created by the Congress of Vienna, but they did not destroy it. None of them threatened the economic or social regime of the countries involved. They were limited wars, in terms both of the resources employed and of the stakes for which they were fought, and they did not stir great public passions. For the most part they were fought by professional soldiers (the second part of the Franco-Prussian War was an exception). The general staffs, prisoners of habit, slowed down the use of new weapons. The superiority of the equipment available to Prussia's infantry contributed largely to Prussia's victory in 1866, while the superiority of its artillery (replacing barrel-loading by breech-loading ordnance) played a similar role in 1870. Prussia's striking initial successes in both 1866 and 1870, due to the disparity between the two military systems, their equipment, and their numbers, made the usual follow-up strategy—of attrition and progressive mobilization—unnecessary. But such fortunate concatenations of circumstance could not continue indefinitely.

After 1815 the principal European powers, out of prudence, fear of the mob, or love of tradition, had gone back to using professional armies. Only Prussia retained conscription, proceeding to become the foremost military power in Europe. This lesson was not lost on the rest. All the other countries, beginning with France, made wise by the bitterness of defeat, reintroduced compulsory military service, which in any case accorded with the

logic of democracy. But on the whole the general staffs remained conservative. They could not avoid replacing rifles, machine guns, and field artillery, but they—especially the French—made many mistakes about the
strategic and tactical consequences of using the new equipment. They
failed to learn some of the lessons of the Russo-Japanese and Balkan wars,
underestimating the machine gun and practically ignoring, up till the declaration of war, the use of aviation and the role of the internal combustion
engine. But in 1914, in spite of everything, nations in arms, equipped by
modern industry, were about to clash. A hyperbolic war could only have
been avoided by a lightning victory on the part of one side or the other.
The battle of the Marne ruled that out. The die was cast.

It is often said that democratically structured and industrially equipped
armies make decisive military results impossible. But as we now know,
nothing could be more mistaken than to think armies made up of millions
of men are incapable, by definition, of dealing one another a mortal blow,
or that they are doomed to fight a stationary war of attrition. The events of
June 1940 shattered that illusion. If the German army had been as superior
to the French in organization and tactics in August 1914 as it was in June
1940, it would have overcome its adversary just as quickly, and Europe
would have remained ignorant, for years or perhaps decades, of the nature
of total war. Perhaps greater numerical superiority alone, which the German high command could have obtained by withdrawing even more
troops from the eastern front, would have been enough. But, as it was, the
conditions for total war were present; all that was needed for it to be unleashed was the right set of circumstances, and this was supplied by the fact
that the forces present were more or less evenly matched.

Because of the state of fighting techniques, accidental and transitory
though it was, total war, especially in the West, took the form for four years
of trench warfare. Techniques of defense became more important than
those of attack. It was not too difficult, by building up formidable firepower, to demolish the enemy's first lines of defense. But the terrain thus
gained was so damaged it became in itself an obstacle to progress. Enemy
defenses, though improvised by hastily summoned reinforcements, were
able to halt the attackers, who lacked support from an artillery, itself paralyzed by lack of mobility and the effects of its own fire.

Until 1917 the amplification of the war was mainly a matter of quantity. The cry for guns and munitions was more than mere propaganda.

Month after month, offensive after offensive, more cannons were massed and more shots were fired. Shortage of guns meant that artillery preparation might last several days, thus giving the enemy time to build up defenses. Later on, the artillery attacks became shorter but more intense. For the Somme offensive in 1916, 900 pieces of heavy artillery and 1,100 pieces of light artillery were massed on a front 15 kilometers long.* Neither side could manage to get the upper hand. Every breakthrough was sealed in relatively short order. After initial successes, all offensives petered out. Even in the last months of fighting in 1918, when the Allies, enjoying considerable superiority in both men and materials, were able to deal the German army some heavy blows, they could not achieve all-out victory.

Of course, amplification in terms of quantity does not preclude qualitative improvement or the pursuit of new weapons and new tactics. The French army had about 100 aircraft at its disposal at the beginning of the war; in 1918 it had several thousand. The use of automobiles for transport, radios for communications, and tanks for combat gradually changed the whole face of armies, especially from 1917 on.

But whatever part tanks are admitted to have played in the Allies' successes, the war was on the whole ended with the help of the same arms with which it had begun. It was machine guns and cannons, improved but above all in much larger numbers, that finished the job. The new weapons such as planes and tanks were not yet dominant, though they had shown that they would be in the next war.

Total war, in the form it took between 1914 and 1918—defined by battles of equipment, strategies of attrition, and fixed fortified fronts—left a memory of horror in people's minds. The sacrifice of tens of thousands of soldiers to gain a few square kilometers, the inhumanity of life in the trenches, the overwhelming importance of technology (in terms of equipment, organization, and quantity) as against personal virtues all combined to destroy the age-old glamour of battle and to foster rebellion. Or rather, revolt against war, which was as old as the human race itself, was reinforced by a revolt against the machines of war, recalling the early protests by artisans against the machines of industry. But so long as the struggle continued, the latent rebellion had to be suppressed and enthusiasm kept up.

---

*At Stalingrad, in January 1943, the Russians massed 4,000 cannon on a 4-kilometer front. The ideal deployment has become 1 cannon for every meter of front.

The geographical expansion and the emotional amplification of war both had their origins in the technological surprise.

~

The extension of the war through Europe followed a classic pattern. As Machiavelli had said, when great powers go to war, smaller ones can neither remain neutral nor gain anything by doing so. By standing aside they only attract the wrath of the victor, whoever he may be, whereas if they take sides they have some chance of earning the good graces of whoever gets to hand out the spoils. The intervention, one after the other, of Turkey, Italy, Bulgaria, and Romania were preceded by the traditional negotiations. Both sides tried to gain additional allies by offering inducements that usually were not theirs to give. The results of this tourney of promises were usually predictable. Italy's hopes could only be satisfied at Austria's expense. It was easy for France and Britain to flaunt a generosity that Germany could only show by sacrificing its companion in arms. On the other side, the Central Powers won Bulgaria over to their cause: Bulgaria's aspirations centered on Serbia, in whose defense the Allies had drawn their swords. Needless to say, the considerations were different in each case: a guess at which side would win, moral affinities, popular feelings, and so on.

In any event, none of these European interventions appreciably widened the scope of the initial hostilities or altered decisively the balance of power. Japan seized the opportunity to take over some strategic positions formerly held by the Germans. The intervention of the United States alone was unprecedented and marked a historical turning point, and the full significance of its role has become clear only in retrospect. And the main cause of its intervention was technological amplification of the war.

It is well known that the United States entered the conflict because of the German government's declaration of an all-out submarine war, despite assurances given to Washington some months earlier. It was the new technology of naval warfare—at odds with human rights as they were understood at the time* (though the British long-distance blockade was open to

---

*As soon as the United States entered World War II their naval chiefs ordered an all-out submarine campaign. A war technique that twenty-five years before had aroused indignation was now accepted as normal.

the same objection)—that precipitated the U.S. decision, making the defeat of the Second Reich inevitable.

Since then, efforts have been made to minimize the importance of this motive. In the isolationist era, it was suggested that responsibility lay with the banks and industrial firms that had supplied the Allies with equipment, raw materials, or credit and, it was said, were afraid of losing clients and money. But this explanation in terms of capitalist machinations (which I regard as superficial, like all of its kind) merely refers us back, in the last analysis, to the same reality. Even the Franco-British alliance lacked the means necessary for fighting a hyperbolical war through to the end. The United States was involved in the struggle, first economically and later militarily, because even the joint resources of the French and British Empires were not enough to keep the monstrous machine of death turning.

Other commentators maintain that the submarine war was merely a pretext: that the threat it represented brought home to the American leaders that Britain's mastery of the seas was something the United States needed, too. The safety of the republic would be in peril if Britain were vanquished, leaving a virtually hostile power dominating Europe free to extend its hegemony or at least its ventures beyond the seas. But would the Americans have awoken to the common interests linking them with Britain if the techniques of submarine warfare had not shaken the Home Fleet and the empire to which it belonged, thus revealing Germany's naval potential and making everyone dread a peace that would, like the war itself, bring destruction?

It would be foolish to underestimate the role played by feelings and ideologies. In times of crisis, the kinship between the British and the Americans does away with mutual misunderstandings, resentments, and irritations. By inscribing on its flags the sacred words *democracy* and *freedom,* the Entente aroused sympathies in every class of American society. Because it echoed everyone's aspirations, the language of the Allies' representatives was understood on every continent. A crusade to make the world "safe for democracy" meant, or seemed to mean, something everywhere. What sense did a defense of German culture make outside of Germany?

Ideology made American public opinion accept the war; it kindled the enthusiasm of a young people and kept the flame burning. That said, the fundamental factor had been, first and foremost, material. The Allies turned to the United States to help them bear the burden of the hyperbolical war. America's economic participation became military when submarines tried to destroy the link that existed between the American and European democracies. The submarine campaign, if successful, would have meant the same as a British defeat: Instead of a friendly fleet, a hostile one, most likely, would have ruled the waves separating Europe from the New World.

~~

People have never stopped pondering the origins of the war. But they have not questioned why it became hyperbolical. Did the peoples of Europe fight one another to the death because they hated one another, or did they hate one another because they fought one another so fiercely? Did the belligerents set themselves unlimited objectives from the first, or only as the violence increased? Was it passionate feeling that produced technological excess, or technological excess that gave rise to passionate feeling? With some reservations and qualifications, and while admitting that the two kinds of phenomena interact with one another, I am prepared to say that the "locomotive" of change, at that time, was technology. It was technology that called for enthusiasm to be whipped up, that doomed to failure all attempts at conciliation, disregarded any appeal to traditional diplomatic wisdom, and helped to spread a crusading spirit. Technology led to a peace that created the situation that started World War II.

There is no doubt that the opening of hostilities was accompanied everywhere by an outburst of national fervor. Patriotism stifled social resentments and revolutionary aspirations alike. In a few days, sometimes a few hours, socialists who had been merciless critics of the diplomacy of the Wilhelmstrasse or the Quai d'Orsay were caught up in the popular enthusiasm and joined in with the crowds. Against German aggression in France, against the Russian danger in Germany, national unity sprang into being.

During the early weeks, victories redoubled the martial ardor of the Germans and defeats tempered the resolution of the French. Far from lowering French morale, the invaders' terrorist tactics and the atrocities they committed—exaggerated but not invented by Allied propaganda—gave rise to a kind of fury, fueled at once by military tradition and the "pacifist" revolt against the horrors of war.

But as the pointless killing dragged on, with no sign of a solution in the foreseeable future, on all sides enthusiasm waned. National unity was broken by a revival of the social demands that had been temporarily muted by the upsurge of ancestral passions. None of the combatants wanted to give in, but resolve became tinged with resignation and constraint took the place of zeal. Propaganda and ideology replaced genuine feelings.

Both propaganda and ideology were addressed first and foremost to civilians. The men involved in the fighting usually killed one another without any hatred or contempt. Sometimes they even felt related to one another through the mystery of a common fate. When they did hate, they hated a being of flesh and blood, an enemy you had to kill to prevent him from killing you. The abstract hatreds that ravage our century are to be found among the urban masses, not among front-line soldiers. What Élie Halévy has called the "organizing of enthusiasm" is a phase in the mobilization of the civil population. It was an unavoidable necessity: The unity of the nation and its will to fight had to be maintained. Defeat needed to seem a total catastrophe, victory an unmitigated good. In other words, the stakes for which the war was being fought no longer had anything to do with the structures and rules of diplomacy. It was no longer a matter of moving some frontier posts a few dozen kilometers. Only such vague and lofty principles as the right to self-determination or a war to end war seemed in proportion to the violence, the sacrifices, and the heroism. It was technological excess that gradually replaced war aims with ideologies. On both sides, people claimed to know *in the name of what* they were fighting, but no one said *what* they were fighting for.

Once general war broke out, its immediate causes were inevitably forgotten and what was at stake no longer had anything to do with the origins. All the relations between European powers were called into question again. Grudges and ambitions were disinterred, by the diplomats from their files, by the people from their memories.

Secret diplomacy was given free rein. The British ministers agreed that Constantinople should belong to Russia; the French ministers persuaded their Allies to recognize France's rights to Alsace-Lorraine. The Great Powers signed secret agreements with Italy, Romania, and Serbia; not all the proposed arrangements were indefensible, but they envisaged a division of the spoils as much as a principled peace. It was easier to proclaim that the war was being fought in the defense of liberty than to publish the results of tangled and sometimes contradictory negotiations.

It was the same on the other side. While it was winning its first victories, the German government did not make known the conditions it would impose on the vanquished. But influential private groups, ranging from industrialists to the Pan-German League, issued extremely high-flown suggestions. Should Germany annex Belgium or merely insist that it make certain guarantees? Should France lose only its colonial empire, or should Germany take part of the home country, too? So long as the leaders of the Central Powers still hoped for total victory, they refused to commit themselves in advance by solemnly setting down their war aims. They left it to the intellectuals to identify the "ideas of 1914" in the name of which Germany went to war, that is, in the defense and for the glory of its unique culture.

Perhaps, after two years, some of the German leaders and, even more, those of Austria-Hungary, wished they could drop "war ideologies" and go back to "war aims"; that they could silence the tumult of propaganda and give the floor back to the diplomats. But it was too late. To the vague note of December 12, 1916, the Entente replied, on January 10, 1917, by a note that, though it did not specify all the details, suggested the liberation of the Czechs and thus seemed to imply the breaking up of Austria-Hungary. The Entente would not accept a peace without annexations or indemnities, as proposed in the motion passed by the German Parliament in July 1917. Secret negotiations with the emperor, Charles, on the subject of a separate peace came to nothing. Everyone went on waiting for arms to decide.

From 1914 until 1918, the idea of a compromise peace encountered particular obstacles. The strategic situation was briefly favorable to whichever party had the least chance of winning final victory. It is possible to bring a war to an end when the party whose superiority is being demonstrated on the battlefield shows modesty and restraint, and, in order to spare itself the trouble of further reducing its enemy, renounces some of the gains that might be expected to flow from victory. Germany had claimed the early successes, and the fighting was taking place outside its own territory. Nonetheless, the longer hostilities continued, the more likely Germany was to lose the war, since the resources at the disposal of the Entente, which ruled the seas, were gradually exceeding those that Germany, hampered by the blockade, could command. In other words, according to the map of operations, it was Germany that had the advantage; according to reasonable forecasts, however, it was the Entente that would win in the end. Neither side could afford to make great concessions.

But quite apart from this accidental argument, it was extremely difficult to end by traditional negotiation a war that had become one of peoples and ideas. No one had set out in 1914 upon a crusade; no one had been thinking of liberating oppressed peoples, of doing away with secret diplomacy, or of spreading democracy. To win world sympathy and keep up the morale of countries being put to the test, ideology had been resorted to, and ideology, after the intervention of the United States and the outcome of the Russian Revolution, played an important part in the Allies' conduct of the war. They had not taken up arms to champion a certain conception of life or society, but as the cost of the war increased they felt obliged to exaggerate the benefits of the victory to come. They declared that there could only be a lasting peace if it was absolute and left the enemy completely crushed. This hardline attitude was not so much the expression of a political philosophy as a reflex to total war itself.

The Treaty of Versailles, much more than its critics have admitted, was the logical consequence of the war, both because of the nature of the causes of the war and because of the ideological significance it gradually acquired over the course of the hostilities.

The Austro-Serbian diplomatic conflict was symbolic of the quarrels over nationalities in southeastern Europe. It became unusually serious, to the extent that it compromised the existence of Austria-Hungary itself. From 1917 on, the statesmen of the Entente added a revolutionary aspect to their undertaking by launching the idea of the liberation of nationalities (who often had no desire to be liberated). They did so without much conviction and without considering the consequences, carried away as they were by the forces that had been let loose. Austria-Hungary was not destroyed by the Versailles negotiations. The recognition of the Masaryk committee dealt it a first blow; the rejection of Emperor Charles's peace offers battered the life out of it; Versailles merely issued a death certificate. Essentially, what Versailles did was register a de facto situation, brought about not so much by men and their intentions as by the war itself and its irresistible dynamic.

Some ministers in Vienna believed Serbia needed to be taught a harsh lesson if the dual monarchy was to survive. They were probably wrong. According to the murdered archduke, federalism was the best way to strengthen the old Hapsburg edifice, which had been proven strong rather than vulnerable by the pressures of war. For two years few people had deserted: Most of the Southern Slavs and even the Czechs fought to the end. Masaryk had as much difficulty persuading his own compatriots as he did convincing the Allied ministers. In the end, Austria-Hungary succumbed to the ideology unleashed by the length of the war. The end resembled the beginning. A Europe of nationalities arose out of a war set off by a quarrel over nationalities.

But the logic of ideas did not correspond to the logic of forces. It had been shown that the national states no longer had the resources necessary to wage total war. Even France and Britain had been able to hang on only with the aid of the New World. To achieve harmony between the size of military forces and that of political entities, the techniques of twentieth-century combat called for larger political entities. The balkanization of Europe, while it probably matched the passions and ideas of the Europeans themselves, contradicted the tendency of economics and war toward gigantism.

And not only that. The crucial problem had appeared as soon as the cannons began to roar: How was the power of Germany to be balanced? The peace treaty would be worth only as much as its solution to the "German question." Would the Reich of Weimar be integrated into a peaceful Europe more durably than that of Wilhelm II?

Everything depended on Germany's resigning itself or being converted to a conservative attitude. That sort of resignation required, at least in a preliminary phase lasting two or three decades, a mixture of contentment and impotence. The Treaty of Versailles created a maximum degree of dissatisfaction and an impotence that was only transitory. Whichever way Germans looked, whether toward Czechoslovakia or Poland, they saw grievances that they could only regard as justified. The clauses on disarmament, and the demilitarization of the Rhineland and the Little Entente, quelled Germany temporarily but did not weaken it irremediably. Having retained its unity and its industry, Germany had preserved intact the springs of its own eventual recovery. In the famous words of Jacques Bainville, "The Treaty of Versailles was too harsh when it tried to be mild and too mild when it tried to be harsh."

All the states, large and small, that had surrounded the Reich feared this above all. But each of them had its own interests, grudges, and ambitions. Poland and Czechoslovakia never managed to resolve the Teschen question.

So long as the Reich remained disarmed, the French system seemed to hold. But as soon as Germany recovered its sovereignty and began once more to prepare for battle, each of the other countries sought their own salvation, until all were swept away in the common disaster.

Such a course of events was not inevitable. It was up to France to bring its allies together to nip Hitler's enterprise in the bud. But the consequences of the previous war were enough in themselves to make it improbable that France should adopt such an attitude.

From the moment Russia's revolution excluded it from the European conclave, and the United States withdrew toward isolationism, the group made up by the victors was potentially weaker than that made up by the vanquished. After ten or fifteen years France found itself more enfeebled by victory than Germany was by defeat. In fact, the 1.5 million Frenchmen who had been sacrificed weighed more heavily in the balance than the 2 million Germans. France, successful, anxious about the future, and satisfied with its place in the sun, was naturally bound to be more pacifically inclined than Germany, strong but bound hand and foot.

A lucid assessment would have concluded that the best way for France to maintain both peace and security was to see that the disarmament clauses, or at least the arrangements providing for the demilitarization of the Rhineland, were obeyed. Pacifism ought to have produced resistance, but for psychological reasons it seems instead to have produced a desire to meet the demands of the dreaded neighbor. Unfortunately, the almost subconscious attempt to appease was directed toward a Germany that could probably now be appeased only by an acceptance of slavery.

World War I had shown that only an alliance between the Western democracies and Russia could muster a force capable of countering the might of Germany. Without the Russian front and the diversion to East Prussia of two German army corps, the battle of the Marne would probably not have been won. To turn a rearmed Third Reich away from its great adventure, Russia would have had to be enrolled on the side of the conservatives. But after emerging from the world war, Communist Russia was not interested in peace, or the status quo, either.

Whether we consider the balance of power between the nations or their internal structures, not to mention their economic organization, Europe at the time of Versailles seems less stable than the Europe of 1914. Territorial redistribution had not ended quarrels over nationalities; it had merely replaced the old disputes with new ones. The nationalism of the new countries increased the number of trade barriers and made everyone poorer. Germany was more bitter and more revolutionary than before, without being, in the long term, deprived of the ability to act.

We obviously cannot tell what would have happened if a compromise peace had been concluded at the end of 1916 or the beginning of 1917. It would be a waste of time to speculate about a (necessarily unreal) past that might have been the future of a different politics. But it remains true that World War II arose out of the extreme prolongation of World War I and above all out of the Russian Revolution and the fascist responses to it in Italy and Germany.

War destroys the traditional institutions that keep Western societies from going down paths leading to social leveling and forms of collectivism. The monarchies that vanished in defeat would not have prevented the "democratization" of the regimes of Central Europe, but they would have lessened the risk of passionate extremism, secular religions, and totalitarian parties. Parliaments are all the stronger when they are born out of transition and consent rather than violence.

It is as if violence, having reached a certain degree, becomes self-supporting. In war, as in nuclear science, there is such a thing as critical mass. Ever since 1914, Europe has been exposed to a chain reaction of war.

CHAPTER II

THE DYNAMIC OF TOTAL WAR

The origin and center of World War II, as of World War I, was Germany. But, like the first war, the second spread out from its European origins to cover a huge territory, affecting, finally, the whole planet and producing not only a monstrous outburst of cruelty and passion but ultimately the atom bomb, which raised the technology of destruction to a height of perfection scarcely dreamed of. And like the first, the second war was lost by the aggressor, and yet again, when the storm was over, the world failed to be converted to the values for which the West had fought. Even more than Germany, democracy, liberty, and European civilization were the victims of a victory won in their name.

In accord with these fundamental analogies, World War II was almost a replica of World War I. Though everything happened differently, the results were much the same. There is no argument about the immediate causes of World War II: Hitler's signature is all over the incriminating evidence. The amplification of the conflict came about not, as in 1914, because the forces opposing one another were more or less equally balanced, but because of Germany's superiority. What was at stake was still the essential makeup of political entities, but one side at least proclaimed that the era of national states was over. Twenty years after its triumph, the national idea was already a thing of the past: The age of empires was beginning. The material consequences of the war created the threat of a new conflict, not because the loser, resentful and intact, was watching out for a chance to get even, but because in Europe and Asia, victors and vanquished alike, equally exhausted, left the two peripheral superpowers to confront one another.

91

From the endlessly debated events of July 1914, public opinion and chancelleries had learned lessons that Franco-British diplomacy did its best to apply. But they now made the same mistake that the French general staff had made before them. Having realized and repented of the folly of all-out offensives, the military leadership switched to a blind belief in firepower and a solid line of defense. By trying to avoid a repeat of the earlier war, it precipitated Hitler's venture.

Britain's political leaders had persuaded themselves that a clear stand by Downing Street, made known in Berlin as early as July 25, might stave off the inevitable. Hence the touching but absurd persistence of Neville Chamberlain, who at every crisis between 1938 and 1939 took care to point out to the Führer and to the world that the British Empire would not remain neutral if France were involved in a conflict with Germany. No one suspected it in Berlin, but times had changed.

In 1939 the equivalent of Britain's warning in 1914 could only have come from Washington.* Roosevelt and most other far-seeing Americans were sure that the United States would eventually be drawn into the war. But the time lag in public opinion and the constraints of democracy forced American legislators to vote not for rearmament, which might have made some impression on Hitler, but for a law prescribing neutrality, which seemed to bar the provision of supplies to any belligerents. This step led Roosevelt to predict a catastrophe that he might otherwise have been able to prevent.

America's inadequacy aside, Britain's warning would have carried more weight if it had been accompanied by different military preparations. Hitler did not believe, either in 1938 or 1939, that Britain would remain neutral, but nor was he sure that the British Empire would get involved in a fight to the death. It was no longer enough to threaten to break off diplomatic relations—this prospect did not worry Berlin at all. What was needed was action demonstrating unshakable resolve. But the Labour Party was opposed not only to appeasement but also to compulsory military service.

The French and British alike were still haunted by the horrors of war. Even their leaders sincerely believed that no one, and above all no war

---

*Politicians still make the same error. An engagement by Washington in 1939 *might* have prevented the last war. But what we need to know is if it would be enough to prevent the next.

veteran, could deliberately initiate a conflict. From this premise arose a series of theories attempting to explain that through some mysterious concatenation of circumstances wars broke out without any of the parties concerned wanting them to do so. To accept war as inevitable, it has been said, may help to make it so. It may well be that the idea prevailing in the chancelleries in 1914, that war was sooner or later inevitable, did indeed paralyze efforts to find a peaceful solution to the Austro-Serbian crisis. But in the face of a regime like that of Hitler's National Socialism, driven by huge, perhaps unlimited ambitions, such considerations were anachronistic. Could Hitler be satisfied? Could he be stopped without recourse to arms? Those were the only relevant questions. Until 1939 the Western democracies tried to appease Hitler, to stop him while they were, at least in the short term, no longer in a position of superiority.

Other observers had been impressed by Germany's argument about encirclement. Seen from Berlin, had not the alliances, before 1914, seemed like a threat to the security of the Reich? Had they not struck German public opinion as a plot against their country's rapid expansion? Hence Britain's continual anxiety over the matter, which led it to assert that the idea of encirclement never crossed its diplomats' minds. In fact, the so-called encirclement had aimed merely at building up an alliance capable of acting as a counterweight to Germany's strength. To abandon such a policy would have been tantamount to increasing the risks of war: The aggressor would only be tempted by the weakness of the prey.

Other commentators have pointed out that after a certain date—if not July 29, then the day after—the mechanism of mobilization took over from the intentions of the diplomats. The generals had given the orders and the civilians had obeyed. Both in September 1938 and in August 1939, quite comical attempts were made to disguise this transition. It was repeated over and over again that mobilization was not the same as war. True, but this claim left out the main factor. Perhaps, in July 1914, the Central Powers wanted merely a diplomatic success backed up by a few local operations at Serbia's expense. Perhaps peace might have been preserved by allowing the Central Powers to get what they wanted. But in 1938 and 1939 the situation was quite different. In 1938 the aggressor wanted to annex Sudetenland—in other words, to destroy Czechoslovakia. In 1939, after the fall of Prague, the existence of Poland was at stake. It was permissible to hesitate over what should be done, but not to seek lessons from the past for a present that was entirely unlike it.

With hindsight the facts of the case seem strangely simple. The advent of National Socialism meant the beginning of an active diplomacy. The new regime would proceed to rearmament and try to get the territorial clauses of Versailles revised. But how far would its ambitions extend? Would it choose objectives attainable by peaceful means? Or would its aims be so wide-ranging that other countries would be forced to choose between submission and armed resistance? In 1933 there was still room for debate, but one thing was already clear: Hitler's Germany must not be allowed any advantages that would make it impossible for the conservative powers to stop him without a general war.

So long as the Rhineland remained demilitarized, France, even on its own, could impose its will. But after March 1936, even France and Britain combined could not stand in Hitler's way by intervening locally. The crucial capitulation, the real watershed in the period from 1933 to 1939, came not in Munich in 1938 but in Paris and London in March 1936.

After that date war was not inevitable (what does that mean when applied to a concatenation of historical events?), but it was probable. It could have been avoided if the forces available to the conservative coalition had been constantly superior to those at the disposal of its revolutionary counterpart. But this could only have been the case with the permanent participation of at least one of the two Great Powers—the United States and Soviet Russia—whose intervention eventually did lead to a victorious issue. However, although Roosevelt encouraged the Western democracies to resist, he also let Congress take precautions against the mechanism that had brought the United States into the war in 1917 (in the New World, too, they enter the future backwards). As for the Soviet Union, its leaders were more afraid of being exposed alone to German aggression than of the possibility of a world war, which favored their own plans for subversion.

Perhaps Western diplomacy could have won over Soviet Russia* had it not been so hesitant; had it not given the Kremlin the impression that it would passively tolerate German expansion toward the East. But I do not propose to talk about what might have been. It was Stalin who in March 1939 took the initiative and sought a rapprochement with the Third Reich. In 1938, in the absence of a common frontier, the Soviet Union was not in

---

*I thought so at the time. I do not think so now.

danger of engaging in total war, at least in the early phase. But once the bastion of Czechoslovakia was removed the situation was different, and Stalin made subtle moves to shift the approaching conflict westward. Moreover, by giving guarantees to Poland and Romania, the Western democracies had given away for nothing what Stalin would have given a great deal for: a promise on the part of France and Britain not to stand by passively if Hitler should commit any act of aggression in the East. From then on it was in Stalin's interest (or at least so he thought then, for the speed of France's defeat upset his calculations) to win, through a pact with Hitler, a respite during which others would fight while he saved up his forces for the final showdown.

But apart from an alliance between the Western democracies and the Soviet Union, made almost impossible by mutual suspicion and conflicting interests, was there no other chance for peace after 1936? Some people still maintain that it would have been impossible to appease Hitler, but such a supposition is at least improbable. After Germany had made Bohemia a protectorate and destroyed or subdued Poland, Hitler had so enlarged German territory and increased its resources that even a leader less hungry for dominance than he was would have found it hard to resist the temptation to go further. A balance of power in Europe was no longer possible. What miracle could have made a regime committed to unlimited action stop short halfway?

By 1939 there was really only one card left to play: that of the "national" opposition inside the Third Reich. Those who opposed Hitler were taken aback by the results of his policies and wondered anxiously what would come next. We know now that just before Munich some generals decided to overthrow Hitler rather than start a general war. What would have happened if the democracies had said "no" right to the end? How far were General Franz Halder and the other conspirators to be trusted? We shall never have definite proof one way or the other. The fact is that, after 1936, there would have been a chance for peace only if a nationalist, but nonrevolutionary, government had replaced the National Socialist regime. A traditional Germany, whether authoritarian or democratic, could be satisfied. Hitler's Germany could not.

It is easy to see why the immediate causes of World War II have given rise to so little controversy and passion. World War I emerged out of a "diplomatic blunder." People could go on arguing forever over whether an explosion would have been more or less likely if the Sarajevo crisis had been resolved peacefully. But World War II arose out of Hitler's plan for conquest. The war could have started a year earlier if the democracies had decided to fight for Czechoslovakia; it could have started later if they had not come to the aid of Poland. But it is impossible to see how Hitler's Germany could have stopped of its own accord, or how France and Britain could have saved their own independence without stopping Germany—in other words, without fighting. That being so, the real question concerns the underlying causes of the war. Where did Hitler's Germany and its thirst for empire come from? Why did the conservative countries give the German Caesar time to amass enough weapons not merely to conquer a civilization but to end up buried beneath its ruins?

Western thinkers contemplating the tragic events of 1914–1918 have concluded that modern war does not pay. There are no longer any victors or vanquished, only death and ruins everywhere. In abstract terms, one might say that the profit of victory can no longer bear any proportion to the cost of the battle. The only possible victory is to avoid war. How can one disagree? As far as France and Britain were concerned, the only victory would indeed have been to avoid war. But such a conclusion, though indisputable, gets us nowhere. How is such a peaceful victory to be won if other countries think otherwise? Some British theorists have thought up another idea. What is absurd is not war itself, but total war. The 185 men who died at Trafalgar did more for their country than the 800,000 who died between 1914 and 1918. Wisdom requires that instead of throwing men and wealth into the flames regardless, we should limit the ante. Accept war in case of necessity, but, as Liddell Hart, the famous English military historian, put it, with limited liabilities.

The Germans drew a completely different moral from their previous experience. According to their reading, hyperbolical war is not the inevitable product of industrial societies. It is due rather to the juxtaposition of accidental phenomena: a rough balance between opposing coalitions; the temporary superiority of defensive over offensive forces; and the difficulty of destroying field fortifications. By isolating their adversaries as one eats the leaves of an artichoke, one by one, Germany's diplomats made it possible for the Wehrmacht to carry out a series of swift and economical campaigns. Weapons tried out at the end of the previous war—tanks and planes—made offensive tactics and strategies attractive again. As Oswald Spengler had famously said, the steam-horse would open up a new era of great invasions, the last one having closed when the Mongolian cavalry lost its supremacy. Finally, the cost of the fighting, even if it was high, would not be excessive if the benefits of victory were lasting. The absurdity of the 1914–1918 war lay in the contradiction between a struggle to the death and the survival of sovereign states. A system made up of independent states is compatible with limited wars, but not with total war. The peace that follows the latter is inevitably the peace of empires.

At first, experience seemed to confirm the German calculations. The Polish and French campaigns showed a cost and profit ratio that reversed that of 1914–1918 and bore out the most optimistic forecasts. Fewer than 40,000 Germans died in the war between May 10 and June 25, 1944, and 66,000 Allied soldiers died before June 6, 1944. Total losses (including dead, wounded, and prisoners) in the French campaign were fewer than 100,000, while the victor, on paper, increased its industrial potential by some 30 to 40 percent—more if the contributions from Czechoslovakia, Poland, and France are all added together.

Just as the bogging down of the armies in the mud of Flanders and Lorraine had prolonged and amplified the violence of World War I, so Hitler, master of Europe from the Vistula to the Atlantic but the prisoner of his own conquests, was led to extend the field of his activities to an inordinate degree and to rush headlong through victory after victory toward the final catastrophe. Between 1914 and 1918 the democracies were loath to negotiate, even when men were dying by the thousands every day. How could Britain treat with a Caesar mightier than Napoleon?

By driving eastward in June 1941, Hitler was trying to make his continental empire safe forever. But from then on, events brought about the coalition he had done his best to prevent. Japan, whose program in the Far East was parallel to his own though with very different causes and significance, defied the giant, the United States. The war at once became not merely European with extra-European extensions, as in 1914–1915, but genuinely worldwide. The fire fed on itself and gradually spread, increasing indefinitely both in area and in intensity. Its successive stages illustrate the uncontrollable dynamic of modern war: strategic bombings, deportations, guerrilla fighting, and death camps.

Theorists had dreamed up beforehand the notion of reducing a country by systematically bombing its cities. The Italian General Giulio Douhet had promoted the idea, and it was plain it would be put to the test during a war between major powers. Uncertainty reigned as to how much damage could be done from the air and what effect raids would have on a people's will to resist. The German air force had been built up and trained to act in coordination with the army; it lacked the equivalent of Britain's heavy bombers, and it did not really anticipate night attacks. During the campaign in the West it struck at communications and transport, army headquarters, and strategic points on the front line and in a zone some 50 kilometers to the rear. But it also carried out "terror raids" in France and Holland (where it wiped out a whole district of Rotterdam), attacking civilian centers in the hope of damaging enemy morale. The German general staff seems to have believed in the physical effectiveness of air raids in giving support to the army—and their psychological effectiveness when directed against other targets—when the attacking force could command mastery of the air in daylight and when the enemy was weak, as in Holland, or disheartened, as in France.

The strategic situation in 1940 persuaded the British, like the Americans after them, to resort to strategic bombing on a hitherto unknown scale. Besieged on their island without any near prospect of a landing on the continent, the only choice the British had was between inaction and air attacks. Daylight bombing was possible only with fighter escort. Technology was not sufficiently advanced to distinguish clearly between area and target bombing. So Britain and Germany embarked on rival campaigns of more or less "indiscriminate" night raids. Blind destruction became one of the habits of war.

Already, in the course of the previous war, firepower had eroded if not abolished the distinction between combatants and noncombatants. The Germans had largely initiated this change, with innovations ranging from poison gas to the long-range guns used to shell Paris. Air raids had added to the risks civilians were exposed to: The definition of open cities, which in principle were to be spared, had become blurred; military objectives, in an age of industrial warfare, might include a wide range of targets; and pilots could and did make mistakes. It was hard for ordinary people to see the difference between a raid on a railroad station and an attack on a town. But with the massive increase in the number, capacity, and range of bombing planes, what in 1914 to 1918 had been a spectacular but relatively minor episode became, in 1939 to 1945, part of a central operation of a strategy whose military efficacy, though doubtful, continues to hold sway.

Ten thousand metric tons of bombs were dropped on Germany in 1940; 30,000 in 1941; 40,000 in 1942; 120,000 in 1943; 600,000 in 1944; and 500,000 in the first five months of 1945. According to the figures of a British economist, the annual loss to German production was estimated at 2.5 percent in 1942; 9 percent in 1943; and 17 percent in 1944. These figures are no doubt approximate. The losses indirectly attributable to the air offensive must have been considerable. Some 4.5 million people were employed to clear away the damage, and in the production and supply of anti-aircraft weapons. But above all, 61 towns with a population of more than 100,000 inhabitants, on which were dropped about 500,000 metric tons of bombs, had 70 percent of their housing destroyed. The part played by strategic bombing in achieving victory seems to have been smaller than its contribution to postwar difficulties.

The Germans had given their enemies the right to make use of these methods, in themselves terrible enough. But two other questions might have been posed, the first regarding military efficiency and the second regarding the long-term consequences of strategic bombing raids. When they were concentrated on certain factories (synthetic petroleum, ball-bearings) or on means of transport, the raids produced incomparably superior results than when aimed at civilian centers. It seems the generals made a miscalculation. The war leaders of the democracies—who were civilians—might also have made a better assessment of their responsibility toward the civilization they were defending. But in our twentieth century they have seemed as incapable of thinking of peace once war has broken out as of preparing for war before the first shot has been fired.

Strategic bombing was in the British tradition of engaging a small force of men, expensively equipped, on terrain where losses could be limited and a decision obtained. Every nation has its own stereotypes. The French like to remember pitched battles and cavalry charges, even failed ones. The British like to honor the "few" of Trafalgar or the Battle of Britain. And did not the answer to the pointless butchery of Flanders lie in the millions of workers in the factories, the hundreds of thousands of ground staff (those squires to the modern equivalent of knights), and the few thousands or tens of thousands of flyers? In any case, will any side that enjoys superiority in *one* method of destruction ever have the self-restraint not to exploit it to the full, when existence itself is at stake? And, when it comes to weaponry, is it possible to envisage any enemies choosing moderation?

Looking at it from another point of view, Hitler's conquests also helped to increase violence and eliminate the distinction between combatants and noncombatants. Wars where the stakes are limited, where the frontiers may change but not the structure of the communities themselves, may be fought by uniformed soldiers alone. But an imperialist war threatening to impose a sovereignty that, in fact if not by law, would rule the belligerents—such a war almost inevitably becomes a war between peoples. A country that submits passively to the law of the occupier might be regarded as sensible (in military terms the "yield" produced by resistance does not always make up for the cost), but would it not lose the will to be a nation? The presence of the enemy revives that will. The mechanism of total mobilization provokes revolt. The victors who recruit labor for the factories at the same time supply new members for the maquis.

One of the most invariable features of imperialistic ventures is for a conqueror's ranks to be strengthened through conquest. Half of the army with which Alexander set out for the East consisted of Greeks who had fought against his father, Philip. Barely half of the army with which Napoleon crossed the Russian frontier on June 21, 1811, was made up of Frenchmen. Hitler had added Finnish, Italian, Hungarian, and Romanian divisions to the Wehrmacht, not to mention the Spanish contingents and the LVF (the Legion of French Volunteers against Bolshevism, founded in 1941 to fight on the Russian front).

In our day, creating such combatants represents at once the most spectacular and the most superficial way for a conqueror to make use of the conquered. Germany's factories needed more workers: Where else should it be found but in occupied Europe? By 1945 there were between 5 million and 10 million prisoners of war and foreign workers in Germany. The technique of total mobilization, applied to such a vast area, took civilized Europe back to the era of great migrations, though the rigors of such a program had since been lessened by administrative methods learned in times of peace.

In eras when armies, in the absence of organized supply, lived off the country they were fighting in, guerrilla fighters would arise as soon as the soldiery's pillage and looting had so encroached on the people's basic resources as to reduce their usual poverty to unbearable want (as in Spain and Russia).* In the twentieth century, guerrilla fighting on the grand scale has been provoked, at least in the West, by the necessities of total war: Diversion of food supplies angered the people of occupied countries by reducing their rations not to below subsistence level but to below the usual minimum; the transfer of workers, too, encouraged tens of thousands of young men to dodge conscription and swell the ranks of the resistance.

In Eastern Europe guerrilla fighting was organized either by the regular government or by a revolutionary party. But General Drazha Mihailovitch, who had witnessed the atrocities committed by the Croats against the Serbs and was struck by the disproportionate losses that could be inflicted on a people engaging in active guerrilla warfare before liberating armies were able to intervene, wanted to hold his forces in reserve. Marshal Tito did not hesitate to carry on a years-long partisan battle, but his object was just as much to take power after the Germans were overthrown as to hasten their defeat.

In Russia group leaders were parachuted behind the lines to carry out specific missions. To maintain feelings of insecurity in the enemy rear was taken to be a military task, one that the general staff had to organize by exploiting or stirring up popular passions. The ferocity of the occupying forces did as much to spread revolt as the patriotism of the civilians or the threats of reprisals issued by the Soviet authorities. (For example, in 1941 the Ukrainians did not dream of rising against the invaders: Legend has since carefully disguised reactions that were quite the opposite.) The atmosphere of national war was to a large extent created by the same methods as those of biological warfare, conceived by certain German theorists and applied, on the orders of a number of Gauleiters, by the SS.

On the pretext that Russia was not a signatory to the Geneva Convention, hundreds of thousands of Russian prisoners were allowed to starve to death during the winter of 1941–1942. Although in the West the German armies behaved "correctly" toward the local populations, making no attempt to increase the burden of the occupation unduly, in the East Poland was subjected to a merciless regime and a reign of terror was swiftly imposed on the occupied Russian territories. Of all the follies committed

---

*This interpretation of the Spanish and Russian rebellions against Napoleon's armies was suggested by Camille Rougeron.

by the Nazis, these provoked the most disastrous consequences for their perpetrators. The Germans ultimately fell victim to the rage they themselves had kindled.

Strategic bombing, deportation of workers, guerrilla fighting, terror, harsh policing—such multiplication of violence arises naturally out of an imperialist war waged with the weapons produced by modern industry. But the whirlwind still did not imply the extermination, coldly decided and scientifically organized, of 6 million Jews; it did not imply concentration camps, with their sadistic imposition of methodical degradation and slow death. We cannot deny the Nazi the sinister distinction of having anticipated and then outstripped the extremist exigencies of total war. In 1871, Joseph Ernest Renan predicted that racial passions would lead the human race to zoological wars, wars of extermination. We have seen it happen.

Anyone looking at the whole range of Hitler's exploits in 1941 would have received the impression that they reflected a preestablished plan methodically applied. In its first phase, Germany rearmed or made a great show of doing so in order to dissuade France from making a military riposte. Even before this policy had put the Wehrmacht on a war footing, Germany sent troops into the Rhineland, supposing rightly that British blindness, French pacifism, and the diplomatic imbroglio of sanctions against Italy would rule out any reaction. From then on, in every crisis, the Western democracies had to choose between capitulation and the risk of a general war. In February 1938 Germany proceeded, without hindrance, to annex Austria. Czechoslovakia, by-passed and isolated, fell in September 1938 after token protests on the part of France and Britain. The Reich then stepped up the construction of the Siegfried Line, designed to discourage any offensive action by France, and turned against Poland, recently its accomplice in the partitioning of Czechoslovakia. At the last moment the Western democracies made a serious attempt to form a common front with Soviet Russia. But Hitler could offer Stalin a better deal: the promise of half of Poland, the virtual certainty of a second world war, and the chance to remain neutral during the early phase of hostilities. What a temptation for an empire still fragile but still full of revolutionary hopes! In the spring of 1940, France, now isolated as well, succumbed in the course of a few weeks. Hitler's empire had come into being, stretching from the Vistula to the Atlantic.

The imperial aspirations that filled German literature seemed miraculously attained. On the military plane, strategies of breakthrough and the exploitation of success seemed to have been given new life by the internal combustion engine, in the form of planes and tanks. Railroads and trucks lent land forces a mobility comparable to that of navies. Economically, operations on a continental scale had replaced the liberal system that had collapsed in the first third of the twentieth century. Politically, nation-states were a thing of the past: They no longer had the resources needed for total war, nor structures suitable for economic rationalization. And people's feelings, though lagging behind events, were already influenced by this irrevocable evolution. External menace was no longer enough to unite all Frenchmen or sharpen their sense of nationhood. The country that had set before Europe a perfect example of the nation-state was now the harbinger of its inevitable decline.

Fifth columns are a characteristic feature of an imperialistic age. They are recruited essentially from among three types of men: pacifists, who are appalled by the moral and material cost of total war, and who deep down would rather see imperialism triumph than live under the sovereignty of bellicose nation-states; defeatists, who despair of their own country; and believers, those who put their political faith above patriotism and are prepared to submit to a leader of whose regime and ideology they approve. The German fifth columns, fewer in number and less influential than has often been suspected, came chiefly from the first two categories. Vidkun Quisling in Norway and Anton Mussert in Holland probably belonged to the third. In France and Britain there were few convinced Nazis willing to work for a German victory because they believed in National Socialism. Some reactionaries saw in their country's defeat a chance to bring about a national revolution. Others with fascist tendencies submitted, perhaps not without satisfaction, to what seemed like the indisputable force of arms. There were few Nazis outside Germany; there could not have been many.

As an imperialist ideology, Hitlerism really defied common sense. An imperialist rule imposed upon old nations proud of their civilization cannot enjoy any stability unless it can persuade its vanquished adversaries to accept their fate. The Roman Empire would have been impossible had Italians, Gauls, and Africans been barred from becoming Roman citizens. Once the Jews had been exterminated (and a few months more would have been enough), racism would have lost its international value. What would have been the point of repeating "Anti-Semites of the world, unite!" when there were no Jews left to send to the gas chambers? When that time came, racism would either disappear or work only in favor of the Germans. And a master race cannot win over the souls of its subjects by proclaiming its own superiority.

The Europe of 1940 presented a pretty good picture of what the empire of tomorrow would be like. It exhibited subtle gradations in subjection. Poland was ruled by the Germans, Czechoslovakia was a protectorate, France (unoccupied) was allowed to have diplomatic relations. Warsaw would have a governor, Prague a protector, Paris an ambassador. The degree of autonomy and the modes of command would vary. The Germans had already shown, in the case of Francolor, for example, how they would "legally" direct the French economy. The slowdown could not be challenged because of France's military impotence. For the rest, the forms of independence would be observed.

But real difficulties remained. Imperial enterprises are easy to start but hard to bring to completion. Hitler, with the unsolicited collaboration of Japan, cemented the alliance among the world's three greatest powers: the British Commonwealth, the USSR, and the United States. As a result, all semblance of careful calculation disappeared. Instead of the unfolding of a plan, contemporaries were witnessing the improvisations of an adventurer.

Even the first phase of the enterprise, which initially seemed guided by the theory and techniques of imperial expansion, was notable more for the run of good luck it enjoyed than for its rigorous strategy. Hitler was consciously applying an ancient rule that prescribed eliminating one's enemies one by one. He tried, not without success, to make sure he was the first to mobilize his troops and even his factories. His theory was that given the efficacy of modern offensive methods, this strategy would allow him to inflict a decisive defeat on the enemies before they had time to muster their own forces: The approach was designed to succeed where a similar operation in September 1914 had failed. So, to the astonishment of his own generals, the master of the Third Reich knocked out Austria and Czechoslovakia without firing a shot and eliminated Poland, Holland, Belgium, and France at little cost to himself.*

---

*In the West, German military superiority, except in aviation, was qualitative rather than quantitative. Even in the matter of tanks the French were outclassed not so much in numbers as in tactics and organization.

But the secret of Hitler's triumphs was psychological rather than military or political. In 1935, when Hitler declared that he no longer recognized the military clauses of the Treaty of Versailles, Germany was defenseless. Hitler's superiority over his generals lay in his intuitive understanding of peoples and of the mob. He was convinced that France would not act, and he was right. The Wehrmacht contingents that entered the demilitarized zone in March 1936 were under orders to withdraw if the French army crossed the German frontier. The Führer had had to make this concession to his chiefs of staff, but it was he who accurately interpreted France's state of mind. In 1938 General Ludwig Beck resigned when Hitler revealed his plans concerning Austria and Czechoslovakia. Generals of the old school, who were nationalist but Christian, too, maintained that such a policy would lead inevitably to world war; though they feared this result first and foremost for Germany, they also feared for European civilization.

In 1938, in Munich, Hitler was right for the last time and for the last time brought off a success without a breach of the peace. What happened belied the fears of the professionals and confirmed the amateur's optimism. The Führer believed more firmly than ever in his mission and his star. And he plunged into what was to prove for him a fatal error. The generals' objections seemed to be refuted by the facts in September 1938, in March 1939, and even in September 1939 and June 1940. The military victories of 1939 and 1940 surpassed the always cautious expectations of the experts. But the latter's ultimate pessimism was well founded. Peaceful victories and blitzkriegs alike were leading necessarily to inexpiable and uncontrollable war—an inevitability that Hitler refused to recognize in advance and refused to accept almost to the end.

When he unleashed his troops on Poland he had no doubt but that France and Britain would declare war. But he did not believe that symbolic act would imply a fierce determination to fight to the end and destroy the Third Reich completely. After the Polish and during the French campaign, Hitler still did not seem to regard the British Empire as an implacable enemy. It may be that at Dunkirk, when he held back his armored divisions for forty-eight hours, thus saving the British army from destruction, he did so in order to avoid wounding Britain's pride and to retain a chance of treating with its leaders.

From that point on, one looks in vain at the Führer's decisions for any sign of a preestablished plan. For a few months he toyed, without much conviction, with the idea of a landing in England. But having failed to gain superiority in the air he abandoned the tempting scheme that had aroused apprehension in his senior staff and in which even he himself could not really believe. He thought of attacking Gibraltar and launching his armored divisions against Alexandria and Suez. Finally, in the autumn of 1940, after his meeting with Molotov, he decided on Operation Barbarossa: the invasion of Russia.

There are plenty of historical precedents suggesting that such a decision was an inevitable sequel to the conquests in the West and the Battle of Britain. Hitler, like Napoleon, was pursuing elusive Albion amid the snows of Russia. Could he deal the British Empire a fatal blow so long as the Russian army and air force remained intact, forcing him to keep part of the Wehrmacht and the Luftwaffe in the East, or at least held in reserve? If the war of attrition were to go on for some years in the West, would not the Soviet Union inevitably become the arbiter of the situation? It is not difficult to adduce arguments of this kind, nor to marshal their opposites. The Soviet Union was scrupulously carrying out its obligations under the Russo-German pact, performing all it had promised and offering more. There was nothing to suggest it might in the near future initiate some warlike action against the Third Reich. But might not Germany, by concentrating its forces against the British Empire in 1941, be able to so weaken the British that they were ready, not to surrender, but to negotiate for peace? During the first few months of 1941, Britain was losing merchant ships at the rate of 500,000 metric tons a month. If the bombing of British ports had supplemented the submarine war, and if the German army had made use of some of the divisions it was holding back "in idleness" for use against Gibraltar and Suez, might not Roosevelt have been able to bring the United States into the war before Britain was overwhelmed with despondency?[*]

But there is no point in pursuing such questions. Our object is not to imagine what might have been but to bring out a simple fact. The master of the Third Reich wanted to build an empire and would probably never have

---

[*]Admittedly, such a compromise peace, in 1941 or 1942, would have been no more than a truce that would have settled nothing. So long as it had Britain, supported by the United States, on one side and the Soviet Union on the other, Hitler's empire, regarded as an enemy by both, would be vulnerable.

reached the limits of his ambitions. But he had not decided on the order in which to carry out the operations involved. The pact with Stalin struck him as a masterpiece of diplomacy at the time. Later he hesitated at the prospect of a fight to the death with the British Empire, either because, out of racism, he deplored the possibility of superior peoples' exterminating one another, or because he had not yet abandoned the hope of a reconciliation.

The extent to which the Reich mobilized its manpower and resources reflects such uncertainties. In 1940, after the fall of France, the rate of production was reduced. Similarly, in October 1941, when it was firmly believed that, as the communiqués issued by the Führer's general staff asserted, the Russian army had been destroyed, production slowed down. It was not until Stalingrad and the first defeats in the East that the Third Reich seemed to acquire a sense of urgency at last. At that point, total mobilization stopped being a theme for public oratory. Moreover, according to subsequent studies, mobilization was less total in National Socialist Germany than in democratic Britain.

Improvisation and amateurism characterize the final phase of Hitler's grand venture. His fundamental mistake was the counterpart of his correct intuitions during the first phase. He refused to admit that despite his theories he had repeated the error of the Second Reich and triggered off a war on two fronts, against the Russians on the one hand and Britain and the United States on the other. Unable to deny the facts themselves, he fell back on what seemed to him an irresistible argument: How could the capitalist democracies and the Soviet Empire stick together through thick and thin to crush Germany? Would it not be an act of folly on the part of the Anglo-Saxons to help to destroy the only bulwark that could defend Europe against the Communist tide? An act of folly perhaps, but one that he himself had led the Anglo-Saxons to commit.

The Allies of 1914–1918 were united against Germany. They could expect the usual difficulties of victory: divergence of interests and competition over the division of the spoils. But France, Britain, Italy, and the United States, once Russia had been eliminated, all belonged to the same universe and had regimes belonging to the same family. None of them cherished inordinate ambitions, and none saw its temporary associates as potential enemies.

Between 1939 and 1945 the member states of the United Nations, bound together only by their common hostility toward Germany, could be divided into two groups: On the one hand was the Soviet Union, on the other the bourgeois democracies. They were bound to come into conflict as soon as the Third Reich collapsed. Rarely has such a clash been so predictable. The Germans never stopped foretelling it; Joseph Goebbels could never see that the more he talked about it the more he forced the Americans to conceal the fact. But the Russians never forgot about it for a moment. The Anglo-Saxons, especially the Americans, often acted as if they did not think the hostility was fundamental.

On the same day that the German armies invaded Russia, Winston Churchill made a speech that automatically created the Anglo-Russian alliance. The war chief of the British Empire was erasing the German-Soviet pact, forgetting that the USSR had committed aggression against Poland, and adhering to the principle that the enemies of our enemies are our friends. It was a natural decision, and it was ratified by the president of the United States and by public opinion in Britain and America. The new allies were determined to destroy Germany: The Soviet Union, bringing its hundreds of divisions into the lists, would offer up millions of dead to the common cause.

Just as natural was the material help that first Britain, then the United States, gave to Russia, which was severely battered by the Wehrmacht's first blows. Both London and Washington feared the Russian army might collapse. They sent Moscow, unconditionally, all the aid they could muster. But after 1942 and Stalingrad, the strategic situation radically changed and the balance of power was in the Allies' favor. The defeat of Germany was only a matter of time. Postwar problems began to emerge. What were Soviet Russia's ambitions? Was the army that was about to liberate Eastern Europe still a revolutionary army? Would it spread communism, or respect the independence of the nations concerned and the rules of bourgeois democracy? The fate of Europe, the Old Continent, depended on the answer to such questions. If the liberating army brought the Soviets and their system with it, one tyranny would merely replace another. The Anglo-Saxon leaders may have foreseen the danger, but they did nothing to prevent it.

So long as the war continued, they had a means of bringing pressure to bear in the form of the Lend-Lease arrangements. General John R. Deane has told how Washington refused to make use of it.* Until 1945 Russia's requests were met without any verification of their validity or demand for compensation, even when the lists of requirements included goods or equipment that would not be needed until hostilities had ended. Britain and the United States accepted the Lublin Committee, made up almost exclusively of Communists; they themselves sent only a few representatives of the London government who were really just powerless hostages. They agreed to the principle of separate zones of occupation, and the Soviet zone, consisting of about one-third of the Reich, advanced into the heart of Western Europe. They recognized the Curzon Line as the frontier between Poland and Russia, and, at least provisionally, the Oder-Neisse Line as the frontier between Poland and Germany. As a result, some 5 million to 6 million Germans driven out of territories annexed by Poland went to swell the population of the Reich itself—70 million people were crowded into an area smaller than France. In order to bring the Soviet Union into the war against Japan, it was granted the Kurile Islands, half of the island of Sakhalin, and Port Arthur, as well as the restoration of special rights in Manchuria (the port of Dairen and the joint management of the railroad sold to Japan). It was as if the Soviet Union, ravaged as it was by invasion, was the stronger party, and the Anglo-Saxon powers, with their inexhaustible resources, were so weak as to have to give way to its demands.

The British and American leaders seem to have been obsessed by the fear of a new German-Russian pact. Stalin had joined hands with the Führer once; why should he not do so again if he thought it was in his own interests? Roosevelt and Churchill, determined to bring down Hitler at as little cost as possible, felt at a disadvantage with Stalin, whose armies bore the chief brunt of the war and whose defection would have forced on the Anglo-Saxons either a negotiated peace or considerable human sacrifices.

Some of the German leaders (Goebbels, for example), if not Hitler himself, had a vague desire to negotiate with Stalin. But it seems that the conversations never got beyond the stage of making an initial contact. At the beginning of 1942, Hitler would not have offered Stalin acceptable

---

*John R. Deane, *The Strange Alliance: The Story of Our Efforts at War-Time Cooperation with Russia* (New York: Viking Press, 1947).

conditions. After Stalingrad, it would have been the other way round. The westerners' fears were probably exaggerated. It was not easy, even for a despot, to forget the blood that had been shed, the atrocities committed, and the insults exchanged and to celebrate a second "meeting of two revolutions." It has been said that Stalin intended to halt his troops at the frontiers and leave the Anglo-Saxons to finish the job. That interpretation forgets the gains Stalin expected victory to bestow on him.

In any event, it is striking that it never occurred to the Western leaders that they might counter blackmail with blackmail. After all, they were best placed if it should ever come to a separate peace. (Or rather, they would have been, if the democracies could ever have envisaged such a possibility, but they probably could not.)

Modern war inevitably involves propaganda. Apart from its more directly military aspects (convincing the enemy of his inevitable defeat, keeping up the confidence of your own forces and civilians), war propaganda tends to become increasingly political. The Germans, by bringing National Socialism with them in their baggage, forced the democracies to broadcast a different, liberating ideology to Europe. To say it bluntly, the Soviet regime, both before and after the war, was no less totalitarian than Hitlerism. Could one praise the courage and the sacrifices of the Russian people, distinguishing the nation from the regime? The Allies chose what seemed the easiest solution. They invented a notion of democracy according to which the Soviet system and a parliamentary regime were two related expressions. In so doing they were echoing the propaganda used by the Communists themselves during the era of the Popular Fronts.

Were the politicians of the West the victims of their own propaganda? Did they really believe that a directorate of the three Great Powers would bring peace to the world? It seems that Roosevelt and part of his entourage, some State Department diplomats and New Dealers sympathetic to the Communists, genuinely believed that Stalin was no longer a prophet of world revolution but the leader of a national regime. They accepted that his war aims were not incompatible with the permanent interests of the United States and democratic Europe. Anyhow, Roosevelt thought the best chance of transforming these optimistic theories into reality lay in playing fair with the master of the Kremlin: by showing him constant goodwill, giving him all he could legitimately want, and treating him as a friend in order to turn him into one. Perhaps, as William C. Bullitt has claimed, Roosevelt hoped to charm Stalin, as he had charmed so many others. Lastly, let us not forget that at Yalta Roosevelt was dying. A statesman who feels that death is approaching is anxious to settle unfinished business. Roosevelt wanted at all costs to preserve the coalition that was to destroy Hitler and the Third Reich; he had scarcely started to think about the conflicts to come.

But perhaps the fundamental reason for the policy followed by the Western powers was neither fear of Stalin's defection nor illusions about the Soviet Union but rather a determination to crush the enemy completely.

The Allies did not need Soviet help to conquer Japan: Perhaps in 1944, but in any case by the beginning of 1945, the Mikado was ready to admit defeat in the form of a negotiated peace. But at Yalta, in order to bring about a capitulation without having to make a landing on the Japanese islands, the westerners asked for and obtained a promise that the Russians would intervene in the Far East. Even in Europe they were afraid Stalin might leave them to complete the destruction of the German armies without his aid. They felt weak when confronting Stalin because they were aiming at something it would be hard to achieve without him. But why had they chosen such an objective?

It was in their interests to weaken Germany rather than to wipe it out altogether. Wanting, as they did, to reestablish the conservative regimes, they should not have wanted the Reich to resist to the death. But they did nothing to detach the German opposition from the regime itself or to hint to the generals or other servicemen that there might be some other way out apart from surrender pure and simple. They acted as if they wanted to see the Nazis and the German nation as one solid and indivisible mass; in other words, they acted against all reason.

Quite apart from the predictable rivalry between the Great Powers, the Allies' attitude toward Germany was indefensible. If the victors had really wanted to do away with Germany as an independent state and to incorporate it into an empire or a federation, crushing it completely might have been necessary. But such was by no means the case. There was no question of restoring a federation, as in the days of the American Civil War. There was no national state in Europe capable of keeping Germany in chains forever. In fact, even if there had been no new imperialist enterprise in the offing, the nonrevolutionary powers for their own sakes should have spared an enemy who was also an indispensable member of the European community. The fact that the westerners encouraged the Germans to persist in a hopeless struggle can only be explained by the seemingly irresistible impetus of total war. If this war was to be the last, it had to be seen through to the end. But by seeing this war through to the end, they were provoking the next.

We do not know what influence the notion of "unconditional surrender" really had on the course of events. No one can say with certainty that a different Allied diplomacy would have avoided the last nine months of war, which compromised the peace so seriously. The plot of July 20 might have failed in the same way anyhow, with or without unconditional surrender. Hitler might anyhow have kept his promise to his people and to himself and never surrendered. The Allies might at least have helped the internal opposition in Germany instead of discouraging it.

Nowadays it is suggested that a different diplomatic policy would not have changed anything. The West had obtained a few promises from Stalin about the liberated countries, but he had not kept them. They might have collected a few more promises in return for Lease-Lend. But would the promises have saved Poland or Romania from sovietization? Similarly, people admit now that the American military chiefs got the campaign against Japan all wrong. They expected to meet fierce resistance from an army that was to all intents and purposes intact and estimated their own losses during a landing at some hundreds of thousands of men. They did not take the atomic bomb into account: At the time of Yalta it was still at the planning stage. Nor did they foresee that the emperor—with his country cut off from all maritime contact with the outside world, and faced with cities in ruins and a war fleet almost annihilated—would manage to impose unconditional surrender even on his hardliners. But even if the American general staff had recognized their mistake at the time, what would that have changed? At the first sign of the Japanese capitulation, would not the Russian army still have invaded Manchuria and transferred the industrial equipment to Russia and the Japanese arms to the Chinese Communists?

It is evident that with or without the West's permission, the masters of the Kremlin would have attempted to do exactly what they actually did. But they would not have been able to play that game in the Far East if Japan had acknowledged defeat before the end of hostilities in Europe. The Soviets, in any case, would have found it more difficult to follow through with their plan had they not been able to conceal their action under the unity of the three Great Powers. How much would the West have gained in moral and diplomatic strength if the sovietization of Poland and Romania had been seen from the start as the breaking of a promise and a proof of imperialism? Lastly, if it had been aware of the danger, might not the West have tried to prevent the arrival of Soviet troops in Eastern Europe by planning an invasion via the Balkans?

The only excuse for the Western politicians is that their war conduct was typical of twentieth-century democracies. They were passively obedient to the dynamics of hyperbolical war. They constructed the simplest and most convincing of propaganda myths: All the United Nations were on the side of what is right; the enemy was the embodiment of evil. Incapable of thinking of peace, which must follow war and is its true object, they kept up the destruction right to the end, not trying to separate the German people from the clique of Hitler's supporters, and not taking any precautions against an ally whose ambitions were scarcely less mysterious than Hitler's. By the time the illusions of propaganda had disappeared and the rulers in London and Washington had public opinion behind them in their determination to resist, the benefits of victory had been lost: Eastern Europe was sovietized, Germany divided in two, and the Chinese Communists armed through the efforts of Soviet troops. World War II laid the foundations of World War III.

As in the case of World War I, it cannot be said that the outcome of World War II was inconsistent with its causes. In 1914 it was quarrels over nationality that had set Europe alight, and the Europe of nationalities emerged from the flames. In 1939 it was the German thirst for empire that precipitated Europe into another inexpiable war. In fighting against the occupier, patriotism reawakened and the victors established independent national states. But the restoration was more apparent than real. In the East, the liberated countries were subjected to the rule of the Soviet Union and of its agents, the Communist parties. In the West, they are paying for isolation with weakness and trying to find their way toward some supranational organization that will respect their pride.

Is it viable, this Europe divided in two by the current influence of empires that are themselves divided into ten or fifteen by grudges and by memories of past greatness?

Ever since, under a July sun, bourgeois Europe entered the century of wars, men have lost control of their history, swept away as they are in the contradictory logics of technology and passion. Out of national war came the first imperialist war. Where will the chain reactions of violence end?

CHAPTER III

THE LENINIST MYTH
ABOUT IMPERIALISM

To many nineteenth-century sociologists the fundamental contrast between industrial and military societies seemed an established fact. From Claude Henri de Saint-Simon to Herbert Spencer they all agreed: Societies based on trade and peaceful labor represented a type diametrically opposed to that of societies dominated by a military caste and driven by a desire for conquest. But Europe knows now that industry, far from preventing war, only makes its scope unlimited.

Twentieth-century historians of philosophy have consciously or unconsciously adopted this state of affairs as their central preoccupation. Arnold Toynbee, after studying Thucydides in 1914 and then going on to Oswald Spengler, put forward a comparative theory of cultures. The success of his monumental *Study of History* is largely due to the fact that it offers an interpretation of the present phase of our "troubles."

But Toynbee's thesis, as regards the masses, has a weakness: It does not suggest any remedies. We are supposed to wait for the peace that emerges once violence is exhausted, when some universal empire will rule the formerly warring states. Only Marxist theory proposes a rule of action as well as an explanation. Industrial societies, we are told, would be peaceful if they were not capitalist. It is the contradictions inherent in a regime linked to private property and free trade that condemn nations to imperialism, and once the whole world has been divided up between them, to bloody conflicts.

~

This theory has appeared in many forms—in the works of Rosa Luxemburg, Nicolay Bukharin, and V. I. Lenin, among others. But the main ideas common to all may be reduced to a few propositions: (1) A capitalist economy, by its very structure, is unable to absorb its own production* and so is bound to expand, though the individuals involved may be unaware of the mechanism in which they are caught up. (2) The scramble by the European nations for overseas territories and colonial exploitation is an inevitable consequence of competition. In Africa, Asia, and Oceania the Europeans are looking for raw materials, outlets for their products, and enterprises in which to invest their excess capital. The period of colonial expansion is a phase of capitalist development typified by the predominance of finance capital and the power of the monopolies. (3) The European wars are the inevitable outcome of imperialism: What is really at stake in them is the dividing up of the world, even when their immediate cause is some European quarrel. They are precipitated by the growing disproportion between home countries and colonial empires and by the fact that the whole world will soon have been shared out. Once that process is complete, the will to power that drove the capitalists to the four corners of the globe turns against itself.

Even in non-Marxist circles the theory enjoys great prestige. It is mentally satisfying. It accounts for a number of facts. Britain, followed by the United States, has taken an interest in the Middle East in proportion to the petroleum resources there. The Boer War is linked to the gold mines of South Africa and the propaganda spread in London by representatives of the major companies. The nations of Europe carved out empires for themselves in Africa in the last twenty years of the nineteenth century, at a time when the chief countries among them (with the exception of Britain) were turning back to protectionism. Before 1914 the big German coal and steel trusts financed a press campaign in favor of an ambitious program of ship-building; they also financed National Socialism before 1933, just as certain American trusts intervened to "torpedo" the disarmament conferences. The war brought about a new distribution of the German colonies among the victors. (Germany would have acted in the same way if it had won: Remember the famous project for a "belt round Africa.")

But if we limit ourselves to these cursory general views, objections at once arise that are as strong as the arguments in favor. The *economic* need for

---

* This was above all Rosa Luxemburg's theory, which Lenin accepted only in a simplified form.

expansion, as premised by the theory, bears no relation to the colonial expansion as it actually was. French capitalism was one of the least dynamic economies in Europe, yet the French Empire in Africa, acquired at the end of the nineteenth century, yielded in importance only to that of Britain. Russia, just entering into a capitalist career, and with vast territories not yet exploited, still maintained an active diplomacy in Europe as well as in Asia. Russia's interest in Manchuria and the Southern Slavs was neither prompted by economic considerations nor engineered by capitalist companies.

If we try to link European expansion throughout the world to some phase of capitalist evolution, we come up against an obvious difficulty: The expansion in question took place, to a large extent, before the development of capitalism. It began in the sixteenth century, and in the twentieth century it seems to be on the wane. So we ought at least to distinguish phases. Monopoly capitalism seems to have influenced at the most the last, late nineteenth-century phase of expansion.

Colonial conflict was not an immediate cause of either World War I or World War II. Morocco provided the occasion for several international crises, but all were resolved by diplomacy: None of the Great Powers regarded such distant rivalries as sufficient motive for resorting to arms. The twenty years leading up to the explosion of 1914 were probably among the most prosperous that capitalism had ever enjoyed. The discovery of gold mines in the Transvaal had triggered off price rises accompanied not by a slowdown of mechanization and technical progress, as in the previous period of price increases, but by an acceleration due to a series of discoveries. Customs barriers remained moderate. Germany's national income doubled in twenty years. International trade went on growing. The idea of a Europe forced to destroy itself because of its own economic inconsistencies is a myth.

Marxist literature is full of extremely abstract controversies concerning the famous Marxist notions of simple and expanded-scale reproduction. Theorists claimed to show, often by somewhat primitive arguments, that capitalism is, by nature, or at least after a certain point in its development, incapable of disposing of its own production. Most of these demonstrations have been challenged by Marxists themselves. It is always possible to follow Rosa Luxemburg's example and choose figures for the factors involved (surplus-value, amount of plus-value expended, amount of plus-value invested, and so on) in such a way that a nonconsumable surplus always emerges after the capital has made a certain number of circuits. But this so-called proof is irrelevant. At the most it would show that the rate of accumulation cannot be the same in both sectors, or if it is the same, that the relative importance of the sectors must be modified.

Marx took care not to deduce from the notions of expanded-scale reproduction the theory that a capitalist regime is incapable of purchasing its own production. He confined himself to showing that random reproduction, not based on a definite plan, creates a permanent possibility of crisis, a possibility that in practice takes the form of crises that are more or less cyclic.

In contrast, on the basis of a Keynesian type of thesis, it has been shown that in certain circumstances a market system does not achieve full employment, or that it cannot absorb all it is physically capable of producing. All that is needed is to give a suitable value to the Keynesian variables—interest rates, marginal use of capital, and propensity to spend. In some cases (given that one accepts John Maynard Keynes's theory), the prospects for profit, as evaluated by entrepreneurs, are not good enough to attract a flow of investment sufficient to maintain full employment. This hypothesis itself gives rise to theoretical debates. It assumes that some variables are recognized as causes and others as effects. Classical economists have objected that the so-called savings surplus would set off reactions tending to do away with itself and so restore the balance. But there is no need for us to follow the controversy further. Even the most optimistic liberal will admit Keynes's possibility of less than full employment, if not as a state of equilibrium then at least as an exceptional case linked to the rigidity of the system. Historically, in certain situations a capitalist regime (based on private property and the market) may therefore be driven to seek foreign territories in which to dispose of its production or invest its capital.

But there is not even any need for such complex and always unreliable theoretical analyses. Empirical study alone is enough to reveal the many well-known economic incentives that exist for expansion. Before the 1914 war, none of the Great Powers possessed all the materials necessary to sustain modern industry: Securing supplies against the possibility of a blockade depended on mastery of the seas. People did not bother much about shortage of currency in an age when states were as ignorant of their balance of payments as healthy individuals were of their blood pressure. But still it cannot be denied that some countries wished that regions producing the materials necessary for industry, and therefore also for military power, might fall into their possession or under their influence.

Nor is it disputed that in certain virgin territories the profits of capitalist companies had more than once reached heights unheard of in the home countries. Countries like France and Britain, which during the half-century before the 1914 war invested hundreds of millions of francs or pounds abroad every year, might have been looking for possessions where their investments would be under the protection of their own flag. While not excluding this possibility, we should remember that before 1914 the French and British colonies absorbed only a small fraction of their respective countries' foreign investments. And the same was true for Germany.

More serious were the incentives to expansion arising out of each country's fear of being excluded from other countries' colonies. As protectionism drove back free trade and the colonies, instead of being subject to an open-door policy, were incorporated into the system of their home countries, the expansion of the French Empire damaged the legitimate interests of the colonized lands. This kind of anxiety reinforced diplomatic rivalry, which obeyed an unwritten law according to which if one country added to its possessions its peers were entitled to compensation.

Even without the essential and permanent excess of production over purchasing power, national economies are bound to compete with one another for markets. All that is needed is for one sector of industry to produce more than the domestic market will absorb. In theory, transfers of the means of production should make it possible to reduce the disparity and to give consumers the goods they want. But such transfers, though easy in the abstract, are difficult and expensive in practice. Heavy industries tend naturally to grow in order to benefit from economies of scale. So in every age they dispose of part of their production abroad, and they are always looking for outlets.

Imperialism arises when violent means are used to open up such outlets and when, as a result, the principals resort to practices belonging to the precapitalist era.* Capitalism does not completely eliminate the influence of force upon economic relations. Whether it is a matter of contracts between employers and employees, marketing companies and farmers, or mining companies and native laborers, the inequality between the contracting parties as to moral and material resources modifies the terms of the agreement in favor of the stronger. Even so, Western companies, by imposing the impersonal laws of the market on economic life, made it increasingly peaceful. The attempt to increase wealth by conquest is typical of military societies: The more characteristics of feudalism a country preserves (as in Germany and Japan), the more it inclines toward imperialism.

Certain twentieth-century institutions have favored such survivals.

The object of cartels and trusts is, at least in part, to use their power to influence the conditions of trade. Through customs dues they corner their own domestic market, in which they sell their products at a price at least equal to that of a marginal producer. The remainder they are then able to dispose of abroad at lower prices. Or else they make agreements with foreign competitors to share world markets. Such international arrangements, though far from covering the whole economic field of operations, represented an important part of the world system.

The struggle for foreign markets is in a way symbolic of capitalism and its particular dynamic. It is connected to monopolies in land and in certain industries that create labor and production surpluses, as well as to the power politics practiced by certain merged interests (militant protectionism, aimed at excluding competitors from the domestic market and at facilitating the invasion of foreign markets; the cornering of colonial markets by home countries; and so on), which put them in more or less open conflict with similar concentrations originating in other countries. (Such conflicts usually end in compromises.)

It cannot be denied that capitalism tends to incorporate unexploited territories into its system. Nor that colonial conquests may be explained in terms of economic expansion. But however valid such arguments may be, two questions remain: Did the formation of the colonial empires in Africa correspond to this pattern? And were the European wars—World War I

---

*Cf. Joseph A. Schumpeter, "Zur Soziologie des Imperialismen," *Archiv für Sozialwissenschaft und Sozialpolitik*, nos. 1 and 2, 1918 and 1919, pp. 1–39 and 275–310, reissued as *Zur Soziologie des Imperialismus*, (Tübingen: Mohr, 1919).

and World War II—a consequence of quarrels over how to divide up the planet into colonial empires? The facts, if we examine them impartially, answer no to both questions.

There were times, between 1870 and 1914, when the diplomats of the various European states put themselves at the service of the capitalists and fiercely defended certain private investments (such as in Venezuela and Persia). This is not to say that the ministers were manipulated by the capitalists: They just saw valid reasons for defending certain economic positions. Similarly, in a regime based on private property, the aims of certain companies may genuinely coincide with national interests. But apart from the Boer War, which to a large extent was triggered off by the intrigues of a big company,* *none of the colonial enterprises that gave rise to really important diplomatic conflicts in Europe was motivated by the search for capitalist profits; all were inspired by political ambitions that the chancelleries disguised by invoking practical concerns.* In other words, the pattern is usually the opposite of that put forward in current theory on imperialism: Economic interests were only a pretext or a justification; the underlying cause was the nations' will to power.

The forestry concessions on the river Yalu,** which lay at the origin of the Russo-Japanese War, was no ordinary business bargain. The shareholders could not expect any early dividends. The 20,000 lumberjacks sent as an advance-guard were really Russian soldiers in disguise. The company had been formed by important personalities who wanted to interest the court of the tsar in a project aiming not at profit but at control of Korea. The object, from the outset, was conquest.

Nor was the French protectorate over Tunisia*** established by governments taking orders from industrialists or financiers. Neither the railroads in Medjerdah, nor the concession granted to the Comte de Sancy, nor the agitation over the Société Marseillaise would have upset the Quai d'Orsay if the latter had not seen the Tunisian protectorate as a suitable complement to the conquest of Algeria.

---

* And even so it must be pointed out that Cecil Rhodes behaved more like a conqueror—there for the glory of his country—than a businessman intent on profit.

** Cf. Eugene Staley, *War and the Private Investor: A Study in the Relations of International Politics and International Private Investment,* with a foreword by Quincy Wright (New York: Doubleday, 1935), p. 55.

*** Ibid., pp. 327 ff.

The same is true of Germany and France in Morocco. The Wilhelm-strasse* protected the Mannesmann brothers' concession not because it took orders from them but because it was glad to have a reason to intervene. It deplored the reluctance of major industrial and banking circles to interest themselves in Morocco. *Die deutschen Banken streiken geradezu alle, sobald man von Marokko spricht.*[2] When, after the 1911 agreement,[3] negotiations began between the capitalist representatives of the two countries, it was objections from the chancelleries and political anxieties that caused them to fail.

The list could easily be longer. The famous Berlin-Baghdad railroad was a political idea, and the German banks only agreed to take an interest (and even then with a good deal of hesitation) under pressure from the Wilhelmstrasse. The Bank of Rome extended its operations in Tripolitania at the instigation of the Italian foreign ministry: It was granted the right to rediscount if it promised to invest there. Once such interests were established, the relationship was reversed and the banks themselves campaigned in favor of active policies. The diplomats cultivated economic interests with the idea that the need to defend them would lead to the acquisition of the territories involved.

The traditional account of all this is easily explained. Colonialist politicians such as Jules Ferry were always invoking economic arguments: the need for naval bases, export outlets, reserves of raw materials, and so on. Nothing could be easier than to take such language literally and transform arguments into causes. Of course it is possible that such long-term interests were included among politicians' motives. But all that the documentation shows is that it was the politicians who took the initiative. And in every era the victors have always found other formulations to camouflage the will to power, which seems to be one of the constant characteristics of European states.

Unquestionably, when some new territory is acquired, companies as well as individual entrepreneurs try to exploit it. Even if exploitation is not the politicians' primary objective, they recognize that it is one of the advantages of conquest. Moreover, in an age when economic considerations are in everyone's mind, the "colonialists" can gain popularity for their cause by

---

*Ibid., p. 178.

invoking them. The public might be put off or even object if the talk were of greatness and glory.

As for the capitalists, is it surprising that their conduct should have been different from that ascribed to them by popular Marxism? For the major industries and banks of the Second Reich, there were enterprises less dangerous and more profitable than Morocco or the Berlin-Baghdad railroad. The more closely Germany was associated with the world market, the more reason capitalist rulers had to fear a European war. In 1911 the collapse of the Stock Exchange and the pressure brought to bear on the emperor by leading capitalists helped to bring the crisis to a peaceful solution. Capitalism had more to lose from a war than it was likely to gain from Morocco.

But neither would it be right to think of German capitalism as committed to keeping the peace. In reality, there was nothing that corresponded to the vague notion of a "German capitalism." There was no one conscious entity, with far-reaching objectives, manipulating governments and people alike for the sake of its own interests. The actions of real "German capitalism" were varied and contradictory, depending on the individuals and circumstances involved. The members of the naval and Pan-Germanist leagues were mostly lower middle class and nationalist. In times of war, groups of industrialists launched peace projects aimed at destroying foreign competition. If Germany had won the war, they would have called for the annexation of Lorraine and the African colonies, just as, between 1940 and 1944, banks and industrial firms colonized the occupied territories. Some sectors were directed toward peaceful trade; others were more spurred on by imperialist ambition. Capitalist circles, with their hesitations and their divergences, really reflected rather than formed public opinion.

~

The central point of Lenin's theory is that the wars of the twentieth century, although fought in Europe and occasioned by European quarrels, were about dividing up the world, and that their significance is to be found in this fact. The main difficulty when one tries to refute this theory is that it is hard even to confirm it. No one denies that World War I broke out over the rivalry between the Germans and the Slavs in the Balkans. Nor does anyone deny that the victors did not give Germany back the African colonies that were occupied during the war and that, according to secret agreements, were to be shared out among the Allies. Nobody doubts that if Germany had won it would have seized at least part of the French and British Empires. It is therefore clear that even if the immediate cause of the war had nothing to do with overseas territories, in its wake would necessarily follow a new sharing out of the colonies. Facts apart, we are in the realm of interpretation.

The burden of proof obviously lies with those who think events have some profound meaning of which the people involved in them are unaware. On neither side did the politicians believe that distant possessions justified a war in Europe, or that the economic system was bound to expand. The fact that the victors took advantage of the situation to seize the colonies of the vanquished introduces no new element to European history. Nor does it in any way prove that the French, the British, and the Germans, who all thought they were fighting to maintain the power or the glory of their respective homelands, were really fighting because the capitalist systems, having reached the limits of the earth, had no choice but to resort to arms to increase their respective shares in it.

Both in the formation of alliances and in the events leading up to the outbreak of hostilities, we can easily discern confrontations of a traditional, or emotional, order. We can see no proof that in our day and age man's fate is decided by capitalist rivalries. France's incursion into Morocco was an additional occasion of discord, but the French and the Germans, whose economies were complementary rather than in competition, had not been reconciled with one another since 1870. The French did not call for war in order to recover Alsace-Lorraine, but neither were they ready to accord a moral ratification to its loss. The most elementary assessment of the balance of power, however, warned them not to get too close to their powerful neighbor. France, allied to a neighboring continental power incomparably stronger than itself, would have almost entirely lost its independence; allied to a maritime power, or a continental one that was not too near, it would retain the essential part of it. This sort of diplomatic calculation applies in every day and age.

Nor does the origin of the conflict between Russia and Austria-Hungary, or between Russia and Germany, seem basically economic. True, Russia's interests in Persia and Afghanistan, which were in any case primarily political rather than economic, clashed more with the interests of

Britain than with those of any other European country. It was the fate of the Southern Slavs that decisively separated Tsarist Russia from the other empires in spite of conservative solidarity, a common concern with the dynastic principle, and a shared fear of revolutionary movements.

The only way to give any plausibility to the Marxist-type theory is to present the 1914–1918 war as having been determined above all by the rivalry between Britain and Germany, and then to present that rivalry as the result of commercial competition. Many German propagandists have defended this thesis for other reasons. To justify their country's actions and make it appear the victim of its wealthy neighbor's jealousy, they have blown out of all proportion articles taken from the late nineteenth-century and especially the early twentieth-century British press inveighing against German expansion as a deadly threat to Britain and suggesting a recourse to arms as the only way to preserve Britain's prosperity.

But these were isolated voices, by no means reflecting opinion in banking, industrial, or political circles. Norman Angell set out the prevailing point of view in his sensational book, *The Great Illusion* (1910). And what was the central point of his thesis? That modern war does not pay. The annexation of a province does not increase the wealth of the inhabitants of the country that wins. It increases the national fortune by a factor of x, but this amount must be divided in proportion to the increased population, and in the end everyone is back where they started. Or perhaps you aim at eliminating a rival? But at the same time you lose a customer and a supplier and suffer the repercussions of the impoverishment you have inflicted. Modern economics gives all countries a common interest. The old idea of spoils to be divided up, of a treasure trove to be raided, belongs to another age. In the century of industry and commerce, war is fatal to victors and vanquished alike. The damage inflicted on the capitalist system would hurt everyone.

This argument, on the whole a valid one if we accept the author's implicit premises (the existence of a world system, respect for individual property on the part of the belligerents),* can be applied to the relations between Britain and Germany (as was shown after 1918). In both countries

---

*It goes without saying that if Germany expropriates Czech proprietors in Czechoslovakia in favor of Germans, or if the Czech government expropriates the Sudeten Germans in favor of Czechs, one national group is getting richer and another is getting poorer. But in 1908 no one dreamed that such things were possible.

the leaderships were well aware of their mutual dependence, despite the real competition between them. Each country was one of the other's most important customers and suppliers.* In 1913 nearly 20 percent of Germany's imports came from the British Empire, which itself absorbed more than 18 percent of Germany's exports. The Reich bought 1,168 million marks' worth of British goods; Britain bought 1,534 million marks' worth of German products. And Britain, as banker, transporter, and insurer, also profited indirectly from German exports.

It is true that the latter had increased by 93 percent between 1904 and 1913, faster than British exports (74.7 percent). But the lead in per capita export of national products remained in Britain (233 marks, as against 150). Moreover, the destinations of the two countries' exports were quite different. Sixty-six percent of British exports went outside Europe, 76 percent of German exports went to Europe. This divergence did not prevent friction: In some places German products drove out British ones. But any British government or capitalist class that saw these marginal annoyances as justification for destroying the competitor by force of arms would have been like the man in the fable who kills the goose that lays the golden eggs. Before accepting an explanation that implies would-be rational but in fact absurd behavior, we would need proof. But there is none; such proof as there is suggests the opposite.

It was between 1880 and 1895, during a period of falling prices, that commercial competition between the two countries was at its most intense, and their diplomatic relations at their best. After the turn of the century, a general expansion of trade lessened the rivalry, but the diplomatic relations deteriorated. There is nothing mysterious about that. Diplomatic alignments are determined not by economic relations, whether they involve rivalry or cooperation, but by considerations of power, racial or cultural affinity, and popular sentiment. Economically, Britain's great rival ever since the beginning of the century has been the United States. Yet the two English-speaking powers have never come close to making war on one another. Hence the comment in a recent Soviet publication: "The peculiarity of this contradiction (between Britain and the United States) lies in the fact

---

*Friedrich Otto Herz, *Nationalgeist und Politik. Beiträge zur Erforschung der tieferen Ursachen des Weltkrieges* (Zurich: Europa Verlag, 1937), pp. 261 ff.

that it exists within a framework of close economic and diplomatic cooperation." The truth is that trade rivalries between nations are one thing, and mortal armed struggles quite another. Despite the myths, millions of men were not sent to their deaths in order to provide outlets for industry.

The hostility between Britain and Germany had one essential cause, and that was Germany's building up of an oceangoing fleet. By threatening or seeming to threaten Britain's naval supremacy, Germany, perhaps unwittingly, precipitated a rupture, and that rupture helped to create the diplomatic context in which the explosion occurred. The whole British nation knows that for them the mastery of the seas is not a luxury or a matter of prestige: It is a matter of life or death. The naval policy of Wilhelm II and Alfred von Tirpitz was bound to be interpreted as a challenge and drive Britain to join the Franco-Russian alliance.

It may be said that Britain would not in any case have allowed France to be destroyed, and that with or without Tirpitz's fleet it would have intervened. We need neither test nor set aside this objection; it does not affect our central argument about the political origins of military alliances. Britain, not without bitterness, has forfeited naval and air supremacy to the United States. To the Germany of Wilhelm II or of Hitler it would never have done so without a fight to the death.

⌒

Although World War I followed a period of rising prices and expanding international trade, World War II broke out ten years after the beginning of the biggest crisis capitalism had ever known. In most countries, recovery had started several years before 1939, with production generally higher than it had ever been before the Great Depression. But the economic revival was peculiar in that it took place mainly within the individual countries. International trade, far from continuing to expand as it had in the nineteenth century, could not even equal its 1929 volume, and the dominant economy, that of the United States, seemed unable to resolve its chronic problem of underemployment. One would have to be either blind or fanatical to deny some connections between the crisis of 1929 and the war of 1939.

One of the immediate causes of the rise to power of National Socialism was undoubtedly the unprecedented economic crisis, with millions of unemployed in its train. But the exceptional acuteness of the slump itself, especially in Germany, cannot be attributed to economics alone. The situation in 1929 and the collapse that followed were due to a series of factors unconnected to economic circumstances in the world as a whole (which included Britain's financial policy; the exchange rate of the pound; the use of the gold standard; the credit pyramid in the United States; the high level of world prices, linked to that of American prices as a consequence of wartime inflation; German inflation; the building up of foreign credits; and so on). One could easily show that the direct or indirect origin of many of these incidental factors was the 1914 war and its consequences. It is nonetheless true that the road that leads from the peace of Versailles to the invasion of Poland in September 1939 passes through the crisis of 1929. If we regard that crisis as to a certain extent a result of World War I, it is even more certainly one of the causes of World War II.

Between 1930 and 1933 Weimar Germany, stricken by unemployment, faced three alternatives: It could either adapt its domestic economy to the world trade situation; it could embark on a program of comprehensive planning under the direction of a labor party with leanings toward Soviet Russia; or it could embark on a program of planning under the direction of "national" parties, a choice that would entail rearmament and a dynamic diplomacy.* The second alternative was ruled out because of the balance of power and popular feeling. Moreover, by concentrating its attacks on socialists represented as traitors, the Communist Party deprived the parties of the Left of the few chances of success they might otherwise have had. As for the first alternative, neither the political parties nor the masses could accept the stringencies involved. Adaptation to the world economic situation would probably have meant a devaluation of the mark; memories of inflation ruled out a Keynesian credit policy unless it was accompanied by a lowering of nominal salaries, and the unions were opposed to that. Recovery looked as if it would be slow and gradual. Logically, the situation called for a few years of diplomatic armistice. But German nationalism had been exacerbated by privation and by propaganda against the Treaty of Versailles. Right-wing circles were eager for Germany to recover its freedom in the

---

*No doubt it would have been possible to construct a policy of full employment on a national scale and without imperialist ambitions. But the proponents of National Socialism wanted an active diplomacy at the same time.

matter of arms. The coalition between Hitlerite and nationalist Germans, symbolic of a rapprochement between revolutionaries and traditional conservatives, was based on certain shared objectives: the elimination of German unemployment, rearmament, and revision of the Treaty of Versailles.

All this is not to say that the former ruling classes favored this solution unanimously: Individual shares in the overall responsibility are a matter for debate. What part was played by the financiers or captains of industry who contributed to Nazi Party funds, or by the Rhineland bankers, the East Prussian landowners, and the politicians who made possible the events of January 1933, when Hitler became chancellor of the Reich? Any explanation attributing a particular attitude to a single "ruling class" must always be more or less mythical. Plenty of conservatives were alarmed by brownshirt demagogy. All we may legitimately say is that the acquiescence of a fraction of the former ruling classes was a necessary condition for the rise to power of National Socialism. These sorcerer's apprentices expected the Führer to discipline the masses, redirect the millions of unemployed into the factories or the army, and give Germany back its sovereignty and power. Neither they nor anybody else wanted what actually happened, what ended in the bunker in Berlin, accompanied by the destruction of their country.

Unemployment, and thus also the economic crisis, lay at the roots of rearmament. To say, as some have done, that it was its cause is an oversimplification. The United States had more than 12 million unemployed, but neither the masses nor the rulers there thought of mobilizing an army or building up a war-directed industry. But recourse to a war economy was an idea that established itself in the minds of the Germans, loyal to their military traditions and anxious to modify, if not to overthrow altogether, the conditions laid down at Versailles. But somehow or other, sooner or later, Germany would have asked for, and obtained, equal rights, and would have asked for, if not obtained, a revision of the peace treaties. And yet, it was not implicit in the permanent features of the German situation that a man like Hitler and a party like the Nazi Party should take power. It was the style and ambitions of the National Socialists, not those of the traditional nationalists, that portended war.

When rearmament had begun and the theory of full employment applied on a national scale, was war the inevitable outcome? Was rearmament leading to aggression just as unemployment had led to rearmament? Did the economic system of the Third Reich preclude peace or even the truce that a British trade delegation offered the Berlin leadership yet again on the eve of the attack on Prague? The debate seems abstract and unreal. Hitler and his entourage always thought in political, not economic, terms. What they wanted was power for their country; wealth for the master race would be a consequence. They never asked themselves whether, economically speaking, they could stop, because after 1939 they never had any intention of stopping. At least occasionally, Hitler actually wanted war: He thought he alone could conduct it successfully, and he regarded it as indispensable to the achievement of his aims. The National Socialist system itself arose out of imperialist ambition.

Would not Hitler have been propelled to conquest, whatever happened, by the economic system he had constructed? This theory is supported by pseudo-Marxists who claim to see in the policies of Hjalmar Schacht, German financier and minister of the economy, the inevitable tendency toward imperialism that they regard as typical of monopoly capitalism. The same argument is put forward by other critics who believe that National Socialism, and so Hitler himself, would have been put in peril by even a temporary lull in the rush to war.

After 1938 and the departure of Dr. Schacht, the economic situation was reversed. What Germans feared now was not unemployment but inflation. Not only had full employment been achieved; there was actually a shortage of workers. An attempt was made to turn shopkeepers, whose votes had been won by demagogic attacks on Jews and department stores, into industrial workers. At this time, Dr. Schacht was in favor of a pause. No more labor vouchers or short-term bonds would be issued now that they carried no guarantee and no longer served to bring unemployed men or machines back into the circuit of production. All that had been achieved would be stabilized. It is thus absurd to suggest that the absence of a recovery in private investment threatened the Third Reich with a collapse that only war could avert.

The "priming the pump" theory had been disproved in 1934, when a limited increase in purchasing power, arising out of new public works, had failed to produce a "multiplying effect" and spread prosperity throughout the economy. The results of priming the pump had been limited. Private investment remained at a standstill. The state had been forced to take on what it had hoped to leave to the initiative of entrepreneurs. But by 1938 or 1939 the situation had changed: After rearmament, the four-year plan, and the annexation of Austria and Czechoslovakia, the Third Reich did not have to choose between military conquest and falling back into stagnation.

But, it will be objected, did not the threat come from another quarter—the lack of currency needed to buy the food that Germany's soil could not produce* and the raw materials that did not exist in its subsoil, even after the acquisition of new territory? Germany's conquests underlined rather than corrected the imbalance. Neither Austria nor Czechoslovakia was self-sufficient. Both had to import part of their food requirements. Both were more closely linked to the world economy than was the Third Reich itself. There can be no doubt that in 1939 German self-sufficiency was as distant and inaccessible an ideal as it had been from the beginning. On what might be called the philosophical plane, it might be said that in the long term Germany still could have chosen to become part of the world economy or even of an expanding supranational one. But the problem did not seem urgent. The Western democracies were ready to make concessions for the sake of appeasement. Once again Hitler was not subjected to any economic constraint.

Might Hitler's authority and even his regime have been shaken by a truce? Would he have lost some of the prestige he had won by his bloodless successes? There is nothing to suggest it might have been so. In September 1938 the people of Germany dreaded a general war almost as much as the French and British did. They would not have blamed their Führer for saving the peace; on the contrary. After Munich, Hitler's Germany was sure of wielding a more complete hegemony over Central Europe than the one that the kaiser's Germany had been refused before 1914. But so long as there was the Soviet Union on one side and the Franco-British alliance on the other, hegemony over Mitteleuropa was still a long way from being a real European empire. Though hidden by alleged political or economic necessities, the truth is that Hitler was not satisfied with limited supremacy. He wanted to use his temporary military superiority to eliminate Poland at least. This he did and so unleashed the juggernaut.

The economy of the Third Reich contained many incitements to imperialist expansion. Norman Angell's arguments did not apply to a system

---

*The Reich imported about 15 percent of its food from abroad.

like that of National Socialist Germany. What does it matter, said the British pacifist, whether a province with mines or factories is inside or outside a country's frontiers? If it is inside, the people in other provinces who want coal or manufactured goods will have to exchange goods of equal value to either indigenous or foreign producers.* But this argument no longer applies when relations between economic units are reduced by non-convertibility of currency and controls on external trade. If coal or iron mines are outside a country's borders, it will have to work its own, possibly poorer and less productive mines and spend more on equipment and labor to exploit them. Or else it will have to buy coal and iron using goods otherwise reserved for other barter agreements.

Inevitably, an advocate of National Socialism inclines toward the theory of *grand espace,* or expansion in areas where for one reason or another borders present no problem. The fewer obstacles the planners encounter, the more smoothly the authoritarian organization of an economic system can proceed. By definition, planners have no power over men and materials on the other side of the customs limits. They cannot foretell the prices of the raw materials they will want to import, or the changing tastes of those who by purchasing manufactured goods provide them with currency. Such forced subjection to a foreign clientele represents the survival of a principle the planners tried to abolish at home. But subjection changes to supremacy when by force of arms buyers and sellers alike have been brought into the same planned economy.

Russia, despite its backwardness in the matter of equipment, was better adapted to the so-called Marxist experiment because it depended less than any other European country on international trade. Because Russia was almost capable, if necessary, of self-sufficiency, it could defy blockades and apply in full the idea of authoritarian planning. And yet, applied to national economies traditionally integrated into the world economy, this same principle was bound to provoke imperialist temptations. Desire for conquest and dreams of rationalization came together in the theory of *grand espace.*

---

*Needless to say, this argument simplifies and schematizes the problem. Even in an era of free trade, territorial borders are not entirely without importance, though their importance is reduced.

So we are far from denying the imperialist possibilities inherent in the economic regime adopted by National Socialism. What we do claim is that the Third Reich was not impelled toward imperialism by the vestiges of capitalism it harbored. The temptation of imperialism would not have been less if Germany's entrepreneurs and private managers had been replaced by state-appointed managers, if the Ruhr had been nationalized, or if total planning had been fully carried out; on the contrary. Heavy industry, owned nationally, would still have been disproportionately massive in relation to the peaceful needs of the domestic market alone. The need to buy more than was needed for keeping people and factories provided with supplies would still have been there, as would the desire to make the plan include as much territory as possible. In short, the contradiction between the essence of modern economics and National Socialism, between political nationalism and the industrial system, would not have been resolved. And it is this contradiction that was the ultimate cause of Europe's suicide.

The contradiction first appeared not at the beginning but in the course of World War I. A traditional conflict expanded into a hyperbolical war because of the weapons that industry provided for the combatants. The paradox had grown more acute before 1939. The troubles that followed the 1914–1918 war and the 1929 crisis had driven the countries of Europe toward the expedients of interventionist trade, in isolation from the world economic context. National Socialism was an extreme form of such withdrawal. Its structure favored neither peaceful trade nor peaceful empires. Although the motives of the protagonists were political, and the conqueror was driven by the will to power, Europe was being torn apart by an absurd setup even before the Hitler escapade began. The nations of Europe failed to provide planning with a rational structure.

⁓

Modern industry has been inexorably linked to military development throughout the centuries of their growth. And although none of the fundamental discoveries that made the Industrial Revolution possible seems to have been prompted by the needs of the military, those needs more than once speeded up or improved methods of fabrication. Mass production of iron, steel, and textiles, adopted partly to meet military requirements, also changed entirely the way battles were fought.

Analogies are often drawn between the style of modern industry and that of an army. Armies take thousands, hundreds of thousands, and finally millions of men away from an organic kind of community and place them in an ordered hierarchy whose single aim is collective action and output. Industry does the same. Discipline is not the same in the factory as it is in the barracks: The worker still has a family life outside the workplace. But there is a parallel, carried to terrible extremes in the labor camps in wartime Germany and in the Russia of the Five-Year Plans.

The evolution of capitalism in the last half of the nineteenth and the first years of the twentieth century opened up a different prospect. The humanization of industrial labor began to seem possible. Improvements in the standard of living gave workers back the personal life of which they had been deprived during the phase of initial accumulation, the period when coal, textiles, and metallurgy predominated. Working-class districts in Sweden and Germany and some recently built areas in Britain no longer conjured up the "damned of the earth." Part, at least, of the proletariat was gradually achieving decent living conditions. A social framework was coming into being. Bourgeoisification was breaking down the isolation of the worker and the amorphousness of the masses. The industrial army was merging little by little into civil society.

The wars did not halt this process. In some ways and in some countries they accelerated it. But they introduced a danger that the middle classes, in the days of their glory, never even dreamed of: the threat of a whole society run like a military organization. Just when economic progress was helping to cure some of the ills arising out of technology, wars have led to the total mobilization of societies.

The reign of the bourgeoisie may soon come to look like a precarious transition between the military order of the aristocracies and the military order of the technocracies.

CHAPTER IV

WAR AND THE TOTAL STATE

Throughout the ages moralists have deplored wars and denounced the destruction they bring. But historians and sociologists, though they do not defend them, acknowledge that wars are of some indirect use: More than once in the past, they have made possible the creation of larger political units, the pacification of wider areas, and the spread of cultures said to be superior. No one, however, has even been able to calculate the cost, in terms of irreplaceable men and values, of empire building, hymned though it may be by the great-nephews of the vanquished. But despite all the uncertainties, we may not unreasonably praise Demosthenes, the belated defender of Athens's independence, without condemning Philip or Alexander. The cities had outlived their historical usefulness. Greece, united by the Macedonian armies, was capable of embarking on the great Eastern adventure. Even *Delenda est Carthago*, the saying children learn at school without realizing its cruelty, is not remembered, as it should be, as a symbol of barbarism, so thoroughly did posterity come to believe in the benefits of Roman peace.

In our own day the historian's optimism, a reflection of the victors' complacency, has rightly been called into question. People are inclined nowadays to defend the victims. Why should the culture of Carthage be considered less valuable than that of Rome? Were the Celts any better off because of Romanization? Simone Weil has carried the reversal of established attitudes to its logical conclusion. Condemning violence itself, she is led finally to condemn all conquerors. But this extreme is no more satisfactory than its opposite. To ratify all the judgments of history is tantamount to saying that might is right, which results in opportunism (unless through some act of faith one is sure of being able to read the future). But to reject them all is tantamount to denying that force may sometimes be necessary to the creation of a state or of a social order, and this way of thinking can lead to a kind of abstentionism.

Sociologists, arguing neither for or against the force of arms, have asked themselves whether the wars of the twentieth century have any credit whatsoever to set against the shattering debit of millions of dead and miles upon miles of ruins.

✐

In absolute figures the wars of the twentieth century probably caused more deaths than any earlier war.* Even if the losses are calculated in proportion to total populations, the wars of the twentieth century rank among the most costly in history. The men who died in action between 1914 and 1918 represented 3.4 percent of the total population of France and 3.0 percent of the population of Germany. If we include indirect losses (deaths in excess of the normal mortality rates and the drop in the birthrates), France lost 7.7 percent of its population, Germany 8 percent. But we should not forget that the 20 million human lives (not including Russia) destroyed by bullets, gas, or the influenza epidemic of 1919 almost equaled the normal population increase for Europe over ten years. Natural disasters, famine, and disease once caused far greater ravages.

Some countries suffered more than others. In France the political and moral consequences of the bloodletting were long-lasting and could be seen throughout the period between the two wars and perhaps beyond. Modern war carries out a kind of reverse selection, sparing the old and sickly and eliminating the brave young men. The demographic balance between the generations may be changed for a long time.** But despite such reservations, the overall conclusions remain the same.

The first war of the twentieth century was more costly than those of the nineteenth (though probably not, for France, than those of the Revolution

---

*Statistics on losses imputable to wars are to be found in Philip Quincy Wright, *A Study of War* (Chicago: University of Chicago Press, 1942), and in Pitirim A. Sorokin, *Social and Cultural Dynamics*, 4 vols. (New York: American Book Co., 1937–1941), esp. vol. 1, appendix 21.

**Between 1914 and 1918, 20 percent of the men in France aged twenty to twenty-four were killed, 15 percent of those of the same age bracket in Germany, and 10 percent of those in Britain.

or the Empire), but it did not inflict incurable wounds on the peoples of Europe. If, as some sociologists suggest, war is to be seen as a way of eliminating population surpluses, it is singularly inefficient in this respect. Epidemics, civil wars, and deportations do the job much more quickly.

Russia and Germany apart, the European countries were less affected demographically by World War II than by World War I. France's total casualties, about 800,000 (including the probable drop in births), were made up in less than three years by the increase of births over deaths. The direct casualties of the United States (some 250,000) were demographically insignificant: The population went on growing throughout the hostilities. In Western Europe the birthrate rose in the postwar years, following a trend that had begun during the conflict. In the face of all arguments, but in accordance with an instinct more profound than argument, disasters and the anguish they bring renew the will to live. The countries that implemented the Marshall Plan (1948–1952) had about 10 percent more mouths to feed than they had had before 1939.

True, these countries did not experience the horrors of total war. Britain was bombed but not invaded,* and did not fight any battles comparable to those of Flanders. The U.S. Army always enjoyed such material superiority that it was generally lavish with ammunition and economical with blood. The big naval and air encounters were fought and won by a few thousand combatants. The costly capture of some strategic positions (such as Okinawa) involved some tens of thousands of men. Only Germany and Russia experienced the extremes of continental war. Only Poland suffered the worst rigors of occupation and attempted a general popular insurrection. And only Yugoslavia saw both ferocious civil conflict and guerrilla warfare. In these places the losses were considerable, both in relative and absolute terms.

The figure of 17 million dead has been given for the Soviet Union (7 million service personnel and 10 million civilians), about 10 percent of the population; for Poland, 4 to 5 million, about 15 percent of the population; for Yugoslavia, 1.5 million, over 10 percent; for Germany, 3 million soldiers and some tens of thousands of civilians, about 5 percent (though to these must be added the German prisoners who died in Russia or never

---

*In 1942, traffic accidents (6,926) caused more deaths than air raids (3,221), and more casualties (147,544) than the total casualties in the armed forces during the first two years of the war (145,012).

emerged from the camps, not to mention the drop in births arising out of various events during and after the hostilities).

Poland's losses are a special case. More than 3 million Jews were purely and simply exterminated. This was not due to the war itself, but rather to a policy devised in advance and put into practice systematically when war provided the opportunity. When Hitler, in 1939, said that if there was a war the Jews would not survive it whatever happened, he was telling the truth for once.

The case of the Jews apart, the effects of these bloodlettings were usually transitory. The growth of the Polish, Yugoslav, and Russian populations was scarcely set back, and certainly not halted. Only the German population had difficulty in recovering. Before 1933 the net rate of reproduction had fallen below the number necessary to maintain population size. But Hitler's policies produced some results, and the net rate of reproduction rose slightly above parity. Between 1939 and 1945 Germany managed to limit the birth deficit. In the western zones the birthrate seems to have reverted more or less to normal, but what will the fertility rate be among the 9 million emigrants in the eastern zone? A population with a falling birthrate may be affected by the consequences of war for several decades (as was seen in France after the wars of the Empire and the war of 1914–1918).

For the Western countries World War II was less costly than World War I. Casualty figures were not determined by the efficacy of equipment alone: Organization and tactics helped to limit them, and sometimes to increase them. The frontline attacks in Flanders and the battle of attrition at Verdun cost the armies hundreds of thousands of dead and wounded. The price paid for the German blitzkrieg in 1940,* as for that of the Allies in 1944–1945, was relatively low.

Medical progress now makes it possible to save a growing proportion of the wounded and to fight epidemics that in earlier centuries killed more people than the fighting itself. The number of men in uniform increases in absolute figures and even in proportion to the total population, but the proportion of losses in relation to the total number of serving soldiers tends to decrease.**

---

*Fewer than 100,000 men, with less than a third of them killed.

**According to Wright, 30 to 50 percent of serving soldiers used to die on the battlefield in the Middle Ages. The percentage seems to have fallen to 20, 15, and then 10 percent in the centuries that followed, but is even lower in the twentieth century.

In any case, even supposing the wars of the twentieth century to be more costly than those of the past, the statistics do not show that they have harmed the nations concerned on the plane of demography. They have made great and sudden changes to the balance of power between nations, they have accelerated the numerical decline in populations that already have a low birthrate, but they have barely slowed down growth in populations where the birthrate is high.

The figures for physical damage and destruction present a similar picture. It is easy to list impressive statistics concerning the cost of the fighting and the scale of the destruction. Between 1915 and 1918 France's extraordinary expenditure rose above 125 billion francs; the peacetime budget was on the order of 5 billion.* The daily cost of the war in Britain was on the order of 35 million dollars a day for the war as a whole. In Germany the daily cost rose from 12 million dollars in 1914 to more than 32 in 1918.

Similarly, there is no difficulty collecting the figures for the destruction suffered by France during the two wars, or by Germany and Russia during the second. For example, the total damage inflicted on France in World War II is calculated at about 5,000 billion 1950 francs, and the total losses, direct and indirect, at 27 billion (about three times the national revenue).

But the real problem does not lie in debates about estimated damage (the cost of reconstructing or replacing a block of flats or machinery, even in partly used condition). The question is, to what extent do wars leave countries permanently impoverished? Is the power to destroy greater now than the power to construct?

Somehow the people always foot the bill for wars. Apartment blocks that have been knocked down have to be put up again. True, the billions spent on dust and smoke are lost forever, when they might have been used for making useful things. But the accounts of modern societies are complex, and an industrial economy can repair some kinds of damage quite quickly.

Let us recall a well-known fact: Ten years after the end of World War I the national income of all the main belligerent countries was equal to or more than what it had been before hostilities began. Agricultural production took seven or eight years to return to its pre-1914 level; industrial production two or three years less. And even this interval was not limited

---

*Cf. Ernest L. Bogart, *The War Costs and Their Financing: A Study of the Financing of the War and the After-War Problems of Debt and Taxation* (New York: Appelton, 1921).

by the physical constraints on production alone; occasional economic crises slowed down the recovery, too.

The fact that postwar national revenue roughly equaled its prewar counterpart does not mean that all classes of the population enjoyed the same standard of living as before. The distribution of incomes within countries had changed. The situations of individuals had often been turned upside down by bankruptcy or by an equally rapid and unwarranted acquisition of wealth. Overall, owners of capital suffered more than those whose income came from the sale of their labor. Holders of government bonds, the real value of which was reduced by four-fifths by inflation, or of Russian government loans, devalued by the 1917 revolution, have no chance of getting their money back. But the countries themselves take only a few years to rebuild their means of production. If harvests are normal and factories turn out the same quantity of manufactured goods, the mass of products offered on the market remains more or less the same. Rough statistics for the standard of living reflect the fact that the volume of goods available remains fairly stable.

In financial terms, modern wars are paid for by the countries concerned partly through taxes and partly through borrowing, or just by issuing paper money. Eventually the money put on the market through budget deficits comes back to the state in the form of subscribed loans. Between 1914 and 1918, the chief belligerents financed only an absurdly small part of their expenditure through taxes. The rules governing a war economy had not yet been learned. For Britain, the least bad example, the figure was only 25 percent. The choice between taxation and borrowing was clearly not equivalent to the distribution of costs between present and future generations. People's annual consumption can only absorb the goods that are actually available. During a war the consumption depends chiefly on the amount of merchandise people can find to buy: Even high taxation does not substantially reduce this amount, since the income in circulation greatly exceeds the value of goods on the market. The method of financing, whether taxation, borrowing, or inflation, affects the ultimate value of the currency, the purchasing power of the public after the war, and the way losses suffered by the people as a whole are distributed among the various groups. Between 1914 and 1918 Britain's national debt rose from 650 million pounds to 7.4 billion; that of France from 33 billion francs to 150 billion. These increases of domestic debts beyond what was strictly necessary prepared the way for monetary inflation, which victimized people on fixed incomes while sparing those with incomes that were revalued when exchange rates collapsed. Where, as in Britain, the value of the currency remained stable, the volume of transfers required to pay interest influenced the functioning of the system to an extent difficult to assess accurately.

In real terms the financing of wars is no longer a mystery. The loss of foreign investments is tantamount to the squandering of accumulated wealth. The French and the British alike received considerable amounts of foreign credits, and as these were never reimbursed, their Allies and neutral countries paid indirectly for part of their war expenditure. During hostilities and the first years of peace, the population paid for another part through a fall in the standard of living. Reducing the margin between normal and subsistence civilian consumption frees resources to be spent on tanks and guns. Neglecting the upkeep of capital, houses, land, and factories is another way of reducing popular consumption. But it produces lasting impoverishment if certain elements of capital (such as houses and chateaux) are never restored.

This method of financing explains the picture that emerges from a comparison of national incomes before and ten years after the war. A country's collective wealth, at least insofar as it can be expressed in figures, seems to be affected only by a reduction in capital, foreign investments, and the value of certain elements of domestic capital. A recession such as the one that afflicted France between 1930 and 1938 can cost a country, economically speaking, as much as a war. If we compare what the French economy would have produced, assuming full employment and normal expansion, with what it actually did produce, the difference amounts to a figure as astronomical as the cost of a war. In 1938 the index of industrial production was 20 to 25 percent lower than in 1929; it should have been 10 to 15 percent higher.

This is why economies with very extensible production capacity can keep their armies supplied without seriously impairing the expenditure of their civilian populations. Thus, in the United States, the industrial system could mass-produce the instruments of war while still providing civilians with most of the usual manufactured goods.* Agriculture, too,

---

*Production of durable goods like cars, washing machines, refrigerators, and so on was suspended.

could increase harvests to such an extent that even while the United States was supplying part of the rest of the world, the authorities in Washington were able to avoid rationing almost entirely. In 1945 the United States was richer, not poorer, than in 1939, with equipment up by some 50 percent. The only burden inherited from the war seems to have been an increase in the national debt. Even so, the servicing of the interest did not call for transfers large enough to endanger the currency or the functioning of the system.

In many ways the case of the United States is so different from that of the European countries as to preclude comparison. Military operations took place far away from American territory, and U.S. reserves of production capacity turned out to be enormous. Yet in Europe, too, the same comparisons may be made concerning national income in the wake of World War II as for the years following 1914–1918. Five years after the end of World War II, agricultural production had almost returned to its prewar volume, industrial production was considerably greater, and in most European countries real wages were higher than they had been ten years earlier. Even in Germany, despite its ruined cities and millions of emigrants, economic activity, two years after monetary reform, was approaching 1936 indexes.

However, the familiar statement that Europe destroyed itself through the two world wars is not disproved by these observations. The statistics adduced so far merely warn against too general a point of view.

Even if we confine ourselves to overall quantities, our conclusions call for a number of qualifications. The extermination of whole populations— genocide, to adopt the United Nations terminology, of which Hitler set the example—takes us back to the dark ages. It is no longer the fighting itself but the fury of the victor that threatens the existence of nations. Just after World War I, when the Germans were rebelling against the demands of the Allies, Delbrück exclaimed: "Let them do what they like to us, there is one thing they cannot do—they cannot kill us." He was assuming there was such a thing as civilization. But nowadays anything that is physically possible is morally possible, too. And it is physically possible to kill, coldly and scientifically, millions of defenseless human beings.

The Nazis taught the world about gas chambers; the Stalinists gave us mass deportations. If these methods have already been used to wipe out or disperse the populations of certain autonomous republics, how can we be sure that peoples belonging to traditional civilizations will not suffer the same fate during or after a third world war? Even if we decline to accept all the apocalyptic prophecies put forward by some experts, it is true that one atom bomb can exterminate tens of thousands of people. It may be that in a World War III the losses in human lives would outstrip the nations' powers of recovery.

Even in World War II such losses were so great in Germany that it will probably be unable, for a decade or two, to play any major part on the political scene. The air raids caused such widespread damage that, for the first time, modern methods of destruction seem to outdo modern methods of production. It will take ten or twenty years to rebuild the houses and apartments reduced to rubble by the bombs. During that time the Europeans, so proud of their culture, will live behind hollow facades or in hovels.

The Old Continent is an artificial concentration, in a relatively small area, of peoples who get only a fraction of their food from its soil. Western Europe is a kind of conversion center that created industrial civilization and, thanks to its technological advance over the rest of the world, was able to absorb a large part of its wealth.

It may be said that a vigorous civilization ought to be able to do without the income from the capital accumulated during the days of its supremacy and adapt itself to a new economic situation. But the peoples of Europe have to pay the price of their comparatively high standard of living, their political democracy, and their social legislation. The economy loses flexibility in proportion as the masses aspire to greater security and governments agree to protect established rights. The sudden changes caused by wars call for adaptations that are not always feasible: Wealthy people ruined by their own extravagance do not find it easy to recover the pioneer spirit and the ardor of their youth.

Wars have not appreciably lessened either Europe's productivity or the size of its populations. But World War I did damage the delicate network of institutions, habits, and beliefs that supported the world economic system. And World War II swept away the Old World's very foundations. You do not need to kill so many million men to stanch the vitality of a civilization.

Serious though they are, the economic consequences of the twentieth-century wars for Europe—foreign debts, loss of foreign investment, loss of markets, slowdown of technological progress—are merely a secondary and superficial matter. Neither the statistics for demography nor for foreign trade or the balance of payments reveal what is most important. Wars give revolutionary parties the opportunity to gain their ends; they break up even those societies that, like France, escape actual revolution.

The ideologies of the parties that came to power in 1917, 1921, and 1933 under Lenin, Mussolini, and Hitler, respectively, all dated from before 1914. The Leninist technique of organization and action was clearly set out in the treatise *What Is to Be Done?* issued just after the riots that were put down in 1905. Against a background of discussions among members of the Russian Social Democrat Party, the essay proposed an alliance between the small but concentrated urban proletariat and the peasant masses as the only way of overthrowing tsarism and ensuring success for a revolution that most Marxists, even the Russian ones, saw as bound to be bourgeois. The denunciation of "pluto-democrats," the praise of violent elites, the application to politics of Nietzsche's inversion of values, the encouragement of state-oriented fanaticism—all the essential themes of fascism are to be found in the counterrevolutionary and nationalist literature. The same is true of *Mein Kampf*, where all these themes are crudely patched together.

But in itself the fact that the ideas preceded the events proves nothing. The twenty years before 1848 saw socialist ideas seething away with the greatest intensity as well as confusion; yet as far as institutions were concerned nothing or almost nothing happened. The revolutions of 1848, even in their most liberal aspect, achieved nothing. It may be, as Max Scheler said, that all philosophies are available in every era and "material factors" open or close the dams that allow them to impinge on reality. War was what opened the dams to antihumanitarian, antiliberal, and antidemocratic ideologies.

It is useless to wonder whether, if the war had been ended by a compromise peace in 1916, the Russian Revolution would have broken out anyway. But, to avoid the retrospective illusion of inevitability, we should remember that the pre-1914 evolution of Russia did not point to the apocalypse of 1917 as the only possible outcome. Russian society was troubled by conflicts at once social and moral. Largely because of the influx of foreign capital, industries were growing up around the towns and cities. Economic modernization and educational advances were making traditional absolutism more and more of an anachronism. The budding bourgeoisie, as well as an aristocracy built on bureaucracy and still subordinated to a state embodied in the tsar, hankered after the liberal institutions symbolized by the West. The workers, most of them recently arrived from the countryside, endured their fate with impatience, like the English workers in the days of Chartism or their French counterparts in the suburbs of Paris in the first half of the nineteenth century. Such social tensions were the inevitable result of the changes arising out of the initial phase of industrialization in a country where only the upper classes were westernized and the masses became less passive as they became more educated.

Clear-sighted observers were aware that the shock of war could demolish this worm-eaten edifice. The crucial reform that might have strengthened the forces of conservation—the creation of a large class of landowning peasants—had still given only inconclusive results. It would have taken ten or fifteen years more for possession of the soil to make the peasants immune to the lure of revolution.

Even if we assume that the Tsarist regime as such would have been unable to survive a long war, there was nothing at the time to suggest that victory would go to a party that in 1914 had only a few thousand members. Apart from its superior technique for propaganda and action, the Bolshevik Party owed its success largely to the decision by the provisional government and the liberal middle classes to go on fighting. The people were tired of the war, which increased shortages, which in turn increased the radicalism of the masses. It is possible to demonstrate a continuity between the old despotism and the new despotism of the Communists and technicians. Nonetheless, the Bolshevik regime betrayed the nation's hopes. It has been asserted, after the event, that a liberal society was impossible because of the weakness of the bourgeoisie and the ignorance of the masses. But whether or not it was determined by the dynamism of the forces unleashed by war, the Bolshevik revolution, inconceivable except in the context created by the conflict, did not complete but rather reversed the movement that was impelling Russia toward freedom and the West.

Beyond Russia, World War I immediately brought about the fall of the ruling regimes in conquered countries while apparently strengthening the institutions of the conquerors. It looked as if the Western democracies—France, Britain, and the United States—had been victorious on the ideological as well as the military plane. But first Mussolini and then Hitler showed that the opposite was true. In fact, the spread of parliamentary democracy through Central Europe, which was thought to echo the movement of ideas and events, took place in circumstances that increased the vulnerability of already fragile institutions.

In this day and age, regimes cannot survive military defeat. This has been true of France ever since the great revolution. Renan rightly saw this as one of France's greatest weaknesses, and hyberbolic war made it true for the whole of Europe. Having adopted as its rallying cry a democratic ideology that was magnanimous rather than precise, Allied propaganda denounced indiscriminately thrones, aristocracies, the junkers of East Prussia, the industrialists of the Ruhr, and secret diplomacy. We shall not try to assess the individual responsibilities of these abstractions or social categories. But it is easy to see that, in the age of the masses, public diplomacy is even less propitious for peace than the diplomacy of the chancelleries. The politicians of the parties were not always capable of replacing the former ruling classes. The elimination of traditional hierarchies and conservative forces, instead of preparing the way for bourgeois republics, opened the door to unbridled demagogy and totalitarian parties.

In countries restored or created by diplomatic decision, the model was the Western-type democracy that had needed a century to take root even in France. But these new countries were riven by nationalist conflicts. Their middle classes, with the sole exception of Czechoslovakia, were small and had no experience of power. So it was not surprising that the large number of parties, adding parliamentary quarrels to the underlying causes of division, soon proved inimical to the survival of the state. Czechoslovakia apart, the small nations typical of the arrangements set up at Versailles took ten years to pass from pseudo-democracy to real or quasi-dictatorship. Political forms are nothing without men capable of bringing them to life.

Inside the larger nations that had won the war, propaganda raised hopes that could only be disappointed by reality. The people had been encouraged to be heroes with the promise that they would eventually be rewarded with the better life they longed for. Countless bad checks drawn on the future were in circulation on the day victory was won. The time had come to build the society of people's dreams. After 1918, vain attempts were made to stifle the desire for something new and return to the past. After 1945, equally vain attempts were made to recreate the myths.

There is no doubt that war imprisons bourgeois societies in an almost insoluble paradox. Such societies naturally adopt a materialistic philosophy. They aim to provide everyone with as high a standard of living as possible. They try to justify inequalities by a kind of proportionality between effort and reward. Economic success is acceptable because it is supposed to be evidence of hard work or intelligence. But such language becomes absurd as soon as the guns begin to fire. Mobilization abolishes just deserts and turns the relative positions of citizens upside down. The family whose head—clerk, artisan, tradesman, or industrialist—is called up goes down several rungs in the social hierarchy. The family whose head remains a civilian rises up the ladder at a time when most of the population is suffering. Reward is in inverse ratio to virtue. We need to reverse the order of values and put sacrifice and devotion to the common good back at the top.

The aristocratic ethic knows nothing of this contradiction. Heroism is valued for itself: For the warrior, honor, glory, and inner satisfaction are recompense enough. The European nations have drawn amply on this reserve of traditional beliefs. The people—peasants, workers, and bourgeoisie alike—showed that their vitality remained intact. The development of industry and the growth of wealth had done no harm to courage and love of country.

After the victory, in both France and Britain, reaction against the horrors of war expressed itself in a fierce desire to resume what was thought of as normal life. In Italy and Germany, politics were affected by the inability of war veterans to adapt to the conditions of peace. Fascism and National Socialism praised the ideology that had been the theme of propaganda for four years. They promised to create a new order based not on the values of capitalism or hedonism but on those of struggle. They were trying to cater to the aspirations of soldiers and factory workers, the two social categories on which the strength of a nation depends.

Middle-class society, like all social orders, was full of injustices. Wealth was often arrived at immorally or by chance. Inheritance, easily justifiable by social considerations, was hard to defend in terms of an individualist philosophy in theory indifferent to groupings that last from one generation to another. In quiet periods, upward and downward movements on the social scale are sufficiently linked to merits and defects to be acceptable. But this is not so in times of war. Redistribution of wealth through inflation multiplies a hundredfold the injustices inherent in a capitalist society. Chance counts more than work; people living on private incomes become the victims of speculators. In the field, heroism represses the middle-class morality, which the racketeers are meanwhile mocking on the home front.*

So-called capitalist society is a synthesis made up of various elements, some of them contradictory. It joins together a bourgeois order (respect for law, work, respectability, savings, and honesty) with an industrial one (technical rationalization and concentration of labor) and a financial one (abstract representation of wealth, money markets, and manipulation of stocks and shares). On the social plane, the bourgeois order limited the tendency of speculative finance toward corruption. It offered a prospect of peaceful integration to workers still more or less excluded from the community.

At the end of the nineteenth century, the Western countries, then at their peak, exhibited a combination of different ethics, just as they included different classes that were rivals but not enemies. If it reigned alone, the morality of material success would doom societies to rapid destruction. An army's soul depends on its respect for heroic values. An administration's integrity depends on its sense of public service. Workers and artisans must believe in a professional ethic; businessmen, tradespeople, and the middle classes as a whole must obey the laws as if they were categorical imperatives. War intensifies at first but later distorts our admiration for heroism, which in peacetime too often turns into a romantic love of violence. It also sharpens the taste for speculation, which by making everything more precarious makes wealth less respected, because it is less respectable, and poverty harder to bear, because it is less acceptable. Moreover, it undermines the professional ethics of workers and entrepreneurs alike. It disturbs relations between individuals and within the hierarchy, makes claims for improvement more insistent while at the same time reducing the means of

---

*During World War II the completeness of the planned economy in Britain and the United States reduced the activities of the racketeers. But in France the defeat and the occupation provided them with exceptional opportunities.

satisfying them, and erodes traditions. It prepares the tabula rasa on which will arise the totalitarian state.

―――

Wars always resemble the societies that wage them. All through the ages there has been a reciprocal relationship between tools and weapons, class structures and the structures of armies. A community's way of life is reflected or expressed in a particular way of fighting, and vice versa. The golden age of chivalry was when knights in armor dominated the battlefield. Archers, who killed from a distance, to the indignation of the nobility, prepared the way for the end of feudalism, which was consummated when castles came to be destroyed in a few days by the artillery of regular armies. Their cannon blasts heralded democracy.

In the twentieth century an ordinary citizen becomes a combatant when the church bells sound the alarm. The drawing of lots, and the system by which recruits could pay to have someone else take their place, are no longer tolerable: One man's blood is as good as another's. If there are not enough volunteers, conscription is introduced (even Britain finally resorted to it in time of peace). In theory only the common good justifies a situation in which some risk their lives while others merely provide their labor or their intelligence.

In the wars of 1914–1918 and 1939–1945, the military virtues—love of danger, spirit of initiative, personal authority, self-sacrifice—retained their meaning and their grandeur. But they were exhibited as lavishly by schoolmasters, teachers, and young men from middle- or lower-middle-class families as by the scions of noble families. And this was true on both sides. At the same time, the new technologies and modern general staffs called not only for the traditional virtues but equally if not more so for engineering and administrative skills. During the second even more than the first world war, the management structure of a nation engaged in combat was very like that of a nation at peace.

It is probable that a corps of professional officers will still be indispensable. That corps will gradually get larger in wartime as tens of thousands of specialists find niches in the armed services. The United States went farther along this road than other countries, demonstrating beyond any doubt that an industrial power has both the human and the material resources needed to create mighty armies.

The two supreme laws for a nation at war apply also to industry and can be summarized in the words *organization* and *rationalization.* In wartime a country applies to the whole of society the rules that in peacetime apply only within certain enterprises or sectors.

Circumstances have encouraged the gradual but irresistible centralization of government. Four years of war did much more to wipe out the vestiges of German federalism than forty-five years of the Hohenzollern empire. Autonomous or semi-autonomous cities or states, local management by local worthies rather than by civil servants—all such surviving habits, irrational but humanly valid, seem unjustifiable to the bureaucratic services that distribute food, raw materials, and orders. To army chiefs they were a nuisance and a cause of irritating delays. Military men and administrators alike protest against any constraint and tend to standardize all constituencies in order to achieve what is to them the only acceptable arrangement: centralized decisionmaking, with administrative areas divided up into units as similar to one another as possible. War hastened the ultimate triumph of the Prussian idea of the state.

Two types of men took charge of Germany's wartime conduct: generals and industrialists, Erich Ludendorff and Emil Rathenau, the army chief and the organizer of industrial mobilization, respectively—a combination typical of modern societies when they cease to be bourgeois and peaceful. The problem of production remains the same whether it is a question of turning out guns or drainpipes, tanks or cars. What does change is the system of priorities. In peacetime before World War II, consumer choices on the market determined step by step the distribution of national resources. After hostilities broke out, the needs of the war-machine came first, and only those popular needs deemed to be irreducible were regarded as binding. The generals give their lists to the industrialists. The industrialists try to provide what is wanted. But how is this to be done without curbing civilian consumption, and how are resources to be shared out economically and in order of urgency? The army is industrialized and industry is militarized. The army absorbs the nation; the nation models itself upon the army.

According to the Hindenburg plan of 1917, the German unions, which had formerly supported workers' claims and were inspired by internationalist ideals and revolutionary aspirations, were also given a public responsibility indispensable to total mobilization. Henceforward the union secretaries were to be treated not as enemies but as colleagues of the state. As delegates of their organizations they were invested with a portion of authority to be used in the service of the country as a whole. According to German philosopher Johann Plenge at the beginning of the war, the guiding principle of 1914, which must be set against the ideals of 1789, was organization. If socialism is to be defined first and foremost as the planning of the life of a people within a national framework, Germany in 1917 was the first to enter the age of socialism on a national scale. From 1939 on, all the belligerents followed its example.

Are Western democratic and industrial societies bound to fulfill or deny themselves through total mobilization? In fact, it all depends on what we regard as typical of these societies. Citizens put on uniforms in the same way as they go to the polling booth. Occasionally, equality between individuals is respected; they are supposed to be indistinguishable before the law. But the citizen-soldier is part of a vast machine over which he has no control. Group autonomy and liberty of opinion and expression become a luxury that a country in danger cannot easily afford. It fritters away material wealth amassed during the years of peace while stinting on the individual rights once generously granted. The liberal bourgeoisie fades away; the masses are ruled by soldiers and organizers. Total mobilization is close to totalitarianism.

The analogy is so close that some historians have seen totalitarianism as merely an extension of total mobilization, an attempt to render permanent the necessities of war. Overall economic planning, covering both men and materials, was tested first during the hostilities. The incorporation of the proletariat into the nation, by means of unions and with the aid of nationalist propaganda, was the guiding principle of the Hindenburg plan. The organizing of enthusiasm, to use Elie Halévy's phrase, seems to be the seed of state monopolization of publicity and ideology, an institution typical of the Soviet Union and the Third Reich.

War provided a favorable occasion for the Bolshevik Party's seizure of power in Russia. The consequences of World War I and the economic crisis of 1929 created favorable conditions for the Nazi Party's seizure of power in Germany. Without the war, the revolutionaries' violence and fanaticism would not have been able to win over the masses and the overthrow of the state would not have been possible. But the example of the Western democracies shows that while mobilization may imply a total state, it does not necessarily imply a totalitarian one. The parliaments went on functioning between 1914 and 1918 in France and Britain, and between 1939 and 1945 in Britain and the United States. A planned economy does not inevitably continue after victory is won. The essential features of totalitarian regimes derive from a quasi-religious doctrine and a will to power.

Planning in the Soviet Union was inspired by a theory or a Utopian ideal, not by the German model of 1917. The Russian leadership denounced private property, market mechanisms, and currency speculation and had a mystical belief in the virtues of centralized organization. The OGPU, later the NKVD (both predecessors of the KGB), was not originally set up to seek out traitors and other suspects in time of war; it was a weapon in the civil war, an instrument of terror, an inquisition necessary to a secular religion anxious to strengthen orthodoxy and convert unbelievers.

The National Socialist regime was probably influenced more strongly by memories of one war and anticipation of another. After the defeat of 1918, Ludendorff drew up a plan for the total organization of the nation that possibly inspired the Hitler regime. In the minds of some of its prophets, National Socialist ideology eventually became like Shintoism, the "national religion" of Japan that Ludendorff so admired and saw as indispensable to the power of societies fighting for their existence.

Centralized administration, economic planning, ideological propaganda, mobilization, and preparation for war were seen by Hitler and his followers as part of a normal state of affairs. The idea of a garrison state belongs to the twentieth century, the century of wars, but it arises out of them indirectly via totalitarian doctrines and parties.

Between total mobilization for war and totalitarianism there remains, despite some similarities in style and institutions, an essential difference. In the first case all that is required is a temporary unanimity limited to one object; in the second, what is aimed at is a permanent unanimity expanded into a comprehensive system of values and thought. In one instance, certain liberties are temporarily suspended and a nationwide war effort is organized; in the other, the masses are taught that service to the community is their primary duty and that the state embodies the highest value and has supreme power over men and things.

But the question remains of how to interpret all this. The hyperbolical wars of the twentieth century broke down social structures and favored the success of totalitarian parties. And will not the threat of a third world war force even the democracies to abandon some liberal institutions?

Modern states now claim the right to mobilize all their national resources, both human and material. Some of them refrain from exercising certain powers in time of peace. But the freedom of consumers to decide through their choices how the means of production are to be used has become no more than a precarious luxury. As soon as defense demands become so pressing that inflation has to be "channeled," this liberty is either restricted or abolished. Totalitarian states are at an advantage in that they need not modify the workings of their system in order to move from peace to war. But this advantage is probably balanced by certain drawbacks: A free economy is more propitious to technical progress than a bureaucratic one. At the same time, democratic states need enough time to muster their forces when danger threatens.

Battles are fought not with steel but with tanks and guns. A country that has steel will, after a year or two, have thousands of tanks, provided it is not wiped out in the meantime. In 1940 the United States had an annual iron and steel potential of more than 70 million metric tons, but not one armored division. Only its distance from a virtual enemy allowed it to do without a large permanent army. The countries of Western Europe will have to live in a constant state of semi-mobilization; the United States will be forced to do the same. But is this state compatible with their institutions?

The affair of atomic espionage in Canada and the case of Dr. Klaus Fuchs[4] have shown even the most skeptical observers that professors of unquestionable integrity and sincerity are capable of betraying their country out of ideological conviction. How can one not take precautions against such elusive enemies? But once you start proscribing certain opinions, individuals, and parties, where are you to stop? The democracies tolerate heresies, but they cannot tolerate *all* heresies, especially when, as in this case, the heresy involves long-term spying and sabotage.

There is little doubt about what must be done in such cases. But we do not ask ourselves what we ought to do. We observe the effects on democratic regimes of the quasi-war that the totalitarian countries wage in time of peace. These effects are obvious: the establishment of a planned economy on a national scale and the tightening of social disciplines.

Between such a state, with its increased powers, and a totalitarian state, the distance remains appreciable so long as those in power do not want to suppress groups and parties, stifle criticism and opposition, or impose some kind of orthodoxy. There is a danger that the victorious democracies might be contaminated by the enemy. But those who put forward this argument in order to deny or quash the moderating influence of an opposition should think how much worse the contamination would be if by some misfortune the democracies were to be conquered.

We can understand that a society might live in one way in peacetime and in another in time of war, but a clear distinction still needs to be made between the two. The Cold War and the risk of surprise attack are in the process of forcing the democracies into permanent mobilization.

However naturally united the free nations may be, and however useful criticism of governments by an informed public may be in promoting efficiency, a third total war would call into play such forces and put so much at stake that the militarization of society would advance in leaps and bounds. And demobilization does not completely erase the traces left on the habits of men and administrative bodies by a period of total mobilization.

If the Cold War continues for some years to come, all countries will become fortified camps unless they prefer the certainties of nonresistance to the uncertainties of effort and struggle. If Stalinist totalitarianism wins and spreads across Europe and the rest of the world, the masses will proclaim their slavish triumph and the benevolence of their tyrants. The police will silence the voices of dissidents reactionary enough to recall past eras when liberty implied the right to solitude and protest. A victory for the democracies would make it possible to save something of political civilization.

But this time men must manage to master the dynamics of violence. If atomic bombs and guerrilla warfare hasten the proletarization of the masses, where will the New Order come from if not from the omnipotent organizers, backed up by the priests of some secular religion? In order to emerge at last from the century of wars, people will happily sacrifice individual liberties and national independence. But servitude has never guaranteed security.

CHAPTER V

NECESSITY AND ACCIDENTS

The Thirty Years' War was the comparison everyone made at the end of World War II, when the collapse of the Third Reich amid apocalyptic disaster left Germany as ravaged as in the middle of the seventeenth century. Whether under the kaiser or under Hitler, the German Empire had still seemed the center of European, and thus of world, politics. It was the German Empire that by its ambitions had twice thrust humanity toward the abyss; it was against the German Empire that the nations had joined together. It was with Germany that the series of wars had originated, and Germany's total defeat marked the end of a historical epoch.

This view of things was not entirely wrong. But we now know that it was, at best, only partially correct. Before 1914 the rulers in Berlin had shown such a mixture of vanity, arrogance, and clumsiness that they had irritated or disturbed all the other countries of Europe. So full of hubris was part of the ruling class and public opinion that Pan-German literature resounded with vague and grandiose ambitions, and these were often interpreted abroad as expressing the secret thoughts of the leaders. But the power of the Second Reich seemed incompatible with the traditional balance of power on the Old Continent of Europe. Indeed, the course of the hostilities showed how far Germany had outgrown its European framework. In this sense the two twentieth-century wars could be seen as wars of coalition against Germany, just as those at the end of the seventeenth century and during the French Revolution and Empire had been wars of coalition against France.

But the events leading up to the explosions, first in 1914 and then in 1939, were quite different in the two cases. In 1914 the main factors were a diplomatic bungle, preceded by a number of conflicts arising out of the rivalry between Russia and Austria in the Balkans, as well as the situation among the multinational empires. In 1939, the cause lay in a deliberate bid for conquest, cold-bloodedly worked out by a gang of adventurers who had gained power thanks to an economic crisis; their plan, which included the destruction of the world economy, aimed first and foremost at capturing a vast territory for Germany to rule. It was not the same Germany that started both wars; the two wars sprang from different causes and were fought for different stakes.

In order to see the two wars as parts of a single whole, episodes in a single struggle, we need to think not of an "eternal Germany" but of the tragic chain of causes and effects, of the dynamic of violence, that we have attempted to analyze. All "monistic" theories, those that accuse the German nation as well as those that blame capitalism, are childish. On the historical plane, they are comparable to the mythologies that took the place of science in the days when men could not understand the workings of natural forces. The history of those thirty years spanning the two world wars can be understood if we follow the effect of World War I on the domestic situation in the countries involved, on popular psychology, and on the breakup of the world economy and if we take into account factors like the Bolsheviks' seizure of power, the personal relations between the tyrants, and such phenomena, partly predetermined and partly accidental, as the exceptionally acute world economic slump in 1929.

It is a history in the full sense of the term, with main threads that we can follow retrospectively without claiming that the outcome was predictable or implicit in the major trends of our time. Through the workings of a diplomacy based on the balance of power, a local conflict was transformed into a European war, which itself, through the influence of industry, democracy, and the rough equivalence between the opposing forces, grew into a hyperbolic war. This war in turn ended by wearing out the weakest link in the European chain. Revolution broke out in Russia, and the thrones of Central Europe, together with the last multinational empires, collapsed. Flanked by a Bolshevik Russia, the Europe of the bourgeois democracies and independent nations tried to return to the pre-1914 world, which it still tried to regard as normal. The 1929 crisis blew up the order that had been painfully restored to currencies and economies. Unemployment opened the floodgates, and a revolutionary movement swept the German masses toward madness. From then on, Europe, torn by three conflicting ideologies as well as the traditional rivalries between the various powers, moved swiftly toward disaster. War, begun in 1939 with the German-Soviet alliance and the partition of Poland, this time girdled the whole world, rekindling and widening the war that had been raging in China since 1931 or 1937. When, after six years, the conflagration died out, the earth had been scorched in Europe and Asia alike. And hardly had the din of the first atom bomb died away than the two sole survivors girded up their loins for a final confrontation.

The whole story is so clear that we are surprised, looking back, that we did not understand it in advance. All the more reason to resist a retrospective illusion of inevitability. In the course of the thirty years in question there were times when destiny was, so to speak, suspended and quite other potentialities could be descried. A few more troops and the battle of the Marne would have had a different outcome. A decisive German victory in the West would probably have shortened the war, whatever policies Russia and Britain had followed after France was defeated. Europe would once again, as in 1870–1871, have been spared the knowledge of what hyperbolical war can mean.

More plainly still, a compromise peace before the Russian Revolution would have brought about two moments of clarity: The Germans would have recognized that they could not, with the help of Austria-Hungary alone, conquer the rest of Europe, and the Allies would have seen that they could not completely vanquish Germany. Or at least both sides would have recognized that they could not come out on top without fighting to the finish a hyperbolic war that would be fatal to everyone. But once passions had been unleashed, would they ever again let diplomacy get a word in?

The shift from World War I to World War II was not inevitable either. It entailed an almost incredible juxtaposition of stupidity and bad luck. The British, a hundred years behind the times, invoked the shade of Napoleon because Poincaré defended France's rights so fiercely and was indifferent to the economic consequences of sanctions. French diplomacy was both finicky and harsh toward the Weimar Republic, when magnanimity and the suggestion of a shared reconstruction of divided Europe might have paid off better. France was weak and resigned in dealing with a Germany that could probably only have understood force and the determination to use it.

There were still some opportunities to ward off fate even after Hitler came to power. In March 1936, a military riposte to the entry of German troops into the Rhineland might at least have slowed down the course of events or even brought about the fall of Hitlerism. It is possible, though not at all certain, that resistance by France and Britain in 1938 could have encouraged the anti-Hitler conspirators (some of them army chiefs) to take action. During the war, the British and the Americans might have maintained or resumed contact with the opposition to Hitler, tried to conquer Germany without destroying it, and avoided driving the war to a point where the annihilation of the vanquished made a clash between the Allies inevitable. To spare your enemy when you are not sure of your ally has always been a tenet of honorable Machiavellian prudence.

Equally incredible was the concatenation of errors that crippled the U.S. victory in the Far East.

History can easily trace missed opportunities, and conjuring up possibilities avoids the mistake of saying that the past was written in advance. Yet for politicians of that time for whom history was really still the future, such a series of errors or bits of bad luck cannot be talked of as accidental. The fact that opportunities were never taken becomes a fact in itself, a dominant element in this historical period. Events were overwhelming, and leaders could not control forces unleashed not so much by their acts as by the automatic consequences of their acts. German inflation could not be stopped before the currency was completely ruined; the slump could not be stopped before the unemployed had to be counted in millions; Hitler could not be halted before he had amassed enough arms to drag Germany and Europe into his venture.

The evidence supplied by History is mysterious. In some periods, events constantly betray the intentions of the people behind them. Peoples make wars, but they never long so passionately for peace. Politicians try sometimes to appease conquerors, sometimes to resist them, now to satisfy them, now to frighten them. And every time we discover that all these diplomatic tactics were misjudged; those concerned resisted when they should have given in, and gave in when they should have resisted. However vast empires may be, they are never big enough to assuage the hunger of a Caesar. Hitler rejected supremacy over continental Europe, which would have met all the wishes of the Hohenzollerns. Stalin turned down an empire stretching from the Elbe to Indochina, which would, at least for a time, have fulfilled Hitler's aspirations. As one war follows another, the stakes grow larger. Now they comprise the whole world.

This is why philosophers sometimes wonder where it will all end and resort to the wiles of reason. Could the unity of mankind be the end and object, dimly wished for, that draws to itself like a magnet not so much the wills of individuals as the dynamic of collective forces; which attracts, through blood and tears, the unhappy peoples whose sufferings appear to be rewarded, after the event, only by some ambiguous good? The gap between the causes and the consequences of events, between men's passions and the results of their actions, between power struggles and ideological conflicts on the one hand and the real cause of contention in wars on the other—all these fascinate an observer tempted sometimes to denounce the absurdity of history and sometimes to sense its overall rationality.

But the only truth available to positive knowledge is recognition of such contradictions. If there is a Providence at work in this tragic chaos it is beyond us. Mythologies replace a multitude of causes with a single factor; they lend an unconditional value to a desired object; they help us to ignore the distance between men's dreams and the destiny of their societies.

Scientists have found out the secret of fire, but not that of History. Lenin, who dreamed of ending class struggle, laid down the foundations of the total state, of concentration camps, and of the omnipotent police. Millions of victims curse and will continue to curse the revolutionary's blindness. Their curses do not help us to predict with certainty the verdict of posterity.

THE SECULAR RELIGIONS

DEMOCRATIC AND
TOTALITARIAN STATES

Syllabus

1. *The formation of a new ruling elite is a fundamental feature of the to-talitarian regimes (German and Italian).* This ruling elite consists of semi-intellectuals and adventurers who are cynical, efficient, naturally Machi-avellian, and violent. Institutions and diplomacy are at the service of their will to power: They wield tyrannical authority at home and pursue unlim-ited expansion abroad. Fascism and National Socialism both subordinate the economy to politics and make foreign policy their priority.

2. *Totalitarian regimes contrast with the democracies rather than with com-munism.* The contrast is between economic and political systems as well as between ideologies: community against individualism, heroism against bourgeois values, character against intelligence, discipline against freedom, faith against reason. Totalitarian regimes deliberately reject not only the transitory political values of the nineteenth century but also the supreme values of Western tradition (respect for the person and for the mind).

3. *Diplomatic conflicts do not arise out of ideological conflicts.* Rich countries, however, inevitably conservative, have to resist the new imperi-alisms. As the imperialist ambitions of Germany and Italy (at least in their extreme forms) are linked to their totalitarian regimes, the conservative powers are ultimately obliged to denounce them while being careful to dis-tinguish the regimes themselves from the peoples concerned.

4. *There is no economic solution to the present diplomatic conflicts.* The totalitarian regimes have deliberately courted or accepted their economic difficulties, which cannot be allayed by other countries so long as these regimes themselves do not give up their imperialist endeavors. However,

should they renounce these attempts, even temporarily, they could partly demobilize their economies; it is politics, not economics, that forbid armistice or peace.

5. *Totalitarian regimes are genuinely revolutionary, whereas the democracies are essentially conservative.* The former, while presenting themselves as the defenders of culture against Bolshevism, have established a permanent state of war in Europe; behind a bureaucratic facade they have destroyed the moral and social foundations of the old order. So it is very strange that they should so long have found sympathizers among the conservatives in France and Britain.

6. *The totalitarian regimes have undoubtedly been technically successful on the economic, political, and military levels.* The passive virtues of their supporters are equally evident. The democracies cannot satisfy their consciences by merely appealing to the values their adversaries despise—they must show themselves capable of the same virtues the totalitarian regimes claim to monopolize. Unfortunately, the anti-fascist movements have so far only shown in exaggerated form those political and moral defects in the democracies themselves that provide the best arguments in favor of tyrannies.

7. *The political and historical optimism of the nineteenth century is now dead everywhere.* There can be no question now of salvaging bourgeois humanist and pacifist illusions. But the excesses of irrationalism do not rule out the need to reexamine belief in progress, abstract moralism, and other ideas typical of 1789. On the contrary, democratic conservatism, like rationalism, can only survive by renewing itself.

8. *A choice between communism or fascism is not inevitable.* Yet it might become so if we misjudge the economic and social conditions necessary to make a libertarian regime possible. The mixture we see now of unbridled and irrational authority, of rationalized technology and demagogic propaganda, presents a caricature of the kind of inhumane society that could come about. The decline of democratic institutions, the crises of capitalist economics, the conflicts between new imperialisms and old complacencies, together with the degeneration of traditional values, culminate in the present situation, where everything remains to be done because everything is called into question.

The considerations that I want to put before the Philosophy Society today may seem very topical—too topical, even, and perhaps ill-timed. So I should like, by way of introduction, to set out two reasons why I am convinced that my choice of subject was not unseemly.

To begin with, for the first time in several years the French are more or less agreed on what their country's policy, at least its foreign policy, should be, so that one may discuss problems without running the risk of unleashing partisan passions.

Furthermore, in this period of suspense between peace and war, in the intermediate stage we are living in, we are enjoying a sort of respite or pause. Everything is in question, and it may be that one of the best ways of throwing off an obsession with war is still to reflect on the problems that face us and that will go on facing us beyond the immediate future and beyond the solution, whatever it may be, that will emerge in the weeks, months, or years to come.

The remarks I propose to put before you are based on three main themes. The first is that the nature of an authoritarian regime depends essentially on its ruling elite, on the character of that elite, and on the revolutionary nature that the elite necessarily imparts to the regime itself.

The second theme concerns foreign policy, and in this connection I want to show the subordination in totalitarian regimes of ideology and economics to specifically political aims.

The third theme deals with the relations between democratic states and the existing totalitarian regimes.

Perhaps the best way to understand the new elites is to look at the theory of revolution worked out by the Italian sociologist Vilfredo Pareto, which seems to me more easily applicable than Marxist theory to the cases of Germany and Italy.

Pareto taught that what is decisive about a revolution is not the class relationships out of which it arises or the institutions it generates, but first and foremost, and almost exclusively, the rise to power of a new elite. (The word is used throughout this paper strictly in its nonmoral and objective sense.)

Pareto went on to say that the nature of a political regime is determined by the character of this elite, and here the word *character* has its psychosociological meaning. In Pareto's view there are basically two types of men and two types of politicians: the cunning politician, parliamentarian, or businessman who prefers scheming to violence, and the politician who despises the humanitarian bourgeois and tends to use violence.

As a result, Pareto's teaching highlights a fundamental opposition between the elite and the masses. He holds that all regimes are based on the masses, but at the same time on scorn for the masses: The rulers always despise to a greater or lesser degree those who bring them to power.

So, when we consider totalitarian regimes, we need to distinguish between the ideologies aimed at the masses, which are current in the country itself and also used abroad, from the radical cynicism of the leaders, which implies quite a different system of values.

Finally, and this is perhaps essential, the function of an elite is to ensure the greatness of the country concerned. But Pareto tends to confuse greatness with power, and for him an elite justifies its position and privileges by its ability to use force as a means of increasing a country's greatness. An elite no longer capable of violence is an elite that is decadent and doomed.

I think all the propositions summarized above apply fairly accurately to totalitarian regimes and to a large extent determine their nature, based as they are both on the masses and on contempt for the masses and put in place by violent elites who assumed that the bourgeois democracies were so cowardly they could be mistreated with impunity.

If we wish to grasp the nature of totalitarian revolutions we should perhaps set aside for a moment this realistic and cynical view of revolution in general. The origins of totalitarian regimes are likely to include other well-known phenomena just as important as those cited by Pareto: for example, an economic crisis that undermines the lower-middle-class masses, or the role played by the former ruling classes, who support the demagogues out of fear of a Communist or social revolution.

This said, if we want to understand the development of these regimes, the "elite" theory is more useful than an analysis of their origins.

In the two countries that we are in a position to study, Italy and Germany, it seems to me that the longer the revolution goes on the more the new elite displaces the old one. The situation is to a certain extent concealed by the fact that among the political leaders in both countries there are still a great many representatives of the traditional classes: senior officials, representatives of the plutocrats. I have even received a letter from Mr. Rosenstock-Franck pointing out that in Italy, in general, the levers of economic power are still in the hands of representatives of the old ruling classes. But I do not think this objection is decisive. One could also say that the landowners in East Prussia have held on to their estates and that "grand capitalism" still exists there. (It is true that in Germany grand capitalism has retained many of its profits and positions.) But as its hold on power continues, the new elite introduces as many of its own men into top posts as possible: In the past two years in Germany, even technicians from the former upper classes have been replaced with striking frequency by members of the new elite.

This new elite is typified not so much by the fact that it is recruited from among the middle and lower middle classes and the former working classes as by the fact that it is made up of men who have a taste for violence—or, in other words, a taste for authority carried to the point of violence—and who are supremely qualified in techniques of influencing people.

These new men do not necessarily have a profession or any other special qualifications, but they do claim to understand human nature. They understand it at the same time as they despise it, since, for the kind of government and propaganda they stand for, comprehension is bound to go with a certain amount of contempt.

In my opinion, the struggle between the former ruling classes and the new elites follows different patterns in Italy and Germany: It is clear that in Germany the new elite is gaining ground more rapidly, and, it seems to me, more certainly. The new elites in both countries are winning, however, for the same reason: Each is successful insofar as it manages to impose its own kind of foreign policy, namely, an imperialistic one. This path entails economic and even social upheavals at home. But the successes won by the totalitarian regimes abroad act as the best possible justification of their power.

The more the "bourgeoisies" in the democratic countries, out of fear of social revolution, allow the elites in the totalitarian countries to enjoy successes that reinforce their authority, the more these elites repress the traditional ones who offer a last resistance to their imperialistic foreign adventures. Hitler's best argument in his quarrels with the Reichswehr and with grand capitalism is precisely that, however rash or implausible his initiatives may have seemed at the outset, they have ultimately been successful.

This analysis seems to me to back up the assertion I put forward in the summary at the beginning of this paper, that is, that totalitarian regimes are genuinely revolutionary, whereas the democracies are essentially conservative.

Here again, however, the facts are hidden by other phenomena that, though real enough, are in my view of secondary importance.

It is certainly true that the property and privileges of the traditional classes are for the most part preserved. Power was given to Mussolini and Hitler alike by a combination of the traditional ruling classes and the new elites. And it is certainly true that, to begin with, the traditional ruling classes fondly imagined that they would make use of the new elites just long enough to solve the social problems that faced them.

But perhaps we mislead ourselves about the nature of revolution by taking as our only model the revolutions of the nineteenth century. We tend to see revolution as in theory a movement to bring liberation. But the revolutions of the twentieth century seem rather to promote servitude, or at least authoritarianism. They establish a power that is harsher and more extensive than the one that was in place before the revolution. They add to the technical organization and the bureaucracy of the state. In this sense, they are the opposite of what we traditionally think of as revolutions.

But if we look closely at the real situation in Germany, we have no difficulty in identifying the revolutionary nature of totalitarian regimes.

On the political plane it is a new, and in my view important, phenomenon in Germany that leaders recruited from the popular classes can override representatives of the old ruling classes. The abolition of respect for legitimate authority and the old aristocracy, together with the transformation of human relationships that in some parts of Germany could still be feudal in nature—all this adds up to a revolution with far-reaching consequences. Six years of National Socialism seem to have done what half a century of social democracy failed to do: It has done away with respect for traditional objects of reverence.

Germany is undoubtedly under the sway of an extreme authority, but that authority depends on an essentially magical principle: the vocation of the Führer. As for the authority of the technical bureaucracy, that tends to be rational, but it could not do without the magic of the Führer.

However, should this source of irrational though ultimately precarious authority disappear, we might see that the German masses have been infinitely more radicalized by the new regime than by parliamentary democracy or socialist propaganda.

The revolutionary effect is equally striking on the economic plane. The entrepreneurs are still there, but initiative, the traditional justification of capitalist enterprise, has been done away with. In present-day Germany, dominated by the system of the plan, the owners of the means of production are still usually the same people as before, but they have lost almost all initiative, all power of decision and choice. Once entrepreneurs have become the equivalent of civil servants, it is easy to replace the head of a business with a genuine functionary.

I believe the revolutionary effects of the regime are equally marked on the moral plane. As everyone knows, the old forms of family, university, and intellectual life have been turned completely upside down in the Germany of today.

Lastly, everyone also knows—so I shall not dwell on this point—that all the old virtues of respect for the individual, for the mind, and for personal autonomy have been deliberately rejected by the new regime. The virtues it cultivates are essentially military ones—the virtues of action, self-discipline, and dedication.

I think I could just as easily justify my other theme: that the totalitarian regimes are opposed directly and first and foremost to the democratic ones.

The opposition of the totalitarian regimes to the Communists is of a different order. Originally they invoke the Communist threat to win over the masses by claiming to be saving the country from the "Communist chaos." It is well known that Mussolini's great successes came six months after the failure of the working-class movements; everyone knows, too, that in pre-Hitler Germany there were fewer than 5 million Communist voters out of a total electorate of 35 million. So it does not look as if the necessary conditions for a Communist revolution were present in either Italy or Germany. But opposition to a Communist regime has been an effective propaganda weapon both at home and abroad.

More important still, I think the totalitarian regimes' opposition to communism is quite genuine, in that it is a rival. The more the National Socialist regime gives rise to a kind of domestic revolution, the more dangerous communism is likely to seem. It looks like an alternative solution to the same problem, another possible outcome of the same process.

Thus, as regards the more distant future, the totalitarian regimes may have increased rather than diminished the likelihood of a Communist revolution.

One word more. I do not think it is for ideological reasons that National Socialist Germany is hostile to the USSR. On the contrary, we know that

Germany holds in reserve, as one of the last resorts of its foreign policy, the idea of an alliance with Russia, improbable as such an alliance may seem.

As for opposition to the democracies, that strikes me as much more spontaneous and immediate. In the first place, as I have said, this opposition in based on contempt, I believe an almost unbounded contempt, on the part of the totalitarians, both for the democratic nations themselves and for the sort of men who lead them.

Second, the totalitarian regimes are hostile to the democracies in order to make their own people lose the habits of the virtues they embody and forget the advantages they offer.

And there is one last reason, probably the decisive one: Both on the diplomatic plane and in the matter of law and order, the democracies are conservative. They are thus bound to be the primary objects of totalitarian enmity.

This point brings me to my second main theme: the problem of diplomacy.

I think everyone in France today on the whole agrees: The dictators' philosophy gives pride of place to foreign policy. One has only to read the theorists of their movements to be sure of this undoubted fact.

Equally indisputable are the imperialist ambitions of these regimes. There again, everyone is well aware of the facts. The only debatable point is, are these ambitions limited or unlimited? The question is really less important than might be supposed, because even the minimum aims of these regimes are such that the democratic nations could not agree to them. Let us suppose that Germany might be "satisfied" with a closed economic area stretching from France to Russia: Even then, it would have such power over Europe that no one could tolerate it. As for Italy, we know what it wants.[1]

What is interesting is to define the relations between these imperialist ambitions and, on the one hand, economics, and on the other, ideology.

First, then, are Germany's demands economic in kind, dictated by economic considerations, or capable of being met by economic concessions? I think the answer to all these questions must be no.

By 1938 the German regime had solved the problem it had inherited from the previous government: It abolished unemployment. Dr. Hjalmar Schacht had put forward a finance plan entailing a gradual return to normalcy: No more short-term bonds were to be issued, and the budget deficit was to be reduced or eliminated.

But since then the plan has failed. Germany created new problems for itself: financial difficulties, difficulties arising naturally out of the economy, and difficulties arising out of foreign exchanges.

All regimes encounter a certain number of financial difficulties in periods of intense rearmament. However, these need not be so great as to threaten the foundations of the system itself. It would be absurd to expect them to cause the collapse of any economic regime, especially the National Socialist one.

As for the problems arising naturally out of the economy, both equipment and the labor force can be worn down if orders are so much increased as to overwork men, machines, and means of transport. Germany's leaders can reduce these difficulties whenever they like by slowing down the orders. Nothing can be done from outside to smooth away the problems Germany creates for itself.

With regard to foreign exchanges, Germany lacks foodstuffs and raw materials because it lacks the currency to pay for them. This is where those economic planners come in who would like to bring about an agreement with Germany. But before foreigners can do anything to help, Germany itself would need to want to solve its problems. In order to do so, all it needs to do is work less for war and more for export. If the regime decides to work almost exclusively to increase Germany's arms potential, what can anyone else do about it?

What is more, Germany neither asks for nor cares about the so-called economic solutions now being bandied about in France.[2] And the simple reason for this lack of interest is that, given Germany's present closed economy, the immediate temptation that besets the totalitarian regime is to enlarge the territory at its disposal—in other words, to embark on conquests that will make further resources in raw materials, industry, and labor available to its national plan.

Thus, for foreign offers of economic help to be of any interest to Germany, the leaders of the regime would have to know they could not succeed in the annexations that for them are at once economic means and political ends. Thus the very condition of an economic solution is that Germany should be assured of a political defeat. As long as Germany is not faced with this certainty, all economic suggestions are beside the point.

Again, as regards diplomatic conflicts and ideology, I think the relations between them are clear enough. Diplomatic differences are not really a matter of ideology: There are states that are governed in an authoritarian manner on all sides of the political arena. What creates a certain connection between ideological and diplomatic conflicts is for totalitarian states to contemplate attacking the democracies because they despise them and see them as easy prey.

A country that turns totalitarian naturally tends to become revolutionary in its foreign policy. Once it has violently suppressed its own social conflicts, it is likely to project the same dynamic toward adventures abroad. The more influence the Phalangists, the party in Spain closest to the totalitarian parties, acquire, the more imperialistic their language becomes. Spain seems to be adopting the same tactic as the totalitarian states, as if when a true totalitarian revolutionary state takes over inside a country, it is bound to embark on foreign imperialism.

There is also another, perhaps more delicate, reason that I think needs pointing out. At the outset the demands of the totalitarian regimes were national in character and supported by the country in question as a whole. When Germany became free to rearm, and even when it annexed Austria, the whole German people were behind the Führer. Now this cannot be asserted so unequivocally: To repeat what I said in my summary, it seems that the democracies must distinguish between the regimes and the peoples. Not that the peoples, up till now, have not followed their masters completely; nor that we could actually separate the peoples from the regimes—I don't know about that. What I mean is that this is the only possible tactic. The democracies have to answer the ruling elites of the totalitarian states, who think they are too cowardly to fight. They have to say, "If you force us to, we shall fight." But at the same time, because they are peace-loving, they have to say, "We are ready to settle all questions by peaceful means." In this way, they can speak to the peoples over the heads of their governments.

I come now to the last point of this rapid survey—the relations between the totalitarian and the democratic states. To start with I want to comment on a phrase that I used in my summary, which some correspondents have objected to, about "being capable of the same virtues."

This is what I mean. Faced with regimes that proclaim that might is right and that they are heroic and the democracies are cowardly, it seems to me foolish to keep talking about pacifism. That sort of discussion will only deepen the Fascist leaders' conviction that the democracies are decadent.

When we speak to people who profess to despise peace, we should explain that loving peace does not imply cowardice. It is absurd to set regimes based on work against regimes based on leisure. It is grotesque to believe you can resist guns with butter or effort with rest.

When the totalitarian regimes threaten them, the democracies should reply that they are capable of being just as heroic and hardworking as the totalitarians. That is what I mean by being capable of the same virtues.

The only difference, and it is an important one, is that in the democracies people must agree of their own free will to the constraints that are imposed on them.

If for a moment we set aside the immediate problem, that of resistance, we may try to push the comparison further and see what there is in the democracies that heralds the coming of totalitarian regimes, suggests their decay, or constitutes permissible borrowings from totalitarian regimes.

The growing decline of the democracies is to be seen not only on the material plane but also in the fact that many of the people who live in them, at least in France, no longer really believe in the value of their own form of government. A large segment of French public opinion reflects a desire for change.

Two phenomena dominate the democracies, two antithetical features that feed off one another: the unbridled demagogy of some and the fascist sympathies of others, each serving as justification for the other.

If on the one hand the parties on the Left show themselves incapable of governing, and on the other the conservative parties start to hope for violent revolution, we shall undoubtedly be drawn gradually toward the false solution embodied by the totalitarian regimes. No need to go on. Everyone knows what I am referring to.

We are aware of the dangers of contagion, and a certain number of totalitarian features can already be seen in embryonic form in our own country. I shall give a few examples out of many.

Orthodox fanaticism, or the spirit of orthodoxy that transforms intellectuals into representatives of a propaganda machine, exists in other places besides the totalitarian regimes. A well-known author recently wrote: "The only war that can be justified is one fought by the very strong against the very weak; the very weak side is eaten up in a night and that is the end of it." A good Machiavellian maxim, perhaps, but if it were adopted as a political principle it is hard to see how resistance to tyrannical regimes could be justified.

Another example is the predilection shown by the parties of the Left for the use of constraints, preferably economic ones, whenever difficulties arise. For years the parties of the Left in France called for currency controls, at first to counter the flight of capital—though the franc was overvalued, as everyone knew—and then because they themselves had made some economic mistakes. This resort to constraints to end crises created or aggravated by politicians themselves strikes me as very typical, not of totalitarian regimes themselves but of the way a country can imperceptibly move toward them. The results achieved in the past six months through very simple and sensible measures in very unfavorable circumstances seem to me to justify my retrospective strictures on the wish for a different policy.

That said, I do not think we need consider totalitarian regimes as such as an absolute evil, nor to speak of fascism whenever anyone proposes to restore some authority or borrow certain methods from the regimes we are fighting against.

On the technological plane, some of the measures adopted by the totalitarian regimes are excellent, and we would do well to imitate them: for example, steps to encourage the birthrate, and some other aspects of social policy.

On a more delicate subject, unemployment policy, I would not say everything is perfect about the methods adopted by the totalitarian regimes, but I think it would be interesting for us to examine them more closely to see whether the democracies might borrow from them.

There is nothing, for instance, to stop us from making use of major public works, though the example of the totalitarian countries shows that if we do we ought at least not to increase marginal wages. It is not sensible to proceed with major public works and at the same time to increase marginal wages. If we want to use the economic methods of the totalitarian regimes we should do the thing properly and not neglect the essential factors. One of the socialist plans that has been put forward, claiming to be based on the German example, simply forgot about the closing of frontiers and the stabilizing of wages.

I doubt if we can fight unemployment successfully just by imitating totalitarian methods. We would need to use other means—for example, transfers of labor—to arrive at the same result. It is absurd to let workers remain unemployed in a region where old industries are dead without trying to get them to go to other places where jobs are available. Such passive acceptance of unemployment could be ruinous for the democratic countries.

Of course, there are limits to state intervention. Freedom entails special economic and social conditions. If you want to maintain political liberty you also have to maintain a certain degree of economic liberty.

The totalitarian regimes of the twentieth century have shown that if there is one false notion it is that the administration of things can replace the government of people. It has emerged very clearly that if you want to administer all objects you must control all individuals at the same time.

Second, it is imperative, if democratic forms of government are to survive, that they reconstruct a ruling elite that is neither cynical nor cowardly, that has political courage without being Machiavellian, and that has self-confidence and a sense of its own mission.

Hardest of all, we need to rebuild within the democratic nations a minimum of common faith or will. And this brings me to the end of my summary: How can we in the democratic countries manage to revive ideas that we can believe in?

I think we have to start by examining the notion of democracy to see what part of it is essential and what is secondary.

The idea of popular sovereignty is not essential: It can lead as easily to despotism as to liberty. And after all, to a large extent it has been popular majorities that have abused their power.

What is essential to the idea of a democracy is legality, governance by laws where power is not arbitrary and unlimited. In my view, democratic governments are those that have a minimum of respect for individuals and do not regard them as means of production or objects of propaganda.

A democratic government is also one where the authority of the rulers is subject to the checks of a system of representation.

Not only do we need to recreate a legitimate authority that is neither magical nor irrational. We must also see to it that those in authority possess the competence necessary to administer present-day societies, which are complex, and where, with the best intentions in the world, the masses call for measures that are directly opposed to their own true interests. Democratic government is difficult. The weight of history tends in the direction of the totalitarian regimes, that is to say of the particular mixture of demagogy, technology, irrational belief, and police state that we see prevailing in other countries.

So if I talk of saving democracy I do not mean that is the most probable eventuality—merely that such and such are the measures I think most desirable. That is the kind of conservatism I am trying to defend.

But that pursuit takes not only the elementary virtues of discipline, acceptance of authority, and technical competence, but also the intellectual courage to call everything into question and to identify the problems on which depends the very existence of France.

The current crisis will be long and profound. However things turn out in the immediate future, we shall not escape lightly. The course of events on which France and the other countries of Europe have embarked can have no swift and miraculous outcome. That being so, I think we teachers ought to play a small part in the attempt to save the values we are attached to. Instead of raising our voices with the political parties, we might try to define as sincerely as we can the problems facing us and the best ways of solving them.

In any case, it is important that we should convince all who hear us and all French people, that the French are heirs, but that to save a heritage one must be able to repossess it.

THE FUTURE OF
SECULAR RELIGIONS

I

"Men will form a society whose goal will be to take from life all it has to give, but solely for the sake of the happiness and contentment of earthly existence. Man will identify himself with God and be filled with divine and Titanic pride. Sovereign lord of nature through knowledge and his own will, man will constantly experience such great satisfaction that it will replace all hopes of happiness hereafter." Thus spoke the Devil to Ivan Karamazov. This was the very definition of temptation: To place the fulfillment of man's vocation in this life is to be guilty of the worst impiety, that of disregarding everything outside the sphere of earthly existence. Lucien Laberthonnière detected the origin of this impiety in Cartesianism: Descartes, good Catholic though he was, cared more about becoming a "master and possessor of nature" than about meditating on eternal life. Socialism, which aims at what the Devil suggests, carries to its logical conclusion this secularization of human thought and ambition. It sees a humanity reconciled with itself and victorious over inequality and injustice, but this reconciliation is clearly dependent on a previous victory over nature. The resources of the planet need to be sufficiently exploited to allow men to dream of an egalitarian, peaceable, classless society.

In this sense, socialism is essentially against religion. In the grandiose expectations of the young Marx, it was to put an end to "religious alienations." Once man is master of his own actions, Marx theorized, he would find complete fulfillment within the real community and no longer seek substitutes for his disappointed hopes in transcendental images.

And yet, insofar as socialism is an antireligion, it is also a religion. It denies the existence of an afterlife, but it brings back to earth certain hopes that, in the past, were inspired by transcendental beliefs alone. I propose to use the term *secular religions* to designate doctrines that, in the souls of our contemporaries, take the place of the faith that is no more, placing the salvation of mankind in this world, in the more or less distant future, and in the form of a social order yet to be invented.

It will, of course, be asked whether it is permissible to use the expression *secular religion* for a phenomenon that excludes the transcendent, or at least sacred, object to which prayer and love have traditionally been addressed. I do not deny that from a Christian point of view, or indeed that of anyone who defines religion by the essential *intentionality* of the feeling it inspires, secular religions seem to have little claim to be so called: At most they might be said to be substitutes for or caricatures of the real thing. But the use of the term can be justified in a number of ways. A psychologist or sociologist might say: "Being religious is not simply a matter of worshiping a divinity; it can also mean putting all the resources of one's mind, all the obedience of one's will, and all the ardors of one's fanaticism at the service of a cause, or making something the end and object of one's feelings and actions." It is a fact that the secular religions are capable of converting souls to the same kinds of devotion, the same kinds of intransigence, and the same unconditional fervor as ever the traditional religious beliefs did in the days of their most universal and authoritarian influence.

This argument alone would not get us far. We could end up using the term *religion* for any doctrine that arouses strong passions and, by the same token, awakens intolerance and the other violent concomitants of faith. But it seems to me that some of the doctrines current today really do deserve to be called secular religions in a more precise sense of the phrase.

Such doctrines set up an ultimate and quasi-sacred goal and define good and evil in relation to this ideal. When a movement like the Deutsche Glaubens Bewegung[3] proclaims, "Everything that is useful to Hitler and the German community is good; everything that is harmful to them is bad," it is simply giving brutally crude expression to the common foundation of all secular religions and the origin of their ruthless Machiavellianism. The followers of these religions of collective salvation know of nothing—not even the Ten Commandments, not even the rules of the catechism or of any formal ethic—that is superior in dignity or authority to the aims of their own movement. That being so, they relate everything—men and things, thoughts and deeds—to that ultimate end, and utility in terms of that end is the measure of all values, even spiritual ones. Partisans of such religions will without any qualms of conscience make use of any means, however horrible, because nothing can prevent the means from being sanctified by the end. In other words, if the job of religion is to set out the lofty values that give human existence its direction, how can we deny that the political doctrines of our own day are essentially religious in character?

Even in their structure these ideologies reproduce some of the typical features of the old dogmas. They give an overall interpretation of the world (the historical world, at least). They explain the meaning of the catastrophes suffered by wretched humanity and vouchsafe a glimpse of some distant outcome to these tragic ordeals. In the present fraternity of the party they offer a foretaste of what the human community of the future will be like, once it is saved. They demand sacrifices that bring immediate rewards; they rescue the individual from the loneliness of crowds without souls and life without hope.

The Religion of Hyper-Rationalism

The reign of socialism, as described in Marx's juvenilia, is the reign of free men who are equals and brothers: This ideal sounds fundamentally very close to the Christian one. The very idea, co-opted by socialism, of man being liberated over the course of history derives from progressivist philosophy, itself a secularization of the Christian vision of mankind on the march toward the millennium. But where Condorcet imagined a continuous movement toward more knowledge and higher civilization, Marxism sees a dialectic—in this case, a chain of contrasting social regimes succeeding one another by means of violent transitions, or revolutions. By negating capitalism, man will overcome the separateness and slavery to which he has been condemned by a system based on private property.

Revolution, then, the crucial element in what might be called socialist eschatology, is not merely a social upheaval, the replacement of one regime by another. It has a supra-political value in that it marks the leap from necessity to liberty. Salvation lies beyond this apocalyptic catastrophe, this Promethean act by which humanity will break its chains and enter again, so to speak, into possession of itself. But capitalism is supposed to lead by spontaneous evolution to this event, initiating a new era. Anything that infringes on this teaching, any interpretation of capitalist development that compromises the directness or necessity of this march toward liberating collapse, strikes the dogma itself at its most sensitive point. Thus Eduard Bernstein's reformism aroused passionate debates and was finally condemned by a congress of the Social Democrat Party (which some Socialist worthies themselves compared to the councils that established Catholic dogmas). His reformist views were treated much more like a heresy than a scientific opinion, or at least they constituted a scientific opinion (concerning the intensifying or weakening of class conflicts and the disappearance or survival of small property) that assumed the character of a heresy because they deviated from the object of Socialist orthodoxy, a certain conception of historical evolution itself. Socialism has gone on producing rival sects that, while appealing to the same prophet and the same sacred book, fiercely excommunicate one another.

It may be objected that these analogies underestimate the scientific character of Marxist socialism. And no one thinks of denying the scientific nature of many of the propositions included in the teachings. Historical materialism, in the brilliantly simplified form it is given in the *Communist Manifesto,* marks a great turning point in the development of sociological theory. Even people who do not accept the economic ideas in *Das Kapital* recognize it as a monument of constructive analysis.

And yet there can scarcely be any doubt that the influence of *Das Kapital* is largely independent of the truth or falseness of the theories it contains. These abstract theories, thoroughly comprehensible only to specialists, have influenced hundreds of thousands of people who are convinced they are accurate solely because they confirmed, with apparently conclusive arguments, the feelings that inspired the socialist masses: moral condemnation of the salaried class; the hope that capitalism, through the crises it regularly engenders, tends naturally toward its own destruction; and so on. Whatever scientific merit we may grant Marxist theories of labor and wages, their greatest effect has been as a demonstration of value judgments, a confirmation of the success the future will accord to people's wills. One might say they have been the intelligence of socialist faith: *Fides quaerens intellectum.*

Almost the same can be said of historical materialism. The notion that societies depend on the means and relations of production has become part of the common consciousness. Even non-Marxists have invariably learned something from it. But if on the one hand it is easy to explain many phenomena in terms of economic data (and even so, we may wonder what exactly is meant by the economic factor—whether it entails the technical instruments or the social relationships of production), on the other, this explanation becomes more and more indirect, uncertain, and even arbitrary as one proceeds from material organization to political regime and then to the intellectual plane. To reduce everything to infrastructure, or to state dogmatically that a certain cause is the ultimate cause, is, scientifically speaking, completely arbitrary. Once we admit that between the different causes there is interaction, by what right and in what sense can we say that one cause is the ultimate one? The truth is that the choice of an ultimate cause depends on the observer's intentions. A Marxist is interested primarily in the economic system, which he is determined to change. Because, according to him, this change will bring about a complete upheaval in human existence, it suits him to see it as the final cause in social evolution. The object of even the exaggerations of historical materialism is to encourage the necessary belief that economic revolution will ipso facto bring with it total revolution.

This conviction lies at the heart of Marxism. It is what lends the ideology its conquering momentum and makes its propaganda so powerful. It creates the crucial confusion between what is necessary and what is desirable; between historical evolution, described as inevitable, and values adopted naturally and unconsciously. Marxism claims to be scientific and to reflect the real changes taking place in society, whereas Utopian socialisms merely wish for an imaginary just order that contrasts with the injustice and disorder that actually exist. But might it not really be more scientific to recognize that there is a fundamental difference between facts and desires, instead of setting them in a vast context that suggests that they are the same? True, prophecies about the gradual decline of capitalism and the advent of a collectivist economy do fall within the sphere of scientific criticism. Such predictions, however uncertain, do not essentially go beyond the bounds of legitimate speculation. It was a useful hypothesis to conjure up the image of capitalism sliding toward death as it developed and grew more concentrated. But the implicit assertion that the postcapitalist economy would give birth to a new, egalitarian human order transcends knowledge and derives from an act of faith. I realize that Marxism, taken literally, admits it does not know what society will emerge after the private ownership of the instruments of production is abolished. But would a single Socialist passionately desire the end of capitalism if all Socialists did not believe in their hearts that the exploitation of man by man would vanish with it?

But the question of whether political and intellectual liberalism is compatible with a planned economy—the central theme of current controversies—calls at least for some sort of demonstration. In other words, the very idea that gives socialism its ability to expand—the identification of what is desirable with what is necessary—far from being self-evident, is now subject to the harsh test of the totalitarian experiments rather than to mere theoretical analysis. Socialist criticism, no matter how keen it is nor how pertinent it may appear when it denounces the present chaos, has not rediscovered the secret source of its former power: the optimistic vision of a future regime that will be both the heir of the present system and its antithesis.

Where did it come from, the anticipation of a radiant future that was to succeed capitalist exploitation? It came from a boundless confidence in man and in human reason. In the eyes of the young Marx, private property, together with the social organization that went with it, was a legacy from the past, an irrationality that it was man's duty to judge and reform. Private property condemns individuals to separateness: Each one is imprisoned inside his own sphere, communicating with others only through the medium of the market for which they all labor, and which, free of any conscious control, tyrannizes over them all and makes them the slaves of their own actions. If this fundamental cause of alienation were removed, man, restored to himself, would emerge straight into freedom. To translate into simple terms what lay behind this belief: Humankind, without God or master and ruling itself by reason, is bound to become peaceable and fulfilled.

The same rationalism can be detected in the notion of historical evolution. Although Marxism no longer explicitly contains the "ruse of reason" that uses human passions to achieve its own ends, nonetheless there is a certain significance to the way events unfold. This meaning may emerge from the chaos of individual actions and not be intended by anyone, but ultimately the overall, irreversible movement of capitalism toward catastrophe seems to have a kind of supra-individual rationality. Reason wins out over time, just as, via revolution, it will win out in the organization of collective existence.

This rationalism has subsequently been given a less Hegelian and more positivist expression. The popularity of the natural sciences has to some degree repressed that kind of historical philosophy. But what lies behind it has not changed.

Of all secular religions, socialism has been and remains the most rationalistic. It has set out in intellectual terms the faith it fosters; rather than exploiting blind passion it throws light on legitimate revolt; and it sees salvation as the outcome of an intelligible history and of the considered will of human beings who are equipped with knowledge and masters of nature.

The Conflicts Between Secular Religions

Socialism's period of greatest expansion came at the beginning of the twentieth century. It was the only, or almost the only, movement that attracted passions without an object. In a world apparently devoted to wealth, comfort, and the spirit of profit, it embodied, despite its materialist philosophy, a principle of spiritual renewal. It had millions of followers all over the world, an imposing mass that gave an impression of strength. The overall unity it managed to preserve in spite of fierce doctrinal quarrels; the quality of its leaders; the enthusiasm of its rank and file—all denoted a movement of liberation destined to build the future.

At the same time, socialism did not conjure up the sense of impending upheaval but maintained a certain balance between revolutionary ambition and a desire for immediate reforms and between a sense of mission, which separated it from the social milieu, and the inevitable incorporation of the working class into its program. The bourgeois world was not driven by fear to give extremist answers to a threatening extremism. The German Social Democrat Party, the pride and model of the International, found a place, despite its dogmatic orthodoxy, inside the kaiser's Reich.

The 1914 war dealt the socialist religion a heavy blow, showing that, despite words and appearances, when it came to a choice, country easily came before party. Patriotism swept through the crowds, even those that had recently proclaimed their indifference to their fatherland and their exclusive devotion to the workers' International. But above all, the war and the Russian Revolution brought about a proliferation of secular religions, a division of the socialist "church" into rival parties, and the emergence of virulent antisocial religions that used similar means for completely different ends.

The similarities between the secular religions are as obvious as the differences. Let us work from the outside in, from form to content.

1. If we compare social democracy with National Socialism, the superficial resemblance is clear to any impartial observer. Nazi gatherings used the same methods as Socialist ones, bringing thousands, sometimes tens of thousands, of followers together in vast halls or arenas. The walls are hung with enormous portraits of great men and with simple slogans written in huge letters. Cohorts of uniformed militiamen goose-step to "political" music amid innumerable flags. (Hitler has never tried to conceal the fact that in matters of mass propaganda, he learned from the Socialists and the Communists.)

When it comes to action, there are obvious differences between the methods used by the humanist, rationalist religion of the Socialists and those employed by the pessimistic, irrationalist religion of the Nazis. All propaganda oscillates between two extremes, one oriented toward education, the other marked by obsession. No one who knows the facts about Germany could be so unfair as to underestimate the moral and social influence of the Social Democrat Party or forget the educational endeavors of the working-class activists and their leaders. Those who experienced it still remember the atmosphere of serious, honest research that characterized the everyday life of the party. The Nazis cared nothing about education—all they thought about was winning over consciences, one might even say unconsciousnesses, spreading their hatreds, and disseminating the slogans that helped create collective obsessions. Both socialism and National Socialism offered their supporters the comfort of a close and fraternal community. But in the case of the Nazis this was a militant, not to say military, order aimed at conquering first the nation and then the world. The church degenerated into a sect, the hope of salvation into a will to power.

2. Nazism, too, has its vision of the world, at least of the historical world. And like all secular religions, it is Manichaean. Out of the confusion of men and things, it identifies two parties, and the struggle between them is supposed to fill the universe; but in the place of the impersonal principles of socialism it puts flesh-and-blood people or groups of people. Socialism was against capitalism (though it recognized its historical necessity and usefulness); Nazism anathematizes plutocrats and Jews. Public enemy number one becomes not a system (for which no one in particular is responsible), but a race, a defenseless minority.

It is easy to explain the Manichaeanism of the secular religions. What need would there be for a savior or a purifier if the world were not doomed to perdition? Moreover, authoritarian parties are born out of and thrive because of the obsessive frenzy they foster. Eager to federate hatreds, convinced that men are linked more by shared hostilities than by shared loves, they are forever showing their supporters new Bastilles to tear down. They have enemies in the plural—Weimar, plutocrats, communism, Jews—but they have one enemy par excellence that they will never finish slaying. Permanent mobilization, which is what crusades for power tend toward, calls for the constant availability that, with the exception of faith, only preoccupation with a hated adversary can produce.

3. Nazism has a doctrine of salvation as well. It heralds a 1,000-year kingdom called the Third Reich, less distant and less perfect than the reign of socialism but therefore more accessible and, for millions of people, more attractive.

True, the differences are not merely those of degree. They concern first and foremost the replacement of an elite class by an elite race. (The distinction is based on historical vocation: The mission of the proletariat is to bring about the revolution and take over from capitalism; the mission of the Germanic race is to found the Third Reich.) They also concern the nature of the ideal goal. The society dreamed of by the Socialists is open to all men and based on universal law, whereas that of the Nazis is confined to one nation and identified with one race. The dialectic that leads to socialism displays a kind of intrinsic rationality. History as seen by the Hitlerites is dominated by a struggle between the races comparable to that between beasts of prey. The ultimate object has nothing to do with the fulfillment of human destiny; it is more like the victory of one species over another.

No doubt the language and the ideology of the Third Reich have some kind of spiritual resonance. They revive the longing that used to torment the Germans when, deprived in the real world of the unity they aspired to, they had to make up for the mediocrity of their innumerable small states by the grandeur of their dreams. They conjure up a Reich that simultaneously ends their divisions and satisfies the desire for community kindled in them by their political humiliation and their religious fervors. In spite of everything, the chiliastic hope has degenerated into what might be described as a stockbreeder's fantasy.

Primitive though it may seem to us, this religion has met with some resounding successes. It is a fact that Germans all over the world, even when not directly subjected to police or propaganda pressure, have responded en masse to the Führer's call. It is a fact this coarse and simplistic doctrine has found partisans at all levels of German society, and that the intellectuals, even the greatest of them, have flocked in thousands to comment on, defend, and illustrate Hitler's philosophy. It is a fact that Nazi-style socialism, or rather pseudo-socialism, has won over millions of people whom orthodox socialism left unmoved.

So why has a national form of socialism, without a doctrine, outdone the Marxist parties? To begin with, rationalism has been more of a hindrance than a help to the socialist religion. By subordinating the realization of a millennial kingdom to a historical dialectic, it tended, willy-nilly, to rule out immediate hopes. In any case, it saddled salvation with terrifying conditions—total upheaval, the reorganization of society under the direction of the proletariat and its representatives—things that millions of men, though outraged by their situation, would not accept and did not even desire. Nazism played on the same hates and loathings that socialism traditionally exploited: It anathematized plutocrats, financiers, and the burden of interest; in short, it carried to its logical conclusion the methods of thought and propaganda, familiar to all revolutionaries, that consist in being *against.*

The divisions between the Marxist parties also did much to favor the purposes of their common enemy. When separated, the Socialists and the Communists lost the advantage of a doctrine that was at once reformist and revolutionary, deterministic and activist. The former ended up relying only on everyday reforms and, in the long term, the notion of a historical dialectic; the latter were concerned solely with direct action and seizing power. The former, taking part in all the institutions of the Weimar Republic, seemed to become bourgeoisified and forgetful of their unique mission; the latter, while seeming to represent revolutionary zeal in its pure form, had to fall in with the decisions of a foreign government and by dint of realistic action were visibly inclined to Machiavellianism—which does not offend the conscience of believers but may repel the undecided.

It might be said that in both its forms socialism was compromised because it was confused with a particular reality—social democracy with the Weimar Republic, communism with the Republic of the Soviets. Nazism thus gained the privilege of novelty. The Nazi Reich was not only nearer and more accessible than the socialist kingdom: It was also free from the flaws of imperfect incarnation.

In addition to all these reasons we can descry another that is simpler and probably more decisive. As early as 1871, Joseph Ernest Renan noted that the life of the peoples of Europe continually alternated between social and national concerns. In his view, France was then dominated by the social question, Germany by national feeling. He expected these roles eventually to be reversed. Clearly, in our own day, those preoccupations are simultaneous and concurrent. But they occur in a variety of forms. Patriotism—or these days, nationalism—survives ineradicably in the depths of people's souls, but it is often all the stronger for being unexpressed. New enthusiasms are directed toward forthcoming conquests and dreams of the future. Unlike Germany, nations that are permanently unified feel no need to be forever defining themselves. But if in exceptional circumstances, for example in an atmosphere of defeat, nationalism becomes overheated, a social doctrine that is nationalistic by nature is much more persuasive than social doctrines in which the idea of a homeland is merely tangential or incidental. In such circumstances the secular religion, with its hope of earthly salvation, merges with love of nation, the highest loyalty to remain intact in a West riven by doubt. The other secular religions are the victims of their own universalism. Real religions must of course speak to each and every individual, but if nothing is known except this world, and if the audience addressed consists of collectivities, is there any reason why particularism, which after all is easiest, should not win the day?

And so the pros and cons are reversed: The religion of hyper-rationalism is succeeded by the religion of biological impulse. The contrast is seen most clearly in the realm of ideology. The Third Reich accords as much importance as socialism does to administrative and industrial rationalization. But the man leading this religion to victory, the man whom this religion takes as its model, is not a man of reason but a beast of prey, triumphant in the animal struggle for life. "The earthly paradise has become the paradise of beasts."[4]

In the last years of the republic, German "democracy" was reduced to a juxtaposition of competing totalities. The complete control of education, youth, sport, and leisure, so strikingly demonstrated by the Nazi regime, already existed within each of the main parties before 1933. The violence of the quarrels between the great organizations, each armed with its own creed, its own prophet, and its own banners, ultimately made it almost impossible for the Constitution to function. Above all it gradually made everyone think that such unbearable tension must resolve itself in an abrupt unification: As soon as one or more minorities had the state at their mercy and were ready to misuse their power, there would be no more real democracy. Everything would be reduced to a choice between the tyrannies on offer. Germany exemplified first a plurality of secular religions culminating in the anarchy of war between them all, then the unity of one secular religion completing the conquest and conversion of the whole nation.

But even in the fateful years between 1930 and 1940, these two extreme forms did not cover all the possibilities. Britain, with its good sense and its privileged stability, escaped the secular religions. No political opinion there took on the pervasive fervor of faith. No party adopted the strict internal discipline and the eternal aggressiveness typical of sects. Nothing has so far destroyed or even seriously undermined the self-evidence of the people's moral and religious imperatives, whether personal or universal. Nothing impaired a long-silent patriotism that awoke as fervently as ever when danger dawned.

France, in this respect, was midway between the Weimar Republic and Britain, though closer to the latter, despite appearances. In France, parties and beliefs became virulently dogmatic only in reaction to external conflicts that happened to be both national and religious. The identification of a country with a creed eliminates rivalry between secular beliefs on a national level but exacerbates them on the international plane. The relations of a democratic country with the totalitarian countries becomes the stake in the struggle between parties. And to conceal his purposes, the conqueror encounters little difficulty denouncing any attempt at resistance as ideological warfare. As long as the secular religions are with us, the doors to the temple of Janus will never be closed.

II

The counterrevolutionary religions will collapse in unprecedented catastrophe amid the ruins of a devastated continent. Fascism is ending in a grotesque escapade that discredits it forever. Never before has a Caesar, even a miniature one, outlived himself in a comedy put on against his king and country. It is a harsh lesson. The Italian people, who never fundamentally accepted the imperial myth, will hate their Duce even more vociferously than they acclaimed him on June 12, 1940, in the square in Venice.

The Germans, in contrast, will go on dreaming of their Führer for some time. They will repeat in the depths of their hearts the comment attributed to a young German to whom someone was explaining the inevitability of his country's defeat: "It was a very good idea, though." But nostalgia for the 1,000-year empire will torture the German masses in vain: This time the peace will be based on the Reich's helplessness, not on its acceptance of defeat. After all, it is not a matter of forgetting dreams, but of time. This question has a wider bearing, for the secular religions are symptoms. Will the great upheaval have torn up the roots of the evil?

Are Secular Religions Inevitable?

It is more than half a century since Friedrich Nietzsche uttered the famous phrase on which our present ordeals are a diabolical comment: "God is dead; anything goes."

The spiritual conflicts of our own day attack men's souls more deeply than any of those that have divided Europe since the Renaissance. It is not enough to say that spiritual unity no longer exists: It has become inconceivable. Christian churches have congregations of millions, but the greatest crises of conscience, including the present one, take place outside the sphere of traditional belief. The Christians in Germany have fought for their Führer without their pastors telling them, or even dreaming of telling them, that they were fighting in the unjust cause of conquest by the sword. Moreover, Nietzsche's inversion of values has been morally accepted and put into practice by millions of people. Despite their different origins, secular morality and the catechism have joined together to form spiritual families akin to one another in their very opposition. The young barbarians trained by Hitler belong to another universe. Can we be sure they will ever be eradicated? What miracle could ever restore peace between them and us?

It is true that men can live without believing in an afterlife. For century upon century, the peasants of every civilization have plowed the earth, bent under the yoke of seasons and myths. How many lives, even today, fail to rise above the unconsciously accepted tradition! How many people are ful-filled, without being driven by atheism into a sense of deprivation and fail-ure! But there are also souls to whom the good news has given a hunger that nothing can satisfy except a plenitude comparable to that which was promised. And even if man can manage to live without expecting anything from God, it is doubtful whether he can live without hope. But there are millions of people, imprisoned in dreary jobs, lost in the multitude of cities, who have no other share in a spiritual community but what is of-fered them by the secular religions. The crowds who acclaim false prophets bear witness to the intensity of the aspirations mounting to an empty heaven. As Bernanos has said, the tragedy is not that Hitler proclaims or takes himself for a god, but that millions of people are desperate enough to believe him. Any crisis, whether economic or political, that severs the mul-titudes from their roots will deliver them yet again to the combined temp-tations of despair and enthusiasm.

At the same time, the secular religions do offer a substitute system of unification. Surprisingly, scientists sometimes discover, as if touched by grace, the virtues of even a watered-down Marxism. Here again it is a mat-ter of an unmet need. When knowledge accumulates ceaselessly but at ran-dom, it increases the desire for a system. Charles Maurras owed his prestige largely to the fact that every morning he added some other example or de-tail to his doctrine as a whole. Whatever one thinks of Marxist materialism, it is certainly better than the ordinary materialism that served as a philoso-phy for the physicist before he or she was converted. Even Nazi racism sup-plies a kind of principle on which to base some sort of philosophy of hu-man existence.

It might be said that these spiritual needs are in a sense created by those who exploit them for their own advantage. But there are times and situa-tions when secular religions seem to fill an abyss into which society might otherwise fall. In short, they introduce a supreme principle of authority when all the others are collapsing.

Today's fashionable formula, according to which the world, in the ab-sence of legitimate powers, is given over to fear and violence, does no more than state a fact. If there is to be social stability, men must agree to obey and recognize that their superiors have the right to command. The reasons for obedience vary according to history and circumstance. Sometimes they are to be found in the depths of the past, in the collective unconscious, inherited from ancient custom; sometimes they are rational and self-evident in terms of a particular technique or function (performed in any given instance by a merely temporary incumbent); sometimes, as in an ideal army, the two kinds of reason coexist and reinforce one another.

Nowadays the traditional legitimacy that sustained monarchies and aristocracies is becoming extinct. In addition, the constitutional forms in which the idea of democratic legitimacy was embodied have lost some of their former prestige. The moral and political ideas that guaranteed them have been undermined by the criticism of counterrevolutionary thinkers and the lessons taught by events. The pessimism of mass psychology has repressed the optimistic notion of a general will. How can we believe that truth or the common good could emerge from free discussion when everywhere we see passions unleashed against one another? Moreover, the mechanisms of democracy have been degraded by the uses to which they have been put, and by the way authoritarian parties have caricatured them. National Socialism gained absolute power by means of repeated elections. Where is the dividing line between plebiscite and election, between votes that are genuine and votes that are rigged?

In France, even before the war, one was struck by the way discipline inside an organization like the Communist Party was much better than that among ordinary citizens or even in the army. Officials at all levels were called *responsables,* reflecting the notion, not confined to the military, that whoever gives orders is the one who assumes responsibility. And the *responsables,* conscious of their position, had no difficulty in winning the trust of the activists. There was none of the ill-humor and continual suspicion that Alain recommended toward all wielders of power, and that the French readily manifest toward their rulers.

Since 1940 we French have been through the tragic experience of seeing first the disintegration and then the restoration of our state. When France collapsed under the shock of Hitler's war machine, when the armistice left us with a government that was "half-prisoner," whose words and decisions might at any moment betray the country and serve the enemy, people clung on all sides to flags, standards, and standard-bearers. One saw the most extreme reactions. Some people, in despair because of their love for their country, became suspicious of everything and everybody and no longer believed in or obeyed anything but their consciences. Others, though often motivated by the same fundamental feelings, obeyed all the more implicitly the orders of their superiors because their authority was so flimsy they feared a social vacuum. Here and there some practically isolated pockets of traditional order survived. For a few months, as Spengler prophesied, armies were known by the names of their generals, as if the ultimate loyalty, amid the collapse of all other values, was fidelity to one person. This phenomenon is more natural than may appear. The "depersonalization" of the state comes about at the end of a long process of evolution: Before a state can be recreated it has to pass once again through the original stage, when power was embodied in one man.

The situations we have just been examining, where a regime is based on the ascendancy of a secular religion, on the fraternity between followers of the same cult, and on the prestige of one man, seem to be poles apart from one another. Prestige is something mysterious and incommunicable, linked to the very being of a leader and to the distance that exists or is artificially created between that leader and his fellow men. It does not in itself offer a rational or even a pseudo-rational justification for the doctrine he espouses. The fact is that in our day and age the adventurers brought to power by popular acclamation reinforce their assumed dignity by the myths they claim to fulfill. Though they derive their authority neither from God nor from history, they never rule in their own name, but always by virtue of a "mission."

Men are tired of obeying "officials" and an authority without a face or a name: In reaction to the anonymity of rational organizations, heroes suddenly emerge. Men are weary of submitting to an order that they do not understand and that, in the absence of any moral inspiration, degenerates into force or inevitability. The hope of salvation can transfigure that order by giving it a spiritual significance. The two kinds of aspiration tend to merge: Collective beliefs generate prophets, and Caesars invent their own religions. Even if all images of an earthly paradise vanished, the primal belief in a man of destiny would remain. When their empire was in decline, the Romans made their emperors into gods.

The Decline of Dogma

As long as men see politics as the vehicle of their fate, they will actively worship the regimes that, dangling before them an illusory future, reflect their desires and console them for their disappointments. As long as troubled masses think themselves betrayed or exploited, men will dream of liberation, and the image of their dream will be the face of their god.

But it seems unlikely that we shall see a repetition of the events that followed World War I. When the current crisis is over, the moral climate will be different from that in which the previous one ended. The messages of President Woodrow Wilson, with his Fourteen Points, created a great illusion; the same cannot be said of the Atlantic Charter. The misuse of propaganda and the excesses of cheap ideology have ended by producing a kind of satiety.

The present phase seems to mark a decline in dogma. At the heart of Marxist dogma, as I have said, was a confusion between socialism and anticapitalism, a belief that socialism would put into practice the values in whose name capitalism was condemned. But what once seemed obvious has become a subject of argument: What human or political regime will succeed capitalism? Assuming that it is bound to have a planned economy, what will be its other characteristics? Socialists probably reject the idea that totalitarianism—with its single party and its abolition of representative institutions and intellectual liberties—is *bound* to accompany state direction of production and trade. But no one denies that the danger exists. Which means that socialism is thrown on the defensive. Victorious religions are not content with repelling attacks; they seek enemies.

Moreover, the Socialist Party is only one of the groups that offer to take on the legacy of capitalism and carry out the task of renewal. Far from uniting the vast majority of the oppressed against the absurd minority of the profiteers, as early predictions anticipated, all these groups merely represent certain masses that are opposed by other masses who may be even more disadvantaged (as in Weimar Germany, for instance).

There is not one large country where parliamentary and democratic socialism has managed by peaceful means to bring about a complete overhaul of the economic system. Communism has managed it, but by violent means of which liberal socialists disapprove. Probably, in the Scandinavian countries and in some dominions in the British Empire, a kind of social democracy has been created; these are based on negotiated relations between entrepreneurs and workers and involve some degree of economic control without eliminating or expropriating the capitalists. But in Germany and France, the socialists have neither, in theory, given up the idea of a socialist revolution, nor, in practice, succeeded in working out a viable system in which the working class could at once modify and be incorporated into society as it exists at present.

Their reformism has been compromised by lack of immediate success, their revolutionary zeal called into doubt by the part they have played in the existing order. They no longer offer the attraction of a new and unknown world. Whatever they may say, they are still half in sympathy with the prewar world everyone professes to reject, even though millions of people secretly hanker after it.

No doubt communism escapes this descent into the prosaic. Throughout Europe it profits from and will go on profiting from the enormous prestige reflected on the Soviet regime and people by the victories of the Russian armies. In France, the Communists have won sympathy in all classes and dispelled some instinctive fears by their heroism in the struggle against Germany. But admiration for the fighters is not the same thing as belief in the message. This belief does exist, vibrant and total, among the officials and the activists of the party, as is shown by their obedience to the numerous and sometimes contradictory orders directed at them and by their loyalty throughout the twists and turns of official dialectics. But in Western Europe they are only a minority, and in the absence of any foreign intervention they have little chance of gaining the upper hand, at least during the first phase after the Liberation.

But if socialist dogmas are in decline, the ideologies common to all forms of socialism are extremely popular. The usual arguments against capitalism—the tyranny of trusts, the scandal of poverty in the midst of plenty—remain in the forefront of people's minds. And few intellectuals will defend an economic system based on the search for profit. At the same time, the efficiency of the Communist regime's performance during the war has refuted some classical arguments on the inevitable decadence inherent in a bureaucratic economy. A preference for a planned economy instead of reliance on automatic market mechanisms, the desire for rational state organization of economic life—all these ideas, more or less related to socialism, are now virtually part of the common consciousness. In this sense, socialism can be said to have triumphed: It only remains to be seen which *kind* of socialists will benefit from this victory.

Despite the differences among countries, a unity did nevertheless exist prior to 1914. I am thinking not so much of international unity—no more than a fragile facade, as events would show—as of the unity within every country, for at that time a single party embodied the socialist hope. Now, however, several groups offer to take over the state and direct its economy. This is the essential and inevitable factor. Will these groups agree to conduct their struggle according to democratic rules? Or will they merely be new candidates for despotism, eager, on the pretext of introducing renovation, to assume absolute power? With the decline of dogma coinciding with the popularity of socialist ideas and the reawakening of nationalistic feeling, is not this a situation propitious to the birth of national socialisms?

Cynicism or Faith in Man?

The future remains to be written. We project on it, in turn, our memories, hopes, and fears. Resignation to a future perceived as inevitable is always a form of defeatism. At present, according to circumstance and mood, we hesitate between two views: Either the age of secular religions will continue as an age of fanaticism devoid of doctrine, or we shall emerge from the war of the nations and myths and rebuild a human order.

Both prospects are logical developments from the present situation. The secular religions have discredited universal ethics, whether Christian or secular. What are justice and truth but "metaphysical prostitutes"? What is the use of teaching us we should respect other people's property unless the lesson begins by defining legitimate possession? Are not rules that apply to everyone, at all times and in all circumstances, necessary meaningless, unable to deal with any bone of contention? What answer could they give to men's urgent and passionate questions about the most humane and efficient modes of production and trade? In this context, feeling attaches not to universal imperatives—which either signify nothing, or else by concealing it justify the established disorder—but to the goals put forward by the secular religions.

But by fighting and imitating one another as they do, the secular religions have helped to discredit themselves. Have not the irreconcilable ideologies revealed the partial similarity of the methods of their groups, which oppose one another all the more fiercely because each one, if successful, would arrogate all rights to itself and deny them to its unsuccessful rivals?

Whichever team wins the state will do as it pleases. The only question is *who* will abuse state power.

Pursuing this line of thought, we can distinguish the main lines of what might be called the cynical view. Half a century ago, in a book that was scorned in France but widely appreciated abroad, Gustave Le Bon declared that we were entering the age of the crowd. "It is no longer in the councils of princes," he wrote, "but in the souls of the crowds that the fates of nations are prepared. . . . For a moment, the blind force of numbers becomes the only philosophy of history." We know now that the age of the crowd really conceals the age of the elites. It is true that without the passive or passionate support of the masses no regime is possible in our own century. But it is also true that the masses are manipulated rather than autonomous. They are maneuvered into worshiping someone they know nothing about. And modern life, complicated as it is, constantly presupposes a mechanism of authority that all must obey, even when they are allowed the illusion of choice. We know now that the industrial age does not produce an egalitarian society, but rather the reign of the engineers, and first among these is he who engineers souls.

As a result, the very image of historical evolution is transformed. In the nineteenth century, most minds were dominated by the idea of a single irreversible movement. In a climate of rationalist optimism, this was an idea of progress. No one doubted that knowledge accumulated and with it grew man's power over nature. But however often economists assert that the standard of living of a worker in the United States today is more or less the same as that of Louis XIV, the nature of man and the organization of societies have not necessarily been fundamentally changed by technical advances. Indeed, this is the essential point. Psychoanalysts find evidence of the same psychological mechanisms in the souls of our ancestors, however distant, as in those of our contemporaries. The reactions of a citizen of a modern democracy are just as shallow as those of a citizen of Athens. Minorities always rule and keep benefits and privileges for themselves, even if their members and methods of governance change. Some people are angry at the thought that politics goes on existing amid the same old confused words in an age when scientists can calculate an eclipse to the seventh decimal point. But the same scientist, with his dazzling but vain triumphs, does not, outside his science, think or act any differently from his lab assistant. Politics lives on myths because the men it manipulates have not emerged from the age of myths.

But even if man remains the same turbulent, passionate, envious being described by Machiavelli, La Rochefoucauld, Pareto, and Freud, and even if the egoism of the elites and the blindness of the masses survive all revolutions, history is not heading toward a fixed end. Either it just goes on, irregular and unpredictable, as chance concerning things, men, and encounters will have it, or it is shaped according to an irrational mechanism: There are but a few types of organization, all imperfect and all attacked by an inner principle of corruption. Authoritarian elites wear out, either because they shed too much blood in combat or because they wallow in self-indulgence. Cunning elites ultimately succumb through lack of energy and resolution. So contrasting types naturally succeed one another, and the more or less regular repetition of such sequences amounts to a roughly cyclical pattern. Throughout the centuries mankind has hesitated between two images of its own history: the inexorable sterility of alternation, or progression toward a more or less determined end. Unable to believe that scientific progress will expand into the progress of humanity itself, people resign themselves to a history that repeats itself.

To look at a different approach, science itself suggests a "realistic" policy. Do not psychology, biology, and sociology all treat men and societies as a kind of matter, with a life and evolution from which causal laws may be deduced? The geneticist proposes crossbreeding, the sociologist talks of creating artificial elites, the psychologist of deliberately exploiting mass passions. They all treat man no longer as a subject but as an object. The philosophy of progress did the opposite. A little while ago we hoped for a humanity grown knowledgeable or at least reasonable. Now we either hope for or dread a humanity subjected to applications of the knowledge of our species acquired by a few individuals.

None of these ideas forces us to be cynical, but all of them taken together encourage us to be so. If in the long run all regimes are equal, the main thing is to be on the right side of the barricade—in other words, a member of the party in power. If ideologies can be regarded merely as instruments for winning souls, the political culture of the elites is more or less tantamount to the art of juggling with words. Such cynicism, which is more widespread than is generally thought, fosters both skepticism and fanaticism. Religions devoid of doctrine are the ones most impatient of orthodoxy and most inflexibly opposed to dissidents, because of the simple fact that they feel more vulnerable than the rest. Their leaders are all the more eager to foster fanaticism because they know they are incapable of defining exactly what the mission is on which their claim to legitimacy is based. Fanaticism and skepticism, although diametrically opposed, fight for possession of the same souls. The masses, like individuals, oscillate between two extremes, sometimes weary of everything and wallowing in passivity, sometimes caught up in a dream of grandeur. National Socialism, as it nears its end, seems to encompass three attitudes: that of the masses, shattered by their misfortune and the painful memory of a once-imminent victory; that of the young Nazis, who, having never known any other universe, are still the same barbarians Hitler dreamed of fifteen years ago; and that of the party leaders, ready to go on desperately playing to the bitter end a game in which they have nothing to lose, because if they fail there will be nothing left.

But another outcome is equally feasible. It, too, begins by discrediting the secular religions because of both their conflicts and similarities. But in this case the decline of dogma, instead of leading to nihilism, would tend to revive what the primacy of politics, common to all the competing ideologies, was ultimately stifling: a sense of universal values.

Such a suggestion may seem paradoxical: Have not the demands of clandestine warfare inevitably made human life cheap and spread contempt for the law (which was that of the oppressor)? This is probably true, but at the same time one observes a completely different reaction: People long for security, national independence, and all those liberties—freedom to think and speak and spend one's money as one pleases—of which a whole continent was deprived by the enemy and his accomplices. It may be that these aspirations include a hankering, impossible to satisfy, after a return to prewar ease. It certainly includes a nostalgia for things only really appreciated after they were lost: Liberty is a "metaphysical prostitute," and theorists will tell us that the formal freedoms of bourgeois democracy—the right to vote, the right of free speech, the right of assembly—are nothing in comparison with the concrete freedom that only a collectivist society can supply. At any rate, there are liberties, whether formal or concrete, that peoples emerging from servitude will soon be demanding, unconditionally and without reservations. They will not tolerate a Gestapo of whatever stripe, nor the abolition of basic individual rights, on no matter what pretext. Or rather, they may endure these things if some tyrannical power establishes itself by surprise and maintains itself by violence; they will not resign themselves to them.

People will try to create a new doctrine on the basis of such feelings as patriotism and desire for freedom and individual rights. This new doctrine may arise, not from a new dogmatism, but from a search for institutions that, while meeting the necessities of the twentieth century, can safeguard the legacy of the nineteenth. The reawakening of rationalism and fundamental liberalism in the occupied countries, for example, demonstrate a persistent vitality in this new era.

There can be no doubt that the revolutions of the twentieth century have prolonged and "normalized" the use of despotic methods. This does not mean these methods are an unavoidable feature of our present epoch, but it does mean that the desire to reconstruct society quickly, via a discretionary authority and in accordance with the preferences of a particular group, inevitably leads to a total state. Before we resign ourselves to an inescapable transition to tyranny, we need to be convinced that there is no progressive solution to the problems of our age.

The search for proof would begin from the fact that also encourages skepticism, that there are similarities between regimes that are verbal enemies. For from that beginning we might be able to identify the things that must be done if we are to avoid a revolution leading to tyranny: These things are the special tasks facing the twentieth century. It is now clear that the quarrels of the nineteenth century led, on the social plane, to a generalizing of the advances made by the revolutions of the eighteenth (equality before the law, abolition of castes and hereditary privileges), and, on the political plane, to a wider spread of parliamentary institutions and individual liberties. Today all regimes, of whatever kind, have to guarantee a minimum of economic security (and, in the first place, security of employment) to every citizen, which means that the state accepts responsibility for some degree of control, direct or indirect, of the economy as a whole. Totalitarian regimes boast of performing this task en bloc. The team that is in power controls all aspects of life and directs the national resources toward whatever end it chooses, perhaps a war of conquest, perhaps an improvement in the standard of living. So in our day and age any revolution will be, and will long remain, totalitarian, for if we transfer to the state responsibility for decisions that used to be made unconsciously by each individual and by all (for example, decisions about the division of labor among different sectors), we condemn the state to act independently of the many competing groups, and thus to become the property of the group in power.

Government that wants to preserve pluralism and liberties must take on such responsibilities as their citizens will not forgive them for refusing and, at the same time, leave room for the play of automatic market mechanisms conducive to the general interest within the operative limits.

No doubt, in the twentieth century, belief in parliamentary constitutions, economic liberalism, and national sovereignty is no longer what it was in the nineteenth. Having been at least partly put into practice, these ideas have lost the charm of novelty. But it would be absurd to underestimate the reawakening of nationalism and a kind of humane liberalism on the ravaged continent of Europe. And some parliamentary institutions and certain forms of free initiative may well find a new justification, even in the eyes of the masses, as the best means of fulfilling the burning desire for personal autonomy.

I firmly believe that an intermediate kind of government, free from the rival dogmatisms, is economically and socially viable. A cloud of the gravest uncertainty hangs over the political future. For in order to produce the infinitely complex mechanisms necessary for such a government, what is needed is nothing less than the prestige of a recognized elite and the collaboration of the masses, mediated by their "ringleaders." Such a collaboration is very likely to develop in Britain. But the prospects are less favorable on the continent of Europe, where popular demands will be sharpened by the sufferings of the occupation, and where the reactionary blindness of the former ruling classes has not always been enlightened by tragic experience.

It would be foolish to accuse the secular religions of organizing intolerance and spreading war. After all, the religions preaching salvation, when they ruled unchallenged over men's souls, were no less intolerant. Acting brutally in the name of purity, they persecuted heretics unmercifully and did not shrink from victories won by fire or sword. Even if temporal motives mingled with the passions of the crusaders, it is true that the Albigensians, among others, experienced cruelty at the hands of those who claimed to believe in the God of love.

I would stress two main arguments against the secular religions. The first is that they are religions of collective salvation. They do not offer individuals the same consolations or hopes, nor do they impose on them the same disciplines, as the personal religions. Moreover, insofar as they are put into practice, they are doomed either to disappear or to prolong themselves through worship of the collectivity or of its leaders. Bernanos saw clearly when he denounced the totalitarian state as the pagan state resurrected.

The second objection is that these substitute religions are undermined from the outset by a secret unbelief. The earthly reality they offer the faithful as an objective ideal gives them no lasting intellectual satisfaction and fills their souls only by the grace of uncertainty and struggle. That is why the enthusiasm they arouse degenerates so readily into blind transports or conscious cynicism. It is not easy for representatives of *Homo sapiens* to believe that Mussolini is always right or that Hitler's words define good and evil.

But whatever the ravages wrought by the secular religions, they alone seem nowadays to possess the secret of arousing the passions that can move mountains and of producing leaders who can send their supporters to death with a word. Nothing great in history is ever achieved unless the masses have faith in ideas and in men. But can we prevent that faith from degenerating into barbaric fury? Will we give that faith monuments to build that bear witness to something other than the sacrifice of millions of slaves? This faith, born out of an aspiration to greatness, out of a desire for devotion to a more than human task, will we teach it to first respect the virtues of mere humanity?

At the end of June 1940, at the Olympia Hall in London, the first order of the day read out to the Free French volunteers ended with the famous words of Tacitus: "One need not hope in order to try, nor succeed in order to persevere." I saw in that phrase, and I see still, the watchword of revolt, always vanquished yet always victorious—the revolt of conscience.

London, July 1944

FROM MARXISM TO STALINISM

The Soviet Union, home of a religion of temporal salvation, attracts both the peasants of Asia, living on the brink of famine, and a handful of atomic scientists, who, in the words of the red master of the Kremlin, have heard the good news given once more to suffering humanity.

The divisions of the Red Army would inspire less apprehension if they were not seen to act in the service of an idea. It is the combination of an empire risen suddenly on the ruins of the European nations and an apparently universal message that spreads a kind of terror throughout the non-Communist world.

Europe is only just emerging from the liberal and bourgeois age and cannot understand by what convolution of thought a doctrine derived from rationalism can have revived the superstitions of the Dark Ages.

Marxism is a Christian heresy. As a modern form of millenarianism, it places the kingdom of God on earth following an apocalyptic revolution in which the Old World will be swallowed up. The contradictions of capitalist societies will inevitably bring about this fruitful catastrophe. The victims of today will be the victors of tomorrow. Salvation will come through the proletariat, that witness to present inhumanity. It is the proletariat that, at a time fixed by the evolution of productive forces and by the courage of the combatants, will turn itself into a class that is universal and take charge of the fate of mankind.

This kind of ideology, which I regard not as a doctrine for the use of philosophers but as a subject for popular faith, brings together three themes that can easily be traced historically and that together provide its explosive force.

First, the Christian theme. All religions of salvation predict in one way or another the revenge of the humiliated. They offer compensation to members of the socially inferior classes, either in the next world or in the present one. Marxism gives the victory of the slaves some plausibility. Are not industrial workers the real creators of wealth? And is not the elimination of parasites and monopolists, who levy an exorbitant tithe on the collective income, irresistibly called for by an immanent logic? Placed in the context of a materialist dialectic, the idea of overturning the social hierarchy is separated from its true origins in Christian aspirations, which atheism has failed to stifle completely, and in the more or less sublimated resentments of those relegated to the bottom of the heap. The positive and scientific camouflage in which the idea is enveloped deludes the faithful as to its true nature without drying up the emotional sources of their belief.

Then there is the Promethean theme. Man, who discovered the secret of fire, is more and more rapidly extending his mastery over the forces of nature. On the horizon already is the era of plenty, which for Trotsky was an accessible objective relatively near at hand. Traditional poverty is gradually sinking into the past, and the curse of labor is a mere superstition surviving in societies with inadequate means of production. The development of socialism still calls for effort and privation, but beyond the purgatory of industrialization lies science and technology, the demiurges of modern times, which will make oppression a scandal and inequality, once a condition of culture, unnecessary. Wealth and leisure, once reserved for the few and denied to the majority, will be enjoyed by all, thanks to the genius of the human race.

Finally, the rationalist theme. Collectivities developed spontaneously, but they must be rebuilt rationally. Spontaneous development itself obeyed an inner logic. The creation of humanity by itself, through the dual struggle of men with one another and with nature, gives meaning to the apparent confusion of events. But a new phase is beginning: Thanks to knowledge of the laws of their own history, men are becoming capable of acting lucidly. Not that they can escape the inevitable troubles that accompany periods of transition. The passage from one social structure to another, the replacement of one social class by another, tend to bring wars and revolutions in their wake. But we know the outcome in advance, and that will be the creation of a new human order, thanks to the conscious action of men. Private property and the anarchy of the market will give way to planning and collective ownership.

Although revolt against inequality and injustice exists in every epoch, the boundless hopes invested in science and technology in our own day are fostered by the industrial achievements of Western civilization. It is the synthesis of this revolt and these hopes, thanks to a pseudo-rationalist interpretation of history, that gives Marxism its power of attraction. Faith in science alone would create only a kind of wait-and-see attitude (want and inequality will disappear in due course) or a reliance on technocracy (the experts will sort things out). Revolt alone would merely revive oft-disappointed illusions (why should the new masters be any better than the old?). The virtues of science will come into their own with the victory of the proletariat.

In the last quarter of the nineteenth century, Marxism became the official doctrine of working class parties on the continent of Europe. (It had only a minor influence in Britain, and an even smaller one in the United States.) But as these parties grew in numbers and influence, there was an increasing divergence between the theory and practice of social democracy. Revolutionary theory was retained, but participation in government forbidden. Eduard Bernstein was excommunicated from both the German and the international Social Democrat conferences, though reformism prevailed in practice. Ideology served to keep up the enthusiasm of the troops and to transform the prosaic nature of everyday political claims. It persuaded the working class that it had a historical role to play. This promise kept it from being completely incorporated into the bourgeois order, on the one hand, and from turning into a permanent and implacable enemy of societies and states, on the other. The social laws conceded by anti-Socialist governments, such as that of Otto von Bismarck, and the improvements in the standard of living gained through union action, had not put an end to the dissidence of the domestic proletariat, but there were signs that this dissidence might vanish without violence or revolution.

Even today there is no proof that the independent development of capitalism will exclude such an outcome. Countries like Sweden and Switzerland, spared by both world wars, show one of the possible issues that was obscured before 1914 by the ideology of the Second International. It was probably implicit in the structure of Western societies, at least within the framework of political democracy, that the working class would organize into unions or even into Socialist parties. But neither unions nor parties prevent the bourgeoisification of the working class, which is encouraged by increasing wealth and redistribution of national income. The Communists' war against what they call capitalism (which includes the British labor movement as well as the Third Reich) was not inevitable.

Stalinism still invokes Marxist ideology, that subtle combination of Christian aspirations and faith in technology. Stalin the Terrible is still seen by millions of men of good will, even in France, as the father of the poor and the righter of wrongs—Stalin, the pyramid-builder, indifferent to the fate of millions of beings "condemned by history," indifferent even to the fate of servants of the revolution once they have ceased to be useful or sufficiently docile. But if we discover the secrets of the party, or read its theoretical and propaganda texts, we see, through the apparent continuity, a radical change. The Stalinists speak the language of the nineteenth-century Marxists, but they belong to a different universe.

Intellectually, it is easy to explain the transition from Marxism to Leninism and then from Leninism to Stalinism. The decisive stages are the invention of the party and of revolutionary action; the role of wars in the origin of revolutions; the doctrine of building a socialist society in a single country (the "socialist bastion"); and the assertion of the leading role of the Russian Bolshevik Party.

Originally, Bolshevism was only one faction within social democracy. It was conspicuous for its extremism, its intransigence, and its tendency to create splits on the basis of apparently minor disagreements. Nowadays, we see Lenin's essential contribution not in the somewhat simplistic materialism of *Materialism and Empiriocriticism*, nor in his interpretation of the global movement of capitalism, but in the theory and practice of revolutionary action. The main lines are well known. The working-class masses, left to themselves, might be content with trade unionism, the mere struggle of here and now to improve living conditions. It is the intellectuals who make the masses aware of their historic mission and who give the revolt of the proletariat its inspiration and objectives. The party, whose officials should include a large proportion of professional revolutionaries, is organized in accordance with the rules of what Lenin called *democratic centralism:* In fact, the real power belongs to the central committee, a kind of senior staff at the head of a clandestine army (the Bolshevik Party was illegal most of the time before 1917).

At the time, in the leading circles of the Second International, the originality of the Bolshevik Party (which was in any case not fully recognized) was seen only as a kind of aberration, something to be explained by the requirements of the struggle against tsarism. The democratic methods were regarded as normal, the technique of violence and clandestinity as a remnant from the past. The 1917 revolution changed all this. It was the Bolshevik Party itself that served as a model for the parties of the Third International.

Once masters of the Russian state, Lenin and his comrades began by awaiting the European or world revolution in the same way as the early Christians awaited the Second Coming of Christ. When they stopped believing in the imminence of the Revolution with a capital "R," they adapted to a situation that they had not foreseen that their theories themselves did not allow them to foresee: The proletariat had triumphed in only one country, and that country, far from having reached the point at which the development of productive forces exacerbates the contradictions of capitalism, was still mainly agricultural, owing its first industrial concentrations, which had sprung up around its major cities, to the influence and capital of the West. On the intellectual plane, a few additional hypotheses were enough to make dogma and reality agree with one another.

First it was posited that conditions favorable to revolution are created not so much by capitalism and crises as by war. The triumph of the proletariat occurs not necessarily in the country that is most industrially advanced, but simply in the country where the regime is weakest and least strongly defended—"the weakest link in the chain." This being so, instead of waiting, like social democracy, for capitalism to mature, one must be continually on the alert for opportunities. Revolution is no longer an almost indefinable, quasi-mythical event that upsets the normal course of human activities; rather, it is a seizure of power. Union action, social laws, economic reforms—all these are no longer of interest except as means to this one end.

The Russian Communist Party and the other parties of the Third International all adopt similar principles of organization and action and are assigned differing but coordinated roles within an overall plan. The first task is to strengthen the bastion of socialism—in other words, to hasten the industrialization of the only country so far taken over by the proletariat. But the theory of "socialism in one country" does not imply that the hope of world revolution is abandoned, only that it will have to be brought about in stages. To begin with, the territory already occupied must be organized and the first proletarian state strengthened. If necessary, the other national parties will be sacrificed to this supreme necessity. Expansion, starting from the basis of the bastion, will take place at a later stage. What circumstances will make this enlargement possible? The only answer is, once again, war. The capitalist world has entered a period of decadence, the symptoms of which are crises and, above all, wars. A first world war made the 1917 revolution possible. A second will give the proletariat an opportunity for further conquests.

The preeminence of the Bolsheviks is justified theoretically. They invoke not only the authority conferred on them by victory but also the real affinity between the destiny of the world revolution and that of the socialist bastion. Confusion between the cause of the revolution itself and the national interests of the Russian state becomes inevitable. Leninist centralization, applied to the International, soon produces similar results: The Central Committee (in fact, the Russian leaders of the Comintern) exercises over all sections of the International the same strict control and uncompromising authority as the Leninist and then the Stalinist general staff wielded over the clandestine sections before 1917 and over the various activities of the party before and after the seizure of power.

If we confine ourselves to this abstract summary we might conclude that the change from the Second International to the Third International was a limited one. We might see communism as a version of Marxism, and indeed, the most reasonable one because it seems to have profited from the experience of the twentieth century. Its chief theoretical contribution is to substitute wars for crises and the ripening of capitalism as the essential factor in the proletarian revolution. In practice, its contribution is to generalize Bolshevik methods of organization and action and recognize the preeminence of the Russian Communist Party, both because it rules a major state and because the fate of the world revolution now seems linked to the Soviet experience. But these novelties leave the traditional doctrine intact—dialectical materialism, class struggle, the contradictions inherent in capitalism, and so on, remain. Yet their influence is more widespread. Communism introduces a foreign body into European societies; in thirty years they have not been able either to assimilate or to eliminate it.

There were two aspects to the traditional teaching: a conception of the world (or at least the human world) and an interpretation of capitalism and its necessary development. The Marxist parties claimed to be acting on the basis of their view of the inevitable future of capitalism. But the Communist parties, in fact, are not interested in what I have referred to elsewhere as "the schema of the evolution of capitalism."* They are not waiting for the development of productive forces to create the objective conditions of revolution; they are adapting to various circumstances, which are different in China and different again in the United States. But everywhere their method is the same: to form a party fostering agitation, espionage, and insurrection. And everywhere their objective is also the same: to undermine the existing government and prepare to seize power. The schema of the evolution of capitalism was a link between historical materialism and the action of the Socialist parties. When that schema disappears there remains, on the one hand, purely opportunistic revolutionary action, and on the other, a justificatory ideology. Only faith connects the two.

But by what miracle could the few thousand intellectuals and workers who are members of the American Communist Party represent the proletariat of the United States? And how could a party composed mostly of peasants represent the Chinese proletariat? It is easy, in the abstract, to describe the Communist Party as the avant-garde of the proletariat and to say its task is to guide the masses toward the fulfillment of their mission. But in practice the party replaces the proletariat; it is the party itself that is invested with the historic mission and regarded as sacrosanct. When a proletariat fails to support the Communist Party, it is the proletariat that is wrong.

The transfer of the historical mission from the proletariat to the party entails another and even more serious consequence. Henceforth there is only one path to the future—the one that passes through the triumph of communism. The world is divided into two and only two camps: on the one hand, the countries where a Communist Party rules, and on the other, all the rest, which are called capitalist even if a labor party is in power, if enterprises are mostly state-owned, or if incomes are more equal than in the

---

*Cf. *Le Grand Schisme* (The great schism) (Paris: Gallimard, 1948), Chapter 5.

home of socialism itself. This Manichaean view of the world is the necessary consequence of the role assigned to the Stalinist party. If that party's seizure of power is the necessary and sufficient condition for revolution whatever the objective circumstances, then logically both a Romania tyrannized over by a few Kremlin officials and a Britain governed by the Labour Party are both still capitalist. (This may be the logic of schizophrenics, but it is a kind of logic just the same.)

In the context of this system, the priority accorded to revolution in what are currently called the underdeveloped countries becomes understandable. As capitalism flourishes and the standard of living rises, the revolutionary ardor of the masses cools. Professional agitators will raise more recruits among the poverty-stricken crowds of Asia than among the workers of General Motors. The Bolsheviks' technique, born in Tsarist Russia, is naturally better adapted to Far Eastern societies shaken by the influence of industrial civilization.

The activities of Communist parties in Western societies, whether in Europe or the United States, no longer have anything in common with those of the Socialist parties. The latter call themselves revolutionary, but they use democratic methods and support the claims of the workers. They tolerate more or less autonomous unions, they try to improve the lot of the workers, and they obtain with more or less difficulty social laws and wage increases. Nothing like this happens with the Communist parties, even when they use the same language and support the same demands. They want the conditions of the workers to improve or regress, according to circumstance, but they are never interested in reform for its own sake. Their aim is to exercise control over the unions and the masses so as to increase their own ability to agitate and subvert, a power they will use in obedience to directives from Moscow. A technique of propaganda and insurrection, in theory in the service of revolution but really in the service of a foreign state—such for thirty years has been the essence of the policy of the Communist parties in the West. This policy is nothing less than a world-scale magnification of the war technique of the first Bolsheviks against the Tsarist regime.

It is not so easy to trace the transition from Leninism to Stalinism as it was to mark the stages from Marxism to Leninism. Neither doctrine nor language has changed fundamentally. The gap has grown wider between the ideology of justification and authentic action, but the widening was gradual. It would be impossible to say when Marxism became a mere "derivation."

Lenin tended to believe that the cause of the proletariat was identical to that of his faction. Several times before 1917 he caused a split rather than bow to what he considered the mistaken opinion of the majority. He manipulated the congresses unscrupulously, convinced that his view of the situation reflected historical truth. He did not hesitate to brand those who did not support him as traitors to the revolution, and never doubted for a moment that the Bolshevik Party's seizure of power was the first stage of the socialist revolution predicted by Marxism. Karl Johann Kautsky—who objected that the seizure of power by the Bolshevik Party was really that of a minority, both of the proletariat and of the country as a whole—was immediately classed as a renegade.

Contempt for formal democracy does not date from Stalin. He imposed the Soviet regime on the nations of the Russian Empire against the peoples' will, but Lenin had earlier dissolved the constituent assembly elected in January 1918 because it did not have a Bolshevik majority. Whatever the intellectuals who anathematize Stalin and still worship Lenin think, the decisive break with the West and with democratic socialism was made by the founder and not by the heir.

From the start the authority of the Central Committee was more like that of the general staff of an army than like that of leaders elected by local sections or their delegates. Today the Central Committee is completely neutralized and obeys the orders of one man, whereas thirty years ago there was a continual struggle, both open and clandestine, of ideas and trends. The leaders of the party and the state manipulate both officials and activists as they please; they have the power of life and death over those whom in theory they represent. In short, Lenin's democratic centralism has ended up as the dictatorship of the general secretary. This setup cannot by any stretch of the imagination be described as democratic: But can the adjective be applied any more appropriately to Lenin's centralism?

Discussions do still take place in the political bureau about the advisability of this or that measure in such and such circumstances, but these consultations are merely technical and are kept secret. The party line is fixed from above; self-criticism is required of executants, not of the leaders—that is, of those who carry out decisions and not of those who make them. Deviationists are brutally eliminated— physically, where the party is in power (by means of prison, deportation, trial, or death), and through disgrace and dishonor where the party has no police force at its disposal.

Stalinism is a logical development of Leninism. It was a great temptation for the general secretary of the party to appoint men he could rely on as officials to ensure that the Central Committee's proposals would always get a majority vote at the congresses. Even Lenin did his best to control the clandestine network, choosing as section representatives, who were supposed to be elected, militants ready to obey his orders. Democratic centralism as applied to the dual bureaucracy of party and state ended by reducing electoral procedures to fictions. Free discussion between the leaders became a mere remnant. The man who controlled the bureaucracy, the real instrument of power, like his predecessor who had controlled the clandestine network, was in fact the supreme leader.

The national parties of the Third International changed between Grigori Zinoviev's day and the "struggle for peace and against imperialism." But the changes in the national parties paralleled those in the Bolshevik Party: Free discussion of trends and ideas disappeared from them all. The Russian leaders of the Comintern have gradually tightened their authority, manipulating the leading elements of the national parties just as they do the Soviet bureaucracy, pursuing the subjugation of the French and German parties with a rigor that recalls the former empire of the tsars, and introducing all over the world the same spirit of orthodoxy that they impose in the home of socialism itself. This process of assimilation is limited, however, as is seen in the contrast between the conservative, reactionary policies of the Russian Communist Party and the revolutionary policies of the foreign parties before they come to power.

On the intellectual level, the party did not immediately claim to be the repository of a total truth, although the premises of spiritual dictatorship do go back to Marxism itself. Historical materialism would seem to suggest a general interpretation for every age. Works of art and of the mind are linked in complex and subtle ways to the relations of production and to class conflicts. The dominant class always influences the whole of society. In a way, the present, bourgeois culture will be swept away or transformed by the proletarian revolution. All Marxists have declared, more or less clearly, that there is a connection between metaphysical hypotheses and political strategy. "Reformism" merged into Kantism and dualism with regard to facts and values; the extremists remained "monists" and materialists. Most Marxists have a vague inclination to see the revolutionary attitude as linked to some sort of moral or philosophical orthodoxy.

Lenin and his comrades would have rebelled against Stalin's practices. They would not admire the party-commissioned official paintings or acquiesce in the state's condemnation of Gregor Mendel's theories.[5] But they, too, had posited the supreme value of the revolution; they agreed that intellectual and cultural freedom should be subordinated to the interests of the collectivity; they also put forward their doctrine as absolute truth and regarded dialectical materialism as a rival of the religions of salvation. As soon as someone simpleminded becomes the master, obscurantism and despotism will prevail.

The world that Stalinism offers its disciples is full of forces that are essentially good or bad. The Soviet Union is, by its own definition, peace-loving and democratic, even when it is attacking Finland, allying itself with Hitler, or opening concentration camps in Germany. France becomes imperialistic merely by participating in the Marshall Plan and receiving a few arms from the United States. Descriptions apply not so much to countries' conduct as to their essence, as defined once and for all by the interpretation of sacrosanct history. It is of no consequence whether the imperialist countries are or appear to be defensive in such circumstances. They are imperialist because they are capitalist and therefore in search of expansion. But even if they were not looking for outlets, they would still be imperialist because they embody the past and the Soviet Union is the future. Events, classes, and nations all take their place in a battle of abstractions that have been transformed into mythical characters (capitalism, socialism, imperialism), a battle whose final outcome is known to the distant prophet.

The dialectic of purification, of purges, is another demonstration of this Manichaean outlook. Marxists, like all men of action, have always tended to value actions more highly than intentions, the consequences of actions rather than their content taken in isolation, and the historic influence of ideas and behavior rather than their motivation. Non-Marxists have more than once suffered from the application of this attitude: Liberals were held responsible for colonial exploitation, and the defenders of formal democracy were blamed for the privations of the workers. But the Communists now blithely use this tactic against deviationists and opponents. Are they weakening the party, yes or no? If so, are they, objectively, enemies to the cause? The argument is familiar and has provided a justification for terror in all revolutionary eras. But it is no longer enough to say that the opponent *behaves like* an enemy to the cause. In order both to discredit him and to restore the prestige of the leaders, he must appear to be not merely the enemy's involuntary ally but his paid agent. Nikolay Bukharin is supposed to have plotted the assassination of Lenin, László Rajk to have spent nearly twenty years as an agent of Miklós Horthy's police or of the Intelligence Service. Through this process of "chain identifications," anyone who ceases to obey the leader will lose both life and honor.

Having reached this point, the Marxist interpreter no longer recognizes any limits or obstacles. He can make anything mean anything, in accordance with an interpretation of the world laid down absolutely by himself. As the supreme interpreter is also the head of state, the dialectic of purification, over which our philosophers quibble so endlessly, results in the sanctification of success and power; the word of the master becomes the sole criterion of good and evil. No one can be sure of sticking to the right line because the line keeps changing, and the master remakes the past and the future just as he pleases. What is orthodox today could be a deviation tomorrow.

We are clearly a long way away from the days of Lenin, who was in favor of making peace with the Germans and was only waiting for events to bring his comrades on the Central Committee around to his way of thinking. With regard to each of the historic decisions—the November coup, the peace of Brest-Litovsk—the Bolshevik leadership was divided. Lenin was several times in a minority. But he never thought of revenge when his opponents finally gave in. He was as quick to make up as he was to quarrel, provided that his adversary admitted his error and, when it came to action, bowed to the law of unanimity.

But Lenin himself did not extend this tolerance to those outside the Bolshevik Party. Already, in his lifetime, the other parties, including the leftist Socialist Revolutionaries who had taken part in the November coup, were banned and eliminated from public life. The chief militants were forced to emigrate, imprisoned, or deported. What happened? Gradually, deviationists inside the party came to be treated like outside dissidents, whether socialist or not. Again, it has to be said that this development was logical, if not inevitable.

It is true that more than fifteen years went by after the revolution before Stalin himself decided to cross the "line of blood" and put party comrades to death. But these apparent scruples of his were merely a relic at a time when millions of kulaks were being killed. In the long run it is impossible to juxtapose two contradictory worlds, one based on respect for one's fellow creatures and the other on the unlimited powers of the ruling party over the vast masses of those who have no party.

Between the Leninist phase, when everyone was free to have his own opinion so long as his actions accorded with party discipline, and the present situation, when any opponent—present, past, or future, real or potential—must confess to crimes he has not committed, there was an intermediary phase. To ensure discipline and eliminate resistance, the job of publicly expounding official decisions was given to those who had fought against them in the cells of the party or in the Central Committee. Men like Zinoviev and Bukharin, after recanting previous positions several times, finally made the ultimate avowal and agreed to proclaim the rightness of the judgment that was to send them to their deaths.

The succession of purges probably conveys what actually happened better than any theory can describe it. Lenin's party was decimated: Three-quarters or four-fifths of its militants were liquidated. Many of the revolutionaries who had been the first to join the Third International in France and Germany after 1917 broke with Bolshevism during the 1920s. The leaders of the Communist parties in exile, whether Polish, Yugoslavian, Hungarian, or Spanish, were almost entirely wiped out. In Eastern Europe, no sooner had the Communist parties come to power than, from 1949 on, such of their leaders (Wladyslaw Gomulka, László Rajk, Traicho Kostov) as had not made a career for themselves in Moscow, or had fought on their native soil, or had relations with the West were eliminated in their turn.

Lenin's comrades had been mostly intellectuals with international backgrounds. They followed Bolshevik practices, but they could not with an easy conscience carry the system to its logical conclusion. Most of them had opposed tsarism because they were heretics by nature and could not tolerate injustice. They were the right men for revolution, but how could they have become good state officials? Victorious Stalinism no longer needed the same men as militant Stalinism had required.

The same mechanism operated in nearly all the foreign parties. Everywhere the revolutionaries had to be replaced by technicians, men of ideas supplanted by men of power. The cross purposes were even more blatant in the case of the foreign Communists. Did Lenin's comrades oppose Stalin out of moral indignation, because they disagreed with his ideas, or out of resentment at having been beaten? We are not sure. But the foreign Communists who ended up breaking away or being executed had all rallied to an ideal Bolshevism; they had no experience of the real thing.

Those who followed Lenin thirty years ago were extremists, hardliners, opponents of social conformity, and great-nephews of Rousseau who believed that man is good and that the evils he suffers are inflicted on him by society. Leninism was the ultimate variation of progressivism—European rationalism in its final form. After World War I, pacifists looked toward that great gleam of light in the east. When the slump came, the country without unemployment became the model and the hope. The Hitler menace made liberals turn to the champion of anti-fascism. From 1941 on, the Soviet regime enjoyed the reflected glory of the Russian soldier, and the country that defeated Hitler was the standard-bearer of peace and of Europe.

The pacifists of 1919 soon found out that the Soviet Union did not condemn war itself; it simply preferred civil to foreign war. The anticapitalists of the 1930s discovered that forced labor is not a satisfactory way of abolishing unemployment. The anti-fascists learned that Stalinism has perfected the techniques of fascism. The anti-Nazis of the 1940s saw that the European unity of Stalin would be as obnoxious as that of Hitler. The renegades or victims of Stalinism are not just idealists disillusioned by reality, revolutionaries incapable of adapting to the new order, nationalists opposing the supremacy of the Kremlin, or westerners taken in by propaganda and ignorant of the true "eternal Russia." In thirty years the very soul of the revolutionary movement has changed.

In the past people wanted justice and accepted violence and party discipline because they were impatient with mere talk. Today that justice is claimed as a right, and the challenge now is to learn to apply it technically. The contrast is not really so clear-cut as that. In Russia, the party is now only a privileged and despotic minority whose main concern is to strengthen the hierarchy. Abroad, the parties still follow a revolutionary policy, trying to destroy the social order and appealing to the emotions that encourage eternal revolt against social injustice. In Europe, every generation supplies Stalinism with new recruits who dream of ending the exploitation of man by man. Today's leaders, who have bowed to the demands of the Stalinist universe, are more likely to be cynical than naive. It is the humble militants who keep the idealist faith. Men like Jacques Doriot or Marshal

Tito, both before and after they broke with Stalin, believed in power rather than in the liberation of man.

⟜

Marxism is a glorification of a postcapitalist future that is unknown and unknowable. Stalinism is a glorification of a society that is unsatisfactory to idealists and alien to the genius of the West.

Stalinism has not dropped the appeal to the future. Russia is going through a phase of socialism (to each according to his work) and has not yet reached the stage of communism (to each according to his needs). To put it more simply, present privations are (or were) explained by the demands of industrial development. Consumption certainly has to be reduced so long as between 20 percent and 30 percent of the national income is devoted to investment. And investment is necessary to end rural overpopulation and to absorb into factories the peasants who, in the field, would not be genuinely employed, even if they actually worked.

It is not the standard of living of the people of the Soviet Union that creates disillusionment, even though it is a favorite target with the anti-Communists. More than thirty years after the 1917 revolution, a social structure has been established on whose characteristic features observers are agreed.

No group or individual has any chance of independence vis-à-vis the state, the power of which is both total and arbitrary. By means of the *kolkhozes*, or collective farms, the peasants are again tied to the land, which belongs to them only in the form of individual lots. By means of the tractor depots, the kolkhozes* are subjected to the authority of planners and collectors. Work logbooks and internal passports limit the worker's freedom to choose his job and place of residence. Movement of workers, purges, transfers of population, and forced labor camps all combine to allow the authorities to move human resources about just as they please, in peace as in war.

Soviet society is made up of groups distinguished from one another by their activities, way of life, and level of income: kolkhoz and industrial

---

*The 1950 regrouping of the kolkhozes represents another stage in the total subjection of the peasantry to the state.

workers; skilled and unskilled laborers; writers and accountants in collective enterprises; managers of factories or trusts; managers of kolkhozes; and union secretaries. But none of these groups has any power or a membership viewing it as a historical unit with its own special interests to defend. The whole structure is an amorphous mass, exposed to a propaganda machine and subject to an omnipresent apparatus of power. The social hierarchy merges into the state hierarchy: Considerable differences in income are the result of a concerted policy. But although privileged people are given what are regarded as superior jobs, they are wage earners just like the unprivileged. This confusion of bureaucracy with aristocracy is not so much an innovation as a return to an age-old tradition. Similarly, directors or managers of agricultural and industrial enterprises, trusts, and ministries are officials of the Soviet state.

The party* is supportive of the regime because of its ideology. It owes allegiance neither to the past nor to tradition, but only to the revolution. Its justification lies in its services to the cause of socialism, but by the same token it must accept the law of orthodoxy. And what socialism requires is leaders—and above all a supreme leader—to proclaim its message unceasingly. The Christian religion is not eliminated, but the supreme truth is that of history in the making. Any leader who betrays that truth betrays the principle in whose name he has enjoyed the right of life and death over his fellow men. The privileged class emerges as at once the bureaucracy of a state that comprises the whole of society, and the clergy of a militant church.

Nothing could be less Western than a society of this kind. Western societies are characterized by their rejection of unanimity. Life in the West, with its distinctions between temporal and spiritual power, Pope and emperor, national church and Pope, nobility and monarchy, bourgeoisie and Ancien Regime, proletariat and bourgeoisie, is made up of tensions not so much overcome as managed, a process that calls for effort, struggle, and creativity. Soviet society aims at unanimity: It no longer permits rivalry between the temporal and spiritual powers, between social classes, or between society and the state. In its merging of temporal and spiritual power, it is a descendant of Byzantium. In placing all men and all resources at the service

---

*There is less solidarity among other sectors of the Soviet elite, such as technicians with no party commitment and even army officers.

of the state, it echoes the essence of all tyrannies. The gradual reduction of the whole population to the condition of the masses may go back to even older models.

Stalinism now presents itself to the West less as a particular version of Marxism than as a particular social order: an authority that, if the Communist Party achieves power or the Red Army is present, will be imposed on a country from on high. But this is a social order that entails the destruction of all traditional ways of life. There are the same professions and occupations in a Soviet and in a bourgeois society, if both have reached a particular stage in their technological development. But in the Soviet Union a tradesman can survive only if he becomes a manager or an official employee of the state. A peasant will sooner or later become part of a collective farm, and collectivization does away with landowners and farmers. The liberal professions will lose their raison d'être (the defense will support the prosecution) and their independence. Craftsmen, tradesmen, small businessmen, and members of the liberal professions will go on doing the work they did before but will lose their former lifestyles and ways of thinking. The Sovietization of a country with a Western culture involves a historical liquidation of social categories that represent up to half of the active population.

Proletarization, not completely achieved under capitalism, will probably be taken to its logical conclusion by communism. The omnipotence wrongly attributed to the owners of the tools of production will really be vested in Stalinist bureaucracy. The neutralization of classes and the intelligentsia will be carried out by violent means by the party that liberated the proletariat. Compared with such total servitude, the issues that give rise to conflict within our own civilization, including that between the bourgeoisie and the working class, look absurd.

⌒

The classical and central theory of revolution in Marx's philosophy is that which sees the society of the future evolving within the society of the present. The 1917 revolution clearly fails to follow this model. The coming to power of the proletariat should have been preceded by the development of productive forces under the influence of capitalism. But scattered among Marx's writings are references to another theory of revolution that gives primacy to the revolutionary party's ability to seize opportunities. Which of the two ideas is closer to Marx's fundamental thinking? One could argue about it indefinitely, but there would be little point because Marx himself tried to effect a synthesis between economic determinism and human will. But as usual, the synthesis has not stood up to experience: Events have forced men to choose. And whatever their choice, to explain it in terms of Marx would be both right and wrong, since he would never have approved of the proletarian party becoming the left wing of bourgeois coalitions (as Social Democrats do every day), nor of its promoting the Russification of Europe (as the Communists are doing, to all intents and purposes).

Is it true that Marx would not see the fulfillment of his hopes in the present realities? He belonged to the nineteenth century, which was humanitarian and liberal. Deep down, he condemned the humanitarian and liberal bourgeois not because of their ideals but because they were incapable of putting them into practice. He dreamed that the community would consciously take over the organization of economic life, not that a minority ruling in the name of the proletariat would wield power just as it pleased.

Lenin believed, or at least wrote as if he believed, in the gradual withering away of the state once class divisions were abolished. Yet never has a police state been more all-pervasive than Russia under the rule of the Communist Party. It is not difficult to show that Soviet society fails to live up to the expectations of either its prophet or its founder. But that is not the real point.

Did not the revolution, as conceived of by the Marxists—with their notions of collective ownership, planning, and power of the proletariat—and, even more, the revolution as realized by Lenin—conquest of the state by a minority party, in a precapitalist country, with forced industrialization—actually imply a society like that of the Soviets?

People often describe Stalinism in terms of a sociological schema derived from the comparative study of revolutions: Thermidor comes after the Reign of Terror, Bonaparte stabilizes the social structure that emerges from the upheaval, the new ruling class increases its power. The Trotskyists combined this interpretation with economic materialism. The victory of Stalinism was inevitable. The bureaucracy, in control of the means of production, sought security and the consecration of its own privileges. Stalin met these requirements ("socialism in one country" rather than permanent revolution); Trotsky did not. Trotsky was historically eliminated and finally murdered by his rival, not because he had played the game unskillfully or neglected the crucial card (infiltration of the party), but because his person and his ideas happened to contrast with what was required by the times he lived in. The bureaucracy, imitating the traditional ruling classes, builds up a hierarchy of wealth and power to suit its own ends, consumes a large part of the national revenue, and imposes an ideology to justify it all—in short, produces the equivalent of the very "exploitation" that Marxism has been denouncing for more than a century.

This account contains an element of truth. Could the seizure of power by the Bolsheviks have led to anything else but the formation of a ruling class and the reconstruction of a hierarchy? Overall planning and public ownership of all the tools of production must entail an omnipotent state. How can anyone prevent such omnipotence from being vested in a minority that in fact owns the state? The Trotskyist version of the Stalinist Thermidor is plausible only if bureaucratic despotism is seen as a passing phase of collective society and not its normal form.

True, we might have recourse to a theory, existing in scattered fragments, that I will call the theory of *economic ages*. Regardless of the type of regime involved (planned or market, based on collective or private ownership), modern economies all pass through typical phases. The phase of capitalism, which in the West extended from the end of the eighteenth to the first half of the nineteenth century, saw the development of industry, or more generally, that of the secondary sector. This expansion of the secondary sector typically takes place via the transfer of populations from rural to urban areas, which is made possible by increased agricultural productivity. The demographic transfer always involves a relative reduction in the agricultural labor force (an absolute reduction is sometimes avoided by a population increase) and the allocation of a large percentage of the national income to investment. In Western Europe, savings were obtained by means of unequal distribution and very low wages. In the Soviet Union, too, collective savings are facilitated by low wages as well as various fiscal devices. The national leaders imitate the moneyed classes of Western Europe in the nineteenth century, enjoying large incomes and spending a fraction of them on their pleasures. Both in Western Europe and in Soviet Russia, it has been the masses who have really been responsible for industrialization, as if the burden of investment must always fall on the shoulders of the poor.

In the case of liberal regimes, it is easy to see the link between large incomes and collective necessities. The leveling of incomes usually tends to reduce collective savings taken as a whole. In the case of the Soviet regime, the need for inequality does not emerge so clearly: Savings are not deducted from the large incomes that remain unspent; instead they are obtained either through limitations on wages, through industrial profits, or through taxes on consumption. (The state thus benefits from a considerable disparity between prices paid to producers in the country and those demanded of consumers in the cities.) Psychological and political excuses are adduced for this sort of thing. A class with absolute power that declined to enjoy the profits it entailed would be made up of angels, not of men. Purity and the rejection of riches do not survive the heroic era. Revolutionaries, once victorious, become middle class. The Thermidorian leader links them to his own fate by allowing them to live. The Soviet elite is merely behaving like all other elites.

It may be that a policy of production at any price naturally leads to growing differentiation. If "the leaders decide everything," perhaps it is in the collective interest that the director of a nationalized enterprise should keep for himself most of the profits he has earned by exceeding the prescribed targets. Perhaps societies in the process of expansion are naturally less concerned with distribution than with creation and therefore tend to be indifferent to the fate of the disadvantaged.

But this theory still does not allow us to present bureaucratic despotism as necessarily linked to a certain phase of socialist construction. Let us admit that constraints tend to relax as poverty diminishes (and it does take time to increase wealth). And why should a ruling minority renounce its privileges of its own accord? How can the masses or the organizations that represent them obtain any kind of liberty vis-à-vis the state? Neither the governing bureaucrats nor the technicians will submit voluntarily to the control of the governed. The regime will evolve, like every other regime in history, but it is impossible to see why the evils imputed to the Stalinist Thermidor should inevitably disappear as productive forces develop and relations of production are transformed.

It would be easy, but misleading, to choose between the various explanations and declare dogmatically that the Soviet Union presents either an image of a society subjected to total planning, or the typical features of a society in the first phase of industrialization, or a variation, typical of our day, on a specifically Russian theme. For anyone who needs to see proof before making an assertion, the choice is impossible.

Some phenomena can be ascribed to several causes. A certain institution might be a natural consequence of planning, but specifically Stalinist in style. Authoritarian control of labor might be inevitable in a given regime, but work camps might not be. All the time, beyond all explanations in terms of the logic of the system or the collective interest, one senses the influence of a mysterious and elusive passion, a kind of frenzy comparable to that which drove National Socialism.

But the uncertainties of choice are more interesting to the historical philosopher than to the man of action. Whether Stalinism is right or wrong in claiming to have its roots in Marxism, it imposes itself on the countries it conquers as an indivisible whole. Its institutions and ideologies are transferred to them en bloc: five-year plans, collectivization of agriculture, authoritarian bureaucracy, cult of the leader, doctrinaire orthodoxy, purges, concentration camps—its satellites gradually get to know the whole of the Soviet regime.

And this regime would be imposed on Western Europe if resistance crumbled or the Soviet armies swept toward the coast of the Atlantic.

The ideology of Stalinism is of Western origin, but no European theorist ever accepted the Bolsheviks' interpretation of Marxism or the practical techniques they derived from it. Stalinism represents a combination of that ideology with certain singular features of Russia, a country that according to Marxist doctrine itself was not ripe for a socialist experiment. The February revolution was born out of a fervent desire for freedom, but after a few months that desire was frustrated by the Bolsheviks' seizure of power, which soon replaced the absolutism of the tsars with an even more brutal (and probably more efficient) authority. The Mensheviks and the cadets represented a party of the West. The Bolsheviks, though using Marxist language, were really carrying on a tradition—that of Ivan the Terrible and Peter the Great.

Stalinism owes the attraction it exercises in Europe to the Western origin of its religion. It owes its sweeping power in Asia to its strange combination of bureaucratic despotism and modern faith in technique. The contradiction between Soviet myths and Soviet reality has paradoxically become a source of strength rather than weakness.

THE EXPANSION OF STALINISM

B efore World War I, Bolshevism represented just a faction of the Russ-ian Social Democratic Party, itself merely one of the revolutionary par-ties in the empire of the tsars. But in 1917 this obscure sect took possession of the Russian state. Soon afterward it created a new International, im-posed the same techniques of organization and action on all the national groups, and set up a network of espionage and subversion across five conti-nents. After World War II, this same Bolshevik Party, which rules over one of the two great world powers, imposed its law on the hundred million Eu-ropeans who had been "liberated" by the Red Army. In Asia, the Chinese Communist Party, following in the footsteps of the Russian Communists, brought the civil war to a victorious conclusion and became master of the former Empire of the Middle. The Stalinist universe now stretches from the Stettin-Trieste line to the frontiers of Indochina.

The extent and swiftness of these successes inspires terror in the rest of the world. Europe, having underestimated or scorned Lenin and his com-rades, is now inclined to admire Stalin and his Politburo beyond all reason. Communism is likened to a religion of salvation and compared to Islam, whose armies laid the infidel low and whose ideas conquered men's souls.

$$\sim$$

Bolshevism made its way by violence. In Russia it took power by means of a coup d'état and was victorious in the civil war that followed. In China the order was reversed. There the Communist Party set up a civil and military organization independent of the state and ended up, after more than twenty years, vanquishing the rival Kuomintang government. In the coun-tries of Eastern Europe the Communist Party, thanks to the presence of the

Red Army, was given key positions under cover of a self-proclaimed National Front. After that it was child's play to acquire a monopoly of power.

The technique of deliberate Sovietization, or revolution from the top, as applied to the countries of the Eastern bloc, can be used anywhere. When the Soviet troops arrived in Romania, the Stalinist Party there had only a few hundred members. The hostility of the Poles toward Russia—Tsarist and Bolshevik Russia alike—is well known. The social structure of Czechoslovakia was like that in the Western countries. But in all these places the Stalinists managed to eliminate allies as well as opponents and to construct a new version of the regime that the Communist Party had taken twenty years to build in Russia. One learns from experience: It takes less time to produce an imitation than to create a model.

It would be foolish to ask what secret affinity—perhaps it was the peasant majority or the Slav community, for example—predisposed the countries of Eastern Europe to follow in the path of the Communists. Any country liberated by the Russian army, even France, Britain, or Spain, would have met the same fate. Only Russia and China show us the circumstances that make a Bolshevik revolution possible in the absence of foreign intervention.

The two great revolutions of the twentieth century that claim to have originated in Marxism came before and not after the full development of capitalism. They took place in Russia and China, mainly agricultural countries suffering, though in differing degrees, from rural overpopulation. In both countries the success of the revolution would have been impossible without the support, or at least the consent, of the rural masses.

True, in Russia, the workers concentrated in the suburbs of Petrograd and Moscow, together with rebellious soldiers in the barracks, played a decisive part in the conquest of the state. But once civil war had broken out, the Red Army probably could not have won had it not been for the peasants' hostility toward the White armies. More plainly still, the Chinese Communist Party, after Chiang Kai-shek broke with it and drove it out of the towns, established itself in the country. It had started in the south. The "Long March" brought it to a remote and primitive province in the northwest. It then introduced agrarian reforms, which at first were moderate (reduction of interest rates and landowners' shares) and later became more radical (distribution of land and elimination of landowners with large holdings).

Neither in Russia nor in China was industrial civilization of native origin. Russia had become Europeanized from the eighteenth century on, under the influence of some of its monarchs, and acquired a bureaucracy in the process. In the second half of the nineteenth and above all at the beginning of the twentieth century, industry had made rapid progress, but it had been largely financed by foreign capital and organized with the help of foreign engineers. Russia had certainly taken a full part in the scientific as well as the literary and artistic movements in Western civilization during the century leading up to the 1917 explosion. But the Europeanization was still superficial and limited to a small upper stratum of society conscious of being different and apart from the masses. This group was torn between a desire to imitate Western institutions and a more or less mystical wish to be faithful to the spirit of the nation.

China has been in a state of crisis ever since European influences hastened the collapse of the ancient empire. For the last half-century the country has been in search of a state that can combine the industrial and administrative technology of the West with the heritage of its own incomparable civilization. The Kuomintang failed. Communism is making another attempt. It seems to be adopting an extreme form of westernization, rejecting more sharply than previous revolutionary movements the family and provincial structures of the past, together with its philosophical and religious ideologies. But the example of Russia should prevent us from jumping to conclusions. Most of the intellectuals who made up the leadership of the Bolshevik Party also believed that they were following the line of the westernizers and not that of the Slavophiles. In 1917, Lenin thought the Russian proletariat was sacrificing itself on the altar of world revolution. Thirty years later, we see that Bolshevism has meant exactly the opposite of what the theorists expected.

Mao Tse-tung's followers seem to have borrowed from the West the "latest thing" in political ideology and mode of action. Marxism allows the Chinese, who suffered such humiliation at the hands of the materially superior West, to overcome their complexes. A country that joins the camp of "progress" and "socialism" suddenly finds itself in the avant-garde of mankind, even if it is going to need several centuries to bring its infrastructures and technologies up to date.

In the long term, both in Russia and in China a revolutionary situation was created by Western influence on a traditional society. In both cases, communism exploits nationalism in its attempt to wrest from the West the monopoly of power, to equal the capitalist countries on the level of industry, and to outdo them in the matter of social organization. In this fundamental sense we may say that Leninism and Stalinism, when addressed not to mature capitalisms but to countries that have been humiliated if not enslaved by Western states, have evolved into a kind of National Socialism.

Leninism, at once borrowing from and challenging the West, does not triumph in quiet times when only nonviolent means are available to militants. In 1914, the Bolshevik faction had only a few thousand members. In 1937, at the outbreak of the war against Japan, Chiang Kai-shek was incapable of liquidating the Communists, but the Communists were even more incapable of conquering the Kuomintang. But just as the 1914 war weakened the Russian state apparatus, so the eight years of war in China helped the Communists to erode the old social and moral structures, at least in the northern provinces, where they waged a guerrilla war against both Chiang Kai-shek and the invader alike.

The Communists take over countries that have disintegrated, and they rely on war to create the opportunities they are waiting for.

The less capitalistic a society is, and the less developed its productive forces, the more favorable are the conditions it offers to Bolshevism. Stalinism is essentially a version of Marxism applicable to what the United Nations calls underdeveloped countries. But is this causal relationship to be regarded as indicating a historical function?

In Europe there is a connection between industrial development, the rise of the bourgeoisie, and the advent of political democracy: The same social class that, following common usage, we may describe as bourgeois directs both the economy and the political institutions. Intellectual liberalism, perhaps necessarily, naturally accompanies this creative impulse. Discussion, criticism, and individual rights seem inseparable from progress in science and the application of science to industry.

In the twentieth century, science does not have to be invented: It is largely a question of using the knowledge acquired by others. Rather than needing to make the effort of discovery themselves, countries may borrow recipes for wealth and power. There is no rule to say that intellectual liberty, representative institutions, and industrial construction must progress together.

It may even be true that industrialization in a context of freedom encounters obstacles that are difficult to overcome. Population increase may precede growth in agricultural resources, and farming methods may not improve swiftly enough to fill the gap. India, with a population that grows by between 3 million and 4 million every year, has not managed to break out of the vicious cycle: Poverty leaves no surplus for investment, without which poverty cannot be conquered. In some countries the influence of Western civilization has so undermined the old order that the masses, held in check by the force of tradition during Europe's Industrial Revolution, lack any such restraints at the very moment when they are needed most. And are the former ruling classes capable, anyway, of playing the part that entrepreneurs have played in the West?

Max Weber has shown how historically singular a human type was the capitalist entrepreneur. Compared with the privileged in most known societies, he is extraordinary: He does not indulge in extravagant expense or fritter away his profits for pleasure or prestige; he saves and invests his savings. He is calculating and likes to rationalize his conduct in terms of money.

Even in the West, engineers are sought out and trained, but entrepreneurs are neither sought out nor trained. In a country like Spain, the privileged classes, whether aristocrats or landowners, have always been more interested in luxury than profit. It may be that Russia will produce a class of entrepreneurs. There are a certain number of them in India. China seems not to have had many. Commercial acumen, speculation, usury, investment in land or banking—these are not as rewarding financially as the activities of entrepreneurs. But the Communist Party makes entrepreneurs superfluous. It is the Communist Party itself that will, through the state apparatus, make the population save, teach it to abandon customs inappropriate to the age of technology, and bring about industrial development.

Yet the Stalinist method is not the only one possible, nor even the most efficient. Its stress on heavy industry arises out of its thirst for power and signals indifference to the people's standard of living. In Asia, it is absurd to declare war on the whole of Western civilization just when assistance from the advanced economies is needed more than ever to reduce the human cost of the initial stage of industrialization.

But non-Communists and their protectors need to show they can perform the task that the Communist parties boast they alone can carry out successfully. And this task is not to spread the parliamentary institutions of Washington and London to the four corners of the globe, but to reform outdated agricultural methods, transform working conditions, and guide the masses during the critical period of their first industrial revolution.

But for political even more than for economic liberty, qualified men are lacking. Most countries that have been colonized or influenced by the West have a number of intellectuals trained in American or European universities—usually lawyers or writers rather than engineers. They aspire to leading roles in government or administration but rarely possess the necessary experience or techniques. Parliamentary institutions, when introduced into societies with a completely different tradition and a mostly illiterate population, tend either to be so manipulated by "feudal" officials that they barely conceal the traditional hierarchy surviving under the surface, or to break up into ineffectual rival factions. It would take a miracle to make a Western-style democracy succeed in such conditions.

⟋⟋

In the twenty years between the two wars, Bolshevism-Leninism had even fewer spectacular successes in Europe than in Asia. Most of the working class rejected the Leninist version of Marxism and remained loyal to social democracy.

When the Red Army entered Polish territory in 1921, the Bolshevik leadership thought revolution would spring up of its own accord as their army advanced; the Polish masses, however, fought fiercely for their barely liberated homeland against their traditional enemy, regardless of the color of its regime. In Germany, after the defeat, only a minority of the Social Democratic Party adopted a revolutionary attitude, in the sense of favoring a seizure of power by violence, and the Spartakists were not even all Communists. (Rosa Luxemburg was extremely hostile to "democratic centralization" and Jacobin dictatorship.) Even in the Germany of 1930–1933, devastated by mass unemployment, communism failed to attract most of the proletariat. The lure of Hitler's National Socialism was much greater than that of international and Soviet socialism. At the end of 1931, the Social Democratic Party, despite its decline, had more voters than the Communist Party.

And today we can safely say that between the two wars no Communist Party anywhere in Europe had the slightest chance of overthrowing the state. Bolshevism's only chance was a second world war, which the Kremlin leadership counted on (in this they were good prophets) and which the Fascists (in theory a bulwark against Bolshevism) crazily precipitated. Social reform and parliamentary democracies were what corresponded to the natural aspirations and the legitimately chosen programs of the proletariats of Western Europe.

European society was shaken by World War I, but it was not overthrown. Except in Russia, the revolutions that broke out in the conquered countries took on a seemingly bourgeois character, standing as they did for the spread of liberal institutions (parliamentary government, universal suffrage, political freedom, and so on). The proletariats had not been denationalized by the war, nor had they sunk into a despair making them open to messianic hope.

In France the Communist Party gained its greatest vote count in 1936, when the Popular Front allowed it to hide behind language that resembled traditional socialism. Communism attracts westerners most when it claims to be the heir of rationalism and the Enlightenment.

Despite World War II, Stalinist communism, though basking in the glory of its victories, was by no means irresistibly attractive to the European masses. The Communist parties would not have won anywhere if their solemnly proclaimed principles had been obeyed: Only when elections were manipulated did they emerge with a majority. They did not gain power through moral ascendancy over the masses; rather, they regimented the masses through gaining possession of the state.

The German armies, the satellite countries of the Third Reich, and the immense majority of Europeans had only one thought and desire: to be liberated by the British and the Americans rather than by the Russians. Although many intellectuals in the West, temporarily safe from Stalin's armies, were singing the praises of socialism's homeland, the peoples destined to enjoy the benefits of the proletarian regime hoped desperately that they would be rescued by the forces of "monopoly capitalism." Czechoslovakia, from which the Soviet army had quickly been evacuated, which had never shared a frontier with Russia, and which dreamed of having a Slav protector against the Germanic threat, voted by nearly 38 percent for the Communists. Yet the Communists did not risk free elections a second time. Central and Eastern Europe feared the Soviet Union just as they had feared, for a century, Tsarist Russia. Marxism did not weaken that fear; it amplified it. It threatened an aggravation of Moscovite tyranny in Stalinist form, but destined this time to last indefinitely. (Admittedly there was a section of the proletariats, usually few in numbers, awaiting Stalinism without apprehension because they felt detached from their own country.)

In the West the Communist parties emerged from their clandestine struggle bathed in a glory that their propaganda never tired of exploiting. But five years later their electoral support had dwindled everywhere, except in France and Italy. The German soldiers had seen what living conditions were like in Russia, and the people in the East had experienced the horrors of invasion: So wherever citizens could cast their ballots freely, the Communist Party received a laughably small number of votes. In Italy and France the Communist parties still had considerable strength. But even there the repugnance of the majority was plain.

In other words, in Europe the attraction of Stalinism cannot survive even a partial experience of Soviet reality. In the absence of such experience, it works with a fraction of the popular masses, but it is a fraction that remains a minority. A differentiated society contains a majority of individuals and groups who believe that if Stalinism prevailed they would be liquidated. Despite two wars, and despite the upheavals caused by German occupation and inflation, the Western Europeans are not yet suicidal. Most of them feel, more or less confusedly, that Sovietization, without serving any historical purpose, would mean the destruction of a spiritual tradition and a social structure characteristic of European civilization.

━━

There is no country where at least one Communist faction could not be founded. Even in the United States some tens of thousands of people were won over, and it seems that the espionage network penetrated the highest levels of the administration. It is not hard to explain such individual sympathies by one or other of the classic psychological mechanisms related to religious or revolutionary conversion. One could list the different kinds of converts: idealists, cynics, and misfits, on the one hand, and members of the bourgeoisie whose successes leave their aspirations unsatisfied or who feel uneasy about their privileges, on the other. Then there are those who take pride in belonging to a tiny minority that is rejected today but may triumph tomorrow; the materialists still hankering unconsciously after the absolute; and the Christians disappointed by the bourgeoisification of the churches. But individual psychology, out of its historical context, fails to account for the essential factor: the strength or weakness of a particular religion at a certain time and in a certain place.

On all five continents the Communist parties' organization, tactics, and ideology are similar, if not identical. But in one country the party may be only a clandestine group, whereas in another it may have hundreds of thousands of members. In one place the Communists are supported by the sympathy and support of people outside the closed circle of the party itself; in another they are the target of fierce hostility. Always and everywhere, Stalinism contrives to recruit enough officials and activists to form a conspiracy. But the efficacy of the party, whether it carries on the struggle underground or openly, depends on its having a large number of militants or sympathizers. And in this respect, it has achieved widely varying results in different parts of the West.

Up till now the English-speaking and the Scandinavian countries have proved relatively immune to the Stalinist virus. Not that there are no Communists at all in the United States, Britain, Australia, or Sweden, but they are few in numbers and meet with resistance not only from the middle classes but also from the popular masses, in particular most of the working class. The resistance is led by the secretaries of the unions, who have realized the dangers to which they are exposed. Stalinism, in its early stages, aims at subordinating union action to considerations of political strategy; then, after the party has seized power, it subjects the unions themselves to the state. The union secretaries are too clever to be taken in by the argument that our intellectuals swallow so readily: Once the state becomes proletarian, there is no place in it for independent unions. The union leaders know, however, that union independence does have a raison d'être, whatever the nature of the government: Political leaders tend by nature to disregard the claims of the people they govern. Whether it is proletarian or bourgeois, a state that encounters no obstacles naturally moves toward tyranny.

One could probably adduce other reasons to account for the inability of secular religion (or secular religions in the plural, since fascism has hardly been more successful than communism) to make a profound impact on privileged countries such as those named above. They all enjoy a relatively high and still rising standard of living, and they all emerged from World War I entirely or relatively unscathed. Despite a fall in its standard of living and the loss of Indonesia, Holland has scarcely felt the temptation of communism. Nor is Britain, vanquished by its own victory and reduced to austerity, any more attracted by the dream of a classless society. And apart from social and economic factors, there is also a moral and historical explanation. Rejection of secular religion as such seems typical of peoples with traditions that are genuinely democratic, in the Anglo-Saxon sense of the term.

Democratic individualism, with its Protestant origins and Christian spirit, is fundamentally incompatible with the message of Stalinism. The habit of local governance and the taste for enterprise and individual initiative are threatened by an omnipotent state. Any group valuing a sense of personal responsibility, and with a preference for freely adopted beliefs, is bound to see the compulsory orthodoxy of Stalinism as an extreme form of clericalism and obscurantism. The Christian faith has not always survived, but it is more likely to continue as a kind of morality than to be denatured into an anti-church crusade.

The same cannot be said of the French democratic tradition. Its Jacobin history makes it tend toward an authoritarian, centralized state. The mythology of the general will justifies not individual rights and the rights of the opposition but the omnipotence of the majority. Rousseau's disciples have often dreamed of a civic religion. Whether the Cult of the Supreme Being or the Comtist religion of humanity, there is a line of non-Catholic thinkers who would like to replace the religions of salvation with a religion directly adapted to the needs of society (of which they consider themselves good judges).

In Western Europe there are two main Communist parties. In France and Italy, communism is the current incarnation of anti-Catholicism, a church rivaling the Catholic Church. In these Catholic countries, in contrast with what happens in the Protestant countries, modern intellectual and social movements have been or seem to have been directed against the Roman Catholic Church, once linked to the prerevolutionary system and now to the bourgeoisie. Things are quite different on the other side of the Channel. Democracy, radicalism, and the labor movement remain steeped in Christian ideas, and these are seen by everyone to justify popular demands for change. And who needs a violent revolution or an orthodoxy when there is neither another orthodoxy to be replaced nor a Bastille to be destroyed?

The Catholic peoples rediscover in the anti-church the universal claim, the dogma, and the discipline* that were or still are the normal form of spiritual action. At the same time, communism, even when temporarily overcome, derives extraordinary strength from the fact that it poses as a rival church. In France, the socialists, radicals, and rationalists who reject Stalinism avoid the direct clash between the two churches. In Italy, the temporary weakness of the liberals left Rome and Moscow face to face during the 1948 elections. It is correct to say that the religion of salvation is still the chief enemy of secular religion. But in our day and age the religion of salvation is stronger when it is not imprisoned within the structure of a church and when it bestows a transcendent consecration on a universe of values shared by believers and nonbelievers alike.

But the spread of Stalinism in France and Italy is not to be explained by such generalizations. A social analysis would reveal other causes. France and Italy differ from the other Western countries in that their economic progress has been abnormally retarded; their precapitalist structure has partly resisted, and so held back, the development of productive forces. They might be described as the underdeveloped countries of the West.

A landless agricultural worker in southern Italy, earning a derisory wage, can easily become a rebel once he ceases to regard his lot as inevitable, stops taking his poverty for the will of heaven, and sees or is shown a gleam of hope. Similarly, workers from the suburbs of Paris in the nineteenth century or from those of Petrograd in 1905 or 1917, badly paid, recently arrived from the countryside, coming from traditional backgrounds, and isolated amid the urban crowds, are easily influenced by the appeal of religion, be it transcendent or secular.

Nevertheless, workers in the major industries of northern Italy and Paris are not usually keen on Stalinism. On the contrary, the example of other countries with Western-type civilizations suggests that their support for reformist socialism would be more in accordance with the evolution of

---

*This is not to say that the dogma and discipline of Catholicism are the same as those of communism.

the West itself. There are many reasons for this apparent anomaly. The level of wages depends first and foremost on the average productivity of labor within the economic unit concerned; overpopulation, or maintaining an insufficiently productive agriculture, pushes wages below what the labor force might naturally hope for. A skilled industrial worker in France often has a standard of living that fails to correspond either to the quality of his work or to what might be called his human worth. The social conditions created by urban overcrowding add to people's dissatisfaction. For some workers and in some countries, labor in modern industry involves a discontent for which the workers themselves hold the regime responsible, though the regime is often a result of the replacement of capitalists by the state. The tradition of the French trade unions is revolutionary rather than reformist, anarchist rather than in favor of state control. Stalinism, once in office, would root out any anarchist tendencies, but while it is still operating in opposition to an existing regime it fosters agitation and favors direct action. It should not be seen as resembling revolutionary syndicalism. In countries other than France, unions with proanarchist leanings (sea-men's and dockers' unions, for example) are the ones most exposed to infiltration by agents of Moscow.

Finally, we should not forget that the Stalinists have not so much converted the masses as colonized the unions with the help of war, the Resistance, and the Liberation. The operation takes place in several stages: First a party is organized, with activists occupying key posts, and from these key posts the masses are manipulated. And here we perceive the essential danger. Communism is at the same time an army and a church. The number of converts is not so important as the strength of the organization.

~

Communism is a theory and practice of civil war in its first phase, and of totalitarian tyranny in its second. The fact that Stalinism has been unable to triumph in the West through the ballot box does not mean it has been defeated. The Stalinists know Europe cannot be converted peacefully, but it can be conquered. And by winning over a minority they are preparing a way for that conquest. The surprising thing is not that Europe refuses to submit to a foreign church, but that so many Europeans expect liberation from a despotism that would destroy an age-old tradition.

In the Stalinist plan, secular religion serves three purposes:

1. It provides a moral training for professional revolutionaries; maintains faith and discipline in the parties during periods of struggle or socialist construction; and wins over enough supporters for the party to be able to paralyze societies doomed by the law of history to disappear;
2. It makes its adversaries uneasy about the legitimacy of their own cause and creates an air of sympathy around the party;
3. Once the party has taken over the state, it is supposed to bring a "new man" into being and to effect a spiritual transformation that will make both the ruling elite and the masses permanently obedient to the rules, values, and way of life of Communist society.

The first purpose, or role, depends mainly on specifically Leninist and Stalinist factors (the mission of the party, the authority of the leaders, and the pattern of purges); the second depends on Marxist ideologies (class struggle, disintegration of capitalism, the inevitable rise to power of the proletariat, and the like); and the third probably exceeds the capacities both of orthodox Marxism and of Stalinism.

Stalinism obviously seeks to win over the masses, but following the example of Bolshevism, it aims first at creating a party—that is to say, a set of reliable officials. Masses without obedience to a network of officials or a general staff are of little or no use to the Communist cause. A party made up of professional revolutionaries, even if they are isolated from the masses, can at least act as an intelligence network, as in the United States. It has been proved countless times that Bolshevik doctrine is extraordinarily efficient when it comes to recruiting a minority of militants who are ready for anything. And why is the Leninist version superior in this respect to the social democratic version of Marxism? The explanation is simple. It is practice, not theory, that calls forth total devotion. The party requires its members to break with the surrounding world and become part of the revolutionary community, and this isolation makes each individual's commitment unconditional and definitive. It is not to the depth or truth of its ideology that communism owes the fanaticism of those who serve it, but to the efficiency of its techniques for organization and action.

For thirty years everyone in Europe who was revolted by the injustices of the bourgeois system inclined toward communism as the only genuinely revolutionary movement. They supported not some particular interpretation of Marxism but a workers party that had not betrayed the cause of the proletariat in a "holy alliance" of church and state and had thrown off the tradition of defeat. It was the glory of the "ten days that shook the world," not the teachings of *Materialism and Empiriocriticism, The State and the Revolution,* or *The Foundations of Leninism,* that attracted all the revolutionaries to Moscow. Doctrine came later, to confirm the act of joining up and maintain the connection between the two elements of Stalinism—on the one hand, the general philosophy of history and the interpretation of capitalism, and, on the other, the attribution of a historic mission to the party. At the beginning, not even of the century but of the 1920s, this connection was extremely dubious: Why should the proletariat of a backward country become the head of the world proletariat? But as the Soviet Union grew stronger and Stalinism spread, the link became more plausible. To demonstrate that the cause of the Soviet Union coincides with that of world revolution, nothing less is needed than the dialectic, that is, the art of justifying any political line whatsoever in terms of the good of the proletariat. In this respect, the vulgarized version of Marxism that is Stalinism has the incomparable merit of providing half-educated minds with an appropriate interpretation of history. It gives simpleminded people the agreeable impression of understanding the world without having to make too much effort. It is a philosophy typical of the age of the masses and of popularization.

This kind of theoretical teaching encourages the rank and file to accept a system of thought, or rather of words, that can explain anything so long as the key to the system is in the power of the leadership. It is easy to call the Social Democrats the proletariat's public enemy number one today, and a fraternal party tomorrow. The masses still have to get used to having such adaptations to circumstance dictated to them from above. Certain turnarounds (the German-Soviet pact, for example) have put party discipline under considerable strain.

So theoretical conditioning cannot be separated from a kind of practical training. The reflexes of the militants are inculcated by a method similar to that by which soldiers are taught to obey orders. Members of the party are indoctrinated to believe that the authority of the hierarchy, from the Kremlin down to their immediate superiors, is more or less sacrosanct. An atmosphere of solidarity and readiness for action becomes as necessary to the faithful as the air they breathe. The feeling of belonging to a sect unsullied by the corruption tarnishing the outside world, the harbinger of the future, overcomes any reluctance caused by the immoral tactics that may sometimes be called for in action. Gradually, the activists come to be influenced not so much by the party's vision of the universe and of history as by the force of the party apparatus. An army can survive for a long time on the battlefield enthusiasm of its soldiers. To enlist, they need to believe in the army, in honor, and in serving the homeland. After that, organization makes up for any lack of fervor.

For some outside the Communist Party, Marxist ideology, seen as a continuation of the Western rationalist and humanist tradition, still generates some sympathy. How can one break with the Soviet Union, says one, when it has laid down the economic foundations of a classless society (in the form of collective ownership of the means of production)? How can one refuse to be in contact with or an ally of the Communists, says another, when their party is bringing about the supremacy of the proletariat? How can one condemn the attempt to build a socialist society when it means that for the first time ever man is taking on the grandiose task of controlling his own economic environment? All the prestige of Marxism works in favor of Stalinism, despite the Soviet reality.

It takes direct experience of that reality to strip away the veil of illusion. A Czech worker subjected to the system of socialist competition and deprived of a union; a peasant threatened with collective farming; an intellectual whose freedom of thought is menaced; a priest who is expected to swear loyalty to the state; freelancers, artisans, and industrialists being turned into proletarians—all become immune to the allure of Stalinism. Hence the paradox of a historical situation in which there are probably more sincere believers on this side of the Iron Curtain than on the other. The Communist faith dissolves as it spreads. It destroys itself through its victories.

In all the Soviet countries a minority supports the regime. But it seems that the faithful come mainly from groups that are privileged by the system—Stakhanovites, government officials, directors—or from among the younger generation, who have known nothing else. Even after twenty years of unrelenting propaganda, the Russian people still did not identify wholly with its masters: It took German atrocities to make them put their hearts and souls into defending their country, and incidentally their fetters. It is the Soviet myth that motivates the masses; the Soviet reality lets them down.

Their disappointment is easily understood when one looks at the disparity between the ideology that reigned during the war and the regime that was set up after the victory. The party promised to give the land to the peasants, and it began to do so, but a few years later it started imposing collectivization by means of force and even terror. To this day the Russian peasants are still not converted or resigned. And the party has now introduced a second round of collectivization, which by reducing the number and increasing the size of the kolkhozes, will probably do away with the peasantry and turn its status into something approaching the condition of ordinary workers. The party encourages nationalist sentiment against imperialism, then imposes the omnipotence of Moscow on the popular democracies. Socialist exploitation by Russia of its dependencies is far more brutal than the worst excesses of capitalism. What miracle could possibly reconcile the new man to his fate?

Yet it seems the Stalinists regard their doctrine as all-embracing. Perhaps that is their aim: to substitute Marxism-Leninism for the religions of salvation. But for the moment, the issues in the battle against the Catholic Church in Poland, Hungary, and Czechoslovakia seem more limited. The Russian tradition calls for the subordination of church to state, for priests to swear an oath of allegiance to the temporal leader. The Patriarch of Moscow attacks the Pope and aligns himself with the "defenders of the peace." What is required first and foremost of Czech and Polish priests is that they recognize the proletarian state. The independence of the church regarded as normal in Western Christianity is seen by the Stalinists as a remnant of European civilization—and as such, something they want to eliminate, at least during their first phase.

Will their second phase, if it ever comes about, aim at eliminating Christianity altogether? It is possible, but in the context of a philosophy of history, one doubts Stalinism has much chance of winning that battle. Stalinism may take Christians back to the age of persecution, but it will not replace religion because it is not a genuine religion, merely a miserable caricature of one.

Intellectually it is extraordinarily poor. Even if one accepted its historical schema of the evolution of societies from capitalism to socialism, its identification of the proletarian cause with that of the Russian Communist Party is childish. Even if one accepted that, against all historical precedents, collective ownership and economic planning fostered a superior civilization and freedom-oriented institutions, the object of Stalinist faith disintegrates as it is put into practice. It can be quite noble to devote oneself to an unknown future. But if a secular religion is to survive its triumph, it has to teach the masses to worship their masters. The cult of Stalin is the first example of this return to the deification of Caesar. Is such an enterprise anything more than just an episode in troubled times?

In Russia itself Christianity has resisted, and the regime is at the moment inclined to compromise rather than resume the war of extermination. This is for tactical reasons: The Orthodox Church is useful to Soviet imperialism. But, such vacillations between atheist propaganda and tolerance apart, I personally think communism is fundamentally incapable of creating a new man.

Western public opinion fears that the young may be attracted by a collectivist system, that generations will soon arise who are conditioned to their fate, unable to understand what freedom is, and ready to bow to party discipline and compulsory labor as part of the natural order of human existence. Certainly, the Stalinists, by exterminating whole classes, will make it difficult to bring back Western-type societies to the Soviet Union and other countries of Eastern Europe. The proletarianized masses, after a slow process of maturation, are supposed to produce a new set of social differentiations, but that will take time. On the political plane, where time is counted in years, the destruction of the old order seems definitive. But I do not believe that centuries of Christianity can be wiped out in a few decades. This is clear if one understands the essence of religious feelings sufficiently to be able to tell the difference between Stalinist fanaticism and a genuine faith. Communism defines for its believers both the enemy and the future, giving them someone to hate and something to build. It arouses passionate devotions; but it does not offer people anything to love.

⌒

While we may exaggerate the moral force of communism, too often we tend to underestimate its political and what may be called its military influence. It does not need to convert the masses. All it has to do, in order to paralyze a country, or even a whole continent, is to keep a hold over an active minority and maintain a virtually passive majority in a state of uncertainty.

In Asia, the imperial powers of Europe have been forced into an inglorious retreat, and rebellion against hunger and the Whites is stirring up millions of illiterate people; a small but well-organized party, led by semi-intellectuals who have become professionals in the field of action, can get itself at the head of the blind crowds and have a chance of seizing power, as happened in Russia and China. In a Europe cut in two by the Iron Curtain and still covered in ruins, Communist parties possess a solid apparatus in France and Italy. They have won the confidence of a section of the masses, who are either tempted by the Soviet myth or simply devoted to those they see as the only interpreters of their anger and their hopes. They have little chance of taking over the French or Italian states by peaceful methods, but to prevent the restoration of world equilibrium all they need do is prolong Europe's weakness. Down the line, launching a few thousand tanks might be enough to destroy a secular civilization.

THE IMPERIAL
REPUBLIC

THE ISLAND-CONTINENT

For the first time in history, said observers twenty-five years ago, a republic has risen to the top without aspiring to rule. As the price of its victory, it must take responsibility for half the world: It must guarantee the safety of the Europeans, too weak to defend themselves on their own; it must interest itself in whole regions of the globe that are on the brink of collapsing into chaos.

This view of things is now called into question. When did the Romans become aware of their vocation to *regere populos?* Do not historians like to joke that the British Empire was founded "in a fit of absent-mindedness"? True, Roosevelt told Stalin (with a rashness that was not unique) that the GIs would not stay on in Europe for more than two years after the end of the war. But after all, the Roman legions left Greece twice before they settled there indefinitely. In 1972, American troops were still guarding the demarcation line in the middle of Europe. And how many Western Europeans, even among those who denounced the Vietnam War, wanted them to leave?

General de Gaulle's philosophy led him to detect in President Roosevelt's idealistic words a will to power that was all the readier to assert itself because it was unconscious. Obsessed by their experience of the years following World War I, the Europeans—the man in the street as well as the statesman—feared isolationism in the United States more than they feared imperialism. They had not forgotten the lateness (from the European point of view) of the U.S. interventions in the world wars (in 1917 instead of 1914; in 1941 instead of 1939), nor the U.S. refusal to ratify the Treaty of Versailles, nor the neutrality laws passed by Congress during the 1930s to prevent what probably most legislators, deep down, thought inevitable, nor the alternation between the crusading spirit ("a world safe for democracy") and withdrawal from a corrupt world deaf to the rallying cry of the United States.

Let us refrain for the moment from choosing between the two interpretations, which are perhaps complementary rather than contradictory, and remember first and foremost the trite but neglected fact that the diplomatic history of the United States did not begin in 1917; rather, it started before 1776 and the Declaration of Independence. It would be worth investigating the part played by the American colonists in the eighteenth-century wars between France and England, which led first to the demise of New France and then, twenty years later, to the Treaty of Paris and the break between the thirteen colonies and the United Kingdom.

The years between 1917 and 1939—or even those from 1898 to 1939—convey a misleading idea of U.S. foreign policy since 1783. And it may be that the years 1941–1968 give an equally false impression, and that the present crisis, provoked by the Vietnam War and the revolt against "the burden of imperialism," heralds a new correction. A historian is in danger of getting things wrong if he concentrates solely on 1914–1939 and the twentieth century. Nothing is more "traditional," more influenced by the heritage of the past, than a country's diplomacy, its way of perceiving international affairs and its role in them. At the risk of shocking professional historians with such a simplistic distinction, I shall divide the diplomatic history of the United States into three main periods: first, from 1783 to 1898, that is, from the Treaty of Paris to the war against Spain; second, from 1899 to 1941 (or 1947); and third, the period beginning with Pearl Harbor (December 7, 1941) or the Truman Doctrine (March 1947) and ending perhaps during the past few years.

Why the distinction between the first two periods? Taken generally, each contrasts with the other in fundamental ways. Whereas the trend of ideas and events from the end of the eighteenth to the end of the nineteenth century leads to an order devised and intended by the founding fathers—a sovereign republic covering most of North America and thus geopolitically insular—after the end of the nineteenth century it is difficult to discern either the logic of the policy or the aims of the politicians. By the end of the nineteenth century, the national project of the founders of the American Republic had been fulfilled. During the next fifty years the republic was looking for a plan, and it passed, according to its mood, from one to the other. American diplomacy today retains some of the habits acquired during the first and second periods.

In 1783, by the Treaty of Paris, the thirteen colonies gained international recognition of their independence; neither the Comte de Vergennes, the French foreign minister, nor the English negotiators, however, were willing to grant them either actual or potential sovereignty over North America as a whole. Two European empires were still present—that of Spain in the south and that of Britain in the north. The territory of the nascent republic was limited on all sides: Navigation in the Mississippi delta brought it into conflict with Spain, and the uncertain border in the north provoked quarrels with Britain and was not finally fixed until toward the middle of the following century.

In spite of these initial weaknesses, the colonists achieved their aim: to occupy, settle, and exploit North America, establishing a single sovereignty that would spare them from the permanent rivalries characteristic of power politics and the curse of the Old Continent of Europe. In the course of a century of expansion, the diplomacy of the thirteen colonies met with no serious setback. It achieved its ends without having to fight a major war.

Nor did it need to annex neighboring states: It was enough that they should be incapable of rivalry. By the end of the first third of the nineteenth century, this condition was understood. Hegel acknowledged, "The free states of North America have no neighbors in the same relation to them as the European countries are to one another. That is to say, there is no country they need to mistrust and against which they have to maintain a permanent army. Canada and Mexico are no threat, and the experience of the last fifty years has shown England that America is more use to it free than subject" (1832). From then on, the disparity between the forces concerned had reached the point of no return, ruling out power politics under the threat of the sword, even in the civilized form of European tradition. As for an alliance between the Spanish and British empires, or later between Mexico and Canada, with the aim of "containing" the expansion of the American Republic, that never seemed conceivable, either between 1783 and Mexican independence in 1821 or, indeed, anytime before the war of 1846.

The success of American diplomacy vis-à-vis its North American neighbors—Spain, then Mexico, France, and England—owes less to exceptional skill than it does to circumstances. During the first phase of the republic, the storm of the French Revolution set the countries of Europe one against the other. Washington was wise and strong enough to restrain the enthusiasm of those colonists who sympathized with France and wanted to rally to its side. The brief war of 1812 did not allow the Americans to achieve their ultimate aim of conquering Canada. Washington was occupied, the Capitol and the White House set on fire. But successes at sea, and Andrew Jackson's victory at New Orleans, counterbalanced the defeats on land.

Meanwhile, in 1803, Louisiana, which Spain had returned to France in 1800, was sold by Napoleon to the United States for $15 million, and the expansion of the thirteen states continued uninterrupted (Kentucky in 1792, Tennessee in 1796, Ohio in 1803, Louisiana in 1812, Mississippi and Alabama in 1816 and 1819, Indiana and Illinois in 1816 and 1818, and Missouri and Arkansas in 1919). Should we call this imperialism? By now the word has taken on so many meanings and carries so many ideological overtones that it would be better to use the more neutral term *expansionism*. Even before independence many Americans genuinely believed that the whole continent belonged to them by virtue of their having been the first to occupy it (in their view the Indians, or Native Americans, did not actually do so), and they had no doubt that they would turn it into an empire or commonwealth the likes of which the world had never seen before. As a text of 1776 put it:

> Empires have their zenith—and their descension to dissolution. . . . The British period is from the year 1758, when they victoriously pursued their Enemies into every Quarter of the Globe. . . . The Almighty has made choice of the present generation to erect the American Empire. . . . And thus has suddenly arisen in the World a new Empire, styled the United States of America. An Empire that as soon as started into Existence, attracts the Attention of the Rest of the Universe; and bids fair, by the blessing of God, to be the most glorious of any upon Record.[*]

---

[*]Richard W. Van Alstyne, *The Rising American Empire* (Oxford: Basil Blackwell, 1960), p. 1. The text is by William Henry Drayton, Chief Justice of South Carolina.

In 1830, Alexis de Tocqueville observed with his usual lucidity the causes and style of that irresistible movement.

> With the aid of their own resources and intelligence, the Europeans lost no time in appropriating to themselves most of the advantages previously available to the natives through possession of the soil. They settled in their midst, seized the land or bought it at a very low price, and ruined them by a competition that they were completely unable to sustain. The Indians, isolated in their own country, became no more than a small colony of inconvenient strangers dominated by a large and alien population.[*]

Tocqueville may sometimes seem angry, but he always explained why. He quoted Washington: "We are more enlightened and more powerful than the Indian nations: we are in honor bound to treat them with kindness and even generosity."[**] But he added: "This noble and virtuous policy was not always adhered to." He attributed the domination of the Anglo-Americans to their superiority over not only the Indians but also the French. He noted that in the small town of Vincennes, founded by the French, the Frenchmen themselves—"decent people but lacking in intelligence and skill"—had practically disappeared. And he concluded:

> The Americans, who were perhaps inferior to them from the moral point of view, were immensely superior to them intellectually: They were ingenious, educated, rich, and self-controlled. I myself have seen in Canada, where the intellectual difference between the two races is much less marked, how the English, masters of trade and industry in the Canadians' country, expand in all directions, forcing the French into very narrow bounds. Similarly, in Louisiana, almost all commercial and industrial activity is concentrated in the hands of the Anglo-Americans.[***]

Tocqueville also saw how and why individual migration paved the way to the expansion of the republic.

---

[*]Alexis de Tocqueville, *De la démocratie en Amerique*, I, 2, 10, in *Oeuvres complètes* (Paris: Gallimard, 1951), p. 349.
[**]Ibid., p. 350.
[***]Ibid., p. 349.

Something even more striking is taking place in the province of Texas. As is well known, the state of Texas is part of Mexico and acts as a boundary between it and the United States.

For some years now, Anglo-Americans have been going individually into this still sparsely inhabited province and buying land, taking over industry, and swiftly replacing the original population. It seems likely that if Mexico does not hasten to stop this trend, Texas will soon be lost to it.[*]

In the same year that Tocqueville's book, *De la démocratie en Amérique,* was published (1835), the Americans in Texas proclaimed their independence, as those in Florida had done in 1810, and proceeded to defeat the Mexicans and request admittance to the Union (this request was not granted until 1844, after lengthy discussions in the Senate).

The style of the expansion was rather different in the case of California (under Mexican rule from 1822 to 1848), where there were not enough colonists to rebel and claim possession of the territory. The federal government tried at first to negotiate its transfer in return for compensation, but the Mexican government, which did not recognize the fait accompli in Texas, obstinately refused. By massing troops on the frontier, it provided the United States with the opportunity for a decisive war. Vanquished and occupied, Mexico ceded all the territories north of the Rio Grande to the United States of America: New Mexico, California, and the southern part of the Rocky Mountains (Utah, Nevada, and Arizona). As was its custom, the Washington government, in order to legalize its military conquests, paid for its territorial acquisitions. In like manner, President James Monroe had in 1818 given back to Spain the part of Florida won by General Jackson; the next year he bought the two Floridas for $5 million. Never did a state buy so much for so little.

Although this continental expansion undoubtedly mirrored the main aims of the founders of the republic and the spontaneous actions of its citizens, public opinion was by no means unanimous when it came to the diplomatic crises caused by events in Europe or the widening of the Union. It was difficult for Washington to get its policy of neutrality accepted when war broke out between Revolutionary France and England. The War of 1812 originated in the blockade imposed by the English fleet and its violation of

---

[*]Ibid., p. 349, n.

the rights of neutrals. The "war" party was recruited largely from people in the western United States, who wanted to improve their frontiers with neighboring British possessions; from those in the south, who had their eye on Florida, then owned by Spain, which was allied to Britain; and from the "hawks" of the day, who had not yet given up on Canada. The merchants of New England, although directly hit by the blockade, tended to be "doves."

Nor did the war against Mexico meet with universal approval: On the contrary, it aroused considerable debate. Was it not a war of conquest, just as blameworthy as the practices for which Americans denounced the predator countries of Europe? In other words, as early as the first half of the period of continental expansion, the historian perceives some features that are still typical of U.S. foreign policy: an unpredictable public opinion (in 1792 and 1812); a desire for legality; a tendency to alternate between the will to power (or expansion) and qualms of conscience; and a strange combination of pragmatism and moralism.

Washington's famous political testament, usually interpreted as a refusal to get mixed up in European quarrels or make permanent alliances, also bears witness to a particular way of seeing international relations:

Our detached and distant situation invites and enables us to pursue a different course. If we remain one people, under an efficient government, the period is not far off, when we may defy material injury from external annoyance; when we may take such an attitude as will cause the neutrality, we may at any time resolve upon, to be scrupulously respected; when belligerent nations, under the impossibility of making acquisitions upon us, will not lightly hazard the giving us provocation; when we may choose peace or war, as our interest, guided by justice, shall counsel. . . . It is our true policy to steer clear of permanent alliances with any portion of the foreign world; so far, I mean, as we are now at liberty to do it; for let me not be understood as capable of patronizing infidelity to existing engagements. I hold the maxim no less applicable to public than to private affairs, that honesty is always the best policy. I repeat it, therefore, let those engagements be observed in their genuine sense. But, in my opinion, it is unnecessary and would be unwise to extend them. Taking care always to keep ourselves, by suitable establishments, on a respectable defensive posture, we may safely trust to temporary alliances for extraordinary emergencies. . . .

The Nation, which indulges towards another an habitual hatred, or an habitual fondness, is in some degree a slave. It is a slave to its animosity or to its affection, either of which is sufficient to lead it astray from its duty and its interest.

Not to get involved in quarrels between European states—that was good advice to a young republic protected by distance and made more secure by the fact that Europe was preoccupied by the intra-European wars. The statement presupposed a compatibility between self-interest and justice, decency, and keeping one's word, reflecting an optimistic ideology that does not preclude what people in the eighteenth century called the *American Empire* and people in the nineteenth called *Manifest Destiny.*

The famous Monroe Doctrine (a message to Congress delivered on December 2, 1823) exhibits both anti-imperialism (as Americans themselves understand it) and an imperial mission (as non-Americans see it) in the Western Hemisphere (a geographical notion invented by the Americans, giving them a zone of influence or responsibility). The British cabinet had suggested to President Monroe that the two countries should cooperate, but Monroe preferred to act alone. He announced a ban on colonization on the American continent:

> In the discussions to which this interest has given rise and in the arrangements by which they may terminate the occasion has been judged proper for asserting, as a principle in which the rights and interests of the United States are involved, that the American continents, by the free and independent condition which they have assumed and maintain, are henceforth not to be considered as subjects for future colonization by any European powers.

The warning was addressed to the powers belonging to the Holy Alliance—France, in particular, which might have been tempted to intervene against the Latin American republics whose independence the United States was anxious to recognize.*

---

*The warning was also directed toward Tsarist Russia, which had owned Alaska since the eighteenth century and was extending its territory toward Oregon. Cf. Franck L. Schoell, *Histoire des Etats-Unis* (Paris: Payot, 1965), p. 150.

But with the Governments who have declared their independence and maintain it, and whose independence we have, on great consideration and on just principles, acknowledged, we could not view any interposition for the purpose of oppressing them, or controlling in any other manner their destiny, by any European power in any other light than as the manifestation of an unfriendly disposition toward the United States.

But at the time the American Republic did not have the military means to impose the decisions it proclaimed so solemnly on the rest of the world. It was the English fleet that thwarted any desires the countries of Europe might have had to apply the principles of the Holy Alliance on the North American continent. Nonetheless, the Monroe Doctrine retains the significance ascribed to it as an expression of the political conscience of the United States. American statesmen have never seen any contradiction between the rejection of imperialism (or colonialism) and the special role, or calling, they attribute to their republic. That republic was setting itself up as the protector of the states on the American continents, declaring them its private hunting ground, set aside for freedom as the United States itself understood it.

The anti-imperialism that inspired the Monroe Doctrine and allowed the leaders of the republic to have a clear conscience served not only to justify or camouflage expansionism or a desire for preeminence. It held in check any temptations to attempt annexation, once it was no longer a matter of territories bordering on those of the Union and inhabited by Indians.

Admittedly, westward expansion did not stop on the shores of the Pacific. It was an American naval officer, Commodore Matthew Perry, who first won the concessions from Japan that allowed the Empire of the Rising Sun to embark on its extraordinary transformation, so rich in almost miraculous achievements, but interrupted by one disaster. The United States did not stand aside from the Europeans' rush toward China, and it made sure it acquired positions among the Pacific Islands for itself. But anti-imperialism raises its head again whenever the population of the territory in view seems opposed to assimilation or appears too far away to become an integral part of the Union.

After the purchase of Alaska* (suggested by Russia itself), a plan to buy the Danish West Indies met with opposition from the Senate. The upper house of the U.S. Congress also disavowed President Ulysses S. Grant when he agreed to make loans to the Dominican Republic; the senators suspected him of preparing to annex the territory. Nor would they let Grant turn the Samoan Islands into a protectorate. It was the Senate again that refused to approve a trade treaty with Hawaii proposed by Secretary of State William H. Seward, because it seemed likely to lead to annexation. But Americans went on settling there just the same. In 1875 a trade treaty was indeed concluded. The base at Pearl Harbor was ceded to the Americans in 1884, and in 1893, there was an uprising on the part of American residents, who forced the native queen to abdicate. The independent Republic of Hawaii asked to be annexed by the United States. This time it was President Grover Cleveland who refused; Hawaii did not become the fiftieth state of the Union until 1959.

The opposition between the president and Congress over foreign policy, like the passionate controversies dividing public opinion on the subject, goes back to long before President Wilson, the Treaty of Versailles, and the League of Nations. The president, made responsible for foreign policy by the U.S. Constitution, does not shrink from taking initiatives and conducting a secret diplomacy. The duality of expansionism and anti-imperialism, of will to power and moralism, is also evident in the very beginnings of the republic. If we see a break in continuity between the first and second centuries of U.S. history, it is because, from 1898 on, the circumstances that used to favor a reconciliation between the divergent tendencies were no longer present. The republic itself had changed more than the ways of thinking of its citizens and statesmen.

Were the Americans, at the end of the nineteenth century, going to be content with their own island, the exploitation of which had scarcely begun? They decided otherwise, or circumstances did it for them. It may be that the reason why the period from 1898 to 1939 (or 1941) gives so inconsistent an impression of U.S. external activities and foreign policy is that the historian hesitates between the two patterns examined above. Perhaps it is because the United States has not been able to stand aside from

---

*Some members of the leadership saw this as another opportunity to include Canada in the Union.

world history, but has not succeeded in taking a full part or defining its role in it either.

$$\sim$$

The war against Spain broke out after a U.S. battleship blew up in Havana harbor, an obscure incident that occurred in the midst of a Cuban revolt and a massive press campaign in the United States against Spanish domination of Cuba. Did U.S. intervention in Cuba constitute a break with the anti-imperialist tradition? Or was it just a further stage in Yankee expansionism at the expense of the Spanish Empire and the Spanish-speaking peoples? Both interpretations have been put forward. Each seems to me to contain part of the truth. The Anglo-Americans' feeling of superiority over the Spaniards and over Spanish-speaking peoples did not begin in 1898. Between the war against Mexico in the middle of the nineteenth century and the war against Spain at the end of the century, the continuity is not hard to trace. The line runs through a pacifist president (William McKinley); a proclamation of neutrality; a war party linked to economic interests (the planters in Cuba), and even more to groups motivated by ideology; and mobilization of public opinion by a press loudly denouncing Spanish oppression; and then an accident acts as the last straw and the president is obliged to act.

Once war had broken out, the imperialists, led by Theodore Roosevelt and Admiral George Dewey, fought it with a view to winning total victory. They extended the field of operations to include Spain's possessions in the Pacific. The peace treaty, which stripped Spain of the last tatters of its empire and granted the United States sovereignty over the Philippines, Puerto Rico, and the island of Guam, ran into opposition from part of the Senate and was ratified by only a narrow margin.

The annexation of the Philippines, a distant group of islands whose people could hardly be seen as constituting a future state in the Union, does not fit into the main outline of U.S. development. The islands, once rid of Spanish occupation, proclaimed their independence, and American troops put down their "rebellion" in a pacification campaign that lasted some ten years and included many acts of cruelty. Theodore Roosevelt himself, in tune with predominant public opinion, regretted the annexation, and despite his own part in it, admitted it had been a mistake.

In contrast, the behavior of the United States in the Caribbean and Central America constitutes a kind of compromise between its rejection of European-style imperialism and its adoption of a broad interpretation of the Monroe Doctrine, which asserts a sense of special U.S. rights and responsibilities. Theodore Roosevelt formulated the latter explicitly:

> Chronic wrongdoing, or an impotence which results in a general loosening of the ties of civilized society, may in America, as elsewhere, ultimately require intervention by some civilized nation, and in the Western Hemisphere the adherence of the United States to the Monroe Doctrine may force the United States, however reluctantly, in flagrant cases of such wrongdoing or impotence, to the exercise of an international police power.*

Cuba, the occasion of the war against Spain, became an independent republic, but the United States obtained a naval base at Guantanamo and, under the Platt Amendment, a permanent right to intervene to restore order and safeguard its interests. The United States practiced gunboat diplomacy at the beginning of the century just as the Europeans did at that time, sometimes to ensure that debts were repaid, sometimes to restore order or to put in place a party or president partial to its own cause. In Colombia the United States favored the secession that led to the creation of the state of Panama and swiftly signed a treaty with the new republic, which in return for a financial indemnity gave it complete sovereignty over a zone 16 kilometers wide running across the isthmus. Although Theodore Roosevelt's successor, President William Howard Taft, believed in the dollar—both as means and end—rather than the big stick, he sent 2,000 U.S. Marines to Nicaragua to support one of his favorites.

Until 1914 the foreign affairs of the United States—the annexation of the Philippines apart—can be fitted without too much trouble into the previous framework and within the logic of the original plan. The right of surveillance over the Caribbean islands is an extension of old practices associated with territorial expansion. The border regions were part of the U.S. zone of influence, and the United States had few scruples and felt little

---

*Quoted by Harry C. Allen, *The United States of America* (London: Benn, 1964).

reluctance about recruiting local supporters in them, stirring up unrest against hostile governments, and if necessary using force. As for the rest, the United States did not choose between its sense of possessing a world role and its preoccupation with trade and investment, between grandeur in the style of Roosevelt and economism in that of Taft. After the war against Spain it counted as an Asiatic power, but it still turned its back on Europe. It was World War I that led the New World to intervene in the old one in order to restore the balance.

Why did the United States enter the war in 1917? This inexhaustibly debated question has not, and probably never can have, any categorical answer. The president had begun, in the traditional manner, by declaring U.S. neutrality; just as in the years between 1792 and 1812, the belligerents, singly or together, disregarded the interests of the neutral powers and interrupted maritime traffic.* Britain, which was operating a blockade by remote control and intercepting neutral cargo ships, was sent protest notes, and Germany, too, received protests about losses of American lives on ships that had been torpedoed. In the end it was against the Central Power that public indignation turned. Was this because of its declaration of out and-out submarine warfare? Because of revelations about the activities of the German ambassador? Due to the bank loans made to Britain and France? Or the feeling of solidarity that prevails, come what may, between the English-speaking peoples? Or was it, perhaps, due to fear of German hegemony in Europe and a crucial weakening of Britain, whose navy had done so much to guarantee the security of the American Republic? No one, I think, can say exactly how all these contributing factors may have interacted.** What is important, if we are to understand what followed, is that public opinion was mobilized once again with the help of a vague but grandiose ideology, and that the president himself presented, and to a large extent conceived of, the U.S. decision as an act of deliverance, and as such as something essentially different from the behavior of the Allied powers and their associates.

---

*Between 1796 and 1798 there was an undeclared hit-and-run war between France and the United States; in 1812 a declared war with Britain.

**I have never been entirely convinced by the so-called realist explanation, that the security of the United States might have been jeopardized if the Central Powers had won the war. The general opinion, which rejected this view and saw America's entry into the war as a decision freely arrived at, seems to me nearer to the truth.

In some ways this difference really existed. The United States never had and never could have territorial ambitions in Europe (any more than Britain had had since the end of the Hundred Years' War). Its hostility toward European-style imperialism had turned it away from colonial conquest. Thus, the countries of the Old Continent were not wrong to believe in the United States' "disinterestedness" and in the president's "idealism," insofar as impartiality and idealism had anything to do with the negotiations. European statesmen, in contrast, saw international relations in terms of the realism (or cynicism) of power politics and the need for a balance of power. Georges Clemenceau feared a desire for revenge on the part of a temporarily enfeebled Germany that normally possessed human and economic resources far outstripping those of France. The American president's good intentions did not constitute a lasting guarantee.

The Senate's rejection of the Treaty of Versailles, the refusal to join the League of Nations, and the withdrawal into isolationism—this series of events, though often recounted, is merely a digression or an interlude in the overall story of the American Republic. Whether the digression is held to begin with the war against Spain, the annexation of the Philippines, or the intervention in 1917 is of little importance and may depend on a more or less arbitrary choice. The important thing is to understand what the novelty of the interlude consists in. I would define it in two complementary ways. The United States, having become both the dominant power in the Western Hemisphere and the chief global power, became, against its will, a participant in world politics. That being so, it now had to deal not with Indian tribes or a decadent Spanish Empire, not with a complaisant or resigned British Empire, but with countries just as determined as it was itself to defend their rights and interests. It was not entering into the European international system, whose corruption it had decried, but into the worldwide system, of which it was becoming a full member exhibiting the same, or even worse, vices.

All in all, the foreign affairs of the United States between 1898 and 1940 were consistent only in their contradictions, turnabouts, and inability to choose a line and stick to it. In short, the United States refused to accept the international system that had existed through the centuries, even though, by playing by its rules, American leaders had, perhaps unconsciously, turned things to their own advantage, to the disadvantage of, in turn, the French, the English, the Italians, and the Spanish. The Americans never acknowledged the similarity between their own continental expansionism and other countries' imperialism. Without any menacing neighbors, with plenty of space still left, they achieved at the end of the century the maturity that Hegel had predicted:

> North America is still at the stage of clearing the ground. But when, as in Europe, the simple expansion of farmers has stopped, and the inhabitants, instead of hurrying outward to new fields, draw back en masse into themselves and toward urban trade and industry, forming one solid system, then and then alone they will feel the need for an organic state. . . . So America is the country of the future, where in future times we shall see, perhaps in the antagonism between North and South America, the real gravamen of world history. It is a dream country for those who find the bric-a-brac of old Europe tedious. Napoleon is supposed to have said, "I am bored by this old Europe." America must break free from the soil on which world history has taken place up to now.

During the half-century that elapsed between its entry into the war against Japan and Germany in December 1941 and its war against Spain (the end of an empire of which the United States gathered up the remains), or between 1941 and the American annexation of the Philippines (an imitation of European imperialism felt both as a sin and as a mistake), the foreign policy of the United States had erred not out of thirst for power but through failure to recognize the role that fate was imposing upon it. The banning of war, embodied in the Kellogg-Briand pact, was in the same vein as Wilson's moralism and legalism, against which, after 1945, George Kennan and Hans Morgenthau in their turn waged a passionate crusade. Other decisions also bear witness to this refusal to recognize the realities of international politics on a world scale. In peacetime the United States did not need a large army because it inhabited a kind of continental island. But as soon as it opposed Japan's ambitions in Asia, or faced the threat of attack in the Philippines, the old U.S. policy of waiting until the enemy fired the first shot before raising an appropriate army became an anachronism.

The same blindness characterized U.S. foreign policy as regards trade and finance. The low Underwood tariff introduced by Wilson in 1913 was replaced in 1922 by the Fordney-McCumber tariff, which raised customs duties. In 1930, when the effects of the slump were already being felt,

Congress voted for the even more protectionist Hawley-Smoot tariff: Despite the advice showered on them by the economists, the elected members did not or would not understand that the United States, a longtime importer of capital, had because of the war become creditor to the outside world. They demanded the repayments of war debts, which were regarded as fundamentally separate from reparations, at the same time as holding down imports through high customs duties. How are such incompatibilities to be explained except in terms of voluntary unconsciousness, perhaps as examples of parapraxis or "Freudian slip"? Similarly, what reasonable explanation is there for the neutrality laws passed by Congress in the 1930s to prevent any repetition of the process that had led to the U.S. entry into the war in 1917? The law of May 1939 banned all sales of war material as well as any loans to belligerents and withdrew the right of American citizens to travel on any ship belonging to a country that was at war. Any belligerent wishing to buy nonprohibited American goods had to pay for them in *cash* and transport, or *carry,* them in its own ships (the famous "cash and carry" scheme). This law, which was passed a year after the annexation of Austria, was thought to encourage "aggressors," and in particular Hitler's Germany, against which public opinion raged furiously. It also coincided with efforts by Roosevelt to maintain the old Open Door principle in China in order to resist Japan's attempts at conquest or expansion. U.S. policy seems to have called for resistance by any means short of war— a policy devoid of sense, especially common sense. Faced with a country like Japan, the United States tried ostracizing its aggressors and banning loans. But by what miracle could these measures act as a substitute for force? As if the United States itself, even in its own brief history, had been able to avoid the use of force!

By voting for supplementary credits for the navy, Congress expressed doubts about its own policy. It was trying to forestall the inevitable. Perhaps the members of Congress hoped that France and Britain, by themselves and without the help of the United States, would manage to overcome the Third Reich, even if it were later allied to fascist Italy and to Japan. But it would probably have admitted that if needed, the United States would once again act to redress the balance of power in the Old World. The combination of the neutrality laws and U.S. moral support of the democracies, if it had any effect at all on the course of events, probably encouraged Hitler to forge ahead regardless and start a war before U.S.

hostility to the totalitarian regimes expressed itself in practical terms. If a historian could, without absurdity, attribute a kind of super-Machiavellianism to the members of Congress, he might ascribe to them a view often thought to have motivated British diplomacy: i.e., that an island power rises as continental powers wear themselves out in wars to the death. But the second European war did in fact transform the potential hegemony of the United States. Europe was achieving the goal for which, through all its discords, it had been blindly striving: in the words of Paul Valéry, to be ruled by a committee of Americans. The leaders of the American Republic would hardly have acted otherwise if they had really wanted to extend over the Old Continent the hegemony they already exercised over the Western Hemisphere.

But no one would ascribe such perversity or foresight to the senators from Arizona or Wisconsin. The island power whose territory remained safe from attack, and which sent expeditionary forces to destinations far away from its own shores, enjoyed—until 1945—the strange privilege of profiting politically from its mistakes. Through its abstention from action, through spreading the illusion that it would stand aside from the hostilities in Europe, through its inability to choose between a compromise with Japan and a resolve to win, which only massive rearmament could have made look convincing, the United States, historically speaking, bears part of the responsibility for the double war in the Atlantic and the Pacific. A quarter of a century's preeminence was the result—reward or punishment—of what everyone now calls an aberration: the paradox by which a Great Power undermines the system as much by refusing to play its part as by taking pride in its power.

After twenty-five years, the Europeans, after complaining about the pride, are beginning to be afraid again of the refusal.

THE UNITED STATES AND
THE INTERNATIONAL SYSTEM

Success and Failure of the Hegemonic Power

The two wars of the twentieth century—taken together, a thirty years'
war—stand as a tragic epilogue to the European age and to the diplomatic system that had been typical of Europe since the end of the wars of
religion. Voltaire wrote:

It had long been possible to regard Christian Europe, Russia apart (for
only since 1716 had that realm been included in the *Almanach royal*),
as a kind of Great Republic divided into several states, some monarchical and the others mixed, the former aristocratic and the latter popular,
but all corresponding with one another since all alike, though divided
into several sects, possessed a religious core and shared the same principles of social and political justice, which were unknown in other parts
of the world. It is on account of these principles that the European nations do not make slaves of their prisoners, that they respect their enemies' ambassadors, that they agree together on the preeminence and
some of the rights of certain princes, such as the emperor, the king,
and other lesser potentates, and that they concur, above all, in the wise
policy of preserving among themselves, as far as they can, an equal balance of power, continuously resorting to negotiation even in the midst
of war, and maintaining in one another's countries ambassadors and
other less honorable spies, not only to warn all their courts of the
schemes of one, but also to sound the alarm to all Europe, thus saving

the weaker among them from the invasions that the strongest is always ready to embark upon.*

Voltaire's analysis as a whole points out, in a neutral style tinged with irony, the distinguishing features of the international system in Europe: the desire to prevent a single power from exercising hegemony (Montesquieu phrased the same idea as "resistance to universal monarchy"); a shared background of beliefs and practices despite the diversity of institutions; and a civilized form of Machiavellianism on the part of statesmen who respect the principles of social justice but suspect one another of sinister designs.

But the countries of Europe did not grant the peoples or constituent states of Asia and Africa the privileges they reserved for one another. The Eurocentric system would only include on an equal footing such extra-European countries as could, by force, impose respect for their existence and their rights. Thus Japan became a full member of the international system, possibly as early as its victory over China (1895), but in any case through its victory over Tsarist Russia. The two Americas stood on the fringe of the system: The United States was admitted from time to time.

The Great Republic described by Voltaire was struck a fatal blow by the 1914 war, which by its apocalyptic nature unleashed passions that made a return to such traditional practices as permanent negotiations impossible. Russia, the last to be included in the *Almanach royal,* left the Great Republic in 1917; Hitler's Germany exited in 1933. From then on, between the main players in the diplomatic game there was neither common faith, nor regular correspondence, nor respect for the same principles. In 1814 and 1815 the allies had imposed a change of regime on France: They drove out the "usurper," the embodiment of a revolutionary idea, a soldier of fortune, glorious but vanquished. In 1918 it was with the legitimate heir of a royal and imperial family that the Allied powers refused to treat, because they held him responsible for the disaster of World War I.

The Europe of the 1930s no longer resembled that of the past few centuries, nor even that of the twenty-five years between the capture of the

---

*Voltaire, *Le Siècle de Louis XIV* (The age of Louis XIV), chapter 2. Quoted by Jean Laloy, *Entre guerre et paix* (Between war and peace) (Paris: Plon, 1966).

Bastille and the fall of Napoleon. There was no longer one "troublemaker," but two. At the time, the Third Reich seemed the more threatening, and indeed it was so. The USSR, too, remained hostile and mysterious to the Western democracies, which, in order to survive, were obliged, whether they liked it or not, to cooperate with one of their enemies against the other. In fact, Britain and France, paralyzed by scruples and by contradictory alliances, endured their fate without ever controlling it.

Hitler and Stalin led the infernal dance. In 1939 they joined together to destroy the Polish army and divide up Poland between them yet again. It was Hitler himself who tore up the pact with Stalin, turning him into the ally of Britain. It was Hitler again who, forced into it by Japan's aggression in the Pacific, declared war on the United States. When he committed suicide in his Berlin bunker and the Third Reich underwent its apocalyptic collapse, the Europe of the past no longer existed. All that was left was a vast field of ruins through which millions of deportees tried to find their way home. The meeting on the Elbe between John the American and Ivan the Russian soldier is pictured in children's history books, a stereotyped image symbolizing both the rise of what Toynbee called "the peripheral countries" and the irreversible decline of civilizations that once spread their influence worldwide.

With Germany crushed, and France and Britain among the victors but exhausted—France by defeat and occupation, Britain by its enormous effort and the weight of the victory—how could there have been a new balance of power in Europe alone? The center of the international system was no longer an equilibrium between the countries of the Old Continent; the United States had become a permanent member of the system, doomed to play the leading role.

At the same time, the old order was heading for disintegration in Asia and Africa. Britain had made India a solemn promise of independence, and no other European empire in Asia would long survive the end of the British Empire. Without the Indian Army, how could Britain have maintained its positions in the Middle East? Little by little, but inexorably, the decomposition was affecting the colonial and semi-colonial possessions of all the European countries, and the process was accelerated by the official anticolonialism of both the Soviet Union and the United States.

The major features of the international system in which the United States played the lead were these:

A world system: The United States could not have limited its actions to one geographical area even if it had wished to; it created organizations, formed alliances, and signed pacts with dozens of countries. Everything that happened, from the center of Africa to the middle of Siberia, was its business.

A heterogeneous system: Peaceful coexistence gradually replaced the anti-Communist crusade, but as I write, American soldiers are still dying to prevent a Communist Party from ruling in Saigon.

A revolutionary system: Europe's withdrawal did not calm the fever that was running through the masses around the world. Neocolonialism, which made a vague attempt to define the influence or economic presence of the West, suffered the same attacks as colonialism; big U.S. companies were held to be just as guilty of "domination" and "exploitation" as the colonial officials of old; and the more westerners denounced the discrepancy between the wealth of some and the poverty of others, the more they added to the resentment of the masses and justified revolt.

A bipolar system: In 1946 the Europeans were afraid the Soviet hordes might advance to the Atlantic; in 1972, only the Soviet Union has the complete armory of deterrence—ballistic missiles buried in silos or carried on nuclear submarines—necessary to balance the arsenal available to the United States.

The history of international relations since 1945 cannot be reduced merely to the rivalry between the United States and Russia. It may well be that in the not-too-distant future, as the implicit agreement between Moscow and Washington grows in strength and scope, the Cold War will come to seem like a spectacular episode rather than one of the most important elements in postwar history. For anyone writing in 1972, however, it is only through the state of relations between the two superpowers that the different phases of American diplomacy can be discerned, for the simple reason that, at least consciously, the officials concerned saw their actions, as they saw the world itself, in terms of the Communist threat. Once this principle is established, the periods emerge quite clearly.

1. *1941–1945.* During this period, which lies outside of the time period under discussion, the United States entered the war against Japan and the Third Reich and made what the American general stationed in

Moscow at the time called its "strange alliance" with the Soviet Union. Roosevelt set the immediate objectives—to destroy the armed forces of the two enemy countries and bring about their unconditional surrender. After the war, haunted by memories of what had happened after World War I, he wanted first and foremost to create an international organization to which both the United States and the Soviet Union would belong (a resurrected version of Wilson's League of Nations), and by this means to reduce as far as possible the risk of a return to isolationism. He dreamed of a triumvirate, or at least a Russo-American condominium, while remaining faithful, along with most of his advisers, to Wilson's legalism and universalism. Such dreams did not preclude agreements, whether entered into out of cynicism or resignation, on the future frontiers of Poland, or the price to be paid to get the Soviet Union to enter the war against Japan.

2. *1945–1947.* This second phase—from the Potsdam conference to the Truman declaration in March 1947 and the departure of Molotov, who set out in July 1947 to take part in the conference that prepared the Marshall Plan—marks the transition from alliance to rupture. As it ended, the United States, and perhaps also the Soviet Union, was wavering between cooperation and hostility. The heads of state no longer met; the Sovietization of Poland, Romania, and Bulgaria, and the way that process was carried out, caused anxiety at some times and at others indignation. Lastly and above all, the division of Germany was becoming more and more of a preoccupation.

These two phases raise a question that will be addressed below in section I. The question is, Was the rupture inevitable? My analysis will concentrate primarily on the strategic aspect of the matter and will subject the military and diplomatic decisions involved to the retrospective query that both Clausewitz and Weber thought legitimate and inevitable: What would have happened if . . . ? That there can be no certainty about any of the answers to such questions does not mean they should not be asked. The critique will also have a moral dimension. Which was responsible for the rupture, the United States or the Soviet Union? Which of the two behaved in accordance with custom and equity? Which had objects in view that a historian must approve of?

3. *March (or July) 1947–March 1953.* These six years cover the Cold War in the narrow sense of the term. Hostile propaganda reached great virulence on both sides. In Eastern Europe, the subjection of countries liberated

or occupied by the Red Army accelerated, and non-Communist democrats were ruthlessly eliminated. In Prague, the Communist Party, which controlled all key posts, liquidated all vestiges of liberal democracy. After the Yugoslav schism, all the other satellite countries in turn witnessed show trials on the Moscow model. In 1949 the Chinese Communists took over the Celestial City. In the West, the French, British, and U.S. zones of occupation were joined together to form the Federal Republic of Germany (FRG), with its capital in Bonn. In 1949 the Atlantic Pact was signed with due solemnities by the United States and such parts of Europe as were still free. In 1956 the Korean campaign triggered U.S. rearmament, the creation of the North Atlantic Treaty Organization (NATO), an invitation to Germany to join in the common defense, and a conflict between China and the United States in Asia. The latter decided to support Chiang Kai-shek in Taiwan and the French in Indochina.

4. *March 1953–November 1958.* The death of Stalin brought about the thaw, and a new attitude toward the outside world developed among the men in the Kremlin. Meanwhile, the organization of Europe into two military blocs continued. It was in 1955 that the FRG officially joined NATO—the same year the Big Four met in Geneva. The Cold War had become less intense. (One armistice was signed in Korea in 1953, and another in Indochina in 1954.) Stalin's heirs were casting their eyes outside Europe, and the context of confrontation was growing larger. The 1956 crisis—involving both the Hungarian uprising and the Franco-British Suez expedition—shook both alliances and revealed a certain solidarity between the two superpowers.

These two phases, dealt with in section II below, call for a complex critique: Its theme is suggested by the title of the section—"From One Crusade to Another." A historian might ask himself two apparently contradictory questions, both of them well-founded. Could the United States have followed an ultimately moderate defensive policy of containment without making a moral commitment? And in the last analysis, did not this commitment conceal the acceptance of a share-out that Stalin wanted and Truman refused?

5. *November 1958–July 1963 (or November 1962).* Between Khrushchev's demand that Berlin become a free city and the Missile Crisis of October–November 1962 (or the signature in July 1963 of the treaty imposing a partial ban on nuclear experiments) came a strange and ambiguous phase

not easily distinguished from the previous one. Soviet diplomacy seemed to be playing a double game of détente and attack at the same time. Khrushchev aimed simultaneously at a favorable arrangement in Berlin and a possible modus vivendi in the world as a whole. Relations between the Soviet Union and the People's Republic of China continued to deteriorate. (In 1959 Moscow denounced the agreement on nuclear cooperation; in 1960 Soviet technicians were withdrawn from China; in 1963 the quarrel between Russia and China was made public at the same time as the Western powers were in Moscow to sign the treaty on the partial suspension of nuclear experiments.) The Cuban Missile Crisis in October–November 1962 marked the end of Khrushchev's diplomacy. In 1963, at the time of President John F. Kennedy's death, the United States seemed to be at its apogee. There were no longer two superpowers—only one. Ten years of détente had led to U.S. supremacy.

6. *1962 (or July 1963)–1969.* The Soviet Union did not resume direct confrontation with the United States, but it did try to catch up in the fields of ballistic missiles and sea power. It, too, became a world power. In 1965, at the culminating point of its supremacy, the United States gradually intensified its involvement in the Vietnam War (though perhaps it had been irrevocable by 1963). For the first time, the U.S. Army was fighting partisans supplied from abroad and regular North Vietnamese troops who often adopted partisan methods. The Americans won most of their battles, militarily speaking, but they were not winning the war. Public opinion, both in the United States and in the world as a whole, turned against the Goliath that could not get the better of David; against the enormous military machine that was devastating the country it was supposed to be protecting; and against the bombing of North Vietnam. President Lyndon B. Johnson gave up the idea of seeking a second term, and Richard Nixon was narrowly elected with a mandate to end the war that was worsening, if not actually creating, a moral crisis (or, to use the expression favored in France, a "crisis of civilization").

The phases of American diplomacy correspond only roughly to the periods I have just outlined. John Foster Dulles's diplomatic policy, though it belonged to the years of détente, exhibited the same main features as the crusading spirit. Moreover, there was often a huge discrepancy between the aims of the people concerned and the results, between impressions and facts (for example, on the subject of the balance of forces). American diplomacy, as experienced by those who practiced it, went through three phases: détente, with its unfounded fear, with regard to public rather than informed opinion, of possible Soviet superiority; the Kennedy presidency, with its desire for action, which after the initial Bay of Pigs disaster led to the Missile Crisis and a sense of world supremacy; and the Vietnam impasse, with the consequent revolt against the burden of empire. In ten years, from 1953 to 1963, as a result of successes that were spectacular rather than lasting, the American leadership gradually convinced itself of a supremacy that in fact has gradually decreased. In a few years, between 1965 and 1969, the cost, the failure, and the horror of the Vietnam adventure triggered a great self-examination. From détente to supremacy and revolt: I shall call the third section *The Tarpeian Rock* (for readers who have forgotten their Roman history, *Rise and Fall*).

Richard Nixon, the former Cold War warrior elected to end the Vietnam War, introduced a new style of policy, resuming relations with Peking and concluding agreements with Moscow. Never has American public opinion thirsted so much after moral purity, and never have American leaders, in the persons of the Nixon-Kissinger team, practiced so resolutely the European art of diplomacy. Theirs was a diplomacy both Machiavellian and moderate—apart from the raids on North Vietnam, which were anything but moderate. A case of Nixon *à la Metternich?*

I

IN SEARCH OF THE GUILTY PARTY, OR THE ORIGINS OF THE COLD WAR

The expression *Cold War*, borrowed from the vocabulary of journalists and politicians, has no one precise content. I distinguish three meanings.

1. In his book, *Histoire de la guerre froide* (History of the Cold War), André Fontaine went back to the 1917 revolution and the subsequent military interventions of the Western countries. He defined the Cold War as the fundamental and permanent hostility between the Soviet Union and the West arising out of the nature of the Soviet regime, the capitalist and liberal countries' fear of it, and the universal mission claimed by Marxism-Leninism and American democracy alike.

But what Fontaine stressed most was the bipolarity. "There would not have been any Cold War," he wrote, "if in the middle of this century there had not been two powers, and two only, big enough, with a sufficiently large population, and with enough confidence in the value of their own beliefs and weapons of all kinds to challenge one another for world dominance, without either one ever being able to be sure of achieving definite superiority."*

But if the Cold War is to be defined as the rivalry for worldwide supremacy, it did not begin, at least between the United States and the Soviet Union, until between 1941 and 1945.

Besides emphasizing the bipolar aspect—the rivalry between two states that outstrip all others in terms of resources and will to power—Fontaine also underlined the heterogeneity of the system—the incompatibility between Marxist-Leninist ideology, on the one hand, and liberal-capitalist notions, on the other. In the first case, the Cold War begins with the 1917 revolution; in the second, with the end of World War II and the collapse of the in-between states.

2. The current meaning of Cold War (or warlike peace) is related, it seems to me, to the following idea: In times of peace, conflicts can become so acute that the countries concerned use against one another the kinds of means normally and traditionally reserved for times of war. Two features, wrote Professor Hans Morgenthau, differentiate the Cold War from many international confrontations of the past: the *impossibility*, given the interests at stake and the positions adopted, for those involved to follow policies that might, through bargaining and compromise, have led to a resolution of their differences, and the consequent *necessity* for them to protect and promote their interests through direct unilateral pressure on their adversaries by every possible means—diplomatic, military, economic, and subversive—other than the actual use of force.** This is the most commonly accepted use of the term *Cold War: war* because the diplomats neither could nor wished to resolve their differences by negotiation; *cold* because they neither could nor wished to resolve them by force. What struck observers was the violence of the opposing propaganda machines, the breakdown or virtual breakdown in communications between the two sides, and

---

*André Fontaine, *Histoire de la guerre froide*, Part 1 (Paris: Fayard, 1965), p. 15.
**Hans J. Morgenthau, "Arguing About the Cold War," *Encounter*, no. 5, May 1967, pp. 37–41.

the seemingly incurable hostility, which, though no war had been declared, became the usual style for international exchanges.

3. But none of these definitions—neither struggle for world superiority, nor bipolarity within a heterogeneous system, nor the impossibility or rejection of both conciliation and resolution by force—allows us to make a clear distinction between periods of so-called Cold War and periods of peaceful coexistence, or, to use another terminology, of tension and détente. "Give and take" negotiations have never precluded direct action or stopped the parties from bringing pressure to bear on their adversary. Thomas Hobbes and Jean-Jacques Rousseau both thought countries lived in a permanent state of war with one another. The proportion of bargaining and pressure varies at different times. According to this view, with which I agree, there is only a difference of degree between "normal" international relations, especially in a bipolar and heterogeneous system, and "Cold War." But between 1947 and 1953, through a combination of the propaganda on each side, the Berlin blockade, the Korean campaign, and various military preparations, this difference of degree became so acute that it seems to me legitimate to use the terms *Cold War* and *warlike peace.*

In this section I shall follow tradition and use the third definition: By Cold War I shall mean the period of extreme tension originating during a war waged simultaneously rather than together against the Third Reich, but becoming overt only in March 1947 with the Truman Doctrine, or even a few months later at the Paris conference held to discuss the plan for U.S. aid.

The literature on the wartime relations among the Big Three—Stalin, Churchill, and Roosevelt—continues to swell. So I could not, even if I wanted to, bring any fresh material or new interpretation to the debate. Moreover, I cannot understand the passion of certain American historians of the so-called revisionist school for rejecting what is seen as the traditional interpretation and trying to prove that the Cold War could have been avoided or was the fault of the United States.

What does "avoiding the Cold War" mean? The phrase seems to suggest that events might have taken a different course after the victory over the Third Reich was won. What different course? Could the Big Three have kept up their alliance? Could they have agreed on a new arrangement for Europe without Homeric exchanges of insults? The word *responsibility* has two meanings. It can signify causal liability: Such and such an act or decision must necessarily and predictably bring about such and such a consequence or reaction. Or it can refer to a political or moral responsibility: Such and such a decision, which entails what is judged to be an undesirable consequence, is regarded by historians not as a mistake but as a misdeed. I shall try in every case to make the necessary distinction.

Today, with hindsight, the disintegration of the Grand Alliance seems just an ordinary development in international relations. We have only to remember what Stalin said to Tito: "This war is not like the wars of the past: whoever occupies a country imposes his own social system on it. Everyone imposes his own system as far as his army can advance. It cannot be otherwise." If that is what Stalin thought—and we have little reason to doubt it—it does not make the search for origins irrelevant (who started the trouble?*), but it does limit its bearing by suggesting where both kinds of responsibility fall: The dividing up of Europe was probably inevitable, but it did not involve guilt on the part of any one participant. Everyone behaved in accordance with his own perception of history, his ambitions, and his values. However, this fact does not oblige the uncommitted observer to abstain from all moral judgment.

1. The Polish Question

In the wartime negotiations among the Big Three, no question loomed larger or was discussed at such length as that of what to do about Poland. In 1946–1947, the affairs of Greece and Turkey, then the future of Germany, took precedence. To put it simply, the moral rupture occurred over Poland, the final break came over Germany, and the Greek crisis and the Soviet demands over Turkey led to the Truman Doctrine and the potential extension of rivalry between the victors to a worldwide scale.

On April 12, 1943, the Germans found the mass grave at Katyn (where some 10,000 Polish officers who had been murdered by the Soviets during the 1941 retreat were buried). On April 16, the Polish government in exile in London asked the International Red Cross to look into the matter. On

---

*The question "Who started it?" obviously does not preclude either the question of causal responsibility or that of guilt.

April 25, the Kremlin replied, blaming the Germans for the massacre and using the Polish government's démarche as a pretext for breaking off relations with it. At the Tehran conference in November 1943 Roosevelt showed little interest in the future and the frontiers of Poland: Churchill and Stalin had heated debates on the subject, but the American president remained silent. Stalin, from his first meeting with Anthony Eden after Hitler's attack, had never concealed the fact that he intended to hang on to the territories he had acquired under his 1939 pact with the Third Reich. Although this claim was never set down in the Russo-British treaty of alliance, Churchill was aware of Stalin's demands and considered it pointless to oppose them. He agreed that the Curzon Line should mark Poland's eastern frontier and that Poland should be compensated in the west at the expense of now-Germanized provinces that had formerly been Polish.

When the Big Three met again at Yalta (February 1945), Stalin had already set up the Lublin Committee (July 23, 1944) and the Soviet armies were occupying Polish territory. The heroic insurrection of the Secret Army in Warsaw had resulted in the total destruction of the city. The Russians were doing just as they pleased, and the West had no practical means of interfering. Churchill, on his own, once again put up a fight for Poland—not now on the subject of the eastern frontier, which had been settled at Potsdam, but concerning the western borders and, even more, the makeup of the government that would take over after Poland was liberated. Britain and France had entered the war to honor their promise to Poland; but Poland was going to emerge bereft of the territories occupied by the Red Army in 1939, though extended in the west as far as the Oder-Neisse Line. Moreover, Poland was in danger of losing its internal autonomy and being subjected to a Soviet-type regime with leaders chosen by Stalin from among the socialists and the survivors of a Communist Party that had been decimated in the great purge. After their lengthy discussions at Yalta, the Big Three agreed on an ambiguous formula: "The government is to be reorganized on broader democratic foundations, to include democratic leaders living abroad." Roosevelt seems to have believed in the promise of free elections—"within a month," Molotov told him. Roosevelt added in reply: "I want them to be like Caesar's wife—above suspicion." According to an unshakable legend, the Big Three divided up the world at Yalta. All the evidence agrees that Yalta represents the peak, not so much of the Grand Alliance as of the Grand Illusion. True, Roosevelt and Stalin concluded a secret agreement by which the Soviet Union was to enter the war against Japan three months at the latest after the end of hostilities in Europe. The American president assented to the territorial conquests Stalin wanted at the expense of Finland (the province Russia had annexed in 1939), Romania (Bessarabia), and Germany (East Prussia). He hoped that the "Three," and even more that the "Two," would go on cooperating with one another after the war.

Perhaps he even believed that the ambiguous agreement on Poland would be applied in the way the West interpreted it, with genuinely free elections. Roosevelt, a politician by training rather than a statesman, with some greatness but with weaknesses, too, a man who could be haughty as well as humane, is too complex a figure to be judged dogmatically. Reservations about him there may be, but ultimately a positive verdict seems to be the right one. Harry Hopkins, one of his closest advisers, said later: "We were absolutely certain that we had won the first great victory of the peace—and by 'we,' I mean all of us, the whole civilized human race."[*] Churchill himself, in the House of Commons, displayed a confidence he may not have felt. "The impression I brought back from the Crimea, and from all my other contacts, is that Marshal Stalin and the Soviet leaders wish to live in honourable friendship and equality with the Western democracies. I feel also that their word is their bond. I know of no Government which stands to its obligations, even in its own despite, more solidly than the Russian Soviet Government."[**] He spoke differently, however, to General de Gaulle a few months later. "When it is time to digest, the surfeited Russians will have their difficult moments. Then, perhaps, Saint Nicholas can bring back to life the poor children the ogre has put in the salting tub."[***]

In fact, everything worked out as if Stalin were still taking the agreement he made with Churchill in October 1944, on the "percentage of influences" in the various countries, more seriously than the rhetoric of the final declaration at Yalta implied. Roosevelt had not approved of the

---

[*]Quoted by Fontaine, *Histoire de la guerre froide*, Part 1, p. 273.

[**]Winston Churchill, *Memoirs of the Second World War*, vol. 6, *Triumph and Tragedy* (Boston: Houghton Mifflin, 1953), pp. 400–401.

[***]Charles de Gaulle, *Mémoires de guerre*, trans. (New York: Simon and Schuster, 1964), p. 728.

Russo-British conversations in Moscow.* He even pointed out in advance that the British prime minister was not speaking for him, though he took care not to express open opposition to the bargaining that took place between Stalin and Churchill, the details of which he may not have known. The respective percentages of influence that Molotov and Eden finally settled on for the Soviet Union and Britain, in theory valid only during the occupation phase, were as follows: Hungary, 80–20; Romania, 90–10; Bulgaria, 80–20; Yugoslavia, 60–40; and Greece, 10–90. Theoretically, this cynical agreement, indignantly denounced by Cordell Hull, the U.S. secretary of state, and never subscribed to by Roosevelt, ceased to be valid as soon as the Big Three solemnly proclaimed at Yalta that they "would by common accord help the peoples of the liberated European states or of the former Axis satellites whose situation in their judgment made it suitable . . . to form governments that would undertake to set up as soon as possible, through free elections, governments answering to the will of the peoples; and wherever necessary to facilitate the process of free elections." Unfortunately this declaration did not say what would happen if the Big Three disagreed. The phrasing concerning the reorganization of the Lublin Committee was also somewhat ambiguous: Stalin read it as meaning that its members would retain their majority and their predominance.

Between the Yalta conference and Roosevelt's death, the pace of events increased without the Big Three's grandly proclaimed entente having the slightest effect on the behavior of the Soviet authorities. Just after Yalta, Andrei Vishinsky went to Bucharest and, by threatening to send in the tanks, forced King Michael to dismiss Nicolae Radescu, his prime minister, and replace him with "fellow traveler" Petru Groza. For the time being, there was no follow-up to the joint decision to reorganize or enlarge the Lublin Committee. The main leaders of the Secret Army and of the non-Communist Polish parties invited to Moscow had been arrested and imprisoned there.

---

*In reply to a letter in October 1944 from Mikolajcyk, the Polish prime minister, asking for his support and quoting Molotov's statement that in Tehran the American president had accepted the Curzon Line as Poland's eastern frontier, Roosevelt wrote that he was unequivocally in favor of a united and independent Poland and of its people's absolute right to organize its domestic life as they saw fit; he was evasive on the subject of frontiers and said he would not oppose an agreement between the Poles, the Russians, and the British. See M. F. Herz, *Beginnings of the Cold War* (Bloomington: University of Indiana Press, 1966), p. 61.

The Secret Army's uprising in Warsaw, ordered by the government in exile in London to prevent Moscow's Polish protégés from seizing power, had ended, after a heroic battle,* in defeat. The officers who were murdered at Katyn; the Secret Army that was exterminated by the Germans as the result of a rash order from London; the non-Communist leaders of the resistance who were arrested—all belonged to the old Poland, and all had to go so that a new Poland could arise out of the ashes and ruins.

On the basis of the facts briefly outlined above, historians have for the last quarter of a century put either Churchill (the Moscow agreement), Roosevelt, or Truman in the dock. Until recently, most blamed Stalin for the breakup of the Grand Alliance. In the past ten years or so the revisionist school has recruited new supporters. After each of the wars in which the United States has taken part—the war against Mexico, the American Civil War, the intervention in 1917—a revisionist school has called in question the orthodox version of events—the version of the people involved and of public opinion itself at the time. Today's revisionism is fostered by political and moral revulsion against the diplomacy that led to the Vietnam War.

This is not the place for detailed discussion of all the problems raised by the revisionists. Our object is merely to understand what Roosevelt and Truman actually did in the decisive years between February 1945—the Yalta conference—and spring 1947—the Truman Doctrine and the Marshall Plan. Two problems strike me as crucial. Did U.S. policy change after Roosevelt's death under the influence of the new president, and if so were the changes responsible, in the morally neutral sense of being its determining cause, for the gradually increasing tension between East and West? Was the mistake or misdeed the refusal on the part of the British and the Americans to let the Russians build a security zone in Eastern Europe? Some commentators call it a mistake, suggesting that abandoning the universalist myth offered the only chance, and a real one, of maintaining the cooperation between the Soviets on the one side and the British and Americans on the other. Others call it a misdeed or moral fault, saying the Russians were only demanding their rights, and that the British and U.S. refusal to agree

---

*Could the Soviet Army have crossed the Vistula and come to the rescue of the insurgents? Historians are hesitant on this point. In any event, for several weeks Stalin refused to agree to the parachuting in of weapons by the Western air forces.

to a legitimate extension of the socialist zone arose either out of culpable blindness or a drive to satisfy the demands of capitalist economics.

2. From Roosevelt to Truman

In Tehran as at Yalta, Roosevelt left to Churchill the thankless task of defending the interests of Poland. He did not want to get involved because of the upcoming 1944 elections and the vote of American citizens of Polish descent. At Yalta he adopted a universalist stance but acted as arbiter or conciliator. His state of mind is reflected in some of the things his son—though an unreliable witness—reports him as saying. "England is in decline. China is still living in the eighteenth century. Russia is suspicious of us and makes us suspicious of her. America is the only great power who can keep the world peaceful. . . . Our role in the future United Nations Organization will be to reconcile the different points of view of the English, who think empire, and the Russians, who think communism."* Some of the most lucid American commentators, including Walter Lippmann himself, believed as late as 1961 that there was still a power struggle going on between the Soviet Union and Britain and that the United States should stay out of it.

Was the United States the only Great Power capable of keeping the peace? Roosevelt was not wrong when he tried to play the arbitrator. Was it possible to hold an even, or almost even, balance between the two sides—on the one hand, an empire that the British were going to get rid of, vanquished by their own victory or constrained by the promises they had made and their own convictions, and on the other hand, Stalinist communism, which was on the point of engulfing half of Europe? To attempt it would be the aberration of a typical politician, unfortunately ignorant of history, and ill-informed into the bargain. In Europe, Churchill was not defending an empire; he was simultaneously defending the need for equilibrium and the values invoked by the Americans.

From 1941 to 1945 Roosevelt seems to have acted in obedience to two main considerations, one concerning the war and one concerning the postwar period: that is to say, on the one hand, the task of obtaining the

---

*Quoted by André Fontaine, *Histoire de la guerre froide,* Part 1, p. 261.

unconditional surrender of Japan and Germany, and on the other, that of doing away with Stalin's mistrust and establishing good relations with him so as to create the United Nations. The latter was intended to prevent both a return to isolationism on the part of the United States and a withdrawal into itself on the part of the Soviet Union. Military pragmatism first, then a Utopian vision. But this Utopia did not exclude a new phase of U.S. "Manifest Destiny."

As the documents show, Roosevelt, in the last weeks of his life, became aware of the impending danger: Events in Romania and Poland, together with anguished letters from Churchill, shook his confidence. He knew that the "strange alliance"* would not survive a brutal Sovietization of the liberated countries by the Red Army. On April 1 he sent Stalin a telegram saying, "Any solution ending in a scarcely disguised restoration of the current regime in Warsaw would be unacceptable, and would lead the people of the United States to regard the Yalta agreement as a failure." In Roosevelt's view, Yalta still stood for universalism, not for the carving up of Europe into spheres of influence. A few days later he was dying.

Had he lived, would Roosevelt have maintained the policy of cooperation with Stalin against all odds? No one can be sure, one way or the other. The records show that, in the period between the Yalta conference and his death, the approach of victory and the behavior of the Russians in Eastern Europe was tending to make him change his mind.

I myself think he would have modified the line of American diplomacy faster than Truman did, not more slowly. And this is not just an unsupported hypothesis, for the arrival of Truman in the White House resulted in neither a break nor an alteration in U.S. foreign policy.

What is Truman accused of? Of having adopted an aggressive tone in his conversations with Molotov on the way to the UN Conference in San Francisco? There is no doubt that he spoke to the Soviet foreign minister in a manner Roosevelt never would have employed, although Stalin, in his letters to Churchill and Roosevelt, did not mince his words. Moreover, that stormy interview was not repeated. At the end of May, to signal the continuity of American diplomatic policy, Truman sent Harry Hopkins to

---

*The title of a book by an American general stationed in Moscow during the war: John R. Deane, *The Strange Alliance* (New York: Viking Press, 1947).

Moscow to maintain or restore U.S.-Soviet cooperation. As usual, the American envoy had little trouble winning a "concession" from Stalin over the voting system in the United Nations. (That is, the veto would not apply to questions of procedure. Since the Security Council's right to raise a particular question was deemed a matter of procedure and not of substance, it would not be subject to a veto on the part of the five permanent members.) The Polish question once again occupied most of the discussion. Stalin once again swore he had not the slightest intention of bringing about a Sovietization of Poland, which would have a parliamentary regime. But he categorically refused to free the resistance leaders who had been lured to Moscow; he merely promised, as he had already done in Yalta, to enlarge the Lublin Committee. He agreed to receive Stanislaw Mikolajczyk, who became vice president of the council. The Americans did not even obtain—and stopped asking for—the elections provided for at Yalta; a Polish government that was practically the same as the Lublin Committee received recognition and official membership in the United Nations. Eighteen months after his return to his homeland, Mikolajczyk was fleeing for his life. So Truman did as Roosevelt would have done, and with the same results. He went on taking the United Nations Charter seriously, and Stalin made legalistic objections that he then withdrew so as to give his opponents the impression that they had wrung concessions from him. In return, he won recognition for faits accomplis in Poland and Eastern Europe that conflicted directly with solemn promises and other commitments that the British and the Americans had made to their Allies.

The sudden suspension of Lend-Lease on May 8, just a few hours after the German surrender, raised a storm in the United States because of the order (later revoked) instructing ships already en route to return to port. The blunder seems to have been the result of bureaucratic automatism based on a literal interpretation of the law. Hopkins assured Stalin that the United States would not dream of exerting that kind of pressure.

In the spring of 1945, Truman, still new to world politics, followed along the line traced by Roosevelt, though with increasing doubts of the same kind as his predecessor had felt just before he died. But he resisted Churchill when the British prime minister implored him not to withdraw U.S. forces at once from the part of Germany that, under the occupation arrangements, was to become the Soviet zone. Truman stuck to his position, and in return for the western sectors of Berlin and Vienna and the establishment of an Inter-Allied Commission in Austria, American troops, followed by hundreds of thousands of refugees, evacuated Thuringia, Saxony, and Mecklenburg. Thus Leipzig, Erfurt, and Weimar belonged to what was to become the German Democratic Republic (GDR). So until the Potsdam conference and beyond, Truman kept to the agreements entered into by his predecessor, while at the same time reproaching the Russians for breaking them.* One cannot help wondering who, apart from American professors, could imagine anyone like Stalin being upset by verbal protests that merely camouflaged a de facto capitulation.

Finally came the historic decision on the basis of which one historian has written a kind of diplomatic novel: the decision in August 1945 to drop the two atomic bombs on Hiroshima and Nagasaki.** Was it the end of World War II or the beginning of the Cold War? A necessary act of cruelty to reduce the cost of the victory, or an attempt to intimidate the Soviet Union? In retrospect, these questions, which nobody raised at the time (*L'Humanité*, the daily newspaper published by the French Communist Party, applauded the deed), have taken on a significance that is both political and moral. Was the decision inevitable or pragmatic? Was it directed against Japan or against the Soviet Union?

The answer, in my view, can be deduced easily enough from the records. Let us first set out the established facts. The U.S. intelligence services knew the secrets of the Japanese codes, and thus American leaders were aware of the real situation: With the Japanese fleet destroyed and most of its merchant navy sunk, the government set up by the emperor and led by Kintaro Suzuki wanted to end a war that was already lost and had instructed Naotake Sato, the Japanese ambassador in Moscow, in this regard, with a view to getting Russia to mediate. Neither Foreign Minister Togo Shigenori nor ambassador Sato knew that their messages had been decoded

---

*Stalin may not have thought he was breaking them. His was a different interpretation of the Yalta agreement on Poland. He may have based his attitude on the agreement with Churchill in October 1944.

**In the copious literature on the subject, one account impresses me as being reliable, scrupulous, well-informed, and dispassionate: See Les Giovannitti and Fred Freed, *The Decision to Drop the Bomb* (New York: Coward McCann, 1965).

in Washington on July 13, four days before the opening of the Potsdam conference, or that Truman and his advisers were well aware of the emperor's earnest desire to see the war end rapidly.*

This being so, why did the United States not negotiate a peace without resorting to the atomic bombs? The simplistic argument—that Japan was already defeated (which is true), so the bombs were really directed against the Soviet Union—contains an obvious inconsistency. Why, in that case, had President Roosevelt asked for and obtained the cooperation of the Soviet Union at Yalta,** in February 1945, when Japan's position was already desperate? The complexity of the general situation arose out of a number of interconnected factors.

1. In Japan, which had been indisputably vanquished, the peace party had to conceal its intentions because the resistance party—the military party—continued to oppose unconditional surrender, that is, a peace based on defeat.
2. In the United States, the advocates of a negotiated peace did not dare either to condemn explicitly the idea of unconditional surrender or to say openly before the senatorial committees that they believed that keeping the emperor in place as an institution would prevent chaos and serve U.S. interests.
3. Inside the U.S. administration, debate centered on how serious the defeat inflicted on Japan ought to be and on future relations with the Soviet Union in Europe and the Far East.
4. The atomic bomb, which Truman had mentioned to Stalin during the Potsdam conference,[1] had been tried out successfully on July 15. It thus became the best, if not the only, means of bringing about a Japanese surrender, without, (1) invading the Japanese islands themselves (the generals thought such an invasion would be

---

*Ibid., p. 48.
**As is well known, Roosevelt, in return, agreed to Stalin's demands for the southern half of Sakhalin; the Kurile Islands; Russia's joint exploitation, with China, of the Manchurian and eastern Chinese railroads; the restoration of the lease of Port Arthur; and the internationalization of the neighboring port of Dairen, subject to the predominant interests of the USSR. The price of Russia's intervention was modestly referred to as "the restoration of Russian rights violated by Japan's treacherous attack." In 1905 the Japanese fleet had destroyed Port Arthur in a surprise attack.

very costly in human lives); and (2) the participation of the Soviet Union, which would deprive the United States of some of the benefits of a victory that it had in fact won on its own.

If we take all these factors into account it is at least probable, and perhaps certain, that the decision to use both atomic bombs arose almost inevitably out of the circumstances. *Despite the bombs,* the emperor in Tokyo met right up to the end with an absurd yet heroic desire on the part of a section of the military party to go on fighting. Phosphorus bombings were ravaging Japanese cities; in terms of the number of victims, the big raid on Tokyo was just as horrific as the nuclear raids. *If* the Japanese peace party, to win out over the military, needed some unprecedented event that would save face for the army; *if* the American president, constrained by the principle of unconditional surrender, was unable to negotiate the modalities of peace, and *if,* finally, the choice came down to "either atomic bombs, or invasion accompanied by the entry of the Soviet Union into the war," how can we be surprised or indignant at what happened? Truman and his advisers expressed in the indicative what we have just set out in the conditional.

But that does not mean to say that American diplomacy was exemplary or rational. Five years later, the United States was asking Japan to take up again the arms it had made its vanquished enemy renounce forever. The United States had itself created the circumstances in which recourse to atomic bombs was almost inevitable: the demand for unconditional surrender; the decision to "reform," "regenerate," and democratize Japan; the timidity of some leaders, far-sighted though they might have been; the crusading language that made even secret negotiations no longer possible; and the hasty judgment of some of the government's military advisers who, thinking invasion was the only way of achieving U.S. political purposes, had persuaded Roosevelt to ask for Soviet support and to pay for it with concessions made at China's expense.

Did Truman, during the summer of 1945, after the success of the Los Alamos experiment and in the light of the deterioration in Soviet-European relations, become apprehensive about the Soviet intervention that his predecessor had purchased? Be that as it may, he was in a hurry to bring hostilities to an end. The decision to use the atomic bombs, *which the U.S. president would probably have taken just to help or to force the emperor to surrender,* also marked the beginning of confrontation with the Soviet Union.

Not that President Truman inaugurated an "atomic diplomacy" with the wish or the hope of terrifying the men in the Kremlin: He simply wanted to have done with Japan as fast and with as little cost as possible, so as to reduce the Soviet Union's share in the operations and guard against the same sort of friction between the victors as was already evident in Europe.

How can we be sure of the intentions of those involved? Of all the innumerable texts and quotations on the subject, which are reliable? How are we to choose among the retrospective accounts and contemporary records of any decision? Clearly we cannot exclude the likely hypothesis that at some point some official or other thought that the terrifying atomic weapon would give American diplomacy more strength vis-à-vis the Soviet Union. But what an objective study shows is that the general situation— with on one side a peace party headed by the emperor, but not yet in charge, and on the other a leadership in Washington constrained by the notion of unconditional surrender and divided over the crucial problem of the emperor—made the dual tragedy of Hiroshima and Nagasaki* logical and intelligible quite apart from the intention of the United States, whether real or supposed, of negotiating with the Soviet Union from a position of strength.

It can also be shown that there is no reason for ascribing to President Truman, during the years that followed, a diplomacy based on the atomic menace. The American leaders did not order a stock of bombs to be produced as swiftly as possible. Neither in Europe nor in Asia can we discern any sudden change in tone or style before and after Hiroshima and Nagasaki. The Americans accepted the dividing up of Korea into occupation zones, as they had done in the case of Germany. They themselves took responsibility** for the occupation of the Japanese islands, having controlled access to them after destroying the Japanese fleet and reconquering the territories making up the coprosperity zone in 1941–1945. In Europe it took two years for the British and Americans to acknowledge the fact that the Allies who had fought together in the crusade against Hitler would not be

---

*Giovanni and Freed's book, *The Decision to Drop the Bomb,* shows that the suggestion put forward by certain scientists for a demonstration in a desert in New Mexico was ruled out before it reached the president. Nor was there a second decision for the bomb on Nagasaki, which was dropped as a result of automatic obedience to previous orders.
**As they had, with the British, for the occupation of Italy.

able to administer Germany jointly. And it was not until Britain, exhausted by its victory, withdrew from the burden of empire, that Truman, in March 1947, made a solemn declaration promising aid and succor to peoples threatened by Communist subversion or aggression. This fortunate decision did away at last with the illusion of a power struggle between Russia and Britain with the United States acting as arbiter. But the president's message distorted a necessary action—support for Greece and Turkey—with grandiose and therefore misleading rhetoric, and the anti-Communist crusade remained verbal. In Europe and even in the world as a whole, U.S. strategy remained defensive.

3. The Division of Germany and the Marshall Plan

More interesting in my view than the indictment of Truman is the accusation brought by certain authors against what they call the universalist idea entertained by the American presidents of that period: Why did they not simply accept the division of Europe into zones of influence, as Churchill seemed ready to do in October 1944? The Red Army brought the Soviet regime with it—but if Stalin used the same words as the westerners, he did not mean the same thing. By protesting Stalinist practices, the British and the Americans created a climate of hostility and provoked the Soviet Union, but they did not improve the lot of the peoples for whom they had entered into engagements they had no means of keeping. This situation raises three questions. Was their rejection of zones of influence a mistake in diplomacy that accidentally had disagreeable consequences for some people or for everyone? Or was it a moral or political misdeed, in the sense that the westerners refused to give the Soviets something to which they had a right? Assuming it was a question of one or the other, either a mistake or a misdeed, could the British and American leaders, given their ideas and the forces acting upon them, have avoided committing it?

Let us begin by using the language of the realists who, at least sometimes, resigned themselves to zones of influence—U.S. Secretary of War Henry Stimson in Washington and Churchill in London. The British and the Americans negotiated the Italian surrender themselves, granting the Soviet representative a place not on the Control Commission overseeing the armistice but only on the Inter-Allied Consultative Council, which had no effective role. The Soviets did not intervene on behalf of the Greek Communists when the British fought against them; they did not even protest. Why not let the Soviets behave in their own way inside the countries belonging geographically to their security zone, that is, their zone of responsibility and influence? Did the British and the Americans condemn the Communist behavior there? Certainly they did, but in terms of their own system of historical thought, the Soviets condemned the maintenance or restoration of the capitalist system in the West. The Soviets, on the one hand, and the British and the Americans, on the other, all acted in the same way in their respective zones: They set up regimes similar to their own with methods and men different from those of the other side. Symmetry, in a context of realist diplomacy, was to be achieved by means of heterogeneous policies. The trouble, according to this interpretation, is that Roosevelt, a universalist at least when it concerned others, and in regard to Europe, cherished the illusion that he had avoided the dividing up of the Old Continent. If that division had been expected and accepted in advance, however, it would not have made the West at once angry at having been duped and eager to embark on a new crusade.

This analysis makes the British and the Americans guilty of a mistake rather than a misdemeanor and derives from a philosophy that modulates from realism into cynicism. It regrets that the West did not drop political heterogeneity altogether and concentrate on geographical and political symmetry. The British and the Americans did not abolish the Communist parties in France and Italy, where they organized or caused to be organized genuinely free elections. In the East, in Czechoslovakia and Hungary, free elections did not produce a majority for the Communist Party.[2] But the latter, using what is known as the "salami tactic," gradually eliminated any people or parties suspected of being hostile to or critical of the New Order. If the ineffectual protests of the West were a mistake, could its leaders have avoided committing it? In other words, could they avert their eyes and betray their friends?

From 1946 on, the Americans took over from the British diplomats. And just as the latter had not regarded themselves as hypocrites when defending equilibrium or the liberty of the people in Europe while conquering an empire in Asia, the American diplomats had no sense of inconsistency when they protested against the Sovietization of Europe while remaining faithful to the Monroe Doctrine. This hypocrisy, if such it was, is typical of the policy of an insular power that aims to preserve the peoples of Europe from "universal monarchy" and that, because of its representative institutions, is an embodiment of liberalism. The Soviet armies brought with them poverty, despotism, and often, governments returning from abroad in railroad wagons. The revisionists of 1970 who compare Eastern Europe with the Caribbean (or even with the whole of Latin America) lack the realism in which they claim to believe: The Europeans who suffered under Sovietization did not think it was comparable to Yankee domination in a region that, in any case, they knew nothing about.

Absurdity reaches its height when the mistake of the protests is seen as a moral fault: According to this view, the United States is supposed to have refused the Soviet Union the legitimate fruits of victory, paid for so dearly by the Russian people—a refusal due to capitalism's irresistible tendency to expand. We shall return later to the overall problems regarding the economic and political objectives of Washington's diplomacy. But in 1945 or 1946, when Truman was calling for the Yalta agreement to be applied to the Polish government, and protesting against the gradual Sovietization of the countries in the East, he was acting in accordance with the feelings of Americans and Europeans alike, as well as following the traditional imperatives involved in the balance of power.

Only a dual transformation, of geopolitical perspective and of moral judgment, would have made it possible to overcome the contradiction between the realism of division and the heterogeneity of the regimes concerned and of their zones of influence. As the European system was replaced by a worldwide one, the impossibility of a continental balance took on a new significance. As soon as the Western Hemisphere became just as much a part of the international system as Europe, the lack of an intra-European equilibrium, lamentable as it might have been with regard to the autonomy of Europe itself, did not preclude another kind of balance—one based on the juxtaposition and coexistence of the Soviet Union, on the one hand, reinforced by the neighboring countries converted to its brand of socialism, and Western Europe and the United States, on the other. Because of the war, the Soviet Union had been able to extend its zone of influence to the middle of Europe, and this development made it inevitable that a bipolar system should emerge across Eurasia and Europe. At least, such a system did emerge as soon as the United States, abandoning the fiction that it could act as an arbiter between Moscow and London, and aware that Britain was growing weaker, agreed to assume the role that the latter no longer had the strength to play.

As for the ruthless methods of Sovietization, they arose partly out of the very nature of the Soviet regime. In the case of Poland, which was the main bone of contention between the British and the Soviets, the Polish government in exile in London obstinately refused to accept the Curzon Line; this position made things easier for Stalin, allowing him with some appearance of justification to create the Lublin Committee. His decision completed the elimination—begun by the Third Reich—of the ruling classes of the old Poland. Stalin knew that the latter, as well as the Polish people, were traditionally hostile both to Russia and to communism. The West, in giving the Kremlin the right to set up governments friendly to itself in the countries bordering on the USSR, in the hope that free elections would be held there, failed to appreciate how incompatible that right was with that hope. Free elections would not have produced governments friendly to Moscow (at least in the way Moscow understood friendship).

That said, even if we concede that the West made a mistake (which it probably could not avoid) in protesting the Soviets' behavior in the liberated countries, that still does not prove the realists' case: The Truman Doctrine on Greece and Turkey had been made known, and the final break between the Soviets and the American and British leaders did not take place until June 1947, when Molotov left the conference that had been called in Paris to discuss the Marshall Plan.

The Big Three had spent relatively little time discussing the future of Germany at the 1943 and 1945 conferences. In Tehran, Churchill and Roosevelt had talked of a possible dismembering of the Reich. Churchill favored the idea that Prussia should be separated off and bear the brunt of the punishment, whereas Roosevelt thought in terms of autonomous regions. At Yalta, the Big Three ratified without discussion the occupation zones proposed by the European Commission based in London. The French zone was taken from the two main Western zones. As for breaking up the Reich, Stalin reminded the other two leaders of what had been said in Tehran, and Roosevelt suggested the problem should be examined in London by a committee made up of the American and Russian ambassadors, with Eden in the chair. The question of breaking up Germany disappeared from the agenda when just after the victory, without consulting anyone, Stalin announced that the Soviet Union had no intention of destroying Germany.*

Unlike the Polish question, the German question did not become a subject of discord between the Allies until after the end of the war. In the last analysis, the British and the Americans accepted both the new frontiers of Poland and its Communist regime. But in Germany, the differences between the two zones, despite the diplomatic symmetry, caused endless quarrels: The Potsdam agreement gave supreme authority to a Control Council made up of the four commanders-in-chief, and the general principles laid down for the political and economic administration of Germany were open to contradictory interpretations.

After the failure of the Control Council conference in Moscow at the beginning of 1947, the West finally recognized the impossibility of arriving at a joint administration for the whole of Germany, and consequently the inevitability, for an indefinite period, of two separate entities, one consisting of the Soviet zone of occupation, and the other of the three Western zones. In fact, if we trace the sequence of events, what is surprising is not the final impasse so much as the two years of hesitation before the unavoidable was accepted. The changes introduced in Eastern Europe—described as advances in socialism, agrarian reform, and nationalization of businesses—had been set in train by the authorities of the occupation as early as September 1945. In the autumn of the same year, the occupation authorities encouraged German socialists and Communists to join together in a single party—a merger characteristic of the Sovietization method used in the other countries of Eastern Europe. In Austria, the merger failed or was not attempted (which made me think, at the time, that the Soviets would end up leaving the country). Kurt Schumacher, who had emerged from the Nazi camps physically exhausted but with his will and moral force intact, headed those socialists who were opposed to any merger. It was he more than anyone else—certainly more than the Americans, who in 1945 scarcely knew what a "unified socialist party" was—who foiled the Communist attempt to take over the labor parties in Berlin and West Germany and saved social democracy in the FRG.

---

*According to Djilas, Stalin made this decision because he hoped to include the whole of Germany in his zone.

Meanwhile, the Russians were dismantling and transferring industrial plants and equipment. At Yalta a figure of $20 billion (of which $10 billion were to go to the Soviets) was considered, though not finally approved, by Roosevelt, despite objections from Churchill. At Potsdam it was agreed that each of the Allies would take its reparations from its own zone by dismantling surplus industrial equipment—the surplus being fixed in relation to an authorized limit on production. To supplement the Russians' share, the West handed over 25 percent of the equipment dismantled in its own zones, 15 percent of which was in exchange for food products from the Soviet zone. In the spring of the following year, the Control Council managed to agree on production levels that Germany was not to exceed. (For example, 25 percent of the 1938 output in the case of machine tools; 40 or 50 percent for industrial machines; and 7.5 million metric tons of steel.) Although the British and Americans had forgotten the Morgenthau Plan's "pastoralization" scheme (which Roosevelt had taken seriously to begin with but dropped on the recommendation of all his advisers), they were not yet entirely cured of their delusions (nor, of course, were the French). The Russians refused to give any information about the reparations they were exacting in their zone, nor did they send the promised food. In May 1946, General Lucius Clay halted deliveries of equipment to Russia until a common program of export and import had been drawn up for the whole of Germany. But this program never saw the light of day. The French representative on the Control Council vetoed the creation of a central administration for Germany as a whole. General de Gaulle stuck to his demand for "no more Reich, back to Germanys," favoring not a restoration of the old particularism with its various different components, but the creation of two new German states.

By the spring of 1947 there were already two distinct entities, and the competition between the Russians and the Americans had produced the speeches of Molotov (July 10, 1946) and U.S. Secretary of State James Byrnes (September 5, 1946). After the Soviet Union refused (at the Moscow conference in 1947) to accede to France's demands about the Saar, Georges Bidault agreed to add the French zone to the dual zone that the British and the Americans had already decided upon. How could the West, after its experience of the Sovietization of Eastern Europe, not resolve to preserve its own three zones, whatever happened, and to see that this part of Germany benefited from the work of reconstruction that U.S. aid was designed to accelerate?

At the time of the rupture—the beginning of July 1947, a few weeks before the creation of the Cominform—the West had already signed the peace treaties with the satellites: They had de facto accepted the Sovietization that had already been carried out in Poland, Romania, and Yugoslavia and was in train in Bulgaria and Hungary. The economic situation was worsening all over Western Europe. There was no prospect of an agreement on Germany, so much did the two parts of Germany differ from one another already, and so fearful were the British and the Americans of the infiltration and subversion tactics used by the Communists in their gradual appropriation of total power. The offer made by the Marshall Plan still strikes me now exactly as it did twenty-five years ago—as generous, enlightened, and efficient. As for the creation of the FRG in 1948, with hindsight, and either because or in spite of the documents that have been published since, I think it was justified: the best decision possible, not in itself but in the circumstances. To put it more clearly, after Russia's refusal to negotiate on the modalities of U.S. aid, the westerners (from then on, the expression is accurate, as the French now gave up playing a lone hand and joined in with the rest) had no choice: The economic recovery of non-Communist Europe, Germany included, was clearly and necessarily the first objective.

Did the Marshall Plan lead to the declaration of a Cold War, as revisionists of the para-Marxist, or populist, school maintain? The offer was addressed to the Soviet Union and the other countries in the East. Even today, historians wonder why Stalin, after hesitating for forty-eight hours and sending his foreign minister and a large delegation to Paris, decided to return an aggressive negative reply. For a few days, the press in the Eastern countries showed mixed reactions, as if they did not know what the master in the Kremlin required of them, as if he himself was hesitating between two approaches. In the end, he rejected this last chance of cooperating with the West. The Communist-led Czech ministers, who had declared themselves unanimously in favor of the U.S. secretary of state's proposal, now realized what their real position was and saw how narrow were the limits of their independence.

Why did Stalin, confounding the expectations of most of the State Department experts, not try to play along, even if only to paralyze the whole scheme? I am still inclined to go for a traditional explanation: that Russia's grip on Eastern Europe was still too recent and precarious for Stalin to risk keeping communications open between the West and the countries he aimed at forcibly incorporating into a different world.

According to the Marxist-Leninist system (which lay behind Stalinist thought), the United States looked to Europe first and foremost for outlets that would help it guard against overproduction and economic crisis.* In an official request for a loan of $6 billion, the Soviet aide-mémoire mentioned American politicians' references "concerning the desirability of receiving extensive large Soviet orders for the postwar and transition period." Stalin, deliberately bound by his own propaganda and ideology, had to denounce the U.S. attempt to camouflage its economic imperialism. Moreover, the Marshall offer confirmed the determination of the United States to have a presence in Europe—which, seen from Moscow, would limit the expansion of Stalinist "socialism" and, by creating another center of attraction, might make it necessary for the Kremlin to reinforce its own grip on power. It is of little consequence whether Stalin sincerely suspected that there were aggressive intentions behind the Marshall Plan or even whether, objectively speaking, the reconstruction of Western Europe really did threaten the Soviet zone. Perhaps the distinction has no meaning for a Marxist-Leninist, whose enemies are always supposed to intend the consequences of their actions.

Perhaps the American president and secretary of state feared rather than hoped that Russia would accept the Marshall Plan. By then they no longer believed an entente with Moscow was possible on a joint administration of Germany. They wanted to put up a barrier against communism and save the peoples of Europe, the Germans included, from the temptations of despair. Dollars could undoubtedly be used as a weapon against communism, an instrument in the so-called policy of containment. It was an instrument that proved effective. A critic can scarcely call it mistaken, and so by what aberration can one manage to see it as wrong?

To arrive at such a gauche interpretation one need only substitute freedom of trade for freedom of humanity and identify it with capitalism and imperialism. Then, in the opinion of William A. Williams, for example, U.S. aid to economic recovery in Europe becomes part of dollar diplomacy, of the Open Door policy, and thus takes on the intrinsic perversity of a foreign policy directed primarily toward expansion of trade. Even in the

---

*At Yalta, Molotov told Harriman that the Soviet Union would be glad to accept credits to help the United States avoid a crisis.

context of such a reading of history, it strikes me as bizarre to condemn on moral or political grounds the unilateral transfer of billions of dollars from the United States to the countries of Europe. Even supposing that because of its own poverty and the hostility it ascribed to the leaders of the capitalist countries, the Soviet Union in 1947 was obliged to react to the Marshall offer by cutting itself off from the West, that does not mean Truman and Marshall made a mistake or did anything wrong when they caused the Kremlin to make such a passionate reply. In the context of our hypothesis, Stalin's reply was just a price that had to be paid. Since the alternative might have entailed the risk of Stalinism stretching as far as the Atlantic, the vast majority of Europeans persist in thinking the price was not too high.

One last argument remains. The form in which the U.S. offer was presented was the one least acceptable to the Soviets. It suggested a jointly established set of needs, together with multilateral relations between Europe as a whole and the United States, instead of bilateral relations between each country and the United States—the arrangement favored by the Kremlin. And were not the Russians bound to have qualms, given the reactions to their earlier requests for loans?

Negotiations between the United States and the Soviet Union concerning a loan for reconstruction—too complex to be described in detail here—began while the war was still in progress. Eugene V. Rostow, who as assistant to Dean Acheson (assistant secretary of state for economic affairs) was responsible for Lend-Lease in the State Department, has recently given some precise information about the first phase of the talks.*

At the end of 1943, Anastas Mikoyan raised the question of a postwar American loan with Averell Harriman, the American ambassador in Moscow. Harriman said he was in favor of such a loan and would pass on the Soviet request to Washington. Rostow thought section 3(c) of the Lend-Lease Act could be used as legal justification for a postwar loan for reconstruction. Under the Lend-Lease provisions, equipment necessary for reconstruction would have been ordered during the hostilities and transferred to

---

*In "The Revisionists," an article later reprinted in *Peace in the Balkans: The Future of American Foreign Policy* (New York: Simon and Schuster, 1972), chapter 4, Eugene V. Rostow highlighted the terms of the law founding Lend-Lease that made it possible to avoid the question of war debts and paved the way for the liberalization of commerce and trade—Bretton Woods, GATT, the Kennedy Round, and so on.

the beneficiary after the war. The Rostow plan was approved by the U.S. services and by the president, and long negotiations ensued concerning the text of a projected agreement with the Soviet Union. Then one day at the end of 1944, a Soviet representative came to see Acheson in the State Department and put an end to that first attempt at postwar cooperation between Russia and the United States. Rostow has concluded that the men in the Kremlin must have changed their minds over the course of the year, adding that the Marshall Plan nevertheless bore witness to the desire for cooperation and offered the Soviets a new opportunity.

A good deal of water had flowed under the bridges of the Vistula and the Spree in the meantime, however, and Soviet requests for loans and problems connected with Lend-Lease had given rise to friction and misunderstandings. Under Lend-Lease, goods and equipment worth $9.5 billion (29 percent of the Lend-Lease total) were sent to the Soviet Union.*

With the Russian army bearing the brunt of the war, Congress enthusiastically supported the dispatch of material to help the Soviets go on fighting for liberty. After the first Lend-Lease discussions regarding section 3(c) were dropped, the USSR made a formal request for a reconstruction loan of $6 billion at an interest rate of 2¼ percent. The answer from the United States was a long time coming. Meanwhile, a new protocol under section 3(c) had to be negotiated, and discussions hit a snag over an absurd quarrel about the interest rate. The Americans refused to go below 2⅜ percent, while the Soviets insisted on 2 percent, suggesting 2¼ percent for the proposed loan of $6 billion. Finally, the fourth protocol was signed in April 1945, but it related to war materials only; the rate of interest concerning industrial equipment was only settled—at 2⅜ percent—on October 13, 1945. Three-quarters of the material asked for by the Soviets (valued about $1 billion) was never delivered. As for the $6 billion loan, it was never the subject of serious negotiations.

The tension between the Soviet Union and the United States over the Polish government in the months after Yalta, followed by the disagreement about German reparations, did not encourage the Americans to be accom-

---

*The equipment included 14,700 planes, 7,000 tanks, 52,000 jeeps, 376,000 trucks, 11,000 wagons, 3.8 million tires, and 15 million boots.

modating or the Russians to persevere. Did the Marshall Plan come too late? Rostow thinks not, but I am inclined to think it came at a time when Stalin had already decided on a diplomacy that excluded even limited cooperation with the West. But on one essential point Rostow has the last word. If acceptance of an American loan meant that the United States would exercise economic domination over the Soviet Union, as some revisionists suggest, why should the United States be blamed for not granting a loan to a country that had suffered so much for the common victory?

4. The Futility of Revisionism

As I said at the beginning of this section, I cannot take the argument of revisionism tragically—I have difficulty even taking it seriously. But let us admit—for it does not present a problem in the context of a certain system of interpretation to do so—that there was a kind of symmetry between the Sovietization of Eastern Europe and the democratization of Western Europe (it can be done if we ignore the feelings of the people involved and the ways in which authority was exercised). *Could* the West have made its ineffectual protests with even more tact than it actually did? In fact, it soon resigned itself to the situation: The idea that Stalin might have been offended by anything Truman or Churchill said strikes me as farcical. At Potsdam, probably, and in any case after the treaties with the satellite countries were signed, Stalin had achieved his minimum objective: recognition of the governments he had put in place in Eastern Europe.

Did the Cold War begin between Yalta and Potsdam? Between Potsdam and the Truman Doctrine in March 1947? Or between Potsdam and the Paris conference in June that same year? There is no way to pinpoint the precise moment. Immediately after Yalta, in the part of Europe occupied by the Red Army, the Soviet authorities behaved without any concern for British and U.S. reactions. In particular, they began the Sovietization of East Germany with measures that made it inevitable for both the former Reich and Europe as a whole to be divided up. If the West had adopted a different diplomatic policy, might it have been able to win concessions from Stalin that would have allowed some degree of cooperation between the former Allies to be maintained? No one can give a definite answer. No one can be sure that Stalin had a predetermined plan setting out in detail the limits of the zone he wanted to have in his power. It is probable that some men in the Kremlin, including Stalin himself, were ready to come to an agreement on Germany provided that it gave Russia partial control over the German economy as a whole, with the hope of acquiring total control in due course. Between the great illusion of February 1945 and the break in July 1947, the tale unfolded as all power rivalries do—through action and reaction, challenge and riposte.

What still seems to me likely, even today, is that in the period 1944–1945, Stalin attempted to ensure a Soviet zone of security, or what some have called an *imperium,* by installing in power, in the countries of Eastern Europe, regimes modeled on his own and men dependent upon himself. Might he have been satisfied merely with "friendly governments" in which Communists predominated, without going so far as complete subjugation? And does it make sense to speculate about such a "possibility"? Of course, no superior force *compelled* Stalin to use the ruthless methods that shocked and terrified the people of Western Europe. The first governments in Czechoslovakia and Hungary, one with a Communist president and the other with elections giving an absolute majority to the peasants' party, would no doubt have been friendly toward Moscow in their actions if not in their hearts. But I still do not see how Stalin could have been satisfied with such a half-measure.

Why should he have allowed neighboring peoples to enjoy better conditions than those he imposed on the Russian people themselves, a people who had emerged triumphant from the Great Patriotic War? That triumph had been dearly bought: Economic decline, mass poverty, and merciless despotism were the realities in the Soviet Union of 1945–1946. Could the Kremlin rely on anything but force to maintain its domination? Monopolistic power was the supreme and obsessional principle of Soviet practice: Was Stalin not bound to apply it to the whole of the zone he regarded as his own? Monopolistic power implied the elimination of men and parties who owed allegiance to Western values and regimes. The half-measure represented by the Czech government between 1945 and 1948 was revealed in the latter year as fundamentally unstable. Another round of free elections would have weakened the Communist Party. Could Moscow suffer such a humiliation without betraying itself and losing face? Stalinism was producing hostility to Russia even in places where such a feeling was not rooted in the past. Even if, as one British historian has said,* Stalin planned to combine a security zone with good relations with the West, the peoples involved made the two aims hard to reconcile. No wonder Stalin opted for the first.

There is no evidence that he even hesitated. As early as 1945 there were signs of a return to a hard line, to open hostility toward capitalism as such, with fascism and liberal democracy regarded as mere variants of the same horror. Jacques Duclos wrote an article inspired by that ideology in the *Cahiers du communisme* (Communist journal), while Molotov, in a speech at the opening session of the United Nations, accused the West of complicity with Hitler. Similarly, Stalin's program for economic growth, and in particular for the development of heavy industry, which he drew up and made public just after the end of the war, was presented as part of the struggle against the capitalist world, renewed after the digression of wartime cooperation.

The revisionists, by ascribing *causal* responsibility for the Cold War to the United States—in other words, by accusing it of being the first or the only side to take actions making it probable or inevitable—are themselves, once again, committing the national sin: subscribing to the myth of U.S. omnipotence. To suppose that by pursuing a different diplomatic policy Roosevelt or Truman might have been able to persuade Stalin to take a different attitude, and to explain Stalin's attitude in terms of what the American presidents said or did rather than in terms of Soviet interests and the Communists' way of thinking, is to ascribe to the United States an inordinate power. When the revisionists want to show that what happened was not mistaken, but wrong, they reverse the roles that the usual account of the Cold War attributed to the two protagonists.

Such a transmogrification can only have an ideological purpose. If a Marxist-Leninist equates the power of the Communist Party with "freedom," and the capitalist regime with evil, U.S. policy becomes guilty of having halted or limited the extension of "liberty" and having secured the survival of capitalism, and thus of evil, in part of Europe. This sort of play

---

*William Hardy McNeill, *America, Britain and Russia: Their Cooperation and Conflict, 1941–1946* (London: Oxford University Press, 1953), pp. 406–408, quoted by Martin F. Herz, *Beginnings of the Cold War* (Bloomington: University of Indiana Press, 1966), pp. 198–199.

on words is of no interest to anyone, not even genuine Marxist-Leninists, who would have admitted at the time, or who admit now at any rate, that they imposed their own regime on Eastern Europe, regardless of the wishes of the peoples concerned, and justified what they had done with a philosophy of history.

Between 1945 and 1947, American diplomats based what *they* did on two principles of legitimacy: first, free elections, and second, a resumption of the traditional role of the "offshore" power, naturally opposed to what Montesquieu called universal monarchy, or the unconditional domination by a single state of the continent of Europe. In the years 1946–1947, it seemed obvious, to anyone who saw international relations in traditional, if not eternal, terms, that it had become necessary to prevent the Soviet Union from filling the vacuum created by the demise of the Reich and by the exhaustion of the theoretically victorious older countries. To criticize U.S. policy in Europe on the grounds that they derived from the Open Door policy is, in the circumstances, laughable, even absurd. Of course non-Soviet Europe remains open to capital and trade: Even Europeans who now question the monetary and commercial system centered on the United States do not—unless they are Marxist-Leninists—regret that Europe has remained "open." The reversal of roles that sees the United States as aggressive because of its social system reflects the same oversimplification and arrogance as are exhibited by extremist views of the Cold War, whether American or Stalinist: All set themselves up as supreme judges of historical good and evil. At the time, Stalinism possessed enough monstrous features to excuse some of the excesses of Western propaganda. That said, the Vietnam War is not an excuse for returning to a black-and-white vision of history that substitutes one devil for another.

While the revisionists denounce the United States, reproaching it for faults of commission and omission that, in their view, may have annoyed Stalin and put an end to East-West cooperation, they neglect the role played by the Europeans themselves. Churchill first, then Ernest Bevin and the representatives of the other countries, begged American diplomats to intervene before it was too late. But U.S. attempts at agreement with the Russians were drawn out too long, in the opinion of the British. It was the behavior of the Soviets in the territories they occupied, and especially in Germany, that gradually led the Americans to take sides with the British and abandon the pretense that the United States was there to act as arbiter in the political rivalry between communism and the British Empire, between two wills to power. Similarly, it was at the request of the Europeans that the North Atlantic Treaty was signed; it was also at the request of the Europeans, as much as at the suggestion of the Americans, that the man who had led the crusade against the Third Reich returned to Europe as commander of the North Atlantic Treaty Organization. If, twenty years later, there is still a U.S. military "protectorate" in Europe, it is because the Europeans themselves asked for it.

The Cold War—if we agree to give this name to the breakup between the Allies, the frenzy of Communist and anti-Communist propaganda, the series of incidents that included the Berlin blockade, and the division of Europe into two zones with radically differing regimes dedicated not to a war to the death but to a Homeric duel—the Cold War, understood in this sense, strikes me as due to a historical dialectic that is probably stronger than the designs of any diplomats.

Let us assume that Stalin did not, as early as 1944, decide to revert to the ideology of two camps—one of peace and socialism and the other of imperialism and war—and to the "hard-line" policy both at home and abroad. Let us assume he expected to receive U.S. aid for reconstruction and hoped that cooperation with the West would last until the end of 1946 or the offer of the Marshall Plan. But the fact is that, inside the zone he occupied, he paid not the slightest attention to the West's inevitable and justified reactions to the liquidation of its friends. And yet, a historian might point out that he did not protest against Britain's policy in Greece, and that the French and Italian Communist parties observed the moderation called for by the doctrine covering zones of influence. This doctrine eventually became the parties' unspoken rule amid the verbal din of the Cold War.

There were three reasons why, even if they had wanted to, the Western leaders could not have remained indifferent to the way Europe was being divided up: the behavior of the Russians on the other side of the demarcation line; Germany; and uncertainty as to what limits, if any, the USSR would set to its own ambitions. Just after a war fought in the name of freedom, the British and the Americans could not willingly accept the Sovietization of Eastern Europe, and above all, the manner in which it was being carried out. Though they could not prevent Russia's excesses, protest was part and parcel of the battle of ideas and propaganda. And Soviet propaganda railed against both the Marshall Plan and the economic reconstruction of Western Europe as fiercely as if Stalin no longer felt bound by the terms of the secret agreement of October 1944.

Two final remarks. Need it be said, in the last analysis, that things could not have turned out differently? Basically, if what we are talking about is the breakup of the alliance and the division of Europe, I believe they ultimately could not have been avoided, though such an assertion can never really be proved. This conclusion does not mean that the fate of all the countries of Eastern Europe was fixed in advance. If Finland had yielded to panic or discouragement, how many historians would have said *that* was inevitable! Tito also showed that Stalin hesitated before having recourse to his armies and did not really get the better of those who were not afraid of him. Nor even now do I see the fate of Czechoslovakia as sealed in advance, in 1948 any more than in 1938 or 1968.

My last observation concerns the very idea of Cold War. The two sides opposing one another in Europe both naturally observed the rules of prudence. Truman chose the technically difficult feat of supplying 2 million Berliners by air rather than using the military to break a blockade that was never officially announced and that, according to the Soviets, was a necessity arising out of reparations. True, there were thunderous insults, there was the Stockholm campaign against the atomic bombs, and the Communist parties did their best to paralyze economic life in Western Europe, but whether Stalin was afraid of an "act of aggression" on the part of the United States (which I do not believe) or wanted to disguise his own real weakness beneath an assumed belligerence, the fact remains: The period of intense Cold War began in the spring of 1947 and coincided with the dividing up of Europe, not with the calling into question of that process. It was the Korean incident that gave the Cold War a military dimension and a worldwide application. Putting it very simply, the Cold War served to conceal the conversion of the United States from a universalist dream to the reality of zones of influence.

Without adopting the usual criticism of Roosevelt's strategy or subscribing to the fundamental argument of his defenders—that resistance to communism would not have been possible had American leaders not tried first by every possible means to bring the Soviet Union into the community of nations—it is still easier to understand than to admire Roosevelt's diplomacy vis-à-vis Stalin during the war years. The American president was not forced to insist on unconditional surrender, which symbolizes a way of thinking typical of a certain American tradition: First vanquish the enemy's armed forces, then sort out the political problems. As if the latter were not bound to present themselves differently according to the way the enemy was conquered.

The situation between the Big Three during the war was as if Stalin held all the best cards, whereas in fact the United States, far from the field of battle and with an industry functioning flat out for the first time since the Depression, was, as hostilities continued, acquiring an overwhelming superiority over Britain, which was entirely dependent on U.S. aid, and over the Soviet Union itself, which of all the Allies was the one making the greatest sacrifices for the so-called common cause. Admittedly, Roosevelt and Churchill may have feared a separate Russo-German peace; they had something of an inferiority complex because of the decisive part played in the battle by the Soviet Union. Stalin had tried, by the Russo-German pact of 1939, to divert Nazi aggression toward the West, but the rapid defeat of France had turned the situation upside down. Why should the Americans have felt guilty about what was due to Stalin's own miscalculation in signing the pact with Hitler in 1939?

Of the Big Three, it was Stalin who regularly got his way, because he knew what he wanted and how to get it. He traded concessions over the United Nations Charter for hard cash, territory, and satellite states. Roosevelt, though paralyzed and almost dying, undertook the long journey to the Crimea and seemed more anxious to appease the Russian despot than to support Churchill. Should we think there was a will to power hidden behind that mixture of pragmatism and idealism? Yes, but the belief that it was up to the United States to ensure peace still does not justify U.S. strategic and diplomatic policy in the years 1943–1945—unless we suppose that the American president accepted in advance that there was to be a Russo-American condominium based on agreed zones of influence. It is possible that Roosevelt had some thoughts of such a condominium, with the United States playing the major role. But I find it hard to believe he would have tolerated the way Stalin actually incorporated Eastern Europe into his zone of power. During the period that followed, American diplomacy gradually resigned itself to, or else resolved on, resistance or even hostility to the

Soviet Union. But apart from one occasion, the United States never managed to stop Stalin from doing as he pleased; it merely tried to put obstacles in his way. Adam B. Ulam* explained the Soviet withdrawal in Iran and the liquidation of the Soviet Republic of Azerbaijan as results of Churchill's speech at Fulton: Stalin was supposedly impressed by the clear affirmation of Anglo-American solidarity. It is possible, though the dates prove nothing. Stalin, confronted with Hitler, was frightened, and his behavior reflected his fears. Confronted with Roosevelt or Truman he was never frightened; not because he underestimated America's strength but because he scorned what he saw as a mixture of hypocrisy, weakness, and blindness. True, the Soviet Union had demobilized its forces to a greater extent than commentators admitted at the time, but the American boys had gone home, too, and in 1950 the strongest country in the world was hard put to it to vanquish a Soviet satellite. Would diplomatic pressure have been effective, in the absence of immediately available military force? I doubt it.

From 1947 on, American diplomacy gave itself a definite objective—and it was a defensive one. The American leaders now knew what they wanted, and they achieved their ends. Roosevelt had not seen the international situation in Stalin's terms. And Stalin tried to shape the world in accordance with his own system of thought. Truman accepted that the world was as Stalin saw it and wanted it. It was a conversion that marked the "finest hour" of American diplomacy in Europe. But it was too radical, for a few years later it led the United States to see international events not so much in their real complexity as in terms of the oversimplifications of Stalinist propaganda. Twenty years ago, critics reproached Roosevelt for failing to understand the Soviet regime. Now they blame his successor for extending to the world as a whole the containment policy that was necessary in Europe.

II

FROM ONE CRUSADE TO ANOTHER

On March 11, 1947, Truman addressed Congress and proclaimed to the world the doctrine that bears his name:

---

*Adam B. Ulam, *The Rivals: America and Russia Since World War II* (New York: Viking Press, 1971).

I believe that it must be the policy of the United States to support free peoples who are resisting attempted subjugation by armed minorities or by outside pressures.

I believe that we must assist free peoples to work out their own destinies in their own way.

I believe that our help should be primarily through economic and financial aid which is essential to economic stability and orderly political processes.

The message to Congress introduced a request for a credit of $250 million for Greece and $150 million for Turkey.

Stalin had not protested against British army intervention in Greece in 1944–1945, but in 1947, Bulgaria, Yugoslavia, and Albania, countries that were now socialist and linked to the Soviet Union, supported and supplied the Communist-led partisans fighting against the monarchical forces. By then Stalin no longer felt bound by the October 1944 agreement—unless in his view it did not impose passivity or reformism on the Communist parties. The agreement merely forbade him to intervene militarily in countries where the governments in power treated Communists as he himself treated liberals. He probably did not treat the Greek Communists, or their Yugoslav counterparts, as Tito's 1948 secession showed, with the unmitigated authoritarianism ascribed to him by Western statesmen and commentators at the time.

George Kennan, who is thought to have initiated the policy of containment, regretted not the declaration, reasonable enough in itself, that the United States would take over from Britain the job of sending aid to Greece and Turkey, but the style and rhetoric of its delivery. The liquidation of the socialist Republic of Azerbaijan had been managed much more discreetly. But it seems to me unwise to exaggerate the significance of the Truman Doctrine of March 1947. Turkey and Greece were part of Europe; the United States was playing the part of an offshore power in the place of a Britain exhausted by victory. The Americans were answering the call of the Europeans and replacing Britain at the latter's own request.

What was the great turning point, then? In Europe, it was the Marshall Plan. In the world as a whole, it was the Korean campaign, the consequences of which the younger generation of historians often fail to perceive. Before the Korean campaign, the U.S. defense budget amounted to around $15 billion. The American divisions in Japan and Germany were more like occupation forces than fighting units. It was the crossing of the 38th parallel by the North Korean army that unleashed a series of consequences, in Asia and Europe alike, that are still with us today and which lent the period from 1950 to 1972 some of its main features. It was from 1950 on that the Cold War took on a military aspect and a worldwide dimension; the United States, for the first time in its history, got used to maintaining a vast military apparatus in time of peace. It was North Korea, supported by the two great Communist powers, that imposed on the United States a limited war and a peace without victory. It was in Asia much more than in Europe that the American Republic took up the imperial burden that the Vietnam War and the revolt of public opinion now forces it to reduce.

1. The Korean Incident

Although most of the events that took place in June 1950 are known, certain points remain obscure (only the Kremlin archives could throw light on them). American diplomacy bears some responsibility* for North Korea's aggression: Dean Acheson's speech placing South Korea outside the U.S. line of defense[3] ran the risk of sending the wrong message to the Kremlin, or at least one that might be misinterpreted. The withdrawal of American troops, without any guarantee of a balance between the armies of the two Koreas, created a vacuum; the North Korean army could not resist the temptation to fill it. If this political responsibility is admitted, the president's decision comes under revisionist scrutiny: Without U.S. intervention, Korea might have been unified under a Communist regime. The republic that the United Nations recognized and in which it supervised the elections would have disappeared (North Korea refused to let UN representatives enter its territory), the victim of aggression in the most basic sense of the word. Such a spectacular defeat would have devalued the U.S. guarantee of protection and intensified the climate of fear. If we compare

---

*Responsibility in the causal sense: conduct that creates some probability of an unwished-for, but not inevitable, event. It is therefore an error.

the advantages and disadvantages of intervention and abstention, the scales still incline in the direction of intervention.

Nevertheless, the American leaders made mistakes in the conduct of the campaign, and perhaps in the interpretation of events and of their rival's intentions. At the beginning of January 1950, they contemplated recognizing the government of the People's Republic of China. The State Department had published an official report criticizing the weaknesses of Chiang Kai-shek's government and announcing that the United States was withdrawing its support from the party that had lost the civil war. The United States certainly surprised the Kremlin by fighting for Korea after having refused to fight for China. It probably surprised Mao Tse-tung when it reacted to the advance of the North Korean armies by deploying the Seventh Fleet between Formosa and the mainland. At the same time, Truman and his advisers decided to send a mission to Indochina to assess the needs of the French expeditionary corps and augment the aid they were already supplying. The diplomatic policy that was drawn up in forty-eight hours between June 25 and 27, 1950, seems to have been based on the hypothesis that the opposition would be a joint enterprise, led by Moscow, with the participation of the Peking regime. It was more or less true that, at the time, the various Communist parties all received the same directives from Moscow, and all followed them. The idea of a worldwide conspiracy, a web spun in Moscow and reaching out all over the globe, never came so close to reality as in the last years of Stalinism. But even in 1950 the image did not entirely coincide with the facts. Mao Tse-tung's negotiations in Moscow lasted several weeks. Ho Chi Minh, though loyal to Moscow, acted also and perhaps chiefly as a Vietnamese patriot; in 1946 he would not have turned down a temporary accord with France.

Whether or not officials in Washington believed there might be a general Communist offensive in Asia after the North Korean attack, they acted as if they did believe in it and embarked on a policy that led to the isolation of China, on the one hand, and to the prolongation of the first and the unleashing of the second Vietnam War, on the other. Together with the decisions made in June 1950, the turns taken by operations in the autumn of the same year form a chain of events indispensable to the understanding of American diplomacy over the next twenty years.

It is now considered unlikely that Mao Tse-tung encouraged the opening of the Korean campaign. Most of the Chinese army was concentrated against Taiwan; the Korean army had been reorganized by Soviet advisers and included officers and men who had fought under the banner of the hammer and sickle. Stalin and Mao Tse-tung, in Moscow, had probably discussed the Pyongyang initiative, but China's attitude until the American troops' advance on the Yalu River and its own frontier was cautious, to say the least. Stalin had ordered, or perhaps merely authorized, the North Korean adventure. (There were movements in support of unity on either side of the demarcation line.) Such an attack seemed to hold few dangers and, if successful, would deal a severe blow to American prestige.

Historians still discuss Stalin's calculations on the subject and the real reasons why, in January 1950, the Soviet representative withdrew from the United Nations,[4] though officially it was to protest the continued presence of the Chiang Kai-shek representative. Did the Soviets already wish to prevent what they claimed to want? Did they hope to allow the United States and the United Nations to save face after the North Korean victory? Commentary still goes no farther than hypotheses. But whatever the truth of the matter, the U.S. leadership asked Moscow to intervene with Pyongyang, and this seems to have reassured the Kremlin and let them allow the campaign to continue. After the Inchon landing and the destruction of the North Korean army, the American leaders, after some hesitation, decided to cross the 38th parallel and in their turn try to unify Korea by force of arms. They did not take seriously the warning Mao Tse-tung had sent them through K. M. Panikkar, the Indian ambassador in Peking, nor did General Douglas MacArthur heed the signal given by the first, limited intervention by Chinese "volunteers" at the beginning of October. When, at the end of November, MacArthur launched the great "end-the-war" offensive, the volunteers attacked, this time en masse, and cut to pieces the South Korean divisions holding the center. The Eighth Army had to make a hasty retreat.

Thus, the officials in Washington missed several opportunities to achieve some success. Perhaps they could have persuaded Stalin to get the North Koreans to fall back. By establishing the U.S. position in the narrow part of the peninsula north of Pyongyang, they might have averted the Chinese intervention and given South Korea a decisive advantage, as well as inflicting a resounding defeat on the Communist camp. Another opportunity presented itself in the spring of 1951, when the Soviets suggested armistice talks and the Americans suspended their offensive.

These errors in the conduct of the war (but who can avoid them?) are interesting insofar as they throw light not so much on American diplomacy itself as on the political system from which it derives. General MacArthur, without formally disobeying the orders of the president and his advisers, carried out a policy of his own, and by his declarations to the press and to members of Congress he also brought pressure to bear on Truman, his own boss. He assured the latter that the People's Republic would not intervene. He reacted with angry words to the intervention of the Chinese volunteers. In Washington, the secretary of state and the Joint Chiefs of Staff dared not categorically forbid the last offensive or order the precautions they thought desirable (for example, not to let American troops advance to the Yalu River).

That said, at no point did President Truman and his advisers contemplate the use of nuclear weapons, despite the legends saying that Clement Attlee dissuaded them from doing so; they did agree to a limited war and a peace without victory. Without General MacArthur's errors of judgment, they would probably have won a limited victory as early as the end of 1950. Because of this, the Korean War marked a break with the American tradition of demanding total victory and making a radical distinction between war and peace. It was in 1950 that the United States resigned itself to the European practice of maintaining a large permanent army in addition to its navy and air force. It was during the Korean campaign that it found, not without regrets and protests, that its formula—first destroy the enemy forces and achieve military victory, then sort things out politically—contradicted the demands of a relationship between political leadership and the military machine and the requirements of a diplomacy with worldwide responsibilities. But it was also the "Korean incident" that widened the setting of the rivalry between the two superpowers and precipitated both the formation of two military blocs in Europe and the quarantining of the People's Republic of China.

2. Rearmament

The Korean "incident"—though *"accident,"* the French word for it, is perhaps a more suitable term, because the decision, either taken or tolerated by Moscow, to launch the North Korean army across the demarcation line was probably not part of an overall plan—caused both the United States and Europe to rearm.

At the time, controversy raged between advocates and adversaries of European and especially German rearmament; the need for the United States to rearm to a certain extent was accepted without reservation by everyone. But it seems to me that in retrospect, all those concerned would admit that rearmament had neither the tragic effects foreseen by those who opposed it nor the benefits hoped for by some of its supporters.

Between 1945 and 1947 the U.S. Army had been demobilized as swiftly as it had been recruited. But the Korean "aggression," however interpreted, gave the United States its first, indispensable lessons in its new role. Peacetime diplomacy calls not only for potential resources but also for troops that can be available immediately. The pressure and menace implicit in ordinary communications between rival states become absurdly insufficient when the need arises for a formal declaration of war, and with it for swift mobilization.

Did the experts in "Kremlinology" overdramatize the Korean incident? Did they see it as a transition from the "by all means short of war" phase of the Cold War to a "war not excluded" phase? Not at all, as far as I can see. The president's advisers, at least those who were experts on the USSR, still thought Stalin feared war just as much as the United States did. But they recommended rearmament just the same, and for two reasons: They were uncertain about the meaning of what was happening, as well as about the intentions of the other parties involved; and in any case, the United States needed to get used to its role as a Great Power. Neither atomic bombs, which could not be used in a marginal conflict, nor the 100 million metric tons of steel yet to be transformed into shells and tanks, supplied American diplomacy with the simultaneously traditional and contemporary instruments that a super-state needed to have at its disposal.

What remains of the objections that were raised at the time? Some people said Stalin would not wait for the United States to muster its forces before he struck. This argument was not only refuted by history; it was also ill-founded. Immediately after the Communist attack on South Korea on June 25, 1950, the U.S. leadership turned to the Kremlin, not to blame it for the "aggression" but to ask the Soviets to use their good offices. So from the beginning, the United States accepted the fiction that Russia was neutral and might act as an arbiter. Yet again, there is nothing to suggest that during all those years Stalin feared anyone as much as he had feared Hitler. He hid his country's poverty from outsiders, pressed on ruthlessly with its economic reconstruction, and exploited every favorable occasion in Europe and Asia alike, pushing forward wherever he encountered no resistance. It seems to me that except on very rare occasions, American diplomacy did not inspire even respect in Stalin, let alone fear.

If rearmament had dangerous implications, they were domestic rather than external. Tocqueville's classical description* of democracy's alternation between indifference with regard to military matters and martial fury is no longer valid.

> I have shown how in the democratic nations, in times of peace, the military career was not much honored and not often adopted. This public disfavor weighs heavily on the spirit of the army. . . . When a long-drawn-out war at last snatches citizens from their peaceful labors and causes their small enterprises to fail, the same passions that make people prize peace so highly may be redirected toward arms. War, after destroying all other industries, becomes the one great industry, and toward it alone are turned from every quarter all the ardent and ambitious desires called into being by equality.

The Cold War has in a way created, in the United States, the modern equivalent of what Tocqueville thought inevitable in time of war—the concentration of popular passions on military matters—but with an important difference: It is war production rather than war itself that becomes the major industry. In the United States today, the existence of a vast fighting apparatus, permanently available, was bound to produce what President Eisenhower called the military-industrial complex.

Was it necessary for the European countries—in particular Germany—to rearm? Again, if the reason for or justification of rearmament was solely anticipation of a Soviet dash toward the Atlantic, we must conclude, with hindsight, that the West got the USSR's intentions wrong, and that its precautions were superfluous. Some people will say those precautions turned out to be superfluous precisely because they were taken. Although there

*Tocqueville, *De la démocratie*, vol. 2, book 3, chapters 22–25.

may be something in this view (what would have happened if Stalin had lived a few years longer?), I do not entirely accept it. Rearmament was necessary for a different reason. I myself would argue that the moral and economic recovery of Europe called for a climate of confidence and security, and such a climate in its turn called for a guarantee from the United States, in the form of the physical presence of American might. And how could that presence be assured except through an organization like NATO? Then how could Europe not have to contribute to the common defense? And how could the FRG be allowed to enjoy the economic advantage of not having to pay its share?

Those who opposed this diplomatic policy at the time will admit that it produced none of the predicted catastrophes. It does not seem to me that the two other policies that were possible, but not put to the test, have become more plausible with the passage of time. Western Europe could not have declared itself neutral and nonaligned without demonstrating a determination and a lucidity that it lacked in 1950 and has not acquired since. A Western Europe such as Kennan described, without either nuclear or traditional means of defense, but confident that its peoples would resist if it were invaded, did not exist in 1950. And even today, more than twenty years after General Eisenhower became the first commander-in-chief of NATO, the European diplomatic policy of the Truman administration between 1947 and 1952 still strikes me as correct, in the sense that it was the best way of achieving the desired end. That end was to reduce the risk of war to a minimum, to promote the recovery of Western Europe in an atmosphere of security, and to pave the way for former enemies to be reconciled, to cooperate, and perhaps even to be united with one another.

One further remark, outside of all polemics. Those who lived through the postwar years have memories that the new generation of historians ought not to neglect. The image presented by the Stalinist regime in the despot's last years was truly horrific. Anti-Stalinists, at least in France, tended to be all the more passionate in their opposition because of the extraordinary blindness manifested by their adversaries and some of their friends. Some of the philosophers of liberty were prepared to go part of the way with a regime in which the only freedom left was the freedom to elect by plebiscite; some humanitarians lauded the goodness of the "Father" of his people despite the purges and the cruelties that, to anyone of sound mind, were a proven fact. True, there was no necessary link connecting

Stalin's alternations between tension and détente at home and the techniques of his foreign policy. Experts knew this and said as much; nonexperts
did not always refuse to admit it. But such analyses were not enough to re-
move entirely the sense of danger and unpredictability created by the terror
emanating from Stalin himself.* Of course, rationally speaking, the West in
general, and the United States in particular, was wrong to reply to Moscow's
frenzied propaganda with language proper to a crusade. Apart from the fact
that Americans have a propensity for that kind of language, the excesses of
one side almost inevitably called forth the excesses of the other. And how
could anyone answer Marxist-Leninist invective and accusations of biological warfare with sensible phrases about the need for the Great Powers to get
along with one another?

But there is another, more important, criticism. The Marshall Plan, the
Atlantic Alliance, NATO—yes, all were well and good, until 1953. Then,
after Stalin's death, politicians and the man in the street alike sensed—correctly, in my opinion—a sudden change. In the course of a few weeks,
Stalin's successors produced numerous symbolic gestures of goodwill. They
halted the propaganda against the use of biological weapons by the United
States. They gave up their claim on the Turkish vilayets of Kars and Arda-
han, which Stalin had raised in his talks with Churchill in October 1944,
at the same time that he had asked for the Montreux agreements on the
straits of Bosporus to be revised. They agreed to the appointment of a new
secretary-general to the United Nations, a post that had been vacant since
the term of its first occupant, the Norwegian Trygve Lie, ended; the Soviets
had blamed him for the part played by the United Nations in the Korea
campaign. The incredibly severe verbal discipline that had been imposed
on activists and intellectuals in Eastern Europe, and that Western converts
to the new religion had imposed upon themselves, suddenly disappeared.
The chief was dead and the ice was melting. The word "thaw," which Ilya
Ehrenbourg used in the title of a book, symbolizes an aspect of what was
then contemporary reality, but even more an aspect of people's consciousness of it. Despite the thaw, American diplomacy in Europe continued as

---

*According to some Western experts, Stalin was preparing, before his death, to modify his
policy in the direction of détente. (Marshall D. Schulman, *Stalin's Foreign Policy Reap-
praised* [New York: Atheneum, 1965].) But according to other evidence and to what Djilas
was told, Stalin thought there would be a third and final war between the two camps.

before. There was a vague gesture toward negotiation with Moscow to prevent the rearming of West Germany; then came the definitive formation of two military blocs, John Foster Dulles's threat of an "agonizing reappraisal," should the French assembly reject the plan for a European army, and finally, West Germany's inclusion in NATO and the creation of the Bundeswehr.

Once again, none of the disastrous consequences feared and foretold by the opponents of this policy happened. In reply, the Soviet Union canceled its treaties with France and Britain and formed the Warsaw Pact, an organization structurally resembling NATO and incorporating its own general staff. Neither the cancellation of the treaties, which had practically fallen into disuse, nor the official organizing of the armies of Eastern Europe under Soviet command made any significant change in the overall situation.

What can be criticized, however, is the rigidity of Dulles's diplomatic policy, with its virtual refusal to negotiate over German unity or anything else. It is true that in 1955 the Big Four met in Geneva, and the phrase "the spirit of Geneva" echoed around the world. But despite the thaw, and despite the détente, the period from 1953 to 1958 seems to me to be characterized in Europe by the crystallizing of the two blocs, and in Asia by the confrontation between China and the United States. The two symbolic crises—the 1956 crisis in Europe and the Middle East, and the 1958 crisis in Quemoy and Matsu in Asia[5]—brought to light the element of entente hidden beneath the exchange of invective between the two superpowers and at the same time revealed the tensions within each of the two camps.

3. The 1956 Crisis and the Defensive Nature of U.S. Strategy

Historians, excluded from the mysteries of the Kremlin, wonder what the chances were in 1953 of an East-West agreement for a unified and neutral Germany. Did Lavrenty Béria, as his enemies alleged afterward, contemplate sacrificing the GDR in the hope of a rapprochement with the West, or out of fear of the troubles that might arise after the death of Stalin? Although there are some signs of a desire for negotiations on Germany in 1953–1954, there is no proof that the USSR would have agreed to the concessions such a settlement would have entailed. Would Stalin's successors have accepted genuinely free elections in the "Democratic Republic," which might have meant losing face and undermining their whole *imperium?* Would the West have risked creating a federation in which the GDR kept its current regime and the Communist Party remained supreme? Once again, I find it hard to believe, even with hindsight.

But American diplomacy can nonetheless be faulted for having taken the partition both of Germany and of Europe for granted from 1948 on. Perhaps Dean Acheson hoped to attain a position of strength from which negotiations could be embarked upon under favorable conditions. But by the time the rearming of the FRG became a reality in 1955, the Soviet Union already had nuclear weapons, had exploded a thermonuclear bomb, and was approaching the levels of production in coal, steel, and electricity that Stalin had set as security thresholds* just after the war. The liberation policy never got any further than speeches and party "programs." Just after he was elected president, Eisenhower, to appease the Republicans who disapproved of Truman's conduct of the war, authorized Chiang Kai-shek to "reconquer" mainland China. That was not the kind of offensive likely to unleash the apocalypse.

As early as 1955 it was fairly plain that U.S. diplomatic policy in Europe was defensive. The verbal refusal of the United States to allow the partition of Germany, together with its nonrecognition of the GDR and the preservation of the Western sectors of Berlin, thinly disguised its resignation to the status quo. The best way to maintain the latter in reality was probably to reject it by word of mouth. At the time, what Europeans feared was not the caution and defensiveness of U.S. diplomatic policy in Europe but, on the contrary, the risk of rash decisions and reckless initiatives. Neither the French, the British, nor the Germans called attention to the double game the United States was playing, with its implicit acquiescence in partition, camouflaged by the propaganda battle. At the most, Churchill, in 1953, before suffering a stroke, sensed that negotiations with Moscow were in the offing.

It was after the two simultaneous crises of 1956, one in Central Europe and the other in the Middle East, that the Europeans became aware of their

---

*Cast iron: 50 million metric tons; steel: 60 million metric tons; coal: 500 million; oil: 60 million. These figures had been given in a preelection speech in February 1946. The figures for 1961 for the same four products were 50.9, 70.7, 510, and 166 million metric tons, respectively.

subjection to Big Brother and of the price that had to be paid for security owed to a country more powerful than their own. The Hungary-Suez phenomenon, reduced not to its essentials but rather to the Europeans' view of it, arose out of two inevitable but incompatible alignments: On the one hand, all the members of the Atlantic Alliance denounced the Red Army's suppression of the Hungarian revolution; on the other, the United States joined forces with the Soviet Union to mobilize the United Nations and world opinion against France and Britain. Western reaction over Hungary remained verbal and ineffective; U.S.-Soviet reaction over Suez achieved its objectives.

We shall not go over in detail the dealings between John Foster Dulles, on the one side, and Anthony Eden and French ministers Guy Mollet and Christian Pineau, on the other. I find it hard to believe that the U.S. secretary of state foresaw and desired the scenario by which the French and the British committed themselves to an escapade and he called them to order and taught them a lesson. I thought then and I think now that the Franco-British operation was doomed to failure and that it promised neither a more accommodating regime in Egypt nor an end to the uprising in Algeria. In any case, without U.S. approval, what was the use of trying to go back to old-fashioned gunboat diplomacy? Just the same, Dulles's behavior was inept, and worse still, exasperating. Trying to defuse the bomb, from the beginning he put forward suggestions in which he scarcely believed himself in the hope of gradually wearing down French and British indignation and finally arriving at a compromise. But why, when he knew of France and Britain's military preparations, did he let them think he would tolerate the use of military force against Egypt?

Once again, the language used by the American leaders made the crisis worse and invited an accusation of hypocrisy. "There should not be two laws, one for friends and the other for enemies," declared President Eisenhower, not even aware of his own black humor. For the law, if one may say so, did indeed apply to friends but spared the enemy, because all the United Nations did was proclaim it. President Eisenhower's now famous saying did not contradict American public opinion. I remember a conversation I had with a well-known judge in which he told me, some years later, how proud he had felt the day the president took a stand against the British and the French. It was a great day in American history, because the president put respect for international law before friendship and self-interest. To sacrifice self-interest to law was not, in 1953, "American." A European, made skeptical by centuries of history, was reminded of how the new state of Panama, created at the expense of Colombia, had granted the United States the privileges necessary for the building and the security of the Panama Canal.

The French interpreted the "dual crisis" in the light of the "dual hegemony." At the same moment, by an irony of history, each of the two superpowers was restoring "order" inside its own camp without the connivance but with the consent of the other. The countries of Eastern Europe were discovering the limits of the tolerance extended to de-Stalinization; France and Britain were seeing how far their independence went outside the area covered by the North Atlantic Treaty. It scarcely matters whether and to what extent the leaders in Washington and in the Kremlin were aware of how others saw the Soviet "victory" in Hungary and the "joint victory" of Russia and the United States in the Middle East. But the dual crisis left its mark on the European consciousness, perhaps above all in France. In Britain, it did not turn either the Conservatives or Labour against their country's close alliance with the United States, but it was a turning point that came to be seen as the end of an illusion, an awakening to the meaning of superpower protection. A country enjoying such protection could not claim freedom of military action abroad. The nuclear duopoly had not restored that freedom to medium powers that had formerly been great ones.

The events of October–November 1956 were spectacular. American diplomacy, through a mixture of clumsiness and moralism, humiliated countries that were its friends and allies; but basically the French and British governments were in the wrong. The Egyptians ran the Suez Canal, which was only closed to traffic as a result of Franco-British action in 1956 and Israeli action after 1967. By then, giant oil tankers had to travel around the Cape, and a major exploit of the nineteenth century no longer seemed a vital factor in world politics. The British had evacuated the Canal Zone only at the insistence of the United States, but their departure fitted naturally into their own policy. The loss of the Indian Empire had meant the loss of the Indian army, and at the end of the war they had admitted that decolonization was necessary in both senses of the word.

Dulles's ineptitude and hypocrisy do not excuse the errors of judgment committed in London and Paris. The British and French leaders had different objectives: The former were preoccupied by the Suez Canal, the latter by Algeria. They did not even know if they wanted to occupy the Canal Zone on a long-term basis or to withdraw after installing a new government in Cairo. Unless Nasser suddenly collapsed (and even then who could tell what would happen next?), they had no reason to expect support or even acquiescence from the United States. Moreover, the timing was bound to exasperate President Eisenhower: How could he fail to suspect the French and the British of relying on the U.S. elections to keep the United States neutral or inactive in the matter?

Like U.S. opposition to the Franco-British adventure, U.S. passivity in Europe seems, with hindsight, to have some justification. At the time of the Berlin blockade, President Truman had shrunk from sending in an armed convoy (as Aneurin Bevan, a British left-wing Labour minister, had suggested, among other things). Today, a historian could scarcely doubt that the Soviets would have let the convoy through and the blockade would have been broken in the course of a few hours.

In other words, in 1948, when the Cold War was at its worst, the American president, with the approval of the European governments, did nothing that would have involved the slightest risk of confrontation with the Soviet Union. Stalin had concealed his weakness behind such a façade of aggressivity that many Europeans, including General de Gaulle himself in 1950–1951, believed war was imminent; the American president never thought, either in 1948 or in 1956, that he could make the men in the Kremlin back down, despite the superior economic and military resources of the United States. In 1956, the United States possessed the means of destroying the USSR's main cities, whereas its own territory was still almost invulnerable. If President Eisenhower had sent even a symbolic detachment over the demarcation line, the European governments would have shaken in their boots and protested. They were more or less hostages of the situation because they were, or thought themselves, unable to defend themselves against the Red Army. By adopting a defensive strategy, the government in Washington recognized the "dual hegemony" but did not betray its Allies. It had used military force in Korea in reply to a military crossing of the demarcation line. It would have done the same thing had there been such a crossing of the line in Europe.

Can we or should we criticize that acceptance of a partitioned Europe? Retrospectively, we see that U.S. diplomatic policy from 1947 on combined effective action in terms of the zone-of-influence theory with universalist language. So criticism alternates between condemnation of deeds and condemnation of words. Should the United States have resigned itself, as far back as 1946, to the Sovietization of Eastern Europe, including one-third of Germany? Should it have spoken of holding the line in 1952, at the time of Eisenhower's election, when the Soviet Union had already set up regimes modeled on its own throughout the Soviet zone, and when "de-Sovietization" would have made the Soviet Union lose face?

Without giving a categorical answer to either question, we should remember that although the Europeans were victims of the partition, insofar as they would have liked to throw off the "dual hegemony," they approved of American defensive diplomacy and observance of the demarcation line. They never wanted the United States to take risks in order to try to "liberate" the Europeans living under a Soviet regime and subjected to the supreme authority of the Kremlin. As for "liberation propaganda," regrettable as it was for arousing false hopes in Eastern Europe, was it not intended to maintain Western claims to embody ordinary people's national aspirations, as against the Marxist-Leninists' pretensions that they were the ones who represented the future?

Leaving aside the immoderate language typical of Congress and of politicians in general, U.S. diplomatic policy, from late 1947 or the spring of 1948 on, was directed toward recovery in Western Europe, avoidance of military intervention on the other side of the Iron Curtain, and refusal to recognize, either morally or politically, the Sovietization of Eastern Europe, in particular of East Germany. The governments of Western Europe, on the whole, agreed in 1949–1950 that the United States should not take risks to "liberate" Eastern Europe; even General de Gaulle* concurred, though he wanted France to take a bigger and more independent part in its own defense. U.S. diplomatic policy, in fact, contained an element of "connivance" with the Soviet Union (military observance of the line of demarcation). It involved, in fact, what the Americans called "leadership" and General de Gaulle called "hegemony" (which originally meant leadership). The U.S. leadership achieved its objective in Europe because, it seems to

---

*Later on, General de Gaulle tried to lessen France's dependence in this respect through better relations with the Soviet Union and the countries of Eastern Europe.

me, they never relied on the Voice of America's trumpeting to bring down the walls.

Of course, both success and failure created problems. The international game never stopped. As soon as fear of Soviet aggression died down, the Europeans found it harder to bear U.S. hegemony and the partitioning of Europe that made it inevitable. As the Soviet Union proceeded with nuclear armament, the United States sought direct dialogue with Moscow; this effort irritated or frightened its European partners, who sometimes lost confidence in the efficacy of American deterrence or lost patience at the idea of an entente being arrived at over their heads. Before examining U.S. diplomatic policy after the success of containment, we must take up again the phase beginning with the Korea incident and deal with U.S. actions in Asia.

4. The Isolation of the People's Republic of China

As I have said, President Truman and his advisers feared that China might intervene when what were called United Nations troops crossed the 38th parallel. It is well known that both the Joint Chiefs of Staff* and Dean Acheson disapproved of the "end of the war offensive" toward the Yalu River and followed it with great anxiety. The Eighth Army's hasty retreat; the UN General Assembly's condemnation of the People's Republic of China for aggression; the Pan Mum-jon negotiations, which went on from 1951 to 1953; then the armistice along a line close to the 38th parallel; the continual support of France in Indochina; the defeat at Dien Bien Phu; and the Geneva conference—all these events marked stages in a crisis that began with a decision either made or simply tolerated by Moscow and that ended in an undeclared war between the United States and the People's Republic of China. At the United Nations, the Nationalist government, which had taken refuge in Taiwan, represented China. At the outbreak of the Korean War, the United States asked Japan to take up arms, though this very thing had been forbidden forever only a few years earlier. The United States made treaties of mutual assistance with the Philippines, Japan, South Korea,

---

*But the committee had also warned against the Inchon landing, which was a total success.

Taiwan, Australia, and New Zealand. After Dien Bien Phu, the Southeast Asia Treaty Organization (SEATO) was set up for the collective defense of the region.*

It is true that, despite the breakdown of diplomatic relations, communications continued: Every so often, an American ambassador would meet a Chinese representative in Warsaw; Americans and Peking Chinese** met in Geneva in 1954, and again in 1962 on the subject of Laos. But twice, in 1954 and 1958, when Chinese Republican troops shelled Quemoy and Matsu and were preparing to attack the outposts of Nationalist China, the Seventh Fleet was put on alert to defend the latter. In 1960, at the time of the Nixon-Kennedy election campaign, those two small islands, a few kilometers off mainland China, figured prominently in the first televised debate between two American presidential candidates.

It is not easy to follow the logic of this diplomacy. By supporting the Nationalist government, which had been defeated on the mainland, the United States was intervening in the last phase of a civil war that a few years earlier it had refused to become involved in (with reason, since it had not had the means to do so). True, geopolitics provided a partial explanation: Taiwan was one of a string of islands that provided the United States with naval bases. But the military argument was an explanation rather than a motive. In any case, even if in 1952 the People's Republic had acted as a satellite or ally of the Soviet Union, why should American politicians try to stir up passions about it among their constituents? Even if it was desirable to contain the expansion of Communist China or of Chinese communism, why not establish the same relations with the Asian as with the European enemy? In fact, McCarthyism and the China lobby paralyzed those responsible for U.S. strategy, who may also have been restricted by their own earlier decisions. Neither of the two Chinas would accept the other's existence, and having opted for Nationalist China in 1950, American diplomacy took twenty years to find the way back to Peking.

Did the men in the Kremlin between 1950 and 1953 want the war to continue, because it prevented any contact between the People's Republic of China and the United States? Did they think it was in their interests to

---

*SEATO was composed of the United States, France, Britain, Australia, New Zealand, the Philippines, Thailand, and Pakistan.
**Chou En-lai said John Foster Dulles refused to shake hands with him on that occasion.

go on monopolizing relations with the standard-bearer of "imperialism"?
Once again, we are watching a boxing match without knowing the tactics
of one of the combatants. If the Soviet leaders rejoiced then at the blindness of U.S. policy, they must now be aware of the difference between what
was aimed at and what was achieved. The immediate objective of the
United States ought to have been to dismantle the Communist bloc—not
in order to provoke a conflict between the Soviet Union and the People's
Republic of China, but in order to restore some flexibility to international
relationships so that countries that had been Sovietized could again enjoy
some measure of autonomy. This objective was not what the leaders in
Washington had in mind, but they nonetheless achieved it. In the coming
years, diplomacy was to produce even more "friction" than military operations. By standing firm in times of crisis in 1954 and 1958, the United
States helped to destroy the unity in the Marxist-Leninist camp.

There is no need to go over the various phases of the Sino-Soviet conflict. (A reconstruction based on press reports and articles in the two countries concerned has already been attempted, but it is necessarily based to a
certain extent on conjecture.) Let us just recall the established facts. Stalin
seems to have been saying what he really thought when he told Roosevelt
that Chiang Kai-shek would rule China for many years and that the time
for communism had not yet come. In any event, after Roosevelt offered
him inducements to enter the war against Japan, Stalin willingly negotiated
with Chiang Kai-shek's envoy, Soong Tze-ven, the Nationalist prime minister. True, the Soviet divisions, after penetrating into Manchuria, handed
over to Mao Tse-tung's armies the weapons they had taken from the Japanese, but according to Milovan Djilas, Stalin had to all intents and purposes advised the Communists to compromise with the Nationalists. In the
main, the party owed its victory to its own efforts, and not to foreign aid or
the help of Big Brother.

Mao Tse-tung, in the course of his visit to the USSR at the end of 1949
and the beginning of 1950, had to negotiate with Stalin over the handing
back of what the latter had been given by Roosevelt and Chiang Kai-shek.
Mao's China, having emerged from a period of troubles, at once made
known its national intention: In accordance with tradition from time im-
memorial, those who had won a mandate from Heaven and were restoring
unity to their country and strength to its central power were endeavoring to
get back what they had been obliged to concede in the days of its weakness.

Stalin seems to have needed some persuading before he agreed to the demands of the fraternal party's leader.

The Korean campaign produced a second bout of tension. At the time that North Korean troops crossed the 38th parallel, the main body of Communist China's troops were concentrated opposite Formosa, where, following a precedent set in the Ming dynasty, Chiang Kai-shek had found an ultimate refuge. Communist China's objective was apparently not Seoul, but Taiwan. Whatever part Peking may have played in the "aggression" of June 25, the American leaders were in danger of failing to distinguish between Peking and Moscow, and of holding the former at least partly responsible for what happened. Given all this, it does not take much—and certain commentators have rushed into the breach—to arrive at the hypothesis that Stalin intended what actually occurred: An insurmountable wall of misunderstanding and hatred built up between the People's Republic of China and the United States.

The "Chinese volunteers" fought in Korea from the end of 1950 to the spring of 1953, a few weeks after Stalin's death. Again, we do not know whether it was Stalin or Mao who rejected an armistice and insisted on the return to mainland China of all Chinese prisoners. The delegates of the People's Republic made the crucial concession soon after Stalin's death—which makes it at least probable that Stalin himself had previously dissuaded the Chinese from accepting the armistice. If his successors could manage to influence the fraternal party, all the more reason to believe that he could, too, since he was the leader of communism worldwide. Perhaps he was not displeased to see the U.S. Army mired in an interminable war, with the Soviet Union in the role of the *tertius gaudens,* the bystander who sells the weapons (to the Chinese) and sees the most of the game.

Certainly the regime in the People's Republic emerged from the three years of war stronger, on firmer footing, and even admired because it had stood up to the greatest economic and military power in the world, which was finally forced to concede a draw. And yet, China paid the price for this battle fought for the common good: Chiang Kai-shek survived in Taiwan, the Seventh Fleet made the Nationalist government's refuge impregnable, and the fury of American public opinion was directed against China even more than against the Soviet Union; the Chinese, not the Russians, had shed their blood. In North Korea, the Chinese had increased their influence at the Russians' expense; the gain, in prestige abroad and in authority at home, counterbalanced the material cost. Nonetheless, to parry the two dangers that threatened—direct confrontation between the Soviet Union and the United States, and the collapse of North Korea—the People's Republic had had, at the end of 1950, scarcely a year after the end of the civil war to embark on an adventure in which, while taking all the risks, it enjoyed only a fraction of the gains. By 1953, despite their Marxist-Leninist convictions, Mao Tse-tung and his comrades no longer regarded their Big Brother with unalloyed friendship.

In 1954, and especially in 1958, it was China's turn to try to attain a national objective; this goal was to drive Chiang Kai-shek's troops out of the offshore islands of Quemoy and Matsu. The United States ordered the Tachen Islands to be evacuated, and to compensate for this Eisenhower promised Chiang Kai-shek he would help him defend Quemoy and Matsu. The U.S. Senate authorized him to use military force for this purpose. After a few anxious weeks of alarming reports in the American press, during which military preparations were taking place in the Formosa Strait, calm returned. Perhaps, indeed probably, the Chinese leadership never really meant to try to conquer the islands by force; perhaps they were swayed by the Kremlin's counsels of caution.

The Chinese artillery started to shell Quemoy and Matsu during the night of August 22–23, 1958. The military crisis lasted several weeks. Eisenhower and Dulles had never formally promised to intervene militarily in the defense of Quemoy and Matsu (the Treaty of Mutual Assistance applied only to Formosa and the Pescadores Islands); nor had they said they would allow the two islands to be taken by force. Khrushchev, who was engaged in negotiations with the United States over the Middle East,* left for Peking on July 31, either to reassert his previous agreement to attend a Big Power conference aiming at a peaceful settlement, or because China, after a military conference lasting from May 26 to July 27, had issued a statement threatening to liberate Formosa. Details aside, subsequent public polemics suggest that the Chinese and the Russians criticized one another. The Chinese thought the Russians had refused to back them up; the Russians

---

*In Iraq, General Kassem had overthrown the pro-Western regime of the Hashemite monarchy in a coup d'état.

thought the Chinese wanted to drag them into an adventure on the pretext that the United States was only a "paper tiger." (To which the Russians replied, "With atomic teeth.") Once again, by standing firm, the American leaders had, instead of welding the Sino-Soviet alliance closer together, exposed its divergences, or, in Marxist-Leninist language, its "contradictions." These consisted mainly of Moscow's indifference to Peking's national interests and the difference of opinion in the two capitals as to the best strategy to adopt toward the United States. Not so much deliberately as by a logic not apparent at the time, U.S. diplomatic policy, by treating the two great Communist powers differently, aroused in them contrasting and incompatible reactions.

The break between the two capitals had many causes, but there can be no doubt that the atomic bomb was one of them. In 1957, the Soviet Union had signed a treaty with the People's Republic of China promising to help it develop its atomic program. But the Soviet Union went back on the deal in 1959, apparently after having, in 1958, asked for a kind of joint command similar to that which the USSR and the United States each operated in its own zone in Europe. In 1960, Moscow recalled its technicians and abandoned the 183 industrial projects already under way.

How are we to interpret U.S. Asian policy? Territorially, it may be compared with the policy of containment in Europe. The United States made alliances with all the offshore countries, including Taiwan, and with the small mainland states that had resulted from divisions between Communist and non-Communist regimes (as in Korea). But this similarity disguised an underlying difference. In Europe, the Western countries, after two or three years of receiving U.S. aid, again enjoyed stable governments and relative prosperity. Unless they were actually invaded by the Red Army, they had no need of outside help to resist Communist penetration. The role of the United States, both on the military and on the political plane, was limited to creating conditions in which the Europeans could live in peace and rebuild a system of cooperation and unity. In the Asian theater of operations, things were quite different.

By refusing to give Mao's China the place that Roosevelt had promised the China of Chiang Kai-shek, the United Nations during the Truman, Eisenhower, Kennedy, and Johnson years deprived itself of the universality about which many of its proponents had theorized. In Taiwan it maintained a regime that had been vanquished in mainland China, and it would allow neither itself nor the West in general to enter into normal relations with what the press called "a quarter of the human race."

Worse still, the United Nations seemed unconscious of the fact that a diplomacy superficially similar to containment policy in the West might call for quite different methods in the East. Since 1947, the non-Communist regimes of Western Europe had assumed the responsibility for containing their own Communists. The United States had hastened the recovery by means of the Marshall Plan and created a context of military security; the French and the Italians did the rest for themselves. But in the Philippines and Malaysia (or Malaya, as it was called until 1963), from the earliest years of the Cold War the authorities faced internal guerrilla warfare. In Malaysia, the British got the upper hand by isolating the Chinese partisans and granting independence to the moderate Nationalists. In the Philippines, too, the partisans were overpowered. But in Indochina, the more or less mechanical application of the containment policy led American diplomacy into a series of errors. When, after the death of Stalin, Eisenhower and Dulles obtained an armistice in Korea,* it did not occur to them to connect the solutions to the two wars. Judging from the course taken by the 1954 Geneva conference, it is at least plausible that Stalin's heirs, engaged in the battle of succession and still capable of leading the Marxist-Leninist bloc, would not have rejected a compromise comparable to that which followed the French defeat at Dien Bien Phu. In any case, why advise the French to carry on fighting in Indochina when they themselves settled for a draw in Korea?

The United States, after refusing to intervene militarily to save the French troops encircled at Dien Bien Phu, also refused to sign the Geneva Accords, while promising not to oppose their execution. A refusal to recognize the People's Republic of China, which the United Nations had pronounced guilty of aggression, was extended by a refusal to have ordinary relations with this new incarnation of evil.** Having for a long while doubted whether the Chinese Communists were real Communists at all, and after resigning itself between 1946 and 1949 to Mao Tse-tung's victory, American officials acted as if the People's Republic was now world enemy number one.

---

*It may be that the threat to use the atomic bomb—a threat said to have been conveyed by diplomatic means—also had some influence.

**In 1955, the People's Republic would not have refused to have normal relations. Chou En-lai made overtures at that time.

The experts seem never to have approved of this interpretation and attitude, but the "Chinese lobby," and the anti-Communist obsession, now directed against Peking, created an atmosphere in which, at the end of 1960, a candidate for the presidency of the United States still had to explain his intentions about Quemoy and Matsu. U.S. foreign relations derived from the passions of the American people, or rather, those of the active minorities who attributed their own feelings to everybody else.

Those passions were to a certain extent understandable. The United States had fought Japan to defend China and the integrality of the Empire of the Middle. Five years after its victory, General MacArthur, in a speech to Congress, suggested that China and Japan had changed places, and that China was now on the wrong side and Japan on the right. That countries are never entirely on either side, and that a change of regime might bring about a reversal of alliances—such commonplaces of European Machiavellianism, though intelligible enough to some diplomats, were apparently not yet acceptable to the people who claimed to reflect public opinion.

The period summarized above may be regarded either as the end of the Cold War or as an extension of it. Stalin's diplomacy, violent though it was in manner and in word, scarcely operated outside Europe. Responsible though it was for the aggression in Korea, it left to the Chinese the thankless task of fighting the American divisions in the field. Sales of arms to Egypt took place in 1955, and Nikolay Bulganin's and Nikita Khrushchev's travels reflect not only a different style but also different aims now extended to the world as a whole.

Moderate criticism of U.S. foreign policy, as frequently formulated by East Coast liberals, is based on arguments that have become traditional. According to this point of view, American diplomacy, bolstered by its successes in Europe, tried to use the same methods in Asia—economic aid and defense of lines of demarcation—arbitrary though these might have been. Unfortunately, economic aid that could help developed countries toward recovery was not suitable for helping underdeveloped countries toward modernization. The kind of intervention that was necessary in Korea, because regular armies had crossed the demarcation line, could not be justified when directed against infiltration by partisans, still less against a rebellion, even one supplied from abroad.

Before we accept this kind of criticism, which comes from Europeans as well as from liberal Americans who are naturally Europe-orientated, let us recall certain facts and the sequence of events. Because of its geographical position, the United States looks both to the East and to the West. It is a Pacific as well as an Atlantic power. Its war had been a war against Japan even more than a war against the Third Reich. Although it had taken over from Britain in assisting Greece and Turkey in March 1947, in June 1950 it took over from Japan in refusing to let Korea be unified under a hostile government.

In Washington, Dean Acheson pondered the intentions of the masters of the Kremlin and those of the Forbidden City alike. He did not rule out the possibility of another Soviet act of aggression. He considered it essential—and I think he was right—that the United States should prove the worth of its pledges by backing up words with deeds.

It was the mistakes MacArthur made in the conduct of the war, more than those made by officials in Washington, that ruled out the limited victory the United States might have enjoyed and forced it to be satisfied with a draw. But the chief consequence of those errors, the break with China, turned out in the end to be advantageous (considered on the level of realistic diplomacy). During the 1950s, observers almost unanimously blamed U.S. policy for its part in forging the Sino-Soviet alliance. American officials usually replied that the United States had no influence one way or the other on relations between Moscow and Peking. In fact, by an irony of history, U.S. policy probably contributed to the breakup of the Sino-Soviet alliance. And in 1971 President Nixon had an opportunity to profit by the rupture, and he used it.

In a way, the United States adopted the same attitude toward China over Quemoy and Matsu in 1958 as the Soviet Union had taken in 1956 over the Franco-British Suez adventure. By holding out against their adversary's partner, the Americans caused a split in the enemy camp: The Soviet Union did not want to fight just in defense of its ally's interests, nor to risk a confrontation with the United States. Similarly, when they were not moralizing, Washington officials told their French and British friends that they did not want to alienate the Third World in the defense of national interests not consonant with their own. The more the superpowers subordinated all other considerations to the desire not to clash with one another, the more resentful their allies became. The Atlantic Alliance withstood the strain; the Sino-Soviet alliance did not.

Let us now turn to the end of the Eisenhower-Dulles era. In 1960, there were fewer than a thousand American advisers in Vietnam. Commentators denounced Dulles's inflexibility and "pactomania," and especially the Eisenhower team's lack of dynamism. Americans had been stunned by the first Sputnik. By way of riposte, the government, the public services, and the universities embarked on vast projects designed to restore U.S. supremacy, which, according to the Democratic opposition, had been lost under Eisenhower. In November 1958, Khrushchev issued an ultimatum: Unless an agreement on Berlin was reached within six months, he would sign a peace treaty with East Germany, which would thenceforth be responsible for communications between West Germany and West Berlin. The deadline had already been put back or even forgotten, however, by the time Kennedy was elected. Meanwhile, the summit conference that was supposed to take place in Paris was abandoned because of the U2 incident, in which a U.S. spy plane was shot down over Soviet territory. What was worrying the Europeans, American public opinion, and officials in Washington was not Vietnam but Berlin, Quemoy and Matsu, and the alleged "missile gap." Looking back, we can say that the time bomb responsible for the 1960s explosion was already in place. In spite of everything, at the time of Dien Bien Phu, the president's caution, together with the objections of General Matthew Ridgeway and some leading senators, finally prevailed over those on the side of intervention, including Admiral Arthur Radford and Vice President Richard Nixon. Now, in 1972, the survivors of the Kennedy clan belong to the George McGovern team, which is more concerned about the moods of popular opinion than about its own consistency. Twelve years ago they wanted to rouse the sleeping giant; they succeeded in making him set out on the conquest of the moon, and they also bear some responsibility for the misfortunes of Gulliver, bogged down in the rice fields of Vietnam.

III

THE TARPEIAN ROCK[6]

Kennedy's arrival in the White House inaugurated American diplomacy's most dynamic period. It contained both failures, of which the most humiliating was obviously the Bay of Pigs fiasco, and successes, of which the second Cuban crisis was the most celebrated. As a whole, this period led up to the apparent world supremacy of the United States in 1963, which was followed by a spectacular fall and the tearing apart of American society over the Vietnam War. The words *apparent* and *spectacular* reflect the uncertainty inherent in our judgments. The known facts concerning these episodes in the rise and fall of the United States have not changed much between 1963 and 1972. But we are still too close to them to define their true significance. Dramatic as they are, they may not rate more than a few lines in accounts written by future historians—unless they turn out to symbolize the fate of the American Republic, which seemed unable to stop alternating between crusade and withdrawal and not fully conscious of the obligations that go with eminence.

1. Kennedy and the New Frontiers

In 1968, when Nixon was elected president, the survivors of the Kennedy team belonged to the camp of the "doves." In 1960, Kennedy himself had launched the "new frontiers" slogan. Eisenhower's America had seemed to wallow in bourgeois comfort, with a low growth rate, relatively high unemployment, and a moderate diplomatic policy. Dulles died in May 1959. Eisenhower received Khrushchev as a guest in the United States in September. In 1960, through the United Nations, the United States, which was opposed to the secession of Katanga, intervened to try to maintain the unity of the former Belgian Congo; it also rejected a suggestion that Berlin be made into a free city, but did not rule out negotiations.

Kennedy was what the Americans call a "doer"; he wanted to give the world a different image of the United States. He spoke the language of the Cold War, or at least of confrontation, as much as that of détente. He surrounded himself with academics from the Rand Corporation and Harvard University, who replaced the businessmen and lawyers who had predominated in the teams of advisers during Eisenhower's and even Truman's presidency. These professors and researchers worked out a philosophy more subtle than that of the admirals and generals. The overall aim of U.S. strategy did not change, but officials were now more aware of the different arenas in which U.S.-Soviet rivalry was played out. The rivalry was military, on both the traditional and the nuclear plane; it was also political and ideological, with results that depended on party struggles within the countries concerned. Rivalry by means of subversion and countersubversion had both military and politico-ideological aspects.

According to the evidence, Kennedy's advisers feared the contempt that service chiefs and CIA officials readily poured on these "eggheads" and intellectuals, alleged to be ignorant of the rough necessities of the international struggle for survival. They wanted to show that they were really "tough guys." This may have played some part in Kennedy's agreement to send Cuban refugees into the Bay of Pigs. At the last minute, having to choose between disaster and using the U.S. Navy and Air Force, the president chose disaster, thus bringing down on his own head blame for both unjustified aggression and inexcusable weakness. Would Eisenhower, who had authorized the preliminaries, have given the green light? The question cannot be answered with certainty. The establishment of a Marxist-Leninist regime in the Caribbean amounted to a rival intrusion in an area that American leaders had always regarded as their private preserve. The CIA-organized attempt to overthrow a revolutionary regime by means of its opponents was reminiscent not only of the earlier practice of the United States in Nicaragua and Panama but also of the subversion (or countersubversion) that had been successful in Iran and Guatemala. How intelligent men could have believed that such an attempt could succeed in Cuba, against Fidel Castro, is still a mystery to me.

So President Kennedy's advisers did not shrink from the sordid and clandestine aspects of power politics. Their own contribution, strangely enough, was made on the military level. They introduced into the Pentagon methods of reasoning that had been worked out under the name of nuclear strategy in the institutes and universities: the idea of a U.S.-Soviet agreement in the joint interests of the two superpowers, with the objective of reducing to a minimum the risks of a nuclear war that no one in his right mind could want.*

The so-called McNamara Doctrine[7]—which Robert McNamara himself may not have believed in—rested on a few simple ideas that I have explained elsewhere and shall only outline here.** Each thermonuclear bomb of a few megatons can destroy a city. The inevitable result is a disproportion

---

*They also introduced cost-efficiency methods into budgeting.
**Ibid.

between what is at stake in any inter-state conflict (and especially in one between the Soviet Union and the United States) and the cost of a nuclear war.* Therefore, the superpowers' first priority is, or should be, to avoid nuclear war. The belief that this common interest united them more than any divergence of interests divided them caused the Kennedy team to work tirelessly for an agreement with the Kremlin that would halt nuclear experiments, as a first step toward arms control. The agreement was not signed until the summer of 1963, after the Cuban Missile Crisis of the previous autumn.

Did the Soviet leaders, Khrushchev in particular, share this belief about nuclear war? In the early postwar years, when only the United States had nuclear weapons, Soviet propaganda operated along two lines: first, by pooh-poohing the atomic bomb, which according to Stalin would frighten only people with weak nerves, and second, by using the Stockholm appeal and popular action to promote moral revulsion against the enemy's use of the atom.

Later, when the Soviet Union exploded its own thermonuclear bomb, official language followed a line midway between disparagement and threat. The Soviet Union would inflict ruthless punishment on any aggressor. It had a nuclear arsenal second to none. The launch of the first Sputnik marked a new phase. In 1967 Mao Tse-tung launched the slogan, "The East Wind overcomes the West Wind." In 1960, at the time of the U2 affair, Khrushchev brandished his nuclear arms, apparently trying to terrify, if not the United States itself, then at least U.S. allies, by suggesting that they might be used. In order to arrive at an agreement symbolizing an "antiwar alliance," both superpowers would have to renounce the hope of exploiting to their own advantage the threat hanging over all mankind.

In the Soviet Union, discussions among Stalin's successors often centered on the subject of nuclear war. Georgy Malenkov had already suggested that the atomic bomb made it necessary to change the whole approach to the final struggle between the "imperialist" and the "peace" camp. Would a nuclear war destroy capitalism, or even annihilate civilization as a whole? Malenkov inclined toward the second answer. Khrushchev did the same a

---

*Applied to a total nuclear war, Alain's dictum is true: "None of the evils we try to avoid through war is as great an evil as war itself."

few years later in his talks with the Chinese. He invented a snappy aphorism: "Nuclear bombs do not distinguish between classes." American leaders probably did not need to convince their Soviet counterparts that both sides had the same attitude about the threat of nuclear war; neither side had ever doubted it. But it was necessary that both sides should see it as in their own interests to say so publicly. Until the end of 1962, Khrushchev must have at least realized that, if there were a confrontation between the two sides, fear and resistance to fear would be different in the two kinds of countries: those with governments subject to constant pressure from public opinion, and those where a few people secretly decided the fate of all. In other words, nuclear arms could always be made use of diplomatically. Did Khrushchev hope to make better use of them than his rival? Who would profit from fear of the atomic bomb? It seems that if American diplomats ever had any illusions about the efficacy of "atomic diplomacy," they lost them in the early 1960s. And they were afraid the Soviets might become deluded in their turn and put the whole world in peril.

Khrushchev's illusions can be explained by the words and behavior of the Americans—politicians, journalists, and servicemen. The Sputnik and the development of Soviet missiles from 1958 to 1960 gave rise to endless speculation about the thermonuclear balance of power. The United States asked its allies to allow it to base medium-range missiles in Europe; it did not have intercontinental ones yet. Turkey, Italy, and Britain agreed, but the last government of France's Fourth Republic refused. Kennedy campaigned on the theme of the "missile gap," the existence of which the experts in the Pentagon privately denied and which President Eisenhower did not take seriously. Strangely enough, the authorities either could not or would not dispose of this fear once and for all. Perhaps they thought the USSR had a production capacity it did not really possess, or at least that it did not make use of at the time.

Once in the White House, the Kennedy team dropped all mention of the missile gap, but it did embark on a huge crash program to manufacture intercontinental missiles (the Minuteman program*) and completed the program for producing 41 nuclear submarines, each armed with 16 Polaris missiles. Though, on the one hand, Kennedy's diplomatic policy aimed at dialogue, on

---

*This program included more than 1,000 rockets.

the other it aimed at being in a "position of strength" and at maintaining a superiority that, all things considered, had always been on the same side.

The arms program could not be dissociated from a nuclear-age conception of international affairs. Officially the initial doctrine of the U.S. Joint Chiefs of Staff, and that of the president himself, deserved its name: the doctrine of massive reprisals. The autonomy of the Strategic Air Command, made up at the time of B-36 long-range bombers, symbolized at once the difference between the supreme weapon and all the rest, and the basic theory of how it was to be used: all or nothing; apocalypse, or abstention from the use of atomic weapons.

During the 1950s, academics and researchers in specialized institutes pondered the lessons of the Korean campaign (the nuclear menace had neither deterred the North Koreans from aggression nor persuaded the Chinese to negotiate) and the consequences of mutual deterrence (which existed long before the rivals achieved equality).* These reflections led to technical developments and a reappraisal of doctrine.

For a long time the B-36s had been concentrated on a small number of airfields, and many of them had been damaged in a storm. Once the USSR had a strategic force, too, the United States had to find a way of keeping its own air power safe from attack. In the case of a nuclear duel, the methods to be used and the targets to be aimed at depended on whether one struck first or second. For the country that made the first strike, the enemy force, if vulnerable, was the logical target. If the enemy force was not vulnerable, the nuclear weapon could be used only against the enemy's goods, resources, and cities. To put it another way, the threat was that an initial act of nuclear aggression, which would likely aim at military targets, would be answered with a destruction of the aggressor's cities. Once the fiction of massive reprisals was ruled out, a choice was possible not only between targets (weaponry or cities) but also between different intensities of riposte. The technicians had gradually succeeded in miniaturizing nuclear weapons so that even the least powerful of the small ones was comparable in explosive force to the most powerful of conventional weapons. At this point it was easy for analysts to set out a variety of hypothetical situations in the case of a nuclear duel. They did

---

*Even when the United States exercised unilateral deterrence against the Soviet Union, a defenseless Western Europe acted as a hostage, allowing counter-deterrence.

so in terms of first-strike capacity (partial or total elimination of the enemy's nuclear weaponry); second-strike capacity (relative invulnerability of one's own nuclear weaponry, and thus the ability to inflict more or less unacceptable destruction on the enemy who had struck first); the variety of possible responses (conventional, tactical nuclear, strategic nuclear, and so on); the risk of escalation in the case of a limited conflict; and so on.

From all these studies, the president's advisers had drawn a few rational, but not compulsory, conclusions: (1) In the case of a nuclear duel in which both adversaries have a second-strike capacity, the threat of massive reprisals does not deter a minor act of aggression. No one would believe that the United States would reply to the entry of East German troops into Berlin by launching ballistic missiles against the cities of the Soviet Union, or even against those of East Germany itself. So, the analysts in Kennedy's entourage argued, what had to be done in Europe was to reinforce conventional weaponry so as not to be forced into the all-or-nothing alternative. (2) The implausibility of total nuclear war increased the likelihood, or at least decreased the improbability, of limited hostilities. To avoid escalation, "crisis management" should be in the hands of one country, with one team grouped around one leader—for example, the president of the United States. (3) Crisis management would be impossible if several countries in the coalition possessed their own nuclear weapons, especially if these were small, relatively vulnerable arms that could only be used against cities, or arms under a different command not answerable to the supreme head of the coalition.

This theory called for military preparations for three possible scenarios, each able to prevent recourse to a higher level of activity. The military had to be ready to react severally against subversion, against a limited conventional act of aggression, and against blackmail threatening a nuclear attack. The Kennedy team began by considerably widening this triple capacity. In retrospect, the cult of the assassinated president made people forget that aspect of his approach to military matters that was at least activist, if not actually militaristic. The slogan "Get America moving again" undoubtedly referred to the military program.

Though this attitude may seem clear enough, it led to some curious consequences. On the subject of Berlin, it aroused in the Kennedy team anxieties that now seem exaggerated. West Berlin was a prime example of a situation that was locally indefensible, and therefore safe—as long as only one of the superpowers unilaterally suspended its nuclear threat against the other—but in danger as soon as the party on the defensive lost its first-strike capacity. It was easy for an armchair strategist to show diagrammatically that the Soviet Union could always concentrate superior conventional forces in Berlin and that, since escalation to the use of nuclear weapons was ruled out, the West had lost in advance in this field of operations. The famous British military historian Basil H. Liddell Hart produced an argument of this kind. At the time of the Cuban Missile Crisis, Kennedy's entourage, on the basis of such reasoning, feared a Soviet riposte in the middle of Europe, where the USSR enjoyed conventional superiority.

By the end of 1962 or early in 1963, the United States had acquired a substantial margin of superiority over the Soviet Union, and the Kennedy team, aware of this fact, thought itself capable of conducting limited conventional hostilities (two wars) and an effective operation against subversion simultaneously.* The professed policy with regard to nuclear war created tensions with the European allies of the United States but served the Kennedy administration well in the Cuban crisis; Khrushchev gave Kennedy the opportunity to pull off a success and at the same time stand by the superpowers' explicit agreement to counter the risk of nuclear war by accident or through escalation. The same thirst for action induced the Kennedy administration to test the antisubversion technique in Laos and then in Vietnam. So the United States took one more step along the path to what became the tragedy of the Vietnam War.

Against Khrushchev, the McNamara Doctrine and the U.S. arsenal succeeded. Against the little men of Vo Nguyen Giap and partisans who carried their own weapons and their own supply of rice, they failed. Even in the nuclear age, man himself can still be the decisive factor in victory.

2. The McNamara Doctrine and General de Gaulle

By its implications rather than by deliberate intention, the McNamara Doctrine offered dialogue to the Soviet Union and imposed discipline on U.S. allies, at least in the matter of nuclear weapons.

---

*The official phrase was "two and a half wars": two simultaneous wars that were local but sizable in Asia and Europe, plus another war against subversion. Hence the policy of "flexible response."

In fact, the buildup of conventional arms worried the Germans, and the French were annoyed by criticism of small nuclear forces as "costly, inefficient, and dangerous." Who was wrong in the controversy over the probable effect of increasing conventional power? Everyone and no one. Logically, the American argument seemed more convincing to me at the time and seems so still: If the enemy is contemplating a limited aggression, the threat of a thermonuclear riposte will not deter him. In the abstract, everyone admits this. It is unwise to overdo what is called "the reasonableness of being unreasonable." Pretending you mean to "do something terrible" whenever you meet with the slightest gesture of hostility may often work, but a single failure is enough to cause a disaster or at least call your bluff. There is an element of bluff in any attempt to use the nuclear threat as a means of deterrence; the commentators were right to point out that you need to know what you are going to do if the other party declines to be deterred.

What was less evident than was claimed by the analysts and the U.S. presidential advisers was the application of this argument to Europe. What message did the reinforcement of NATO troops send to the men in the Kremlin? Did it make them think the West would not let itself be forced into the all-or-nothing alternative, but would acquire the means of meeting all threats at all levels? Or did the Soviets see it as proof that the United States, whose territory would not this time be spared the ravages of war, no longer guaranteed Western Europe the same protection as before? Did preparing for limited wars in Europe mean you made them more probable at the same time as you reduced the risk of escalation? Or did it mean you made them less probable because they did not necessarily lead to escalation?

I still refuse to choose dogmatically between the various arguments. Experience alone would make such a choice possible—and fortunately these differences of opinion have never been subjected to the only decisive test, that of events. The Europeans naturally leaned in one direction and the Americans in the other. A so-called limited war in Europe would not have had limited consequences for Western Germany: No part of the FRG would have been spared its ravages. A theory that seemed to increase the risk of local hostilities in order to reduce that of wars involving the two superpowers was in the interests of the United States, not of Europe. It provided a partial confirmation of General de Gaulle's hypothesis, which supposed that Europe was to serve as a field of battle while the Soviet Union and the United States became, so to speak, "safe havens."

Perhaps the heart of the controversy concerns the attitude toward the use of tactical atomic weapons. Both sides of the argument agreed that the simplest dividing line, the one that did most to facilitate an implicit entente between enemies, lay between conventional and atomic weapons. So long as atomic weapons, even those of small caliber, were not used, the intention of not going beyond the bounds, not crossing the threshold of the irreparable, was plain for all to see. But did this demonstration, assuming it lessened the risk of escalation, also lessen the force of deterrence through nuclear menace? Such questions brought to the fore the problem of priorities. Was the first objective to prevent through deterrence any kind of hostilities in Europe, or was it to minimize the probability of a resort to extremes?

Everyone agreed, finally, about generalities such as the importance of avoiding a choice between surrender and apocalypse; of not taking into account threats that were not really plausible; and of acquiring methods of riposte that were not out of proportion with the initial attack. But at what point should one take into account the danger of escalation arising automatically out of the use of tactical atomic weapons? Or, more precisely, at what point should one announce that one was going to create such a danger? The answer varies according to whether priority is given to the efficacy of deterrence or to precautions against escalation.

The argument of McNamara and his advisers against French atomic weapons had two disadvantages: It prevented nothing, and it increased mutual recriminations and general bad humor. It seems, according to objections made by the Chinese in later polemics, that the demands the Kremlin made on its Chinese allies were similar to those made by Washington on the Europeans: After promising to help China with its atomic program, the Soviets apparently had made their aid conditional on a single system of command, the equivalent of the central management of nuclear weaponry, which Robert McNamara considered the only acceptable arrangement. Walter Lippmann memorably likened it to the situation where, since everybody is in the same automobile on a dangerous road, the West must trust the driver to make the necessary decisions in moments of danger—the driver being the president of the United States.

It is not our business here to say whether General de Gaulle and the French government were right or wrong to devote a substantial part of the military budget to the production of atomic weapons and the means of delivering them (the Mirage IV, ballistic launching equipment on the ground or in nuclear submarines). In the current context of the Atlantic Alliance, one could say that a reinforcement of conventional weaponry would have increased joint security more than a nonintegrated force would have; though the latter might have resulted in a marginal increase in deterrence, the enemy would have been unable to predict its applications. The French government was looking to its own national interest, and the case of the United States was not so convincing that its representatives could lecture the French government and openly accuse it of irrationality or irresponsibility. To look beyond the situation that had prevailed from 1945 or 1949, did not the French government have the right to think of the security situation it would have to deal with after American troops were withdrawn from Europe? As for the deterrent power of a "small," relatively vulnerable and admittedly not very strong force, who could say it would be nonexistent? Insofar as nuclear deterrence is founded on fear, how could one admit its danger while denying its effectiveness?

President Kennedy admired General de Gaulle. He hoped his trip to Paris and his conversation with the French president would be followed by talks to work out the modalities of a cooperation between the United States and France similar to the one between Washington and London. Consciously, President Kennedy seems to have seen only advantages to putting an end to the "special relationship" with the British government, and even to making U.S. relations with Paris as similar as possible to those he entertained with London. But he did not succeed in this, and could not have done so, because in 1961 General de Gaulle, on the point of winding up the Algerian War, was critical of the Atlantic Alliance and advocated a policy based on a fundamentally different idea that was unacceptable to Kennedy. It derived from an aspiration formerly favored by some officials of the Fourth Republic but abandoned by them under the pressure of the Cold War.

What General de Gaulle wanted was an independent diplomacy. He did not wish France to be just one member among others of the Atlantic coalition, automatically supportive of U.S. policies. Arguments over nuclear strategy and the organization of the Atlantic Alliance were just a smoke screen to disguise this aim. The word "independence" kept cropping up in everything the French president wrote or said. In domestic affairs, France under the Fifth Republic had undergone a change since the time of the Fourth Republic; its government, with a surplus balance of payments, was now more sure of itself and of its future. This confidence allowed it to reject more easily any attempts at foreign interference. On the whole the French had managed their own affairs as they pleased between 1946 and 1958. After that, the Americans felt little need to supply anti-Communist parties and unions with moral and financial assistance.* Between 1947 and 1952 they had shown some hostility toward the RPF (Rassemblement du peuple français—French People's Rally), founded by General de Gaulle. But they played only a small part in the Gaullist Party's defeat in the 1951 elections.

In the matter of foreign policy, during the Fourth Republic it looked as if France would have to rely on the United States because of colonial wars and the foreign trade deficit. But until 1950, the French ministers' desire for aid in Indochina was outstripping the U.S. leadership's willingness to pursue the struggle. It was after 1950 and the Korean campaign that France's struggle in Indochina became a confirmed part of the general fight against Communist expansion. From 1950 to 1954, French ministers "depended" on the goodwill of the United States, but neither in Indochina nor in North Africa did they behave as if they were servants of the United States or representatives of a satellite state. More than once, Georges Bidault led or tried to lead the United States farther than it wanted to go (such as the request for them to intervene to save Dien Bien Phu). In the three countries of North Africa, none of the governments of the Fourth Republic did as Washington wanted; the administration of Pierre Mendès-France was an exception, though it, too, showed great concern about its own national sovereignty.

In granting Algeria independence, General de Gaulle was acting in accordance with Washington's wishes. He recognized the legitimacy of popular liberation movements in Asia and Africa. World War II, even more than the anticolonialist ideology of the Soviets and the Americans, had lent these movements a force that was all the more irresistible because the ex-colonial powers no longer believed in their mission, in their right to rule, or in the value of their former predominance. By his style, words, and manner, General de Gaulle gave Frenchmen and the world the impression that he and he alone was the decisionmaker, whereas the governments of the Fourth Republic had seemed subservient even while

---

*As they had done in the late 1940s.

objecting to the rearming of East Germany and the ratification of the European Defense Community.

In the long run—and for General de Gaulle this was the main point—France's diplomatic policy only became independent when it dissociated itself from that of the United States, and incidentally from the Atlantic Alliance. The latter applied only to a limited area. Every so often, the Gaullists emphasized this paradox and expressed a wish for the regional alliance to be expanded into a worldwide one. In a letter to General Eisenhower in 1958, General de Gaulle pretended to advocate a policy he really rejected: He proposed what has been called a "triumvirate," something he certainly did not want to obtain. NATO had been founded in 1950 at the request of the Europeans themselves, with the joint high command structure organized in such a way that French troops would not be under foreign orders in time of peace. The Atlantic high command wielded that sort of authority only in wartime. Nonetheless, General de Gaulle saw historical significance in the series of decisions by which he reduced France's participation in NATO. He finally rejected the very principle of central command, though France remained within the Atlantic Alliance. In a spectacular gesture, he requested the United States to evacuate their troops from their bases in France by a given date.

In fact, ordinary participation in NATO would not have prevented General de Gaulle from making any of his moves, going on any of his journeys, or taking up any of his positions. It would not have stopped him from allocating his military expenditures as he wished, or from setting up his own strategic force of deterrence. But independence, regarded as a good in itself, ruled out membership in an organization in which an ally typically took a leading role, and which undermined the traditional idea of sovereignty (the presence of foreign troops on national territory in time of peace), even granting that the terms of the alliance were freely negotiated.

If this analysis is correct—and I do not think sincere Gaullists would seriously challenge it—there was no way that President Kennedy could have changed the mind of someone he regarded as a hero of historical stature, glad and proud though he would have been to bring him back into the atomic fold. The Kennedy team, because of its determination to act, because of the persistence of the spirit of confrontation with the Soviet Union, and because of its strategic and nuclear policies, was bound to clash with General de Gaulle. The "grand design" of advocates of the new frontier contradicted that of the erstwhile leader of Free France. Washington's aim—an Atlantic community consisting of the United States and a Europe enlarged by the entry of Britain into its ranks—amounted, in the eyes of General de Gaulle, to increased subordination of Europe to the United States, and to the subordination of all European citizens to the Anglo-Saxons. Kennedy's diplomatic policy, reduced to its main principles, was a combination of the great Atlantic design and dialogue, especially nuclear dialogue, with the Soviet Union. And this approach was diametrically opposed to Gaullist diplomatic policy on two points: It deprived France of its freedom of maneuver, and so of the very essence of independence, and it contained the threat of another Yalta.

It is not a question of condemning either Kennedy's diplomatic policy or General de Gaulle's view: Some French people more or less agreed with the U.S. stance, and there were a few Gaullists in the United States. What concerns us here is the inevitable transformation of a most powerful ally into a leader, and the reaction of the protégé country to this new hegemonic pattern. It was difficult for most American officials to understand the Gaullist point of view, traditional though it was: The desire of a country to have a free hand and not be reduced to the role of a protégé has always been seen as the very essence of an independent diplomacy. However, at the end of 1962, President Kennedy renewed, to the advantage of British Prime Minister Harold Macmillan, the special relationship concerning nuclear matters that President Eisenhower very much regretted having granted. Then Kennedy was both surprised and shocked by de Gaulle's famous press conference in January 1963.[8] He could not see that the attempt to exclude France from the atomic club, or to include it conditionally (the incorporation of France's military forces into the Atlantic system) was bound to make the French president reject the British government's candidacy to join the Common Market. After the United States abandoned the Skybolt missile, it was in an entente with the American president where Macmillan sought an alternative solution that might in the coming years provide—or keep up the fiction of—a semi-autonomous nuclear force.

We should not forget what emerges from a detailed study of the period: the elements of bureaucratic confusion and improvisation in these diplomatic games. The U.S. secretary of defense gave up the Skybolt missile for reasons of cost and effectiveness, not to humiliate Britain or close the question of Anglo-American nuclear cooperation. According to his own tenets, President Kennedy should have stood firm and not have made the Polaris missile agreement. Still less should he have added an offer that seemed to put Britain and France on an equal footing, an arrangement both technically and politically unacceptable to General de Gaulle (technically because France would have had to make sudden changes to its nuclear program; politically because the Anglo-American formula seemed to involve incorporation into the U.S. system). At Nassau, Kennedy resigned himself to a decision prescribed not by his overall policy but by the desire, which came over him during his tête-à-tête conversations with Macmillan, to maintain a friendly atmosphere between the United States and Britain.

General de Gaulle backed Kennedy up unreservedly during both the Berlin crisis and the Cuban Missile Crisis.[*] The French president fully recognized the need for deterrence and containment of communism through the American exercise of power. It was the resulting equilibrium that allowed France to play its own game. As the United States was obliged, in its own interests, to maintain this balance, France did not have to pay for the security it was getting for free. To have joined the ranks of the "good Atlantic powers" would have been to sacrifice the political and moral advantages of going it alone and standing, in the eyes of the whole Third World, for nonalignment.

3. The Cuban Crisis and the Rise of American Influence

In July 1963 the Kennedy team must have felt triumphant. During their first two years they had encountered failure and disillusionment. In the Bay of Pigs fiasco they had lost face, but above all they had lost self-confidence. Since the interview in Vienna in which Khrushchev had tried, not without some success, to intimidate the young president, Kennedy had tried whenever possible—for example, in Laos and Vietnam—not so much to avenge the slight as to show his rival how firm he could be. He tried not to seem weak, unsure of himself, or unaware of his own power. But the negotiations on the suspension of nuclear tests, which had begun on October 31, 1958,

---

[*]Publicly he was hostile to Kennedy's move to negotiate with the Russians. As for France's position on what was to be done if there was a military crisis in Berlin, that was never officially known.

were getting nowhere. On August 29, 1961, the Soviets, without warning, resumed their tests. A few months later, the Americans, too, embarked on a new series of tests. It was not until October–November 1962 that the stationing of Soviet missiles in Cuba provided Kennedy with the opportunity for a spectacular success and allowed him to achieve the more closely held of his two diplomatic objectives. All things considered, dialogue with the Soviet Union mattered more to him than the Atlantic community did.

So many books have been written already about the Cuban Missile Crisis there seems no point in adding another account.* I shall confine myself to a few remarks that throw light on certain aspects of American diplomacy. In the atmosphere that prevailed in 1962, no president of the United States could have stood by and watched Cuba being turned into a Soviet nuclear base. The argument that a Soviet base in Cuba merely balanced U.S. bases in Turkey would have been indignantly rejected—justly, in terms of power politics (why not compare Cuba and Finland?), though

---

*The most recent book published on the Cuban crisis—Graham T. Allison, *Essence of Decision, Explaining the Cuban Missile Crisis* (Boston: Little, Brown, 1971)—should be read carefully by anyone interested in international relations. As well as making use of all the literature and adducing all the available information, Allison also pointed out the gaps in our documentation and the impossibility of knowing for certain what Khrushchev's intentions really were. Allison used three successive models of interpretation: first, that of the agent who uses various means with an end in view; then, that of the agent who calculates costs and benefits; and finally, to correct oversimplification, taking recourse to organization and political theory. What happened in the crisis in question cannot be wholly explained in terms of the thoughts and decisions of an individual agent, by definition assumed to be identified with a state.

A historian must also take into account the modes of perception and action of large organizations as well as differences of opinion between groups presenting the president with alternative courses of action.

Among the most striking conclusions and bits of information to be found in Allison's book are the following: (1) The stationing in Cuba of 48 MRBMs (medium-range ballistic missiles) and 24 IRBMs (intermediate-range ballistic missiles) doubled the first-strike capacity of the Soviet Union. And so, despite current opinion in Europe, and especially in France, the crisis had a military significance. (2) Although it is impossible to say with certainty how such a risky decision could have been made in Moscow, the beginning of an explanation is provided by the fact that the ballistic missiles were checked by a specialized section of the army. At this point, those responsible for the missile program had 750 medium- or intermediate-range missiles trained on European targets. But they had neglected to produce intercontinental missiles. So it was natural for them to think of using MRBMs and IRBMs to make up for U.S. superiority in intercontinental missiles. (3) The delay in informing President Kennedy of the presence of offensive weapons in Cuba also arose out of bureaucratic friction: It was decided not to order U2s to overfly the western

not in terms of international legality. In the special committee set up to advise the president on the various options, there were, as usual, some people (military men, in this case) who recommended the immediate bombing of Soviet bases. But once again the president opted for a moderate solution. During the talks he secretly promised to withdraw the missiles stationed in Turkey and not to attack Cuba (the latter portion of the promise fell through because it was conditioned on an inspection of the island, which Fidel Castro refused to allow). The Kennedy government felt it had followed the experts' advice: to impose its will on the adversary by sending messages backed up by acts—blockading Cuba, making military preparations on the mainland—showing that the words were to be taken seriously. Between nuclear states, threat of violence took the place of violence itself. Clausewitz wrote that war does not interrupt diplomatic dealings. In this case, the latter seemed to replace the former and almost to become its

---

part of the island between September 19 and October 4 because the land-air missile bases already observed made a military incident possible in which the apparatus of observation might be destroyed. Arguments between the CIA and the U.S. Air Force postponed U2 flights even longer, so that the decisive photographs were not taken until October 14 and did not arrive on the president's desk until October 16. (4) One of the reasons that the president was against a surprise air attack on the bases was that the pilots had refused to guarantee the destruction of *all* the missiles. They would only guarantee that they could wipe out 80 percent. (5) The Soviet decision to withdraw the missiles was made under the threat of imminent military action—in fact, as a result of an ultimatum that, though secret, undoubtedly existed.

It seems to me that doubt still exists on three points. (1) To what extent were the officials in Moscow aware of the risks they were taking? How far was an unflattering assessment of President Kennedy an element in their reckless policy? (2) As long as we have no further documentation, we shall be restricted to hypotheses on the intentions and motives of Khrushchev and the various services involved in his decisions. Was Soviet policy a riposte to the U.S. intercontinental missile program, or a testing of the Kennedy team? A move to protect Cuba, which the Soviets had never explicitly promised to defend against U.S. aggression, or an ostensible act of aggression undertaken with the real object of forcing negotiation? (3) Was the world really on the edge of the abyss, as the president and his advisers believed? Kennedy very nearly ordered an air attack on the bases: If he had done so, how would the men in the Kremlin have reacted?

I still think it very unlikely that the bombing of the bases would have unleashed a nuclear war: The circumstances in which the crisis took place were too unfavorable to the USSR. Of course, this theory cannot be proved. We should therefore note Allison's conclusion: We could be more certain that there would be no nuclear war if all states were more like the model of the rational agent. Several months before the crisis, President Kennedy had ordered the withdrawal of missiles from Turkey; they were still there when the crisis occurred.

equivalent—so long as your adversary believed you were physically and morally determined to use violence if it came to the point.

The policy of adequate response and escalation had not been designed for a situation such as the Cuban Missile Crisis. The American analysts were indeed apprehensive, either in theory or out of convention, of aggression coming from the other side. In their mind's eye, the United States was on the defensive, and they tried, in theory, to have available as many measures as possible that meant neither apocalypse nor passivity. The somewhat vague and ordinary idea of a gradual application of force proportionate to the situation nevertheless had some novelty in the United States. It contrasted with the national character as expressed toward the Indians and the Spaniards in the nineteenth century and in both world wars in the twentieth. It was this idea, however, that apparently inspired the strategy that led to the satisfactory and peaceful resolution of the Cuban crisis. It was probably this crisis that led Thomas Schelling to invent the notion of *compellence,* by way of a parallel to deterrence. In both cases the point is to impose one's will on the other party, in the case of deterrence, by dissuading him from doing something, and in the case of compellence, by making him do (or desist from doing) something. But in international relations the distinction between defensive and offensive actions is often blurred. Was the Cuba incident a case of compellence or of deterrence? If the missiles had already been operational, U.S. strategy would have counted as a counteroffensive designed to restore the status quo ante. If, as official accounts confirm, the installation of the missiles was not complete, U.S. strategy was more in the nature of deterrence, even though the operation it aimed at preventing had already begun. In any event, the United States enjoyed such advantages in the battle of wills that its success is self-explanatory; the only difficulty is how to identify the parts played by the various people involved. Did Khrushchev give in because of America's superiority in conventional weaponry in the Caribbean, or because of its overall nuclear superiority? What did Khrushchev really want? To deter the United States from attacking Cuba, to restore a nuclear balance that had been upset by American superiority in intercontinental missiles, or to force Kennedy into general negotiations on a modus vivendi in conditions favorable to the USSR?

Some points still remain obscure. No one knows whether the nuclear warheads were ever actually delivered to Cuba. The Western part of the island, in which the rockets were installed, was never overflown during the decisive period in October. Conflict between the services involved—the CIA and the U.S. Air Force—over how the different tasks were to be shared out is supposed to have put air operations back for several days. If the Americans received any intelligence from Colonel Oleg Penkovski,[9] who was subsequently shot, they must have known that the men in the Kremlin were not putting their strategic or any other forces on alert. So was armed conflict between the Soviet Union and the United States over Cuba really a possibility? Cuba meant something to the American people; to the people of the Soviet Union it meant nothing. It goes without saying that it is easy for a commentator who knows the outcome to discuss such matters dispassionately; such coolness is impossible for those in the thick of things, whose decisions may affect tens of millions of people. Nonetheless, the French,* and with a few exceptions Europeans in general, seem not to have shared the keen anxiety felt by the members of the Kennedy team and a large proportion of their fellow Americans.

Kennedy had won. But Khrushchev had not suffered any *material* loss. Had he lost face? By his account of the matter, he got what he wanted—America's promise not to attack Fidel Castro's Communist regime. The Chinese suspected Khrushchev had gotten what he wanted and accused him of "strategic capitulationism" and "tactical adventurism." World opinion, on the whole, concluded that the United States had brought off a success. The debate continues. Was the Cuban Missile Crisis an isolated incident, or a turning point in postwar history?

Khrushchev's diplomatic policy, unlike that of Stalin, was conducted on a worldwide scale. According to Fidel Castro, it was Khrushchev who suggested the stationing of ballistic missiles in Cuba, an offshore island near the coast of Florida. The American president had been advised by some of his military chiefs to order an immediate air attack on the Cuban bases: Had he done so, the Kremlin would have had to choose between nuclear war (the least likely scenario), a military riposte in the middle of Europe (dangerous and therefore improbable), and ineffectual protest. Soviet leaders took a huge risk that is still hard to understand even today. Work on the bases could not have gone unnoticed (U2s were overflying Cuba), and

---

*The French press, on the whole, was more favorable to U.S. strategy, as well as less anguished, than the British.

although Andrey Gromyko, the Soviet foreign minister, denied what President Kennedy already knew, Khrushchev could hardly delude himself. What did he think? That President Kennedy would tolerate the bases? I do not rule out this theory, because Khrushchev did not have much respect for Kennedy after the Bay of Pigs fiasco and the Vienna meeting. Perhaps the Soviet leader thought the missile bases would force the American president to negotiate about Berlin, and perhaps about other problems, too.

If we follow the sequence of events, what resulted from the crisis in October–November 1962, apart from the fall of Khrushchev (no one can say what part the Cuban failure played in his overthrow), was the final abandonment of the November 1958 ultimatum about West Berlin, and less than a year later, the signing of the Moscow Treaty partially suspending nuclear tests, followed four years later by the Non-Proliferation Treaty. So it was as if the confrontation between the two superpowers had made the leaders on both sides take measures (such as the telephone hotline) or make agreements (slowing down the arms race, such as the Non-Proliferation Treaty) symbolizing a joint resolve to eliminate as far as possible the danger of nuclear war—the first war in the history of mankind prepared for with the firm intention of never fighting it.

At the same time as the Missile Crisis, another event on the other side of the world indicated a new power alignment. In the Himalayas, Chinese troops inflicted a severe defeat on the Indian army, then halted of their own accord and a few weeks later freed their prisoners, whom they had indoctrinated while in captivity. The Soviet press took care not to support China's position openly. U.S. and Soviet diplomatic policy in Asia tended to converge on the subject of China.* At the least, the myth of a single Communist or Marxist-Leninist camp was becoming incompatible with the actual behavior of the two great countries, empires in the traditional sense of the word, which both claimed to be inspired by socialism.

By a second coincidence, the significance of which must have been clear to all observers, it was in July 1963, when the British and the Americans were in Moscow to sign the treaty partially suspending nuclear tests, that the two central committees of the Communist parties, of the Soviet

---

*In 1972, at the time of the Bangladesh War, the United States found itself on China's side against India, which was supported by the Soviet Union.

Union and of the People's Republic of China, published letters setting forth their ideological differences. So the West's quarantining of Mao's China had not prevented the breakup of the socialist camp; Western observers wondered whether the formulation of their quarrel concealed or revealed its causes. Did the Chinese object to the Soviet Union's collusion with the United States, the "capitalist" aspects of its regime, its abstention from revolutionary activism, and its "bourgeoisification"? Did the Soviets blame the Chinese for their adventurism, for the arrogance with which they tried to cut corners so as to arrive in one fell swoop at a higher form of society than socialism, and for their refusal to accept the unequal terms of the treaties that had fixed the borders between Russia and China? Did they suspect the Chinese of wanting to draw them into an armed confrontation with the United States? In 1972, after Nixon's visit to Peking, an observer is inclined to dismiss both sides equally: Each accuses the other of "colluding" with imperialism, which both, realistically, are bound to do in some circumstances and within certain limits.

This does not mean that differences over the strategy to be adopted toward the United States played no part in the gradual estrangement between the Russian and Chinese leaders. The latter never accepted the Kremlin's tutelage or slavishly imitated the Soviet model. The 1958 crisis over Quemoy and Matsu, the recall of Soviet technicians and the halting of Soviet aid in 1960, the 1963 agreement with the enemy against both the Chinese and the French—all these had made Mao, who in 1957 still talked of the wind from the East conquering the wind from the West, and was even ready to recognize Moscow's leading role, gradually come to hate Khrushchev and his successors. In fact, there was one more bone of contention between the two Great Powers that claimed to be inspired by the same ideology: Besides failing to agree over strategy, they also favored different interpretations of dogma. And as soon as they were no longer entirely at one over theory, it exacerbated the difference between their interests. Since 1917 the Bolsheviks had enjoyed a monopoly of revolutionary messianism, as well as unconditional power, at home in Russia. Under Stalin, they had tried to wield a similar sort of power over the countries of Eastern Europe. They were incapable of compromise either in their party, their empire, or their ideological bloc; that being so, quarrels became inevitable and insoluble. Russians and Chinese alike found they had more to fear from one another than from the faraway United States. Their two empires had a common frontier thousands of kilometers long, and the populations of the frontier provinces, neither Russian nor Chinese, offered a fertile field for subversion.

But my enemy's enemy is not always my friend. American diplomacy could not choose between the two Marxist-Leninist powers, both of them hostile to "imperialism" and to the values and political systems of the West. What still strikes one as surprising is that Washington did not change its attitude toward China or its strategy in Vietnam. The Vietnam War and the Cultural Revolution held back for nearly a decade an evolution heralded in July 1963 by the signature of a U.S.-Soviet treaty and the public trading of invectives between China and the USSR.

When Kennedy was assassinated and replaced by Lyndon B. Johnson in the White House, the United States was reaching the peak of its power and glory. Even sober observers said there was only one superpower now. In every field the United States enjoyed unquestionable supremacy. In the military sphere, it had at least five times more intercontinental missiles, stored in silos, than the Soviet Union. The Seventh Fleet in the Pacific and the Sixth Fleet in the Mediterranean made the Pax Americana rule the waves. Between 1961 and 1965, U.S. economic growth speeded up and the United States caught up with the USSR in the race to conquer space. After the challenge of Sputnik, science and technology leaped forward. Soviet-type authoritarian planning turned out to be less and less adapted to complex modern industry. Triumphant Russian forecasts based on comparative growth rates fell into disuse. Significantly, U.S. agricultural surpluses paralleled USSR requirements for agricultural imports, owing to low yields. The Soviets of socialism needed the American Midwest.

4. Bogged Down in Vietnam

In the twentieth century, the Tarpeian rock is still close to the Capitol. In 1972, President Nixon preaches modesty and a "low profile." Between rise and fall, supremacy and humiliation, one event stands out amongst all others: the Vietnam War, begun by the French army in December 1946 and taken over by the Americans in 1954 after the Geneva Accords.

The United States has lost its finest title—that of champion of the right of countries and individuals to self-determination. But it is not only abroad that its image has been damaged. Of the tens of thousands of young men, well-fed and over-equipped, who have fought for a year in the rice fields against men, women, and sometimes children whose thin bodies and reproachful looks constantly asked why they were there, how many have gone home cynical, rebellious, drugged, or at any rate disillusioned with the American dream in which they were brought up? Nothing has played a bigger part than Vietnam in the profound crisis the United States has been going through in the past few years.[*]

Whether or not historians find this judgment exaggerated, no one will doubt the effect of the Vietnam War on the American people. All, even the fiercest hawks, will admit that entering the war was a strategic and political mistake. To let communism spread over the whole region—Vietnam, Laos, Cambodia, and Thailand—would have been less costly[**] in every sense of the word, material and immaterial, than the containment of North Vietnam. The decision entailed, between 1965 and 1968, an expeditionary force of half a million men, and then their withdrawal, accompanied by intensified air bombardments. Two million metric tons of bombs were dropped on Germany during World War II; 1 million on Korea; and about 6 million on Indochina up to the end of 1971. A study published by professors at Cornell University in November 1971 reported that about half the annual tonnage of bombs was dropped on Laos (the Ho Chi Minh trail). According to the official Pentagon figures,[***] the tonnage amounted to 2,865,806 metric tons between 1966 and 1968 and 2,916,997 from 1969 to August 1971. In 1972 the tonnage amounted to more than 6 million, of which more than half was dropped after Nixon's arrival in the White House and the decision to "withdraw." Again, there is no need to point out the "mistake." Let us just ask how the inconceivable became a fact, in order to understand and analyze U.S. diplomatic policy.[****]

---

[*]André Fontaine, "Ce qui est mort au Vietnam: Fin d'un grand rêve" (What died in Vietnam: The end of a great dream), *Le Monde,* May 13 and May 14–15, 1972.

[**]At least to the United States: Some Vietnamese think otherwise.

[***]*New York Herald Tribune,* November 10, 1971, according to the same report.

[****]The *Pentagon Papers,* published by the *New York Times* in 1971, is an invaluable source. Reprinted in Neil Sheehan, ed., *The Pentagon Papers as Published by the New York Times* (New York: Quadrangle Books, 1971).

The first phase of the commitment arose out of the well-known conversion from anticolonialism to anticommunism in the United States. Roosevelt, who was hostile to French colonialism (which in his view treated Indochina like a milch-cow), laid down that the South should be occupied by the British and the North by the Chinese. The expeditionary corps, prepared with the final offensive against Japan in view, managed to restore French authority in the South, not without fighting but without a negotiated agreement with the nationalists. The latter made a treaty with the French in the North; both sides were eager to see the Chinese occupation troops leave. Ho Chi Minh* did not reject the idea of belonging to the French Union; General Leclerc de Hauteclocque, for his part, was against any attempt at reconquest by the expeditionary force. The Vietminh (League for the Independence of Vietnam), though led by Communists, acted as interlocutor.

The war began on December 19, 1946, at the instigation of Vo Nguyen Giap, after incidents (such as the bombing of Haiphong) for which the French were largely responsible. The objective then was not to contain the expansion of communism, but, at least in the eyes of the leaders in Paris, if not to maintain full French sovereignty then at least to find more accommodating interlocutors than Ho Chi Minh and the Vietminh. After unsuccessful discussions between the French government envoys and the leader of the Vietnamese resistance, the officials in Paris made the fateful decision to create three associate states—Laos, Cambodia, and Vietnam—and to make a treaty with Bao Dai, ex-emperor of Annam, to be head of the independent state of Vietnam. By then, June 1949, the Truman-Acheson team had already decided to support "the French 'presence' in the area as a guide and help to the three states in moving toward genuine independence within (for the present, at least) the French Union."** From this point on, first France, supported by the United States, and then the United States directly looked for non-Communist Vietnamese rulers to whom "genuine independence" might be granted.

---

*The *Pentagon Papers* tell us Ho Chi Minh wrote several times to President Truman asking for his help in the cause of his country's independence. The American president seems not to have replied.

**Dean Acheson, *Present at the Creation: My Years in the State Department* (New York: Norton, 1969), pp. 671–672. The French Union was the name given to the group formed by the French Republic and its associated overseas territories and states from 1946–1958.

The refusal to treat with the Vietminh, originally motivated by France's desire to save something of its empire, took on a different significance when the worldview arising out of the Cold War in Europe and North Asia was extended to Southeast Asia. Acheson and Bevin would have liked Bao Dai to be recognized by the Asian countries before they themselves decided to do so. They did not make the decision until February 7, 1950, in response to the recognition of the Vietminh by the Soviet Union. (Mao Tsetung, who had done the same, was on a visit to Moscow.) The Korean War was not the cause of U.S. engagement, but it did help to strengthen American resolve: The dispatch of a military mission was announced at the same time as the intervention in Korea and the defense of Taiwan. Between 1950 and 1954 (the Geneva conference), the United States took on an increasing proportion of the cost of the war (up to 80 percent of the total). The money came from the United States, the army from the French Union. But the officials in Paris and those in Washington were not fighting the same war. The former were primarily interested in keeping their empire intact, even in the modified form of the French Union; the latter thought only of containment and exerted constant pressure for the independence of the associate countries to be made complete.

Georges Bidault thought "withdrawal" in Asia would precipitate the same thing in Africa: The new imperial structure, the French Union, would not survive the collapse of even one of its props. This view became a self-fulfilling prophecy. The North Africans fighting in the French expeditionary force in Indochina learned both of France's weakness and of the strength of guerrilla warfare. As for the Americans, they were applying the policy of containment, and this ruled out negotiations with Ho Chi Minh. Talks had already been rejected with indignation and contempt by General de Gaulle in March 1949, even before the Korean campaign:

> The military situation in Indochina has gradually been allowed to deteriorate. But that situation is absolutely fundamental. I am well aware that some benighted souls claim, as they put it, to replace force with politics. But there can never be any politics, especially not any grand, magnanimous politics, if a country ceases to be strong. Some people advocate what they call the Ho Chi Minh solution in Indochina; in other words, and in actual fact, surrender, and after a few more or less long-drawn-out formalities, the destruction of all that France has achieved in

Indochina, and of Indochina itself, with all its liberties, its culture, and its traditions.*

So it is wrong to say that American diplomacy got involved in Indochina and then gradually got bogged down in it inadvertently—unless one is prepared to suggest that Truman and Acheson would have acted otherwise if they could have foreseen the long-term consequences, and that does not make sense. To start off with, around 1948–1949—at first hesitantly, so as not to clash with France, a necessary ally in Europe, but later with determination, to prevent a Communist-led Nationalist Party from coming to power—the United States wanted an independent, non-Communist Vietnam: The Bao Dai solution was the first one proposed. And in spite of everything, there is a connection between that early recourse to the ex-emperor of Annam and the 1969 Vietnamization. Did the United States, as André Fontaine has suggested, lose its finest title, that of champion of the rights of nations and individuals to self-determination? If so, it was France that set the example: General de Gaulle and General de Lattre de Tassigny, too, had justified resistance in Vietnam in terms of the "domino theory" (where would communism stop after it had conquered Indochina?), the balance of power, and the nature of the Communist regime itself.

From 1950 to 1954, American diplomacy, under Eisenhower and Dulles as under Truman and Acheson, stuck to the same line. The Americans were afraid the French might throw in the towel and did not encourage them to negotiate. Dulles** saw no contradiction between the Korean cease-fire and the pursuit of the war in Vietnam. He supported and financed the plan put forward by General Henri Navarre. After Dien Bien Phu, the French, forced to choose between sending in the draft and pulling out, opted for the latter. The American diplomats did not oppose the peace talks or the Geneva Accords,*** but they did not take part in them. On July

---

*Press conference, March 1949.
**The Pentagon records show the pressures the United States put on the French government to prevent them from giving up the struggle.
***Were the leaders of the Vietminh deprived of a total victory that was within their grasp, as is generally thought, or, as Khrushchev suggested in his memoirs, were they exhausted and pleasantly surprised to get as much as they did? I find the Khrushchev version unconvincing.

21, 1954, they took note of the cease-fire and undertook to observe its provisions but declared that the United States would regard any resumption of aggression that violated the accords with the utmost gravity, as a serious threat to international peace and security. In 1954, at the time of Dien Bien Phu, American leaders had to choose between two undesirables: preventing a Communist victory and avoiding another land war in Asia. They chose the second alternative. They could tolerate the Communist victory because the Vietminh* got only half the country, and American diplomacy once again showed its loyalty by transferring to the Republic of South Vietnam the financial and military aid hitherto given to the associate states via the French.

Before 1954, in the eyes of the Americans, the French, by clinging on to the last tatters of the imperial purple, were endangering the cause that the NATO governments had proclaimed as common to the whole free world. After that year, by supporting Ngo Dinh Diem,[10] then the series of generals who seized power, and finally President Nguyen Van Thieu,[11] were the Americans betraying for their own advantage the ideals they claimed to follow? Legally, they could justify themselves in terms of the Southeast Asia Treaty (1954).

Both the South Vietnamese and the Americans broke the Geneva Accords: the Saigon government under President Diem by pursuing the Communists, whereas the accords forbade reprisals; the Americans by carrying out acts of sabotage in Hanoi even before the Vietminh arrived, and by undertaking commando operations organized in the South. The *Pentagon Papers* show that the CIA continually engaged in clandestine activities against the People's Republic in the North.** The regime in the North, for its part, followed the current Communist model, which had little in common with the liberal principles embodied in the final declaration at Geneva.

Who started up the war again? According to the *Pentagon Papers*, the Vietminh had taken most of its officers and men with it to the North but

---

*Discussions on the possibility of intervention continued within the administration well after the fall of Dien Bien Phu. *Pentagon Papers*, pp. 10–12.

**Pentagon Papers*, pp. 54–99. Colonel Edward G. Lansdale (pp. 19–20) was in charge of the earliest operations in Hanoi, including an attempt to destroy a large printing press; publication of propaganda leaflets made to look as if they were issued by the Vietminh and designed to spread panic; contamination of gasoline to destroy the engines of trucks.

had left behind in the South a minimal organization capable of acting as the nucleus of a subversive movement. From 1954 until 1958, activists in the South were ordered to limit themselves to political methods. It was not so much North Vietnam as the repressive activities of the Diem government that made Communist officials and activists, threatened with being wiped out, decide to resume the armed struggle in 1956–1957. Still, as early as May 1959, at the 25th Congress of the Central Committee of the Lao Dong (Vietnamese Communist Party), a decision was made to supply* and direct the insurgent movement in the South until the two Vietnams were united. Instances of infiltration into the South, which had never entirely ceased, became more frequent. The 4th Congress of the Lao Dong in 1960 openly proclaimed in a resolution: "The immediate task of the revolution in the South is to overthrow the dictatorial clique in power in South Vietnam and to form a democratic and national coalition government there." The resolution was conveyed to party officials in instructions dated January 26, 1961: "In executing the decision of the 4th Congress of the Lao Dong, the National Liberation Front was formed in order to unify the revolutionary struggle, overthrow the American-Diem regime, and set up a popular democratic union government for the peaceful unification of the country. Without the leadership of the Lao Dong, the revolution for the liberation of the South can never succeed."

There can be no doubt that from 1958–1959 the leaders in the North played a decisive part in organizing and leading the subversion in the South. In a report of June 2, 1962, the Indian and Canadian members of the Control Commission denounced the violation of the Geneva Accords: "It has been proven that armed and nonarmed personnel, ammunition, and equipment have been sent from the north zone to the south zone." But the infiltration of these militants (natives of the South, in the first phase) would not have been enough to trigger off so swift and powerful a rebellion if part of the southern population had not been alienated by the methods of the Saigon government.** The number of officials, activists, and soldiers infiltrated rose from a few hundred in 1959 to 2,700 in 1960, and to more

---

*This decision was probably made after Le Duan, former political commissioner of the Vietminh forces in South Vietnam in 1951–1952, returned from a clandestine mission in the South.

**In 1955, in the course of the campaign against the Communists, between 50,000 and 100,000 people had been put in the camps.

than 6,000 in 1961; starting in 1965, it increased dramatically in response to the installation of the U.S. expeditionary corps. In short, neither the verdict of the 1956 elections nor even the persecution of the Communists* in the South (how was the Hanoi government treating dissidents or the peasant victims of agrarian reform?) are enough to justify political and moral condemnation of U.S. diplomatic policy. There are three main reasons why that policy came to seem more and more deplorable:

1. The way the war was being conducted, the disproportionate violence of the weaponry used, and the effect of the hostilities on those who were becoming victims, despite the fact that the official objective of the U.S. intervention was to defend them;
2. The role played by the Americans in the politics of a country they had undertaken to protect;
3. The disparity between American action and the language of the U.S. leadership, and between this ever-recurrent war and the new climate in international relations.

An army always resembles the country it comes from and of which it is an expression. The U.S. military machine has the power of the industry that produces it. Nowhere else in the world would soldiers have worn the armband supporting the antiwar movement, and yet not refused to go to the front. Of these two features of American society—technology and the individual right to dissent—the first was more visible than the second. The military machine, with its B-52s, its hundreds of helicopters, its artillery barrages, bombing raids, and defoliation, was crushing a people and disfiguring a landscape. According to official figures, 23,360 square kilometers were treated with defoliants before the end of 1970; 13 million metric tons of explosives—bombs and ammunition—had been used by the end of 1971. All these death-dealing weapons against a population of 17 million, most of them peasants! The disproportion of the means** disqualified an

---

*Of course, the persecution was absurd, and its effects were the opposite of those intended.
**The *Pentagon Papers* (p. 536) speak of "limited means" to achieve "exaggerated ends"; the American presidents never engaged all the means proposed by their advisers. Still, the end—a strong non-Communist regime in Saigon—turned out to be unattainable. I see no point in calling it "excessive"; it was not so in itself, only in relation to the situation.

end that was strategically as moderate as usual: to keep a non-Communist government in Saigon.

Rarely has the image of David and Goliath seemed so apt as for that long trial of strength between enormous machines and little men. Both sides committed atrocities. During the first phase of subversion, the Vietcong carried out a systematic campaign of assassination attacks against representatives of the Saigon government. When it occupied Hué in the course of the Têt campaign of 1968, it did not shrink from massacring local dignitaries and government officials alike; hundreds of them were found buried alive in common graves. American troops, too, were guilty of atrocities (the My Lai case was the subject of wide publicity). There had been a large number of such acts during the ten years it took to pacify the Philippines at the beginning of the twentieth century. There was no radio or television in those days, and in the eyes of those who bore the white man's burden, the "natives" were not yet quite human.

The strategy adopted exacerbated the inevitable effects of the American war machine. Between 1965 and 1968, General William C. Westmoreland, commander of the American forces in Vietnam, resorted mainly to two methods, which required a minimum of cooperation from the Vietnamese themselves*: One involved "punishing" North Vietnam in the hope of making the Hanoi leaders give up the fight; the other meant concentrating military effort in the sparsely populated regions just south of the 18th parallel so as to destroy as many North Vietnamese units as possible. Some military and civilian advisers, long before President Johnson agreed to it, considered bombing North Vietnam to "punish" it for helping the rebellion in the South. This thinking was nothing very new: The British had often used air raids against rebellious tribes in the Middle East. But in the context of the Cold War and revolutionary wars, and compared with the previous twenty years, it was an innovation because it broke the rules of the game that the French had agreed to abide by in Indochina and Algeria and that the Americans themselves might be said to have laid down in Korea. Tunisia and Morocco had offered Algerian partisans logistical bases that were attacked neither by French troops nor by French planes. President Truman had not agreed to the bombing of bases in Manchuria; nor

---

*And which kept American troops away from the most heavily populated areas.

had the Chinese hindered the traffic between Japan and Korea or bombed the airfields on the Japanese islands. So the American strategists were going back to the old method of "punishment"*—of attacking enemy territory as much to weaken morale as to destroy resources—common throughout history. (Take Thucydides, for example, who told how the Athenians and the Spartans, masters of sea and land, respectively, went every year and ravaged each other's lands.)

The American bombings did not break the spirit of the leaders or the people of North Vietnam any more than blanket bombing had crushed the German people in 1942–1945. The courage and ingenuity of the North Vietnamese won admiration from everyone, including the Americans. Life went on: Scattered, the factories, businesses, and institutions continued to function as before. Despite their rivalry, both the Soviet Union and the People's Republic of China increased their aid. If the bombings were supposed to stop infiltration to the South, the results were at best limited—too limited to have any decisive effect on the course of operations in the South.

The same formula of the progressive use of force, which, at the time of the Cuban Missile Crisis, had shown how political victory might be won at minimum human cost, led President Johnson and his advisers to make decisions that were both detestable and pointless. In Cuba, mere threat had been enough to make the enemy withdraw; in Vietnam, millions of tons of bombs only strengthened the determination of the North Vietnamese—as if to warn armchair analysts of the dangers of oversimplification. The notion of a duel between two nuclear powers applied more or less to the Cuban crisis, but not to the conflict between the United States and North Vietnam. Between giants, escalation is possible; it is not possible between a giant and a dwarf. Moreover, any man or any country may prefer death to surrender. American public opinion, preoccupied with technological arguments, discovered with admiring astonishment the mystery and greatness of human nature.**

---

* Thomas Schelling set out the theory of it in his book *Arms and Influences* (New Haven, Conn.: Yale University Press, 1966).
** Service intelligence reports had *all* predicted the bombing would not force North Vietnam to surrender. But only a few advisers believed them. Moreover, the services also said that bombing would not be materially effective unless it took the form of single massive attacks. Gradually increasing the pressure allowed North Vietnam to adapt to the raids.

While the bombers were "punishing" North Vietnam and armored divisions were harrying the troops infiltrated from the North, neither the government nor the army of the South was approaching the goal of being able to resist subversion on their own. Yet in the eyes of the world, and in their own eyes, the Americans were fighting to guarantee South Vietnam's right to choose its own destiny. Did South Vietnam really exist as a sovereign state? Who represented it? Who possessed legitimate power? Those parts of the Pentagon records that threw light on the part played by Ambassador Henry Cabot Lodge and the agents of the CIA in the overthrow of Diem startled readers unfamiliar with affairs of state and the language of officialdom. So the United States hatched conspiracies and installed politicians: True, unlike the French, they were not trying to save some imperial authority; no, they were actually exercising it. The more shaky and unpopular the South Vietnamese regime became and the less possible it was to win the war, the less it seemed justified. The French had abandoned Bao Dai before the Geneva conference and had given a chance to Diem, who, during the first few years, did better than even the most optimistic of observers had hoped. In 1963, the Americans gave the green light for a conspiracy among the generals. For several years there was a game of musical chairs, with generals and coups d'état succeeding one another. The political vacuum in Saigon did not mean that most South Vietnamese wanted to throw in their lot with the regime in the North, but it did undermine both the chances of victory and the political and moral bases of U.S. intervention.

The defense of Vietnam, started in the 1940s as a Cold War reflex, began, with the passage of time and the accumulation of horrors, to seem anachronistic and even monstrous. No longer was a Communist camp united under the rule of the Kremlin setting itself up in opposition to a free world united in the defense of Western values. Underneath the confrontation between the two superpowers and the balance of power on the nuclear plane, countries living under different regimes were forging new links and exchanging goods and civilities. Between 1963 and 1968, while hostilities were intensifying in Vietnam, Europe basked in a more peaceful climate favoring cooperation. The Missile Crisis at the end of 1962 had dealt Khrushchev's adventurism a mortal blow. With the Moscow Treaty of 1963 and the polemics between China and the Soviet Union, Washington and Moscow adopted a new kind of dialogue. Against whom was containment to be directed? Against communism, seen as an absolute evil? Against the imperialism of North Vietnam? Against Chinese expansionism, of which North Vietnam might be regarded as only an instrument?

From 1948 to 1968, U.S. diplomatic policy was once more extraordinarily consistent: It confined itself, though with determination, to preventing communism from spreading to new countries. Once North Vietnam was "lost," the South still had to be saved. But what were the arguments for this? The first, invented by the French and used by General de Lattre de Tassigny, was the domino theory.* Where would the flood stop if the first dam broke? At the Suez Canal? San Francisco? As late as 1963, Lyndon B. Johnson, just back from a visit to Saigon, declared: "We must decide whether to help these countries to the best of our ability or throw in the towel in the area and pull back our defense to San Francisco and a 'Fortress America' concept." The theory may seem absurd in such an extreme form, but it contains an element of truth—an element larger today than it was in 1954. The U.S. withdrawal and the collapse of the South Vietnamese regime would probably lead to a Communist victory in Laos and Cambodia, perhaps in Thailand, too. In 1972 the prime minister of Singapore apprehensively expected the advance of communism in Malaysia and in his own city, in the case of a U.S. withdrawal.

A second argument was a moral one, or at least arose out of the American philosophy of international relations: It had to do with the crossing of the demarcation line and the use of force to change the territorial status quo. Was it a civil war rather than a foreign one? The North Koreans, the Soviets, and the Chinese had also talked of civil war when Mr. Malik resumed his seat at the United Nations. Why should something be tolerated in Vietnam if it was not tolerated in Korea?

To counter the objection that containment was becoming meaningless in the context of the Sino-Soviet conflict, some of Kennedy's and Johnson's advisers, in particular Walt W. Rostow, worked out their own interpretation of contemporary history. The Chinese Lin Piao[12] and the North Vietnamese Ho Chi Minh were the last prophets of revolutionary romanticism; Vietnam was a crucial test of counterinsurgency; and the United States had finally deterred the advocates of the revolt of the country against the towns, the last to believe in the expansion of communism by force.

---

*Often encountered in the *Pentagon Papers*, used by officials in secret documents.

Whether or not, and to what extent, the presidents and their advisers really believed in these arguments or excuses, the war created its own logic. The importance of Vietnam increased in proportion to the scale of U.S. commitment because it called in question the credibility of the U.S. guarantee. Truman and Eisenhower had favored containment, and Eisenhower refused to send GIs to fight in Asia. Kennedy did not want to lose the war, but he did not want to send in the GIs either. Johnson, forced to choose between the two alternatives, chose the second. But like his predecessors, he was, though much less than has been alleged, led astray by his services. Daniel Ellsberg,[13] the man who handed over the Pentagon archives to the *New York Times,* declared, on the basis of these documents, that the presidents always refused to "lose" Vietnam but never completely accepted the demands of their services. In 1968, when the Joint Chiefs of Staff called for 200,000 more men, Johnson was persuaded to refuse their request by Clark M. Clifford, McNamara's successor, because to agree would have meant calling up the reserves. This he always opposed. After anguished deliberations, he chose the other alternative: to reduce or halt the bombing, and negotiate.

The talk of defending South Vietnam and respecting international law did not ring true, even if a few officials did manage to believe in it. Clearly, the Americans were not sacrificing so many thousands of GIs and billions of dollars just for the South Vietnamese: They refused to contemplate defeat; they wanted to preserve the value of their guarantee and their prestige as a Great Power; and they wanted to prevent communism from spreading all over Indochina and perhaps throughout Southeast Asia. The generals were appalled at the idea of a defeat, or anything short of victory, being inflicted on them by these little yellow men, among the poorest in the world and yet apparently invincible. Who had been the first to cross the demarcation line? Who had been the first to violate the Geneva Accords? In 1968, no one was any longer interested in such questions. Faced with an expeditionary force of half a million men, the North Vietnamese and the Vietcong, a group made up of the Communists and their allies, continued to embody nationalism—Ho Chi Minh as against Bao Dai. The United States was reluctantly playing the same part as the French had fourteen years earlier.

What frequently strikes a French reader of the *Pentagon Papers* is the U.S. leadership's tendency toward half-measures. Kennedy agreed to the intensification of the clandestine war against the North in May 1961. But he refused to send in units of GIs. He increased to more than 15,000 the number of American "advisers," though historians cannot understand clearly the significance or the use of this increased commitment.* In this respect, the American way of doing things, despite all the differences, resembled that of the French governments during the Fourth Republic. Perhaps it arises out of the nature of democratic government when it has no outstanding personalities at its disposal.

Just as striking was the contrast between the accuracy of the analyses supplied by the intelligence services, in particular the CIA, and the frequent mistakes made by the civilian advisers, especially the academics. The CIA had foreseen that the bombings would strengthen the determination of the North Vietnamese leadership, that they would not prevent infiltration, and that every reinforcement of American troops would produce an increase in help from the North. Before launching air operations, President Johnson had sent a threatening message, a virtual ultimatum, via the Canadian member of the international Control Commission. This attempt at compellence was met with an implacable resolve that the intelligence experts, unlike the armchair theorists, had correctly appraised, exactly predicting its implications. Similarly, the intelligence experts had indefatigably told the presidents and their advisers, who would not listen, that the main cause of the war and the key to victory, if it existed, lay not in the North but in the South. In other words, it was up to the United States to establish a government in Saigon that was capable of winning and retaining popular support and of making the South Vietnamese desire to be independent of the Communist North.

George Ball[14] was the only one of Kennedy's and Johnson's chief advisers to counsel disengagement and the negotiated acceptance of a coalition government in order to limit the costs and camouflage defeat as effectively as possible. As for the Joint Chiefs of Staff, which had had reservations in 1954, realizing that if there was to be a South Vietnamese army there first had to be a national government, by 1968 it had joined the hawks. While Robert S. McNamara had gradually become aware of the mistakes that had been made and of the military ineffectiveness of the bombings, the Joint Chiefs of Staff, including General Westmoreland, were still looking for a

---

* *Pentagon Papers*, p. 116.

"military victory," in the sense of the destruction of the armed forces of the Vietcong in the South. In the spring of 1968, Lyndon B. Johnson changed his strategy and gave up on the idea of a military victory—a meaningless objective from the very outset. Even if it had been attainable, it would not have guaranteed the political end in view, which was the maintenance of a non-Communist government in Saigon.

How, in the last analysis, can we imagine the unimaginable and understand the disaster, that twentieth-century version of the Sicilian expedition?[15] First, there was hubris, the overweening pride that destroyed the heroes of Greek tragedy: The officials in Washington would not believe the reports submitted by the secret services, which as early as 1949, and again in 1954, insisted on the link between nationalism and communism in Vietnam, pointing out that it would be extremely difficult, if not impossible, to arouse any other kind of nationalism. Another factor was a naive belief that the techniques of subversion could be turned back against the Communist enemy. Like the French colonels in Algeria, many of the president's advisers believed that the techniques of subversion and persuasion could be effective in any circumstances. The commando operations ordered by President Kennedy in May 1961, by way of a riposte to infiltration, then resumed on a larger scale* by Johnson, had nothing in common with the organization of parallel hierarchies. Then there was the conviction, sincere in many cases, that the United States would jeopardize its role all over the world if it accepted defeat in any part of it: This theory was proved by events to be a self-fulfilling prophecy. Last, we must take into account the perhaps inevitable corruption of the men who conduct high politics. In private life they may be good fathers, good husbands, and good citizens, but they end up "objectifying" situations and formulating "options" as if they were dealing with pawns on a chessboard or raw materials in a factory. To be able to order such bombings in cold blood, and then enjoy a good night's sleep, calls for a kind of transformation. Such a transmogrification may be necessary, but it takes place so easily that it always amazes me when I encounter it in men I used to know before they went into public life.

---

*Johnson did not tell the senators that U.S. torpedo boats had been attacked by North Vietnamese gunboats while the South Vietnamese were carrying out commando operations in the same region.

We are still in the spring of 1968: Johnson announces that he will not be a candidate in the presidential election and initiates the policy of de-escalation. At the end of 1968, Nixon, formerly Kennedy's rival, is elected. Four years later André Fontaine writes: "To save a country that, but for them would not have existed, they changed their policy in Europe, destroyed their own finances, devalued the dollar, stood idly by in 1967, despite the clearest commitments, when Egypt challenged Israel, and in 1971 looked on and let Pakistan, their ally, be crushed." But the United States did not alter its policy in Europe fundamentally; if it did change, it did so in the right direction. The inflation was partly attributable to the Vietnam War. The devaluation of the dollar was long overdue. The Israelis replied to the Egyptian challenge, and the United States reacted in the best possible way by dissuading the Soviet Union from intervening. The United States had no alliance with Pakistan against India, and the independence of Bangladesh, after the repression ordered by Marshal Yahya Khan, was both just and timely, and in accordance, I am sure, with André Fontaine's own wishes.

It is nonetheless true that the United States, as a nation, was torn and wounded by the Vietnam War. Even in 1972, no one can foresee the long term effects of this tragedy. Are we to conclude, with André Fontaine, that "the Vietnam affair may have played a similar part in the history of the United States as the Suez expedition in the decline of France and Britain"?

IV

BACK TO METTERNICH—OR TO GEORGE WASHINGTON?

With President Nixon's visits to Peking and Moscow in 1971 and the entry of the People's Republic of China into the United Nations, a period of diplomatic history—the postwar era rather than the Cold War—came to an end. Although all commentators agree about this obvious fact, on every other aspect of the matter they differ.

How important in this development was the policy followed by the Nixon-Kissinger team?[16] Did it constitute a break with the policy of Nixon's four predecessors—Truman, Eisenhower, Kennedy, and Johnson— or was it no more than a shift in direction? Did the objectives change, as well as the methods and the style? Will Nixon's "realism," based on the old European tradition, shape the world of the future in the same way as Stalin made the world of yesterday mirror the image he derived from his own ideology?

For the first time in twenty-five years, Americans and Europeans alike are talking of isolationism—mistakenly, if the word is used to mean the same kind of foreign policy as that of the United States between 1921 and 1939. History does not repeat itself, and the American Republic can no longer withdraw into itself. But that does not mean it has to continue in the imperialist role that it has been playing for the last quarter of a century. At a time when North Vietnam and Israel are demonstrating the autonomy of small nations, why should a world power be denied a measure of the same privilege?

After eight years as vice president, Richard Nixon, the former Cold-War warrior just beaten by Kennedy in 1960, is embarking on a second term with the blessing of Chou En-lai, Leonid Brezhnev, Golda Meir, and Georges Pompidou. Toward what kind of future will he direct the foreign policy of a country that no longer identifies its own fate with that of the West as a whole, but still acts as the laboratory of a humanity uncertain of its destiny, and as guarantor of a still precarious balance of power both in Europe and in Asia?

1. Richard Nixon: The Legacy of Vietnam, and Two Projects

When Richard Nixon moved into the White House at the beginning of 1969, he inherited a much more onerous legacy than the one Truman bequeathed to Eisenhower. The two bequests did have something in common: an unpopular war that was dragging on with no military triumph in sight. But there were many differences, some local, some relating to the international system as a whole.

In Korea, regular armies confronted one another along a continuous front. The Pan Mun-jong talks seemed endless: Mao Tse-tung's plenipotentiaries refused to let Chinese prisoners choose whether to be repatriated to Taiwan or to mainland China. American public opinion would no longer accept the idea of GIs fighting on faraway battlefields in intermittent operations with no possibility of a clear-cut outcome. The old tradition—do the job as soon as possible and get back to normal life—was forcing the hero of the "European crusade" to accept that his real task and duty was to settle for a cease-fire, since peace was not to be won, and accept an end to the fighting instead of victory.

President Eisenhower did not lack the means to achieve the end dictated by circumstances both at home and abroad. The United States enjoyed a crushing superiority over the Soviet Union in industrial production as well as in nuclear weaponry. Was it Stalin or Mao Tse-tung who refused to make the minor concession needed to bring the fighting to an end? We cannot be sure. It was more in the interests of Stalin than of Mao to prolong a conflict that drove a wedge between Washington and Peking. But could not Mao have agreed to make peace if he had really wanted to? Be that as it may, two months after Eisenhower was installed in the White House, Stalin disappeared from the scene, and a few weeks later a cease-fire was agreed in Pan Mun-jong. Stalin's successors in Moscow performed a number of symbolic acts indicating a change of style, if not a change of heart.

The Vietnam War, even if it was justified on the grounds of respect for lines of demarcation, differed from the Korean campaign in two main respects. In the summer of 1950, the Soviet representatives at the United Nations argued that what was taking place in Korea was a civil war. In fact, the invasion had followed unsuccessful attempts by the North to stir up guerrilla operations in the South. No one could rightly have denied the existence or the legitimacy of the Seoul government and of the army that defended it. The North Koreans and the Soviets may once have used the same vocabulary to anathematize the Seoul regime—the "clique" of Syngman Rhee, the "puppets," the accomplices of imperialism—as the North Vietnamese use now to castigate the regime in Saigon. In 1950, the only people who believed them were their friends, though there were plenty of those in the West; today, any impartial observer must wonder. Neither in Vietnam nor abroad does President Thieu stand for patriotism and nationalism, as did Synghman Rhee. The Vietcong is taking over from the Vietminh, who fought the French in the name of independence. Synghman Rhee fought the Japanese all his life, whereas many South Vietnamese generals once served in the French army. Although the Saigon regime is upheld and to a certain extent legitimized by anticommunism and the fear felt by the population in the South of the ruthless regime in the North, it is not strong enough to face up unaided to the combined assaults of the partisans, the North Vietnamese army, and the "progressivist" propaganda in the world at large.

On the military level, too, there are more differences than similarities. In the early days, the Vietcong, recruited on the spot, rattled the Saigon regime and would probably have overthrown it if the United States had not sent in an expeditionary corps in 1965. To this, North Vietnam responded by increasing its aid to the rebels and infiltrating some units of the regular army. Though it had not lost any battles, the American forces had not won the war.

How was it to be won? To adopt the language of Clausewitz, the *Zweck,* or political objective, of fighting the war was, for the United States, the maintenance of a non-Communist regime in Saigon. What military objective leads to or is equivalent to this end? As we have said earlier, a strategist might hesitate between several answers to this question. One answer would be to inflict on the North Vietnamese such "punishment," in the form of suffering and destruction, that the Hanoi leadership would decide to stop, or be forced to stop, supporting the rebels in the South. The bombings were designed to achieve both these ends, the material and the moral: They achieved neither. A second answer might be to search and destroy the regular units of the North and the partisans: The problem with this answer was that the expeditionary force had no hope whatever of eliminating *all* the units or *all* the rebels. And partial successes got nowhere. Sometimes, in a revolutionary war between partisans and an established government, the partisans can win simply by not losing. This possibility exists when the established government either depends on a colonial power or represents a regime that is too weak to fight alone. In the former case, the home country loses patience and ends by opting for the rebels. In the case of Vietnam, American public opinion lost patience, just as French public opinion did at the time of the Algerian War, and called into question the legitimacy, even the practical justification, of the struggle.

I now come to the third answer, and to the only rational strategy. The military objective was, or should have been, inseparable from the strengthening of the Saigon government and army. Because the political goal of the war, as seen from Washington, was the survival of a non-Communist Saigon, and because the expeditionary force could not stay in Vietnam indefinitely, U.S. intervention should have aimed above all at gaining enough time to set up an order in South Vietnam that could withstand both subversion and a possible attack by North Vietnam. There is no evidence that the United States could have achieved this, but it did not even try to achieve it, or not as a matter of first importance, at least until early 1969.

President Johnson made an irreversible decision when he halted the bombing and agreed to negotiate. His successor had to find a solution in order to reconcile a divided nation with itself and give it back the freedom of action in the world that had been hampered by the impasse in Vietnam. How could the war be ended with honor? What did "with honor" mean? From the American point of view, the North Vietnamese were fighting outside the limits of their own country, and evacuation of the GIs called for withdrawal of Hanoi's troops in return. But neither Ho Chi Minh nor his comrades, who had tried in vain in 1945–1946 to get the French to grant the union of the three Kys (provinces) of Vietnam, saw it this way. Moreover, the rebels who had risen against the Saigon regime would not negotiate with it except under conditions* that guaranteed their own supremacy and the final disappearance from the scene of their enemy. In Korea, the cease-fire had at least enabled the Americans to achieve their minimum objective. How could they retire from Vietnam without conceding total defeat, even if that defeat was political and not military?

President Nixon *could* have negotiated the withdrawal of American troops with Hanoi if he had been prepared to forget about the regime in Saigon.** He could have accepted Hanoi's arguments in favor of a "coalition government." But in fact, he rejected this "shameful" way out. He wanted to win (or not lose) the war, and at the same time placate the American people.

The legacy of Vietnam was very different from that of Korea, and when Nixon inherited it the balance of military power was changing in favor of the Soviet Union; U.S. domestic inflation, largely due to Vietnam, was weakening the dollar and reducing year after year the apparent*** trade surplus (which officially went into deficit for the first time in 1971). President Nixon's arrival in the White House coincided with a moment of truth both within the Western world and in relation to the Soviet Union: The Europeans (in particular the Germans) and the Japanese had progressed more rapidly than expected, had partly made up their lag, and were emerging as

---

*This at least is what American officials maintain, both in public and in private. I am inclined to believe them, though I cannot be sure.

**In exchange for this he could have obtained the release of U.S. prisoners.

***I say "apparent" because the trade balance had been in deficit for several years, if purchases due to tied loans are taken into account.

competitors in all the markets, including the U.S. one. In addition to the urgent task of winding up the Vietnam War, there was the vaguer and more long-term problem of how to restore an international system in which the United States would no longer enjoy pride of place, which would not exclude opposing or even conflicting interests, but which would still permit, if not an equilibrium comparable to the European consensus, at least traditional kinds of relations between all the powers, including the revolutionary ones.

The Nixon policy can be interpreted in various different ways because of the evident contradiction between its two objectives: the refusal to lose the Vietnam War, and the desire for normal relations with *all* other countries, Communist states included. The two aims were not fundamentally incompatible: Henry Kissinger would no doubt argue that to accept a "humiliating" defeat would deprive the United States of the authority it needed if retreat was not to be transformed into rout. The maneuvers involved in withdrawal call for moral force as well as adaptability. And Richard Nixon was obliged to embark on such maneuvers. Nonetheless, the inconsistency was obvious to disconcerted commentators and to the man in the street: In April 1972, the president's spokesman announced progress in the negotiations on limiting strategic weapons at the same time as television screens were showing long processions of Vietnamese refugees and the formidable armada massed in the Gulf of Tonkin.

Nixon's policy marked a historic break with that of his predecessors. For the first time since 1947, there had been an attempt at disengagement and even modesty: Neither Eisenhower, Kennedy, nor Johnson would have talked of keeping a low profile. It was an approach that would mean not lowering one's guard, but rather trying to avoid hubris, the overweening pride that destroyed the heroes of Greek tragedy. Before analyzing the temporary significance and the long-term effects of U.S. disengagement, let us look at the coups d'éclat, the spectacular moves, that have characterized Nixon's diplomatic style over the past four years.

By focusing his interest and action on a few hot spots—above all, Vietnam—Nixon seems to me to have continued the practice of his predecessors. The novelty of his policy lies in its method and organization. What strikes observers both at home and abroad is the role played by Henry Kissinger and his brain trust. The customary institutions provided for in the U.S. Constitution and subject to the control of Congress have been replaced by an ad hoc organization created by the president and staffed with men chosen by him and his adviser. In short, a kind of royal cabinet has been superimposed on the secretary and the department officially responsible for diplomacy.

It seems to me that this novelty is no more than the intensification of a trend that has been especially visible since Kennedy's arrival in the White House. The president, the supreme elected member, has always been free to choose his own staff. At the time of the Great Depression, Roosevelt recruited a team of reformist intellectuals. During World War II, Harry Hopkins, as an adviser, played a much more important role than Secretary of State Cordell Hull. There is a tradition of "presidential secrecy" comparable to the "secrecy of the king." This creation of "parallel bureaucracies" is facilitated by the diminished prestige of civil servants in a country where the "spoils system" survives and where the president, on the day of his inauguration, still appoints people to hundreds of posts. There is no reason to suppose that this trend is irreversible. As in the past, so in the future, another Eisenhower could employ another Dulles both as secretary of state and as his own "private adviser."

Henry Kissinger certainly plays many roles that his predecessors, National Security Council chiefs McGeorge Bundy and Walt W. Rostow, did not have a monopoly on and may not have filled simultaneously. Kissinger gives the president daily reports on the world situation. He sets out the various possible decisions among which the president may choose. In a crisis, he chairs a special action group, and he regularly presides over the National Security Council. As an expert on both the real state of events and the desired outcomes, he also directs or organizes, in accordance with the president's directives, at least in very serious circumstances, the activities of the services. He carries out secret missions in Peking and Moscow to prepare the way for Nixon's negotiations with Chou En-lai or Brezhnev, and in Paris to negotiate with the North Vietnamese. Can Kissinger himself go on carrying out all these tasks indefinitely? The organization responsible for U.S. foreign policy varies in accordance with who is in the White House. A Kissinger presupposes a Nixon: An adviser like the one presupposes a president like the other. Kissinger occupies the foreground because he has forged special links with Nixon, a man of suspicion and a loner, and also because they have both had to solve a perhaps insoluble problem: how to combine an "honorable" withdrawal from Vietnam with a world diplomacy conducted without a crusading spirit, without a bogeyman enemy, and without allies of unblemished virtue.

The Vietnam War troubled American consciences and at the same time exasperated the realists. Was the Saigon regime really part of the "free world"? Could dropping millions of tons of bombs on North Vietnam be called defending the free world? What was the point of containing communism when each of the two chief Marxist-Leninist states regarded the other as its main enemy and ideological allegiance no longer determined political alignment? Moreover, when Nixon arrived in the White House, anticommunism, far from providing the war with a political or ethical foundation, was itself emerging discredited from the conflict. By a kind of mental confusion, anticommunism was coming to be seen as the principle of evil because it had led to evil in the form of the horrors of Vietnam. Only one argument remained: The United States, responsible as it was for worldwide equilibrium, could not accept a humiliation that would undermine the confidence of its allies and deprive its promises, and its utterances in general, of all credibility.

Nixon and Kissinger seem to have decided early on that the North Vietnamese and the Vietcong would not agree to negotiate for peace unless they were assured that General Thieu's team, the only one capable of offering some resistance to the Communists' attempts to seize the country, was to be eliminated. That being so, Nixon was obliged to conduct the war with a view to a political victory and a military defeat. If the Saigon government managed to survive, it, and with it the United States, would thereby have won, in the sense of having attained its objective. But to make such a strategy acceptable to American public opinion, the president had to undertake to phase out the expeditionary force, thereby leaving responsibility for land operations to the South Vietnamese army. The "Vietnamization" policy exactly paralleled that of Dulles after the Korean War. It could be called cynical if taken to mean that the Vietnamese were to kill one another for the benefit of the United States, but it was acceptable if it meant making the people of the country concerned responsible for their own defense. (Would Europeans regard the "Europeanization" of the defense of Europe as cynical or natural?)

The strategy of trying to achieve political victory through reduced military means gave rise to the crises in Cambodia and Laos in 1970 and 1971, respectively. Whether the overthrow of Prince Sihanouk was due to CIA intrigues or to factions hostile to him among the Khmer oligarchy, it provided an opportunity for striking at the Vietcong by penetrating the parts of Cambodia it used as a refuge, a logistical base, and a regrouping center. Nixon succumbed to the temptation, but the violence of the reaction in the United States showed him the limits of his room for maneuver. The incursion by a South Vietnamese division into Laos in 1971 was part of the same plan: to give the Saigon regime and its army time to reinforce and slow down preparations for the expected North Vietnamese offensive, which did not take place until April 1972, more than four years after the Têt offensive. At this point, Nixon had practically no soldiers* in Vietnam capable of taking part in land operations. He massed an armada in the Gulf of Tonkin; American planes, setting out from bases in South Vietnam and Thailand and from aircraft carriers, could carry out as many as 600 missions a day.

At the beginning of the offensive, President Nixon could boast of having achieved two results. First, the North Vietnamese offensive was taking on the appearance of conventional warfare, and Hanoi's regular divisions were crossing the demilitarized zone and thus the demarcation line, too. The offensive was not a popular uprising against the "puppets," but an out-and-out invasion—a legitimate one, if the Hanoi leadership had the right to use force to impose its authority on the country as a whole, but comparable to an act of aggression if the Saigon government was considered neither more nor less legal than those of Seoul or Hanoi. The fact that the North Vietnamese offensive might be regarded as an act of aggression gave the president back some of his freedom of action; this was the second result.

Calm returned to the universities; the students were no longer threatened with the draft. The timing—between the president's visit to Peking and his projected trip to Moscow, and when the evacuation of American troops from Vietnam was entering its final phase—was seen by the American public as proof that the North Vietnamese offensive was indeed an act of aggression.

In the course of the weeks between Nixon's two journeys, the offensive gave rise to a crisis at once in the field and in Washington. It suddenly appeared that détente between the two main Communist countries might be incompatible with an honorable solution to the war. Nixon and Kissinger

---

*Two battalions, at most a few thousand men.

clearly hoped that both Soviet and Chinese influence would work in favor of their plan. They were looking beyond the Vietnam War, which, in the context of the inauguration or restoration of a worldwide international system, was no more than an episode. Nonetheless, the Soviet arms used by the North Vietnamese army, and North Vietnam's first victories in the Quang Tri area, placed a question mark over the Nixon-Kissinger strategy as a whole. Should the United States take extreme measures to save the Saigon regime, thus running the risk of having to give up the meeting in Moscow? Or should it allow the Saigon regime to collapse, and thus risk arriving in the Soviet capital weakened and humiliated by the defeat of a country for which the United States had expended so many dollars and so many lives in vain?

In April 1972, it was once again time to resort to arms. In order to reconcile the demands of public opinion with the need to avoid defeat, the president's strategy had aimed at the withdrawal of the expeditionary force, reinforcement of the South Vietnamese army, and support of the latter by U.S. naval and air power. When the fall of Quang Tri and the rout of a South Vietnamese division threatened a military disaster, the president sent the Kremlin both a challenge and an appeal. In the short term, the mining of North Vietnamese ports could have no effect on the outcome of the fighting. At the worst, it put Nixon in a position of equality, if not of strength, for the talks in Moscow. At best, it might force the Politburo to choose between temporarily suspending the negotiations with Washington and exerting increased pressure on the North Vietnamese to abandon the idea of total victory. Brezhnev opted for a third solution: to receive the American president as if nothing had happened.

Why should he have regarded supplying the North Vietnamese with heavy weapons as breaking the rules governing the modus vivendi, or détente, between the superpowers, when the United States had sent thousands of men to South Vietnam and was still intervening with its navy and air force? For his part, Nixon, by deciding to mine the North Vietnamese ports on the eve of his departure for Moscow, was addressing three arguments, two explicit and one implicit, to Brezhnev: Each of the superpowers should respect the principal interests of the other; the accords that were about to be negotiated were more important than the fate of Vietnam or any other small country; and a superpower should not lose face, and thus neither of them should directly or through its allies seek to humiliate the other. Brezhnev probably accepted the first two arguments. Would he, could he, listen to the third?

The way Nixon reacted to the crisis of April–May 1972—that is, the North Vietnamese offensive being fought with Soviet arms just before he was to make the trip to Moscow to conclude an agreement—illustrates the president's two objectives and at the same time the two sides to his character. His two aims were to end the war honorably and to negotiate with Peking and Moscow without losing face. His dual personality made possible, on the one hand, his prudence regarding the withdrawal and the low-profile policy, and on the other, his acceptance of risk and his firmness, verging on bluff, in a crisis. (Other examples of this combination include the overthrow of Prince Sihanouk in Cambodia, the stationing of Russian SAM missiles on the Suez Canal, the use of a Cuban port by Soviet nuclear submarines, and the entry of Syrian tanks into Jordan.)* Nixon's opponents say that the Cold War crusader can still be seen behind the prophet of "peace for a generation"; they add that on the excuse of the withdrawal, he dropped more bombs on the three countries that made up Indochina than Johnson dropped in the attempt to win the war. Commentators from the Left speak of the Kissinger mystery: How can this university professor, who is not devoid of either humor or humanity, sleep peacefully at night after giving orders that entail the deaths of so many men? I have asked myself the same question, but there is only one answer. Only someone not born to become a prince, or perhaps just a prince's adviser, can even ask himself the question. At most he may teach those who *are* born to such eminences.

The visit to Peking also symbolized both the substance and the style of Nixon's policy. He had probably wanted since early 1969 to resume contact with Peking, or more precisely, to free the connection from the clandestinity that marked, and rendered ineffectual, the conversations in Warsaw. For their part, the leaders of the People's Republic of China—after the check to the leftists that followed the sacking of the British Embassy, and after the fighting on the Ussuri (Wusuli) River in March 1969—wanted to regain their place in the international community. From among the three kinds of relations that a Communist country may maintain simultaneously—between country and

---

*These crises were listed in the president's report to Congress on foreign policy as signs of a new period of confrontation preceding the progress in negotiation.

country; between party and party; and between country or party, on the one hand, and a people or rebels in another country, on the other—the Chinese leadership was to emphasize the first, that between country and country. The idea of a worldwide insurrection of the country against the towns was dropped, or at least was no longer officially sanctioned by Lin Piao's signature. The moderation usually shown hitherto in the actions* of the Chinese leaders was now manifested in words and diplomatic moves. In July 1971, President Nixon announced officially that he was going to Peking and that Kissinger, his adviser, had already been there secretly to make arrangements for the visit. Nixon's visit took place in March 1972.

Let us pause for a moment to examine "style" and "substance" here. The style is revealed in the fact that Nixon announced the visit to Peking without consulting the Asian allies of the United States or even informing them in advance. It is also revealed by the decision to cast the resumption of Sino-U.S. relations in the dramatic form of a journey by the president himself, who spent an hour with Mao Tse-tung, the new emperor of the Kingdom of the Middle, and several hours with Chou En-lai, the second most important person in the regime. Should we try to separate the politician from the statesman in all this, the candidate for a second term from the prophet of "peace for a generation"? What would be the point?

No doubt Nixon intended the coup de théâtre, and this annoyed the Japanese very much. On the one hand, it showed a lack of the tact and regard for other people's "face" that are indispensable in a Great Power wanting to remain part of the Asian scene. On the other, the journey to Peking, which in Asian eyes had something humiliating about it—the United States had quarantined the People's Republic of China, yet it was the American president who initiated the rapprochement and asked to be invited there**—was a most spectacular, if not the only, way to symbolize in the eyes of the whole world the beginning of a new era. President Nixon neither could nor would have overturned at a blow the policy that had brought about alliances and security pacts between the United States and Taiwan, and between Taiwan and Japan. Chou En-lai neither could nor

---

*With two notable exceptions: their determination, during the Pan Mun-jong negotiations, to obtain the return of *all* Chinese prisoners to mainland China, and the bombing of Quemoy and Matsu.

**Did Nixon ask for an invitation, or did he merely accept the offer of an agreement?

would have paid for the seat at the United Nations to which the government that had ruled mainland China for twenty years had a right. So neither Nixon nor Chou En-lai were in any position to conclude an agreement of any great substance. The desire of the United States to maintain diplomatic relations with Taiwan ruled out U.S. recognition of the Peking regime, and thus also the possibility of setting up an embassy.

Reduced to its essentials, the outcome of the Peking meeting was more or less as follows. The People's Republic had emerged both from the Cultural Revolution and from isolation. After the fighting on the Ussuri River and the concentration of Soviet divisions on the frontiers, the Soviet Union had become the main enemy, at least for the moment, for it represented the threat of a preemptive strike, if not an invasion, just when the United States was showing a desire for partial and phased withdrawal. So the Chinese leaders saw it as logically in their interest to agree to a visit from Nixon, which might dissuade the Soviet Union from aggression, facilitate their taking a seat at the United Nations, and favor a change in Japanese policy toward them. The People's Republic, despite Lin Piao's ideological messianism, had already followed a realistic diplomatic policy in Southeast Asia, where it was on good terms with Pakistan and on bad terms with India.

On the brink of election year, Nixon was overtaking his Democratic opponents on their left. Dubbed a "peace warrior," he was reawakening the American people's old sympathy for faraway, fabulous China, providing the Soviets with a further reason for treating with him, and also giving the Americans a lesson in both the new and the traditional diplomacy: the new, because for twenty years the Chinese and the Americans had been carrying on only an intermittent dialogue in Warsaw through ambassadors; the traditional, because, according to historic practice in Europe, communication between states meant nothing more than the acceptance of reality. To recognize a state is not to approve of its regime or its activities: Nixon, though not breaking overnight with the U.S. policy of nonrecognition, took the first step (the only one that counted) on the path toward recognition. He visited the capital of a country that the United States pretended not to see.

The Peking trip was a stage on the road to Moscow: The negotiations with Peking were a beginning; negotiations with Moscow would crown the whole. In the case of Chou En-lai, the mere fact of having conversations with him was, for the moment, what mattered. In the case of Brezhnev, what mattered was the agreement on strategic arms limitation and the final declaration on the rules governing coexistence, symbolizing the end of the Cold War and the dawn of a new era.

Since 1960, all American presidents—Kennedy, Johnson, and Nixon—have tried to free direct relations between the two superpowers from the ups and downs of local conflicts and untimely interventions on the part of the smaller powers. The American Republic and the Soviet Union go on aiming at incompatible objectives and contrasting with one another in their visions of the world and their own ultimate goals. What has to be done is enlarge the area of common interest, to formalize and defer to the implicit accord, and perhaps to deduce from it some rules acceptable to both sides. Détente at the top should at best make it possible to settle local conflicts peacefully, and at least to stop them from spreading or escalating. The negotiations on limiting strategic weapons (which was to result in a treaty when Nixon went to Moscow) followed interminable negotiations on the halting of nuclear tests and on non-proliferation. They also led to treaties (partial suspension of nuclear tests in the Moscow Treaty of 1963, and a Non-Proliferation Treaty signed but not yet ratified by the main countries concerned).

The conclusion of the SALT negotiations[17] represented a step forward in relation to the two preceding treaties. The Moscow Treaty limiting nuclear tests and the Non-Proliferation Treaty chiefly inconvenienced the countries that do not belong to the nuclear club or those which, like China and France, are only secondary members of it. Establishing a fixed number of interception and offensive missiles represents not gradual disarmament, but rather a slowing down of the arms race (perhaps a change from quantity to quality, as reflected by the MIRV),[18] a limitation on the weaponry that the two superpowers let each other possess. This first agreement on limitation was made possible by the U.S. acceptance of the principle of equality, and by a change in the Soviet Union's favor of the balance of nuclear (and conventional) forces. It thus illustrates the continuity of Nixon's policy in comparison with that of his predecessors, while at the same time revealing new factors more or less camouflaged by his rhetoric: These include not only the rise of the Soviet Union, perhaps the weakening of American resolve, and the maintenance of communication between the two superpowers, but also their pursuit of confrontation, direct or through allies, in various parts of the world.

2. The World System and the Autonomy of Subsystems

Let us now go back to the question we asked at the beginning of this section: How does the diplomatic policy of Nixon and Kissinger differ from U.S. diplomatic policy in general since World War II? Its novelty is due in the first place to circumstance and the need for withdrawal and disengagement dictated by American public opinion. Second, it arises out of the fact that the style of diplomacy changes in accordance with the personalities of the current president and his advisers. It is also related to the combination of two objectives, one local and the other global: an honorable solution in Vietnam, and reasonable dialogue at the summit. The major initiative of the president's term—the visit to Peking—was innovative, too. Does the novelty of Nixon-Kissinger diplomatic policy ultimately derive from the philosophy of international relations prompting the president and his adviser?

It is a philosophy that belongs to European rather than to American tradition. Kissinger, who came to the United States from Germany during the 1930s, might, thirty years later, have been teaching his adopted country the doubtful wisdom of Metternich or Bismarck. This is an oversimplification, but perhaps not too far from reality.

The influence of this gray eminence, the little German professor, would be inexplicable if the two men, the president and his adviser, did not see the world through the same spectacles.

But we should not exaggerate the contrast with the past. All presidents of the United States have practiced Realpolitik—in the same way as Molière's fictional Monsieur Jourdain—without knowing it. When Roosevelt "bought" Soviet intervention against Japan at the expense of China, he was doing what statesmen everywhere have always done. He was also spontaneously reverting to impure practices that Americans have never formulated, though they have always been aware of their advantages and disadvantages. As for Nixon, the rhetoric of his words often disguises and transforms the prosaic nature of his deeds. When he returned from Peking and Moscow, he presented himself as a pilgrim for peace.

Moreover, his predecessors—Kennedy and Johnson for certain, Eisenhower probably—wanted dialogue with Moscow and made efforts to achieve it. Why has Nixon been able to go further than they were? Above all, because he had the courage to go to Peking. For twenty years, from the

Chinese intervention in Korea until the Sino-U.S. negotiations in 1970–1971, the United States excluded Communist China from the United Nations and communicated with the People's Republic only through intermittent meetings in Warsaw (at the level of ambassadors). This attitude on the part of the United States did not, however, prevent a rupture between the two main Communist powers; it might even have helped to bring it about. Nonetheless, it is to Nixon that the credit must go for the "Machiavellian" feat of breaking the taboo that had made China untouchable, for helping Peking reenter the great international game, and for giving the Kremlin a further reason for entente with Washington.

In both Peking and Moscow, Nixon found interlocutors ready to speak the language of reason and reality. The Cultural Revolution was a thing of the past. After Lin Piao was gone, Chou En-lai took command, and the worldwide revolution of the country against the town joined other myths in the oblivion of history. In Moscow, Brezhnev and his comrades were more like bureaucrats or managers than prophets. They had achieved virtual equality with the United States on the military level, though they were aware of their economic and technical inferiority. Soviets and Chinese alike wanted dialogue with the American president, the former chiefly for economic reasons, the latter for fear of encirclement or a preemptive strike on the part of the Soviet Union.

Why did the Soviet-U.S. condominium that Roosevelt had dreamed of thirty years ago come to nothing after the war? Why the Cold War instead of cooperation? Revisionists blame Truman and the hypocrisy of universalism; others accuse Stalin and the ruthless Sovietization of Eastern Europe. There is no need to choose between the two: After Yalta, the Americans neither prevented nor accepted the Sovietization of Eastern Europe and of part of the former Reich. Some spectacular episodes apart, the origin of the Cold War, and its significance, lay in this mixture of protest and tolerance—moral protest and actual tolerance. Today, the ratification of the German-Soviet and German-Polish treaties[19] embodies the moral recognition, by the last country that had protested against them, of accomplished facts. Dialogue between Nixon and Brezhnev does not run the same risk of misunderstanding as that between Stalin and Roosevelt once did: Today's interlocutors understand one another better because they are more alike. The Americans and the Europeans have lost their illusions and no longer deny the Russians the right to intervene militarily in a country belonging to the socialist community.

Are we to conclude that the philosophies of Roosevelt, Truman, Nixon, and Kissinger have had less influence on their decisions than current circumstances, as perceived by themselves and reflected in the views and wishes of their adversaries? Nixon is undoubtedly meeting the wishes of the nation that elected him when he seeks an accommodation with the Soviet Union past and present, and at the same time tries to limit U.S. foreign commitments. He gives both friends and foes the impression that he thinks and acts differently from his predecessors—perhaps even in a way that is not American. What makes exact appraisal difficult is the complex interaction between circumstances and men.

Nixon and Kissinger both certainly start out from the notion that the world of international relations naturally and permanently involves opposing interests, and consequently conflicts. They believe in neither collective security nor the rule of law; the international system toward which they incline would result in a balance of opposing forces rather than a community of countries or peoples. Nothing could be less like the Holy Alliance formed after 1815 than Nixon's dialogue with Brezhnev and Chou En-lai, Brandt and Pompidou. The historiographer of Metternich has certainly not retained either the dogmatism or the rationalism of that implacable defender of an empire doomed by the evolution of ideas. Commentators who refer to the Realpolitik of European tradition see it as the replacement of the gradual nurturing of communities by an interplay based on the balance of power. It entails ever-changing relationships between participants all jealous of their own freedom of action and therefore disinclined to engage in permanent alliances. If this is indeed the case, is the policy modeled on old-school European cabinets or on George Washington's warning against "entangling alliances," which tend to produce paralysis and involvement in other people's quarrels (neither of which inconveniences is merely temporary)?

The world system is so different now from the European system of the past few centuries that the old rules have taken on quite new meanings. The widening of the field in which diplomacy operates, nuclear weapons, instantaneous communications, the great differences between regions, contempt for civilized customs and "traditional courtesy"—all these things and many others make it as impossible to compare the practices of the Republic of European states as described by Voltaire in a passage cited above with those of the United Nations as it would be to compare them with the practices of cold-blooded monsters in some jungle. In the European Republic of the past, countries close to one another geographically and culturally used to join together in temporary coalitions in order to prevent a universal monarchy or the hegemony of a single country. Periods of unrest occurred when internal quarrels, religious or ideological schisms, and rivalries between states overlapped. In 1815, the Holy Alliance was based both on the restoration of the military balance of power and on an attempt to chain up the monster of revolution, with its train of conscription and war to the death. If Nixon and Kissinger want, to quote the title of a well-known book, to save the world, what kind of world would that be?

The world system is still militarily bipolar. There are still only two world powers, the Soviet Union and the United States of America, each with its complete panoply of arms, each present on every continent and every ocean. The Soviet Union has not only achieved nuclear equality; its land forces enjoy superiority in Europe, and it now has a modern navy that gets stronger every year.

It does not yet have aircraft carriers comparable to those of the Sixth and Seventh Fleets. It still suffers the disadvantages of a geopolitical situation less favorable than that of the United States. Must we then conclude that the equalization of the two world powers' military forces and the vulnerability of U.S. territory fundamentally alter the structure and functioning of the world system, and that the changes involved determine the style of the dialogue between Moscow and Washington?

I do not deny the existence of these changes and their consequences. But as I have shown in previous sections of this chapter, the people in charge of U.S. diplomatic policy have always treated their rival with caution, never trying to force it into a humiliating retreat. In times of crisis, they have treated their allies more harshly than their enemies. For their part, the men in the Kremlin have carefully calculated the risks they have taken, even during the two Berlin crises, with the single exception of the stationing of ballistic missiles in Cuba. Until now, the Soviet leaders seem to have drawn greater self-confidence from their strength, and while claiming a status comparable to that of the United States—that of a world power present at all the crossroads of history—they are behaving less aggressively toward their fraternal enemy.

If there is still such a thing as bipolarity—in the sense of the concentration of military forces in the hands of two states, both much stronger than all the rest—what then is the multipolarity that all the commentators see in the present system, a quarter of a century after the Truman Doctrine?

I perceive three differences:

1. The relative autonomy of certain subsystems;
2. The rivalry between China and the Soviet Union, which in some ways is more virulent than that between the United States and the Soviet Union;
3. The many different planes on which relations between states (and societies) take shape, so that military force does not necessarily ensure a proportionate amount of political power or moral influence.

The autonomy of some subsystems is seen especially clearly when military conflicts arise between countries in the area concerned. In 1967, Israel, threatened by the blockade of the Gulf of 'Aqaba and the Egyptian divisions massed in the Sinai, went to war and in six days won total victory over its three neighbors, Egypt, Jordan, and Syria. The Soviet Union had armed the first of these and was closely linked to the third. But it intervened in the conflict only at the United Nations, in order to hasten the cease-fire to which Israel would not agree until it had gained all its objectives. Each of the two superpowers, whose leaders kept in touch with one another throughout the week that the crisis lasted, insisted that the other should not intervene directly. So thanks to the isolation of the subsystem, Israel was able to use its military superiority freely, in the traditional way.

In 1971–1972, the Indian subcontinent provided another example of a crisis resolved militarily by the stronger of two local powers. In 1970, General Agha Muhammad Yahya Khan of Pakistan had ordered free elections in the country's two provinces. Voting in the eastern province gave 167 out of 169 seats to candidates belonging to the Awami League, the party in favor of autonomy rather than independence for the province. After negotiations came to nothing, Yahya Khan chose the path of violence: Sheikh Mujibur Rahman, head of the Awami League, was imprisoned; troops sent to East Bengal struck at autonomists, politicians, intellectuals, teachers, and students. A few Awami League militants on the frontier with India proclaimed the independence of Bangladesh. Millions of Bengalis, fleeing the excesses of the soldiers from the Punjab, crossed the border and crowded into refugee camps. Guerrilla warfare broke out in Bengal. On the frontiers, the Indian authorities gave material aid and moral support to the partisans.

So here, again, the world situation made it possible for the country that was locally the stronger to resolve a crisis by force of arms. Yahya Khan's government, responsible both for the free elections and for the refusal to accept their verdict, could not send reinforcements into the eastern province, which was separated from West Pakistan by more than 2,000 kilometers of Indian territory. So on the eastern front, India enjoyed a superiority that guaranteed an easy victory. All Indira Gandhi had to do was sign a "reverse treaty" with the Soviet Union and she was free, without fear of Chinese intervention, to "conquer" or "liberate" the eastern province, which was soon transformed into Bangladesh. Did Mrs. Gandhi's India violate the United Nations Charter when its army crossed the frontier to come to the aid of an oppressed people? It certainly did. Would it have served mankind better if she had obeyed the charter and kept the partisans supplied for years and years? I take leave to doubt it. However reprehensible it may be to break quite openly the rule forbidding recourse to arms, and although the hypocrisy of aiding partisans strikes me as generally preferable to formal and flagrant invasion, in this case I cannot bring myself to blame Mrs. Gandhi for her expeditious solution to the problem.*

It was a solution that brought about a curious alignment, together with accusations and defenses that were even stranger. Since 1962 the People's Republic of China had been in conflict with India over the demarcation of frontiers in the Himalayas (experts are divided over the respective merits of the two points of view). China had maintained cordial relations with the military regime in Pakistan, however. The Peking delegate to the United Nations, while not denying the claims or complaints of the Bengalis, argued against India's interference and the dismemberment of a sovereign state. The representative of the Soviet Union argued in favor of a people's right to self-determination, while the United States pleaded for respect for the United Nations Charter, suggesting that the military action was standing in the way of a political settlement already being negotiated. Here again, as in the Middle East, recourse to regular arms was made possible by

---

*An imperfect one, however. Minorities hostile to the Bengalis or guilty of collaborating with the Pakistani soldiers were, in their turn, the subject of persecution.

the isolation of the battlefield and the superior strength of one of the belligerents, and the foreign powers were forced to stand aside because of their distance from the scene, their different points of view, and the fact that their strengths were more or less equally balanced.

The two subsystems in question have certain characteristics in common. In the Middle East, the Soviet Union could only have prevented the local power from gaining a victory over its neighbor by intervening physically. So, too, with the United States in India and Pakistan. In the current world system, countries no longer obey the rules of diplomatic courtesy requiring small states to bow either to the will of a greater ally or to the consensus of the superpowers. To throw down the gauntlet is becoming the modern method. Small countries use it vis-à-vis large ones, whether friends or enemies: President Thieu uses it in his negotiations with Washington; the Israeli government uses it in its dealings with the Soviet Union. When the masters of the Kremlin received Nasser's anguished appeal, they had to send fighter squadrons and anti-aircraft batteries to defend Egyptian territory against in-depth raids by the Israeli air force: Neither direct (if scarcely credible) threats nor indirect messages via Washington would have dissuaded the Jerusalem government from its course.

Did the arrival of aircraft carriers in the Bay of Bengal dissuade Mrs. Gandhi from complementing her victory in the east by settling the Kashmir conflict in the same way? President Nixon said it did, attributing the end of the hostilities both to the movement of his own fleet and to the good offices of the Kremlin. Is this just a retrospective justification of an unreasonable attitude? Probably, though one cannot be sure. Anyhow, the main point is that Nixon could no more impose his will on Mrs. Gandhi, the ally of the Soviet Union, than Brezhnev could impose his will on Mrs. Meir, who could be sure of U.S. support. The shared paralysis of the superpowers, assuming they are not physically engaged in the subsystem, makes weaponry supreme and teaches that might is right.

The case of the Indian subcontinent is different in many ways from that of the Middle East. What does the fate of the Bengalis matter to the superpowers? What do they care even about the balance of power between India and Pakistan? For the foreseeable future, India will remain a regional, not even a continental, power, unable to project its strength beyond the limits of the subcontinent. In the Middle East, behind the prolonged conflict between Israel and its Arab neighbors, the superpowers see an issue vital both to Japan and to the United States: the world's most enormous oil reserves, upon which Atlantic and Pacific states alike can draw. So there they stand, the Soviet Union and America, face to face, agreeing to avoid collision, but unable, despite Chinese invectives, to achieve real collusion.

On the Indian subcontinent, whatever the exact words of its guarantees and promises, the United States never undertook to fight against India in order to maintain the integrity of Pakistan. In 1965, Johnson avoided taking sides during the second war between India and Pakistan, and he seems to have been quite happy to let the Kremlin take the credit for the mediation symbolized by the Tashkent meeting. Was Richard Nixon carried away by his feelings about the two protagonists, Yahya Khan and Mrs. Gandhi? Did he think he had been deceived by the Indian prime minister? That he owed a favor to the man who had facilitated Kissinger's trip to Peking? Was he hoping for a show of respect for the United Nations Charter and the appearance of an agreement with China? Did he want to teach the rulers of India a lesson and prevent them from developing a sweet tooth for power politics? In the present state of our knowledge, no one can choose between these many explanations, which are not all incompatible with one another.

What interests us in our search for the exact meaning of multipolarity is the involvement in a subsystem of two rivalries, one continental and the other worldwide: the Sino-Soviet rivalry, which for the present does not really extend outside Asia, and the U.S.-Soviet rivalry, which operates all over the world. On the highest nuclear level, the two world powers remain alone and unequaled. Because of this, and thanks to their air forces, navies, and conventional weaponry, they are capable of intervening anywhere, though paradoxically enough, one of them is less and less tempted to intervene, at least militarily, while the other has so far not gained much from having reached the rank of superpower.

Nixon's trips to Peking and Moscow, with their dual objective of helping to wind up the war in Vietnam and ending the absurd situation of noncommunication between the Soviet Union's two rivals, were inspired not only by realism but also by good sense. There is no need to invoke Metternich, Talleyrand, or Bismarck, nor even to stress the decline of ideologies: The quarrel between the Soviet Union and the People's Republic of China, too, has ideological causes and an ideological dimension. The schism in the world of Marxism-Leninism confirms the lesson of history: Friendship between socialist states is no better than friendship between Christian countries at resisting the depredations of time and diverging interests. But at least conflicting interpretations of the common faith can be used as diplomatic weapons, assuming they do not actually kindle passions.

Accidentally or because of Stalin's Machiavellian ways, relations between Peking and Washington had broken off at the time of the Korean campaign. The Kremlin had obtained a virtual monopoly on contacts with the White House. The visit to Peking was the major event of Nixon's first term because at a blow the American president secured, in his turn, the advantage of dialogue with two states that for the time being were unable to communicate, let alone agree, with each other. So long as the Sino-Soviet conflict remains or seems to remain insoluble, the United States, once it has got out of Vietnam, will be in the position of the third party, the onlooker free to do as it likes—the very freedom as was prized by traditional diplomacy.

What justifies the use of the term *multipolarity* in Europe is not the split between China and the Soviet Union, but the many levels on which relations—whether international or transnational, military, economic, political, or ideological—operate between states and societies, though there is no intercommunication between the different planes, and the nuclear plane does not determine the others. At the end of the 1940s, Stalin lowered an Iron Curtain in the middle of the Old Continent of Europe. He was installing regimes akin to his own in the countries of Eastern Europe, directed by men who believed in Marxism-Leninism, many of whom were returning from exile abroad. In the West, the old nations—whether victorious or vanquished, ravaged or weakened—seemed an easy prey for a conqueror. Only the American Republic seemed capable of erecting a barrier against the ambition of a tyrant or the spread of what the Europeans then called the *New Faith*. So each of the two superpowers surrounded itself with a bloc—the free world ranged against Eastern despotism. The nature of a country's internal regime determined its diplomatic allegiance. In this sense, inter-state relations were dominated by ideology, with each bloc constituting a kind of Holy Alliance (one that joined together established regimes against revolutionaries).

These blocs had no equivalents outside Europe. Outside its own backyard, the Soviet Union has never wielded unconditional authority over other countries inspired by Marxism-Leninism. Even between 1949 and 1953, the

People's Republic of China did not accept the status of a satellite nation. Ideological kinship or affinity between regimes was a characteristic of the two European blocs.* The countries that support the United States in Asia, the Middle East, and Latin America have nothing in common other than the fact that they are not ruled by a monopolistic party inspired by Marxism-Leninism. So there has never been a Soviet bloc or a free-world bloc in Asia, Africa, or Latin America. If some commentators now refer to a period of bipolarity, they do so in a special sense. The policy of containment, carried to an extreme, would have meant that the United States could not accept any territorial or ideological loss: No country, however small, could switch its allegiance and adopt the language of Marxism-Leninism. Hence the tendency of Washington diplomats to undertake responsibilities anytime and anywhere, even when no specifically U.S. interest was involved.

Whether in Europe or in regions outside the field of U.S.-Soviet confrontation, the Nixon-Kissinger policy is characterized by a lesser degree of activism, with regard both to allies and to the Third World, than that of previous administrations. The Gaullist veto on Britain's candidacy for the Common Market in January 1963 annoyed Kennedy and was regarded in the United States as rather shocking. In 1971, Nixon did not come out as either for or against Britain's entry. Though no doubt he was officially in favor, he refrained from bringing any pressure to bear, either in London or Paris. In short, he performed the hegemonic role with more discretion than Kennedy had. Although like his predecessor, he claimed a monopoly when it came to negotiation or action in the matter of nuclear arms, he kept his European allies regularly informed. In this he was continuing a trend begun by Johnson, who had already abandoned Kennedy's great designs.

The Congo crisis had given rise to U.S. intervention via the United Nations and a confrontation between the United States and the Soviet Union. The civil war in Nigeria, in contrast, had been settled locally; the fact that the Soviet Union sent arms to the central government left Washington unmoved. The British, too, supplied the Lagos authorities with weapons. In the natural logic of things, accelerated by the tragedy in Vietnam, Nixon's election was preceded by the decline of globalism.

Similarly, Nixon's team did not really break new ground in Latin America or the Caribbean. Any innovation consisted merely in a lesser degree of

---

*With the exception of Portugal, and later of Turkey and Greece.

activism and intolerance toward revolutionary regimes, even when the latter were inclined to indulge in socialist or even Marxist-Leninist language. It seems that Washington refrained from calling on either the CIA or its friends against the nationalist generals in Peru or the Allende experiment in Chile. It is as if Nixon left U.S. involvement in Africa and Latin America to the State Department and refrained from directing the professionals. The shift from activism to abstention may seem like the beginning of phased withdrawal.

3. Nixon and the European Tradition

We still have not found the answer we were seeking. We have said, but not proven, that Nixon's policy owed its novelty to the philosophy of international relations that lies behind it—unless we ascribe the trip to Peking to that philosophy. As for the rest the return to a moderate doctrine of containment; the pursuit of dialogue with the Soviet Union, begun by Kennedy or perhaps even Eisenhower; the reduction of foreign commitments in order to appease public opinion and adapt to the new balance of power did it call for anything more than common sense or an ability to seize opportunities? This approach leaves out two aspects of Nixon's policy: on the one hand, the sort of language he uses occasionally, and, on the other, the decisions of August 1971 and the economic and monetary quarrels within the capitalist world market. Only time will tell if these aspects are fundamental or secondary.

In an interview published by *Time* magazine on January 3, 1972, President Nixon said:

> We must remember the only time in the history of the world that we have had any extended periods of peace is when there has been balance of power. It is when one nation becomes infinitely more powerful in relation to its potential competitor that the danger of war arises. So I believe in a world in which the United States is powerful. I think it will be a safer world and a better world if we have a strong, healthy United States, Europe, Soviet Union, China, Japan, each balancing the other, not playing one against the other, an even balance.*

Time, January 3, 1972.

A strange, almost absurd definition of an ideal system for world peace. Even if there were five main players on the European scene between 1815 and 1914 (Britain, France, Germany, Austria-Hungary, and Russia), there is nothing magical about that number. The European order established by the Congress of Vienna survived the limited conflicts of the nineteenth century for a number of reasons that had nothing to do with how many principal countries were concerned. Moreover, the five participants listed by the American president exist only in his imagination, or at least the differences between them are of altogether another kind from those between the main countries involved in the nineteenth-century European system. Nixon names two world powers, one great economic power that is not armed (Japan), one continental power that is poor but possesses an embryonic nuclear force (China), and a group of industrialized nations without a common government and without either the ability or the will to assert itself abroad (Europe).

Furthermore, the main participants in the nineteenth-century European setup really did constitute a system, with each taking all the others into account when calculating its own place in the balance of power. There is nothing like that in today's world system. On the political and strategic level, the countries of Europe, even if they were unified, would stay out of Asian conflicts; similarly, Japan would stay out of conflicts in Europe. Because of its prestige and its ideology, China exercises, or would like to exercise, some influence on the European countries that belong to the socialist community. Chou En-lai privately encourages Western Europeans to unite in order to prevent his main enemy, the Soviet Union, from concentrating its forces in the East. Once again, it is clear: There are only two world powers, but that does not make the system bipolar, unless bipolarity means the formation of two blocs or camps, one around each of the world powers. Japan, because it lacks weaponry and nuclear arms, in particular; Europe, because it lacks unity and resolution; and both, because of the physical proximity of one world power, continue to depend on the alliance and protection of the United States.

So the idea of a five-sided equilibrium alarms the Japanese even more than it does the Europeans: It amounts to a refusal to differentiate explicitly between allies and adversaries, which would represent a fundamental departure from postwar diplomacy. It could eventually lead to the posture reflected in a famous expression, not so much cynical as natural, identifying offshore power as a guarantee of stability: "England has no allies; it has only interests."

True, President Nixon has publicly stated over and over again that the United States would respect its alliances and would not sacrifice its friends for the sake of rapprochement with its enemies. But not long before the *Time* article, another event—the measures taken on August 15, 1971[20]— astonished the Japanese and the Europeans alike and revealed a paradox: If the world economy is divided between two markets, one socialist and the other capitalist, economic rivalries or quarrels will arise within each of those markets, and thus among allies. Romania's opposition to the Comecon plan and its decisions illustrates the type of quarrel characteristic of the socialist community. The Europeans, the Japanese, and the Americans argue with increasing vehemence over the international monetary system, the causes of Japan's and West Germany's trade deficits, rates of exchange, discriminatory measures, and overt or covert protectionism. The devaluation of the dollar, which, like the visit to Peking, is taking on a historic significance as a moment of truth, nonetheless creates technical and economic disagreements on the plane of high politics. It must have struck first the Japanese and then the Europeans that the enemies of the United States— China and the Soviet Union—are becoming its interlocutors, perhaps its partners, within the world market at the same time as the European community and Japan are becoming its rivals, almost adversaries. Is there not a danger that the two chief alliances constructed by American diplomacy since 1950—Japan on the one hand and Western Europe on the other— could fall into disuse, the victims at once of détente between the United States and its enemies and of tensions between the allies?

In Asia, once the Vietnam War was over the United States was in a happy position as not only a world power in the theater of operations but also an offshore power free to act and to choose its connections as it pleased. So long as Mao Tse-tung reigns in the Forbidden City, any reconciliation between Peking and Moscow is ruled out, and American diplomats, though not playing one great Communist power off against the other, have regained room for maneuver—something they had been deprived of in the era of obsessional anticommunism. It may even be that Chou En-lai would like the United States to maintain a residual presence in Southeast Asia to save China from being encircled by the web of connections woven by Soviet diplomacy. The latter make Stalin's and even Lenin's old dreams come true by obtaining credits and techniques from the world's most advanced economy. But, seen from Tokyo, Nixon's and Kissinger's doings present a major ambiguity: For more than twenty years, Washington officials were glad to shoulder all responsibility; now they want to delegate it. How far will this go? What will Japan's role be in all this?

Of course, Prime Minister Kakuei Tanaka, successor to Eisaku Sato, whose coups de théâtre in 1971 precipitated his own fall, followed in Nixon's footsteps and soon outstripped him. Nixon could not break off diplomatic relations with Taiwan, but Tanaka did so at once and without hesitation. He, too, receives economic offers from Moscow and Peking— the Soviet ones are more substantial (the development of Siberia) but also more compromising; the Chinese ones start modestly but have potential. The Japanese premier does not have to choose between them, though it is not easy to remain at a strictly equal distance from Moscow and Peking.

The uncertainty hanging over the Japanese leadership concerns Tokyo's relations with Washington. What is left of the military alliance? What turn will the economic rivalry take? Does Nixon differentiate between the Land of the Rising Sun and the Empire of the Middle, the first an ally, the second a former enemy that still denounces imperialism, supports Prince Sihanouk of Cambodia, and fights against the clients and protégés of the United States? Can Japan, sure of the U.S. guarantee, extend its power abroad by economic means, without any other military ambition than protection of its own neighborhood? In Vietnam, Asia for the Asians meant the withdrawal of the U.S. expeditionary corps. What does it mean in Northeast Asia? Should Japan resume its former role as a Great Power on the military plane as well as others, or should it rely on the nuclear guarantee of the United States?

In Europe, both the situation and the question are at once similar and different. The Soviet bloc still exists, as first Czechoslovakia and then Hungary have learned, at a cost, in the sense that the Kremlin continues to set the permissible limits of national autonomy and ideological heresy. Within the bounds prescribed by the Kremlin, Romania and Hungary display their own personalities, the former in its diplomacy, the latter by its internal organization. The United States has never, in Western Europe, exercised an influence comparable with that wielded by Stalin and his successors in Eastern Europe.

Nonetheless, the recovery of the older countries and the development of the Common Market have gradually modified the relations between

Britain, France, and West Germany and between these countries and the United States.

All the Western European countries have forged links with most of the countries in Eastern Europe. When General de Gaulle traveled in Poland, while he spoke of the traditional friendship between that country and his own, he asked his hosts (in vain, as it happens) to look beyond their own environment—a discreet reference to the socialist community on which Wladyslaw Gomulka (leader of the Communist Party and head of state from 1956 to 1970) wished to focus their attention and their loyalty. Though there is no longer an Iron Curtain in the matter of cultural diplomacy or sport, there are still two separate worlds: The Soviet Union goes on enforcing doctrinal conformity and forbidding ideological coexistence. National organization and partial economic integration proceed quite differently in the two sectors into which Europe is divided. The exchange of goods between them has increased and may continue to do so. It is in the Soviet Union's interests to exchange raw materials and energy for ready-to-use factories and often technically advanced manufactured goods. The countries of Eastern Europe also find it worthwhile to foster trade, not only for its own sake but also in the hope that interdependence will promote peace. The government of the FRG, too, cherishes the hope that the GDR will absorb some of its own ideas and democratic freedoms. The East German government replies with what it calls *Abgrenzung*, or demarcation. If East Germany is to survive, as such, in a Europe crisscrossed by the movement of people and goods, the most immaterial frontiers (*Grenzen*), those of the mind, will need to be strengthened.

So where does the United States stand now in a Europe still divided but apparently at peace, a Europe no longer resounding with clashing propagandas? What will the U.S. role be in the coming decade?

Richard Nixon has described his diplomacy, both in Europe and in Asia, as "low profile": a comparison between Kennedy's attitude in 1961–1962 over Britain's first candidacy for the Common Market, and the open refusal of American leaders to take a stand on the subject since 1969, highlights the change that has taken place since Nixon took office. I do not think the president and his advisers were really immediately in favor of Chancellor Willy Brandt's policy of opening to the East (*Östpolitik*). But they did officially approve it, only joining the French and the British in negotiating those parts of the accords on Berlin that directly affected the Big Four. In short, Nixon's

United States allows the Europeans to take responsibility for their own fate: It is up to them to organize themselves as they see fit.

Western Europe, despite its physical proximity to the community of socialist states, belongs to the Atlantic group as regards both ideology and economics. The transnational currency there is the dollar. Many American conglomerates have branches there. The supply of energy in the region depends on relations with oil-producing Middle Eastern countries where American companies have invested billions of dollars. Western Europe is continually affected by all that happens on the other side of the Atlantic, including inflation, interest rates, and movements on the Stock Exchange. No decision made in Moscow by the planners or the Politburo is as influential in Western Europe as the variations in the economic situation of the United States. There is now a transnational economic society that knows no frontiers; its symbol is the eurodollar, and it places limits on the national sovereignty of its members and on their ability to pursue independent policies in the matter of currency or credit.

In the language of the Marxist-Leninists, Western Europe belongs to one world market, the capitalist market, and Eastern Europe belongs to another, the socialist market. Relations between the two markets and between countries belonging to each of them are on a limited or marginal scale in comparison with exchanges within the two markets themselves.

Can the countries of Western Europe have, and do they want to have, closer links to the other half of their continent while continuing to be part of the Atlantic transnational society? Certainly. Can they have, and do they want to have, a Europe "united from the Atlantic to the Urals"? Certainly not. Politically, such a Europe, without the United States and with the Soviet Union, would bring about what is called the "Finlandization" of Europe,* the replacing of one protectorate by another—one that might well prove more invasive than the first.

Economically, exchanges with Eastern Europe can complement and enrich, though they cannot replace, exchanges within the Atlantic or capitalist market. Politically, unless it could make a great effort in the direction of unity and determination (and this seems unlikely), a Western Europe

---

*Though if the Western Europeans found themselves in a situation comparable to that of the Finns, I doubt if they would show the same courage and preserve the same degree of liberty.

detached from the United States, or in which the United States ceased to be interested, would drift into a state of subordination that would in the long run turn it into a satellite state.

And so two crucial questions emerge. In Asia, does the U.S. alliance with Japan, which prevents the latter from rearming, confirm the limited but necessary role of ideological kinship in diplomatic alignments? And in Europe, will the U.S. military presence guarantee that détente is compatible with security?

The answer to both questions will be provided by Richard Nixon during the course of his second term of office. The postwar world that he is helping to create is not like the world of Metternich or Bismarck. Admittedly, Nixon, through Kissinger, borrows something from the wisdom of the European tradition. He accepts a certain dissociation of international relations from ideological conflicts; he does not dream of crusades or collective security; he recognizes that conflicts of interest between states are only natural. He neither hopes for nor expects a worldwide condominium, an inflexible delimitation of zones of influence, or summit bargaining to resolve every crisis, however small. The words that recur most frequently in reports to Congress are "restraint" and "self-restraint." Prudence and moderation are Aristotelian virtues that the immoderate proliferation of arms in the world today makes more imperative than ever.

This being so, what would remain in the diplomatic policy of Nixon and Kissinger of the skeptical wisdom of the old Europe, except the rules of common sense; of reality, if you will; of cynicism, sometimes—though, the bombing raids in North Vietnam apart, of restrained cynicism? Equilibrium between the two world powers on the nuclear level; relatively separate subsystems in which the two world powers assume various roles in association with participants from the same region or continent; a situation where every country defends its own interests while showing the necessary respect for the vital interests of others—all this has nothing in common with the dogmatic rigidity of Metternich. The monster of revolution is not chained up by a Holy Alliance of counterrevolutionaries. Revolutionary states refrain from spreading their beliefs by force, and the United States refrains from seeing a threat in every revolutionary movement.

So why, in spite of all, does doubt persist? Will Nixon and his successors go on being flexible and moderate? If the United States is no longer faced with a monstrous enemy, what need has it of allies? What is the point of permanent ties? Why should it protect commercial competitors who are ungrateful enough to invade the U.S. market? How long will a United States dependent on trade put up with the paradox of partners who are also adversaries—partners in a strategic and diplomatic system, adversaries in economic competition? Will the crusade of the dollar be followed by the diplomacy of the dollar?

What is to be feared is not the teaching of Realpolitik, but a translation that misrepresents and betrays it. Perhaps, to American eyes, Metternich's wig resembles that of George Washington.

SUCCESS OR FAILURE?

Let us look at Robert E. Osgood's verdict on U.S. diplomacy in his preface to George Liska's book: "America's foreign policy in the first two decades of the cold war has been a striking success, judged by the normal standards of national security and power."[21] Would Osgood say the same thing five years later? What is left of the expectations that backed up his verdict?

> Even though the world of the mid-1960s bears no resemblance to American ideals of international harmony, the United States has achieved its proximate goal of containing the expansion of Communist control. The moderation of Soviet policy, the loosening up of the Soviet bloc in Eastern Europe, the disruption of the Sino-Soviet bloc, the frustration of Communist China's expansionist ambitions, and the failure of either of the principal Communist states to extend their domains by exploiting revolutions in the backward areas—these developments fulfill the most critical objectives of the policy of containment enunciated twenty years ago. The United States is now clearly the most powerful state in the world by any criterion; it is the only truly global power.

That last sentence, typical of the years that followed the second Cuban crisis, has plainly ceased to be true, even if it was so at the time it was written. The SALT agreement of 1972 grants the Soviet Union superiority as regards the number and megatonnage of ballistic missiles. Assuming that superiority at a higher level remains with the United States, and that its number of targeted nuclear warheads balances its inferiority in the number of missiles and the power of its warheads, the Soviet Union has now achieved equality. At the same time, it is developing its navy so swiftly that when it brings aircraft carriers into service it will become a global power in the full sense of the word, although in many respects its geopolitical situation seems less favorable than that of the United States.

It is true that the United States has not lost its advance with regard to production, productivity, technical innovation, and standard of living. Despite the chiefly verbal anti-American violence in many countries around the world, it is the American Republic that goes on attracting immigrants, intellectuals, and scientists. The Soviet Union's bureaucratic despotism is less fascinating than the monstrous face of Stalinism was—it neither terrifies nor attracts. Brezhnev seems in his turn to be embarking on an imperialist venture outside Europe, or at least he has all the old will to power, whereas the leaders of the American Republic, denied approval by both political parties, are battling with the senators who, jealous of their obsolete prerogatives, would limit the president's freedom of action just where he particularly wants it, as commander-in-chief of the armed services. In the international system, power depends as much on will as on resources. Western Europe, taken as a whole, has the resources but not the will. France and Britain both lack the resources. So the question arises: Of the two countries capable of playing an imperial role throughout the world, is not one undergoing a weakening of its will?

Let us change Osgood's last sentence to bring it closer to present reality. The United States, after twenty-five years of predominance, still has the most productive economy in the world: It is still at the head of technical and scientific progress; it has not, however, been able to prevent the Soviet Union from rising to its own level in the military sphere, even if the Kremlin pays for this equality by having to devote a larger portion of the gross national product to defense. In 1947 there was only one "global power"; now there are two.

Osgood's other expectations are still valid in the context of the philosophy he explicitly invokes. Almost everywhere the United States has achieved its proximate goal, the containment of communism; it has limited the expansion of Communist power. But not all critics of American diplomacy would call containment a genuine success. The interventions in Guatemala (1953) and Santo Domingo (1965) did succeed, but do they deserve either moral or political approval? Assuming the intervention in Vietnam succeeds, in other words, that it ensures a non-Communist government in Saigon, does that allow us to say that U.S. diplomatic policy in Southeast Asia has been a success? To arrive at a more impartial judgment on the meaning of containment, we need to use at least two other criteria: the means employed, and the kind of regimes that containment has saved from communism.

If we use the second criterion, a first distinction emerges, crude but valid: In Europe, success has not involved limited war, counterrevolution, or CIA agents. For Western Europe, communism, whether of Stalin's brand or of Brezhnev's, would mean economic, political, and moral "regression," a lower standard of living, and a loss of liberties. The word *regression* does not imply an evolutionist theory of history but is a reference to the aims of the people of both camps, even the dogmatists among them. The Marxist-Leninists do not want to reduce productivity, but they do reduce it through a crude method of planning. They want total power for the Communist Party, but individually they know very well that only by a dialectical play on words can total power be reconciled with personal freedom.

"Revisionist" critics can only condemn U.S. diplomatic policy in Europe by renouncing the values of American civilization, even of Western civilization in general. Economic aid and the Marshall Plan have speeded up reconstruction and allowed the nations of Europe to acquire institutions that the immense majority of their people wanted. If in this case it is possible to speak of "the failure of success," it is merely insofar as the European economies have become trade rivals of the U.S. economy. The same can clearly be said of Japan as well.

What arguments could a denigrator bring to bear? He could say that success was easy because the Soviet Union never harbored the ambitions ascribed to it by Cold War crusaders. In the last analysis, Soviet diplomacy, too, probably achieved its proximate, if not its maximum, goal in Europe, which was the maintenance and recognition of the faits accomplis of 1945–1946. Instead of asking the revisionists' childish question, "Who is the guilty party?" it would be better to give up using the phrase *Cold War* once and for all, or to admit that it was at least partly a sort of shouting match that reached epic proportions. The British and the Americans could not allow the Sovietization of Eastern Europe without protest. Stalin, even if he did not fear military action on the part of the Americans, had to isolate his *imperium,* shield it from Western influence, and prevent it from comparing Sovietization with Marshallization.

It may be that such an interpretation will ultimately be accepted when the Kremlin archives are opened. But for the moment let us merely conclude that American diplomacy in Europe, since it took over from British diplomacy, has been both prudent and defensive, resolute and efficient. Some people will reproach it for resigning itself too quickly to the partitioning of Europe: But I do not think either the Americans or the Europeans have ever given their leaders a mandate to "liberate" the countries of Eastern Europe, whether through threats or negotiation. For the time being, rivalry leads to compromise or accommodation. Maintaining the partition is a kind of draw in which the rivals simultaneously succeed and fail, and spheres of influence are accepted under the camouflage of universalist language.

Others criticize the contrast between the exaggerated rhetoric that politicians use and the modest proportions of their actions. What is the point of employing crusading language and turning Uncle Joe into a second Hitler when in fact Washington has never really taken seriously the words of the order of release? This point relates to another aspect of American diplomacy that we have scarcely touched on. It is as if leaders, Congressmen, and journalists sometimes thought it necessary to muster popular passions against an absolute evil lest public opinion refuse to support diplomatic action that was as rational and realistic as that of other countries. McCarthyism, verbal hysteria, and polemics in the country as a whole, but above all within the political classes, ended up misleading the world about the Americans, and the Americans about themselves. The "McCarthyist reign of terror," as some Europeans imagined it, fortunately did not exist; the excesses of McCarthyism, however, did pave the way for the present excesses of revisionism.

Officials in Washington may not themselves have been inspired by the crusader spirit, but that spirit was nevertheless reflected by a general adoption of the policy of containment. This attitude resulted, on the one hand, in an obsessive anticommunism (though during this period the Soviet Union was seen as the main rival, and although the United States naturally opposed the expansion of Soviet power, this was confused for too long with the power of any Communist Party), and on the other hand, in the Korean campaign.

At the time—in 1950—diplomats in Washington were bound to make Stalin partly, if not wholly and entirely, responsible for the aggression in

North Korea. European public opinion still had doubts about the value of the U.S. guarantee. It was prepared to judge the United States on its reaction to what seemed a direct challenge, the violation by a regular army of a dividing line established by agreement between the two superpowers. The trouble, both for the United States and for the world as a whole, was not that Truman and Acheson decided to intervene militarily, but that they decided at the same time to intervene in China, in the last phase of the civil war, by placing the Seventh Fleet between the mainland and Taiwan, and to increase their support for the French in Indochina. These decisions, made in June 1950, contained the seeds of the whole of U.S. diplomatic policy in Asia over the next twenty years, including the Vietnam tragedy, still not over as I write this (in the summer of 1972). Truman's mistake in the conduct of operations, an error instigated by MacArthur, led to the entry of "Chinese" volunteers into Korea and caused a break between Peking and Washington, the isolation of Mao's China, and a fierce desire, shared by Truman, Eisenhower, Kennedy, and Johnson, to halt the spread of communism in Asia.

Here again, the officials concerned soon resigned themselves to a defensive policy in the region where they faced, or thought they faced, their rival, even if only via satellite states. After the Eighth Army's defeat on the Yalu River in the autumn of 1950, Truman and Acheson in fact agreed to a draw. They halted the spring offensive of 1951 as soon as negotiations began. It was probably Stalin who saw an advantage in prolonging the hostilities, or who at least allowed his then allies in the Forbidden City to demand the return to mainland China of all Chinese prisoners—a demand the Americans could not accept. Finally, American diplomacy made do with maintaining the demarcation line in Korea, though as a result it became all the more determined to apply the policy of containment, even if that meant resorting to arms.

Until 1962–1963, by a historical irony, U.S. diplomatic policy in Asia, though in itself misguided, brought, in the short term, more advantages than disadvantages. It fueled the quarrels between Peking and Moscow and created situations in which the national interests and strategic designs of the two main Communist powers were likely to diverge or conflict. For the United States, the Sino-Soviet quarrel was a success. Should we, like Osgood, give Washington's diplomatic policy the credit for it?

Once the Communist camp was split, traditional and conventional wisdom would have suggested a resumption of relations with Peking so as to reinstate normal procedures in the sphere of communications between states. According to Clausewitz, diplomatic relations never stop, even when soldiers fight. So much the more, then, in a period of peace, it makes no sense to refuse to communicate. It may be that between 1963 and 1966 Mao would not have agreed to a dialogue with Washington unless the United States abandoned its alliance with Taiwan. It may be that Nixon and Kissinger were lucky to come on the scene after the fighting on the Ussuri River, after the Cultural Revolution, and at the time of Chou En-lai. Even if this theory is confirmed later, the determination shown in Vietnam by all the American leaders, one after the other, demonstrates another aspect of American diplomatic style, one that has nothing to do with either the "Wilson syndrome," or crusading rhetoric, or the contrast between words and deeds. Truman did not answer Ho Chi Minh's letters. Acheson saw fit, after the triumph of communism in China, to put up a barrier and say, "Thus far and no further." Dulles brought pressure to bear on the French government to carry on the struggle. Eisenhower and Dulles decided to support South Vietnam and do away with what remained of French influence so as to establish at last a non-Communist Vietnamese nationalism. According to the books written by his friends, Kennedy considered the United States already too deeply committed for him to refuse the legacy: There were fewer than 1,000 American advisers in Vietnam in 1960 and more than 15,000 at the time of the young president's assassination. Kennedy, beset with contradictory advice, opted for a half-measure: no more ground troops, but a substantial reinforcement of the military presence without any clear definition of the status of the adviser combatants. Johnson, even more than his predecessor, saw himself as a prisoner of the legacy. In this tragedy, American democracy showed what exceptional and fatal steadfastness it was capable of carrying out.

This constancy did not exclude the reversal of pros and cons or an alternation between one extreme and another, as, for example, shown by the U.S. attitude first toward the Soviet Union and then toward Communist China. In 1971, Red China was all the rage in the United States, as if twenty years of ostracism had been a mere interlude that could be ended by a couple of games of ping-pong. Such perseverance in an undertaking that, even if it had been successful, would not have been worth its human costs, first in Vietnam and then in the United States itself, illustrates the defects in the diplomatic policy sustained by the United States over twenty years. Containment was not, as such, a wrong or unreasonable objective outside Europe. If Europeans tend to think it is, they do so out of egoism or Eurocentrism rather than out of lucidity. What *is* unreasonable is to interpret containment as a kind of categorical imperative and the coming to power of any Marxist-Leninist party as a defeat. Thus, in 1965, Washington resigned itself to the emergence of the Communists in Indonesia. In so doing, it won a victory without intervening, perhaps *because* it did not intervene. The refusal to admit defeat, together with the tendency of all presidents to adopt a moderate position; unbounded confidence in the ability of the greatest power in the world to solve any "problem"; the application of abstract schemes without adequate knowledge of the local situation; excessive violence and a disproportionately large war machine—all these ways of thinking and acting were seen at their worst during the years in question. It was absurd to seek military victory via a search-and-destroy policy instead of helping the South Vietnamese army to defend itself.* It was absurd to think Chinese expansion could be contained by forbidding North Vietnam to unify the three Kys by force. Absurd, too, was the idea that one final and decisive test could show these last romantics that wars of national liberation were pointless. Likewise, the wager that bombing the North would destroy the resolve of the North Vietnamese was branded in all the intelligence reports as doomed to failure.

General Maxwell Taylor now admits that the advisers of the American presidents knew nothing about Vietnam or the Vietnamese people and their history and traditions. They argued in the abstract, on the basis of models. They asked for the gimmicks of a counterinsurgency strangely redirected against the North in 1965 at a time when even halting infiltration would not have been enough to restore security in the country or reestablish the authority of the South Vietnamese government.

Just as the leaders in Washington failed to put themselves in the shoes of other people—those of the North Vietnamese, who saw Vietnam as one country and not two—so, too, the negotiations on arms limitation could not

---

*All in all, an expedition against the North might have stood a better chance.

succeed so long as the balance was so unequal that Robert S. McNamara, the U.S. defense secretary, could say he was in favor of attacking the enemy's forces rather than its cities, adding that the United States was temporarily in a position to do so. How could the Soviets accept such a situation?

The Soviets took advantage of circumstances to achieve parity in nuclear weapons and to approach, perhaps even to reach, parity at sea. In 1964, the Soviet Union had around 100 intercontinental missiles, six or seven times fewer than the United States. But whereas the latter did not exceed its 1967 total of 1,054 intercontinental missiles, by 1969 the Soviets had more than that number. The SALT agreement signed in Moscow recognized that the Soviet Union had a superiority of 40 percent in the number of intercontinental missiles (1,408 as against 1,000) and of missile-launching submarines (62 to 44), and a superiority of a third in the number of submarine-launched missiles (950 to 710); its megatonnage of nuclear power was three times that of the United States. At present, the Americans have 5,700 nuclear warheads, the Soviets 2,500. If the Soviets perfect the MIRV (multiple independently targeted reentry vehicle), they could easily outstrip the United States in the matter of nuclear warheads, so much higher is the weight of warheads that their authorized rockets can carry.

The consent of the United States to this agreement bears witness to the opposite of its usual perseverance. Perhaps, at this level, equality and superiority do not mean anything any more. Perhaps the idea of mutually assured destruction is enough to maintain a balance of terror without weakening the resolve of the weakest player in a moment of crisis. The Moscow agreement on strategic arms is a kind of compensation for American steadfastness in Vietnam: Massive reprisals, flexible riposte, and arms control are stages in the evolution of American thought, ending in a treaty the Senate would never have ratified before the Vietnam tragedy and the turnabout in American public opinion. Osgood's idea of the United States as the only world power sounds out of date these days.

At this point, perhaps historical irony will help us find success in failure once again. After twenty-five years, containment in Europe led not to the victory of one camp or the other, but to accommodation. Should the westerners have hoped for more, at least in the short term of a generation? Similarly, without the frustrations of the Vietnam War, would American diplomacy have had the courage to break with the past and turn again to Peking? It seems clear that we are witnessing the formation of an Asian subsystem in which four states—the Soviet Union, Japan, the United States, and China—will be linked to one another by a set of complex relations. In South Asia, India is in the process of joining the list of Great Powers; Japan will take care not to join the list, at least for a while. One result of the ubiquity of American diplomacy was not so much a will to power as a centripetal movement, a turning in on itself by the United States. Failure becomes success because it encourages this withdrawal, teaches modesty, and paves the way to international equilibrium.

History has not, by a wave of its magic wand, undone the expectations that supported Osgood's verdict. Freedom fighters have not repeated Fidel Castro's achievement in any country in Latin America. Both civilian and military governments there have become more and more nationalistic, sometimes more and more anti-American, but none has turned Marxist-Leninist. In Chile, Allende's government has not abandoned the constitutional path. During the 1960s, when the United States had the Vietnam millstone around its neck, nations were riven by internal conflicts, and urban and rural violence became endemic in rich and poor countries alike. The Soviet Union presented a facade of order and authority, if not of law, but it no longer sent a message of salvation to young people searching for an absolute. Much less than twenty-five years before, it aroused hope in the disinherited and faith in the revolutionaries. With a new equilibrium in the international system has come a less virulent messianism. Did Kennan, when he wrote his article on containment, open up a new prospect?

The United States, while dominating the world, has not ruled it. Like all strategists, it has made strategic errors—for example, in Korea and Vietnam. In Yugoslavia and in China it has profited from the mistakes of its rivals, just as the Soviets have profited from America's own mistakes. The American ambassador's support, over several years, for Fulgencio Batista, followed by a swift abandonment of the Cuban dictator, allowed Castro to win power. But Castro made the Missile Crisis possible, and his regime, with its unsuccessful Five-Year Plans, has degenerated into a kind of mini-Stalinism that discourages the Latin Americans from following in his footsteps. If Washington resumed relations with Havana, that would be enough to make Castro's regime lose whatever prestige it has left. Another success through failure.

Two questions remain before we close this balance sheet. How will the Soviet Union use its military power? And will the United States, when the time comes, agree to play its necessary part in the international system, which will call for the traditional methods of European (or eternal) diplomacy, without adopting a crusading spirit and without exploiting its own omnipotence?

American diplomacy succeeded in Europe not only because it contained communism but also because it fostered economic progress and human liberty. The Bay of Pigs landing was a double failure—political and moral. The intervention in Santo Domingo was a military success, and a political success in the short term, but the moral loss was probably greater than the political gain. Even leaving aside such spectacular episodes, does the success of containment represent success for other nations, too, or failure? When one and when the other? It all depends on the regime that manages to survive, with or without U.S. help. The Eastern Europeans acclaim the president of the United States: They are sorry that they, too, do not live in the sphere of influence and responsibility of "imperialism." Where are the countries in which Leonid Brezhnev would be acclaimed?

THE END OF
COLONIAL EMPIRES

WHAT EMPIRES COST AND
WHAT PROFITS THEY BRING

(address delivered April 20, 1962)

Mr. President, Ladies and Gentlemen:

When you did me the honor of asking me, who am not an economist, or only an amateur one, to speak to an audience of professionals, I thought I should choose a subject with two characteristics. On the one hand, it ought to be connected with current events and give rise to semi-political arguments; and on the other hand, it should be a subject that lends itself to relatively objective analysis. I think the problem I have posed, about what empires cost and what profits they bring, does have those two characteristics. Mr. President, Professor Baudin has said that the subject is rather vague and difficult to analyze. I shall try to prove him wrong, and I shall begin by saying what I mean by an *empire.* I use the word to refer to nonindependent territories—nonautonomous territories, to use the United Nations jargon—which are, for the most part, underdeveloped, and which are under the sovereignty of a developed country. This definition does not apply to all the historically known empires—the Roman, Soviet, French, and British Empires, for example, which all present special features of their own. But what interests French people today is what is called the French Empire, or the French Union. The question I shall ask is, To what extent can one draw up a balance sheet of the advantages and disadvantages of that empire? It goes without saying that I do not claim to be able to draw up a complete account in the space of forty minutes. I would just like to point out the main variables involved and the kind of argument that may be used to help solve the problem.

First, a caveat, in the hope, probably vain, of soothing in advance any passions my words may arouse. Whatever anyone may think, I have never for an instant thought that economic considerations should determine policy in any given case, and especially in the case of Algeria. As some of you know, my opinions on policy in Algeria are heretical. I expressed them a year ago, and if it was to be done again, I would express them again. I still think that the least bad policy, that which would save most of what can be saved, is the one I set out in a pamphlet a year ago. In it, contrary to most critics' accounts of what I said, I never supported my suggestions with purely economic arguments. What I did say is that it is absurd to claim that France would be ruined if it lost its sovereignty over Algeria, because it is not true, and we ought not to justify a battle fought in the name of greatness, or honor, or for the sake of our compatriots in Algeria, with economic arguments that are devoid of truth. The second economic argument I used is that it is probably impossible, and in any case would be extremely costly, to raise 8 or 9 million Muslims to the French standard of living, or at the least to bring the Algerian and French standards of living close enough together to make feasible a policy of integration. Let me repeat, moreover, that the considerations I shall put forward today do not imply any assertions about what ought to be done in Algeria. That depends essentially on an actual situation and on political arguments that I have no wish to enter into, unless by some unlikely chance objections from the audience oblige me to do so.

So let us examine the attitude of French public opinion toward the problems of the empire, or of the nonautonomous territories belonging to the franc area.[1] I would say that French public opinion is obsessed by and torn between two complexes, which I shall call the *Dutch complex* and the *Spanish complex*.

Those who are affected by the Dutch complex are those who remember that, before the war, Holland derived 17 percent of its national income from Indonesia. Since the war, Holland has lost Indonesia, but it is still richer than it was before the war. In other words, even a small country with a rapidly increasing population has been able, by concentrating its investments on its own soil, to make good its losses and demonstrate a proposition that is self-evident to you economists but unrecognized by the greater part of French public opinion: namely, intensive expansion is possible in the twentieth century for developed countries if they have the necessary physical infrastructure and enough technical staff. There are no limits to such expansion either in theory or in practice (or at least no Western European country has reached them yet, assuming they exist). Growth is possible even within the same territorial limits. In the twentieth century, a developed country does not have to acquire extra space. Those affected by the Dutch complex point out that what Holland has done, other countries can do; some of them go so far as to explain many of France's difficulties by the fact that the home country is still responsible for underdeveloped territories in which we invest large sums every year.

If the whole of French public opinion had the Dutch complex, we would have a policy: It might be either a good one or a bad one, but at least it would be *a* policy. Unfortunately, the other half of French public opinion—and for the time being this second half is more eloquent than the first and has more press outlets—is obsessed by the Spanish complex. This complex is not so widespread as its Dutch counterpart, but I think it is just as intelligible. It may be summarized in the statement, Spain has been in decline ever since it lost its empire.

As Lucien-Anatole Prévost Paradol pointed out about a century ago, for a country that has known power and glory there is no middle way between preserving its former greatness and total impotence. Many Frenchmen today, especially if they are in the army, believe that what is called "the loss of the empire" (and Algeria represents the last part of the empire in M. Baudin's sense of the word: that is, the empire of power, domination by power, with power increasing through domination)—many excellent Frenchmen, with whom for many reasons I sympathize, are convinced that the loss of Algeria would be such a political and moral disaster that it would bring about France's inevitable decline. The worst of it is—and I shall try to be objective about this—that while sufferers from the Dutch complex may be right, sufferers from the Spanish complex may not be wrong. The former are clearly right economically. But the latter could be right politically and morally. It is possible that an event experienced as a disaster could actually become one, with psychological consequences such that what is not factually inevitable comes to pass all the same via a human, a historical, mechanism. Moreover, the two theories underlying the complexes belong in different contexts. All anyone can do, and what you economists must do, is help our fellow countrymen to think the problem through as accurately as possible. But I add this coda: Although an economist may set out the pros and cons inherent in a situation, he cannot tell us what alternative to choose because economic pros and cons do not show the way to a political solution.

The first and most natural advantage of dominance, as we all know, is plunder. There are cases in which conquest makes it possible simply to rob the conquered country of its wealth. In its most elementary form, this means taking its gold and other precious metals, but, as we saw in 1944–1945, there are other, scarcely more subtle, methods. In modern jargon, there is the "equipment levy." The Soviet armies in Manchuria and Eastern Europe, and even the Western armies in West Germany, were not above such a primitive form of looting as dismantling machinery at great expense so that it could be reassembled somewhere else, also at great expense, only for it to be noticed in the meanwhile that . . . Need I go on? This kind of booty does not usually get anyone very far, and nowadays such direct plundering of existing assets abroad is unlikely to lead to expanding wealth at home.

A second possible advantage of dominance arises out of the practice by which a conquered people is allowed to occupy only inferior positions in its own country, the senior posts being reserved for the conquerors. This is what the whites in South Africa are currently attempting as they try to make use of a black labor force while denying its members any possibility of rising up through the technical or social hierarchy. Countries that adopt such policies are forced to live in a kind of fortified camp—a repetition of the ancient Spartan experiment, and one unlikely to produce any examples of humane civilization. Even if such methods were admissible, I doubt if Frenchmen or any other Western Europeans would contemplate adopting them. We are not overburdened with qualified staff in France, and the idea of forbidding a subject people to acquire qualifications strikes us as not only absurd but also despicable. In my view, no Frenchman dreams that his country's dominance should take anything like that form. The official notion of French dominance sees it as leading in due course to the autonomy or independence of the territories concerned, or else to assimilation. In either case, discriminatory practices such as those I have described above are ruled out.

The third possible advantage of dominance, and here we approach current realities, lies in the supply of raw materials. It cannot be denied that nonautonomous territories can be very useful in this respect. But distinctions need to be made. A primary factor, which is military or political rather than specifically economic, is security of supply. In this respect, it is necessary, or at least desirable, that the needs of the home country should come first. It is a further advantage that such raw materials can be paid for in the home country's national currency. This does not mean its sovereignty has to be maintained at all costs; it does mean that the unity of the monetary area needs to be preserved. Admittedly, it might become necessary to assert the home country's sovereignty if one of its formerly dependent territories wanted to leave its monetary area. But if the object is to pay for raw materials in one's own national currency, the example of the sterling, and temporarily of the franc, too, shows that sovereignty is not indispensable. Two further factors are the profits from raw materials and their purchase price. It is certain that when very rich oil deposits are found, it is very useful if the soil beneath which they lie is subject to the sovereignty of the dominant power, which can then retain a higher proportion of the profits. If that sovereignty has been lost, the oil can still be paid for in the national currency, but part of the profits will have to be handed over to local peoples in the form of royalties. A fourth advantage lies in the possibility of buying raw materials at a reduced price. All countries have made use of this system. Soviet Russia did so in Europe, but not after 1956, the time of the rupture. We know that up to 1956 the Soviets bought Polish coal at less than the world price, and although Poland was not under Soviet sovereignty, the USSR's political dominance allowed it to buy this raw material at reduced cost. But this exploitation through political dominance came to an end in the eastern zone in 1956. It is extremely interesting to recall that when the Soviets arrived in Eastern Europe, they began by trying to conduct two operations together—economic exploitation and ideological and political propaganda. But after ten years they noticed something that you economists knew all along, namely, that it is impossible to exploit a country and at the same time make your regime popular. After ten years of exploitation, and in particular, of underestimating the value of the region's raw materials, the regime had become so unpopular that the Soviet officials radically changed their policy. Like me, you have probably read the economic studies showing that, since 1956, Eastern Europe has cost the Soviet Union more than it has brought in. To digress for a moment, this does not mean that the USSR is in a hurry to get rid of Europe's eastern zone. It does mean that, like everyone else, the Soviets have failed to find the miracle recipe that would make an empire a paying proposition in the twentieth century. Even for the Soviet Union, which has political means at its disposal that we in our democracies have not, the contradiction between exploitation and domination has emerged as self-evident.

Trade outlets are the fourth advantage usually adduced to justify empires and other forms of dominance. We are always hearing about outlets. I did bring some propaganda pamphlets about Algeria with me that tell us how many days French workers used to spend toiling for Algeria—but I would not want us to get overexcited. As for outlets, the first thing to say about them is that in the nineteenth century, in the first phase of growth, the existence of foreign outlets was probably useful in most cases. It is easier to launch economic growth if you have foreign territories available where you can off-load industrial goods that cannot all be sold in the home country because of limited purchasing power there. Second, in the twentieth century, again outlets present advantages that are particularly attractive to entrepreneurs, among them the virtual certainty of being able to sell goods in protected markets. A supplementary point: Political dominance makes it possible to impose on nonautonomous countries a commercial regime that, to put it mildly, does not necessarily work against the interests of the home country. This possibility undoubtedly often makes the sale of manufactured goods easier than it would have been without protected markets, which leads entrepreneurs to think that, in the case of a world depression, the repercussions on their business would be mitigated. I must add, of course, that protected markets can also involve disadvantages. They are too kind to entrepreneurs. If you want to encourage entrepreneurs to produce more cheaply, protected markets have the opposite effect. It amazes me that people so often forget the scale of French exports to the French Union when trying to explain France's balance-of-payment difficulties. The fact is that more than 40 percent of our exports of manufactured goods go to the French Union, and that the industrial raw materials that come to us from the franc area amount to 15 percent of all our imported raw materials. If more than 40 percent of our exports of manufactured goods go to an area that supplies so small a fraction of our necessary imports, it is not surprising that we have difficulties with our balance of payments.

The last advantage of dominance, which is substantial but difficult to discuss briefly, is dealt with by Pierre Moussa in his interesting book on the economy of the franc area:[2] It is the ability to construct an integrated supranational economy. There are undoubted benefits in belonging to a large monetary area: Intensive expansion is possible, but surface expansion is often easier. The pros and cons cannot be reduced to figures, but it is clear that in the twentieth century the existence of a large monetary area counts as a favorable circumstance.

What conclusions can be drawn from all this?

1. Military power or sovereignty is still useful for ensuring security of supply as regards raw materials. This is an advantage that cannot be expressed in figures, because the cost of the risk of insecurity is different in every case.

2. Sovereignty or dominance is still useful for making sure a country enjoys a suitable amount of the profits from rich oil or mineral deposits. Take the case of Kuwait. Kuwait is not under British sovereignty. It is an emirate protected by Britain, with an astonishing ratio between its millions of tons of oil and its mere thousands of citizens. There are 150,000 Arabs there, and it produces 50 million metric tons of oil a year. Dominance over such a territory is an enormous advantage. One day I played a practical joke on an English-speaking audience: I said that the ideal twentieth-century colony was a desert with plenty of oil under the surface and as few people as possible above it. But what I said is economically true: The closer an empire gets to this ideal, the better it is for it. But as you know, Kuwait is an extreme case.

As for protected markets, let us say they present a mixture of advantages and disadvantages to which it is hard to put a figure. An exporter of cotton or cotton goods is sure that it would be disastrous for him to lose his outlets. But an economist, seeing often inefficient industries hold on to protected markets within the French Union, is not sure that the overall outcome benefits our society as a whole.

The last factor, the enormous franc area, is not dependent on sovereignty. All it requires is monetary unity.

Now let us turn to another aspect of the subject. Why are we so ready to talk about the "cost" of empires, the "cost" of dominance?

When people believed that dominance paid, either they had no intention of developing dependent territories or they did not know what development costs. The first alternative is conceivable: One can, or one could, exercise dominance over a territory with the sole object of extracting from it raw materials directly useful to the home country, perhaps also with the idea of selling some manufactured goods in the dependent region, though without intending or feeling obliged to raise the people's standard of living there. But in the twentieth century we know it is no longer possible to exercise dominance over dependent territories without promoting their economic development. But that immediately involves costs. First, an infrastructure has to be created to provide for transportation and administration, and that is expensive. Then, it is necessary to set up the educational and technical institutions on which the process of development largely depends. Finally, the home country needs to invest capital, often considerable amounts of it, in the local industries. In most cases the local population is increasing rapidly; in the twentieth century, the cost of the economic development that the home country feels obliged to shoulder has therefore become increasingly high. A further point. Supposing the dominant power's investments abroad are profitable. Keynes's opinion on this has always struck me as self-evident, though it is frequently forgotten. He says that if one lends money to facilitate investment in Africa, Asia, or Argentina, there is obviously a danger that these debts may some day be repudiated. The investment itself thus would remain in the country of the borrowers. True, even if you invest in your home country, there could be a political change or the state might confiscate your capital. But in that case, though the individual would lose out, the community would still have the factory, the bridge, or the school in question. In contrast, in the case of nationalization or repudiation of debts, the material benefit of capital invested abroad passes to a foreign country. In my view, there is also another reason why the cost of empire is underestimated. I think people used to underrate the major disadvantages of economic integration for both the home country and the dependent territory. The attempt, within the same political community, to bring about simultaneous progress in regions that are at different stages of economic maturity and that have fundamentally different economic structures is still bound to encounter obvious, but often unrecognized, obstacles.

What is the disadvantage from the point of view of the home country? It is faced with a dilemma in which both alternatives are more or less unacceptable. Either the home country wants to introduce its own standards into the dependent territories—educational and social norms, for example, and organizational standards in general—in which case the transposing of

French norms into an underdeveloped territory involves it in liabilities that are in the long term intolerable, or the home country introduces different norms, in which case its policy of assimilation or integration is immediately denounced as discriminatory, in spite of theoretical denials. Algeria is a striking example (although the dominant powers just might, and indeed do, get away with introducing different norms in Black Africa). In Algeria, because of the size of the French population there, it was almost impossible not to introduce French standards, especially in education. But these standards were quite unsuited to the needs of a community like the Muslim community there, which is basically an underdeveloped one, requiring not an inferior educational system but one that is not unduly expensive.

The disadvantage, from the point of view of the underdeveloped country, is the great difficulty, if complete political and economic integration is to be achieved, of applying to the dependent territory a political economy suited to the early phases of development. As has often been said, the complete freedom obtaining in commercial transactions between Algeria and France has never furthered Algeria's industrialization. The fact is, in France, as in Europe, industry tends to follow industry. It is difficult to get private individuals to invest or industrialize in less developed regions where conditions are relatively unfavorable. That being so, there are two fundamental objections to any attempt at economic integration involving countries of different ages: For the home country, the cost soon becomes prohibitive, and for the underdeveloped country, there is a danger that the necessary measures will not be taken until it has achieved a minimum amount of autonomy. I consider it in the fundamental interests of both parties that differences in the matter of legal norms and adequate economic autonomy be taken into account in this context.

Given these economic issues, what kind of policy is desirable for the French Empire, in particular, and for European empires in general? What factors should policymakers take into consideration?

I myself think that our own first rule should have been to reduce wars to a minimum: They are very costly in economic terms and from many other points of view.

The second rule or aim would be to see that as many resources in raw materials as possible are paid for in the national currency.

Third, it is both legitimate and natural that France should spend some hundreds of billions of francs in the French Union, but it would make more sense if governments would give some thought to how much they really wanted to spend and set some limits on the figures.

When I say this sort of thing I am often told that I talk like a capitalist. I should like to point out that none of the hundreds of billions that the French state spends comes out of my pocket. So, being on the right side of the fence, I lose less from that expenditure than ordinary French workers do. It seems to me quite extraordinary that real or self-styled men of the Left should think it unworthy of an economist to count the costs, which have to be paid by the whole community and not just by capitalists. It is the whole community that deprives itself of part of its resources when it invests them overseas. The community has a perfect right to decide to do so, but I doubt if economists have the right to say that the French community is going to get richer when it spends hundreds of billions in Africa. It seems to me highly probable that there are more profitable possibilities for investment in France itself.

What is the present situation in the French Union? At the moment, it has relatively few resources in the form of raw materials, apart from the oil deposits in the Sahara, where the expenditures on investment and arising out of sovereignty are relatively high. It is difficult to arrive at exact figures, though I am as familiar as you are with the published statistics. Taking the good year with the bad, the cost of investment in Africa, excluding special expenditure in Algeria, must have reached some 200 billion francs per annum. Taking into account all the investment financed by the French state in North Africa and Black Africa, France has every year spent a greater proportion of its national revenue on the French Union than the United States has allotted in economic aid. But I see no evidence that France has won any admiration from the world as a whole or any gratitude on the part of its protégés. This ought to serve as a lesson. Trying to help dependent territories, or even actually managing to do so, is not enough to solve the problem of good relations between them and the home country. Why? Because nowadays there are political and emotional factors that count more than strictly economic phenomena do. The fact is that in a large part of Africa those who claim to speak for the masses—I do not say the masses themselves because I do not know what they want—are more attracted by the myth of independence than by the aid we send them.

What ought to be done? On the economic plane, I myself would advocate trying to maintain the franc area as long as possible. Contrary to the opinion attributed to me, I consider that, all in all, to maintain a franc area with Africa is more favorable than otherwise to the development of the French economy.

Further, leaving aside the special case of Algeria, I believe we ought to impress the governments we have established in various places with a sense of their own responsibilities; that is to say, we ought to tell them we are ready to help them, but within certain limits. Above all, let us not give them the impression that we want to make use of millions of francs to forbid them independence; we shall never have enough millions to buy their dependence if they want independence. Our only chance of keeping them from becoming too impatient for independence lies in assuring them that they can have it when they want it. I am thinking explicitly of Black Africa, leaving aside the very special question of North Africa. But whether or not we promise Black Africa independence, let us not forget the first necessity of both political and economic policy. This is to give African governments a sense of their responsibilities, which means we cannot provide them with subsidies designed to maintain French-style standards in their territories. Their countries' achievement of autonomy, or even sovereignty, would require overcoming the two difficulties that I have mentioned in connection with the simultaneous development of poor and less poor countries: the need to avoid imposing French norms on dependent territories and the willingness to allow these territories to develop their own economic policies. We are in the process of creating in Africa what Monsieur Moussa, an enthusiastic advocate of the project, calls "Big Schemes," that is, the development of mineral deposits, dams, and so on. The peoples of Africa will certainly benefit from them.

But such projects represent, first and foremost, and this is perfectly legitimate, the interests of France. They are complementary to the development of the French economy. But, as they simultaneously involve a good deal of investment in the territories, the local populations also profit from them.

I fear, however, that such projects may strike the local governments as another form of colonial exploitation, unsuited to the sort of development needed by the native peoples.

I have two more observations that it is just possible to mention without arousing passions. First, where there are unusually rich deposits of raw materials, as in the case of oil in the Sahara, the possibility of exploiting them for our own advantage depends on our agreeing to share the profits. Disregarding the demands of what I view as blind nationalism, we are more likely to do well out of the proceeds if the three countries that make up North Africa believe that they will do well, too, and if the big anonymous oil companies have a stake there. I know that is one of the things one is not supposed to say, but as you have done me the honor of inviting me to speak, and I have a well-known reputation as a heretic, I shall venture to say what I think. Only myopia disguised as patriotism can overlook anything so obvious.

Finally, the territories dependent on metropolitan France are still extensive. Whatever the outcome of the Algerian War, the development of Algeria, Tunisia, Morocco, and Black Africa will call for amounts of capital and numbers of technicians that France alone cannot supply. I believe that it is in France's interests, at the same time as it endeavors to maintain the franc area, to involve other countries in that task.

The economic remarks I have put before you are marginal in comparison with politics. I have deliberately left aside the problem that overshadows all the rest: The problem of Algeria is too complex to be analyzed in the space of a few minutes. All the rest—the preservation of the franc area, relations with Black Africa, everything else—is to a certain extent dependent on the Algerian problem. But, again, the solution of the Algerian problem does not depend on economics, and this evening you decided that I should be an economist.

INDOCHINA

In France, the desire to preserve the status quo at all costs does not derive just from the class responsible for "collaboration"; former leaders and representatives of the Resistance, moved by the spirit of greatness and passionately eager to preserve their heritage, ended up losing it amid another disaster.

Unfortunately, the question of the empire presented itself immediately after the liberation of mainland France, even before the end of the war with Germany. Indochina had undergone a strange fate, remaining under a French administration that took orders from Vichy. Admiral Jean Decoux, the governor general, was ardently loyal to Marshal Henri Philippe Pétain and introduced some ideas and organizations inspired by the regime of the National Revolution. (Vietnamese youth, after being made to parade in honor of Pétain and French patriotism, eventually went on to discover Vietnamese patriotism.) On the diplomatic plane, Admiral Decoux did the only thing he could. There was no way of preventing the Japanese from using the naval and air bases. In 1940, the Unites States and Britain were incapable of helping the absurdly inadequate forces at the French authorities' disposal. By accepting a collaboration that the Japanese could easily have forced on them, the government of Indochina, following instructions from Vichy, did no harm to the Allied cause and preserved its own chances for the future.

The war of the airwaves between the Vichyists and the Gaullists raged in Asia, too. Admiral Decoux, adopting the slogans and sometimes the practices of Vichy, and the Gaullists, pursued by the admiral's police and denouncing "collaboration" elsewhere, carried on French quarrels in drastically different circumstances. After General de Gaulle arrived in Paris, the secret organization moved into the interior of Indochina, and French radio attacked the admiral with redoubled vigor. In the army and in the administration, the number of "Resistance" members sincerely eager to fight the Japanese, or simply to "clear" themselves, increased massively. The Japanese replied to this resistance* with a forcible takeover on March 9, 1945.[3] Not only were the French unable to prevent the Japanese occupation, they were also publicly humiliated by the Japanese soldiers, and on that day, in the eyes of the Vietnamese, they lost their mandate from heaven.

The expeditionary force, which originally had been intended to take part in the final campaign against Japan, was ordered to restore French authority in Indochina. It succeeded, after some fighting, in the South (Cochin-China was legally a colony). In the North, General Leclerc prepared the way for a landing by making an agreement with the Chinese generals commanding the occupation forces and Ho Chi Minh, an old Communist militant presiding over the Vietminh government set up in Tonkin after the Japanese capitulation. The outcome remained in suspense throughout 1946. General Leclerc had returned to Indochina convinced that its reconquest would call for an army of 500,000 men and long years of fighting. He was in favor of treating with the nationalists. Admiral Georges Thierry d'Argenlieu,[4] an officer in the marines turned monk who was appointed governor by General de Gaulle, initiated a conference in Dalat with southern politicians, while Ho Chi Minh was negotiating in Paris. Ho Chi Minh left France for Hanoi empty-handed. After a number of incidents, the most serious of which was the French artillery shelling of Haiphong, the Vietminh unleashed hostilities on December 19, 1946. A surprise attack intended to wipe out the Hanoi garrison failed. The war began, with the French gaining ground in the towns and the Vietminh seeking refuge in remote regions or underground. Throughout 1947, the socialist foreign minister Marius Mouter let slip the last chances of a peaceful settlement. From 1948 on, events followed their inevitable course.

From the beginning, what was evident was not so much a resolute decision to fight as indecision leading to war—the kind of situation that was to recur so often in recent years. In Paris there was a divided government in which the advocates of Resistance regularly had the last word. In Indochina

---

*It is possible that the Japanese might not have tolerated the continuation of the French administration even if the resistance had remained passive.

there was a proconsul who took initiatives (such as the Dalat conference and the shelling of Haiphong) that went beyond or against instructions from Paris. When initiative and indecision combined to bring about an explosion, the official order was to "hold firm" (as at Verdun). For Paris, to continue the war was politically the easiest solution.

Indochina was not a populated colony. Apart from officials and soldiers, there were only a few merchants, engineers, clerks, planters, and so on. Independence did not entail any serious or problematical transfers of population. The only argument against withdrawal—but a weighty one—was that the Vietminh leadership was Communist. To treat with Ho Chi Minh was to hand Vietnam over to communism. But I doubt if that was the only reason why the political class was so loath to give it up. If the only objective of the war had been to put up a barrier against Communist expansion, the French government should have mustered the forces of non-Communist nationalism and promised others what it denied Ho Chi Minh. Under pressure of circumstances, it did make an attempt at such a policy, but with much delay and an air of giving with one hand what it was taking away with the other. The great majority of French leaders, whether soldiers or civilians, could neither imagine nor accept a war like the one the British had fought for years against Communist guerrillas before finally granting Malaysia independence. There was no future for former officials in an independent Indochina, and most politicians, on both the Left and the Right, including some who had acted heroically against the Germans, refused to apply the British Commonwealth model to the French Union. The evolution of the French Empire was not to emerge through the independence of the overseas territories.

Although the communism of Ho Chi Minh was not the only, or even probably the chief, cause of the outbreak of war, it was behind the "revival" in 1950. In 1945, the American authorities, in accordance with Roosevelt's instructions and frame of mind, were hostile to the return of the French. In 1950, when the North Korean armies had crossed the 38th parallel, all was suddenly reversed. Ho Chi Minh was no longer the hero of an anticolonialist struggle; he was turning into the leader of a party that was hand in glove with Soviet imperialism. The war in Indochina, which the spokesmen of the French government had had such difficulty "selling" to the U.S. administration, was now taken over almost with enthusiasm by the latter when it decided to intervene in Korea. From then on, the war went on costing francs, but it brought in dollars. In 1953, the Korean armistice opened a new phase. For the last time, there was the chance of an honorable escape from the trap: Instead of trying to persuade the U.S. government to link the Korean armistice to an armistice in Indochina, Monsieur Bidault aimed at victory, whereas the United States was content with a draw. The territorial clauses of the 1954 armistice were no different from those that might have been signed in 1953, but this armistice followed the defeat at Dien Bien Phu, which could not fail to have consequences all over the world. In North Africa, especially, the old order was threatened.

THE ALGERIAN TRAGEDY

This booklet is made up of two notes, the first written in April 1956 and the second in May 1957.

The first was intended for a few friends who were responsible, to some extent, for French public opinion and policy. I was trying to persuade them that our military activity ought to be accompanied by a program of reform leading to the constitution of an Algerian state. Six months later I began to write the second note, but I kept it in a drawer: People had taken up their positions and it had become impossible to make any of them change their minds.

I would not have published the pamphlet at all if my last book, *Espoir et peur du siécle* (Hope and fear of the century), had not contained a few pages on the "Algerian impasse." Supporters of M. Robert Lacoste and Monsieur Guy Mollet have criticized me for encouraging the rebellion and giving it "crazy hopes." But the Algerian War is not an ordinary war. Its objective is not victory but peace. Whatever the outcome of the fighting, conditions allowing Muslims and Frenchmen to live together must be restored. There are 9 million Muslims there today, and their number is increasing fast. More and more insistently, they ask for government jobs and demand to be able to govern themselves. Even if huge sacrifices were made, and even supposing that the oil reserves in the Sahara turned out to be exceptionally productive, the standard of living of too large a population on too poor a land can improve only slowly. Inevitably, however the fighting turns out, the status of the French minority is bound to change. After examining the facts, we are entitled to decide on a policy of what is called *pacification*—the maintenance of a large army in Algeria over a number of years, despite the independence of Tunisia and Morocco, despite the blueprint law in Black Africa, and despite the United Nations and Soviet, U.S., and Afro-Asian propaganda. If French public opinion is convinced that the future of our country depends on retaining unconditional sovereignty on the other side of the Mediterranean, it will go on supporting a struggle that is not physically beyond us. But as all agree, the worst possible thing would be to give up on it out of weariness, instead of holding out, perhaps grudgingly but also lucidly.

France must choose between the two alternatives. And it would be best if it chose with its eyes open. What would it be like if the conformists conspired to prevent us from acknowledging unpleasant facts? I recently happened to come across a passage by Montesquieu: "Be true in everything, even on the subject of one's country. Every citizen is obliged to die for his country; no one is obliged to lie for it." We live in a country that does not oblige anyone to lie for it, and where the search for a truth, no matter how unpleasant, cannot be against the common good.

Paris, May 6, 1957

I

I admire the Frenchmen everywhere who take an uncompromising stand on Algeria. There exist indissoluble links between Algeria and France, say some of them. But if free elections were to be held, who is to guarantee that the elected representatives of the Algerian people would approve of those indissoluble links with France? Negotiations are necessary, say the others. But the first condition that the leaders of the maquis would lay down, assuming they could agree amongst themselves long enough to stop fighting and start making peace with the French, would be recognition of Algerian independence. And does anyone imagine that the Algeria of the Front de Libération Nationale (FLN, National Liberation Front) is going to let a million French Algerians stay on there? Negotiations may lead to Algerian independence, but so may free elections. It might be worth fighting for months or years to be able to talk to moderates instead of extremists. Is it right to fight without looking where we are going, shouting slogans that seem to contradict one another?

Even those who do no more than criticize the means, which in any case are unlawful, are guilty of a certain amount of hypocrisy. Civil war is a dreadful thing; so is guerrilla fighting; so is repression. Anyone who objects to the atrocities of repression in a country ravaged by guerrilla warfare is logically asking for the whole population to be evacuated. Of course, there are certain methods, such as torture, concentration camps, and intensive searching, which one is bound to reject on grounds of conscience, and which are not even effective. But any kind of repression brings with it some useless "atrocities." It is all very well to appease one's conscience by denouncing them. But would there be fewer of them if the FLN came to power? It would be easier to watch intellectuals ignoring the consequences of their denunciations if the latter seemed to serve any useful purpose.

In the wake of this self-examination, let us honestly try to analyze for ourselves the fearful problem that hangs over France's future.

1. Is France being unfaithful to itself and its principles when it tries to maintain "indissoluble links" between Algeria and itself, when it tries to maintain "its presence" on the other shore of the Mediterranean?

If we are to give an honest answer, we must first do away with the ambiguity about "principles." In Europe, the right to self-determination may be seen as an application of the idea of liberalism. The unity of Germany and Italy called for by the liberal bourgeoisie could or might have facilitated the progress of liberal institutions. But even in Europe, the national and liberal ideas did not chime together for long. Absolutist nationalism ravaged Central and Eastern Europe, so much did the intermingling of nationalities preclude an equitable solution for all, and so widely did the demand for national unity finally stand in the way of individual rights. The deportations and transfers of population that the European policy of nationalities produced in the twentieth century were a shattering disavowal of the values that had inspired the liberals. Finally, the individual had no more rights as such, but only as a member of a national or racial community.

The revolt of the peoples of Asia and Africa against the West is not primarily a demand for individual rights, but a revolt against foreign domination. Whether independent Indians or Egyptians enjoy more or less liberal institutions is up to them. People of color, whom the westerners have humiliated, use a Western vocabulary to voice their claims, but if they were given the choice between liberal institutions under Western tutelage or tyrannical ones in an independent state, the fact is that most of them—or at least the intellectuals who claim to speak for them—would choose the second alternative.

When the French argue that the leaders of the FLN would set up a theocratic or totalitarian regime, they are missing the point, even if they are right. Or at least their argument does not touch their interlocutors, most of whom rate national independence above respect for the rights of the individual. The argument does not convince the French themselves, who find it hard to admit that there is a contradiction between nationalism and liberalism and do not know how to overcome it when they see it. Most of them would probably make the same choice as the Algerians and put national independence before liberal institutions.

No doubt they would hesitate first and feel some guilt as they made the choice. But they would do it all the same, persuaded by two arguments. You cannot use force in the name of liberal ideas in order to hold out against a national insurrection, because to maintain a position by the use of force rules out liberalism. The Muslim communities of Algeria have not been integrated into a liberal civilization. (Only a minority of Algerians have become acquainted with its advantages, and then only more or less partially.) It may be that future rulers of an independent Algeria will *faire suer le burnous,* that is, exploit the workers there worse than their French masters of yesterday and today. The people of Kabylia have probably suffered more at the hands of local administrative officials than from French settlers of whatever rank. Many Algerians may even come to miss the French regime in the future. But these arguments, whether true or false, do not affect the rights and wrongs of the present situation. The French will never really make up their minds to put down the revolt in Algeria until they believe they are justified in imposing their own civilization on its people.

Let me make myself clear. The France of today and tomorrow is magnificently governed if we compare it with Saudi Arabia or Yemen, or the government an independent Algeria would likely get. But that is a defensive sort of comparison. The French Revolutionaries had no qualms when they mulcted a conquered Europe in the name of liberty. The Soviet Communists are equally untroubled when they force their regime on Eastern Europe in the name of the liberation of peoples. But *we* are no longer easy in our minds when we use force in Africa, even though we invest hundreds of billions there every year.

There is no direct relationship between bad behavior and bad conscience. In the nineteenth century, Europeans behaved much worse (vis-à-vis their principles) than we do, yet their consciences were clear. In the twentieth century, we behave better and blame ourselves more. The reproaches of those who were the victims yesterday teach or remind us of what our fathers did, and we no longer believe enough in ourselves.

Have we left principles behind and shifted imperceptibly toward mass psychology? Yes, indeed. But political principles are a transposition of practice, a justification of people's will to power. Carried to their logical conclusions, they are bound to be contradictory. The conquering peoples who dominate history have always broken their principles, sometimes for their own good and sometimes for that of their victims. When someone keeps invoking a principle that proves him wrong and his opponents right, his prospects tend to look dim. In such circumstances, it is better to be resolute than resigned.

2. When France grants independence to Morocco and Tunisia, the French, even those who had sided with the Moroccan and Tunisian nationalists, experience a sense of defeat. And yet, if the protectorate was illegitimate or out of date, should we not celebrate the courage that makes us put our ideas before our interests and sacrifice power to principle? In fact, apart from a minority of progressives (and perhaps not even them!), left-wing Frenchmen feel scarcely less humiliated by the "loss" of North Africa than right-wing Frenchmen do. When Prussia was working for German unity, French consciences were troubled both when they tried to oppose it and when they were inclined to put up with it. Some urged a realistic policy; others promoted the idea of the nation; others again wanted France to sacrifice its position in Europe. All were divided within. The war that was lost in 1870 only brought them all together in the belief that France should have either declared German unity justified in advance or opposed it while there was still time, at the latest in 1866. They lacked the courage to admit that, in a regime so much influenced by public opinion, their opposition helped to create the in-between policy that they all, with hindsight, condemn.

Similarly, today the advocates of friendship with nationalisms criticize the advocates of strong arm tactics for having compromised the policy that was eventually adopted. If France had voluntarily granted in 1954 what it finally conceded under the pressure of terrorism, it would not have felt so intolerably humiliated. Britain does not feel it has lost India, because Britain gave India independence of its own free will. Britain *will* feel it has lost Cyprus, because it will remember the deportation of the archbishop.

The argument is not without weight, but it is not decisive. Nehru spent plenty of time in prison: The British could have had doubts. (The massacres that followed the proclamation of independence could have been put down to India's former masters.) But that is not all. The supporters of "friendship with Tunisian and Moroccan nationalism" have never suggested granting independence pure and simple; they have never written that independence implied the departure of a considerable number of the French people hitherto living in Tunisia and Morocco. If a bad conscience comes from not being able to decide on a policy, or an inability to give voluntarily what one finally must concede, the people in favor of rejection are not the only ones to blame; nor is the division of opinion among Frenchmen. Neither the Left nor the Right told the truth. Neither said that internal autonomy called for independence in the short term, or that independence involved the departure of many of the French people previously settled in North Africa.

Would things have turned out differently if we had negotiated with the nationalists sooner? It is possible. And it would certainly have been better to come to an agreement with Monsieur Habib Bourgiba in 1946, or at a pinch in 1952, before the disasters in Indochina and the irrevocable decline of French prestige. But let us not forget that the British administration in India was almost completely "Indianized," and this did not prevent the demand for independence. If the Tunisian administration had been staffed entirely with Tunisians, the shock, when it came, might have been less, but de facto cosovereignty would not have prevented the demand for exclusive sovereignty, de facto and de jure alike. The mechanism that drives nationalist movements to keep raising their bids would have been set in motion whether we anticipated their claims or turned a deaf ear to them.

When we give something away we are criticized for taking the credit away from those who need to win arguments and gain points to please the crowd. When we resist, we are blamed for playing into the hands of the extremist. Perhaps there is a happy medium; I am prepared to let our rulers alternate between extremes. Perhaps, by its very nature, the happy medium exists only in the words of our interlocutors. Perhaps we necessarily agree with one another too soon or too late; perhaps both at the same time. Deep down, the Moroccan nationalists are surprised at having "grabbed" complete independence; they expected it to come later, after many years in which nationalist struggle would have acted as a mode of government because its demands were not completely satisfied. They were surprised by how quickly we gave in—a decision hastened by the deportation of the Sultan, followed by Dien Bien Phu. But it must be said that slow, gradual evolution was perhaps even more difficult than a sudden break. The Neo-Destour Party in Tunisia could not have been satisfied for long with domestic autonomy or with the possibility of being overtaken on the Left if it showed too much moderation. *Independence* is a magic word; nationalism is the mortar that holds the Islamic masses together. From the moment when the French government started treating with the nationalists—and unless it wanted to cut them off from the people as a whole, as it would have been bound to do eventually—the movement leading to independence was irreversible and entailed a change in the local situation that the French were almost bound to feel as a defeat.

Modern Morocco is 90 percent a French creation. Enclosed within the traditional Morocco is a Western economy directed and managed by Frenchmen. The money, the experts, and the administrators are all French. From modern Morocco emerged an educated minority that called for independence in the name of our principles, at the same time as protests against "modernism" were heard. At present, Morocco has neither the capital nor the managers to run the Western-style economy we have built up there. The leaders of the Istiqlal (the Moroccan nationalist party), aware of their need for outside help, may help interdependence become a reality. In any case, the future of French influence is uncertain. Any non-French influences that make themselves felt, particularly if they come from the United States, will inevitably be resented. The French invested so much effort in Tunisia, and even more in Morocco, and became so linked to the soil, alien though it was, that they are bound to find it painful if they, members of what was formerly a dominant minority, find themselves merely tolerated as guests.

How many French people could bear to stay on just as guests or friendly colleagues? Let us not try to be dogmatic. Minor civil servants or employees will have to go "home," and the Neo-Destour government will have to find jobs for its own supporters. If things go well, people like engineers, senior civil servants, and teachers will for some years be valued and kept on. I doubt if that will apply to the ordinary settlers, those who own or work the land. To begin with, the French will probably be allowed to hold on to their property to maintain agricultural production. But it can hardly be doubted that foreigners will seem increasingly out of place in an independent Islamic state.

In the case of Morocco and Tunisia, we might at a pinch forget the events that led to independence, resign ourselves to the repatriation of a portion of our fellow countrymen who had settled there, and not see as a historical defeat our acceptance of a change that the spirit of the age seems to render inevitable. But can that be true of Algeria? Can we really grant Algeria independence in April 1956, hoping that interdependence will follow, while at the same time glossing over the need to repatriate large numbers of Frenchmen and abandoning friends and fellow countrymen alike to the tender mercies of a fanatical minority?

3. On two points all observers agree, whether they are on the Left or the Right, in favor of resistance or of negotiation: In Algeria there is no equivalent of the Neo-Destour Party in Tunisia or the Istiqlal in Morocco; in other words, there is no "valid interlocutor" capable of controlling and calming the masses. Those who lead the maquis on the military and political level are not organized in a single party, they have no single chief, and they are more intransigent than the nationalists in Tunisia and Morocco.

Honest upholders of dialogue think, even if they do not write, that negotiation would strengthen the moderates, allow the leaders of the insurrection to emerge into daylight, and at the same time distance them from Cairo. Perhaps those who think an Algeria governed by the FLN would be a wholly Islamic state, in which only Muslims would be full citizens, are exaggerating the religious or racial fanaticism of our possible interlocutors. I do not know a single sincere observer who is not privately apprehensive about what the fate of the Algerian Republic may be after elections take place that are manipulated by the FLN.

In financial and economic terms, it is quite possible that a credit of 500 billion francs to repatriate the French from Algeria would in the long run be a less expensive solution than a prolongation of the war, even if it were to end in victory. Let us pause for a moment here. To persuade the French of the need to hold on to Algeria, it is said that hundreds of thousands of Frenchmen would become unemployed as a result of a break between North Africa and the mother country. I regard this argument as false and harmful to the cause it claims to serve. A people does not fight to keep jobs. The defense of markets may sometimes be presented as a matter of honor, but to disguise a matter of honor as the protection of vested interests defies common sense, intellectual honesty, and the laws of mass psychology.

Algerian independence, following that of Tunisia and Morocco, might result in a decrease, but certainly not in an interruption, of trade between the home country and its African departments and protectorates. Some industries, particularly those dealing in textiles, would be affected. But in the long run France would not be poorer if it stopped investing 200 to 300 billion francs per year in Africa. Industry would lose some protected markets, but in economic terms, these encourage laziness and in the end cost more than they bring in. Indonesia was more important to the Dutch economy than North Africa is to the French one, and Holland has gotten over the consequences of Indonesian independence. Even if the French economy did not manage to overcome the consequences of African independence, that would be the fault of the former rather than of the latter. An economy unable to cope with international competition without the benefit of private preserves is a victim of its own inflexibility, not of the events that merely showed up its ossification.

We should stop saying it would cost too much to "repatriate" the French from Algeria and that French workers would be laid off for one day a week if we "lost" North Africa. The war is currently costing 200 or 300 billion francs a year. And if we win the war and decide to incorporate Algeria into the republic, it will cost us almost as much every year in investments. Investing the same amount of money in France would be of more benefit to most French people. And, above all, the Left should stop dangling before us the idyll of an independent Algeria welcoming French experts and French capital. Why should the French be willing to go on covering the deficits in the Tunisian, Algerian, and Moroccan budgets indefinitely? The truth is, we would naturally prefer to leave that to the Americans, even as we denounce them for being bad allies and driving us out of our colonies faster than our enemies.

The Algerian War is an economic burden, but the industrialization of countries with populations that are growing too rapidly is and will continue to be an economic burden. Even if Algeria remained part of the republic, and even if France, Tunisia, and Morocco were to become interdependent, the amount of investment required would be too much for us alone. It would be better to interest the U.S. government in the business right away, instead of leaving it till later to complain that the dollars are too few and wrongly timed.

But all that is for tomorrow. What ought we to do now? What do we mean by winning the war? The officially proclaimed policy of the socialist government may be summarized as advocating military action to create the conditions for free elections, followed by dialogue with the elected representatives of the Algerian people on the country's future status. There are two objections to such a policy. Is it possible to restore order sufficiently to make free elections possible? If the elected representatives demand independence pure and simple, shall we be ready to grant it, or will the dialogue be limited to details of Algeria's status inside the French Republic or the French Union? The socialists would probably dismiss these questions, not because they underestimate their importance, but because they do not want to fight on two fronts. Right-wing opinion likes to hear about unbreakable ties; it would not hear of granting independence after victory was won. Free elections seem impeccably "left-wing" (it is undemocratic to admit that an aggressive minority might be representative of the population as a whole). No one asks if the army will ever be able to create the conditions necessary to make democratic procedures possible.

But if peace is not achieved after a few months, and there is nothing to indicate that it will be, what is likely to happen in France? How long will public opinion go on supporting the war effort? Will the argument between the French people who favor resistance and those who advocate dialogue become so fierce as to make legitimate government impossible? I am not sure I know the answer to all these questions, but at least we can examine the problem. Tunisia and Morocco are independent. Algeria, though it lacks the national tradition of the two ex-protectorates, must be growing increasingly self-aware. Any day it could be endowed with a status different from that of Tunisia and Morocco. But it cannot go on being an integral part of France. The creation of an Algerian political unit is inevitable. Integration, in any sense of the word, is no longer practicable. A proportional representation of the Algerian population in the French National Assembly would be the surest way of bringing down the regime. The difference in the birthrates on the two sides of the Mediterranean is too great for these two peoples, with their different races and different religions, to form part of one community.

To say that Algeria is not France, and to recognize Algeria's political personality, is basically to admit that there is bound to be an Algerian state at some time in the not-too-distant future. And that being so, whether it comes sooner or later, it is bound, in theory, to be independent. Politics has a logic of its own, whatever happens. A protectorate tends toward independence because a protector cannot strengthen its protégé state without giving it additional claims to independence. By ruling out integration, the protector starts a process that will end in independence. Soviet-type integration presupposes a strong state and a supranational ideology.

Is it not possible to admit that Algeria will be a state tomorrow and an independent state the day after? Why should the French fight if the result is the same, win or lose? The British fought for years in Malaya to give independence to moderates, not extremists. Will the latter get the upper hand after the British have left? Possibly. If it is absurd to fight and not keep the fruits of victory, is it any less so to fight for an end that cannot be achieved?

The French are ready to accept the fact that 400,000 soldiers are in Algeria for one simple reason: We cannot abandon our compatriots, some of whom belong to families that have been living there for generations. Attributing the various responsibilities is neither here nor there: Responsibilities exist, but I do not feel I have any right to apportion blame. If the French of Algeria have stood in the way of reforms, the French of France have shown little interest in what was going on so far away. When disaster is already upon us, it is too late or too soon to draw up a balance sheet and sort out the rights and wrongs. To the elementary reason that a country cannot without dishonor abandon a million of its own people, the politicians may add two other considerations.

It would not be very honorable to sacrifice the Muslims who were our friends and leave them to the fury of a violent minority. Nor would it be sensible to ignore the fact that the way Algeria achieves independence may have an enormous influence not only on its own future but also on that of North Africa and of the West as a whole. According to whether Algeria becomes independent in three months or three years, ten months or ten years, the rulers of independent Algeria will be different, and so will the future destiny of North Africa.

So the only war aims that France can reasonably set before itself are these: to allow Algeria to achieve independence without resorting to a policy that the French themselves see as degrading and that leaves them with an intolerable feeling of humiliation; and to strengthen the chances of those in Tunisia, Morocco, and Algeria who wish to set up Islamic states enjoying friendly relations with the West.

There is more to strategy than deciding on war aims, but if you do not know your ends you have no chance of finding the right means. The Americans lost the war in Europe because they thought their objective was to destroy the German army, whereas they ought to have targeted a new equilibrium. We want to restore order in Algeria, but we may be unable to achieve that goal unless we know what we are going to do next. In any case, we shall have a better chance of gaining our military objective if we do not neglect the political one.

4. Even if these analyses are accepted—and I am not sure that any Frenchman, on the Right or the Left, would accept them—doubt remains about the means by which we are to achieve our ends. What methods would we *genuinely* recommend to Moroccans and Tunisians who would like to retain links with France and the West?

Publicly, they denounce the blind repression exercised by the French. Privately, as far as one can judge, they fear France's surrender as much as its resistance to Algeria's demands. In seeking a peaceful solution that will not strengthen the extremists and the fanatics, they, too, may be trying to square the circle. So long as the war continues, neither Monsieur Bourgiba nor the Sultan can stop making speeches in support of Algerian independence, even if they think certain aspects of it would be as difficult for them as for us.

Is there a way out? Can negotiations that would give power to the fanatics be avoided? Can we fight without discouraging the moderates? Which path gives the nationalists not yet won over to Islamic extremism a solution—fighting or talking? No one can answer these questions with certainty. The least bad solution, the one that strikes me as offering the least negative prospect, is based on the truth: that we are determined to fight rather than be dishonored, but that we are not fighting to prevent the Algerians from becoming independent if that is their wish.

Even if we openly declared our aims and the means by which we were trying to achieve them, a military effort would still be needed to convince our adversaries that weariness will not win from us the capitulation they expect despite our martial declarations. We would then need to get the

National Assembly to approve the principle of compensation for the French people who would be leaving the Algerian Republic. We would also have to convince everyone of the sincerity of our resolve and our promises through votes in the National Assembly and perhaps through declarations to our allies.

What does our proposed policy amount to? We would have to make progressive methods as attractive as possible to the rebels, and the prospect of a long war as unattractive as possible. Many objections to this program may be made. Is it worth going to so much trouble just to surrender the stake in the end? Will not our policy meet with paralyzing opposition? Isn't this policy ultimately the same as that of the government, except that the latter, instead of admitting its final goal, obstinately denies it?

It is possible, probable even, that if it were officially recognized that Algeria would one day become independent in character, many of the French in Algeria would be furious. The Left would go on, in spite of everything, denouncing colonialism and the horrors of repression and disguising the real meaning of its policy by representing our interlocutors as peaceable Muslims who are friendly to the West and steeped in French culture. Everyone says no policy can succeed in Algeria without the support of public opinion. Unfortunately, no policy, whether of resistance or of giving in, will get the full support of public opinion. Any effective policy divides France, and perhaps even individual Frenchmen are not sure what to think. A policy that seemed to have every class and every party against it would perhaps divide them least.

Be that as it may, it seems to me necessary to break the taboos. The links with Algeria are not indissoluble. If we recognize the Algerian character, we can stop ruling out the Algerian state. If we recognize the Algerian state, we can stop ruling out Algerian independence. "Losing" Algeria does not mean France is finished. Economically, Algeria is a burden. The sole objective of the war, after the independence of Tunisia and Morocco, is to find "interlocutors" (yes, I dare use the word) in Algeria who are nationalist without being xenophobic. It is possible that we have no choice between simply giving in and fighting on indefinitely. If that is so, we shall sooner or later have to be brave enough to propose a radical solution, offer to evacuate Algeria, and vote for spending the millions of francs that would be necessary to repatriate the French or maintain a French enclave on the coast, which is safe against the rebels. Would we leave chaos behind us?

That is possible, even probable. But there are limits to the responsibilities a society as a whole can assume with regard to its parts. Would Algeria, evacuated by France, be nonviable economically, and perhaps politically, too? Again, it is likely. But neither is it possible for France, disavowed by half its people as well as it allies, to go on fighting without a definable aim, even if its adversaries are unwittingly acting against their own interests.

5. Everyone agrees that the Algerian War endangers what is left of the French community. The government will be disowned by half the French people, whatever it decides. None of the factions has the courage to face up to the consequences of what it claims to want.

France's financial and economic equilibrium is threatened by the war. We cannot fight and yet allow our military effort to be sabotaged, but we cannot try to prevent that sabotage without resorting to methods that French anarchism, disguised as liberalism or communism, would denounce as fascist. I cannot produce a miracle solution any more than anyone else. But in spite of everything, one can avoid adding to our troubles by fostering hysteria.

I do not know how the French would react to the "loss" of Algeria. It is best not to deepen our dissatisfaction by talking as if our own incompetence were responsible for all that is going on in the world. It is best, too, not to blame foreigners for the results of our own weakness, or to arouse xenophobia just by denouncing it, or to predict that France will turn Communist if North Africa becomes independent. We should beware of the blind reactions of a people that has been humiliated. That humiliation could be made worse if we were to ignore the role of historical necessity, or if we used apocalyptic terms to describe how fatal a blow would be dealt the French economy if it were left to its own devices.

France would be different without North Africa. A crisis that turns our country from a world power to a continental power cannot leave us unmoved. Each of us feels it intensely, and it causes us to lash out against ourselves and one another. The primitive fury with which every party attacks every other merely reflects the misery we all share. As in June 1940, so again today, our only choice is between great evils. And no one can be sure that his chosen alternative would lead to the lesser ills.

I tend to think we would make our countrymen's ordeal easier to bear if we told them the plain, unvarnished truth. France cannot fight off Algerian independence once and for all. We are fighting to grant that independence in a certain way and to some interlocutors rather than to others. If the French refuse this kind of language and will only fight to maintain their dominance (which I do not believe), then the heroic choice of surrender and repatriation would be better than a war fought reluctantly, half-heartedly, and with no chance of success.

April 25, 1956

II

A year has gone by since I wrote the note above. As all sincere observers foresaw, the so-called pacification policy resolved nothing and made everything worse. The two communities are farther away than ever from "peaceful coexistence." Relations have been broken off between the resident minister and the Algerian elite. The middle classes, the ulemas, students, intellectuals—all those who might be able to control the Algerian masses and prevent them from succumbing to the temptation of blind violence, all the viable interlocutors, all who might negotiate a compromise, are taking refuge in a wait-and-see attitude or joining the FLN. The time has come, in the face of a conspiracy of cowardice, to speak out and tell the whole truth, unpalatable as it may be, without sparing certain feelings that I find quite legitimate, that I may even still share, but which must be silenced when the future of France is at stake.

Before asking ourselves what is possible in our present situation in May 1957, let us first ask ourselves what is desirable. "Algérie française"—all you who give such thrilling expression to the delusions of national amour-propre, look first at the facts and study the figures before you start dreaming about the wealth buried under those burning sands.

The first fact is that the population of France itself and the Muslim population of Algeria do not belong to the same demographic type and are not on the same economic level.

Integrating two such radically different populations would meet with insurmountable obstacles, including economic and social legislation that suits one people and cannot be made to suit the other.

The Muslim population of Algeria has a death rate of 15 percent and a birthrate of 43 percent. The infant mortality rate, which is 15 percent as against 4 percent in France, will lessen as hygiene improves. Demographers calculate that the Muslim population of Algeria will rise to 3,373,000 between 1960 and 1970, and to 4,527,000 between 1970 and 1980. By the latter date the total population will reach about 18 million.

So rapid an increase produces an exceptionally young population: Only 5.5 percent are now over sixty years old, as against 11.6 percent for the non-Muslim population of Algeria and 16.4 percent for the population in the home country. The number of men of working age rose from 2,048,000 in 1948 to 2,365,000 in 1955. Nearly 800,000 young men are today practically unemployed. Sixty-seven thousand new jobs a year would need to be created between now and 1960; 98,000 between 1965 and 1970; and 127,000 between 1975 and 1980. (These figures are not forecasts: Events will probably slow things down. But they indicate what would happen if nothing happened to modify the factors presently at work.)

Inevitably, the European population of Algeria will be dominated numerically more and more by the Muslim population. There are now 1.04 million non-Muslims as against 9 million Muslims. By 1980, at the present rate, the non-Muslims will scarcely have increased in number at all (1.2 million), while the Muslims will double to reach 18 million. The net reproduction rate of the non-Muslims is only 113 percent, as against 210 percent among the Muslims.

All the solemn declarations of France to commit itself to raising the Algerian masses' standard of living to a level closer to that of the French are meaningless so long as whoever governs the country is unwilling or unable to impose Malthusian measures. This is the first major objection to the maintenance of French sovereignty in Algeria: France would be condemned by world public opinion if it imposed such measures, whereas an Algerian government would be praised for its wisdom if it did the same thing. Nor could any French resident do as Monsieur Bourgiba has done and forbid polygamy.

Nor is that all. In order to create jobs, it is necessary to industrialize. But industries in France have no interest in building their factories in Algeria. From the economic point of view, being located in France itself, where previous industrialization favors new enterprises, offers every advantage (with a few exceptions). For the emigration of French industry to Africa to be conceivable, the French state would have to grant huge concessions to industries willing to locate in Algeria; because of the differences in productivity in the two countries, the minimum wage would have to be even lower than it is now. As for industrialization through local initiatives, the common market between France and Algeria has the effect of paralyzing any such attempts. Goods made in France are usually cheaper. Now there is a war on, and whatever the outcome, a doubt is bound to hang over the future: What Frenchman is going to invest his money in a country ravaged by racial hatred?

As long as Algeria is subject to French sovereignty, we shall tend to transfer our standards there, whether for schools, hospitals, or social legislation. We shall be more concerned about the old than about the young. The gap between the two countries' standards of living will remain. Any policy inspired by egalitarian justice will be disastrous, ruining France without saving Algeria. Algeria is not a part of France. It ought not to be, and it cannot be. Its surplus population and its poverty make it an underdeveloped country, and it ought to be treated as such. Is it conceivable that the French, rational and legalistic as they are by nature, should apply legislation fundamentally different from that of France itself to "French departments"? Recognition of Algerian nationhood is made necessary by the demographic and economic facts as much as by the demands of its elite and its passionate guerrilla fighters.

From several other points of view, Algerian autonomy has become desirable in itself, quite apart from events. The free entry into France of Algerian workers is now a serious problem and will soon be much worse. Between 1945 and 1956, the number of Algerian workers in France has risen from 60,000 to 330,000. French industry needs them, and many believe we should have taken on more. The growth, since 1960, in working-age French citizens does not suggest a decline in the need for Algerians in industrial settings. But the gap that will inevitably remain in the standard of living between the two countries might well result in a flow of Algerian emigration that, if not controlled, could produce violent reactions from public opinion, especially among the working classes, at the first signs of even limited unemployment. The circulation of workers between countries with different standards of living cannot be completely free, particularly when the peoples' religions and customs are different, too.

In Algeria itself the application of a policy of assimilation has in some ways produced disastrous results. The transfer there of our primary and secondary school system is absurd. It makes children start school later and reduces the number that receive secondary education. It would be easier to teach Algerian children to read in Arabic rather than in French.

Though it is meant to demonstrate equality, it is really quite unfair to ask them, at the age of eleven and twelve, to take sixth-grade examinations in competition with French children. What is needed is an educational system designed for the Algerian masses, not one aimed at the French in Algeria and the minority of Algerians capable of being included with them.

Thus, whether it is a question of industry, education, or social legislation, Algeria *must* have a different regime from that of France. For one thing, the necessary measures can be taken only by Algerian governments. It is not the rebellion, but, first and foremost, the facts that make recognition of Algerian nationhood necessary. It is no accident that Monsieur Fernand Boverat,[5] who can hardly be accused of being either a Communist or a progressive, spoke in the following terms:

> If we do not want to condemn France before long to maintaining its presence in Africa by no other means than force of arms, and at the cost of indefinite military operations, we must accept—for demographic reasons—a rapid transformation of the French Union into a federation of territories, each with an autonomy in proportion to its political and economic capacities. That is the best and even the only way for France to maintain substantial outlets for its industries, outlets that will be all the more likely to survive the less the populations concerned have had to struggle for their autonomy. The more blood flows, the fewer will be our future customers. . . . If France had not exhausted and ruined itself for the past ten years by making war in Indochina and Algeria, and if it had not crushed its industries with taxes to pay for its military operations, then the cost of goods produced in our factories would be much lower than they are today, and the volume of foreign exports would be doubled.* But these exports are much more valuable to France than those that go to our colonies, for these, especially those destined for Algeria, are paid for largely by means of the subsidies and investments that we arrange for our overseas territories. In other words, they are paid for to a large extent by the French taxpayer, and thus by the manufacturers themselves.

---

* This statement is arbitrary: No one can say what the figures would have been.

Two contrasting answers are usually made to this argument. Some say you want to destroy the French economy; others charge that you want to abandon the Algerians to their poverty. The first group thinks I care nothing about my country's prosperity; the second thinks I am hardhearted and mean-spirited. The Right takes care of the material charge; Monsieur Etienne Borne[6] heads up the emotional one.

"French workers work one day out of every nine for Algeria," says a headline in a bulletin supporting the French cause in Algeria; 20 percent of French exports go to North Africa (307 billion francs, of which 172 billion go to Algeria). Without North Africa, the cotton industry would lose 43 percent of its foreign markets; the car industry, 43 percent of its exports; and so on.

Such statements are meaningless. Let us suppose France recognized Algeria's right to independence. Let us even suppose Algeria became independent tomorrow. It would need to buy and sell. But it would have more trouble than France would finding new export markets to replace the old. No one can say for certain if and how far the economic links would survive between a sovereign Algeria and France, or if and to what extent France's industries would export elsewhere the goods they no longer exported to Algeria. No one can calculate exactly the cost and the sufferings involved in the conversion. But what a strange aberration for the home country to regard as an indispensable source of wealth departments with a population that doubles in thirty years and in which every year we spend, in investments and expenditure arising out of sovereignty, capital that could produce a better return in France.

At this, I am attacked from another quarter. But if the population of Algeria doubles every thirty years, how poor it will become if it is left to itself! I do not consider it either kind or realistic to "abandon" Algeria. But to save the Algerians from poverty by sending in an army of 400,000 men does not seem to me an ideal solution. To do something that would justify our presence, peace is the first requisite. But the rebellion has been going on for nearly three years now, and no end seems in sight.

Étienne Borne, who accuses me of typically conservative hard-heartedness, sees no point in talking of the guns and planes that spread so little prosperity (not to mention other even more painful facts). In answer to those who praise France's generosity and at the same time say that Algeria represents a good bargain, there is no point in my saying they must choose, for the two arguments cannot both be true. Given the poorness of the soil, the high birthrate, and the lack of motivation or spirit, it is impossible for France to derive profit from its possessions there and at the same time raise the people's standard of living. The truth is that France has invested hundreds of billions of francs in Africa, money that came from the home country and could have been invested there. It does not follow that the French Union is a burden from the economic point of view. It provides markets, and in the long term it may open up prospects for expansion for French products. In any case, every Western state should consider it a duty to help underdeveloped countries. Personally, for reasons both moral and economic, universal and national, I believe in France's "mission" in Africa. I believe France has an "African vocation." But neither that mission nor that vocation is compatible with refusing the peoples of Africa the right to rule themselves.

Today France is held responsible for the suffering of the Algerian masses. The sums it invests in their country is not regarded as foreign aid. World opinion attributes to "French exploitation" what is really due to growth of the population and lack of resources. Given that raising the standard of living is now held to be one of a colonizer's duties, the task represented by Algeria is beyond the powers of France alone. On this score, American public opinion is typically naive: It blames France for the poverty of the Algerians, but it does not blame Mr. Nehru for the poverty of the Indians or the condition of the untouchables.

The policy of integration, which is doomed by demography and perpetuates a war that cannot be won, is not a safeguard of French greatness, but rather its ruin.

Let us be clear: The cause of the war is the FLN's demand for self-government and the French government's refusal to grant it. The French government wants to preserve unconditional sovereignty over Algeria. The FLN wants the recognition of Algerian nationhood.

⌒

The most serious question here is the one hardest to answer. What would be the consequences of recognizing Algeria's right to independence? What would France really "lose" if, to use the usual jargon, Algeria was "lost" in the same way as Morocco and Tunisia—that is to say, if it was independent?

Could the French minority stay on in an Algerian Republic? No one can answer dogmatically yes or no. But some possibilities can be discussed. The longer the pacification-cum-war lasts, the smaller the chance of peaceful coexistence between the two communities. The rulers of an Algerian Republic could not, unless they went out of their minds, ignore the fact that they will need France when they take up the responsibilities of power. The symbiosis between the Algerian and French economies and between the Muslim and French populations is so strong that the bonds will tend to last in spite of passions.

That said, it would be dishonest not to face up to the painful consequences and the risks involved in a transformation that I regard as inevitable. The French population is mainly urban, with a high proportion of managerial executives working in industry, commerce, and administration. For a long time, the Algerian Republic will need technicians; it will not need minor officials of the kind the Algerians themselves could easily replace. The repatriation of the sort of officials who, like their counterparts in Tunisia and Morocco, would no longer have a place in an Algeria governed by Algerians must be organized and financed by the home government.

Will the other French people, those who, because of their qualifications, are still useful in Algeria, be able to adapt to the new conditions? Will they feel secure? Will their rights be respected? I do not know and cannot say. But who imagines that the million French people who make up one-ninth of the present population, and will make up one-eighteenth of the population twenty-five years from now—who imagines that they will go on governing, administering, and managing the country? It would be best if the unavoidable "decolonization" took place gradually. Perhaps it is not yet impossible to restore dialogue with the Algerian elites, to find interlocutors who will accept the transitions and give the French minority the guarantees they need. But how can we do these things if we set ourselves an impossible and undesirable goal—the retention of France's unconditional sovereignty?

It may be said that the examples of Tunisia and Morocco are not encouraging. True, but the prolongation of the war in Algeria does not encourage the moderates, that is, the nationalists who would like to work with France as friends. And yet, in neither of the former protectorates do the rulers wish to break with France. They cannot avoid declaring their solidarity with the Algerians, so they try to teach the rebel chiefs moderation while pleading the cause of Algerian nationalism with French ministers. I do not deny that sudden independence may propel Morocco into chaos. But I am sure that sending an army of 400,000 men to Algeria after granting Morocco independence is crazy. We are ready to sacrifice 600 billion francs in French investment in Morocco for the right to invest more hundreds of billions in Algeria. We do not hesitate to undermine our future chances in Morocco on the pretext of saving our future chances in Algeria, whereas a French presence in the middle of North Africa would make no sense if both of the former protectorates became hostile to us.

Does the discovery of oil in the Sahara[7] change all future prospects? If only we knew the real figures! But let us suppose that the oil wealth of the Sahara is as great as people say. It would still be a mistake to think the oil profits would be enough to solve the economic problem of a rapidly growing population. A hundred or so million tons of crude costs about a billion dollars. The hoped-for profit, if the wells are exceptionally rich, comparable to those in the Middle East, might amount to some hundreds of millions of dollars. But have we any idea of the millions of francs of investment required to produce an annual output of several tens of millions of tons of oil? The oil of the Sahara does for the first time offer Algeria economic prospects that are not desperate, but it is not a magic wand transforming the harsh realities of underdevelopment into paradise.

Besides, the richer the Sahara, the more necessary and inevitable becomes an agreement with the Tunisian, Moroccan, and Algerian nationalists. Does anyone imagine we could invest millions of francs in pipelines while the guerrilla war is still going on? Or that the two independent states of North Africa and the Algerian nationalists take no interest in a desert whose inexhaustible resources are always being dinned in their ears? The surest way to lose all the oil of the Sahara is to try to keep it entirely to ourselves.

To return to the situation at hand, what are the possibilities before us? I think there are four of them.

1. To continue with the policy of Monsieur Robert Lacoste, the so-called "pacification policy."

2. To modify not so much its objectives as its methods.
3. To proceed with partition.
4. To accept the principle of an Algerian state, while realizing that the implementation of this decision may take various forms, including negotiations, a proclamation on the part of the French government, and agreements with the governments of Tunisia and Morocco.

Will the policy of pacification, as conducted at present, lead to success? I have never met anyone, even in the entourage of the resident minister, who shares his confidence. Anyhow, pacification is expected to take two or three years. Let us take an optimistic view and imagine that three years from now the guerrilla army will not be thoroughly eliminated, but exhausted. There may be terrorist attacks here and there, both in the countryside and in the towns, but the reconstruction of an autonomous Algeria on the French model, with municipalities, general councils, and elected local and regional assemblies, will be on its way.

France could spend 300 billion francs a year in Algeria for the next three years. But let us look at the risks. A change of minister could bring a reversal of policy, and this, if imposed through foreign pressure or because French public opinion lost patience, would seem like a defeat and lead to consequences much more dangerous than a cool and resolute decision taken now would entail.

France's own determination is not the only factor. What is going to happen in Tunisia and Morocco during the next three years? A military effort had to be made last spring in order to strengthen the moderates in the two former protectorates. From now on the prolongation of the war works in favor of the extremists. In any case, the *immediate* independence of Morocco compromised France's undertaking. The Moroccans lack the executives necessary to manage the economy that we built up in their country. The sudden transfer of sovereignty to the Moroccan government was bound to provoke mass demands, cause disappointment (independence worsened all the economic difficulties), encourage the people toward extremism, and push their rulers toward demagogy. The war in Algeria only amplified the expected reactions. The speeches of Monsieur Bourguiba and the Sultan, regarded as anti-French by French public opinion, were considered lukewarm by the people of Tunisia and Morocco. Nationalists in the two former protectorates who did not want to break with France, and who knew what a rupture would cost, felt increasingly trapped between moral solidarity with the combatants in Algeria and the desire to maintain contact with the French government. What will our position be in Tunisia and Morocco three years from now if peace has not returned to Algeria?

The plain truth, which many leaders admit in private but deny in public, is that Monsieur Lacoste's policy in Algeria is in contradiction with that of Monsieur Alain Savary[8] (or that of Monsieur Maurice Faure[9]) in Tunisia and Morocco. The arrest of the five *fellagha* (rebel) chiefs[10] brought out this contradiction, though French public opinion, satisfied with the cape-and-dagger exploit, did not realize its true significance. Monsieur Bourgiba and the Sultan, having contacted certain circles in Paris, had tried to force the hand of the French government while urging moderation on the Algerian leaders. The arrest may have been initiated solely by the special services. Perhaps those who wanted to pursue the pacification policy at all costs, without negotiating or exploring political possibilities, saw this spectacular episode as a way of forcing Monsieur Guy Mollet to take a "hard line" and making Monsieur Bourgiba and the Sultan become more intransigent. Whether the outcome was due to chance or calculation, the consequences were inevitable: massacres at Meknès, the emigration of the French from Morocco and Tunisia, and a stiffening of the attitude of the Moroccan and Tunisian rulers.

Let us still take the optimistic view: Neither Tunisia nor Morocco have intervened officially in the conflict. Nonetheless, both countries act as supply bases for the Algerian combatants, as China did for North Vietnam. Ten years of experience have taught us that the chances of overcoming a guerrilla army that has outside help are generally poor (unless you use methods like those the Soviets employed in Hungary). As the length of the war forces Tunisia and Morocco into intervening more and more, their rulers will grow increasingly hostile to us and the French will leave their countries. Why would France want to hang on to sovereignty in Algeria, and what would that sovereignty signify, if it drags the two independent states of North Africa into chaos and leaves them with the United States as their only Western contact?

In short, a pacification program that is going to take another three years to carry out cannot succeed, because in the meantime the situation will have deteriorated irreparably in Tunisia and Morocco. But whether we like it or not, North Africa is a whole. Any policy we try to apply in Algeria must be compatible with those we pursue to the east and to the west. We cannot "win back" Algeria at the same time as we finish off the process of "losing" Tunisia and Morocco. The objectives we aim at in North Africa should be defined generally: Our goal in Algeria cannot be separated from our goals in the two neighboring countries. Do the advocates of pacification really think that refusing to negotiate in Algeria will be conducive to maintaining French influence in Tunisia and Morocco, independent countries that can, if they wish, choose chaos rather than friendship with their former masters?

＊＊＊

If the psychology of the officials in Algiers, and the ideas in the various headquarters, could be changed, would that be enough to make pacification work, to restore contact between Frenchmen and Muslims, and to initiate a dialogue between the French and the moderate nationalists?

At this point, as all the evidence agrees, the war is helping to harden positions and separate the two communities from one another. It may be that the great majority desires, above all, an end to the terror that the FLN inspires in their coreligionists and to the repression with which the French army replies to the attacks and other activities of the partisans. Too many Muslims are being killed by the terrorists for anyone to believe that Algerian public opinion is unanimously anti-French. But how can a proud people fail to sympathize with those of its sons who are fighting?

Would reforms, or the announcement of a constitution, improve the chances of the pacification policy? We need to separate moderate nationalists from the FLN. Would partial reforms, based on French departmental administration, do the trick? But would any of the nationalists be tempted, if we ruled out in advance any prospect of an Algerian state? Or might the offers be regarded as the first step on a long path, and would our "interlocutors" reserve their positions while they waited for the next phase? Or perhaps the government will merely fix the point of arrival and rule out any hope of further development, and the FLN will continue the struggle despite the combatants' growing weariness.

The feelings of the Kabyle or Arab populations, and the hopes and fears of the nomads, are hardly relevant: In a national insurrection, active minorities are more influential than the majority. And can we reach the operative minority, which has become aware of itself in contradistinction from the French, if we exclude forever the magic word, *independence?* A few years back, it might have been possible to envisage at least a long period of transition. But the lamentable series of errors that led to the immediate independence of Morocco was bound to produce consequences in Algeria.

Some people say that by rejecting free elections, the FLN admits it is not sure of winning a peaceful contest. Unfortunately, there are other interpretations. Are the leaders of the FLN convinced that the offer of elections is genuine and that the promises will be kept? How long will the interval be between the cease-fire and the elections? The FLN's organizers may be afraid that, by agreeing to a cease-fire, they would be putting themselves at the mercy of the French government; once having suspended the guerrilla war, they would have difficulty starting it up again. It may be, too, that they want to gain independence by force of arms. Some Algerians want the French to recognize them as equals—in other words, as fit to rule themselves. The fact is, in Algeria we are confronted not with the Neo-Destour Party, as in Tunisia, but with the FLN, and there is no civilian leader there like Monsieur Bourguiba, and no religious leader comparable to the Sultan. Let us hope the leadership of the FLN will agree to a procedure similar to the one the French government has offered. But just to wait for their consent as we pursue pacification does not amount to a policy.

꙰

Various politicians have considered partitioning Algeria as a solution. Monsieur Maurice Allais has recently taken up this possibility again. Most of the French residents would be concentrated along the coastal region between Algiers and Oran. Muslims representing up to a certain percentage of the total population would be allowed to live inside the resulting "French Republic," enjoying complete equality as regards civil rights, and possibly even political rights; but the principle of French sovereignty would not be called into question. The rest of the country would be an Algerian Republic, in which the French would have equal rights but with the title of foreigners (at a pinch, with a special status). Another version of the partition idea would provide for Tunisia to annex the eastern part of the country, and Morocco to annex the western part, while the center, including an area jutting out toward the Sahara, would be made up of French departments.

This second version of the partition would be the most difficult of all to put into practice. It would threaten the already delicate balance of

Tunisia and Morocco. The frontiers are ill-defined: In the west it is difficult to separate Algerians from Moroccans, and Tunisia's absorption of the eastern provinces would probably cause serious unrest. There is no Neo-Destour Party or Monsieur Bourgiba ("the supreme fighter") there; Algerians and Tunisians have never belonged to the same country. Neither Tunisians, Algerians, nor Moroccans would willingly accept a settlement that increased the difficulties in the former protectorates without promising reconciliation between the French and the Muslims.

The first version of the partition described above—two republics in Algeria, one with French and the other with Muslim sovereignty—is not much more practicable. It amounts to applying to North Africa the same solution as that which obtains in Israel in the Middle East: not a precedent that encourages imitation. But there are many other objections, too. At present, the proposal would be rejected both by the French and by the Muslims—by the former because it would involve painful changes and look like a first step toward giving in, and by the latter because it would announce the certain continuation of hated colonialism. The French of Algeria are not a population capable of self-sufficiency with a wide enough range of skills and occupations to make up a complete community: They mingle with the Muslims and provide them with a management framework. A partition would destroy this symbiosis and strike all concerned as unnatural and wrong.

Finally, such a plan would not appeal to public opinion in France. Currently, supporters of resistance and advocates of reconciliation in North Africa alike would be hostile to an idea that, whatever happened, would call for prolonged effort.

―✺

And so we come to the last policy listed at the beginning of this section: the acceptance in principle of an Algerian state, not ruling out its "vocation for independence." In the end, we are confronted with a choice: either a combination of the policy of pacification, with reforms and the promise of a constitution; or a policy similar to the one applied to Tunisia and Morocco, which led to independence for the two former protectorates. The argument turns on just one point: Does France accept the fact that one day it may lose its "sovereignty" over Algeria?

As we have seen, Algeria's autonomy is not incompatible with France's long-term interests. On the contrary, the demographic and economic disparity between the two countries makes inevitable the creation of an independent authority specific to Algeria.

The most rational points of the argument opposing this concept relate to the uncertainty hovering over the future of the Algerian state. Will it give our fellow countrymen, settled on African soil for generations, the opportunity to stay on? What kind of regime will this improvised country have? What will be the influence there of the Communist Party? The dangers invoked by such questions are real. The creation of an Algerian state is a difficult undertaking, and there is no guarantee of success. But we are now faced with a choice of evils. The pacification policy leads not to peace but to the perpetuation of a ruinous war that tends to make itself inevitable. The less the two communities can coexist peacefully, the greater the temptation for both sides to give in totally to war. If we accept a policy leading to Algerian independence, at least there is a chance of a solution that lies between indefinitely continued violence and sudden capitulation. It is because we rejected the independence of Tunisia and Morocco in principle, even in the long term, that we ended up, in fact, conceding it from one day to the next. By rejecting an Algerian state in theory, we are standing in the way of the federal or confederal solution that might not be ruled out if we stopped being frightened of words.

On all sides, rational arguments are used to justify passionate attitudes. The fate of Algeria arouses passions not only in the French who live in Algeria but also in the French who live in France.

The passions of the former are comprehensible and legitimate, but not necessarily clear-sighted. These French people created the Algeria of today—they fertilized the soil, dug, built, struggled against man and nature, and sacrificed themselves magnanimously for the liberation of France itself. They cannot imagine themselves leaving the land they have lived in, and where their dead are buried, or living under a government or administration made up of Algerians. Algeria is their home country as much as it is that of the Muslims.

I do not propose to argue about principles. I would probably feel the same way that my compatriots in Algeria do if I were in their shoes. But the nationalist claim, with its mixture of religious and racial fanaticism, combining Western ideology of self-government with the human desire for equality, is a fact that cannot be ignored without disastrous results; it can, however, be recognized without hurting our main national interests.

Among our compatriots in Algeria, the desire to hold on to the present state of affairs is based on basic feelings that inspire both individuals and communities. The passions of the French people in France are many and contradictory. The slogan "Algérie française" derives from the history lessons that children are taught at school, fostered thereafter by the press. People's pride is invested in the possession of Algeria, as if France's wealth, greatness, and future were all at stake.

Wealth? We have seen the view we need to take about that. Future? That depends on the French themselves—on their vitality, their unity, their adaptability. Sovereignty over the Muslims of Algeria would be a burden, involving certain duties to humanity. But you would need to be completely ignorant of twentieth-century history to suppose that raising the standard of living of millions of Muslims is indispensable to the prosperity of our own country.

France no longer possesses the greatness that belongs to power and will not again. But France still has enough power for its philosophy to influence the world, so long as it does not ruin itself in pointless escapades. It is by refusing to recognize the conditions of wealth, greatness, and a future that the French risk hastening their decline. As Renan said in 1870: "What we lack is not heart but a head."

May 6, 1957

The above text, finished on May 6 of this year, may now seem out of date. The Algerian War becomes more of a tragedy every day. Every character plays his part, and fate drags everyone along, the lucid and the blind, the fanatics and the moderates, toward a common catastrophe. But let us refuse to bow to this inevitability of blood and death.

The FLN has chosen to make use of all the most horrible forms of guerrilla war. To ambushes and surprise attacks on military units are added reprisals against Algerians guilty or suspected of sympathizing with the French or lacking zeal for the national cause. The FLN does not shrink from the most extreme terrorist methods: random bombs that kill women and children, liberals, and extremists indiscriminately. At Mélouza, the FLN exterminated a whole village, apparently because it supported the Mouvement National Algérien (MNA, National Algerian Movement).

It is as if these madmen wanted to encourage, not the Frenchmen who argue for reconciliation, but those who believe only in repression.[11]

Whatever the cause of these atrocities, and whether the FLN leadership decided on such methods in cold blood or out of exasperation generated by the pitiless struggle, any return to the idea of giving priority to the restoration of law and order would mean an end to any kind of policy and, in the long run, an end to hope. There are more rebels in the maquis now, and they are better armed, than at the beginning of the rebellion, or even compared with a year ago. Despite the rivalry between them, the FLN and the MNA share the same objectives, and both include extremists as well as moderates. Now more than ever, we cannot abandon the French people of Algeria and the Algerians loyal to France to the fury of the fanatics. Now more than ever, there can be no promise of peace through the policy of pacification as practiced for months. Today, as in the past, there is but one solution: to stop opposing in principle the demands of the nationalists, and to prepare for the inevitable development toward an Algerian state, as well as setting a timetable for its creation.

This may be France's last chance to take an initiative of its own. If the new government follows in the footsteps of the previous one,[12] the Algerian War will, a few weeks or months from now, no longer be an exclusively French affair. Currency shortages will force austerity measures that public opinion does not yet suspect. The Algerian War, together with an economic crisis, will put a great strain on a Parliament without a majority and a regime without authority.

So all of us will soon be facing what could be a decisive test. No miraculous solution will spare us the effort and pain of adapting to a changed world. Do we mean to face the ordeal clear-sightedly, seeking peace with the nationalism that is stirring up the Muslim masses and cannot spare Algeria? Or shall we cling to the theoretical positions disavowed by half our fellow countrymen, and by almost all our friends in Europe and the United States, and accept the fate that drags us toward an interminable war, foreign intervention, a confused battle in which we shall react to our own misery by turning and rending one another?

What can an ordinary citizen do but express the anguish he feels and appeal to everyone to have the courage to face the truth?

June 6, 1957

ALGERIA AND THE REPUBLIC

The attempt to turn the Muslims of Algeria into French citizens, which might have been conceivable some decades ago, is now anachronistic. Even disregarding the unanimous opposition of the governments in Tunis and Rabat and of the FLN, the idea comes up against innumerable obstacles. Economically, it would involve the home country in sacrifices it would not willingly enter into. Nor would there be any certainty of achieving the desired result—a reasonably rapid reduction in the gap in the two countries' standard of living. Socially, it would call for the transfer to Algeria of the administrative standards that obtain in France. Politically, it would bring into the National Assembly a number of Muslim deputies, precluding any hope of rehabilitating the French parliamentary system. Morally, it would not stifle the nationalist claim, stronger in the elites than in the masses, that is fueled by the sense of injustice born of competition for equality with the French.

Integration is neither desirable nor possible. Foreign observers all wonder what mixture of ignorance, pride, and myth it is that makes so many French people enamored of a project that is as pretentious as it is far-fetched.

We are told that any other solution leads to secession. But breaking the links with the home country would result in total disaster for Algeria, which itself can feed only 2 or 3 million of its 8 or 9 million sons.

Germaine Tillion's *L'Algérie en 1957* (Algeria in 1957) was published a few weeks before *La Tragédie algérienne* (The Algerian Tragedy). Asked to write a study by friends who had been deported or interned, she described Algeria's great suffering in a style moving in its sobriety. She was neither for nor against pacification: After examining the economic problem, she observed that Algeria could not manage without France (not the opposite). She seemed to provide arguments for those who say France can only save Algeria in the context of a single state. Thierry Maulnier[13] concluded that Algeria's choice was simple: "France or famine."

But Maulnier's conclusion is doubly unjustified. It is not what Germaine Tillion concluded. She was well aware of the political ideas and passions behind the rebellion, and in the final pages of her book she wrote: "It may be asking a lot of us, it may be asking a lot of the Algerian elite, but if neither side can or will make any concessions, then we should lose no time in making room here for all those we want to save in Algeria, whatever their blood or religion. For Algeria's ship is sinking, and there is no time to lose before it is wrecked. But it could have been avoided, and perhaps it still can."[14]

The alternative is inadmissible for another reason. If we must help Algeria in order to save it from famine, we cannot set our continued domination as a condition. Would Monsieur Thierry Maulnier ever have expressed his point of view in the words, "Either you accept the French regime or we wash our hands of you"? How could he fail to realize that his choice between "France or famine" would inevitably be interpreted in this way by any Algerian nationalist?

Even with these reservations, there is still a serious problem. Is there not a contradiction between political liberation and economic development? To repeat Tillion's words: "Is anti-colonialism becoming an excuse for pauperization?" For rich countries, giving independence to a colony has become a cheap way of getting rid of an unprofitable business. It is also a somewhat cynical method of abandoning in midstream peoples whose archaic modes of living you have destroyed without providing them with the means of adapting to modern civilization.

There is some truth in this argument. If a colonial power washes its hands of those it has just made independent, its seeming liberalism may be a mere cloak for self-interest. In the case of Algeria, both explanations are possible. Those who suggest dialogue with the Algerian nationalists may be idealists invoking the people's right to self-determination or aspiring to be friends with the Muslims. But they may also be capitalists anxious to cut costs and indifferent to the poverty of an independent Algeria. (It goes without saying that all those on the Left belong to the first, noble category, while all those on the Right are in the second, sordid camp.) Each side may attribute base motives to its adversaries and claim sublime inspiration for itself.

It is out of love for Ali and Mohammed, for love of the most deprived of the Kabyles and the Arabs, that the generous former governor of Algeria[15] finds himself miraculously in agreement with such superior minds and distinguished souls as Monsieur Roger Duchet,[16] Monsieur Alain de Sérigny,[17] and other writers on the *Écho d'Alger* (Echo of Algiers).[18]

If Monsieur Georges Le Brun-Kéris[19] and Monsieur Étienne Borne[20] condemn my cynicism, it is because Christian compassion imposes on them the need to shield the Algerians from the suffering and tyranny of the FLN. Tillion's book showed it is possible to speak honestly against Algerian nationalism in the interests of the Algerians themselves or to plead for Algerian nationalism in the interests of the home country alone.

Why, all over the world, have the Left, the foreign governments who judge the situation, and most economists decided in favor of anti-colonialism? For some fundamental reasons that it may be worthwhile setting out, since French public opinion tries to ignore them.

1. Refusal to move toward autonomy or independence logically implies a choice in favor of integration, or, in other words, economic or cultural alignment. But when one is dealing with large populations, alignment demands that the home country make efforts and sacrifices that no democratic regime can or will force upon its citizens. We should not forget the conditions that Tillion considered necessary for the saving of Algeria: "None of these three conditions is optional: 2,000 billion francs' worth of investment over five years; two years of compulsory civilian service for graduates of some state-run schools of higher education; and special preference for Algerians in French factories. By this means, and by this means only, we can reverse the trend and guide a whole people away from the future misfortune toward which it is drifting." But if this plan were put into practice, what resources would France have left for the other territories of the French Union? If help on this scale were offered to underdeveloped countries all over the world, what would be the total amount of aid that the rich countries would have to give the poor ones?

I doubt whether those 2,000 billion francs are really available, not financially but practically: in order words, whether the goods those billions are in theory intended to buy really exist.

I personally mistrust such grandiose and unworkable plans and such dogmatic choices (the idea that it has to be 2,000 billion in five years or nothing, because half-measures would only make matters worse). In fact, sensible governments and economists alike have concluded from the figures that the cost of alignment would be prohibitive, so the choice has to fall on autonomy or independence.

2. Economists have put forward another argument in favor of this theory: It is rarely in the interests of an underdeveloped territory to have its economy managed by a developed country. Admittedly, in the nineteenth century the Europeans helped to bring industry into some colonies and protectorates. There is no point in speculating on the relative costs and profits for the colonized and the colonizers in a colonial era that in its previous form is coming to an end. Inevitably, the rulers and administrators of a home government always see the economy of a dependent territory in relation to the interests of the home country. The absence of customs duties paralyzes the industrialization of underdeveloped countries. What democratic government would have the farsightedness and the strength to introduce duties that would protect its colonies' budding industries against competition from those in the home country? The economic argument in favor of anticolonialism is that steady economic development calls for at least the autonomy of countries that were formerly colonies or protectorates.

Is Algeria an exception to this rule? In some ways, yes. The Algerians need to keep their privileges in the French labor market. In other ways, no. Say what you like, it is doubtful that Algeria could develop its industry and create jobs for all its workless in the context of complete symbiosis with France. In any case, Algeria needs an administrative system that is different from that of France, and this implies a certain amount of autonomy, if not actual independence.

3. Even in exceptional cases, where the economic development of dependent territories is helped rather than cramped or diverted by union with the home country, integration becomes impossible as soon as there is a nationalistic revolt. At a pinch, France might spend hundreds of billions of francs a year to raise the standard of living of the Algerian people, but it could not do that and at the same time spend more hundreds of billions on

pacification. Even if the latter were successful, such success is never more than temporary because the nationalists go on receiving outside aid. It is worth fighting to transfer sovereignty to moderates instead of extremists, that is, to nationalists with whom cooperation is possible. But there is no point in fighting against *all* nationalists, because integration itself only produces more of them in every generation.

Algeria is certainly an extreme case. Advocates of integration there have better arguments for their view than their counterparts elsewhere. The number of Algerians who would like to remain French is probably greater than in any of the other countries that have gained their independence since the war. Yet most observers are convinced that, for Algeria, autonomy of some kind, and not integration, offers the only possibility of success.

But independence won in opposition to France, an independence breaking the ties between Algeria and the home country, would be a disaster for the supposed victors. For no one would take over from France: not the Soviet Union, nor the United States. The labor market would be closed to Algeria's unemployed. Without capital from abroad and without the 350,000 salaries paid by French enterprises, Algeria would collapse into total catastrophe.

In this war of passion, each side is fighting against its own economic interests. The Algerian nationalists are fighting to the death to win back their ancestral right to poverty. The French are struggling fiercely to retain the right to devote part of their resources to improving the lot of their adversaries.* Algeria's poverty and the loyalty that the French in Algeria have toward France are combining to produce a horrible tragedy.

The Algerian minority, grown aware of its desire to be a nation, has been able to recruit enough fighters to carry on a guerrilla war. The mass of the population is trapped between the partisans and the French army, now tortured by the one group, now liberated by the other. Can this tragedy be transformed into something positive? Might France's attachment to Algeria be expressed in the form of economic aid instead of repression? Might Algerian nationalism build schools instead of burning them down, and

---

*It goes without saying that it is in the interests of the nationalist leaders to create an Algerian state, and in the interests of all the French people of Algeria to maintain French sovereignty.

respect both the conditions necessary for France's presence and those necessary for Algeria's salvation?

Let us borrow our conclusion from Germaine Tillion:

> Between absolute independence and blueprint law, there is a whole series of intermediate solutions that force from us only concessions that we are already willing to make and that in any case cannot be avoided. So why should we not take the trouble to examine them? Because it would amount to admitting that our adversaries have a right to exist, and rather than that we would prefer to continue the war indefinitely, ruin our country for good, and sacrifice both the security of our compatriots in Algeria and our hopes in the Sahara. We and our adversaries alike each have in our hands half of the remedy that could save the heroic and unfortunate people of Algeria. If, out of blind hatred, stupidity, or weakness, we abandon one another and take the easy way out, which is total war carried on indefinitely, then woe to them, to us, and to our neighbors.
>
> And yet the resources we need have built up, on the level both of material means, which we possess, and of desire for progress, the undoubted heritage of rebellious youth. Those resources have accumulated in the midst of the cruel sufferings of the past three years, in spite of them, even because of them.

MORE THAN ANYONE ELSE

More than anyone else, General de Gaulle has the power to restore peace, because he can also make war, and because he has a reputation for magnanimity.

Peace does not presuppose the "loss" of Algeria; it does presuppose, sooner or later, dialogue with *some* of the Algerian nationalists. The objective is not to prevent the Algerian people from one day using their right to self-determination, but to create the conditions in which they might do so without breaking with France. However many Algerian Muslims took part in "fraternization," it does not make the nationalists cease to exist, or change the Muslims into Frenchmen, or make it possible for Algeria to be represented by deputies sitting in Paris.

Rarely has any man been backed by such a consensus of goodwill. Setting aside the extremists who brought General de Gaulle to power but would like to install a military-cum-fascist regime, the immense majority of French people passionately wish success for this strong and liberal government. Far from all the world being in league against us, our allies and enemies alike are on the whole in favor of our presence in Algeria—the Soviets for fear lest the Americans establish themselves there, the Americans out of unwillingness to take on further responsibilities, the Europeans out of hostility to Nasserism, and all the West out of its need for France. Although our own nationalists lapse into xenophobia and tell us of dark plots hatched by the intelligence services and foreign oil companies, we have in fact remained almost unscathed. Neither the Soviet Union nor the United States has sacrificed its Arab policy to win our favors. If no one has come out strongly in our support, it is because no one has believed in our success, for the simple reason that there was nothing to guarantee it. When France has a policy likely to work that is framed in terms compatible with Western values, then abstention may well be transformed into support.

If that happens, the army officers, who are not all won over to the ideologies of the activists, may gradually forget the wild ambitions of May 1958 and be content with what is their proper place, not merely in a republic but in any industrial society. Even in South America, at least in the most advanced countries, the generals and the colonels have recognized that law and order are impossible without respect for the constitution. If the colonels in Algiers, with the help of the parachutists, seized power, they would not be able to govern by themselves, and the civilians they called in as leaders would at once do their best to put them in their place. In this respect, General de Gaulle has done nothing since June 2, 1958, that any other president of the council would not have done in his place. In the atomic age, an army that does not obey the government destroys a nation. In the century of urban masses, a wholly military power can never be anything but a transitional stage toward either a fascist regime or a return to constitutional procedures. I am sure that our officers have not yet, for the most part, been won over to the ill-digested doctrines of Mao Tse-tung or the legendary but out-of-date traditions of South America. They will not try to make up for their disappointments at the expense of the republic and their fellow countrymen.

It is difficult to obey a government that one does not respect. A British historian who is a good friend of mine ended a book on France with these words: "A people which, in one hundred and fifty years, had astonished the world in every field of achievement, which had known every form of glory, in war, in sanctity, in all the arts and sciences, had yet failed to find institutions that united the French people and gave them a political way of life worthy of their genius, their courage, their legitimate hopes."[*]

No one can say for sure what institutions will unite the French people and answer their aspirations. But there are plenty of negative certainties: What the extremists and the conspirators want is contrary to historical necessities and to the lasting hopes of most Frenchmen. The May revolution could be the beginning of France's political renewal, on condition that it makes haste to devour its children.

---

[*]Denis W. Brogan, *The French Nation from Napoleon to Pétain* (London: Hamish Hamilton, 1957), pp. 302–303.

THE DAWN OF
UNIVERSAL HISTORY

A few words may be needed to explain the title of this lecture and to re-move the bad impression it has probably made on you. A publisher, together with the chairman, is responsible both for my being here and for the subject, which I shall survey rather than treat in depth.

A year or so ago, this same publisher, who is responsible for a series of books on the different eras of civilization, asked me if I would write a history of the world since 1914. I replied at once that no serious historian would agree to take on such a task. We have all lived through part of history since 1914, each one in his own place and with his own passions and prejudices, but none of us has experienced it all. Nobody has wholly mastered that huge and fragmented mass of material or yet raised to the level of consciousness events weighed down with so much human pain, so many unheard-of crimes and boundless promises. Then, after some thought, I added: No serious historian would be conceited enough to try to do what you ask, but I am not a historian. I do not know whether I am a philosopher or a sociologist, but perhaps I might be able to write a piece bringing out some of the special characteristics of our time and putting particular stress on what I call *the dawn of universal history*. For the first time, what are called the *higher* societies are living through one and the same history. For the first time, we may perhaps speak of "human society." This lecture will set out some of the ideas that figure in the introduction and the conclusion of the book I have undertaken to write.

I realize that a study like this will probably be judged harshly by many of my colleagues, whether they are philosophers or historians. Sociology has not yet been given an established place in traditional English-speaking universities, or else it hides under less American names (such as anthropology). As for the philosophy of history, whether it derives from Bossuet or Hegel, Marx or Toynbee, it is at best regarded more as a literary than a scientific exercise, fit perhaps for writers but not for respectable thinkers.

What can I say in my own defense? First, that I am more conscious than anyone else of the precariousness and vulnerability of the essay I intend to write. Let me make it clear in advance. It will not be a narrative like that of Thucydides: There are too many events and they are too disjointed. Nor will it be a synthesis, like Jacob Burckhardt's book on the Italian Renaissance. It will be an essay and presented as such, restricted in its scope because of the inevitable limitations inherent in the author's personality and influenced by the experience and aspirations of a particular man, involved in a particular country, in a certain generation, and in a certain intellectual system.

Why should I be criticized for writing such an unambitious work? Unconsciously or otherwise, we all do it. A scholar may be able to look with an innocent and impartial eye on past centuries. Perhaps a historian writing of Athens or Sparta, Rome or Carthage, pope or emperor, the Holy Roman Empire or the French monarchy, is uninvolved by the passions of the people he is dealing with. Perhaps he manages to understand equally impartially the combatants on all sides in a battle, the beliefs they share, the interests that oppose them, and the disasters and the successes they unwittingly bring about between them. But when we open our morning newspaper or vote for a candidate in an election, we do not hesitate to place ourselves in our own age, or to situate our age in time itself. Anyone who tries to discover what life, active or endured, has been like for an Englishman or a Frenchman in the twentieth century is presenting himself with "an interpretation of the world since 1914." I shall try to make my interpretation as coherent and impartial as I can. And this is how I shall set about it.

I

Every succeeding generation in Europe since the beginning of the twentieth century has felt it was living in an unprecedented era. Does the very constancy of the convention show it was unfounded? Or was it a kind of premonition, confirmed by our own experience as false for our predecessors but true for us? And even if we hesitate to say every generation has been wrong except perhaps our own, is there not a last hypothesis suggesting that all of them may have been right, but all together rather than each one separately, and not in the way they thought?

In other words, it strikes me as true, or at least probable, that in the nineteenth century, mankind lived through a kind of revolution, or perhaps a mutation, which went through its early stages in past times but has increased its pace in the course of recent decades. Since the beginning of the nineteenth century, each generation and each individual thinker has tried to define that historic mutation. Claude Henri de Saint-Simon and Auguste Comte spoke of an industrial society; Alexis de Tocqueville of a democratic one; Karl Marx called it capitalist. Our own ideologies, if not our ideas, derive from the work of the great doctrinarians of the first half of the nineteenth century. If we compare their diagnoses and predictions with what has happened between their time and our own, we shall arrive at a first definition of what I have called a *historic mutation.*

Let us start with the school of Saint-Simon and Comte, which for immediately understandable reasons seems to be coming back into fashion. The emergence of two great and in some ways similar industrial systems on either side of the Iron Curtain has finally made observers realize that there are two species, or versions, of a certain type of society: the Soviet regime, on the one hand, and the Western regimes, on the other. Why not call this type of society an *industrial society,* since it is characterized by the development of industry?

This in fact was Saint-Simon's and Comte's central notion. Both saw, coming into being before their eyes, a new society, which they called "industrial" and which was created in Europe. Comte set out even more precisely than Saint-Simon or his school the main features of this new society, and although the founder of positivism is rarely read these days, and even more rarely studied seriously, his definition of industrial society provides us with a starting point.

Like Saint-Simon, Comte contrasted producers—industrialists, farmers, bankers, and the like—with the political and military elites who, in a society engaged in peaceful labor, are relics from a feudal and theocratic past. Like all human societies, the industrial society has a primary objective, in this case the exploitation of natural resources. The age of wars, conquests, and Caesars is over. Napoleon, for all his genius, was guilty of what, in the eyes of philosophers of history, is the worst of crimes: anachronism. The Roman conquests were meaningful and productive because they prepared the way for the unified world in which Christianity could spread; communities devoted to war were bound sooner or later, when might proved its right, to achieve peace. In our own day, conquests cannot be justified because they no longer serve any purpose, and because the people, through their spontaneous—and finally successful—resistance, proved that the heir to the revolution was wrong to change to hatred the sympathy they once felt for the enterprise the French nation had embarked on alone for the good of all.

Arguing with a dogmatism that some saw as typical of sociologists, Comte drew the consequences, all of them, of that change of aim. Henceforward, not war but labor became the supreme value. It is labor that creates managers, who are the rulers of modern society; it is from labor that everyone derives the status and prestige accorded him by public opinion. Labor defines every individual's place in the hierarchy. So labor is, or should be, free: The more families become rooted in a class or occupation, the more mobility between generations becomes the rule. Individuals may now aspire to a rank in proportion to their merit, regardless of what their parents did. Comte saw wage-earning not as a modern form of slavery or serfdom but as a promise of personal freedom.

Europe, or more precisely, the nations of Western Europe—Britain, France, Italy, Spain, and Germany—were, in the eyes of Auguste Comte, the avant-garde of mankind. They were ahead of other peoples in what was ultimately a common task: the development of the planet, the creation of an industrial society, and the gathering together of all the groups scattered over the five continents into a peaceful community. But according to the high priest of positivism, Europe's advance carried with it more duties than rights. Comte warned his contemporaries against the temptation of colonial conquest. He repeatedly denounced the occupation of Algeria and even expressed the hope that the Arabs would "vigorously drive out" the French if the latter were not intelligent and virtuous enough to withdraw of their own accord.

It is easy, and many have taken advantage of the facility, to make fun of Comte's prophecies. When he said the age of European wars and colonial conquests was over, he was certainly wide of the mark. But if we consider him not as a prophet but as an adviser to princes and peoples, we see he was wiser than the events themselves. He did not foretell the future as it was, but as it would have been if history had unfolded in accordance with the wisdom of men of goodwill.

He said that industrial society, then spreading through Western Europe, was acting, and would continue to act, as an example for all mankind. He was wrong, certainly, to concentrate on Europe and underestimate the original contributions made by other civilizations; to believe that forms of belief and political organization were strictly linked to social type; and to disregard the durability of ways of thinking that he dismissed as theological or metaphysical. But in such matters as the relations between labor and war, the exploitation of natural resources, and the exploitation of man by man, he understood with undeniable lucidity the revolution that had taken place and that rulers and peoples alike are at last painfully acknowledging today. That is, he saw that wars between industrial societies are both ruinous and pointless, while nonindustrial societies—which we call underdeveloped—are bound to take industrial societies as models. And, in this sense, Europe has been exemplary. But, said Comte, Europe would be wrong to impose that example, taking advantage of a temporary "advance" in order to reopen the age of great invasions. What is the use of killing, enslaving, and looting? Gold and silver are no longer real wealth. The only wealth is labor, rationally organized. Slavery was necessary in the distant past to accustom men, with their tendency toward sloth and absentmindedness, to regular effort. But European man has been so well trained in rational labor that constraint is no longer necessary. So wars should be as out of date as colonial conquests are.

There have been both, but nowadays they strike us as irrational, at least if we agree with Comte in thinking men make war neither for its own sake nor just for the exhilaration of victory. If the main objective of industrial societies is labor as a means to well-being—as the spokesmen of both Soviet and Western societies now vie with one another in proclaiming—then the two European wars of the twentieth century have been pointless, and the third should not take place.

Let us now turn to the other great doctrinarian: Karl Marx, who was born a generation later than Auguste Comte. Marx, too, observed a historic mutation, and although he used different words and concepts, he stressed the same main facts. The development of productive factors, for which he gave credit to the bourgeoisie, has been more rapid in recent times than in any other age. In a few decades, the triumphant middle classes have done more to change the conditions and techniques of labor in common factory work than the elites of feudal or military societies did in the past 1,000 years.

The high priest of socialism and the high priest of positivism agreed in stressing the essential difference between traditional societies and modern society. Both identified the distinguishing characteristic of the latter in the primary importance it accords to labor, together with its application of science to techniques of production and the resulting increase in collective resources. The main difference between the two doctrines is that, for Marx, the conflict between employers and employees is fundamental, whereas for Comte, that conflict is secondary, a symptom of social disintegration that will be corrected by improved organization.

Marx tended to explain everything in terms of the conflict between employers and employees and the class struggle between capitalists and the proletariat: want in the midst of plenty, despite the growth of productive forces; the alienation of workers; and the despotism of the propertied minority. So he had an apocalyptic view of the capitalist future, foreseeing a worsening of the major conflict between capitalists and the proletariat until the final explosion. At the same time, he sketched an idyllic portrait of the postcapitalist regime: He never actually described it, but he suggested its attractions by way of contrast. If social inequalities, the exploitation of man by man, the class struggle, and the alienation of the workers are due to the characteristic features of capitalism—private ownership of the means of production and possession by the capitalist minority of economic and, indirectly, of political power—then the elimination of private property, together with the proletarian revolution, will bring the prehistory of mankind to an end and begin a new era in which social progress will no longer have to be achieved through the violence of political revolutions.

It seems to me that on the main point on which he disagreed with Comte, Marx was perhaps right in the short term, but wrong in the long term. Conflicts between employers and employees inside enterprises or over the sharing out of national revenue have not been decisive. On the whole, conflicts have been fiercer in societies still in the initial phases of industrialization than in mature industrial societies. The working classes, organized in unions and often represented in parliaments by powerful socialist parties, still make claims, but they have gone over to methods that are legal and peaceful. They do not want revolution, which might usher in a dictatorship of the proletariat; they have no clear idea even of what a dictatorship of the proletariat is. It has been proved, for them as for most observers, that private ownership of the means of production, as practiced in Western societies today, forbids neither the development of productive forces nor the raising of the standard of living for the masses. However one judges the relative efficiency of the Soviet and Western regimes, it is clear that one does not signify want and the other plenty. The difference between the two regimes themselves are more marked than those between their enterprises, and those between their state structures and public authorities are more striking than those between their two societies. As Comte remarked, industrial societies incorporate their workers into a technico-bureaucratic hierarchy.

The conflicts that have dominated the twentieth century and determined its course have been national or imperial rather than social. Comte and Marx, as theoreticians, were aware of the historic mutation taking place before their eyes, but they underestimated the durability of the traditional aspect of history—the rise and fall of empires, rivalry between regimes, and the beneficial or baleful exploits of great men.

They both underestimated, too, the power of the specifically political factor. Marx wrote as if the political regime of capitalism could be adequately defined in terms of the power of the bourgeoisie and as if the political regime of socialism could be adequately defined in terms of the semi-mythological slogan "the dictatorship of the proletariat." Comte ascribed power to those who managed labor and were solely concerned with lessening the harshness of toil and preventing excessive demands on workers by making use of public, feminine, and proletarian opinion. Both Comte and Marx overlooked the alternative put forward by Alexis de Tocqueville: a commercial and industrial society promoting both equality and mobility. These things are indeed called for by the fundamental trends of modern societies, though the latter may still choose, on the one hand, a despotism of one, with a single person ruling over millions of individuals whose differences are blurred into the uniformity of conditioning and servitude, or, on the other hand, liberty for all, with everyone perhaps much alike in their comfort and a kind of mediocrity, but retaining their right to exercise choice, initiative, and belief.

The theorists of sociology, underestimating the partial autonomy of politics, argued as if history, in the sense of the succession of wars and empires, victories and defeats, was over and done with. Today, in 1960, the century we have lived through seems a dual one to me. It is traversed by the intellectual, technical, and economic revolution that, like some cosmic force, sweeps mankind along toward an unknown future. But in some respects, it resembles much that has gone before; it is not the first century to have seen great wars. On the one hand, we see the need for progress; on the other hand, it is history as usual, and the drama of empires, armies, and heroes.

It is in the statistics of intellectual or industrial production that the groundswell becomes visible. At the beginning of the twentieth century, men used a few tons of oil a year; they now consume nearly a billion. Consumption increases at 10 percent per annum. Fifty years ago, a few million tons of steel represented the annual production of a Great Power; today it represents the annual increase in its production. Ninety percent of all the scientists who have ever existed are living today: This figure was given to me by Robert Oppenheimer, and I was very struck by it. The acceleration of history is reflected in such statistics, and these in turn illustrate the growing accumulation—what Comte called the ever more rapidly growing accumulation—of knowledge and power.

Let us now turn to traditional history. It is perpetually astonishing: what has happened has happened and cannot not have been, but how easily it could have been otherwise! If the Germans had not sent two army corps to the eastern front on the eve of the battle, would the miracle of the Marne have taken place? If the world slump had not dragged on for years, or if the French and British had given a military reply to the return of German troops into the Rhineland, would the last world war have happened? Without Churchill, would Britain have held out alone against the Third Reich? What course would the greatest of wars have taken if Hitler had not attacked Russia in 1941? Traditional history is action—it is made out of decisions made by people in certain times and places. These decisions could have been different if they had been made by other people in the same situation or by the same person in another mood. And no one can say, either in advance or in retrospect, the limits of the consequences arising out of some of these localized and dated decisions.

In traditional history, accident appears to reign, and greatness rubs shoulders with cruelty. Innocent blood is shed everywhere, and the victories of princes are paid for by the peoples' sacrifices. The law of necessity seems to rule in the evolution of knowledge and power, and quantity triumphs over and mocks the achievements of individuals or the few. Sometimes I muse on the wonderful history Thucydides might have written of the Thirty Years' War—the one that lasted from 1914 to 1945. Toynbee and Thibaudet compared its first episode to the Peloponnesian War. (But did they know, in 1918, that the peace of Versailles was only the Nicias armistice?) We would probably have to get someone like Marx or Colin Clark to finish the account, not with a narrative but by an analysis of the irresistible process of worldwide industrialization. In a way, this progress is no less dramatic than the rise and fall of the Third Reich. Like a torrent it carries all before it, uprooting age-old customs, throwing up factories and sprawling cities, covering the whole planet with roads and railroads, and offering the masses a prospect of the abundance to which privileged nations already bear witness, confirming its possibility; but it starts by tearing men away from the protection of beliefs and practices handed down over the centuries, and then hands millions of them over, bereft of faith and law, to the uncertainties of an incomprehensible system driven by mysterious machines.

I do not know if I shall be able, in this as yet unwritten book, to give the reader the dual sense of human action and necessity, event and process, history as usual and the novelty of industrial society. Allow me, in this short lecture, after pointing out the differences between these two aspects of the century, to show how, in various ways, accident and necessity, event and process, have combined to weave the web of real history as it has unfolded. Let us try to detect the law of industrial necessity at work in the drama of wars and empires, as the actions of certain people give form and shape to the process of industrialization. After this dual dialectical inversion it will be time to wonder whether, in the future, the process will be able to go on without dramas.

II

There are three ways—not mutually exclusive, it seems to me—of arranging the succession of events or incidents in a necessary sequence and discerning the law of industrial evolution in the drama of great wars. Through the state of the industrial system, a historian may explain the origin of wars, their course, or their result. I do not believe in the first of the three ways, but I make considerable use of the second and third.

The first way, that of Lenin and the Marxists, sees in the drama of history only spectacular episodes in process. For them, the 1914 war was not an expression of the traditional nature of human history, but rather the inevitable consequence of capitalist contradictions and of rivalries between capitalist states. This is not the place to analyze in detail a theory I have discussed many times before.* But so that the present account may not be too incomplete, allow me to summarize, in three propositions, a classic theory that still has more supporters than it deserves.

1. Colonial imperialism was only an extreme form of capitalist expansion in what is now called the underdeveloped world; it operated across continents with traditional economies that were so weak as to be defenseless against the greed of big companies and the domination of the European states.
2. Peaceful partition of the world into spheres of influence or colonial empires was impossible: An ineluctable necessity forced capitalists and capitalisms into a feverish search for profits, outlets for their products, human labor to exploit, and reserves of raw materials to develop. It was no more possible for capitalist economies to make a lasting arrangement to carve up the planet between them than it is for individual capitalists in separate countries to share the market out amongst themselves or get together to suspend competition.
3. The cause of the Great War, and the stake for which it was fought, was really the desire to partition the world, though the hostilities took place in Europe and apparently arose out of specifically European conflicts. Without realizing it, Frenchmen, Germans, and Britons died to increase their own country's share of the spoils in the rest of the world.

But in my opinion these three propositions have not been proven, and in some ways they have been disproven by the facts, or at least made improbable by an unprejudiced examination of the facts.

Economic expansion in its various forms (the quest for profit through developing rich reserves or exploiting human labor; the search for outlets for manufactured goods; and the attempt to corner privileges and exclude competitors), even if one assumes it to be linked to the essence of the capitalist

---

*See, for example, *La Société industrielle et la guerre* (The industrial society and war) (Paris: Plon, 1959).

regime, does not automatically entail colonial acquisition or the assertion of political sovereignty. The latter is only useful or necessary, economically speaking, in order to exclude competitors or to acquire special privileges without having to compete for them fairly. But the African territories that the countries of Western Europe managed to conquer without difficulty at the end of the nineteenth and the beginning of the twentieth century represented only an absurdly small proportion of the foreign trade of the capitalist states; they absorbed only a very small percentage of the capital that Europe, the world's banker, invested abroad. All this being so, how can we go on regarding colonial conquest as merely an extreme form and necessary expression of an expansion inseparable from the capitalist economies?

The second proposition also seems arbitrary to me. We know only too well that rivals often manage to share out markets amongst themselves, thus suspending the allegedly inexorable law of competition. All the more, how much easier would the division of the world into spheres of influence have been, as well as the friendly settlement of Asian and African disputes among European nations, if the origin of such differences had been only commercial interests! The European economies, precisely because of their industrial development, were one another's best customers. In the view of the big capitalist companies, west and equatorial Africa, Algeria, and Morocco were only marginal zones of activity. German banks were less interested in Morocco than the Wilhelmstrasse could have wished. But it was the chancelleries that made it impossible for French and German capitalists to work together in Morocco. The diplomats thought in terms of power, not because they cared about commercial interests or because the spokesmen for commercial interests pressed them to, but because they had read the history books, and such had been the law of politics for thousands of years.

I am still waiting for someone to show me how a war that arose out of German-Slav rivalry in the Balkans, with Europe as its main theater, and with the balance of power within the diplomatic system of Europe being the thing at stake in the minds of the participants from the day the first gun was fired, could really have some other origin or some other meaning or cause. By what subtle reasoning can anyone make out that Africa or Asia was the cause of World War I, when what started it off were the revolver shots that struck down the Austrian archduke and the shelling of Belgrade? How could those far-off countries constitute a more authentic point at issue than the political status of Central and Eastern Europe?

In reality, for anyone who examines the past without preconceptions, all the facts point in the same direction and suggest the same explanation. The 1914–1918 war, as to its origin, was as much in conformity with historical tradition as the European wars that preceded it, and as the great war that Thucydides recorded, which involved all the cities in the Hellenic system (for example, in the way the continental countries made up the international system of Europe). A system based on balance inevitably drifts toward interminable war when it splits up into two coalitions or when one of the political units involved seems about to establish its hegemony over the historical area as a whole.

At the end of the fifth century B.C., Athens threatened the liberties of the Greek cities. At the beginning of the twentieth century A.D., Germany caused a similar danger to hang over the nations of Europe. War to the death was not inevitable, but it was inevitable that if war did break out, the other Great Powers would immediately feel they were fighting for their very existence and for their liberties. The immediate cause of the explosion, the status of the Balkans, was neither a mere occasion nor a pretext. Austria-Hungary and Turkey were multinational empires, one a legacy from the days when provinces belonged to kings, the other from conquests that had no other foundation or justification than the sword. But the ultimate disintegration of these empires, especially that of Austria-Hungary, was upsetting the balance of power. Germany was losing its main ally: Millions of Slavs were in danger of going over to the other side. It is understandable that the Reich should have supported the dual empire in an adventure where the latter sought salvation but found death. It is also understandable that, from the beginning of August 1914, the British, and, even more, the French, should have feared a German victory, which would have meant the loss of their independence, or in any case of their Great-Power status.

The 1914 war came along like an ordinary war in the age of industry. It is in its evolution and its consequences that it bears the mark of the century to which it belongs, and of which it is a tragic expression.

Thucydides' great war was fought from beginning to end with the same weapons, and apart from a few subtle tricks during the Sicilian expedition, the Greeks seem not to have produced so many technical inventions as acts of heroism in the course of their innumerable battles. The Thirty Years' War of the twentieth century, which opened with the revolver shots at Sarajevo or the Austrian shelling of Belgrade, ended with the thundering of atomic bombs over Hiroshima and Nagasaki. Between 1914 and 1945, the technology of production and destruction alike had made great strides.

The early battles were symbolized by machine guns, light horse-drawn cannon, and heavy artillery. The second phase, which saw the continuous front, trenches, the massing of artillery, artillery preparations, and the use of ever more guns and ammunition, resulted in bloody but sterile battles in which tens of thousands of men died for the gain or loss of a few meaningless kilometers of ground. The thousands of planes, tanks, and trucks used in the last phase of the hostilities introduced the technique of motorization and cooperation between air and armored power that together brought Hitler's Wehrmacht its spectacular successes between 1939 and 1941. The age of oil had succeeded, though not replaced, the age of coal; light metals joined together with steel. But qualitative superiority shifted precariously between one industrial power and another. And the race for quantitative superiority in men, weapons, and ammunition that had been a main feature of World War I (and of the first phase of the Thirty Years' War) was resumed even more fiercely in World War II. Germany, with 4,000 tanks and almost as many planes, put first Poland and then France hors de combat, winning a series of shattering victories in the summer of 1941. In 1944–1945, the industrial machine of the anti-German coalition was working flat out, and the Soviet and Anglo-American armies were victorious thanks to a numerical superiority comparable to that of 1918.

It had been the kind of war waged by industrial societies capable of mobilizing all their men and all their factories. Workers and soldiers alike, all citizens, contributed to the collective effort. It was a mass rising such as had been called for by the decrees of the Convention during the French Revolution. It was a triumph of organization, including what Elie Halévy has called "the organization of enthusiasm," for which survivors of the massacre criticized the veterans later. This industrial war, fought by uniformed civilians, was to fuel the pacifist revolt, which reflects, rather than contradicts, eras of conflict.

The second phase of the Thirty Years' War can, like the first, be explained in terms of the categories of traditional history. The side that was vanquished, which had long seemed the stronger, remained, perhaps excessively but understandably so, sensitive to the conditions imposed upon it and had a second try. There could be no real peace unless all the countries concerned were satisfied, or else we would have only truces. Any kind of

Germany would have broken the truce. Hitler's Germany broke it cynically and with boundless ambitions.

But this interpretation, though traditional, is also partial and in many respects inadequate. Admittedly, Jacques Bainville foresaw most of the events that led to the catastrophe of 1939 without referring to the economic consequences of the war and of the Treaty of Versailles. German rearmament, the reoccupation of the Rhineland, the dissolving of alliances, the break between France and the countries that succeeded Austria-Hungary, the German-Soviet alliance for the partitioning of Poland, the German attack on the West, the breaking of the German-Soviet pact—all these episodes in the continuing drama recall precedents and are in conformity with the logic of power politics. But it took the Great Depression of 1929, the millions of unemployed, and the complete disintegration of the politico-economic unity of Central Europe to enable a passionate movement like National Socialism to mobilize millions of Germans by giving them back some hope of a future. It took the evil genius of a Hitler to embody the desire for restitution in a monstrous orgy of crime.

A war between industrial societies was bound to take the form of a battle of equipment. The Great Depression was not the inevitable consequence of the nature of these societies; we know it would have been relatively easy to limit their ravages. No, the depression was a dramatic accident only made possible at the time by the nature of our societies. Thirty years ago, commentators would have denounced the way the people who drew up the Treaty of Versailles neglected the economic considerations. Since 1945, an even more irrational territorial arrangement than that of 1918 has not ruled out prosperity. Meanwhile, the Thirty Years' War has developed consequences we are still pondering, and about which we keep asking, Were they tragic or necessary? Tragic *and* necessary? Or necessary rather than tragic?

We are very familiar with these consequences—*weltgeschichte,* as the Germans call them: Europe has lost its preeminence. Yesterday, it was the center of world politics; today, it is divided between a zone ruled over by the Soviet Union and a zone dominated by the influence and protected by the power of the United States. The colonized peoples have achieved independence. The industrialization that gave Europe its superiority has become, or is in the process of becoming, common to the whole human race. All sections of mankind have access today, or will have access tomorrow, to the same tools, so will not the merciless law of quantity apply to peace as well as war and reduce Europe to the dimensions it has on the map?

"The Rape of Europe," "the decline of Europe"—the present situation can no doubt be expressed in historical terms. For us Europeans, who have lived through two great wars, witnessed the worst outrages ever inflicted by men on the honor of humanity, and now observe the end of empires, it is tempting to lament the evanescence of history. But should we really give way to the temptation? The spread of the industrial society, the unification of mankind—were not these two things caused or hastened by the Thirty Years' War inevitable, dictated by the law of necessity? And has not the whole tragedy, seen in the light of this outcome, been the means of fulfilling a predestined fate, as foreseen by Auguste Comte: an industrial society that would set an example for all human communities and unite mankind for the first time ever?

III

Now let us turn to the other aspect of the twentieth century and examine the accumulation of knowledge and power. Economists and sociologists nowadays are in the habit of studying long-term trends in production and productivity. Since the publication of Colin Clark's *Conditions of Economic Progress*, the calculation of growth rates (whether of gross national product or of income per capita), together with comparisons of the labor force employed in each of the three sectors, has become the normal method of measuring the development of different economies. But it seems that the statistics concerning national revenue or employment reflect the results of dramatic events as much as a regular process. The spread of industry throughout the world has taken place despite wars, revolutions, and catastrophes.

This is so evident that it need only be illustrated; proof is superfluous. First let us consider how different are the reactions of China and of Japan to the influence and threat of the West. In Japan, a section of the ruling class initiated the historic mutation without which the Empire of the Rising Sun would have been doomed to a kind of slavery. In China, the great majority of the bureaucratic class was unable either to understand or to carry out the necessary change, and it was only after a long series of civil wars and the seizure of power by the Communist Party that the Chinese state had the strength and the ability to implement an accelerated program of industrialization. The whole history of Asia since 1890 has been shaped by the disparity between the degree of modernization in the Japanese and Chinese empires. It was the former's advance over the latter in borrowing Western techniques of power that inspired in Japan the crazy ambition of conquering its vast neighbor on the mainland. And it was the Sino-Japanese War that gave the Communist Party its best opportunity. In each case, industrialization began with a dramatic phase of the conflict between past and present, tradition and the West.

The evolution of this dramatic phase not only determines the moment of take-off and the rate at which the process of industrialization develops; it also influences the choice of methods and decides which social group will take the initiative or the responsibility for the new direction. In Japan, it was a class steeped in the aristocratic spirit that brought about the change and tried to maintain a synthesis of national values and Western techniques. In China, it was ultimately a class shaped by Marxist-Leninist ideology and totalitarian practices that took charge of industrialization and the organization of the teeming masses. In Russia itself, the process began in the last quarter of the nineteenth century, while the absolutist political regime was still in place. War and revolution interrupted progress and produced a new elite that was inspired by a Western doctrine but opposed to the liberal West. Without the 1914 war, and if customary history had not toppled the Tsarist regime and provided Lenin and his comrades with their long-awaited opportunity, it is conceivable that the industrialization of Russia might have followed a different course, under a different power and at a different pace. What seems to have been inevitable, when we look back from the point of view of 1960, is that Russia, unless the unity of its empire had been destroyed from within or without, would become the premier power in Europe. If all peoples have the same capacities to produce and destroy, the law of greater numbers will prevail, within certain limits. But whatever answer we give to our questions, we are entitled to ask them. So what would have happened if Aleksandr Kerensky had eliminated the Bolshevik leaders in July 1917? What would have happened if Russia had had another two or three decades of peace in which to get over the crisis of the first phase of industrialization?

If Russia did not have that period of grace, if China was not spared by the ambitions of the most advanced countries in Asia, America, and

Europe, it was not because the capitalist economies were inexorably bound to imperialism but because industrialization provided both the means and the temptation to embark on conquest and military glory. For the statesmen and nations who went on thinking in the old categories, the chief significance of industry lay in its power to increase the ability to mobilize resources for war. It did not open up a new era; it provided new cards with which to play the old game.

In a way, that is the meeting point between history as usual and necessary history: Are knowledge and power at the service of power politics, or do they foretell, as Comte prophesied, the end of power politics and the beginning of a united mankind engaged in the only worthwhile struggle, the one for mastery over nature and the well-being of all humanity? Japan and Germany, the two great disturbers of the twentieth century's peace, gave yesterday's answer to this question of today. The masters of those two empires thought nothing had changed except the number of soldiers and the effectiveness of arms. Industry was a means to power, and the object of power was conquest. Is it the same today?

At the risk of being accused of naïveté, I would say that the present generation understands better than its predecessors the world in which we live, and which the thinkers of the nineteenth century intuitively recognized as something new. And I think my optimism is based on certain facts.

The first and best known of these is the revolution in arms. Between 1914 and 1945, the power of destruction remained less than the power of production and construction. The armies of 1914 used weapons that were less efficient than those that scientists and engineers were capable of inventing and manufacturing, if the best minds were devoted to the task. The infantry of 1914, which moved at walking pace, and the horse-drawn guns belonged to tradition. Even the armored divisions and the air squadrons did not yet really upset the calculation of profit and loss. The revolution dates from nuclear explosives. A war fought with thermonuclear bombs is no longer rational for any of the belligerents. Since 1945, industry has finally arrived at the first condition of peace, peace for fear of war—an eventuality announced prematurely by so many writers. The result is not that peace is assured, but merely that war is no longer the continuation of politics by other means. Thermonuclear war, unless one of the combatants is not really vulnerable, can only be the result of an accident or a misunderstanding.

Nevertheless, world public opinion has understood more clearly than in any other age the nature of modern economics and the possibilities for the peace it implies. Between classes and peoples alike, the causes of conflict seem weaker than the reasons for solidarity. True, there is nothing fundamentally new here. Liberal economists have been telling us for centuries that both parties gain from a bargain, that the essence of economics is exchange, and that wars and conquests are always pointless and often ruinous for everyone.

But recent facts have helped to spread these beliefs, which were once confined to quite narrow circles, to the general public. West Germany, with half the space of France, has had to absorb some ten million refugees, yet it enjoys unequaled prosperity. For West Germany, the price of defeat is not poverty, as it would have been in the past: It is well-being. The whole of Western Europe, including Britain, has lost its colonies, its power, and its diplomatic prestige, yet it has never before reached such levels of production and productivity.

During the 1930s, the West, obsessed by the Great Depression, thought in almost Marxist terms. It was looking for outlets and ended up convincing itself that growth was or might be paralyzed by lack of markets. Now it has recognized, almost with surprise, that despite recessions and temporary halts, expansion, as the economists have always said, creates outlets by and for itself. The progress made by the Soviet Union with a technique of rigid planning, by the Federal Republic of Germany with a relatively liberal strategy, and by other European countries with mixed techniques has weakened the influence of these so-called doctrinal quarrels. The scientific, social, and human requirements for growth—a sufficient number of technicians, incentives for entrepreneurs and administrators, and techniques of persuasion or pressure to get the masses to agree to change—these things are now more important than methods of regulation. The emphasis is on features common to all growth rather than on those particular to one type of regime.

Similarly, ideologies are less important than in the past and have lost their emotional power. In the West, and perhaps even in the Soviet Union, people no longer think that one regime is by nature imperialistic and exploitative while the other is peaceful and fair. All regimes are imperfect; none can ensure protection from injustice or is bound to make people poor. Even the most intemperate enemies of communism do not deny that the Soviet economy is growing rapidly or that the people's standard of living is rising. The severest opponents of the liberal West or of capitalism will admit that there has not been a major slump since 1945 and that the exploited proletariat lives better than ever before.

Does this mean that the industrial society, as imagined by Auguste Comte and being put into practice in various forms, really is exemplary, and that the human race is becoming socially alike at the same time as it is in the process of becoming diplomatically unified? Such a conclusion would be premature. I believe the dawn of universal history is on the point of breaking. It will have some novel features in comparison with the provincial histories of the nations and civilizations that belonged to the 6,000 years of the immediate past. But there is nothing to tell us that universal history will not be tragic, too.

What do I mean by *universal history?* To begin with, I mean the unification of the field of diplomacy. China and Japan, the Soviet Union and the United States, France and Britain, Germany and Italy, India and Ghana—all these states now belong to a single unique system. What happens on the coasts of China is not without influence on relations between Europe and the United States, or between the United States and the Soviet Union. Never before have so many states recognized one another's right to exist; never before have Europe and Asia, Africa, and America felt so close. What the main countries once did in Europe and Asia, the main countries of to-day, at present the United States and the Soviet Union, do across the five continents. It is a platitude to say that the means of communication and transportation have abolished distance. The accumulation of the means to knowledge and power in these state-continents is also one of the conditions of planetary diplomacy and of a change in the scale of power.

Diplomatic unification is accompanied by the worldwide diffusion of certain forms of technical and economic organization. No community that wants to survive can deliberately reject the development of productive forces, as the Marxists say—the rationalization of labor and the extension of technical equipment. How can anyone refuse the means to achieve strength and well-being? Thus, from Tokyo to Paris, from Peking to Rio, the same airports and the same factories meet the eyes of the visitor. The same words—*capitalism, communism, imperialism, dollar, ruble*—ring in his ears as soon as he engages in conversation with an intellectual or politician. A traveler, if he goes by superficial impressions, might think the whole human race lived in one world of machines and ideas.

But such impressions are largely deceptive. The human race, insofar as it is diplomatically united, is also divided, as all the diplomatic systems of the past have been. Two coalitions meet and oppose one another in the center of Europe. Around them, more and more, other states boast of their noncommitment. Relations between the Soviet Union and China are shrouded in a certain mystery. The United Nations provides a symbolic forum for the spokesmen of the states of the universal age, but most of the speeches express not the real condition of the states, which weakness condemns to impotence, but the ideology they indulge in so as to feel they are taking part in the history of mankind.

Perhaps the traditional divisions inherited from the provincial past weigh less heavily than the divisions typical of an age in which one kind of society has become the model. For of the two versions of the industrial society—the Soviet and Western versions—one at least claims to be the only valid one for everybody. Two states, in two different historical zones, embody the two ideologies typical of the West, and to this great schism is added another division—fleeting in terms of centuries, but long in terms of decades: that between rich and poor nations, those which have almost everything and those which have almost nothing, those which are called underdeveloped and those which already harvest the fruits of productivity. In a humanity on the way to unification, inequality between nations takes on the significance that inequality between classes once had. The condition of the masses varies more from continent to continent and from country to country than ever before. At the same time, the awareness of inequality is spreading, and resignation to poverty and fate is getting rarer.

The motives for hostility between the different sectors of this unified humanity are not repressed by any common spirituality. The unity is merely material, technological, and economic. The power of the means of production, destruction, and communication has filled oceans, leveled mountains, and overcome distances. Vague ideologies derived from European doctrines of the nineteenth century provide a few words that are common to men who do not worship the same gods, observe the same customs, or think in the same categories. Never have countries belonging to the same diplomatic system been so different from one another; never have the partners in a single enterprise been so devoid of fundamental solidarity.

For a decade or so we have been obsessed by the great schism between the Communists and the free world. How could it have been otherwise, when the Soviet armies are stationed 200 kilometers from the Rhine and Soviet propaganda proclaims that the final and universal triumph of communism is inevitable—in other words, tells the West it must choose between being killed and dying of its own accord!

That is not all. The clash between the two blocs is twofold. It is not only a rivalry for power but also a competition of propaganda; it is a foreign war, but it also has some characteristics of a civil war. Economic planning under a state ruled by the proletariat and aiming at abundance and equality: Such a regime, whether realized or not by a country like the Soviet Union, is a Western dream, a Utopia, through negation of the real that has dominated political if not doctrinal discussion in the West for decades. It may be that Orthodox Russia, heir to Byzantium and the monolithic traditions of oriental bureaucracy, belongs to a different sphere of civilization from Western Europe. But the Russia that invokes Marxism and socialism belongs to the Western sphere of civilization, at least by the language it uses and through its proud claim to have accomplished as much as any of Europe's greatest reformers to set an example to humanity.

Perhaps, too, the intensity of the conflict is already waning. The irrationality of a war to the death fought with atomic and thermonuclear weapons is evident to the leaders of both blocs. The similarities between the two productive forces and between the methods of organization of labor, even in industrial enterprises with different legal statuses, becomes increasingly apparent even to those most blinkered by their chosen ideologies. True, there is still room for real debate. The societies concerned have different ways of living and thinking, and this is reflected in type of ownership, mode of regulation applied to the economy as a whole, and style of authority. Let us not repeat the mistake of some Marxists by denying the different repercussions of *economic regimes* themselves on communities on the pretext of occasional similarities between their productive forces and organization of labor. That would be as great an error as that of the Bolsheviks when they exaggerated the implications of the different regimes: one, according to them, guaranteeing peace, justice, and plenty; the other inevitably leading to imperialism, exploitation, and want in the midst of accumulated excess. We know both myths are false. So let us not indulge in another myth, which though preferable to the old ones, is just as misleading. Moral similarity between industrial societies that have matured under different regimes can no more be guaranteed than moral conflict. Even if, as is probable, such societies do increasingly resemble one another, they will not necessarily be friends. How many times in history have great wars seemed, in retrospect, to have been fought between fraternal enemies?

Even if we followed the interpretation currently in fashion, which has the two superpowers gradually moving closer together, it would be wrong, even in the age of universal history, to reduce the problem of unity to the confrontation between the United States and the Soviet Union, or even the contradiction between a regime of one-party, state-controlled planning and a semi-liberal government with several parties. Nor should we forget the two other principles of division that I mentioned a short while ago: inequality of development and diversity of customs and beliefs. Inequality of development is partly a heritage from the past, characteristic of a phase of transition. But even if the peoples of Africa and Asia manage to catch up some day, and that cannot happen soon, the indispensable condition for a balance between populations and the space they occupy is the limitation of their numbers—in other words, because the natural control mechanisms (famine, epidemics) are no longer operative, the determination of desirable social volume is left to the collective or the individual conscience. Either societies succeed in managing their own growth rationally, or disparities in number and standard of living will continue indefinitely, with all the suffering and incitation to violence they bring in their train.

But perhaps the last principle of division is even more important. Insofar as the human race is now living through a single history, it needs to acquire a more rational control, not just over its biological instincts but over its social passions. The more men of different races, religions, and customs live in the same world, the more they must learn to be capable of mutual tolerance and respect. They must recognize one another's humanity without ambition to rule or desire to conquer. Those are obvious requirements with which no one will disagree. But on reflection, we see that they call for man to exhibit a new kind of virtue. What separates men from one another most is what each holds sacred. A pagan or Jew who will not convert is offering a challenge to a Christian. Is someone who is ignorant of the God of the religions of salvation our neighbor, or a stranger with whom we can have nothing in common? But it is with him that we shall have to build a spiritual community, which is the superstructure or foundation of the physical community, which tends to be created by the unity of science, technology, and economics, a unity imposed by the historic destiny of a mankind more conscious of its differences than of its solidarity.

The diplomatic field has unified itself via the tragedy of two world wars. Industry has spread through a series of revolutions—French, Russian, and Chinese. Violence has made a path strewn with millions of innocent victims. The wiles of reason invoked by the followers of Bossuet, Hegel, and Marx have not been sparing of men's suffering and blood. We have no proof that things have changed, or that from now on the rational process will reign in peace. But it is possible that, in this respect, universal history will be different from the provincial histories of past ages. It is just a hope, supported by faith.

This sketch will probably have no other conclusion than the above, ambiguous as it is.

The philosophers of history popular with our contemporaries emphasize one or another of the joint aspects of historical evolution. Optimistic philosophers of liberal or Marxist inspiration see the process of accumulating knowledge and power stretching out indefinitely into the future. Through fair exchange or rational planning, the whole human race will share out equitably the benefits of the progress due to the genius of scientists and engineers. Pessimistic philosophers, such as Spengler, note the resemblance between the disasters that swallowed up the civilizations of the past and those we have witnessed in the twentieth century. Western civilization is dying as ancient civilizations died before it, in wars and revolutions, sprawling cities and uprooted masses, the refinement of impotent elites, and the triumph of money and technology. Is not the Europe that has lost its empires already decadent? Does not the passing on to other races of the instruments by which the white minority secured its dominance signal Europe's inevitable degradation?

Optimists or pessimists, these philosophers neglect some features of our age as well as the potentialities of the universal era. Interpreted in the light of the past, Europe's present might well arouse gloom. But how much do the great powers of yesterday weigh in the balance—Britain, France, and Germany, with their 50 million people eager for happiness—against the state-continents of today, for whom a hundred million constitutes a unit? Yet, have not the European nations, in losing their empires, lost their historical being, so to speak, and should they not give up any pretensions to greatness? Such a traditional view may be anachronistic. In our century, dominance brings loss more often than gain. The source and measure of wealth is rational labor in common. Europe, contemplating a world in the process of adopting a civilization that Europe itself generated, need not feel vanquished by its own victory. Greatness is no longer indissolubly linked to military force, because the superpowers can no longer use their weapons without causing their own destruction by way of reprisal, and because no society need rule over others in order to give its children a decent life.

Europe has two reasons for refusing to feel decadent. It is Europe that, first by its achievements, then by its warlike follies, helped humanity cross the threshold into the universal age. In this age, when because of the exploitation of natural resources men need no longer tyrannize over one another, Europe can still be great while conforming to the spirit of the new era and assisting other peoples to cure themselves of the childhood illnesses of modernity. Realizing its ideas at home, with a task to perform abroad— why should Europe brood over a bitterness that is explained by the recent past but for which the prospects of the future give no reason?

Never have men had so many reasons to cease killing one another. Never had they had so many reasons to feel they are joined together in one great enterprise. I do not conclude that the age of universal history will be peaceful. We know that man is a reasonable being. But men?

After a long journey, I end with some propositions with which the wisdom of the nations will not disagree. After having evoked Hegel and the wiles of reason, I now find myself drawing close to Candide and the language of Voltaire. But after all, when philosophy agrees with common sense, is that a compliment to the first or to the second?

ENDNOTES

[All endnotes in this book are translated from an edited selection of the editor's notes of *Une histoire du XXᵉ siècle*.]

NATIONS AND EMPIRES

1. The Third Rome (after the original Rome and Constaninople) was Moscow, symbolizing the fusion of both the Orthodox and the Slavs.

2. Vladimir Ilich Lenin, *Imperialism: The Highest Stage of Capitalism*, written between January and June 1916, published as a pamphlet in Petrograd in 1917. Lenin's preparatory notes were published in 1939 as *Notebooks on Imperialism*.

3. Czar Nicholas II and Kaiser Wilhelm II met at Potsdam on November 5, 1910, and there followed a period of Russo-German negotiations concerning the Baghdad railway and the Balkans. The Potsdam Agreement of August 19, 1911, authorized the construction of the railway. At the beginning of 1911 the British Foreign Office suggested to the Wilhelmstrasse that the German colonial empire be extended at the expense of Portugal's overseas possessions.

4. Alfred T. Mahan (1840–1914), professor of history at Newport Naval Academy and close friend of Theodore Roosevelt, has shown that maritime supremacy is the key to world power in a work published in three parts: *The Influence of Sea Power upon History, 1660–1783* (Boston: Little, Brown, 1890); *The Influence of Sea Power upon the French Revolution and Empire, 1793–1812* (Boston: Little, Brown, 1892); and *Sea Power in Its Relation to the War of 1812* (London: S. Low, Marston, 1905).

5. Captain Matthew C. Perry (1784–1858) sailed his four ships into the Bay of Edo in Japan on July 8, 1853, and sent the Shogunal authorities a message from the American president demanding the opening of Japanese ports. In February

1854 Perry returned with eight ships to bring pressure to bear on Japan, and on March 8 he concluded the Treaty of Kanagawa, which opened the ports of Shimoda and Hakdate to U.S. ships.

FROM SARAJEVO TO HIROSHIMA

1. The trialism of Franz Ferdinand consisted of complementing the Austro-Hungarian dualism that resulted from the compromise of 1867 with a Yugoslav component. The 1867 compromise arrived at by the house of Hapsburg and Hungary recognized the internal political autonomy of the latter within the dual monarchy. In 1871, a trialist project involving the kingdom of Bohemia failed because of opposition from, on the one hand, the Sudeten Germans, who felt threatened by the Czechs, and, on the other, the Hungarians, who considered their position to be endangered. The project of the Archduke Franz Ferdinand, nephew and, after 1896, heir to Franz Joseph I, was adopted by the Croats and the Serbs in the empire, meeting in a Congress held in Fiume in 1905. But this new attempt at trialism met with hostility not only from Hungary but to an even greater degree from the kingdom of Serbia, which feared it would be marginalized.

2. "The German banks all froze immediately at the mere mention of Morocco."

3. Under the Franco-German treaty of November 4, 1911, Germany renounced its claims to Morocco in return for a part of French Congo, which was incorporated into the German Cameroons, and for France's abandoning its preemptive right if the king of Belgium ever relinquished the Congo; France received the strip of land connecting the Congo with Lake Chad, and, most important, recognition of its protectorate over Morocco.

4. In March 1950, Klaus Fuchs (1911–1988) was tried for espionage in London and sentenced to fourteen years in prison. A German Communist, Fuchs had sought refuge in England in 1933 and received his doctorate in physics from the University of Bristol in 1936. He afterward became a laboratory researcher at Edinburgh. Following a stint in Canada from June to December 1940, he resumed his research at the University of Birmingham and received his British citizenship in June 1942. At the end of 1943, he was among the delegation of British nuclear scientists sent to the United States in the wake of the Quebec conference of August 1943. He worked at Columbia, then at Los Alamos, where on July 16, 1945, he was witness to the first atomic explosion. Like Julius Rosenberg, he was attached to the GRU, the Soviet Union's military intelligence service. In 1946, he left Los Alamos to direct Harwell, England's leading nuclear laboratory. The FBI discovered his spying in 1949 following the successful decoding of World War II–era messages transmitted by the Soviet embassy in Washington. Arrested in January 1950, he was released in

1959 for good behavior and sent to East Germany, where he held the post of associate director of the Rossendorf Institute for Nuclear Physics until 1974.

THE SECULAR RELIGIONS

1. On January 22, 1939, Mussolini made a speech threatening France. On April 1, in Capua, he repeated his demands for living space for Italy. Seven days later, Italian forces invaded Albania. On May 7, Italy and Germany concluded a political and military pact.

2. After Munich, French foreign minister Georges Bonnet, following the policy of appeasement advocated by Chamberlain, cultivated a trade policy aimed at bringing Germany closer to the democracies, and to France, in particular, by means of economic agreements.

3. The Deutsche Glaubens Bewegung, "German Faith Movement," campaigned for a German Church organized on the model of the Nazi Party. For the beginnings of the "German Christians," see *Revue d'Histoire moderne et contemporaine,* October–December 1965, pp. 287–308.

4. Georges Bernanos, *Lettre aux Anglais* (Rio de Janeiro: Atlantica, 1942), p. 287.

5. "Mendelism is an erroneous, metaphysical theory of heredity dreamed up by an Austrian monk, Gregor Mendel, in the middle of the last century and accepted by present-day reactionary genetics." So states the *Soviet Dictionary of Philosophy.* According to the theory of the two sciences, one bourgeois and one proletarian, the geneticist T. D. Lyssenko "definitively refuted Mendelism and its pseudo-laws." His theories also provided Stalin with the justification in 1949 for embarking on a "Major Plan for the Transformation of Nature," which quickly proved disastrous. In France, from 1948 to 1952, Communist intellectuals like biologist Marcel Prenant and philosopher Jean-Toissaint Desanti defended Lyssenkoism.

THE IMPERIAL REPUBLIC

1. On July 24, 1945, after a plenary session of the conference at Potsdam, Truman informed Stalin of the existence and refinement of a new weapon. According to Truman's *Memoirs* (Garden City, N.Y.: Doubleday, 1955–1956), Stalin did not seem very interested in the news. It was not new to him: He had been informed of it by his intelligence services.

2. The Communists won 38 percent of the votes cast in the legislative elections held in May 1946 in Czechoslovakia. In Hungary, they obtained 16.9 percent in

the legislative elections held in November 1945 (57 percent of the votes went to the independent Peasants' Party), and 22.3 percent in the legislative elections of August 1947; in the free elections for the Constituent Assembly in January 1918, the Bolsheviks had obtained 17 percent of the votes cast.

3. On January 12, 1950, Dean Acheson, U.S. secretary of state, did not mention Korea in referring to the U.S. "defense perimeter" in the Pacific. Acheson (1893–1971), a lawyer who had been undersecretary of the treasury in the early months of the 1933 Roosevelt administration, assistant secretary of state for relations with Congress from 1941 to 1945, undersecretary of state from August 1945 to June 1947, and secretary of state from 1949 to January 20, 1953, returned to his law practice after the election of Eisenhower. Under Kennedy and Johnson, he was chairman of the working party on NATO.

4. Jacob Malik, USSR delegate to the UN Security Council, withdrew in January 1950 in protest against the continued membership of the representative of the Republic of China. The latter was now reduced to Taiwan: The Chinese Communists had captured Peking, and Mao Tse-tung had proclaimed the People's Republic of China on October 1, 1949. Malik resumed his post on August 1, 1950. On June 27, during his absence, the Security Council, following a request from Truman that it examine the consequences of North Korea's aggression, adopted a resolution recommending that the members of the UN "provide the Republic of Korea with such aid as may be necessary to repel the armed attack and restore peace and international security in the region." A UN expeditionary force was then formed and sent to Korea.

5. Between August 22 and October 6, 1958, Communist China resumed its bombardment of the coastal archipelagos of Quemoy and Matsu that were occupied by the Nationalists of Chiang Kai-shek. The raids began again after October 20, the eve of Dulles's arrival in Formosa. Chiang Kai-shek issued a communiqué reaffirming that his policy was defensive and declaring that the Nationalists' reconquest of China would not be affected by force. Peking then announced that air raids in the future would take place on odd days only. They were later suspended. Four years earlier, on September 3, 1954, the Chinese Communists had bombarded Quemoy and Matsu. On December 2 of the same year, Washington replied by signing a treaty of assistance with Formosa. On January 18, 1955, the Communists landed on the Taichen archipelago. Eisenhower declared that the United States would defend Formosa and the Pescadores, of which Quemoy and Matsu were part. See Camille Rougeron, "Les Matsu et les Quemoy: Test des armes atomiques tactiques" (Matsu and Quemoy: A test for tactical atomic weapons), *Forces aériennes françaises*, no. 105, June 1955, pp. 991–1005; Morton H. Halperin and Tang Tsou, "The 1958 Quemoy Crisis," ed. M. H. Halperin, *Sino-Soviet Relations and Arms Control* (Cambridge, Mass.: MIT Press, 1967), pp. 265–303; Jonathan T. Howe, *Multicrises: Sea*

Power and Global Politics in the Missile Age (Cambridge, Mass.: MIT Press, 1971), pp. 166–263.

6. Aron wrote, in, "Récit, analyse, interprétation, explication: Critique de quelques problèmes de la connaissance historique" (Narrative, analysis, interpretation, explanation: A critique of some problems concerning historical knowledge), *Archives européennes de Sociologie* 15, no. 2 (1974), reproduced in Raymond Aron, *Etudes sociologiques* (Paris: Presses Universitaires de France, 1988), pp. 104–105:

> In the chapter devoted to the fall—from the Capitol to the Tarpeian Rock—I availed myself freely of the privileges of pragmatic criticism: (1) Who would have made the decision to intervene in Vietnam if he had foreseen the consequences—the nation torn apart, the impossibility of victory, the compromising of the prestige of the United States and the damage to its moral authority? In short, the evolution of events on the ground demonstrated the strategic error—no need to go on about it at length: The facts speak for themselves. (2) Study of the Pentagon documents reveals both how the American authorities meddled in the internal affairs of South Vietnam and the clumsy and childish ploys they resorted to in the clandestine war in the North. How could the United States say it wanted to preserve the freedom of the South Vietnamese to choose their own destiny when the political vacuum between the overthrow of Diem and the consolidation of Thieu was filled by mere phantom governments? (3) The Pentagon documents also reveal the series of half-measures with which the presidents responded to the demands of their services. In particular, it is hard for a historian to understand what John F. Kennedy meant by the increase in the number of advisers—from fewer than 1,000 to more than 15,000. (4) America's conduct of the war and the bombing raids on the North ranged the whole of world public opinion against the U.S. Goliath and his storm of steel. Its conduct was at once inefficient and, on the plane of humanity, obnoxious.

7. The McNamara-Kennedy doctrine, based on the principle of graduated deterrence, was expounded to the members of NATO meeting in Athens on May 6, 1962, by Secretary of Defense Robert McNamara. According to Raymond Aron, "The doctrine of graduated deterrence includes not only raising the atomic threshold and enlarging the field of operations conducted by means of classical weapons, but also, in the version presented by Mr. McNamara, a phase of counterforce strategy, even in a second strike, before the total catastrophe of counter-cities strategy" (Raymond Aron, *Le Grand Débat* [The Great Debate] [Paris: Calmann-Lévy, 1963], p. 83).

8. At a press conference on January 14, 1963, General de Gaulle said he was against Britain's possible entry into the Common Market and rejected the U.S. proposals made in Nassau to supply Britain with Polaris instead of Skybolt missiles on

the condition that they would be incorporated into NATO's nuclear force (British Prime Minister Harold Macmillan had asked that the same proposal be made in parallel to France). (Charles de Gaulle, *Discours et Messages* (Speeches and Messages), vol. 4, *Pour l'effort, août 1962–décembre 1965* (For trying, August 1962– December 1965) (Paris: Plon, 1970), pp. 66–76.)

9. Oleg Penkovsky (1919–1963), colonel in the Soviet State Security, and assistant chief of the foreign section of the State Committee for the coordination of scientific research from 1960 to 1962, was arrested on a charge of spying for Britain and the United States on October 22, 1962. (The arrest was made public on November 11.) He had been in contact with the British intelligence services since April 1961 and had supplied information on, among other things, the Soviet ICBMs (intercontinental ballistic missiles). He was executed soon after a public trial held May 7–11, 1963. Michel Tatu thinks Penkovsky "could not have informed the Americans about a possible state of alert in the USSR armed forces during the Cuban crisis, because he was arrested before Kennedy announced the blockade." The *Washington Post* published extracts from Penkovsky's diary in 1965. The Soviet government demanded that publication cease, and when the *Post* refused, its Moscow office was closed and its correspondent expelled. See Oleg V. Penkovsky, *The Penkovsky Papers* (Garden City, N.Y.: Doubleday, 1965).

10. Ngo Dinh Diem (1901–1963), minister to Bao Dai in the 1930s, refused to join the government formed in 1945 by the Vietminh, which saw him as a means of rallying the Vietnamese Catholics to its cause. In 1954 he became head of the South Vietnamese government supported by the United States. His autocratic and nepotistic regime became unpopular and paved the way for the Communists. The United States permitted the military putsch in which Diem died.

11. Nguyen Van Thieu (born in 1923) joined the Vietminh in 1945, then the French forces, and then Diem's army. As commander of the 5th infantry division, he played an important part in the 1963 putsch. In 1964 he became minister-president in the military government of Prime Minister Nguyen Cao Ky, then head of state in 1965. In 1967, after the reform of the constitution, he was elected president of the republic, and in 1971 he was reelected. Despite the authoritarian nature of his regime, he was supported by the Johnson and Nixon administrations. In 1975 the retreat before the Communist offensive against the northern provinces turned into a rout, and Saigon was encircled. Thieu found refuge first in Taiwan and then in England.

12. Lin Piao (1907–1971), a Communist since 1925, took part in the Communist military expeditions in 1927–1928, joined Mao Tse-tung in April 1928, and became a strategist in the guerrilla war against the Nationalists. He was a member of the leadership of the young Soviet Republic of Kiangsi in 1931 and led

the advance-guard of the Long March to Shensi in 1934–1935. From August 1945 to October 1949, he was largely responsible for the operations that brought the Communists to power: the invasion of Manchuria and the capture of Peking and Canton in 1949. In 1955, he was the youngest Chinese marshal. As vice president of the Central Committee from May 1958, he was a main figure on the political scene. With China mobilized to confront international tension, he became minister of defense in September 1959, and in 1962 he directed operations on the Indian frontier. In the 1960s, he applied the principles of guerrilla warfare to diplomacy and politics. With the advent of the Cultural Revolution he became an advocate of the cult of Mao. The triumph of Mao and his prophet Lin Piao was celebrated in April 1969 at the Ninth Congress, and their hegemony over both party and state was confirmed. But after August 1970, his star began to wane. He died in a plane crash when trying to flee the country, perhaps after a failed coup.

13. Daniel Ellsberg, an expert on decisionmaking (*Decisionmaking Under Uncertainty*, honors thesis, Harvard University, 1952; *Risk, Ambiguity and Decision*, Ph.D. thesis, Harvard University, 1962), was a member of many strategic bodies, including the working party of the Executive Committee of the National Security Council during the Cuban Missile crisis in 1962. His research on "patterns in high-level decisionmaking" in periods of crisis gave him access to the archives of many government bodies concerning the Missile Crisis, Suez, the Skybolt decision, Berlin, and the U2 incident. He was special adviser to the assistant secretary of defense in charge of affairs of international security during the period of escalation in 1964–1965. He was posted to the State Department to work with the U.S. military authorities in Vietnam until 1967, then made assistant to minister-adviser William Porter. He made public the archives concerning the escalation in Vietnam; part of this material was published by the *New York Times*. See Daniel Ellsberg, *Papers on the War* (New York: Simon and Schuster, 1972).

14. George W. Ball (1909–1994), undersecretary of state for economic relations under Kennedy, then undersecretary of state, resigned in September 1966 because of a disagreement with President Johnson over Vietnam. See George W. Ball, *The Past Has Another Pattern: Memoirs* (New York: Norton, 1982).

15. Nicias, though he had advised the Athenians against it, was obliged to lead the Sicilian expedition, which proved a disaster and in which Nicias himself was murdered by the Syracusans.

16. Henry A. Kissinger (born in 1923) was President Nixon's special adviser on foreign affairs and national security, then secretary of state. He later became a professor at Harvard's Center for International Affairs. He is the author of *Nuclear Weapons and Foreign Policy* (New York: Harper, 1957), which envisages the use of tactical atomic weapons in a limited conflict, and of *The Necessity For Choice:*

Prospects of American Foreign Policy (New York: Harper, 1961), which reverts to the previous theme and makes a clear distinction between limited and total war. Raymond Aron met Kissinger when he was at Harvard in 1960–1961.

17. SALT, Strategic Arms Limitation Talks, were held between the United States and the USSR from 1968 on. The SALT I agreements were signed in 1972.

18. MIRV, the Multiple Independently Targetable Re-entry Vehicle, is a multiple warhead with elements that can be aimed at different targets. The SALT agreements recommend that in the case of the MIRVs, each of the multiple warheads counts as one, as distinct from the case of the MRV (Multiple Re-entry Vehicles) warheads, in which all the elements are aimed at the same target.

19. On August 12, 1970, in Moscow, Chancellor Willy Brandt signed a treaty between the FRG and the USSR implicitly recognizing the existence of another German state (article 1, paragraph 2). It stated that "peace can only be maintained in Europe if no-one undermines present frontiers" (art. 3). West Germany recognized the Oder-Neisse Line: The territories east of the Oder were regarded as "given up," and the "demarcation line," according to Bonn, between the Federal Republic and the Democratic Republic was designated as a "frontier." On the day the treaty was signed, Walter Scheel, the West German foreign minister, sent Andrey Gromyko, his Soviet counterpart, a "letter relating to German unity," saying, "The treaty was not inconsistent with the Federal Republic's political aim of working for a state of peace in Europe in which the German people may recover its unity and dispose freely of itself." The Bundestag ratified the treaty in 1972. On December 7, 1970, a treaty was signed in Warsaw between the Federal Republic and Poland recognizing the Oder-Neisse Line. This treaty had the same structure and references as the previous one. Both consecrated the Östpolitik—the establishment of new relationships between the Federal Republic and the countries in the East—initiated by Willy Brandt in October 1969 when he became chancellor. This diplomacy was completed on December 21, 1972, by a fundamental treaty concluded between East and West Germany. Though there was no formal recognition, the treaty recognized the full and entire sovereignty of both countries (art. 4), and permanent representations, though not embassies, were to be exchanged (art. 8). The Federal Republic sent the Democratic Republic a "letter relating to German unity," as it had previously sent to the USSR. The two Germanys joined the United Nations on September 18, 1973.

20. On August 15, 1971, President Nixon announced the suspension of dollar convertibility, the introduction of a 10 percent surtax on imports, and a three-month freeze on U.S. prices and wages. All this was so that the United States might "protect itself against the speculators who have declared war on the dollar, the pillar of world monetary stability, and at the same time to improve the balance of payments and create jobs."

21. Robert E. Osgood, "Preface," in George Liska, *Imperial America: The International Politics of Privacy* (Baltimore: Johns Hopkins, 1967).

THE END OF COLONIAL EMPIRES

1. That is, the area using the franc as its currency.

2. Pierre Moussa, *Les Chance économiques de la Communauté franco-africaine (Cahiers de la Fondation nationale des Sciences politiques,* no. 83) (Paris: Armand Colin, 1957).

3. On the morning of March 9, 1945, after issuing a threatening ultimatum, the Japanese military authorities abolished the French administration. Admiral Decoux was imprisoned, together with most French officials and military personnel. Military installations were taken by force, though there was some resistance. Of the 12,000 metropolitan French people in Indochina in 1945, 2,000 were killed.

4. Georges Thierry d'Argentlieu (1889–1964), a naval officer who fought in the Moroccan campaign and in the 1914–1918 war, left the navy in 1920 and entered the Carmelite order as a monk. He became its provincial superior in 1932. In 1939, he was mobilized and took part in the defense of Cherbourg. Taken prisoner on June 19, 1940, he escaped and joined de Gaulle in London on June 29. He carried out various missions in Africa for the Free French (Dakar, Gabon). After serving as a member of the Defense Council of the empire, then on the National Committee, in July 1942 he was appointed French high commissioner in the Pacific as a rear admiral based in Nouméa. Early in 1943 he was promoted to admiral and put in command of the Free French Naval Forces in Britain. At the Liberation he was made northern admiral and assistant chief of staff. He attended the San Francisco conference in April 1945. On April 16, 1945, he was appointed French high commissioner and commander-in-chief in Indochina, but after carrying out a much-debated policy there he was recalled to France on March 5, 1947. He withdrew to the Carmelite house at Avon. He remained a chancellor of the Order of the Liberation until 1958.

5. From the second decade of the twentieth century, Fernand Boverat (1885–1964), demographer and advocate of an active policy for increasing the birthrate, organized the National Alliance for Increasing the French Population, which at the end of the 1930s became the National Alliance against Depopulation. During World War II, he took part in the work of Alexis Carrel's French Foundation for the Study of Human Problems, and in this context he published *Une doctrine de la natalité* (A theory on increasing the birthrate) (Paris: Librairie de Médicis, 1943).

6. Etienne Borne (1907–1993), a disciple of Jacques Maritain, the philosopher, was involved in the founding of *Esprit* and contributed to Dominican reviews

such as *La vie intellectuelle* (The life of the mind), *Temps présent* (The present tense), and *Sept* (Seven). He also wrote for various Christian Democrat publications, including Georges Bidault's *L'Aube* (Dawn). Borne taught in Toulouse and took part in the Resistance groups Liberté and Combat.

7. Petroleum appeared in the Sahara on June 26, 1956, at Hassi-Messaoud. Drilling revealed considerable reserves. On November 8 a natural gas deposit was found at Hassi-R'mel.

8. Alain Savary (1918–1988), a member of the Assembly and the secretary of state for Moroccan and Tunisian Affairs in the Mollet cabinet, resigned from his post on November 3, 1956, following the rerouting of an FLN transport plane. Pierre Mendès France resigned from the government on May 23, 1956, to protest the Algerian policy. Savary went on to establish the independent Socialist Party in 1958.

9. Maurice Faure, a radical member of the Assembly and the secretary of state for foreign affairs, attempted to reestablish ties with the Tunisian and Moroccan authorities.

10. Five leaders of the FLN (Ahmed Ben Balla, Mohammed Boudiaf, Hocine Ait Ahmed, Mohammed Khider, and Mostafa Lacherf) were arrested by French officials on October 22, 1956, when the Moroccan Air Atlas plane they were taking to a secret preliminary meeting with French representatives in Tunis was rerouted to Algiers with the complicity of its French pilots. Max Lejeune, the secretary of state for national defense, was the only member of the government to know about the operation in advance. Guy Mollet, though disapproving of the mission, protected the responsible parties.

11. There was a new wave of FLN terrorist attacks—the "spring offensive"—especially in May and June 1957, at the time of the Battle of Algiers, that was directed against Algerians. On May 26, 1957, Ali Chekkal, former vice president of the Algerian Assembly, was killed as he came out of the stadium at Colombes in Paris, after watching the final of the French football cup with René Coty, the French president. During the night of May 28 and 29, at Mechta Casbah near Melouza in Grande Kabylie in Algeria, 303 villagers were massacred by the Armée de Liberation Nationale (ALN, National Liberation Army). On the night of May 30–31, thirty-six Muslim workers were murdered at Wagram, near Saïda. On May 31, René Coty broadcast a radio message asking "all civilized peoples to refuse to listen to the troublemakers and other agents of this hideous terrorism, which tramples underfoot both divine and human laws and sets at naught the conscience of us all." On June 1, three bombs exploded at bus stops in the middle of Algiers, killing ten people and injuring about a hundred more. On June 4, the FLN attacked the center of Tlemcen. On June 9, a bomb killed nine people and injured eighty at the casino on the Corniche in Algiers.

12. The Guy Mollet cabinet, installed in office on February 1, 1956, resigned on May 21, 1957, after the French Parliament refused to approve its financial plans in 1957. The formation of a new government proved difficult. Maurice Bourgès-Maunoury succeeded in doing so, however, and in his investiture speech on June 12 adopted an attitude of resistance on the subject of Algeria. He said: "Our apathy is the rebels' last hope. But there, too, they are mistaken. I solemnly declare to the whole population of Algeria that our country will keep up its effort as long as is necessary. It can and it will." The Bourgès-Maunoury cabinet resigned on September 30, followed by the Félix Gaillard cabinet, which was installed on November 6, 1957, and resigned on April 15, 1958. The Pflimlin cabinet was due to be installed on May 14, but the events in Algiers were scheduled for May 13 to prevent it from taking office.

13. Thierry Maulnier published a long report on Algeria in *Le Figaro* from April 23 to May 5, 1957. It was called "The Army Defends France's African Opportunity in Algeria" and presented Algeria as a region of economic expansion comparable to the American West. He criticized *La Tragédie algérienne* in an article entitled "The Offensive of the 700 Million" in *Le Figaro* on December 5, 1957. He consistently argued that France should maintain its position in Algeria. Thierry Maulnier—a pseudonym for Jacques Talagrand (1909–1988)—graduate of the Ecole Normale, contributed to Henri Massis's *Revue universelle* and to *L'Action française* between 1930 and 1944. He wrote political essays such as *La crise est dans l'homme* (The crisis is in man) (Paris: Alexis Redier, 1932); *Mythes socialistes* (Socialist myths) (Paris: Gallimard, 1936); and *Au-delà du nationalisme* (Beyond nationalism) (Paris: Gallimard, 1938). In the summer of 1940, while still contributing regularly to *L'Action française*, he began writing in *Le Figaro*. After the war, he started *La table ronde* (The round table) with Mauriac, took part in the Congress for Liberty and Culture, and contributed to *Preuves* (Proofs). His articles against communism are collected in *La Face du méduse du communisme* (The Medusa's head of communism) (Paris: Gallimard, 1951). Sartre caricatured him as one of the characters in *Nekrassov*. He kept his penchant for authoritarian regimes. In his memoirs, Raymond Aron observed: "In 1967 Thierry Maulnier brought back from Greece a series of articles favorable to the colonels' regime. But *my* Greek friends, Kostas Papaioannou and the imposing figure of Constantin Carmanlis, would, if necessary, have protected me from any weakness" (*Mémoires* [Paris: Julliard, 1983], p. 594). See Jean-Louis Loubet del Bayle, *Les Non-Conformistes des années trente* (The Nonconformists of the thirties) (Paris: Le Seuil, 1969); and Etienne de Montety, *Thierry Maulnier* (Paris: Julliard, 1994).

14. Germaine Tillion, *L'algérie en 1957* (Paris: Editions de Minuit, 1957).

15. Jacques Soustelle, former governor-general of Algeria, criticized *La Tragédie algérienne* in a pamphlet: "Monsieur Aron has the necessary weapons to attack on

a new front, that of the moderate bourgeoisie. When addressing them one should speak not so much of grand principles as of what is and is not possible. One should at once reassure and arouse their patriotism, at the same time as troubling their economic instincts. These are tasks that the ordinary crowd of liquidators are incapable of handling, but Monsieur Aron acquits himself splendidly" (*Le Drame algérienne et la décadence française: Réponse à Raymond Aron* [The Algerian drama and French decadence: A reply to Raymond Aron], Plon, *Tribune libre,* no. 6 [1957], p. 5). In an account of Soustelle's *Réponse* in *France-Forum,* a review close to the Mouvement Republican Populaire (MRP) and on the whole favorable to the maintenance of French sovereignty in Algeria, the author comments:

> Faced with the formidable arguments of Raymond Aron, one might have expected to see Jacques Soustelle defend point by point the policy of integration he himself advocates. Just to say that Aron "recommends the evacuation of Algeria" or to ascribe to him the argument that "Algeria is a burden and must therefore be dropped" . . . is not mere simplification or even caricature of his opponent. . . . There is no reason why argument about France's Algerian policy should not become heated, as long as reason is not replaced with blackmail and threats. With all its faults, and I have not overlooked them here, Raymond Aron's book at least has the virtue of making us think about the aims of our policy. It is a pity that Jacques Soustelle doesn't follow his example in this; instead, rather than, like Aron, trying to help people understand a difficult problem, he simply rehearses his own prejudices and myths. His "reply," that of a respected leader determined not to change his mind, risks providing Aron's pessimism with an unhoped-for and inopportune justification. (Pierre Decamp, "Polémiques et témoignages sur l'Algérie" [Polemics and evidence on Algeria], *France-Forum,* no. 6, October–November 1967.)

Jacques Soustelle (1912–1990), governor-general of Algeria from January 1955 until February 1956, sided with the French of Algeria. He was minister of information from July 7, 1958, to January 8, 1959, and the only member of de Gaulle's government directly involved in the Algerian uprising of May 1958. In October 1959, he tried to gather together the Union pour la Nouvelle République (UNR) deputies in favor of a French Algeria. In January 1969, he supported the rebels during the week of the barricades and as a result was dismissed from the government on February 5. On April 5, he was excluded from the UNR. He then got even more involved in promoting a French Algeria, took part in the conference at Vincennes, founded the Rassemblement pour l'Algérie Française, and as a result had to live in exile for several years. See Bernard Ullmann, *Jaques Soustelle: Le mal aimé* (Jacques Soustelle: The unloved) (Paris: Plon, 1995).

16. Roger Duchet, reacting to *La Tragédie algérienne,* wrote to its author: "You refer to Montesquieu: But he never said that, hiding behind the citizens who do their duty, others may have the privilege, without risk, of easing their consciences and choosing renunciation. The right to seek and speak the truth is inalienable and belongs to all who fight. And that is why I take their side." Aron's reply contained the following: "Permit me to observe that the very terms in which your letter is written makes your claim farcical. If I thought there was any point in entering into discussion with you about the problem itself, it would be easy to show that invective cannot take the place of ideas, and that willful blindness is a sign of cowardice rather than courage." (An exchange of letters, June 1957, quoted in N. Baverez, *Raymond Aron* [Paris: Flammarion, 1993], p. 350.) Roger Duchet (1904–1981), senator for the Côte d'Or from 1946, founder and general secretary of the Centre national des Indépendants from 1947 to 1961, and political director of the weekly *France indépendante* from 1950, occupied various ministerial posts from 1951 on, including that of head of the mail services in the cabinets of Edgar Faure, Antoine Pinay, and René Mayer. After March 1958, with Gaullists Soustelle and Debré, the radical dissident André Morice, and Bidault of the MRP, Duchet called for a "government of public safety." His articles in *France indépendante* from January 1956 to June 1958 are collected in *Pour le Salut public: Les indépendants devant les grands problèmes internationaux* (For the public safety: The independents and the great international problems) (Paris: Plon, 1958). On June 18, 1960, he organized a conference at Vincennes on the theme, "Algeria is a country subject to French sovereignty and should remain an integral part of the republic." He was a member of the Vincennes committee appointed on November 3, 1960, and dissolved by the Council of Ministers in November 1961. Duchet lost his position as general secretary of the CNIP because of his marked sympathy for the revolt of the generals in April 1961.

17. Alain de Sérigny (1912–1986), editor of *L'Echo d'Alger* (The Algiers echo). See A. de Sérigny, *La Révolution du 13 mai* (Paris: Plon, 1958); and *Echos d'Alger,* vol. 2, *L'Abandon, 1946–1962* (Desertion, 1946–1962) (Paris: Presses de la Cité, 1974).

18. "It was the mouthpiece of the most egotistical of interest groups and campaigned successfully against Clemenceau, Violette, Léon Blum, de Gaulle, and Châtaigneau," Mendès-France wrote in *L'Express* on January 24, 1956.

19. Georges Le Brun-Kéris (1910–1970), MRP adviser of the French Union from 1947 to 1958, and assistant general secretary of the MRP from 1951 to 1958, contributed to *Forces nouvelles, Terre humaine, La Croix,* and *France-Forum.* From 1958 on, he was African representative of the French Cotton Industry Union. Le Brun-Kéris was the author of *Mort des colonies?* (Are the colonies dead?)

(Paris: Le Centurion, 1953); and *Afrique, quel sera ton visage?* (Africa, what will you look like?) (Paris: Fleurus, 1964).

20. Raymond Aron gives extracts from Etienne Borne's criticisms of *La Tragédie algérienne* in *Mémoires*, p. 372:

> This kind of realism, which is quick to give new privileges to those who are already prosperous and to snatch chances from those about to give up; this positivism, which recognizes only the verdict of scales and calculators; this sort of stoic fatalism, so concerned with accepting the fait accompli; and even this analytical intelligence, so skillful at dismantling in order to understand—I can't help seeing in all this the typical features of a right-wing mentality, probably a constant element in the history of ideas. It is a right-wing attitude that sometimes, via the reasonable paths of resignation, leads to defeatism.

This passage echoes the account of *La Tragédie algérienne* in *France-Forum*, Borne's review:

> For Raymond Aron, the problem is "tragic" in the Greek sense of the word. Beneath the apparent rigor of his thinking, the author implicitly accepts the myth of Fatality, which philosophically cannot be demonstrated. No doubt, in the absence of meaning, a certain historical weight comes into play. And it would be a mistake to underestimate the influence today of unbridled nationalisms. But other fundamental developments are also emerging, which more rapidly than we suppose may overtake contemporary conflicts: Among so many contrasting trends, humane action, even in Algeria, may yet catch on and change the course of events. Of course, one's first reaction, confronted with such an accumulation of mistakes and so many stoked-up hatreds, and sometimes with pathetically inept official pronouncements, is to yield to discouragement and accept the old adage, "Those whom the gods would destroy they first drive mad." But the gods are dead, and so should our ancestral doubts and fears be, too. The faith of a few people, in mainland France and in the two communities living in Algeria, could at any moment suspend the journey into absurdity and create conditions favorable to the trying out of new kinds of coexistence. It wouldn't be the first time in history, or the last, that reason triumphed. (Jean Aubry, "La Tragédie algérienne by Raymond Aron," *France-Forum*, no. 5, August–September 1957.)

Etienne Borne, a former fellow-student at the Ecole Normale, later wrote to Aron:

> It seemed to me at the time that in opting for independence pure and simple, when all was not yet finished, you were not really being yourself—in a nutshell, not being a

centrist. But in terms of a kind of realism that weighs up forces and masses, you were probably right, and that was what I was trying to say in that unfortunate and polemical short-cut of a phrase—"typical right-wing philosophy." The dream of a Franco-Algerian federation making coexistence and cooperation possible between the two communities was no doubt Utopian. But you were one of the first to see it, and I am very willing to give in to you on the subject. (Quoted by Aron in *Mémoires*, p. 388.)

PROVENANCE
OF THE TEXTS

NATIONS AND EMPIRES

"Nations et Empires," in *Encyclopédie française*. Paris: Société nouvelle de l'Encyclopédie française, 1957. Vol. 11, *La Vie internationale*, col. 11.04.1–11.06.8. Reproduced in Raymond Aron, *Dimensions de la conscience historique* (Dimensions of the historical consciousness), chapter 6, "Recherches en sciences humaines no. 16," Paris: Plon, 1961, pp. 171–259. Reissued by Presses Pocket, 1985, pp. 151–224.

FROM SARAJEVO TO HIROSHIMA

"De Sarajevo à Hiroshima," in Raymond Aron, *Les guerres en chaîne* (One war after another). Paris, Gallimard, 1951, pp. 13–112. Lengthy extracts were published in *Liberté de l'esprit* (Liberty of mind), no. 10, May 1950, pp. 65–68; nos. 11–12, June–July 1950, pp. 136–141; no. 19, March 1951, pp. 69–73; and no. 20, April 1951, pp. 101–104.

THE SECULAR RELIGIONS

"Etats democratiques et Etats totalitaires" (Democratic states and totalitarian states), paper delivered to the Société Française de Philosophie (French Philosophical

Society) on June 17, 1939, and published in the *Bulletin de la Société Française de Philosophie,* 40th year, no. 2, April–May 1946, pp. 41–55. Reproduced in *Commentaire,* vol. 6, no. 24, Winter 1983–1984, pp. 701–719, and in Raymond Aron, *Machiavel et les tyrannies modernes* (Machiavelli and modern tyrannies), text established, presented, and annotated by Rémy Freymond, Paris: Editions de Fallois, 1993, pp. 165–183.

"L'Avenir des religions séculaires" (The future of the secular religions), *La France libre* (Free France), vol. 8, no. 45, July 15, 1944, pp. 210–217, and no. 46, August 15, 1944, pp. 269–277. Reproduced in Raymond Aron, *L'Âge des Empires et l'avenir de la France* (The Age of Empires and the future of France), Paris: Défense de la France, 1945, pp. 287–318. Reissued in Raymond Aron, *Chroniques de guerre* (War chronicles), *La France libre, 1940–1945* (Free France, 1940–1945), edition revised and annotated by Christian Bachelier, Paris: Gallimard, 1990, pp. 925–948.

"Du Marxisme au Stalinisme" (From Marxism to Stalinism), in Raymond Aron, *Les guerres en chaîne* (One war after another). Paris: Gallimard, 1951, part 2, chapter 6, pp. 136–158.

"Expansion du Stalinisme," in Raymond Aron, *Les guerres en chaîne* (One war after another). Paris: Gallimard, 1951, part 2, chapter 7, pp. 159–177.

THE IMPERIAL REPUBLIC

"Les Etats-Unis dans le système interétatique" (The United States in the international system), in Raymond Aron, *Les Dernières années du siècle* (The last years of the century), final text prepared by Jean-Claude Casanova, Pierre Hassner, Stanley Hoffmann, Pierre Manent, and Dominique Schnapper. Paris: Julliard, 1984, part 1, chapter 2, pp. 33–62. Reproduced in a presentation by Raymond Aron of the 8th edition, *Paix et guerre entre les nations* (Peace and war among the nations), Paris: Calmann-Levy, 1984.

"D'un plan Marshall à l'autre ou aller et retour des dollars" (From one Marshall Plan to another, or the return trip of the dollars), in Raymond Aron, *République impériale: Les Etats-Unis dans le monde, 1945–1972* (Imperial Republic: The United States and the world, 1945–1972). Paris: Calmann-Lévy, 1973, part 2, chapter 2, pp. 199–227. The work was inspired by a course of lectures delivered at the Collège de France in 1970–1971 and published also in an English version, *The Imperial Republic: The United States and the World, 1945–1973,* Englewood Cliffs, N.J.: Prentice-Hall, 1974.

THE END OF COLONIAL EMPIRES

"Coûts et profits des Empires" (Costs and profits of empire), lecture delivered in Paris to the Cercle de la France d'Outre-Mer (French Overseas Club), dinner-debate on May 12, 1958, and published in the *Bulletin d'information de l'Association des docteurs ès sciences économiques* (Bulletin of the Association of Ph.D.s in economics), new series, no. 18, 3rd trimester 1958, pp. 2–30.

"Indochina," extract from Raymond Aron, "Liberté de l'esprit," in Aron, *Immuable et changeante: De la IVe à la Ve République* (Immutable yet changing: From the Fourth to the Fifth Republic). Paris: Calmann-Lévy, 1959, chapter 4, pp. 135–139.

"Tribune libre no. 2," in Raymond Aron, *La Tragédie algérienne.* Paris: Plon, 1957, p. 76.

"Tribune libre no. 33," extracts from Raymond Aron, *L'Algérie et la République.* Paris: Plon, 1958, pp. 39–47 and 130–133.

THE DAWN OF UNIVERSAL HISTORY

"L'Aube de l'histoire universelle" (The Dawn of universal history), lecture delivered in London 1960 under the auspices of the Société des Amis de l'Université hébraïque de Jérusalem (Society of the Friends of the Hebrew University in Jerusalem). Published as "Recherches en sciences humaines, no. 16," in Raymond Aron, *Dimensions de la conscience historique,* Paris: Plon, 1961, chapter 7, pp. 260–295. Reissued by Presses Pocket, 1985, pp. 225–254.

INDEX